In late 1990, I ventured off to Los Angeles in the belief it was the only place in the US where Rave Culture was happening on a scale even slightly similar to the UK. I was an active participant in the Alternative Dance Music scene of Tampa, Florida (anything from Industrial Dance, Post Punk, Acid House, Hip Hop and Grunge) since sneaking into 21+ nightclubs in 1987, and started DJ-ing by early 1990. As mind-blowing as it all was, I had expected to be wow'd beyond any notion of being able to exclusively play house & techno in its ever mutating iterations. Instead, I heard records I knew, I heard records already owned and I even heard DJ's make mistakes! The rose-tinted glasses had come off and I felt emboldened to return to Florida and put my own thumbprint on the culture.

By the end of 1991, I'd gathered up a crew and began throwing some of the first one-off raves in the Southeast, including the first to bring Moby and Doc Martin to Florida. In Tampa, we'd become known for being the 'black sheep' of the Florida scene for what was already an uncommon trait: doing things our own way. Our particular group of people had all orbited around that same Alternative Dance Music scene and inevitably converged upon each other more purposefully throughout 1991. However, one acquaintance named Peter Wohelski had left his radio show at 88.5 WMNF to spend the year across the pond experiencing UK Rave Culture first hand. When he returned by 1992, he quickly caught wind of what we'd been up to and got in touch with myself and Grumptronix about a new DIY 'zine he'd started called TRiP MAGAZEEN.

Our previous histories uniquely informed our eclectic tastes in Rave, and we were resolute to push that mindset onto a scene that had quickly begun to define itself by musical cliques. TRiP covered everything from Hardcore Techno in all its global forms to Ambient Electronica and House.

Keeping a keen eye on American scenes got us nods from the likes of Mad Mike of UR and John Acquaviva & Richie Hawtin of Plus 8 Records (the only magazine Plus 8 had advertised in). We conducted ome of the first ever US interviews with Laurent Garnier, The Future Sound Of London, Aphex Twin and the late, great Caspar Pound of Rising High Records which still inspire to this day.

From 1992 to late 1994, things grew exponentially for each of us within our contributions to TRiP. Having become an established touring DJ, I was offered the job of Dance Music Buyer at The Alternative Record Store where I further encouraged people to find their own voice rather than follow the heard. Grumptronix was invited to the UK to DJ at Megadog and Megatripolis parties and kickstarted his production career at Mr. C's Watershed Studios. And most notably, as the founder of the 'zine, Peter was offered the position of Director Of A&R at Astralwerks in New York which effectively ended TRiP's short, but impactful run. To have the full volume of TRiP MAGAZEEN be published by Blurring Books for the world to peruse over 30 years later brings me so much joy.

–

DJ THREE

Looking back on the 30th anniversary of the end of TRiP MAGAZEEN, its beginning in 1992 feels like a lifetime ago.

I spent the Fall and Winter of 1991-'92 in London, living with an American friend who had scored a music publishing deal and was trying to get signed to a label. Over the previous few years, I had already been introduced to the sounds of Chicago and Detroit in the Tampa alternative clubs and Belgian 'hoover' rave tracks, UK hardcore breakbeats, acid jazz, and 'ambient house,' were starting to make their way over to the US as imports and finding themselves in heavy rotation on my radio show at home. I was reasonably sussed, but I couldn't wait to soak up the vibes of London!

That Summer, Prodigy's "Charly" went #1 on the UK Pop Charts, and as I arrived in the capital, Nirvana's culture-redefining *Nevermind* album and the drama around Kurt Cobain and Courtney Love's Sid & Nancy-esque romance was dominating the UK music press.

Upon arriving in the capital, I was quickly neck-deep in dance music culture, hanging out in Soho and West End record shops like Black Market and Quaff, raving in legendary spots like Corsica Studios, listening to DJs like the Shamen's Mr.C, Kid Batchelor, Fabio & Grooverider, and Colin Faver whilst scouring the late-night radio dial for pirate radio stations and religiously listening to Colin Dale's legendary KISS-FM show, Abstrakt Dance.

Months later, I returned to Tampa from London with literally 8 pence in my pocket. I felt like I went from drinking from the firehose of this culture to a tiny trickle, onging for that vibrant buzz that I'd gotten used to.

Identifying with the scene's DIY punk ethos, I thought, what was the most punk rock thing I could do with my journalism degree to spotlight this music and culture here in the US?

A fanzine.

Think of a fanzine (or a 'zine) like a physical blog, but one that was written, photographed, and produced by fans. You'd finish it and go to Kinko's to make your copies. Again, this is before the internet as we know it existed. We communicated by hardwired telephones, snail mail and faxes. Access to BBS message boards and listservs was happening for some via dial-up internet, and eventually, email would become a thing.

Taking cues from legendary American punk fanzines like Flipside, Maximum Rock'n'Roll and the early days of UK dance music bibles Mixmag and DJ Magazine, I called in some favors from my record label connections to score an interview with The Shamen who were on tour in the US that Spring. I cobbled together the first issue and distributed it to some of the record shops in town.

I quickly discovered that some acquaintances from the Alternative club scene had kick started rave culture in Tampa while I was gone. With kindred spirits Christopher Milo aka DJ THREE (soon of Hallucination Recordings and Second Hand Satellites fame) and Wayne Consiglio aka Grumptronix in tow, along with my then-girlfriend Jackie, we set out to highlight an eclectic array of what we thought was the most important underground music, as well as the most pivotal happenings in Florida, around the US, and the globe.

TRiP covered the Florida scene from Orlando's seminal AAHZ club and Simons in Gainesville to one-off parties and chill-out rooms all over the Sunshine State and published some of the first US interviews with the likes of Aphex Twin, Moby, Orbital, The Orb, The Shamen, The Prodigy, Richie Hawtin, Laurent Garnier, Autechre and loads more that you may have never heard of or, even heard.

At the end of 1994, TRiP published its final issue. I left Tampa for New York soon after, accepting a role as Director of A&R at Astralwerks and truly starting my journey on the business side of electronic dance music.

Fast-forward 30+ years, and looking back on my long career, dance music culture has come a long way, baby.

Going back through the back issues, I found myself in a space of nostalgia for when this music and culture was shiny, fresh, and new. Before it all became fully monetized and more about social media followers rather than the dancefloor. They captured a positive sense of both the pre and early internet community at a time of wide-eyed excitement and optimism in what felt like a movement for cultural change.

With gratitude and profound thanks to the following for your love, support, inspiration or friendship during those years (and beyond), I'd like to thank: Glenn Boothe, Sioux Z & formula PR, Brian Long, Richie Hawtin, John Acquaviva, Marci Weber, Ramon Wells, Matt E. Silver, Stace Bass, Doc Martin, Mr.C, Hallucination Records/ Rabbit In The Moon crew, The Stickmen, Alan D. Oldham, Mad Mike Banks, Sunshine Jones, Moby, Rob & Sean (Autechre), Laurent Garnier, Jackie Rosquete-Dwyer, Jonah & Billee Sharp, Phil & Paul Hartnoll, Mark Gage, Gavin Hardkiss, Mixmaster Morris, Charles Uzzell-Edwards, Tom Middleton, Raymond Roker, Grumptronix, DJ THREE and Jay Ahern.

Very special thanks to DJ DB and Sean from Blurring Books for making this project come to life.

RIP Pete Namlook, Caspar Pound, Terence McKenna, and Scott Hardkiss.

–
Peter Wohelski

01

PREMIER ISSUE!!!!
PREMIER ISSUE!!!!
PREMIER ISSUE!!!!
PREMIER ISSUE!!!!
TRiP
SHAMEN
PROGENY HITS TAMPA
Vinyl Solution
Rave Effects
Record Reviews
N-Joi
Altern 8
Saint Etienne
LFO
Del
Tim Dog
Galliano
THE BAY AREA'S FIRST UPFRONT DANCE CULTURE FANZINE!

CONTENTS

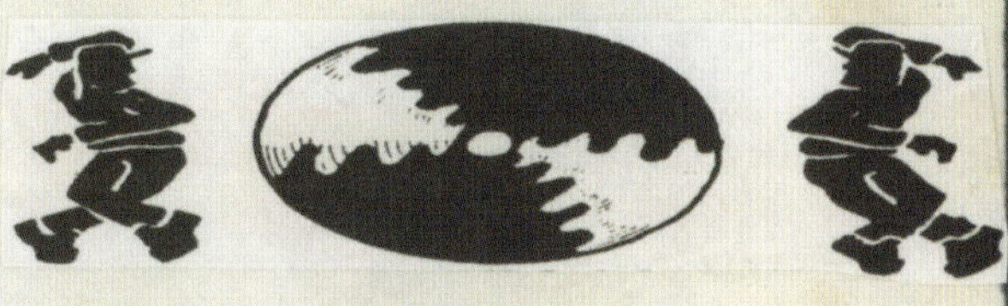

TRiP MAGAZEEN
100 E. Martin Luther King Blvd.
Suite # 10
Tampa, Florida 33603
U.S.A.
(813).238.0310

FEET ff FIRST

Welcome to the first issue of **TRiP MAGAZEEN;** I hope you enjoy reading this as much as I have enjoyed putting it together. It's definitely been a labour of love.

The Bay Area's underground dance scene has always, for the most part, been very small but strong. It's not Miami, New York, or Los Angeles, but there are a few handfuls of people dedicated to cultivating a fruitful scene here. The success of recent upfront dance events in the area over the past six months (808 State Raven Productions' one-nighter over the holidays, The Shamen' Progeny tour, and Quadrophonia) has certainly proved that there is a growing audience looking for an alternative to "alternative".

"Alternative" music as we know it is dead. With major labels scouring the States for the next Nirvana that they can crossover to rock radio, the musically adventurous are searching for that "Next Big Thing". They will have to look to dance music to find that edge. The 1990's are the the Decade of Dance-Indie, Techno/ Rave, House, Hip-hop, reggae/ world beat... It is this music that **now** has the edge, that punk esthetic and a Do-It-Yourself mentality.

It is this new cutting edge that **TRiP MAGAZEEN** is dedicated to reflecting, regardless of whether it comes from Tampa

continued on Page 2

continued from Page 15

still dissing Compton, your favorite Niggaz 4 Life-NWA, and dropping the facts that East Coast rappers aren't all new school daisy-wavers.

BLACK SHEEP-"Wolf In Sheep's Clothing" (Mercury)

The Native Tongues finally air thier dirty laundry and let the lowlives of the family out to play-the Black Sheep. Their massive debut has all the qualities of their higher profile siblings-jazzy, funky fresh beats, dope breaks, and clever rhymes-until you get to the subject matter...

INDIE-DANCE/ALTERNATIVE 12"/ep

AQUANETTAS-"Whoa!" (Major Label)

continued on Page 6

FEET ff FIRST

the U.S., or abroad. If you have any comments or suggestions, please feel free to write them down and send them to the address listed. It's your 'zine too.

Respect is due to these people/orgaizations for helping to bring **TRiP** to fruition: my mates at **RaveSeen Magazeen/UK** for agreeing to hook up with us to bridge the gap over the Atlantic, making both scenes stronger (we'll be sharing some advertising, information, and feature stories); **BOYS' OWN, GEAR, the Housin' Authority @ Eastern Bloc, Rosee at KISS**, and **Juan Kerr and the "Uranium Orchids" posse** (you know who you are!) for their advice and support. Cheers!!!

HYPE HYPE HYPE HYPE HYPE

...Rave Flash!!! **N-JOI** ("Mind-flux") will be doing a P.A. in MIami during the Winter Music Conference, March 24-28. Call WMC for more information: (305)-563-4444....As the rumours have suggested for months, **THIRD BASS** have broken up. **MC SERCH** has already begun work on a solo lp with **MUGGS** of **CYPRESS HILL**, and the **SD50's** working on tracks. **PRIME MINISTER PETE NICE** and **DJ RICHIE RICH** will stay together, producing other acts and culling material for a possible solo project for Pete....At press time, word was that a licensing deal involving U.K. indie **VINYL SOLUTION** and **SONY MUSIC** had been completed. Details were not available, but look for domestic releases from **EON, BIZARRE, INC., MIDI RAIN,** and other acts on the London-based indie soon. (Also check out the profile on the label elsewhere in this issue!)....**LEEDS** is the current club capital of the U.K. with several kickin' club nights like **ORGANIK, BACK TO BASICS, THE GALLERY,** and**THE ARK.** The North Rises Again!....Holland's **FIERCE RULING DIVA** ("Rubb It In") will be doing P.A.'s across America in late March/early April-hopefully they'll reach Tampa. Fingers crossed!....**HUMAN RESOURCE'S** essential rave track **"DOMINATOR"** just got picked up by **LONDON RECORDS** for some serious duckets....Cleve land is the site for **RAPFEST '92,** a convention designed to promote and encourage the growth of hip-hop music. To be held June 17-21, early registration is an affordable $150. Call (216)-292-9492 for info....Germany's rave communities are holding chillout nights with new age and classical music on Thursdays and Sundays-a nice prelude to the massive raving madness on Fridays and Saturdays....The rage for some U.K. ravers is taking an air mask and smearing it with **VICKS VAPO-RUB** and wearing it wearing it while raving. It apparently produces quite the top buzz....Sheffield's **LFO** are busy remixing **AFRIKA BAMBAATAA'S** classic **"PLANET ROCK"** for their U.S. label **TOMMY BOY;** the duo are also preparing to remix tracks for **THE SUGARCUBES(?), YOUNG GODS,** and **DEPECHE MODE(!)** as well as doing a project with the legendary **KRAFTWERK....**

Vinyl Solution

Initially starting out as a rock-music shop in Hereford Rd W11 about 12 years ago, Vinyl Solution has grown into one of the most respected and creative innovators amongst London's independent record labels. The shop is now on the Portobello Rd with the label based upstairs. John Saul Kane arrived at Vinyl Solution about five years ago with a demo from which came his first single "Grim Death". He has since then been instrumental in giving what was once a rock label, equal status and recognition as an indie/dance label.

During the last twelve months Vinyl Solution have come and come again with a succession of releases which regardless of how many records were sold, have made people stand up and take notice. **John Saul Kane** works as an all-round consultant for the label and has along the way signed a number of artists including **Cash Crew** who have since been signed to Virgin Records & **Johny Rocca aka Midi Rain** who has also played a key part in furthering the name of the label.

GUNSHOT

Midi Rain have recently released their third track for Vinyl Solution **"Always"**. The first two tracks were **"The Crack Train"** which was released back in July, shortly followed by **"Eyes"**.

VINYL SOLUTION

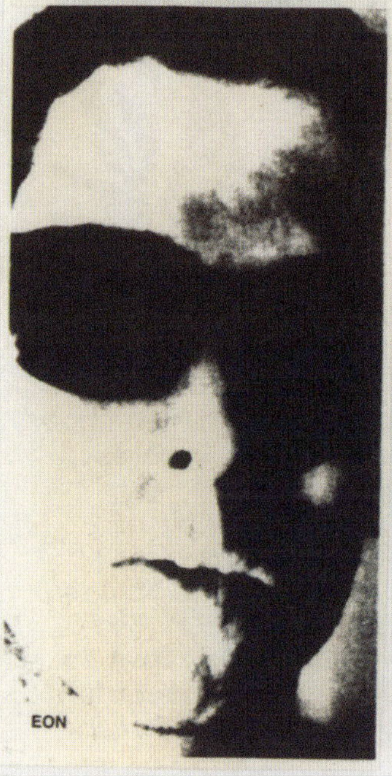
EON

John Saul Kane's creativity and slightly macabre imagination have assisted his more recent signings in developing strong musical identities of their own. Artists such as Depth Charge, **Gunshot** and **Eon**. He has also worked with artists outside the label such as **S-Express** and **Bomb The Bass.**

The Depth Charge vs Silver Fox 12" released back in August was boldly original with sampled extracts from a Japanese B-movie and featuring rapid fire vocals from MC Alkaline of Gunshot. The record didn't do that well, probably because it was hard to bag. This scenario seems to be stunting the creativity of would-be musical innovators throughout the industry. If Vinyl Solution can stand firm and continue to produce the same quality and original sounds, they're in serious danger of creating a whole new scene of their own.

JOHN SAUL KANE

cont. next page

VINYL SOLUTION

Maybe when the flood of formularised raver-friendly music dies down, we can replace it with simply 'good music'.

John Saul Kane: *Part of the problem lies in the fact that all the people that work in the record shops are dj's, and dj's are real snobs who only play their own particular type of music. The same records are getting played in the clubs, played on the radio and are plugged by the same dj's in the shops. So anything that's a bit different or unusual gets passed over.*

Another Vinyl Solution prodigy is **Eon**. Eon has been around for a long time as a house dj and is highly respected as such. He gained recent recognition as a recording artist following the release of his first single this year which was the 12" **"Fear/The Mindkiller"**. He has since been working on the new S-Express 12" **"Trumpets"** as well as his new single "Basketcase", both of which are due for release very soon. Eon has also just done the remix for Midi Rain's "Always".

VINYL SOLUTION

East London-based **Gunshot** are another example of the broad music policy now being adopted by the label. Gunshot's latest single **"Clear From Present Danger"** was released mid-November. This followed their previous 12" **"Crime Story"** which achieved high indie and dance chart placings, a number of TV appearances and a Peel session.

The huge success of northern chartstorming **Bizarre Inc**. will hopefully open the way for the other acts to come through. Their style of commercial rave-friendly music is unusual for Vinyl Solution but has placed them in the top 10 Network chart twice, first with **"Such A Feeling"** which reached number 9 and more recently with the re-release of **"Playing With Knives"** which reached number 4.

During the past 12 monthS Vinyl Solution have gone from strength to strength and I'm sure this is just the beginning.

BIZARRE INC.

On their new single New York' Aquanettas go for a looser, more jangly indie feel compared to the Stones-y 1989 lp "Love With The Proper Stranger". Primal Scream's Andrew Innes turns in a psychedelic, almost "Loaded"-like remix that will definitely turn the heads of both college radio and alternative dance floor jocks. A fresh-sounding pleasant surprise worth a couple spin for sure!

SAINT ETIENNE-FOXBASE ALPHA
(Warner Bros.)
Team up two ex-Melody Maker journos wotha pristinely pure female vocalist, stir in cool beats, mesmerizing grooves, senseless soundbites, top with a liberal serving of indie-pop sensibility, and sprinkle lightly with English dance culture. Voila! You have Saint Etienne. This is one of the landmark records of 1991, along with "Screamadelica" and "Blue Lines".

A Raver's Guide To Lights and Lazers

Lights, lazers and effects are an integral part of any rave. The wise promoter knows that the company he chooses (from nearly 100) must be capable of using all the effects to their full extent and be able to install the system safely as lighting can be very, very dangerous. However, it seems to be common practice for some organizations to list as many effects on their flyer as possible, to try to fool their public into believing that the light show is worth seeing. After all, how many of you actually know what all those terms mean?

ROBOZAPS - An intelligent light with a beam that can be rotated, via a mirror through 360 colour and brightness can be altered. All intelligent lights can be programmed to suit the venue, sweep to the music and make patterns.

GOLDENSCANS - The state of the Art Lighting effect for raves, as it is very bright and very fast. A standard MK 2 Goldenscan has 6 colours, 6 patterns and the beam can be adjusted from a pinhead to a full flood. They will also stobe and a good operator can use them to create an excellent show.

SUPERSCANS - As above, but even better as they have prisms which defract the light.

GOBOSCANS - Like a roboscan but with gobos (pieces of plastic) inside that make a pattern.

FANS - A single light that comes out as a flat sheet. Quite effective when used with a smoke machine.

STROBE FLOWERS - The rave effect - lots of fingers of light but nothing special.

ARCLINES - Tubes 1.8 or 1.0 metre long that glow in U.V. light with mini strobes inside giving a pulsing light. They are arranged in patterns or used to accentuate certain areas such as the stage. They give the best effect when hung just out of sight above head height.

STROBES - unnecessary to list on a flyer as everyone has them.

TERRASTROBES - The brightest, smallest, most controllable and most reliable of the strobes.

U.V. GUNS - A rave isn't a rave without ultraviolet light. The guns are the brightest.

VARI-LIGHTS - A trade name for the ultimate effect. They differ from other intelligent lights as the whole light moves, not just a mirror. They are the brightest the fastest and the most progammable with the most patterns and colours. The company is owned by Phil Collins and as they are supplied with an operator they are very expensive to hire. Therefore only the best raves will have them.

MULTI-COLOURED-LIGHT SHOW - Everything is even if you only have 4 coloured light bulbs that you flick on and off.

MULTI-COLOURED LAZERS - A lazer is a tube that electrifies gases that put out a beam of light. The effect given depends on the skill of the operator. Lazers are usually coloured green, blue and cyan but more are possible. The Omnicron system is probably the best.

3-D HOLOGRAPHIC SYSTEM - Hasn't been invented yet, but an excellent effect can be obtained by projecting the lazer onto a fine mesh. True holographs are projected into thin air.

FIBRE-OPTIC SYSTEM - Very thing glass tubes that are very expensive and not very reliable.

BUBBLE MACHINES - The bubbles look wicked but they burst and make the dance floor dangerously slippery. Everything (including you) becomes horribly sticky. A good production company would not use them.

A good light show should be carefully planned and installed, by a company that understands how a rave works. The lights and lazers should work with the music to get you up and keep you moving all through the night.

SHAMEN hit Tampa with Pl

Nineteen ninety-one was a year of both agony and ecstacy for the **Shamen:** the group's latest U.K. lp **En-Tact** was both a domestic and import smash and licensed by Epic Records for a Fall release; their nightlong traveling rave/live concerts-"**Synergy**"- was wowing audiences throughout the U.K., Europe, and even the Soviet Union; and were preparing to release what was expected to be the Scottish dance outfit's most successful single to date, a remixed version of "Pro-gen" entitled "Move Any Mountain".

Then it all shattered. Bassist and cofounder **Will Sin(nott)** drowned in a swimming accident in Tenerife after shooting the video for "Move Any Mountain". A tragic blow to a band that was on the verge of changing the face of music in the States, a blow that left founder **Colin Angus** with the decision to pack it in or continue on.

Angus chose to continue on. "The plan was there, and the positive spirit had been there for the past two years. I know that Will would have wanted the Shamen to go on, as the name meant a lot to him. It's been tough...I honestly believe Will would've wanted all this."

"This" was a Number One UK single with "Mountain"; the reformation of the group with London DJ/rapper **Mr. C** joining as well as a new female vocalist, **Cheryl Melder**; the

U.S. release of **En-Tact**, "Mountain" yielding a #1 Club hit and Top 40 crossover cut; and the updating of the Shamen live experience, now called **"Progeny"**. The gigs toured the U.K. to massive reviews and packed venues with special guests **Cabaret Voltaire**, **Meat Beat Manifesto**, and **Orbital** playing some dates.

Nineteen Ninety-two. The Shamen bring **Progeny** to the States for almost three weeks of raving madness. "We got the idea when we moved out to London in '88 and met Mr.C at some acid house parties he was doing," Colin explains, "seeing the basic model of that at his and other events

ROGENY'S techno madness

where the club had a high-tech light show and the beat went on all night..."

This cavalcade of DJ's, MC's, and artists made its way to the Bay area at the beginning of February, giving Tampa's rave community more than a taste of the U.K. Rave Experience. Manning the wheels of steel on the night were local guest drivers **DJ Steve(DNA/Evolution)**, Miami's **DJ Chang**(who got the headstrong crowd kickin' with a serious set of bangin' 'ardcore) cooling things down on the house tip was **DJ3**(Tampa) with a surprise p.a. from **Machine Said's Dave Christophere**, who captivated the punters with a gyrating belly dancer during their set.

After a short break, New York's **Moby** came on and whipped the hardcore throng into a frenzy with a selection of his tracks-**"Go!"**, **"Drug Fits The Face"**, **"Mobility"**, **"Voodoo Child"**, and others. Most people in attendance came away from the night buzzing about this raging p.a. Look for anther massive set from Mr. Hall at the upcoming **Raven Productions** one-nighter at the end of March in Tampa.

The Shamen's Mr.C then took to the decks with a groovin' selection of house and garage right up until the Shamen hit the stage. Not like a typical p.a., with performers lip-synching to pre-recorded tapes of their hits, a fully-equipped Shamen came on about Midnight and jumped into an hour-long wave of tracks from **En-Tact** and two new songs.

After the Shamen's set, **Moby** returned, this time on the decks, for a short set of bodyburning hardcore to move the crowd into the morning hours with the big beats.

Techno/Rave is exploding across America at a rapid rate thanks to groups like the **Shamen** and the **Progeny** live concept. Exposing the alternative crowd as well as the already initiated to the true rave concept can only fare well for the rave community.

RECORD REVIEWS

TECHNO/RAVE

12"/ep

SHAMEN-"Make It Mine" (Epic)
Glasgow's finest is back with another kickin' set of remixes on this CD5". Nine mixes in all; 2 from the original import, 2 by **Pro-gress**, 3 from **Moby**, as well as self-produced club and radio mixes. Moby radically reworks the tracks, taking a more bleepy, subsonic almost Detroit approach; Manchester's Pro-gress slows it down a touch-mixing up the guitar for an industrial feel.

N-JOI-"Mindflux" ep (RCA)
The most successful techno act to date returns with "Mindflux a serious bass-burning galloper for the whistle posse-no sell out here. Also included is another version of the now-classic "Malfunction" and two tracks from the "Adrenalin" ep "Phoenix" and "Rhythm Zone", both strong midtempo chewns. Nice one, top one... already sorted.

BASSHEADS-"Is There Anybody Out There" (deConstruction/UK)
With all but one sample re-recorded from its white label day this atmospheric, moody, episodic, twittering, jangling, rock-riffed, Pink Floyd sampled, Afrika Bambaataa chanted track makes you want to "Just get up and dance." A top 10 U.K. hit.

ALTERN 8-"ACTIV 8" ep (Network/UK)
An ancient MC Crazy Claire sample kicks off this surging, bleeping 130 bpm raver in its thunderous Belgian style; also check out the stark frantic Vix-Vapo Mix, plus the droning "Move My Body". Fuckin' 'ardcore innit, mate?

U.H.F.-"U.H.F." ep (XL/UK)
Richard M. Hall=Moby=U.H.F. Yes, the prolific Moby is at it again, churning out another blasting ep; this time under the name U.H.F. The title track is a scratching, synth-buzzing chugger with a nice italo-piano break; "Peacehead" is a wicked thumper with a wobbly male vocal sample; "Everything" kicks right in, manic as hell with a coolin' piano line, noting everything will be all right. Chuck D urges "come on" and the shit hits again; "Protect Write" goes minimal with a pulsing techno groove, crashing cymbals sizzling over the top. A very crisp biscuit.

LFO-"Love Is The Message/Tan Ta Ra" (Tommy Boy)
This latest offering from LFO features two remixes from the Sheffield duo's debut lp, **Frequencies**. Eric Kupper does a nice job with "Love"'s Beware of Bass mix, turning in a more melodic and pumping vocal-oriented track, while Moby delivers a brilliant chunk of bouncy E-funk for the insomniacs with "Tan Ta Ra".

X-101-"X-101" ep (Mute/Tresor/ Black Market-UK)
This purely instrumental rave six-pack comes from Detroit's UR label by way of Tresor Records, Berlin. A UR/The Vision produces ep, X-101 ranges from burbling tracks like "Sonic Destroyer", the smoothly pumping "Rave New World", a wobbly "G-Force", and the jittery, throbbing "Whatever Happen To Peace". Not overly Detroit to be too cold, yet just Belgian enough to push to groove. A fine ep.

SHAFT-"Roobarb and Custard" (Great Asset/ffrr-UK)
The first release from **ffrr**'s new hardcore label, **Great Asset** is a pounding "Charly"-like track with its cartoon sample and frantic piano break and "gonna make it better" diva wail. The Dr. Trip and Bob Bolts mix moves while the flip side's Apple Crumble mix is a bit more atmospheric. A right good tune.

SUPEREAL-"Body Medusa" (Tribal America)
This fierce hi-hat and wah-wah chugger builds gradually into a mesmerizing jittering track. In three forms: a surging mix by hot-at-the-moment **Leftfield,** the group's own industrial/rave Out of Your Body mix (with Die Warzau samples), and a whispering reggae flutterer by ex-RSW mate Karl Bonnie. A recommended biscuit.

KA-22-"Metamorphism" ep (Radikal)
Ok, so they nicked samples from KLF, N-Joi, and Quadrophonia; I still like this derivitive driver. There is good and bad derivative hardcore and this is pretty good, I'm ashamed to admit. The bleepy flip nicks a Sweet Exorcist sample... A nice ep, but certainly not essential.

RECKLESS-"Reckless Karnage" (Pulse 8/UK)
The crowd noise grows and the voice says, "We're going to do a song you've heard before," yeah, no kidding. The first hardcore offering from the label that brought you Rozalla and Friends of Matthew isn't bad, although the seasoned ear easily locates the nicely programmed Quadrophonia samples and makes it hard to find this one a stunner.

LP/COMPILATIONS

VARIOUS ARTISTS-PAROXYSM (Mute/ Black Market)
Par-ox-ysm: A sudden fit, attack, or convulsion (like dancing?). This compilation from the Black Market label, licensed by Mute, features 6 artists from the U.K. and U.S. that reflect the many variations of house found at London raves: techno, acid, bleep, hip-hop, and ragga. A strong, diverse compilation that is a must listen for a true perspective on the U.K. dance scene.

RECORD REVIEWS

V/A-CHAMPION SOUND: THE BEST OF KICKIN' RECORDS, VOL. I (Kickin' UK)
A storming collection of top tracks from one of the U.K.'s up-and-coming hardcore techno labels. Only for the headstrong, **CHAMPION SOUND** features massive cuts from **Messiah, ZeroZero, Wishdokta,** and **The Scientist.** A not-to-be-missed compilation for the non-posing insomniacs.

QUADROPHONIA-COZMIC JAM (RCA)
After several months of availability on import, Quadrophonia's highly anticipated debut hits record racks domestically- and pretty well worth the wait. The full-length offering from this half-Dutch/half-Belgian duo, Oliver Abbeloos (also 1/2 of techno innovators T-99) and Lucien Foort, serves up a selection of bangin' Belgian 'ardcore here. All in all, a record chock full of chewns to keep the techno- boffins jumpin' and pumpin' for months to come.

ORB-AUBREY MIXES: THE ULTRA-WORLD EXCURSIONS (WAU! Mr. Modo Big Life/UK)
Released in Late November 1991 and deleted the day of its rel ease, this Orb collectors item and companion to the double lp/cd/cassette, "Adventures..." features alternate versions and never released remixes of your favorite Orb tracks. With mixes by Steve Hillage (Gong, System 7), Youth, Jimi Cauty of KLF, Pal Joey, and Ready Made, **Aubrey Mixes** explores the universe travelled by **Adventures** and reaches deeper into musical bliss. **(Editor's note:** As we went to press, Caroline Records licensed **Aubrey Mixes** for a U.S. release**)**

V/A-Techno/Rave, Phase One (Invasion)
This compilation, licensed primarily from the **Lower East Side** and **Midtown** labels, showcases 11 (13 on CD) tracks from where many say is the techno capital of the world-Holland. **Phase One** is a whirlwind of Techno hits featuring **Turntable Terror's "Break"** (the first indie label track to go Top 10 in Billboard's club chart), the U.K. smash from **Fierce Ruling Diva-"Rubb It In"**, as well as cuts from**Frequency** and **Incubus** The liner notes are by DMR's Matt E. Silver and is a veritable who's who in U.S. rave culture... Hardcore that is strictly underground- if you know the score you'll pick up this comp.

HOUSE/GARAGE/ACID JAZZ/R&B

12"/ep

REESE PROJECT-"Direct Me" (Giant)
Techno innovator Kevin "Master Reese" Saunderson is back with this hot slab licensed from his KMS label. "Direct's" 5 mixes range from

RECORD REVIEWS

Joey Negro's garage-y Disco Blend Mix to the original stunner by UR. The headstrong may prefer the Reese Riot Mix or the bonus track, "Station of the Groove."

HELEN BRUNER-"Gimme Real Love" (Cardiac)
A smooth, garage-y, piano-driven groover from this soulful sister from Philly. Produced, arranged, and mixed by Helen and containing **no** samples, this track is climbing the **Mixmag U.K. Buzz Chart.** The **TRiP** jury is out on this one, it could sneak up on you...

KYM SIMS-"Too Blind To See It" (Atco)
Yo, this record is the shit! A bouncy midtempo cut, it was made for radio and garage dj's with its smooth pop feel. It has a hook that will grab you by the shorts and I guarantee you'll be singing the chorus of this Top 5 U.K. smash for days! Steve "Silk" Hurley does it again...

ROBYN SPRINGER-"Forever And Ever" (Cardiac)
Hot and funky is the best way to describe Robyn Springer's debut single on Cardiac. Smooth, colorful vocals, a strong drum groove, swwet harmonies, and a jazzy flute solo make this track a winner **TRiP** gives thumbs to the Raw Mix.

GALLIANO-"Jus' Reach" (Talkin Loud/4th & Broadway)
One of the hottest musical trends coming out of the U.K. at the moment is Acid Jazz. Acid jazz is a fusion of jazz hip-hop, and rare groove. Labels like Acid Jazz and Gilles Peterson's Talkin' Loud have brought these cool sounds into the limelight with artists like **Brand New Heavies Young Disciples, Omar, and Galliano.** Their latest 12", "Jus' Reach"; released domest ically, is lacking the usual amount of jazz rap on previous releases as the song jogs thr ough girls hollering and a "Nah na-na Na Nah" chant. The remixes, by Nellee Hooper (Soul II Soul) and Mick Talbot(The Jam) are much cooler on the jazz-funk tip. If you like this, you may want to check out Galliano's lp, **In Search Of The 13th Note.**

RECORD REVIEWS

LP/COMP.

CeCe PENISTON-FINALLY (A&M)
This virtual unknown emerged from the Phoenix, AZ heat and stormed onto the scene with her debut 12" "We've Got A Love Thang" (a #1 U.K. and U.S. club hit) and the recently released second single, "Finally"- also the title of her debut lp. **Finally**-the lp features the production and remix talents of Steve "Silk" Hurley and Daviv Morales, but it's Peniston's angelic, yet soulful voice that shines throughout slower cuts like "Inside That I Cried" and set the uptempo tracks apart from the pack.

MUSTO & BONES-THE FUTURE IS OURS (Citybeat/RCA)
Solid and diverse. That's how one describes the debut of remixers extraordinaire Tommy Musto and Frankie Bones **THE FUTURE IS OURS**. After truckloads of remix and production work, this dynamic duo put their reputations on the line and crank out an upfront diverse lp-from almost hardcore techno("Passion Devotion) piano-driven house("Don't Give Up on My Lovin"), to downtempo tracks("Time Is Running Out"). While cohesive and tight, this record will be sorely underappreciated and overlooked, buried in the soul or rap sections of your favorite record shop. That's sad because although **FUTURE** isn't the biggest sound around, it's an offering that deserves a listen.

HIP-HOP

12"/ep

PUBLIC ENEMY-"Shut 'Em Down" (Def Jam/Columbia)
DJ Pete Rock remixes the mighty P.E. on the jazz tip with "Shut 'Em Down." Pete goes subtler than the original, but Chuck D kicks the ballistics just the same. The CD5" also includes mixes of the controversial "By The Time I Get To Arizona," and a cool Breakapella remix of "Shut" that's perfect sampling fare.

SISTER SOULJAH-"The Hate That Hate Produced" (Epic)
Public Enemy's newest member Sister Souljah (aka Lisa Williamson) minces no words and drops some heavy science with writing and production assistance from the Bomb Squad's Eric "Vietnam" Sadler.

DEFINITION OF SOUND-"Moira Jane's Cafe" (Cardiac)
On the debut, "Love and Life" U.K. musical chameleons Definition of Sound adapt Van Morrison's "Gloria" to a hiphop beat in their funky ode to what may be a restaurant or soul kitchen of legend, Moira Jane's Cafe. But this is a remix and also where the comparison ends. E-Smoove turns in a somewhat rammed and mellow Groovy Mix, but the house-treated track loses

its soul.

TRUE CULTURE-"It's So Good, It's Bad" (Cardiac)
Hailing from the Bronx but with roots in Kingston, Jamaica, rappers True Culture exp lore the intermingling relationship between hip-hop and reggae. Their debut 12", "It's So Good..." nicely handles both styles with the hard rap and well-coordinated samples of the Hip-Hop Mix while the duo's spicy ragga vibe comes through loud and clear on the Club Mix.

LP/COMPILATIONS

DEL THE fUNKee HOMOSAPIEN-"I Wish My Brother George Was Here" (Elektra)
This lp, co-created with his cousin Ice Cube, is no hype. Delbert is definitely one funky homosapien; matching some of the dopest loops around to some serious but fun rhymes there are lots of good tracks here. The highlight has to be the jaunty "Mistadobalina", about an uncool bloke named Mr. Bob Dobalina. This record is a winner and shows that new schoolers can flow and not be from New York.

TIM DOG-"Penicillin On Wax" (Ruffhouse/Columbia)
Striaght out of the motherfuckin' Bronx and takin' no shorts, "Penicillin On Wax" proves that Tim Dog's no one-trick pony, picking up where "Fuck Compton" left off. He's

continued on Page 2

Clubbers DIARY

If you have an event or a club night that you would like listed in TRiP's Clubber's Diary, please send along a flyer or release about your event or night to the usual address.

ONE NIGHT EVENTS

SENSORY OVERLOAD-Saturday, March 21 @ Ritz Theatre, 1503 E. 7th Ave, Ybor City. Featuring a State-of-the Art light and sound system, smart bar, performance art, and more DJ's on the night: DJ3, Brian Brite, DJ Chang, and guests. 18 and over. $5 on the night.

MANIC TAMPA-Friday, March 27 Venue TBA. Featuring P.A.'s from **MOBY**. DJ's on the night: Moby, Charlie Casanova(NYC), Doc Martin(LA), and Florida's hardest DJ's. Price to be announced so keep your ears to the street. A Raven Production

WEEKLY CLUB NIGHTS

SUNDAY-

911, 911 N. Franklin St., Downtown Tampa, 224-0911. Upfront dance with DJ Bill Ward. 18 and over. $2 on the door.

BENNIGAN'S, @!@¢ Tyrone Blvd. St. Petersburg, 343-1075. Alternative dance. 21 and over.

MONDAY-

??????

TUESDAY-

M-PLODE@BOYS VIDEO & DANCE, $(!) E. Busch Blvd., Tampa, 985-2837. Techno/Rave with DJ Joe Billi. 18 and over. $3 on the door.

DISCO INFERNO@RITZ THEATRE, 1503 E. 7th Ave., Ybor City, 247-3319. Disco and Acid with Mido on the decks. 18 & over. $1.00 on the door.

BIARRITZ, 23138 U.S. 19 N., Clearwater, 799-3063. Alternative dance with DJ Bill Ardiff. 18 and over. $1, 21 and over on the door.

WEDNESDAY-

??????

THURSDAY-

TRACKS, 1430 E. 7th Ave., Ybor City, 247-2711. Techno/ Rave. $3.00 on the door, Free before 10 pm for over 21 18 and over.

FRIDAY-

CHANNEL ZERO @ CLUB DETROIT, 16 2nd St. N., St. Petersburg 896-1244. House and Techno/ Rave. 18 and over.

DNA, 14975 N. Nebraska Ave, Tampa, 971-DNA1. Alternative dance with DJ Steve. All ages. $5 on the night.

SATURDAY-

EVOLUTION, 1902 E. 7th Ave., Ybor City, 248-8888. Alternative dance with DJ Steve. 18 and over. $5, 18-20; $3, 21+ on the door.

TRiP MAGAZEEN
100 E. MLK BLVD.
SUITE #10
TAMPA, FLORIDA 33603
U.S.A.

POSTMASTER: DATED MATERIAL....PLEASE RUSH

02

The Bay Area's First Upfront
Dance Culture Fanzine!!
TRiP
Vol. I, # 2
A conversation with
MOBY
Instinct Records
Ybor City Gets Mental
Record Reviews
SL 2
Church Of Extacy
Yothu Yindi
Phuture
Massive Attack
F.U.-Schnickens
Inter-Mix
Win A Vinyl Solution Label Sampler CD! Details Inside!

Win a Vinyl Solution Label Sampler CD

Last issue **TRiP** reported that London-based indie **Vinyl Solution** had signed a U.S. licensing deal with Columbia Records Courtesy of Columbia, **TRiP** has one (1) copy of a **promo only** CD sampler with tracks by **Eon, Bizarre, Inc.**, and **Midi Rain** to give away to the lucky raver who can name **one song** from **each** of these acts. Simple, huh?

Send your answers to **TRiP** HQ at the address on the next page, **Attn: Vinyl Solution Contest.** The first person to correctly answer will win this nifty promo gem. Make sure to include your name,address and phone #! The winner will be notified by phone and their name will be announced in the next issue of **TRiP MAGAZEEN...**

Instinct

cont. from page 7

eper and more ambient side of house; one of its anchor acts is the soulful **Optimystic.**

What's next in the plan for World Domination with this multi-faceted dance label? Currently, the label is "aggressively seeking and signing acts" for its roster. With the hardcore techno boom here in America, is the label looking to sign more U.S. acts? "Definitely. It's just been within the past two months that I've been reeiving demo tapes (from good U.S. acts)." states Hoffman.

Also "look for some big announcements between Instinct and **Kickin'/U.K.** in the near future," baits Jared. A U.S. licensing deal, maybe? "Big announcements," is all he'll say, not wanting to give too much away.

As far as new music, **Moby** is putting the finishing touches on his debut album, to be released at the beginning of June. Instinct will also be releasing a second **This Is Acid Jazz** compilation. **Sonic** will also be releasing several compilations including **Techno Sonic, Vol.2**, in addition to new signings **Ground Level** (Australia) and **Visual Attack** (U.K.). **Optimystic** will release more music on **Liquid** for Summer 1992.

Athough Instinct has come a long way in three years, the artist-oriented, big label approach of this indie is sure to be just the beginning of grander things to come out of this versatile dance label.

CONTENTS

Vol. I, Number 2

TRiP MAGAZEEN
100 E. MLK Boulevard
Suite #10
Tampa, Florida 33603
U.S.A.
(813).238.0310

EDITOR: Peter Wohelski

FEET ff FIRST

Here we are again, Round Two of this thing called **TRiP Magazeen...** To everyone who rang and all the mental Tampa Bay ravers I spoke with that gave feedback on **TRiP #1**- A big cheers and thanks!

Some random observations; In the past six weeks alone there's been three one-night events, a few good club nights and a bangin' promo party. We're not London, but I'm st- arting to believe that we got it goin' on here. It's only a matter of time before we're really kickin'.

Nuff respect go out to the **Raven Productions** massive for their **Manic** one-nighter. I don't think they drew the crowd they expected, but the talent in the house was blind ing. Both **Doc Martin** and **Ch- arlie Casanova** tore shit up on the 1's & 2's and **Moby** was strong as usual. A top night.

Scene queen **Mother Tucker** hosted **"Mother's Rave"** at the Ritz in Ybor City a couple of weeks back. A much better ni ght than the **Sensory Overload** event The Ritz hosted almost a month previous, Mother and Her Children booked some ser- ious drivers that turned it out and grooved the party into the wee hours.

Apparently **Mother** will be hosting a weekly rave on Fridays at The Ritz begin- ning May 1. I've been saying this should happen since **808 State** came to town, although I'm not sure the scene is ready to support this on a weekly basis. I hope I'm wr- ong.

HYPE HYPE HYPE HYPE HYPE

....Funky 1991 breaktrough artists **BRAND NEW HEAVIES** have cut their second lp "completely live" to be released later this Spring. Called **BNH ULTIMATE BREAKS AND BEATS**, the lp features the lyrical talents of **GANG STARR, BLACK SHEEP, DE LA SOUL, MAIN SOURCE**, and **3RD BASS**....Congrats to **KEVWON** and **THE DON** of **DEFINITION OF SOUND** for their recent Billboard Dance Club #1 for "Moira Jane's Cafe"....**CHARISMA RECORDS** has acquired the entire catalog from **BOY GEORGE**'s **MORE PROTEIN** label The first release is a compilation of U.K. singles entitled **CLOSET CLASSICS VOL. I** featuring tracks from **e-zee posse, MC KINKY**, and **EVE GALLAGHER**....Gangsta rappers **ICE-T** and **ICE CUBE** co-star in a film called **LOOTERS**, set for a July 3 release....U.K. Techno whiz **THE PRODIGY** have signed to **ELEKTRA.** NO release date on the first U.S. 12", but rumour has it **TODD TERRY** may do the remix(?)....From London comes loads of news fromthe "Sound System Called **THE ORB**"; **DR. ALEX** and company have a new lp, **U.F.Orb** coming out shortly and is supposed to be Stateside in May with a new show of epic proportions; Alex also has projects in the works with some **dub reggae** artists and a collaboration with **KRAFTWERK** called **ORBWERK**....This year's **NEW MUSIC SEMINAR** (June 17-21, NYC) will have an expanded focus on dance music and a cap on registrants for a **"more promotionally effective atmosphere"**. Always an event, NMS is to be experienced at least once. For registration info, call (212) 473-4343....Rumour has it that techno pranksters**ALTERN 8** have/will sign with **VIRGIN AMERICA....L.A. RAVE PROMOTERS** have been selling balloons filled with **NITROUS OXIDE** for about $5 at events; unfortunately the L.A. rave community has had a dark shadow cast over it as authorities found rave flyers at the scene of a recent nitrous-related death.. Rapper **TIM DOG** is doing a remix of "Bronx Nigga", a track on his **PENICILLIN ON WAX** debut with **BLASTMASTER KRS-1**....Detroit Techno founding father **DERRICK MAY** is now a free agent in the U.S. and the inside track says he has an armload of top chewns ready to drop at the right offer....**RAVEN PRODUCTIONS** go back underground with **THEE RAVE-IN** on **MAY 31, 1992.** Keep your ears to the street for more info....Zimbabwean diva **ROZALLA's** just released debut lp may get scooped up by **EPIC** for a domestic release....**BHANGRA HOUSE**, a melding of **HOUSE** and **INDIAN** music has been popping up in London clubs, a reflection of the U.K.'s large Indian population....**EVOLUTION** brought in **XL RECORDINGS A&R MAN/DJ RICHARD RUSSELL** from London recently Russell is ½,along with XL's **NICK HAWKES**, of **KICKS LIKE A MULE** ("The Bouncer"); he mixed up the big beats along with regular DJ **STEVE MC CLURE....**

Raving Madness Storms Ybor

HARDCORE, YOU KNOW THE SCORE...-Moments from a raving weekend in Ybor City: From topleft, The E-implied flyer from **Mother's Rave,** DJ Chang (Miami) rips it on the 1's & 2's at Mother's Rave, At Evolution's XL Recordings Party, DJ Wayne C (St. Pete), XL's Richard Russell, and Evolution's Steve Mc Clure pose for **TRiP** before hitting the decks that night.

Instinct, Sonic, Liquid Music Beat The

Over the past three years New York-based Instinct Records has launched itself into the elite of American independent dance labels. Although known for spearheading the Techno/Rave explosion in the States with the breakthrough of singles by **Moby, Voodoo Child, Barracuda, and Brainstorm**(all created by one Richard M. Hall), Instinct is much more than just only a techno label but one with several identities.

Founded with a "naive, well-intentioned thought" out of "insanity" and "a lack of common sense" in 1989 by dance music writer/club runner/DJ Jared Hoffman and his partner Dave Brubaker, Instinct was originally an alternative indie-rock label. But seeing that indie-rock was already happening and, according to Hoffman, "Being a DJ, I was hearing so much great (dance) mu-

sic that we decided to focus on licensing tracks."

The label's first-ever release in Spring 1990 was "Never Stop" by seminal acid jazz group, **K-Collective.** The group soon split up, some members forming a band called **Brand New Heavies,** who re-recorded the track with a female vocalist for their debut lp. Instinct has continued to license and release this fusion of jazz, hip-hop, and rare groove music, although Hoffman feels it won't really take off on this side of the Atlantic. "As much as I love it, it's not really a breakthrough sound. It's too based in a retro movement, which is happening in England, but not here."

The success story of this young label, however, is **Moby.** Discovered on a tip from **Brand X** tipsheet editor **DJ Moneypenny,** the label signed him up in Fall of 1989 and a year later released the single **"Mobility"**; but it was the b-side, **"Go"**, a U.K. Club #1 that really placed Instinct on the map. **Moby** has also released projects for the label under the pseudonyms **Voodoo Child, Barracuda,** and **Brainstorm.** Why

Majors With A Big Label Approach

all the secrecy? Jared Hoffman explains, "We used all the different names as not to step on our own toes. There were such strong responses to each track that we wnated to be able to develop and build our own buzz for each record. By using the different names, we were able to do that and not kill the previous release"

In the three times **"Go"** has been released, (as a B-side, as an A-side, and its remixes), it has sold approximately 25,000 copies to date. Not bad for a strictly underground track, considering that on a popular level, **Right Said Fred's "I'm Too Sexy"**- a Billboard Pop Singles #1- has sold around 30,000 copies.

It is this sort of success in the past year that has allowed Instinct to make what Hoffman calls, "A massive leap forward." New distribution and the subsequent penetration into retail chains has only helped establish the label as a force in the marketplace.

So you may ask, despite this presence, how does an independent label like Instict compete against the major label's dance departments? It

doesn't. "With what we are doing, the majors would get no return on. They need a 5-15,000 copy committment for an artist to make their overhead. We are an artist-oriented, artist-driven label; we don't put out cheap releases with no promotion and no artwork. Everything we do is big label!", expounds Jared.

Besides acid jazz releases and Moby's amalgam of aliases, Instinct has licenced and released tracks from labels like **Low Spirit** (Germany), **Kickin'** (U.K.), and **Antler/Subway** (Belgium) among others. Not wnting to strap the Instinct imprint into one type of music, Hoffman and Brubaker began two raincoat labels to channel releases through- **Sonic Records** and **Liquid Music. Sonic** focuses on hardcore techno, recently releasing records by **Praga Khan, Church Of Extacy**, and **U.H.F.**- another Moby alias. **Liquid Music** concentrates on the de-

Instinct cont. on page 1

Socially Conscious Raver Gives A Breath

Richard Melville Hall. Not necessarily a name burning on the tip of every blissed out raver in America's tongue, is it? Let's try his nickname, derived from his relation to author Herman Melville- **Moby.** Ring a bell now? If not, it should.

Within the past two years this modest, somewhat soft-spoken, slight, white New Yorker has made a name for himself with dancefloor stormers like **"Go"** and tracks under such pseudonyms as **Voodoo Child, Barracuda**, and **Brainstorm.** Most successful as just Moby, he plans on killing off his aliases. "I may use them again, but for the time being, it's going to be Moby only. I want to encompass all my different types of music- from the really hard stuff to the garage-y, piano stuff; even the more atmospheric, non-rhythmic things.", replies Moby.

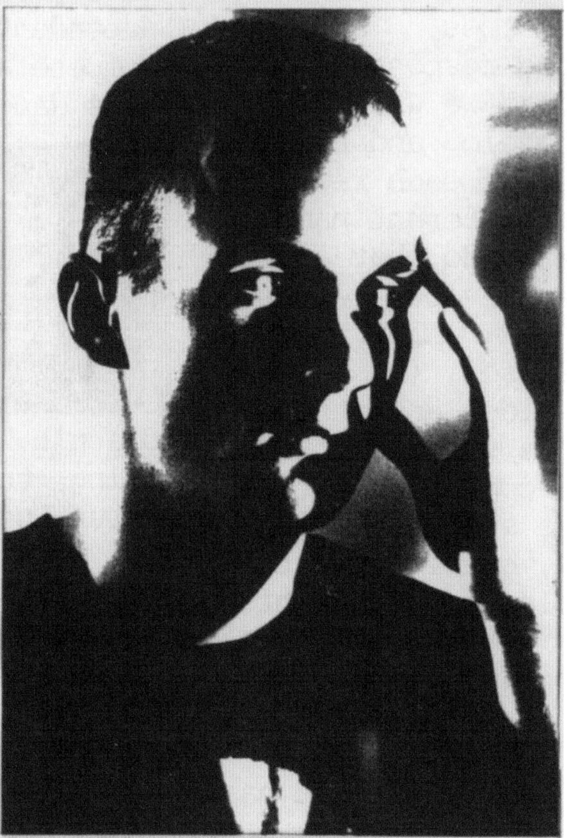

Atmospheric is a word that comes up quite often when talking with Moby, or even describing his music. Melancholy, too. Influenced by electronic music innovators **Brian Eno, Jean Michel Jarre,** and **Kraftwerk** along with early alternative fare such as **Echo & The Bunnymen, A Certain Ratio,** and **Joy Division,** it's easy to see where a track like **"Mobility"** gets its roots.

Not exclusively into one type of music, Moby was also brought up on old punk rock like **Bad Brains, Minor Threat,** and **Black Flag's "Damaged".** At 16, he also played bass for a New York punk band, the Vatican Commandos, and guest sang with **Flipper** when their singer was thrown in jail. "House music, or techno is the perfect synthesis of all these things. It's energetic, atmospheric, and intelligent at times. A lot is really stupid but at its best, it's a good introspective genre.", explains Moby.

After dropping out of college, Moby started DJ'ing about seven years ago. "I started off playing more alternative things, then industrial things. Then with house happening, I really got excited about that..." During that time he also lucked into a job spinning at New York's **Mars** club. "...I used to play a lot of hip-hop too- until I started actually listening to the lyrics.', admits Moby.

He doesn't DJ now on a regular basis, although he does do a taped monthly guest spot for Osaka, Japan's **Radio MARS.** "Some of the early shows, I'd be totally eclectic...now it's

Of Fresh Atmosphere

mainly the really hard techno and the really atmospheric. And some of the more disco-y stuff, like **K-Klass.**", reveals Moby.

Despite his busy schedule Moby goes out qiute a bit when he's home. When asked about DJ's that he likes, Moby replied, "I can't think of any off hand. (pause) **Repete** at **Limelight,** I have a good time dancing to him. He's not a very imaginative DJ but he works a crowd so well, almost like a craftsman."

The Top 10 popularity of "Go" in the U.K. has made this ex-philosophy major a most sought after name for remix work, having done tracks for recent tourmates **The Shamen, Pet Shop Boys, Orbital, LFO, Erasure, Fortran 5, N-Joi,** and **Recoil.** He also did a rap for a track on the Recoil album. "It was really fun, we did it in the studio with **Alan (Wilder of Depeche Mode-** Recoil is his solo project). It's sort of a socially conscious rap... I didn't see the point in having an opportunity of doing a rap on a record without using it as a way to communicate. It's very emotional.", Moby explained.

His remixes have a very distinct quality, sampling small bits of the track, recreating the rest himself. The end result is usually minimal as well as the "M-word" and the "A-word"- melancholy and atmospheric. "No matter how hard I try, I can't get away from it; I really like atmosheric things. So, I'm most satisfied with something that creates atmosphere.", admits Moby, almost apologetically.

Having been all over the U.S. and Europe in the past year or so, Moby has experienced dance culture virtually worldwide. He likes the U.K. for its energy, "although some things really bothered me... they're always looking out for the next new thing", but has found America to be the best. "The calibre of people in America into techno is the highest in the World.", percieves Moby.

For a long time critics have dismissed dance music as a reputable genre in the States, arguing that it's disposible and lacks artists or personalities behind the music. To allow techno to establish itself in the U.S., Moby feels this must change, "People aren't gonna go crazy over <u>**just**</u> songs. People like hype people like personality, people like videos. I know for me as a fan, I tend to like records that I know something about the person creating them. I gravitate towards... a **Derrick May** record or a **Joey Beltram,** where you know there's a personality attached to the music."

MOBY

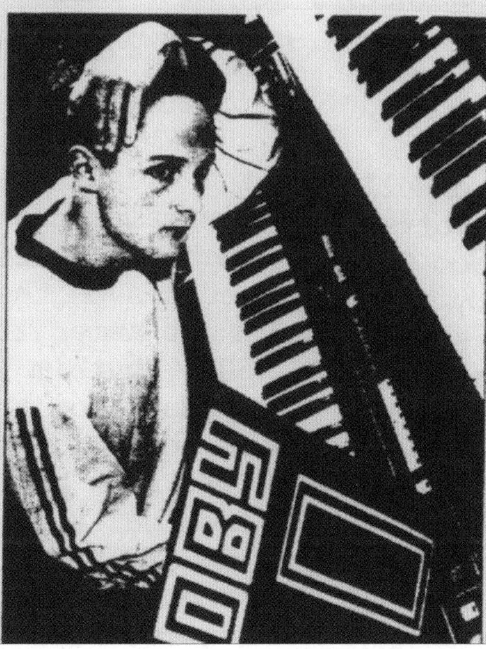

With that concept in mind, where does this lead the Techno Explosion in the future? "In America, a big crossover will come from the alternative and industrial communities... I sort of see Techno as being a little more sophisticated and Rave Culture as being a lot more fun. Recently I went to Gothic club and its was so depressing because the people were so pretentious. With Rave culture, if you're out there waving your hands in the air, hugging people- hopefully that'll appeal to people and it'll develop."

Although you wouldn't know it through his music, Moby is a very socially conscious artist. He takes the role of a concerned citizen very seriously, "Americans are so dishonest now. We're all like smiling happy people, but inside, dying.", states Moby.

It is this social conscience, combined with the unpretentiousness of rave culture that could possibly help change our way of thinking and heal this world we live in. Moby perceives himself as an example for the Rave Community "One of the appeals of Techno is that its so aggressive and so raw that it has sincerity, and people respond to that."

"We could have a subtle shift, like in the 60's, towards thinking outside of a Western, capitalistic framework. I think people need to realize that it's not uncool to be a concerned citizen and to take social action. That's kind of what I'd like to accomplish, and in the meantime make good music.

Nuff said, Moby.

RECORD REVIEWS

CHURCH OF EXTACY-"Church Of Extacy" (Rising High/UK)
Yet another **GTO** side project, Newman and Wells have created their most menacing driver to date. Adding new meaning to the hard in hardcore, this apocalyptic winner lurches, snarls, and-dare I say-grinds its way to the altar of raving madness. Only for the headstrong, you know the score! **(Editor's Note: At press time, Sonic Records licensed this 12" for a domestic release.)**

LP/COMPILATIONS

V/A-Instinct Dance (Instinct)
From one of America's leading techno labels comes this massive collection of eleven 12" on one CD. All written and produced by one **Richard Hall** under several aliases-**Barracuda, Brainstorm, Voodoo Child**, and of course, **Moby**-Instinct Dance covers the spectrum of underground dance music. Barracuda leads with an Italo rave trio-including the funky "Drug Fits The Face", followed by Moby's smash "Go" and the ambient "Mobility". Hall's hardcore pseudonyms then slam into gear with "Rock The House", "Move The Colors", and a remix of the Hendrix-sampled "Voodoo Child". Call it a label compilation or the debut Moby lp in disguise, I don't give a toss, but **Instinct Dance** is a brilliant offering of classics capable of kickin' in windows and knockin' down doors.

N-JOI-Live At Manchester (deConstruction/UK)
Fuckin' 'ardcore! London's N-JOI totally turn it out on this well-pressed import lp at an import 12" price. Recorded live at the Manchester Academy, this shows why this band is one of the best in techno; all the chewn are in the house-"Adrenalin", "Malfunction", "Mindflux"... and its all wicked. Totally for the headstrong, throw this on and go fuckin' raving mental!

V/A-retrotechno/Detroit Definitive (Network/UK)
Influenced by **Kraftwerk** and **"Planet Rock"**, high school mates Juan Atkins, Kevin Saunderson, and Derrick May began fooling with drum manchines and keyboards, pioneering in the Mid/Late 80's the deep minimal sound known as Detroit Techno. Releasing their own records on their own labels under names like **Reese, Model 500, Rhythim Is Rhythim,** and **Mayday,** the trio began a stir in the acid house-influenced U.K. Now Network Records brings out this amazing collection of seminal tracks! As the name implies, this is the definitive word in the Detroit sound- an essential compilation for those who know or the open-minded.

HOUSE/GARAGE/ACID JAZZ/R&B

12"/ep

YOTHU YINDI-"Treaty" (Hollywood)
Think of digeridoo music set to a balearic house beat, throw in a piano break, tribal chants and you have this monster smash from Australian Aborigines Yothu Yindi (Yoo-too Yindee). Originally an Australian import, this multi cultural octet's first release holds two mesmerizing remixes by William Orbit in addition to the organ-bursting Filthy Lucre Mixes. This was hot all Winter in the U.K., topping DJ's like Sasha and Danny Rampling's Top Of 1991 charts.

PHUTURE-"Rise From Your Grave" (Strictly Rhythm)
Yes, it's that Phuture! Chicago's DJ Pierre is back to drop a message of social conscience and jack the party in full Phuture effect. Minimal drums and keyboards, the trademark hypnotic bassline and the ominous voice of Cocaine, "Rise..." is a superb chunk o E-funk served up by one of the innovators. Top.

MASSIVE ATTACK-"Be Thankful" ep (Circa/UK)
Massive returns, following their groundbreaking debut with an ep of remixes and a new track, the atmospheric "Home Of The Whale". The once ambient "Hymn Of The Big Wheel" gets the **Nellee Hooper** treatment and transforms into a rammed and mellow thumper driven by a serious groove and Studio One crooner **Horace Andy's** brilliant voice. **Paul Oakenfold** turns out a jazzy, flute-driven remix of "Be Thankful...", while **Larry "Mr. Fingers" Heard** serves up a soulful, pulsing reworking of the b-side "Any Love". If you missed **Blue Lines**, here's a second chance to discover the musical melting pot known as Massive Attack. A top one worth the import dosh.

POSITIVITY-"Out Of This World" (Fokus)
A swirling, jazzy, atmosheric groover from this group of Londoners. The bouncy Vocal Mix chugs along housily with a sizzling sax solo, but the true winner is the gradually building, airy, trace-inducing Dub Mix. A record for whistle blowing, hands-in-the-air, and blissing out.

HARDRIVE featuring L.G.-"Sindae" (Strictly Rhythm)
The Masters At Work (Kenny "Dope" Gonzales & "Little" Louie Vega) got it goin' on with this jumpin' and pumpin' choon about a 'round the way girl. Nicely complimented by new school style rapper L.G., "Sindae" avoids the usual hip house rubbish; the deeper instrumental mixes are also kick in' for the late night dance floor as well. A versatile biscuit worth a spin.

RECORD REVIEWS

MARATHON-"Movin'" (Ten/UK)
Revived by a handful of taste making British DJ's, the re-release of this blinding club classic features remixes from garagemaster **Joey Negro, Youth** and **ReadyMade.** Joey Negro/ Dave Lee's massive house, dub and vocal mixes fill the A side, sticking close to the magic of the perfectly piano-driven original. The B-side, however, is all naff hardcore remixes that destroy the uplifting quality of the origin al. A must have for the A side alone.

HIP-HOP

12"/ep

QUEEN MOTHER RAGE-"Key Testimony" (Cardiac)
This Afrocentric sister from the Black Watch/X-Clan posse attempts to drop science with some production help from X-Clan and a Dr. John sample. Despite the solid production, QMR's whispered rap doesn't feel right on the Clan Side. The flip's electric piano and drum groove Bassmood Mix seems to help this sister's conscious lyrics flow much better.

CYPRESS HILL-"Hand On The Pump" (Ruffhouse/Columbia)
Describe hardcore funky Latin spliff-smoking, under-the-influence hip-hop? Cypress Hill fool! This single displays DJ Muggs' (ex-7A3) mastery on the decks, using "Duke Of Earl"'s vocal line as the bassline of this hardcore joint from a Latin perspective. A wicked track from a tuff debut

LP/COMPILATIONS

FU-SCHNICKENS-FU-Don't Take It Personal (Jive)
It seems as if 1992 is going to be another massive year for great debut hip-hop. 1991 brought up Main Source, LONS, Pete Rock & CL Smooth; so far '92's dropped Black Sheep and now the Oriental-garbed, ragga-flavoured FU-Schnickens. Lyrically skilled, **Chip, Moc,** and **Poc-FU** kick the fast ragga hip-hop rhymes and the beats are slammin' too! With some production spice from **ATCQ** ("La Schmoove"), **Dres** from **Black Sheep** ("Check It Out"), and **Lyvio G** (the kickin' "Ring The Alarm") as well as holding their own, **FU-Don't...** offers 10 funky and unique tracks that will keep the jeep pumpin' in '92. Essential.

SISTER SOULJAH-360 Degrees Of Power (Epic)
Surrounded by Eric "Veitnam" Sadler's hard-as-nails production, **Sister Souljah's** debut lp comes correct on the hardcore Black female's perspective. Unfortunately her trebly delivery is more suited to public speaking than fast rapping, but lyrically she cuts through hypocrisy like a knife. It's not how Souljah says it, but what she says about the state of Black Ame-

rica that is most important here. A passionate plea to the women of Black America to stay strong.

INDIE/ALTERNATIVE

12"/ep

BASEHEAD-"2000 B.C." (Imago)
Combine the mellow indie guitar sensibility with new school hip-hop funkiness and you have Washington D.C.'s Basehead. About the morning after a drinking binge, "2000 B.C." (B.C. standing for brain cells) is the first 12" from their remixed major label debut **Play With Toys**, originally released on tiny San Francisco label, **Emigre**. Led by Michael Ivey's organic creative vision and ironic, humourous songwriting Basehead have sort of a "Galaxie 500 meets De La Soul on quaaludes" feel that meshes musical racial barriers. A fresh sound capable of redefining boundaries in the Post-Nirvana era, "2000..." is just a teaser for a massively brill lp.

LP/COMPILATIONS

INTERMIX-Intermix (Third Mind)
Yet another side projest from **Front Line Assembly's Rhys Fulber** and **Bill Leeb, Intermix** is a coagulation of FLA's industerial pounding, Delerium's chill-out ambience, and the fierce pulse of Techno/Rave. Obviously influenced by Enigma The Orb, and RSW, Leeb and Fulber have created a massive effort tapping into the under ground dance scene while retaining a fresh viewpoint. A perfect bridge between alternative and 'ardcore sets for the +8 Brigade.

A.R. KANE-Americana (Luaka Bop/Warner Bros.)
Dreampop innovators and "Pump Up The Volume" co-creators, A.R. Kane release **Americana**, a domestic anthology of music culled from 2 ep's and 2 lp's released on Rough Trade/UK. With tracks that range from extraterrestrial pop-dance ("Love From Outer Space", "Snow Joke") to woozy sonic experiences("Baby Milk Snatcher" "Up"), the Kane's show a horde of musical influences and reference points that create their visionary sound. Also included is "Water", a new track. Two thumbs go to David Byrne for having the brains to release this body of musical innovation. Brilliant!

YELLOW MAGIC ORCHESTRA-Kyoretsu Na Rhythm (Restless)
Japan's Yellow Magic Orchestra was a pioneering early '80's force experimenting with pop music and technology in a dance framework. Too electro to be rock but not weird enough for New Wave, YMO lent a refreshing Japanese perspective inmusic that garnered some critical acclaim but went virtually undiscovered by the U.S. public. Kyoretsu Na Rhythm is their first ever domestic release; an overview of the group's career-from quirky electro-pop songs("Lighten Up") and more sophisticated sequenced and sampled tracks("Rydeen"), to post-Kraftwerk/pre-synth pop gems like "Cue". YMO have influenced the likes of **LFO** and **Nightmares On Wax;** this is a wonderful re/introduction to one of alternative music's true pioneers.

Clubbers DIARY

If you have an event or a club night that you would like listed in TRiP's Clubbers Diary, please send along a flyer or release about your event or night to the usual address.

ONE NIGHT EVENTS/CONCERTS

YOUNG GODS-Thursday, May 7 @ Ritz Theatre, 1503 E. 7th Ave Ybor City. All ages. $5 on the door.

YOTHU YINDI, FUNKY GROOVY CAT APILLARS, GOG, and others-Saturday, May 9 @ Cuban Club & El Pasaje Courtyard, Ybor City. All ages. $15 in advance, $17 on the night. Call 238-8001 for more information

THEE RAVE-IN-Sunday, May 31, Venue and Price to be announced. Keep your ears to the street for more information. A Raven Production.

WEEKLY CLUB NIGHTS

SUNDAY-

911, 911 N. Franklin St., Downtown Tampa, 224-0911. Upfront Dance with DJ Bill Ward. 18 and over. $2 on the door.

RENE'S, W. Kennedy Blvd., Tampa, 872-9631. Underground Dance with DJ Infinite Beat. 18 and over. No cover on the door.

MONDAY- ???????

TUESDAY-

M-PLODE @ BOYS VIDEO & DANCE, 4910 E. Busch Blvd., Tampa, 985-2837. Techno/Rave with DJ Joe Billi. 18 and over. $3 on the door.

WEDNESDAY-

RENE'S, W. Kennedy Blvd., Tampa, 872-9631. Underground Dance with DJ Infinite Beat. 18 and over. $5 on the door.

THURSDAY-

TRACKS, 1430 E. 7th Ave., Ybor City, 247-2711. Techno/Rave with DJ Rick West. $3.00 on the door, free before 10 pm for over 21. 18 and over.

FRIDAY-

CHANNEL ZERO @ CLUB DETROIT, 16 2nd St. N., St. Petersburg 896-1244. Deep house and Techno/Rave. 18 and over. $3 on the door.

MOTHER'S RAVE @ THE RITZ THEATRE, 1503 E. 7th Ave., Ybor City, 247-3319. House and Techno/Rave hosted by Mother Tucker. DJ's to be announced Beginning May 1, 1992. $5 on the night.

SATURDAY-

EVOLUTION, 1902 E. 7th Ave., Ybor City, 248-8888. Alternative and Techno/Rave with DJ Steve Mc Clure. 18 and over. $5, 18-20; $3, 21+ on the door. Free before 10:30.

RECORD REVIEWS

TECHNO/RAVE

12"/ep

RHC-"Fever Called Love" (R&S/ Belgium)
Hypnotist/Rising High major domo Casper Pound along with pal Marc Williams and ex-Shamen vocalist Plavka turn out this smooth, bleepy, pulsing techno driver on Belgium's bangin' R&S label. Originating from **R**ising **H**igh **C**ollective's Friday residency at London's Brain club, Pound & Co. drop two additional mixes a firing instrumental break-beat oriented London Mix and the fierce Alternative Vocal Mix. A top chewn with serious tranceability on the dance floor.

ISOTONIK-"Different Strokes" (ffrreedom/UK)
Originally on Orange Records and licensed to ffrr, this ambient synth and crowd noise washed piano jangling, "Mentasm"/"Charly"-like jitterer is on the commercial rave tip The Grooverider Remix is reccommended-hard but not hardcore.

MOBY-"Go" Remixes (Instinct)
New York punk-turned programmer serves up six- count 'em- six versions of the now-classic "Twin Peaks" influenced U.K. Club #1, "Go". They're all here; a raging radio-friendly edit, the swirling Subliminal Mix, the chugging Woodtick Mix, a rising, ambient, piano-driven Soundtrack Mix, and its Original Mix-a "Twin Peaks"-less, Detroit-like thumper. The headstrong will prefer the rampaging Rainforest Mix. Totally crucial and essential!

HARDWAX 001 (Hardwax)
Hard to the fuckin' Core, mates! Rumour has it that the **UR** massive in involved with this bangin' label from Detroit. Both tracks on this debut 12", "Onslaught", and "Rave To The Maximum", meet in between Detroit and Brussels and the results are,well, fuckin' menacing. An ultra-crisp bisquit.

ORBITAL-"Mutations" ep (ffrr/ UK)
An ep of guest remixes from the Brothers' Hartnoll's debut lp. As with the lp, each format contains different tracks; the CD5" carries the stuttering "Chime Crime", **Joey Beltram**'s frantic slammer "Oolaa", the strong,chugging "Fahrenheit 3D3", and **Moby**'s bounding "Speed Freak". The vinyl also has remixes from **Meat Beat Manifesto, Dave Dorrell(MARRS)**, and **Dave Angel** worth checking. **(Editor's Note: ffrr/London recently relesed the Orbital lp domestically.)**

SL2-"On A Ragga Tip" ep (XL/ UK)
"Smokey Joe, Merry Chreesmass" Pass that mighty spliff over

RECORD REVIEWS

here as we groove to the raggacore of London's SL2 (Slipmatt & Lime). "...Ragge Tip" is along the same line as "Way In My Brain" from their last ep-mixing dub and breakbeats to massive results-while "Pleasure" is a pumping midtempo piano-driven track. The flip carries the top "Changing Trax", abouncy chugger; and the bleepy, subsonic, jungle-beat driver "Bassquake" (which was the b-side of "The Noise" on Awesome/UK). A superb sophomore effort from these Chigwell lads!

2 UNLIMITED-"Twilight Zone" (Radikal)
2 Unlimited's follow up to the ultra-massive "Get Ready For This" is a fierce commercial raver with its T-99 synth stabs and farting acid bass line. The flip's Rio & LeJean Remix is the pick of this 5 pack with more of a frantic vibe and true hardcore flavour

MINDCONTROLLER-"No Sense" (80AUM/Radikal)
"I control your mind when I get a little deeper, make your heart pump like the sound of a beeper" kicks the rhyme from the bloke who dropped on "Dominator" (Lorenzo Nash) in this seriously wicked bass burner licensed from Holland's 80 AUM label. Also featured is the slammin' synth screeched, ragga-toasted "Teknophobia". Hardcore... you know the score!

HOMEBOY, HIPPIE, & A FUNKY DREAD-"Start Da Panik" (Rising High/UK)
HH'nFD are "on amission from God" and kickin' shit on this fierce breakbeat raver on the same thunderous line as "Total Confusion". Also check out the pulsing, stark Top Buzz Mix, plus the rumbling, rock-riffed "Get Wild".

PRAGA KHAN featuring JADE 4U-"Free Your Mind" (Sonic)
Techno innovators Praga Khan return with a serious bodybending blaster of the Belgian sort. Produced by **MNO**("God of Abraham"), an Ernest Angley sample kicks of this synth-buzzing chugger with its bouncy piano break. The flip slows it down a bit with the Original piano-driven mix and Jared Hoffman's Ultra Sonic Dance Mix. One for the box.

QUADROPHONIA-"Schizofrenia" (RCA)
For the fourth single from this 1/2 Belgian/1/2 Dutch duo's debut lp **Cozmic Jam**, New York's Mark Kamins serves up a mixed bag of remixes-some good, some mediocre. Things thunder into gear as Flavor Flav tells you to "Get That Shit!" on the Electrik Chair Mix, whilw the frantic, pounding Omen Mix turns it into "Techno Time Motherfucker!". A fairly wicked chewn that will please the brain burners.

ECCENTRICITIES

DARE TO BE DIFFERENT!

Everything from sterling silver jewelry to Doc Martins.
With fashions by:
Lip Service • Lust • Ercoli • Tripp
Vox Pop • Blaxx • Betsy Johnson
and many others.

ECCENTRICITIES
935 ½ S. Howard Ave.
Tampa, FL • (813) 254 - 8080

TRiP MAGAZEEN
100 E. MLK BLVD.
SUITE #10
TAMPA, FLORIDA 33603
U.S.A.

POSTMASTER: DATED MATERIAL....PLEASE RUSH

03

SUMMER OF RAVE ISSUE
TRiP
Vol. I, #3
DJ's Take Control
Profiling the Bay's Tastemakers
Controlled Bleeding
Record Reviews
Speedy J
Future Sound Of London
Optimystic
Kym Sims
Hiphoprisy
Jah Wobble
Recoil
TRiP Talks Trash With
FIERCE
ruling
DIVA
THE BAY AREA'S FIRST UPFRONT DANCE CULTURE FANZINE!

DIARY

ONE-OFF EVENTS

HANDS 2 HEAVEN, Thursday, June 25 @ The Edge, 100 W. Livingston, Orlando. Featuring P.A.'s by **Sonz of A Loop da Loop Era, MSM, Q-Bass, & Run Tings.** Drivers on the night include **Danny Breakz (UK), DJ Icee, Bruce Wilcox, Steve Mc Clure** and others. 18 and up. $5 b4 11, $7 after.

The Death of AAHZ, Saturday, July 4 @ Beacham Theatre, 46 Orange Ave., Orlando. 18 and up. VIP Package Admission, $10, or $5 on the door.

SIR MIX-A-LOT W/BRONX STYLE BOB, Thursday, July 2 @ Ritz Theatre, 1503 East 7th Ave., Ybor City. All ages. $10.50 adv. @ Ticket Master

WEEKLY CLUB NIGHTS

SUNDAYS-
911, 911 N. Franklin St.. Downtown Tampa, 224-0911. Upfront dance with DJ Bill Ward. 18 and over. $2 on the door.

RENE'S, W. Kennedy Blvd., Tampa, 872-9631. Underground Dance with DJ Infinite Beat. 18 and over. No cover on the door.

MONDAYS-
BENNIGAN'S, 2126 Tyrone Blvd., St. Petersburg, 343-1075. Alternative and Techno/Rave with DJ Bill A. 18 and over.

TUESDAYS-
ALTERNATIVE SOUNDS @ STATE THEATER, 687 Central Ave., St. Petersburg, 821-9584. Alternative and Techno/Rave with DJ Bill A. 18 and over. $2 on the night.

WEDNESDAYS-
RENE'S, W. Kennedy Blvd., Tampa, 872-9631. Underground Dance with DJ Infinite Beat. 18 and over. $5 on the door.

THURSDAYS-
TRACKS, 1430 E. 7th Ave., Ybor City, 247-2711. Techno/Rave with DJ Rick West. $3.00 on the door; free before 10pm for over 21. 18 and over.

FRIDAYS-
EUPHORIA @ RITZ THEATRE, 1503 E. 7th Ave., Ybor City, 247-3319. Techno/Rave and House with DJ Gary Ann and special guest drivers. Hosted by Mother Tucker and Her Children. 18 and over. $5 on the night.

SATURDAYS-
EVOLUTION, 1902 E. 7th Ave., Ybor City, 248-8888. Techno/Rave and Alternative with DJ Steve Mc Clure. 18 and over. $5, 18-20; $3, 21+, free before 10:30.

DJ 3, continued from Page 9

YOUR IMPRESSIONS OF THE BAY AREA'S RAVE SCENE? **"I'd like to say there isn't one Some good things have happened as well as some half-hearted attempts.** (XL's) Richard Russell **at evolution was better energy than most everything since April and it was in a club. Alex Machine and myself, along with a third party started** Raven Productions **in December. I set the flyer so "Fisher-Price" and everything was simple to set a standard-show people what's up-sort of. It was great; cool cops, cool crowd, perfect atmosphere.** DMR **coverage and the** Shamen **show set us up with** Moby **and** Matt E. Silver; **in only 3 weeks we put** MANIC **together to hit people big-Moby,** Casanova, Doc Martin, **smart drinks, virtual reality, etc. We got over 600 and I knew the drawbacks but I counted on the sound and lights to accomodate and it didn't. Overall it was great-we made no money (again), but people were there and we made a lot of "tech-heads"...The goal was to start a scene & we did, and already a backlash. The Ritz trying to cash in, alot of people with attitude trouble.** Raven Productions **is not anymore. "Thee Rave In" was our sound & light man using the name-no new ground broken except cool cops in Tampa. There is no self-indulgence or pretension in the music that is changing.** Tribal, hardcore, house, **it's all one thing. Now that there are divisions being made, I hope DJ's keep people open minded.**

McClure, continued from Page8

YOUR IMPRESSIONS OF THE BAY AREA'S RAVE SCENE? **"My opinion on the whole thing is if people keep a positive outlook on it, it can only get better. If people take a negative attitiude and try to take any form of this music and make a buck off of it, not caring about the music, people will know. It's not a money thing, it's a unity thing. Techno should be taken seriously, not as a joke or just a trend.**

WHAT ARE SOME OF YOUR FAVORITE CURRENT RECORDS? **"Anything on** Suburban Base,
SHUT UP AND DANCE-"Raving, I'm Raving"
4 HERO-"Cookin' Up My Brain" (Sonz of A Loop Da Loop Remix)
ACEN-"Close Your Eyes" (Production House/UK)
Jam And Spoon-"Stella" (R&S/Belgium)
OPUS III-"It's A Fine Day" (East/West America)

CONTENTS

VOL I, #3 JUNE 1992

TRiP MAGAZEEN
100 E. MLK Boulevard
Suite #10
Tampa, Florida 33603
U.S.A.
(813) 238-0310
(813) 876-7473 Fax

EDITOR: Peter Wohelski

ADVERTISING: Ad rates are gladly given on request.
BACK ISSUES: Back issues of TRiP are available for $1 postpaid. specify issues please.
SUBSCRIPTIONS: **$8** yearly for 8 issues plus TRiP Posse Bonuses. Make checks/ m.o. payable to Peter Wohelski.

FEET ff FIRST

I hate bringing economics and politics into things, but it's cold hard reality... When one shells out their hard-earned dosh for a top night out, one expects to be looked after properly and treated like a human being, not a lower life form by the staff.

Granted, not everyone is a raver. Yet, with hardcore techno's popularity on the playlists of club DJ's, maybe I'm expecting too much that a club's staff would be clued-up? I was at a club night recently where I was treated as a head of cattle by the club's neanderthal, steroid-popping security staff.

What was I doing to warrant this abuse? Fighting? **No.** Moshing? **No.** What then? I was **blowing a whistle** and getting mental on the dancefloor! I was surrounded by other mad ravers and a whole crew of Biff & Buffy's that kept putting the thing in my mouth when I stopped.

I wasn't bothering any of the punters, so what **was** the reason I was tossed out? **I was annoying this neanderthal!** Too fucking bad, mate! By patronizing this club, I help pay his paycheck. I'm sure this specific establishment has quite enough clueless geezers to replace me if I never return.. If these so-called "alternative" clubs run techno/rave nights, they need to hire or schedule clued-up staff who respect ravers and rave culture!

continued on Page 15

HYPE HYPE HYPE HYPE HYPE

....In the latest of their wild pranks, **ALTERN 8's CHRIS PEAT** ran for Prime Minister in the U.K.'s recent elections. The **"ALTERN 8-IVE HARDCORE PARTY's"** platform? Raves on every corner, Ecstacy in the milk every morning, and a Techno awareness campaign for disabled people....Manchester's legendary **HACIENDA** celebrated its 10th year this past May 13, the night featured a P.A. by the **PET SHOP BOYS** and other guests. The club is also publishing a book tracing its history....A recent issue of **DANCE MUSIC REPORT** proclaimed Florida as having the most exciting rave scene in the U.S. next to Los Angeles!....**EPIC RECORDS** has bought the rights to Belgian industrialists **FRONT 242**'s back catalogue from Chicago's **WAX TRAX RECORDS** and will be reissuing them with new artwork and extra bonus tracks. The first two re-releases on Epic will be **FRONT BY FRONT** and **GEOGRAPHY....BRAND NUBIAN** have their second lp ready to drop this summer on **ELEKTRA**. The album features an appearance by both **BLACK SHEEP** and **CYPRESS HILL.... APOTHEOSIS' "O FORTUNA"** has been banned in Benelux! Seems the estate of composer **CARL ORFF** felt that the hardcore versions of **CARMINA BURANA** were a defacement of the original work. The record is available domestically on **RADIKAL RECORDS....**Look for a new underground club to be opening this summer in Tampa. Called **WONDERLAND**, the club will be in a renovated Downtown Tampa warehouse....New York based **INSTINCT RECORDS** has finalized their licensing deal with London's **KICKIN' RECORDS.** The first releases under the new **KICKIN' U.S.A.** banner will be by **MESSIAH** and a Kickin' compilation.. From Detroit comes news that **"MAGIC" JUAN ATKINS** is working with **N-JOI** on an upcoming track and the lads from Essex will return the favour by remixing an Atkins classic....The latest rage in U.K. club accessories are **BIBS.** First diapers and pacifiers, the masks and snorkels, now **BIBS??!!....MUTE RECORDS/UK** has started a new hardcore techno label called **NOVA MUTE.** The label will only press a limited amount of each release. No word on whether or not any of these releases will be made available through Mute here in the U.S.....The bay Area's own **DJ 3** called in recently to tell us about his recent trip to **ATLANTA**, spinning at a **SONY MUSIC/VINYL SOLUTION** promo party. Apparently 3 ripped it up on the 1's and 2's in front of a packed hardcore-starved massive at **WEEKENDS** until the wee hours....Orlando-based techno act **RADIOACTIVE GOLDFISH** recently cracked the Top 10 on **BILLBOARD's** dance chart with their debut single **"LSD Is The Bomb"**.

FRD rides "Trance Europe Express" to U.S. success

Native New Yorker **Jeff Porter** and Dutchman **Jeroen** (pronounced **Yer-oon**) **Flamman** are the "hardcore party music" duo known as **Fierce Ruling Diva.** Based out of Amsterdam, **FRD** have taken Europe and the U.K. by storm with manic tracks such as **"Whipped Cream", "Rubb It In"** (a U.K. Club Chart smash), and **"Atomic Slide".** Signed to **Invasion Records** here in the States, Fierce Ruling Diva recently completed a P.A. tour of the U.S. and are about to fire their next hardcore salvo on America- a 1992 remix of "Atomic Slide", called **"You Gotta Believe"** remixed by both **Charley Casanova** and **Moby. Jeroen** and **Jeff** took some time out as heads of **Lower East Side Records** to do an interview with **TRiP Magazeen** via the fax machine. Prepare to get sorted by **Fierce Ruling Diva!!!**

TRiP: How long has Fierce Ruling Diva been together? One of you is from New York, the other Amsterdam; how did you meet and decide to work together?

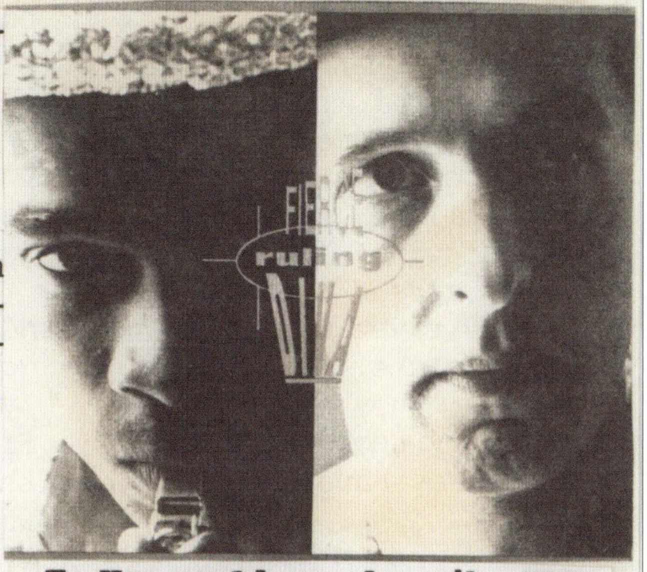

Fierce Ruling Diva: We've been together for five years, started DJing 3 1/2 years ago, started producing tracks 1/2 a year after. Jeff was on holiday in Europe after finishing his study at Boston University, we met in a gay bar, lived in New York for a year and then returned to Amsterdam to bring the Dutch people the sound we got hooked on while living in New York.

T: What is your association with Lower East Side Records?

FRD: Fierce Ruling Diva **is** Lower East Side Records. Our address in Amsterdam features two apartments, a home studio & an office. Besides **LESR**, we started a sub-label called **Subtopia 12" Diskettes.** It's named after our famous after-hours-club on-a-barge that the police closed down 3 weeks ago after 1 1/2 year of after-hour madness.

T: How would you describe FRD's **sound and the Dutch sound in general, as compared to Belgium, U.K., etc.?**

FRD: FRD's style is more trashy, informal, opportunist and humourous, due to our lifestyle. Amsterdam is a bit more liberated & trashy than England or Belgium...and so are we!

T: What are Fierce Ruling Diva' influences?

FRD: We are both DJ's, and we a very much influenced by what we play. Before '87, Jeff used to be more into the **New Order**-style, Jeroen was into punk only.

T: Many people have been saying Holland is the Rave Capital of the World. Truth or hype; and if true, why?

FRD: House/Techno/Rave is universal, there is no rave capitol. Amsterdam, however, has always been a city with a high energy level and certainly a place where changes can be made. A lot of the excellent Dutch techno comes from outside Amsterdam, though.

In Holland, there is a weekly crowd of +/- 75,000 ravers that spread over an average of 40 raves a weekend and 100's of clubs. Dutch DJ's are very good; they hardly leave the country though, 'cause usually they have a full agenda!

T: FRD **recently returned from a P.A. tour of the States. What are your impresions of the rave scene here in the U.S.?**

FRD: American ravers should have more interest & respect for their own producers; **Joey Beltram, Moby, +8, U.R., Techman One, Charley Casanova, Kevin Saunderson, Kenny "Dope"** All of these people get lots of respect in Europe. Don't forget, in Europe Rave=Techno=House=Acid.

T: Why a '92 remix of "Atomic Slide"? Any particular reason why you chose Charley Casanova and Moby to remix it, as compared to a Joey Beltram of some one from Europe?

FRD: "Atomic Slide", like "Rubb It In", was previously released on Lower East Side Records. LESR did not reach all those people we wanted to reach. When bigger record companies got interested in pushing FRD worldwide, we decided we wanted to rerelease our own personal favorites, to make a good base for new productions.

Moby and **Charley** are friends of ours and they gave us a good deal, but more importantly, they are both **FRD** fans. We figured it was better to have the track remixed by people who already had been loving the song for months! Nothing against Joey Beltram!

T: What's up next for Fierce Ruling Diva? Tour plans? Album? ???

FRD: At the same time our 12" comes out, the album will come along with tons of exciting new tracks. The hard hooligan-techno is dying out in Europe. It is up to FRD to show there is life after it! We have a UK tour in July and a tour in the States for August/September. Late September, we are hoping open a new after hours club; maybe legal, else illegal.
We will continue to produce & promote other artists.

'Bleeding resurfaces with "Penetration"

Over the past ten years, Controlled Bleeding has been one of the most interesting ex perimental/industrial acts ev- er. Going through different phases of sonic development, from pure noise, to ethereal, medieval pieces, to more song-oriented "mainstream" industr- ial dance, 'Bleeding has cover ed the full range of aural ex- perience.

In 1988, the band signed with Chicago's Wax Trax! Reco- rds- a mixed blessing. Althou- gh Controlled Bleeding became recognized by a generation of industrial music fans that we- re unaware of their past, the label began to run into finan- cial difficulties and the gro- up decided to depart and reev- aluate themselves.

In that time, group found- ers Paul Lemos and Chris Mori- arty began **Skin Chamber**, a br-

utal, metal project that Lemos describes as "venomous" as we- ll as an independently relea- sed lp, **Golgotha**.

continued on Page 15

RED 356 to release homegrown hardcore

As the Bay Area prepares for the "Summer of Rave" some mental ravers are stepping off the dance floor and into the studio to create their own bangin' rave tracks.

One of the more visible acts is Red 356. Formed in 1990 from the ashes of two area syn- th-pop groups by vocalist Mitch Dupre and keyboardist Sergio Balsera, the band released a demo to positive reviews but left them unfulfilled.

Influenced by underground acts like **Inner City** and exci- ted by the energy of the hard- core techno coming into Ameri- ca, Balsera and Dupre changed direction and added turntable technician Mini Mix Mario and plunged into creating new chewns.

The group's upcoming ep, Technotopia, to be released la- ter this summer is full of sla- mmin' tracks that reveal two di- fferent sides to Red 356; one hard but not hardcore, the ot- her firing and headstrong.

In the meantime, Red 356 is currently doing P.A.'s thr- oughout Central Florida, hav- ing recently done blinding sets at Gainesville's Innermind, Tracks in Tampa, and the Happy Sunday Rave-In.

Look for Red 356 at the upcoming Suncoast Pride '92 event at Tracks, June 21.

DJ's Take Control, Part I

Tastemakers Mc Clure, DJ Three

DJ Steve McClure could very well be the Techno Ambassador of Tampa. A longtime fan of the more progressive side of house music, Steve was among- if not the first area turntable terrorist to fill dancefloors with wax from acts like **KLF, 808 State,** and **LFO** as well as other urban sounds. Having worked in several other cities in Florida gives this tastemaker a different perspective on putting together and moving the crowd on his club nights

HOW LONG HAVE YOU BEEN DJ'ing? **"I've been playing for a long time; probably about four or five years seriously."**

WHERE HAVE YOU WORKED IN THE PAST? **"Late Night Library** (Tallahassee), **AAHZ** (Beacham Theatre, Orlando)**."**

WHERE ARE YOU CURRENTLY WORKING? **"DNA Fridays,Evolution Sat. "**

HOW WOULD YOU DESCRIBE YOUR STYLE? **"I don't really have a certain style, it's hard to explain. You have to just hear it. I watch the crowd and try to play music that makes people feel good and want to dance. I try to take an entertainer's standpoint and build a show every week."**

WHAT DJ's/REMIXERS/ARTISTS DO YOU ADMIRE? **"On the top of my list would have to be** Sonz Of A Loop Da Loop Era **(Suburban Base Records'** Danny Breakz**). They're real uplifting. Above and beyond that,** Moby, Joey Beltram....

ARE YOU WORKING ON ANY MUSICALLY-ORIENTED PROJECTS BESIDES DJ'ing? **"Right now, I'm just concentrating on what I'm doing and thinking and planning new things in the future. My personal interests are getting to work with video...and I think that a DJ's ear will help me get my foot in the door with that.**

WHAT IS YOUR FAVORITE ALL-TIME RECORD? **"Lords Of Acid-'I Sit On Acid'-it may be played out, but it's a classic."**

McClure, continued on Page 2

share insights on Rave Scene

DJ THREE is one of the area's true progressive DJ's. As 1/3 of the **Raven Productions** collective, Three was instrumental in putting Tampa on the map in the worldwide rave community by organizing our area's first rave parties which were covered by **Dance Music Report.** "DJ Three is for the underground and nothing else," he states,"Alternative, hip-hop, 'underground', I play good records. I'm not just a techno DJ."

HOW LONG HAVE YOU BEEN DJ'ing? **"I've been goofing around with tapedecks,turntables, and other gear since '84"**
WHERE HAVE YOU WORKED IN THE PAST **"Rene's, Manchester, PROGENY Raven Productions' one-offs, THE RAVEN, MANIC, EUPHORIA"**
WHERE ARE YOU CURRENTLY WORKING? **"I'm doing one-offs through out the Southeast, like Miami and Atlanta; I'm also planning a party for later this summer."**
HOW WOULD YOU DESCRIBE YOUR STYLE? **"Technically, I'm more hip hop oriented, because I do more than just mix, but musically I lean toward House and Techno culture."**
WHAT DJ's/REMIXERS/ARTISTS DO YOU ADMIRE? **"As DJ's,** Andrew Weatherall, Frankie Bones, Derrick May**; as far as remixing, again** Weatherall, Joey Beltram, **and** Moby.
ARE YOU WORKING ON ANY MUSICALLY-ORIENTED PROJECTS BESIDES DJ'ing? **"I'm currently remixing a progressive dance project for a local act, I did two tracks with** ALEX MACHINE **for the PROGENY event; I'd like to do my own projects in the future."**
WHAT IS YOUR FAVORITE ALL-TIME RECORD? **"I don't know the name of it, but there was always a song that gave me the chills from Day 1. I like records that make you feel."**

DJ 3, continued on Page 2

RECORD REVIEWS

FUTURE SOUND OF LONDON-"Papua New Guinea" (Jumpin' & Pumpin/ UK)
A massively hooj choon this pa
st Fall/Winter in the U.K., al
most singlehandedly responsible
for setting off the trancy, sp
liffed out , dub-influenced pr
ogressive house movement. Bril
liantly remixed by Boys Own's
Andrew Weatherall, who stretch
es it out into a pulsing, swir
ling 11-minute opus, and **808 State's Graham Massey**, turning
in a bass-burning chugger, com
plete with tribal chants and
trademark **808** production. A su
perb offering that will leave
you mashed!

APHEX TWIN-"Digeridoo" ep (R&S/ BELGIUM)
This is Techno-The Next Genera
tion! From the haunting digeri
doo of the title track (an alm
ost 160 bpm thunderer) and "An
alogue Bubblebath 1"'s ambient,
mesmerizing breakbeat groove,
to the brutish "Flaphead" and
"Isoprophlex"'s fierce and fra
ntic thrashing, this apocalyp-
tic ep takes you into the futu
re of dance music. This unique
creative offering is a must for
the bodyburning, headstrong
massive!

ALTERN 8-"Evapor 8" (Network/ UK)
The hardcore nutters from Staf
ford return with **"Evapor 8"** a
Top Of The Pops live introed,
"Strings Of Life" sampled jitt
erer, but the winner here is
the fierce, but episodic "Arm-
ageddon" with its firing break
beat and **Fini Tribe** chime samp
les. Also check the bass-burn
ing new mix of "Infiltrate 202"
and the bleepy Hallucin8 Mix of
"Frequency".

SPEEDY J-"Pullover"/"Something For Your Mind" (Remixes) (+8)
From the +8 crew comes this
remix ep by Germany's **Jochem "Speedy J" Papp**. "Pullover" is
a pounding minimal Detroit dri
ver with a wiggling synth line
The flip delivers "something
for your mind" and body with
the slammin' headstrong Speedy
J Mix and the storming, trance
inducing Exposure Remix. A cr
isp biscuit for the true insom
niacs.

EDDIE "FLASHIN'" FOWLKES-Inequality ep (430 West)
Detroit's 430 West drops a wic
ked chunk of e-funk for the
non-posing party people with
this brilliant ep from Eddie
"Flashin'" Fowlkes. Kickin'
strictly underground tracks
like "Electricity" and "Under
standing The Groove", Fowlkes
defines the phrase hard and
funky. This true techno-no rav
ing here, mate! A massive one
for the box.

ARAKNOFOBIA-"Arachnophobia" (Guerilla/Tribal America)
Is it "Dominator"? No. Is it
"Mentasm"? No. Is it "Quadro-
phonia"? No. This **Friends Of Matthew** produced Belgian style
techno nightmare wants to be
all of these, creating a pump-
ing commercial raver that will
get the techno boffins firing.

The flip's Black Widow Mix is the pick with its bizarre flute solo in the middle of the hardcore madness.

UNDERGROUND IN MOTION-"Antedote" (Atmosphere)
From the producers of **Toxic 2** ("Rave Generator") comes this trancy, pulsing driver reminiscent of "French Kiss". In two forms; a very minimal Club Mix and the Dances With De Wulf Mix, a swirling, Kraftwerkian techno chugger perfect for late night bliss outs.

0733-"Record Bass Story" ep (Probe)
"Close your eyes and think of England" is written in the grooves of this acid-inspired instrumental ep on this **+8** sub label, **Probe.** +8's **Richie Hawtin** and **Casey Tucker** strip it way down, keeping things minimal but still hardcore. The Dis side's 33 rpm "Record Bass Story" rumbles along nicely, but the Dat side's fierce acid bassline farting, hi-hat chugging "Loser" and the sizzling "Alternative Roots" are this ep's gems. Worth a spin for dead cert!

TEMPERANCE-"Phantasy" ep (Hi-Bias/Canada)
Ranging from garage to techno, dance pop to rave, this diverse six pack showcases the talents of one **Mark Ryan.** The ep opens with the nice garage-y pop of "LOsing Touch", featuring the strong vocals of Lorraine Reid; "Purity" is a nice trippy slice of late night deep groove, while "Exortium" is an undeveloped bit of bonus beat raving. The flip goes techno with the piano/organ driven, bass-bleeping "The Theory", "Hipnonsense", a hi-hat sizzling breakbeat driven chewn, and the pulsing, **Inner City**-esque, techno-garage of "Phantasy".

ODYSSEY 2000-"Odyssey" (Exist Dance)
Via Los Angeles, the rave capital of America, comes this storming 12" from the Exist Dance label. "Odyssey" is a slammin' and wicked breakbeat raver with two headstrong mixes. "Hop On Pop" is a midtempo, sliding synth, siren wailing chugger with a cool organ break. A massive effort that shows that Americans can drop rave tracks as well as anyone else.

LP/COMPILATIONS

V/A-TECHNO CLASSICS, VOL. I (Rising High/UK)
In a year's time, London-based Rising High has firmly established itself as one of the UK finest hardcore labels. Set up by the original hippie of **HHFD Caspar Pound**, Rising High is well respected for its experimental, purist approach to hardcore techno. Featuring storming tracks from **The Hypnotist, Project One, HHFD, Interface, RHC,** and other label favorites, **Techno Classics** reflects this purity, owing more to good old Chicago acid than

RECORD REVIEWS

Eurotechno. A kickin' sampler of this label's beginnings and a launch platform to its future. Essential.

V/A-FUCK OFF AND DIE (Shut Up And Dance/UK)
Formed in 1989, Stoke Newington based Shut Up And Dance Records has quickly become one of the most adventurous labels on the UK dance music scene. A compilation of SUAD's first 20 singles, __Fuck Off And Die__ features the diversity and innovation of this top purveyor of vinyl. From the cheeky choons of label **heads PJ and Smiley** 's **Shut Up And Dance,** the **Ragga Twins'** fusion of the hardest house and their ragga chat, to the brutal and manic **Rum & Black,** the gospel-like **Ade,** and **Nicolette**'s Billie Holliday on Acid vocals, this collection comes correct with the freshest chewns around. Play very loud and "dance before the police come!"

V/A-THE THIRD CHAPTER: BREAKBEAT HOUSE (XL/UK)
Always the frontrunner of what up, XL Recordings presents the next edition in its kickin' series of compilations, this third chapter dedicated to breakbeat house. Converting many of hardcore techno's skeptics, the breakbeat house sound has brought together the old hip-hop b-boy posse, the raggamuffin crew, and the conventional four-to-the-floor crowd with it's speeded-up hip-hop beats combined with reggae basslines and motifs. Chock full of manic tracks, __**Third Chapter**__ gets you sorted with top chewns from both the **XL** roster (**SL2, Prodigy, Liquid, NU-Matic**) and other firing UK labels (**Project One, Tronik House Kicks Like A Mule**). A serious stunner.

HOUSE/GARAGE/ACID JAZZ/R&B

12"/EP

OPTIMYSTIC-"Trust Me" (Liquid)
This blinding piano-punctuated ambient synth washed deep house groover jogs along beautifully with a soulful female vocal riding throughout. "When" is a colourful instrumental midtempo garage track with a hype drum groove, jazzy organ/piano break, and a diva wailing "When", while "4 A.M." is just that, a perfect chill-out chewn or post-party jam. Brilliant.

PEACETIME-"The Truth Will Set You Free" (RCA)
Capitalizing on the current gospeltrend set by **Sounds of Blackness** comes this garage-y female choir chorused, organ-driven, male vocal carryin' on uplifter from Peacetime. "Truth" tries hard to duplicate what SoB succeeds at so wonderfully, being genuine, but it comes off as just a lame imitation.

HELEN BRUNER-"Missin' You" (Cardiac)
From her upcoming debut album,

this second single is more imm ediate than her last; this smo· oth groover chugs along nicely with a sweet vocal performance and a clever piano-driven bre- ak. Ultra fresh.

ROBYN SPRINGER-"Makin' Moves" (Cardiac)
Robyn springer is back with a fresh and funky follow-up to "Forever And Ever"... Ditch the played-out rapper on the LP Mix and go for whotcha know with the Up Mix for a steamin' slice of bouncin' uptempo jazz funk. Thumbs up.

LP/COMPILATIONS

KYM SIMS-TOO BLIND TO SEE IT (Atco)
From the House Of **ID** comes the latest voice in **Steve "Silk" Hurley**'s quest for World Domin ation. **Too Blind...** is a fine collection of ballads, uptempo and midtempo tracks from this wailing Windy City diva. Hurl- ey's production is so telltale that he can probably produce tracks in his sleep, but it works! Worth a listen...

V/A-CLOSET CLASSICS, VOL. I/ THE MORE PROTEIN SAMPLER (Char isma)
After several years of import- only status and an aborted U.S licensing deal through Virgin, **Boy George**'s More Protein lab- el returns to these shores thr ough Charisma Records. With this debut release, **Classics** reveals that George is as able an A&R Man as he is a popstar. All the label's UK hits are here, opening with **E-zee Pos- se**'s thundering "Everything Starts With An E", to the rag- **ga**-influenced **MC Kinky** and **I-**

RECORD RD REVIEWS

sus Ad, to **Jesus Loves You** and the garage-y piano-driv- en soul of recent signing **Eve Gallagher.** Mostly unavailable here until now, this compila- tion delivers the goods while touching on some of the genres of music the Karma Chameleon loves most.

HIP-HOP
12"/EP

TRUE CULTURE-"Rude Boys Come To Play" (Cardiac)
Merging hardcore hip-hop with raggamuffin basslines and rhy- mes, new York's True Culture Drops their latest single, the title track from their debut album. The Hip-Hop Mixes emp- hasize a **P.E.**-like drone in the background along with a walking reggae bassline, the multi-cultural duo bustin' da lyrical on gangsta life, ragga flavoured. Changing direction on the Raggamuffin Rude Boy Mixes, True Culture rocks the dancehall riddim with a tuff, horn-driven version that deli- vers the big beats.

LP/COMPILATIONS

KRIS KROSS-TOTALLY KROSSED OUT (Ruffhouse/Columbia)
Yo G, I admit I was skeptical, really skeptical, when I saw these two kids all tricked out with their backwards gear.

RECORD REVIEWS

"Not another street-smart R&B/ Rapper kid act," I said. Then I heard the record; not bad, not bad at all. Bloody wicked, in fact. Catchy, too. Ignore the skeptics, these "Lil' Boys In The Hood" can get wreck. Respect to 'em!

DISPOSABLE HEROES OF HIPHOP RISY-HIPOCRISY IS THE GREATEST LUXURY (4th & Broadway)
It's been five years since **PE'** landmark **It Takes A Nation Of Millions...** dropped science on an unsuspecting world; now pre pare for **Hiphoprisy**! Like the-ir caucasian counterparts **Con-solidated**, DHH also tells the story of a country gone awry, but from a Black perspective. **Michael Franti**'s tales of our society's racism, media manip-ulation, homophobia, etc., flow over bangin' industrial/ hip-hop beats; this is the al-bum that Consolidated wish th-ey could make.

INDIE/ALTERNATIVE

FRONT LINE ASSEMBLY-TACTICAL NEURAL IMPLANT (Third Mind)
Industrial innovators **Front Line Assembly** have always be-en known for a hard-driving, yet melodic style that has en-deared them to their fans wor-ldwide. **Tactical Neural Implant** the group's sixth lp, is a si-gn of maturation of their sign ature sound. Over the past year FLA has spent a great deal of time working on more melodic side projects-**Delerium, Will,** and **Inter-Mix**- all influences one can see enhancing the FLA project. It is this melodicism that makes **TNI** a step ahead of the typical brooding, angst ridden, doom-and-gloom indus-trial dirge.

RECOIL-BLOODLINE (Sire/Reprise)
Musical mutation and guests galore are the order of the day on the latest installment of Depeche Mode member **Alan Wild-er**'s solo project, **Recoil.** Wh-ere past Recoil efforts have focused on soundscapes, song structure is the aim of **Blood-line**, starting right off with **Nitzer Ebb**'s **Douglas McCarthy** vocalizing on a cover of **Alex Harvey**'s "Faith Healer". Curve chanteuse **Toni Halliday** trans-forms into a techno/diva on cuts like "Edge To Life", whi-le **Moby** makes his vocal debut rapping on "Curse". Stretch-ing out of the pop framework of **Depeche**, **Bloodline** creat-es refreshing listening for both the **DM** fan and the music-ally curious.

KMFDM-MONEY (Wax Trax!)
After the success of 1990's **Naive**, German expatriates **KMFDM** return with a slightly harder edge to their latest lp, **Money**, Some tracks are obvious singles material, although no-ne are as catchy as on the la-st lp. I used to really like KMFDM; I still have a soft sp-ot for them. But it seems as if they're using all the best qualities of their better kno-wn contemporaries to raise th-emselves to that level.

JAH WOBBLE'S INVADERS OF THE HEART-RISING ABOVE BEDLAM (Atlantic)

Former **PiL** bassist and ex-London Underground employee **Jah Wobble** makes another foray into music with a new band that deftly weaves threads of indie pop sensibility with dub reggae, Latin, Indian, Arabic, and other forms of World Beat. **Rising Above Bedlam** is a complete joy to listen to: challenging, intriguing, imaginative, every thing a 1990's record should be. This is a record that deserves your attention. Top.

Controlled Bleeding
continued from Page 7

1992. Controlled Bleeding resurface into the marketplace with a new lp, **Penetration**, on Third Mind Records. The lp comprises all the elements of 'Bleeding into one comprehendable package, although Paul Lemos feels that the album was not intended to be that way. "It was not conceived as a complete album, as we worked on frag ments and ideas of it during our hiatus."

For now the group is preparing to embark on their first-ever tour. "We've always played live," says Lemos,"but we've never really toured before." The group then plans to return to the studio for a much more developed album that will "expo se the true Controlled Bleeding

Last issue's Vinyl Solution Promo CD Winner!!!!!!!

The winner of last issue's **Vinyl Solution Promo CD Contest** was Christopher Smith of Tampa.

CONTROLLED BLEEDING-PENETRATION (Third Mind)

One of the first American proponents of industrial music, but not highly recognized by their contemporaries, **Controlled Bleeding** finally steps into the spotlight with **Penetration**. Co produced by **Bryan Martin** of **Swans** fame, **Penetration** encompasses the entire spectrum of 'Bleeding- pure noise experiments, mournful ethereal overtures, thrashy industrial-metal workouts, and ambient, almost brass-driven tracks- all into a cohesive, comprehendable form. An excellent substitute for your **Ministry** fix.

FEET FIRST

continued from Page 3

Here we are, the beginning of the **"Summer Of Rave 1992".** Already there's been quite a few club nights and parties, some good, some half-hearted. **Euphoria, Amnesia, Thee Rave-In, Brainrave '92,** Thursdays @ **Tracks-** if you're sorted you know the score on all these. The scene here is growing quickly and it's already adopted a strange feel to it. There's no room for pretensions, so if you've got one, fuck right off This scene is about good music fun, peace, and unity. Don't tarnish it...

Some people who deserve big shouts out: **Matt E. Silver, Jason @ URB, Heather @ Under 1 Sky** (a great Brooklyn-based 'zine, write or call **TRiP** for the address), my mate **Ishai**, and the true ravers. Peace, Rave, Unity!

TRiP MAGAZEEN
100 E. MLK BLVD.
SUITE #10
TAMPA, FLORIDA 33603
U.S.A.

POSTMASTER: DATED MATERIAL....PLEASE RUSH

04

The Bay Area's First Upfront
Dance Culture Fanzine!!
TRIP
DIGITAL BOY
TALKING IN FUTURISTIK TERMS
NEW MUSIC SEMINAR RECAP
SUBURBAN BASE RECORDS
RECORD REVIEWS
PROJECT ONE
X-102
SCOTTIE DEEP
MILES DAVIS
BRAND NEW HEAVIES
BOBBY KONDERS
OUTSIDE N
WIN A HOUSE OF PAIN SCHMOOZE PACK! DETAILS INSIDE...

TRIPPERS DIARY

ONE OFF EVENTS

Bozo Productions presents **RAVING ON RAVING**, Sat., Sept. 5 @ Club Carousel, 8550 Arlington Expy., Jacksonville. Featuring P.A.'s from **AUDIO FM**; scheduled DJ's on the night include **Kimball Collins, DJ Three, DJ Chang, Chris Gallagher.** Hosted by **MC IKE** and **MC MR. CLEAN.** 18 and up, $8 w/ flyer, $10 without. For more info, call 1.800.512.3966.

New Culture and Kali Productions present **PSYCHIC ENERGY**, Sat., Sept. 19 @ Ground Zero, 2581 Piedmont Rd Atlanta, GA. Featuring P.A. by **AUDIO FM** and **ROMEO ROMEO** Drivers confirmed include **DJ Repete(NYC), DJ Three, Kimball Collins, Bruce Wilcox.** 18 and up, $10 at TicketMaster and on the night. For more info call 904.336 0305.

WEEKLY CLUB NIGHTS

SUNDAYS

911, 911 N. Franklin St., Tampa, 224.0911. Upfront dance with DJ Bill Ward. 18 and over, $2 on the door

TRACKS, 1430 E. 7th Ave., Ybor City, 247-2711. Techno/Rave with DJ Rick West. $5 on the door; free before 10:00 for over 21, 18 and over.

THURSDAYS

TRACKS, 1430 E. 7th Ave., Ybor City, 247-2711. Techno/Rave with DJ Rick West. $5 on the door; free before 10:00 for over 21, 18 and over.

SATURDAY

EVOLUTION, 1902 E. 7th Ave. Ybor City, 247-0888. Techno, Rave and Alternative with DJ Steve McClure and occasional guests. 18 & over. $5,18-20; $3, 21+, free before 10:30.

WIN A HOUSE OF PAIN SCHMOOZE PACK!

TOMMY BOY RECORDS' LATEST SIGNING, HOUSE OF PAIN KEPT SOUND SYSTEMS PUMPIN' ALL SUMMER LONG WITH THEIR DEBUT SINGLE, "JUMP AROUND". NOW THE FULL LENGTH IS OUT AND TOMMY BOY ANF TRIP MAGAZEEN HAVE TEAMED UP TO HOOK YOU UP WITH A HOUSE OF PAIN SCHMOOZE PACK. IT'S AS SIMPLE AS ANSWERING THESE THREE QUESTIONS ABOUT THE HOUSE OF PAIN!

1) WHY DO THE HOUSE OF PAIN HAVE SHAMROCKS IN THEIR LOGO?

2) WHICH MEMBER OF HOUSE OF PAIN WAS IN ICE-T'S RHYME SYNDICATE?

3) WHO PRODUCED "JUMP AROUND"?

THE FIRST THREE WITH CORRECT ANSWERS WINS SCHMOOZE PACKS; THE NEXT 100 ENTRANTS WILL RECIEVE POSTERS, STICKERS, OR "JUMP AROUND" CASSETTE SINGLES. SEND ENTRIES TO THE ADDRESS ON THE NEXT PAGE, ATTN: HOUSE OF PAIN CONTEST. DON'T FORGET TO PUT YOUR ADDRESS, PHONE# AND WHERE YOU GOT THIS COPY OF TRIP!

HOUSE of PAIN FINE MALT LYRICS

TommY BOY TRIP TommY BOY

HOUSE of PAIN FINE MALT LYRICS

CONTENTS

VOL. I, #4/SEPT. 1992

TRiP MAGAZEEN
100 E. MLK Boulevard
Suite #10
Tampa, Florida U.S.A.
(813) 238-0310
(813) 876-7473 FAX

EDITOR: Peter Wohelski
CONTRIBUTING EDITOR: Chris Milo
CONTRIBUTING EDITOR: Chris
ADVERTISING: Rates given on request-call or write for details.
BACK ISSUES: Back issues of TRiP are available for $1 postpaid.
SUBSCRIPTIONS: Available by sending a SASE to the above address.

FEET FIRST

Some Post-Summer of Rave thoughts and miscellaneous brainwaves...

Apologies to **John Landsman,** formerly of Raven Productions for any misinterpretation of the **"DJ's Take Control"** profile of DJ Three in last issue. We know you got it goin' on, John!

I'd like to announce the addition of **Chris Milo** to the TRiP Posse as a contributing editor. He'll be writing stories, reviews, and helping to bring some special projects to fruition (like a TRiP Magazeen DJ tape series!).

Total NO respect goes out to Miami's **Blue Cow Productions** for the fiasco called **Exxon.** Many ravers from Tampa Orlando, and Melbourne drove several hours to find out that inability to properly secure the correct permits kept the event from even starting. This promoter had the balls to even use the name and similar graphics for a party in San Diego the week previous! **A word to Out-of Town promoters:** You better be on the up-and-up, just because you got rich in Cali, don't be coming here thinking we don't know what's up... We **will** take you down!

On a positive note, respect is due to **Verb Productions** in Gainesville for a top night at their **B-IN** event at Florida Theatre 28 August. A fine space, killer lights, kickin' sound, a jumpin' PA from **Audio FM** and firing sets
continued on Page 6

HYPE HYPE HYPE HYPE HYPE

....In a statement issued to the U.K. press, **THE KLF** have called it quits. **KLF COMMUNICATIONS**, the group's label, informed their distributors that all the label's releases have been deleted, effective immediately. As to whether this is just another of the duo's infamous scams remains to be seen. ....**THE SHAMEN** return with a new single, **"L.S.I."** featuring vocals from new vocalist **JHELISA**, ex-vocalist of labelmates **SOUL FAMILY SENSATION**....The soundtrack to the film **"COOL WORLD"** features new music from **MOBY**, along with **FUTURE SOUND OF LONDON, MINISTRY,** and **MY LIFE WITH THE THRILL KILL KULT**.. ..From L.A. comes the report that the City of the Angels' 24 hour Techno/House/Dance radio station, **MARS-FM**, has dumped it underground format for a more mainstream "alternative" rock format. **MARS** gave techno its first commercial radio exposure breaking loads of import dance records and sponsoring rave events....Rave events in the U.K. are falling in attendance this summer due to the **SPIRAL TRIBE** collective's free travellers raves. Earlier this summer, the collective reportedly drew over **25,000** ravers to a gathering on the town common of thetiny town of **CASTLEMORTON** that lasted **5 DAYS**....It's a long story, but **TRiP MAGAZEEN** is eluded to as part of **TOP ALTERN 8 PRESS SCAM** in the liner notes of the Stafford duo's debut lp, **FULL ON MASK HYSTERIA!!**....North Florida techno act **AUDIO FM** is preparing to release their debut 12" on their own Gainesville-based **EUPHONIC RECORDS**. The duo will be performing at upcoming one-off events in Gainesville and Atlanta....What a difference a year makes as the acclaimed **DISPOSABLE HEROES OF HIPHOPRISY** go from releasing their debut single **"TELEVISION"** this time last year, to opening act on the **U2** stadium tour....Is that really **CHARLES BARKLEY** kickin' the lyrical ballistics in those new **NIKE** adverts? Or maybe **CHUCK D**??.... Speaking of adverts, check out **FRANKIE KNUCKLES' "WHISTLE SONG"** in the new **NESTEA ICE TEA** advert soundtrack....**ROCKPOOL** Dance Music Editor **JONATHAN KADISH** is heading up a new label, **GYROSCOPIC RECORDINGS**. The label's first release is a trancy biscuit called **FREQUENCY SEX"** by **TRANCE MEDIA**; the label will be distributed by **EMOTIVE RECORDS**....**RHYTHM KING** has closed its **OUTER RHYTHM** and **SPLISH** (run by **MARK MOORE** of **S'EXPRESS**) labels due to the apparent decline in 12" sales in the U.K....**ROZALLA** has been the opening act on **MICHAEL JACKSON'S** current European tour. Wonder if she lip-sync's as bad as she did on **ARSENIO** recently?....

SUB BASE TURNS HIP-HOP INTO BOOGIE TIMES

After making a decent effort to get a good seat at the sanctioned techno panel during this year's **New Music Seminar**, **TRiP Magazeen** contributing editor **DJ Three**- thoroughly bummed at how non productive it was- ended up in conversation with **Dan Donnelly**, owner of **Suburban Base Records**, one of the U.K.'s most upfront dance labels. **Donnelly** shed some light on the label's philosophy, techno in America, and the Sub Base agenda at NMS...

Started out of Donnelly's successful **Boogie Times** record shop in **Romford, Essex**, outside of London, a few years back he and some friends began by moving their own tracks via Boogie Times white labels and eventually the positive demand gave birth to the label.

Complete with studio and "a great engineer", **Sub Base** has been consistently pumping much better than average U.K. techno tracks for quite awhile; "I Feel This Way" by **M&M featuring Rachel Wallace**, "Far Out" by **Sonz Of A Loop Da Loop Era**, **Run Tings'** "Fires Burning" and most recently **Krome & Time**'s "This Is The Sound Of The Underground" and the U.K. singles chart-topping "Sesame's Treet" from **Smart-E's** are just a few of the choice chewns that have come from the Sub Base posse.

Working within their groove seems to be the **Suburban Base formula, as it** seems to work well for them considering the continual popularity of their tracks. As of late, the label has expanded their parameters, moving into Progressive House with **Acorn Arts** as well as other offshoot labels.

The **Sub Base** Crew, keeping jeeps pumpin',via Essex to you........

Asked to describe the sound of **Sub Base**: techno, hardcore, jungle?? Dan Donnelly commented, "We think the "jungle" label is a bit racial really..." agreeing that racial tension is much worse and prevalent here in the U.S. than in England, adding that "Our music is our own interpretation of hip-hop."

Sub Base continued on next pg.

Ironic then, that New York gives more props to England than other foreign hip-hop scenes, as more often than not, the U.K. seems to copy rather than expand upon the structure of hip-hop.

Donnelly and Co., while attending the Seminar, expressed little, if any interest in any of the techno-oriented night-time happenings; opting instead for some of the great hip-hop events during NMS week.

On the growing American scene, "It's fucked up how separate everyone seems to be...", Dan Donnelly noted, as on a dance music level the U.K. is more unified, noticing that all tha labeling of this music here is "Stupid...it's all under house music..." True, or at least true enough.

As an artist (**Q-Bass**) as well as label owner, are there any other labels or acts he likes? "**Reinforced** is more or less on the same tip as we are **Moving Shadow**...we also like **The Prodigy** for how well he's handled his success."

A large contingent of the Sub Base Posse hit Orlando four days after NMS (25 June) for a club rave at **The Edge** with approximately 2000 ravers in the place, getting mental to a good, but too early and too short set by **DJ Danny Breakz** and P.A.'s by a very talented **Rachel Wallace**, Run Tings, Q-Bass, and Sonz Of A Loop Da Loop Era, in addition to some of Central Florida's top DJ's. But if you missed it, the Suburban Base crew won't mind, they'll just keep giving you kickin' U.K. chewns... by DJ Three

FEET ff FIRST

continued from page 3

by DJ Chang and DJ Three made this a memorable close to Florida's Summer of Rave. Cheers!

Go buy the new **Inner City** lp, **<u>Praise</u>**! An outstanding effort from Kevin Saunderson and Paris Grey, uplifting, moving... Who says techno has no soul?

Like I mentioned before, TRiP is going to be doing some special projects in the near future. The first is to be a DJ Tape Series (ala **MIX MAG**) featuring American DJ's If you're a DJ and you're interested in being on one of the volumes, call or write.

The main point though, is that for us to decide on these projects, we need some feedback from you. Drop us a line and let us know what you like about **TRiP**, what you don't like, and what we could do to better serve, inform and educate all of you.

Big ol' shouts go out to Albee! @ Tommy Boy, Erin @ Formula, everyone's fave hardcore turbo-nosebleed headstrong raver, Ishai, Max @ Movement, "Juan Kerr" in the U.K., and everyone who reads this mag. Peace...

ITALY'S DIGITAL BOY BREAKS TECHNO'S FACELESS TAG

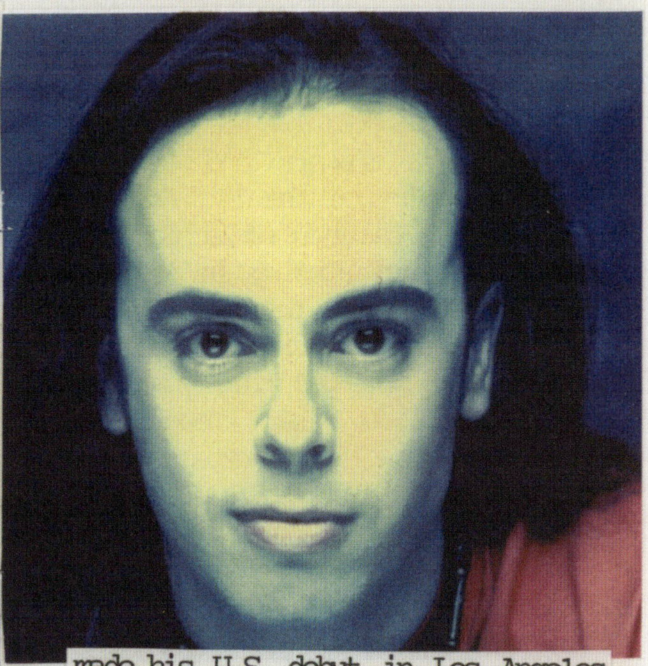

At the age of 22, Italian hard core renaissance man **Digital Boy, aka Luca Pretolesi** has already conquered his home country of Italy and has set his sights upon the raving madness going on here

Known as **Italy's #1 Dance Artist**, this composer/producer/performer/label boss began as a DJ in his hometown of Genova, Italy. Saving money from his gigs, he purchased some musical gear and put out a track called **"Kokko"** on his own **Demo Studio** label. The underground success of this stormer brought the attention of **Flying Records**,

Digital Boy's debut full-length LP **Technologik** led to massive club and chart success, spawning a Italian #1 Top Single, **"Gimme A Fat Beat"**, as well as a #1 Top Single, **"OK Alright**. "Gimme A Fat Beat" also grabbed the attention of Los Angeles' underground dance music radio station, **MARS-FM**, who made the record its anthem and playlist- ed it for 8 months!

Futuristik, Digital Boy's second LP, a much more hardcore effort spawned the singles, **"This Is Motherfucker"**, and **"1-2-3 Acid"**; two tracks that brought Italian magazine **Dance Italia di Leopardo** to write this about Digital Boy,"This is the heavy metal of dance...leave **Iron Maiden** behind and throw yourselves onto this frequency!"

Despite all his chart and studio success, Digital Boy prefers to emphasize his fierce live show, breaking down the faceless barrier around techno music. Fronted by **MC Fresh** and surrounded by a mountain of gear, Digital Boy's live techno experience has won him P.A.'s opening for **Adamski** in Italy and he made his U.S. debut in Los Angeles this past April in front of over 4000 people- the second largest turn out ever for a techno artist.

Although hard to tell when speaking through an interpreter, Luca Pretolesi seems like a very passionate man about his music and techno/rave in general. Based on his observations halfway through the American leg of his **Futuristik** tour, he likes what he's seen of America's growing scene, especially Los Angeles and Dallas, as it reminds him of back in the day when techno was just starting out in Italy.

What did bother him about the American scene is the prevalence of drug use among ravers here. Digital Boy feels that there is no reason to use any artificial stimulants to enhance raving, that the music's positive vibe and energy should be more than one needs to take them to the top. Possibly not a bad idea, considering the dodgy state of most substances these days...

The Futuristik Tour will take Digital Boy throughout the rest of the world until January 1993.

NEW MUSIC SEMINAR 92 AN

New Music Seminar. For thirteen years, an excuse for the music industry's movers, shakers, and wannabe's to descend upon the Big Apple for a weeklong festival of schmoozing, boozing, and abusing in search of the next year's **next big thing.TRiP Magazeen** contributing editor **Chris Milo** attended this year's baccanalian feast, also known as NMS 13- here's his perspective.

New Music Seminar #13, my third time around. For me its an opportunity to meet and establish relationships with other people who do what I do in other areas to keep a global scene perspective...and hook up some vinyl. (NMS) gets worse every time; weak panels, poorly represented music styles, and less **"new"** music. Maybe its biggest obstacle is that is its own obstacle.

After fully copping out on rap in 1991, this year had some good acts- **Das Efx, Main Source, House Of Pain** (with **B-Real of Cypress Hill**), **Yo-Yo.** After a year's absence, **Clark Kent** and **Dr. Dre** brought back the **DJ Battle For World Supremacy** with top class judges like Main Source's **Sir Scratch** and **Premier** from **Gang Starr** as well as some smokin' and some fully not on it DJ's. **DJ Rock Ryder** of NY's **X-Men** was an early fave, then **DJ Honda** (no joke) from Japan ran 'tings hard but in the end, S.F.'s **Mixmaster Mike** took it with his lightning deck work.

Live band of the Seminar? An unlisted **Jah Wobble** performance, although **Sinead O'Connor** never showed to do backing vocals for **"Visions of You".** Who' s Jah Wobble? Here's a clue...ex-**PiL** bassist, did session work for the **Orb**, world mu-

OBSTACLE IN AND OF ITSELF

sic pioneer, etc., etc. **Disposable Heroes Of Hiphoprisy** were no dissapointment live- much hip-hop flavour with live drums and guitar

Nightlife? **Detroit Night** at **Limelight** was great; **Derrick May, Jeff Mills** (a wicked DJ) of **Underground Resistance, Kevin Saunderson,** and others on the decks along with P.A.'s from **Tronik House** and Italy's **Digital Boy.** May even dropped **Vicious Pink**- playing what <u>you</u> want, see? Limelight again- highlighting **Bizarre, Inc., Bon** DJ'ing, and the best live techno act, Underground Resistance. **Fierce Ruling Diva** was great, **Moby** and **Rozalla** was a good night.

Once again the hip-hop panels had decent panelists (I think no one boycotted like **KRS-1** last year- he did the right thing) and a lot of issues. Racism, media, selling out but they always end the same; "How do we fix that?", "First we have to fix ourselves...", "OK, I'm a rapper who's trying to get signed...", and so on. I think this year at least, a tiny beam of light was shed upon the fact that you can't rely on the "Everyone work together, let's do this..." blah, blah plea, when everyone needs to work on themselves. Strong **<u>units</u>** are made of strong **<u>individuals</u>:** you want something done right, (fill in the blanks)!

As for the techno panel, I can't explain how sad it was. I'm curious why some of the people were on the panel; not that they weren't qualified, but there were some far more rooted, prominent, and influential people. The vibe of the panel I thought would be amazing- so many at the heart of a common interest in one room...not even. I left

continued on Page 15

RECORD
REVIEWS

TECHNO/RAVE
12"/ep

V/A-"Fourplay" ep (XL/UK)
The first in a series from XL featuring tracks from 4 different acts on one ep at the price of 1 12". **DJ's Seduction** and **Phantasy** team up on "DJ's Unite", a wicked hi-hat sizzling, synth blown pounder, **Glide's** "Alright" is a pulsating, high-heeled Sheila cooed, bass bangin' breakbeat blinder. **Noise Factory's** "Be Free" brings the riddim with lots of ragga chat, sped-up dub bass lines, and thundering breakbeat while **Mike Gray's EQ** "gave you true devotion" with it's buzzing synth-driven, ultra-frantic offering. Top.

BELTRAM-"Demo EP Part One" (MetalManiac/Belgium)
Out on his own **R&S** sublabel, this self-produced six-pack slammer has its ups and downs "Get Into Life" is a fierce bassburning chugger with urging "Get Into Life" samples; "She Ain't Coming Home" opens ambient before exploding into searing synth droning and sizzling cymbals, while "Warning is a trademark Beltram driver Turbo nutters will delight in the flip's "Jacob's Ladder"/ "There Is No Law" sampled "Fuck You All Motherfuckers", "Machines", and the speed metal/techno planker, "Metal Maniac".

PROJECT ONE-"Don Gargon Comin'' ep (Rising High/UK)
Marc Wiliams and posse deliver yet another pumpin' set of roughneck breakbeat for those who know the score! If you liked the last two, you need to own this one too; if you missed them, get sorted and buy this. Tuff.

TERRORIZED-"It's Just A Feeling" (KMS)
Licensed from Hamster/UK, KMS locks onto this wicked "**Inner City meets TronikHouse**", piano driven, diva-wailing, string synth soaring stunner with its fierce acid bassline farted, jungle beat break. The b-side "It's A Tough Beat" is a rumbling dub-influenced breakbeat biscuit with a buzzing bass line and drill sample from **Van Halen's "Poundcake"**.

FIERCE RULING DIVA-"You Gotta Believe (Atomic slide '92)" (Invasion)
Holland's **FRD** launches their second shot into the U.S. with the follow up to "Rubb It In", a 1992 remix of "Atomic Slide" by the ambassador of Techno, **Charley Casanova**. Also featured is a dope Garage Mix, Deep House, and the two original mixes. Worth it for the Garage Mix alone!

EUPHORIA-"I Like Noise" (Quark)
A pair of **N-JOI-like** synth-stabbed midtempo commercial winners feature on this second ep from Euphoria. The title cut drones "I Like Noise",

while "Genocide" is a "Mind-Flux" sampled, frantic siren wailing rumbler in two mixes.

ALEX ALOT-"Jacob Your God" (White)
A thunderous biscuit from Bronx, NY DJ **Alex Alot** full of analog synth stabs and **Art Of Noise** trademark drums over a frantic driving breakbeat. The track slows down to a sli thery synth ala "Mentasm" bef ore jumping back into high gear with samples from **Ministry "Nature Of Love".** For more info, fax 212.288.4835.

V/A-"Industrial Strength Sampler" ep (Industrial Strength)
From one of the U.S.' best up-and-coming techno labels comes this 4-track split ep by two **Lenny Dee** projects. Running forwards, **English Muffin**'s two cuts buzz along, jungle techno style, the best being "Dust Muffin"-a fierce bassline buzz ing, hi-hat chugger with sped-up **Opus III** vocal samples and driving piano break. **Crowd Control,** spinning backwards, delivers two menacing headstr-ong Belgian/Detroit pounders for the insomniaks and non-posing party people. A must.

BLAME-"Music Takes You" (KMS)
Domestic release of this kick-in' breakbeat stunner from Moving Shadow/UK in four mixes; Original, Music Takes Two, ext-ended Kaotic Chemistry Takes You, and buzzing Ecstacy Takes You. Unfortunately, no **Seal** samples or **Two Bad Mice** remix es; nonetheless a nice one if you missed the import.

LP/COMPILATIONS

THE ORB-U.F.ORB (Wau! Mr. Modo Big Life/U.K.)
Ambient explorer **Dr. Alex Pat-terson** and his band of merry men embark on their latest sonic excursion, this time to the outer reaches of our own universe. Wafting in deli-cately, **U.F.Orb** is more dance-able (?!) than its predecessor enveloping one in its hallucin atory, dub-influenced haze. In typical Orb fashion, grooves flow in and out of the mix, generating a pulsating symph-ony of beats, sounds, voices.

ALTERN 8-FULL ON MASK HYSTERIA (Network/UK)
Now all on one LP/CD/CS; more **Altern 8** than one can toler-8! Seriously though, all the Staf-ford pranksters singles, etc. are all here , great liner not-es outlining how the duo has managed to scam all the press, record companies... the chem suits, the masks, the bass, the noise, its all here. Just buy it!

V/A-KAOS THEORY3 (Telstar/UK)
With cuts from such heavy hit-ters such as **Smart-E's, Manix, Acen,** and others this is a ser-iously upfront collection of in-demand tracks for the non-vinyl pursuing raver. Most of the tracks are full 12" length but some are edits; a compila-

RECORD REVIEWS

tion to keep punters of all persuasions jumpin' and pumpin' into the Fall of 92.

X-102-...DISCOVERS THE RINGS OF SATURN (Underground Resistance-Tresor/Germany)
Hardcore techno and a science lesson to boot, **UR** and **The Vision** strike out against the "Teenage Mutant Ninja Ravers" with a blinding 36-minute mass of molten conceptual Detroit madness. Menacing, mesmerizing minimal, massive, and a must for the turbo nosebleed headstrong motherfuckers!

HOUSE/GARAGE/ACID JAZZ/R&B 12"/ep

SCOTTIE DEEP-"Fathoms" (Aztonk)
From the Motor City comes this emerald vinyl deep house gem by **Scottie Deep**, aka **Scott Kinchen** Very deep, rammed and mellow, "Fathoms" pulses along with hihats smokin' and a bit of electric piano, hand claps, and female singer scatting over the top. Perfect for the late nigh chill and trance session.

GALLIANO-"Skunk Funk" (Talkin' Loud/UK)
Acid jazz poet **Robert Galliano** and his funky crew are back wi th more funk for your soul on this single from their new lp. "Skunk Funk" takes Galliano in a **Tom Waits/Leon Redbone**-esque voice to "Harmony Village" in three distinctly different mixes, all produced by **Style Council's Mick Talbot.** The Brave And Strong Mix hits hard with a driving hip-hop groove, pumping horns, wheezing organ, and soulful female background vox; the Soldiers Mix shuffles more on the jazz-funk tip, mixing up the organ, while **Andrew Weatherall** spliffs things out on his Cabin Fever Mix adding an echoey dub bassline, timbales and radio frequencies. A serious crisp biscuit.

QUE SERA SERA-"You Don't Know" (KMS)
James "VICE" Denham drops this bouncy piano-driven chunk of feel good garage. In four forms; 12" Vocal, Instrumental, the more techno-y VICE Mix, and the radically reworked Alternate Mix. Not necessarily blinding, but I like it....

LP/COMPILATIONS

MILES DAVIS-doo-bop (Warner Brothers)
For a few years now, rappers have been incorporating jazz samples in their music, merging the two truly American musical styles both past, present, (and future?). **Gang Starr, ATCQ Main Source,** and **Dream Warriors** are just a smattering of acts that have brought jazz to hiphop, but it took an innovator like the late **Miles Davis** to bring hip-hop to jazz. Miles' final studio lp, **doo-bop**, showcases his fine horn against streetsmart beats provided by **Rappin' Is Fundamental's Easy Mo Bee.** The purely instrument-

al tracks here are clearly the
best with the raps being a bit
played on the lyrical, but all
in all, a stunning, innovative
close to a master's career.
Fusing jazz, hip-hop, and funk,
doo-bop could be the definitive
"acid jazz" lp.

**V/A-TRACKS FROM THE FOURTH FL-
OOR/THE FIRST TEN YEARS (RCA)**
From deep house to early tech-
no, Latin freestyle to jazzy
bits New York's Fourth Floor
Records has been one of the mo-
st influential street labels
of the past ten years. **Tracks**
showcases some of the best cuts
from the label's history and
the careers that were launched.
Producers like **Todd Terry, Len
ny Dee, Frankie Bones, Tommy
Musto, Yvonne Turner, and Omar
Santana** are just a few of the
innovators that started out
through the label. Full of
classics, this comp. provides
an excellent resource to some
of the most important tracks
in clubland.

THE DAOU-HEAD MUSIC (Columbia)
The brainchild of keyboardist/
producer **Peter Daou** (pronoun-
ced "Dow"), this debut is an
astounding hybrid of deep hou-
se, avant-garde jazz, freeform
keyboard ambience, dark-themed
prose, and surreal vocals. To
call them "alternative" would
be a true definition of the
word. A record that fits in
many catagories and none at
all, **Head Music** is just that-
music for your head that also
moes your body. A different
sort of chill-out record.

**RONNY JORDAN-THE ANTIDOTE (4th
& Broadway)**

RECORD REVIEWS

Co-produced by **Longsy D** (remem
ber "skacid"?), the debut from
guitarist Ronny Jordan reflects
a new age in jazz fusion comb-
ining cool jazz with hip-hop
overtones, rap, pulsating bass
lines, and heavy dance rhythms.
Educated in the "Groove Academy"
and influenced by the likes of
Wes Montgomery, Miles, and **Geo
rge Benson**, Jordan takes jazz
guitar to new territories on
tracks like a funked-up version
of Miles' "So What", "Get To
Grips" (with a conscious rap
by **I.G. Culture** of **Dodge City
Productions**), and the cool
"After Hours". Glad to see 4th
& Broadway had the vision to
release this in the U.S. If
you miss this, you're missing
one of the best records of 1992.

**HIP-HOP
12"/ep**

**LIVE SQUAD-"Murderahhh"/"Hear-
tless" (Tommy Boy)**
Ruff, raw, and real describes
the hardcore debut tracks from
new Tommy Boy signing **Live Squ-
ad.** "Murderahh" comes on the
roughneck tip, spouting gangsta
rhymes about cop killin', homi-
cide for fun, and gangbanging.
"Heartless" hits full on with
phat beats, double barrel rhy-
mes, and a fresh-ly loaded **Mo-
town** sample. A real eyeopener
to hip-hop's new gangsta's

RECORD REVIEWS

BRAND NEW HEAVIES-HEAVY RHYME EXPERIENCE, VOL. 1 (Delicious Vinyl/Atlantic)
If you're looking for the smooth, soulful follow-up to the Heavies' stunning debut, you're in the wrong place. That comes out in late 1992/early 1993. **This** is the jam-of-the-jam, super phat, long-awaited phunky joint teaming up the amazing BNH with the new school's finest. Stemming from an impromptu freestyle jam during the Heavies' NY debut **Heavy Rhyme Experience** features the band live in the studio with **Main Source, Gang Starr, Black Sheep, Ed O.G.,** gettin' live over the funky grooves. This is already classic. Essential!

HOUSE OF PAIN-HOUSE OF PAIN (Tommy Boy)
After a stint with **Ice-T** and **Rhyme Syndicate** and a debut lp that wasn't, **Everlast** returns alongside Irish drinking mates **Danny Boy** and **DJ Lethal** like a pint glass upside the head with the **House of Pain.** Besides the Irish flavoured smash, "Jump Around", this debut is deep with slammin' beats, dope rhymes, and phat production from the **House** and guests **Grandmaster Muggs** of **Cypress Hill.** A serious debut sure to keep you blunted and your system pumpin'

REGGAE

BOBBY KONDERS & MASSIVE SOUNDS (Mercury)
Longtime **WBLS-FM** (NYC) DJ **Bobby Konders** moves from behind the mic to the studio mixing desk on this self-titled debut collection. Best known for his radio shows full of dancehall, hip-hop, and other urban sounds, Konders successfully rolls all of these elements into one big fattie, an intertwining of fresh grooves with exposed roots. Whether it's comin' ruff and direct with tracks like "Mack Daddy" or smooth and rootsy like "Rising To The Top"-even housey with "You Don"t Know", Bobby Konders run tings round here...

SUPERCAT-DON DADA (Columbia)
The second in a recent series of dancehall DJ's to sign with American major labels, Kingston's **Supercat** hopes to follow in the success of labelmate **Shabba Ranks** with **Don Dada**. Unlike Shabba, Supercat stays pretty true to the hardcore dancehall massive with a rougher, less crossover vibe; chatting about drugs, guns, and lots of slackness like his hard rhyming American gangsta counterparts. Co-produced by longtime producer **Rupert Livingston** this debut also enlists the talents of rapper **Heavy D, Frankie Paul, Trevor Sparks,** and reggae legends **Steely And clevie** to give the record some much needed spice.

INDIE/ALTERNATIVE

OUTSIDE N-OUTSIDE N (Demo)
Altough bound to be lazily tagged as **Consolidated** or **Hiphop-**

risy clones, Brandon, Florida's **Outside N** present a solidly produced and programmed 3 song demo that shows lots of vision and promise. Like the aforementioned acts, Outside N combine socio-political topics with industrial-edged hip-hop beats and samples forging a pounding mass of in-your-face hysteria. Recommended. For more info, (813).684.5336.

IN THE NURSERY-DUALITY (Third Mind)

Sheffield's **In The Nursery** have spent almost 10 years refining their elegant, sophisticated sound. Melding classically-based horn and string arrangements with military snare drum and timpani into lush, post-industrial orchestrated soundscapes, **ITN's** twin brothers **Klive** and **Nigel Humberstone now** bring forth **Duality**, a project essentially six albums in the making. Finally reaching that pinnacle of perfection, **Duality** is not overdone or geandiose ib its cinematic texture.

NMS continued from Page 9

fully unhappy, feeling things like "Thank God this music **is** faceless!"

The unsanctioned techno panel at Limelight hosted by key representatives from the whole techno nation turned out much the same, patching the sanctioned panel's wounds. With the exception of a few rational conclusions- i.e.: there **are** good breakbeat records, there are DJ's that **shouldn't** be, techno as a labeled dance music form is from Detroit, U.S.A. This panel sadly went nowhere.

The underground keeps going, but here's a thought or two. **So what** if 90% of breakbeat records suck and that England is out of hand bec ause of no quality control- at least they have their **own** scene. So the "Suburban Knights" think rave tracks from a year and a half ago are techno, **who cares**? They'll burn like the fad they rode in on! What about the day they think **+8** is cool? **Scary**...

I agree with **Jeff K.** of **KDGE-FM/Dallas** in the notion that U.K. techno has enabled DJ's to transform a mundane racially-tinted alternative scene into a decent , almost-educated underground. The alternative kids like the hardness, the hip-hop kids like the flavour...now they're "under one sky", raving. Where I couldn't play "F.U." by FUSE a year ago in most cases people are checking the deeper stuff now. In the U.S., it's going backwards in a way; as far as England, if **Aphex Twin, Future Sound of London, ragga,** and **progressive house** (a term that does more harm than good, maybe) are a sign, it's alive on its own. (In the U.S.), it's up to the DJ's and the "Johnny Bought A Sampler"'s to push the levels (of awareness and creativity). The biggest problem with break records, for me personally, is that most DJ's are boring. Pure techno is on an upswing- once it gets very popular, we've got to avoid the rave record syndrome of "Hey, just like **"Anasthasia, cool."**

Perhaps Derrick May summed it all up in one quote: "You've got one chance to make a change, that's it."

by Chris Milo

TRiP MAGAZEEN
100 E. MLK BLVD.
SUITE #10
TAMPA, FLORIDA 33603
U.S.A.

POSTMASTER: DATED MATERIAL....PLEASE RUSH

05

TRiP
Vol. I, #3
A Look Inside
XL
RECORDINGS
2 BAD MICE
ROMEO ROMEO
DJ MARK KAMINS
RECORD REVIEWS
APHEX TWIN
INNER CITY
MR. FINGERS
MC SERCH
AUDIOAFTERBIRTH
Liam Howlett
The Prodigy
THE BAY AREA'S FIRST UPFRONT DANCE CULTURE FANZINE!

DIARY

ONE-OFF EVENTS

FUNKY FRIDAY HIP-HOP FEST, Thursday, October 23 @ Club Detroit, 16 2nd St., N., St. Petersburg. Featuring **Black Saturday, Funky Groovy Catapillars, Outside N, Lost-N-Found,** and **Kenny K.** 18 and up. $5 on the door. For more info call 896-1244.

Digital Domain Productions in association with **Unity Promotions** presents **INFONET**, Saturday, October 24 @ Orange County Convention Center, 9800 International Drive (Across from the Peabody Hotel), Orlando. On the decks: **Guy Ornadel** (UK) **Kimball Collins** (Orl), **DJ Three** (Tpa), **Chris Gallagher** (GVL), and others. 18 and up, $14 in adv., $16 on the night. Call 287-8844 for more info.

GUAVAWEEN @ EVOLUTION, Saturday, October 31 @ Evolution, 1902 E. 7th Ave., Ybor City. Drivers include **DJ Steve McClure, DJ Three, DJ Alex Machine, DJ Mit** (Tal), **DJ Andy Hughes** (Daytona). 18 and up.

WEEKLY CLUB NIGHTS

TRACKS, 1430 E. 7th Ave., Ybor City, 247-2711. Techno/Rave with DJ Rick West. $5 on the door; free before 10:00 for over 21, 18 and over.

THURSDAYS

TRACKS, 1430 E. 7th Ave., Ybor City, 247-2711. Techno/Rave with DJ Rick West. $5 on the door; free before 10:00 for over 21, 18 and over.

SATURDAY

EVOLUTION, 1902 E. 7th Ave. Ybor City, 247-0888. Techno Rave and Alternative with DJ Steve McClure and occasional guests. 18 & over. $5,18-20; $3, 21+, free before 10:30.

THE FACTS ABOUT AIDS

AIDS (Acquired Immune Deficiency Syndrome) is an equal opportunity disease. It affects men, women and children regardless of race, age, or sexual orientation. AIDS is caused by a virus called HIV (Human Immunodeficiency Virus). To date, there is no conclusive data to explain how AIDS got started or where AIDS came from. People with AIDS—regardless of their sexual orientation—deserve compassion and support, not violence and bigotry.

- ***You can get AIDS by having vaginal or anal sex with an infected partner.***
- ***You can get AIDS by sharing drug needles with an infected person.***
- ***You can get AIDS by being born to an infected mother.***

The simple act of putting on a condom can save your life, if they're used properly and every time you have sex. For more information about AIDS and condoms, call *1-800-342-AIDS.*

AIDS IS NO PARTY!

the alternative record store

TAMPA'S PREMIERE ALTERNATIVE STORE ANNOUNCES ITS NEWLY ESTABLISHED 12" DEPARTMENT!!!

THE MOST CURRENT TECHNO,

HOUSE, AND ALTERNATIVE

IMPORTS AND DOMESTICS

11900 N. NEBRASKA AVE.,
TAMPA, FL, 33612, U.S.A.
813.977.6383

CONTENTS

VOL. I, #5/OCTOBER 1992

TRiP MAGAZEEN
100 E. MLK Boulevard
Suite #10
Tampa, Florida U.S.A.
(813) 238-0310
(813) 876-7473 FAX

EDITOR: Peter Wohelski
CONTRIBUTING EDITOR: Chris Milo

ADVERTISING: Rates given on request-call or write for details.
BACK ISSUES: Back issues of TRiP are available for $1 postpaid.
SUBSCRIPTIONS: Available by sending a SASE to the above address.

FEET FIRST

All sorts of crises and tragedies have struck our part of the world the past couple of months; the tornadoes in Pinellas Park and of course the massive devastation of the South Florida tribe with Andrew, most notably.

When one is faced with that sort of crisis, we tend to look inward for a positive, uplifting source to draw some sort of optimism from. A mental therapy, a spiritual healing to envelop yourself in momentarily shielding us from the weight of overwhelming external forces.

Some look to religion, some look to the closeness of friends and relatives. Some in the House Nation find their solace within the positive vibe of techno. Especially with the influx of all the good deep soulful, spiritual trance tracks lately, techno is a blinding medium in which to find that inner source and exorcise demons. Nothing clears your mind better than a high-volume, substance-free, deep-as-your-soul, trancendental bliss out.

A HYPE! addendum- As we went to press, **TRiP**'s L.A. sources report that **MARS-FM** has now gone off the air, replaced by an easy listening format station. **R.I.P.**

The **TRiP** Vibe keeps on rollin' nationwide as this mag is now available in selected safe record shops and clothing boutiques in **Baltimore, Brooklyn, Gainesville,** and **Orlando** as well as the true hardcore headstrong Tampa Bay area.

Big 'ol shouts go out this month to the following: Marcy Weber @ MCT, Art Payne @ KMS Detroit, Sean Deason @ **Matrix**, Kathy Gillis @ Virgin, the ever short and annoying Annie P., DJ Chang, DJ Bruce Wilcox, the one and only Matt E. Silver, and DJ Icee.

....Opening on a sad note, **MICHAEL OVA**, one-half of Toronto-based **HI-BIAS RECORDS** passed away recently of an AIDS-related illness. An exciting young label, Hi-Bias will carry on as he would have expected....If you can find one, pick up a copy of Plus 8 Records' **COMIC BOOK. PLUS 8019** includes a **F.U.S.E.** flexi-disc and is illustrated by **ALAN OLDHAM**, who did the label art for **TRANSMAT** back in the day....Didya know that before he joined **FU-SCHNICKENS, CHIP-FU** used to be known as **K.C. FLIGHTT**?!?....Reliable sources tell **HYPE!** that **RCA** is close to working a licensing deal with **MOVING SHADOW/ U.K.** (**TWO BAD MICE, BLAME, KAOTIC CHEMISTRY**) in the States.. ..After last month's dramatic music shift, L.A.'s **MARS-FM** has returned to an urban/underground dance format, playing Techno/Rave and House along with funk, rap and alternative dance tracks....Going their separate ways: **LARGE PROFESSOR** and **MAIN SOURCE, ERIC B.** and **RAKIM....GUERILLA RECORDS** has unceremoniously dropped **REACT TO RHYTHM** from the label after the band was brought to Los Angeles for several live gigs and refused to play....With the closing of Orlando's **AAHZ**, look for Tampa's **Evolution** to go to an all-nighter format with **DJ STEVE MC CLURE** and guests driving the wheels of steel on Saturdays....**MCA** has secured a deal with London's **BLACK MARKET RECORDS.** Run by Chicago house pioneer **LARRY "MR FINGERS" HEARD**, the label first group of releases include **DJ MASSIVE** and **JUAN ATKINS**....Last year's brilliant **STEVE HILLAGE/ALEX PATTERSON/DERRICK MAY/YOUTH/PAUL OAKENFOLD** ambient deep house collaboration lp, **SYSTEM 7**, has now been released in the U.S. through **CAROLINE.** The lp has been renamed **777** as not to conflict with **APPLE MACINTOSH**'s new operating software of the same name....In what seems like forever, **NINE INCH NAILS** have released a new ep on their new label, **INTERSCOPE.** Expect **TRENT REZNOR & CO.**'s full-length major label debut in Early 1993....It's rumoured that the rights to quite a chunk of Jamaica's legendary reggae label, **STUDIO ONE** is now in the hands of **SONY MUSIC.** The thought of all those long out-of-print gems reissued on CD makes **HYPE!** very tingly. Massive!....As we go to press, **808 STATE** are completing their **SPINMASTERS** DJ Showcase Tour to promote their new lp **GORGEOUS.** The group plans to return to the States in November for a full live audio assault....Former Tampan, now American ex-pats **FLOWER SERMON** are set to release their debut single **"LULLABY"b/w"FLOW"** through the reorganized **ROUGH TRADE SINGLES CLUB** in October limited to 1000 copies..

Two Bad Mice 'Hold It Down' in Orlando

Overheated and looking a tad exhausted, Moving Shadow head mouse **Rob Playford** hops onto the dressing room counter after his **Two Bad Mice**'s storming P.A. at Orlando's **The Edge**, and breathes a short sigh of relief.

2

"Fucking hell," the short, ponytailed Brit Playford spits, "while they've been running around with Mickey Mouse, I'm working my arse off!", refers Rob Playford to the rest of the **Moving Shadow** crew present on this hot Labor Day eve.

Working their arses off, indeed. Rob Playford and Two Bad Mice partner **Sean O'Keefe** have come out of nowhere and positioned their Moving Shadow label as one of the most wicked U.K.

MICE

underground dance labels and themselves as quite sought after hardcore remixers. "Actually we've been doing this(the label) for a couple of years now, but we're just getting recognition for what we've done," clarifies Playford.

Starting as DJ's (like most English kids), Playford and O'Keefe made the natural transition from spinning tracks into creating their own and putting them out. Still, the time spent behind the mixing desk has not eroded their skills on the decks. While at The Edge, both Mice drove the crowd hard with fierce sets of "rumbly, rumbly" chewns. "I've only been DJ'ing a lot lately, I'm usually too busy and we don't do many P.A.'s at home," reveals Rob.

As remixers Two Bad Mice have made quite the name for themselves, reworking tracks by, among others, **Phuture Assassins** (Suburban Base), **Dream Frequency** (CityBeat), **Blame**, (Moving Shadow), and their own releases to massive results. Well, almost; the Mice' remix of Dream Freq-

BAD

uency was rejected by CityBeat and Playford is trying to license the track for release on Moving Shadow. "We ripped everything out of the track except the vocals and made it real deep dub; I don't think that was the type of mix they wanted, really," admits Rob.

The softspoken Brit is also looking forward to some upcoming projects with both Suburban Base and Reinforced; remixing some of each other's tracks. "We all know each other, we're good mates, and we do about the same type of work."

Perhaps Moving Shadow's success can be attributed to the label's attention to making good quality tracks and getting them pressed and out into the shops quickly. "It's getting the music out that's most important. We get the records out in the shops first and worry about the paperwork later," stressed Playford,

continued on Page 15

NY MC TAKING TECHNO TO NEXT LEVEL

Whether he's working the crowd into a frenzy as House MC at Manhattan's techno strongholds **Limelight** and **Palladium**, throwing down tracks with the likes of **Charley Casanova** and **Program 2**, or spreading the word of **R.A.G.E.** throughout the world, New York's **Romeo Romeo** is about positivity and taking techno to the next level.

Perhaps best known for his work with DJ Charley Casanova's **Turntable Hype ("Revolution"), Romeo began** ("Revolution"), Romeo began his career with Charley doing freestyle records. A trip to Belgium and Holland opened Romeo's eyes to the techno vibe; he and Casanova cutting a track for **R&S** called "Gonna Make You Move". A return trip to Rotterdam later solidified Romeo's belief in the power of techno.

In addition to his work with Casanova, Romeo has collaborations waiting in the wings with **Lenny Dee** (We've got two slammin' tracks done but Lenny's been busy with his own label, **Industrial Strength**."), **Joey Beltram** ("You'd never know it by looking at him, but Joey, when he gets in the studio...you could say he doesn't have arthritis in his fingers...", and **Lorenzo "Dominator" Nash** ("A few months ago, we brought Lorenzo over for a Battle of the MC's contest in New York. We worked on the vocals and some of the music, and now I'm about to send the DAT to Lorenzo's people to finish.")

An artist in his own right, Romeo Romeo has just finished an ep and has been touring the U.S. and Europe with his **R.A.G.E.** (**R**hythmatic

continued on Page 15

Ambassador shocked by raving Russians

The techno-starved youth of the Commonwealth of Independent States were treated to a unique slice of "World Techno-beat" recently as New York-based international DJ **Mark Kamins** played to 2000 manic ravers in Moscow 26 September.

Joined by an African and Algerian band as well as a Russian DJ who worked on reel to reel tapes instead of turntables, Kamins came on to spin his brand of Tribal and Trance with a pair of **Technics 1200**'s borrowed from a Moscow radio station.

"I'm still in shock," said a still disbelieving Mark Kamins, "I was sort of expecting all the kids to just be standing around, **not** knowing what to do- but they were just mental!" The event, which was held in an old movie theatre, cost almost an average Russian's month salary to get in, according to Kamins.

In addition to the rave, Mark also DJ'ed a party on a boat for some St. Petersburg club kids on the night previous 25 September. "They freaked me out, because they went more for the **Strictly Rhythm** New York House sound than techno," commented Mark.

He also reported that both of the parties he worked had good sound and equipment, two complaints that plagued previous Techno Ambassadors like **Adamski, The Shamen,** and **Westbam** on their goodwill visits to the then Soviet Union.

One of Manhattan's most in-demand DJ's, Kamins can be found doing guest spots at New York clubs **NASA, Meat,** and the soon-to-open **U.S.A.** between his frequent trips to Japan and an upcoming jaunt to Rio de Janeiro and Sao Paolo in the month of November.

Florida ravers can catch Mark Kamins behind the wheels of steel at the grand opening of **Hell**, a new club in Miami on Halloween night.

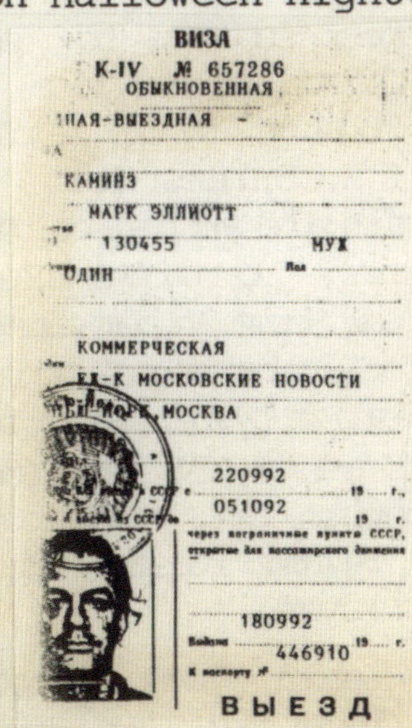

Mark Kamins' TOP 5

Sunscreem-Perfect Motion (Sony/UK)
Shift-Havanna (23 rd Prescinct/UK)
Diss-cuss-Pissed Apache
Trance Porter-Open Your Mind
Trance Form-Transporter

Pictured: **Mark 's Russian Visa**

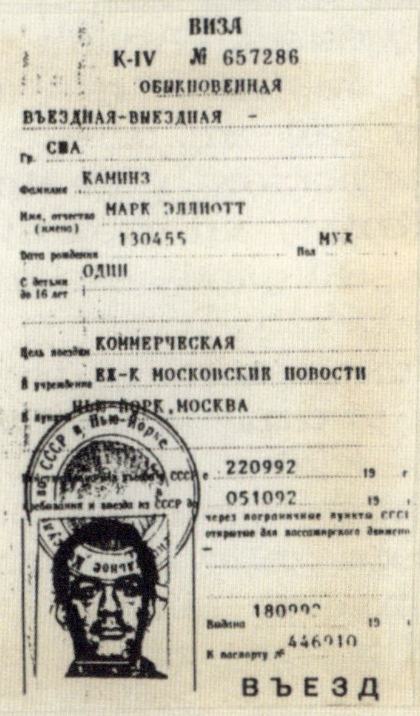

DJ credibility, not chart success t

From its initial releases of American House tracks by **Brooklyn Funk Essentials** and **The Flowmasters** right up to the mad chart success of techno whiz kids **The Prodigy** and **SL2**, London's **XL Recordings** has been one of the U.K.'s most consistent and reliable underground dance labels.

Founded in 1989 to operate alongside the already-established **Citybeat Records** by Citybeat manager **Tim Palmer** and **Nick Halkes**, the force behind XL was to create a rave music friendly label.

In a scene dominated at the time by U.S.-oriented tracks, XL first broke through when **Frankie Bones** and **Tommy Musto**- two respected American innovators, over to play one of the **Energy** raves- were corralled by the fledgling label into a recording studio. The result was the **"Energy Flow"** ep; Musto & Bones using the alias of the Flowmasters. Previous releases such as the **"Looney Tunes"** ep (Bones & **Lenny Dee**) and subsequent house music explorations by the **Moody Boys, Bobby Konders,** and homegrown talent **Fantasy UFO** quickly established the label's identity.

With a clear policy entailing no editing to comply with **Gallup** chart criteria (kind of like a U.K. **Billboard** chart), only pressing at 33 rpm for maximum quality and duration, XL has managed to maintain a musical credibility and upfront direction that has kept the label in the front of DJ's record boxes worldwide- in the wake of rave's commercialization.

"The major role for XL is whether the track has DJ credibility and will it kick the dancefloor. If it doesn't pass these two tests, we've failed.", Tim Palmer told **Clubland** Magazine, "Record companies are always too concerned with chart positions. If they feel the track has no chance to make the Top 40, they won't release it. Our concern is to release good dance music, music for DJ's."

The label has had its share of chart success however, beginning with Belgian blaster **"Anasthasia"** by **T-99**, released in April 1991 and reaching #14 in the charts. Similar chart success closely followed with **Cubic 22**'s **"Night In Motion"**, another Belgian creation.

XL's biggest success to date though, was the unheralded rise of **The Prodigy**'s **"Charly"** to the #1 position on the U.K. Singles Chart in August 1991. With the arrival of this **"Mentasm"**-sounding, cartoon-sampled, sped-up Breakbeat House Anthem came a succession of bandwagon-jumpers trying to capitalize by releasing tracks with children's TV programme samples, prompting an underground backlash that **MixMag** recently proclaimed "killed rave".

Prodigy leader **Liam Howlett** responded to **Check Dis**, "We could

he key for 'rave friendly' XL

have just done another "Charly", but everyone would have just branded us as the group that samples children's television. We wanted to get away from that, so we released **"Everybody In The Place."** I'd like to see the scene go back underground really."

"Everybody In The Place" debuted at #2 behind **Queen's "Bohemian Rhapsody.**

Chigwell lads **SL2** (**Slipmatt** and **Lime**) are also well respected; Slipmatt being a DJ for the **Raindance** organization, both founding pirate radio station **Awesome Radio** and their own **Awesome** record label, before XL signed them up. The duo's releases **"DJ's Take Control"** and **"On A Ragga Tip"** were recieved to rave club play and solid upfront shop sales.

The discovery of The Prodigy, SL2 and other XL signings like **John + Julie**, (aka **GTO, Church of Extacy, Signs Of Chaos**, etc.), **Nu-Matic,** and **Liquid** are due to the label's on-the-ball A&R staff Nick Halkes and **Richard Russell** and their "ear-to-the-ground" policy. Both can be found at various club nights and events throughout the Capitol and the U.K. Halkes and Russell also stay upfront musically with their project, **Kicks Like A Mule**, that has sprouted two singles to date, **"The Bouncer"** and **"Number One."**

The label has started a singles series that reflects this "ear-to-the ground" philosophy; the **Fourplay** series features one-off tracks from up-and-coming DJ's and producers. XL has also founded a new hardcore hip-hop sublabel, **Ruffness**, dedicated to releasing quality hip-hop flavours.

As far as America, where the label took its first tracks and the techno scene is exploding nationwide, Xl maintains a presence with their

New York office. Housed in Tommy Musto's **Northcott Productions**, the label keeps influential DJ's hooked up with upfront vinyl and aware of what's going down on the other side of the Atlantic.

XL has also worked a licensing deal with **Elektra Records** for The Prodigy. In this exclusive agreement, Elektra has already released the Essex group's previous singles with domestic remixes by **Joey Beltram** and **Moby** as well as the current **"Fire"** ep and the upcoming full-length album, **The Prodigy Experience** (**Editor's Note:** As we went to press, Elektra released the Prodigy lp). How extensive this agreement will stretch remains to be seen.

With such strong prospects in the future, an foothold in the American market, strong commitment to the underground, and the XL's recent singles successes, the future looks bright for the U.K.'s most successful underground dance label.

RECORD REVIEWS

TECHNO/RAVE
12"/ep

MOBY-"The Ultimate 'Go'" (RoughMix)
Seems many wondered "What's up?" after his last releases through **Instinct,** but out of nowhere comes a 1000 copy pressing of "Go" mixes... two incredible mixes by **Jam & Spoon**, hard raver by **PCB,** and three by **Moby** himself. Jam & Spoon's Delerium Mix and Moby Arpothoski Mix- deep trance and hard techno respectively- are my picks as fully brilliant. The others are quite good, including J&S' killer slow pure ragga dub version. Get it while it lasts and Moby- keep it coming! **(CM)**

808 STATE-"Timebomb" ep (Tommy Boy)
The world of techno has changed greatly since these Mancunians released their second lp, **EX:EL**- the "Belgian Hoover" sound, "Dominator", "Charly", breakbeats, ragga, etc. Now in late 1992 and beyond Vicks, **808 State** respond with the "Timebomb" ep, a way to play catch-up and show that the innovators haven't fallen off. But by not fully grasping the current trends, they have. "Timebomb" and "Nimbus" are weak break tracks with now tired trademark 808 sounds (the group, not the machine). Showing the most promise is "Reaper Repo", a balearic/tribal/progressive house mover full of congas and samba beats Here's hopin their upcoming **Gorgeous** lp will restore my faith in 808 State as innovators.

SONZ OF A LOOP DA LOOP ERA-"Peace & Loveism"/"Freedomism" (Suburban Base/UK)
Sorry, but Sub Base has been falling off lately. A bit formula to say the least, but I'm sure the masses will approve. "Freedomism"'s got trademark sequenced scratches and the same synths as before with a Latino-style breakdown. "Peace & Loveism" is a bit better with a clever use of **Enya** strings and better beats. **(CM)**

LIQUID-"Future Music"ep (XL Recordings/UK)
Much different than the Spring's happy "Sweet Harmony" ep, Liquid flows deep with this moody 4-tracker. "Liquid Is Liquid" is a trancy deep dub bassline and echoey piano groover with intermittent slices of fluid breakbeat to push things along, "Music"'s deep piano-driven, "don't stop the music" crooned, breakbeat stunner, and the bass burning, hi-hat chugging, late-night mesmerizer "House (Is A Feeling)". The only loser of the lot is the directionless piano-jumping filler "The Year 3000". Not as immediate as its predecessor, but "Future Music" grows into a superb bisquit with each spin. Brilliant.

NIKO-"Oh Yeah" (Instinct)
This debut single on Instinct for **Frequency X** member **Niko** is expected to follow in the footsteps of his new labelmate, **Moby**. In three forms; the fierce, frantic Final Fury Mix, the stonking Pressure Mix, and the hard trance of the Dark Treatment Mix. Also included is "Axiom", a flute-driven, bassline wiglling trance stormer. Nice one, better than I expected.

N2O-"Nitrous Oxide" (EX)
A searing cymbal sizzling, synth buzzing, raging Belgian breakbeat stormer in two mixes, produced by **Tim** "The Horn Track" **Taylor** and **Toxic Two**'s **Damon Wild.** The flip's "Lazer Worshippers" comes along the same hardline with it's frantic synth, crashing cymbals, and mental rumbling bass, while "On A Rize" is a "Planet Rock" drum groove, whale sampled, synth swirling slice of pulsating trance dance. Choice

DEMISE-"Demise" ep (Fokus/UK)
This **Ralphie Dee/Dino Blade** produced fourpack ep serves up a diverse selection of styles; the A-side moves to Detroit with "Mental Asylum", a hard, frantic, bass-bleeping chugger with **MC 900 FT. Jesus** samples and "Playground Memories" a happy, pulsing, midtempo acid groover. On the flip, "New York City", a wicked bassline buzzing, pinging "1,2, New York City" shouted stormer, and the uninspired ragga of "Culture Assassin".

G DOUBLE E-"Asylum Seeker" & CHEEBA WIZARD-"Jump The Devil"

RECORD REVIEWS

(Hardcore Urban Music/UK)
Hardcore Urban Music, the **Genaside II** famed label is back after somewhat of a hiatus with two 100% kickin', ragga-core releases. No gimmicks submitting to the charts here...just deep vibed breakbeat madness. Underground. **(CM)**

APHEX TWIN-"Xylem Tube" ep (R&S/Belgium)
The Aphex Twin brings his next apocalyptic slab of thundering stomach quaking mental techno. From the hard trance of "Polynomial-C" to the mind-numbing turbo headstrong planking of "Phlange Phace", this is one devastatingly trancendental experimental mindphuq! Totally essential for the true hardcore

TRANCE MEDIA-"Frequency Sex" ep (Gyroscopic)
The first release by **Emotive Records** distributed **Gyroscopic Records** is a ultra-fierce digital/analog monster that builds and breaks, full of fat trippy acidic synth-buzzing riffs. Pitch it up and drop it with **Aphex Twin** or anything on **Rotterdam.** Slammin'!

ANARCH-E-"Punk Rock"ep (Hall-uci-Nation)
"One Nation, Underground... Invisible" says the fine print on this very brainy (for lack of a better word) Tech-

RECORD REVIEWS

no-Rave 12". "Hardcore Mutha Fucker" starts with "1984, Punk Rock...Hardcore is dead" and a guy saying "When the music gets so fast it's like it has no beat-you can't dance to it" and **Ice-T** sample responding "Shit ain't like that", into a cool track with unfamiliar breakbeats and stabs topped with the gentle female sampled "Hardcore Mutha Fucker". "Give It Up Punk" is a deeper track with a not too quick rap sample from? Eerie melody breaks and **Tone-Loc**'s "I'm blazin' the joint" sample not overused and twice as loud as the track without ear damage. Get it-only 1000. Someone said it might be **Altern 8-DJ Three** doesn't know. **(D3)**

WORLD POWER ALLIANCE-"Belgian Resistance"/"The Seawolf"/Kamikaze" 3X12" (Underground Resistance)
The first in a series of "Techno/Rave" tracks these triple simultaneously released, single A-sided dub plates each share a common military theme; declaring war on the "Teenage Mutant Ninja Ravers", perhaps? Techno-pure, hard, and fast, "The Seawolf" is the most havoc-causing of the three, ala **+8**, with its fathoms deep bubbling bassline, pulsing dive alert samples, and warp-speed hi-hats.

LP/COMPILATIONS

INNER CITY-PRAISE (Virgin)
After 1990's dissapointing **Fire**, **Kevin Saunderson** and **Paris Grey** return in '92 with a vengeance, making the Inner City album that they wanted to make. **Praise** is a perfectly balanced, full-on thumping convocation of uplifting garage/techno and hardcore-influenced breakbeat tracks. Opening with a Detroit meets breakbeat driver, "One Nation" to the soulful "Pennies From Heaven", the **Altern-8** produced "Let It Reign", and the spiritual "Faith", Inner City successfully creates their most definitive album to date and resoundingly answers techno's critics with a reverberating, "Yes techno does have a soul!"

EON-VOID DWELLER (Vinyl Solution/Columbia)
Almost two years after the import smash **"Spice", Eon** (aka **Ian Loveday**) lets loose **VoidDweller**, the first full length project via **Vinyl Solution/UK**'s licensing deal through **Sony.** For those who missed them the first time around, the hits are here-albeit a bit tired-but the gems are the handful of all-new tracks. Assisted ably by **J. Saul Kane** (and on one track, **Baby Ford**), Eon demonstrates equal ability with breakbeat rhythms, hard Detroit-style pounders, and deep trance grooves; as individual tracks Void Dweller succeeds but as a unit, it doesn't mix well.

SHAMEN-BOSS DRUM (Epic)
Recovered from the tragedy of

1991, the Shamen pick up where **En-Tact** left off;spreading their message of positivity to a wider audience with **Boss Drum. Mr. C** and **Colin** interact well; C's cockney accent lending a bit of fun to the lyrics while new vocalist **Jhelisa** more than adequately fills **Plavka**'s empty shoes. Although not as strong as its predecessor, this underground techno record with pop appeal will not alienate the hardcore massive with its "techno-tribal" instrumental workouts as the more accessible radio friendly tracks subtly communicate these Scots' message to the mass populace.

HOUSE/GARAGE/ACID JAZZ/R&B 12"/ep

REESE PROJECT-"Colour Of Love" (Giant)
With remix and co-production from Motor City mates **Underground Resistance, Mark "MK" Kinchen,** aad **Juan Atkins, "Master Reese"** comes through with a smash follow-up to this Spring's "Direct Me". In six forms; Underground Resistance's uplifting, bouncy piano-driven, horn-stabbed 7"/12" house stormer, the UR Jazzed Up Mix with its deep female scat vocal, a vibraphone punctuated, bassline pumping groover; the smooth, whirling Juan Atkins Techno Mix, MK's female vocal stuttering deep dub mix, and **Saunderson**'s own dark **"Rock To The Beat"**-like 808 bassline driven Reese Deep Mix. Safe.

P.D.Q.-"Again" (Fourth Floor)
A version of **Sly Stone**'s **"Thank You"**, this Italian licensed production comes in three

RECORD RR REVIEWS

versions; a classic Italo-house piano mix, the **"French Kiss"** sounding Deep Club Mix, and "Tribal Again", an unrecognizable, but effective **Sheffield**-meets-**Tribal Trance**, jungle chanted rumbler.

AIRTIGHT-"Housewerk" (Fourth Floor)
This **Psychotropic** produced energetic acid buzzer pleasantly pulses along with just enough ambience to keep the punters happy. Also check the FXTC Mix on the back, a summery pianosynth stabbed, female vocal cooed dancefloor sizzler A right good tune.

V/A-"Murk Records DJ Sampler" (Network/UK)
The Brits go buck whyle over U.S. Garage tracks and this three track DJ promo sampler import licensed from Miami's **Murk Records** just proves that the English repackage our ideas and sell it back to us at twice the price. Seriously though, this fiercely deep and cool as ice sampler is a bargain, fully worth the import dosh- American homegrown Garage at its best! Essential.

LP/COMPILATIONS

MR. FINGERS-<u>INTRODUCTION</u> (MCA)
Sensual, jazzy, and intelligent Chicago House Legend **Larry "Mr**

Fingers" Heard delivers one of the classiest collections of chill chewns I've heard in awh ile. Smoothly flowing a laid-back true house vibe through-out, **Introduction** takes the more sophisticated, clued-up clubber to another level of spiritual healin , not spliff ed out bliss. If you're not sorted already, this is an lp worth investigating.

HIP-HOP

BROTHERS LIKE OUTLAW-THE ONE-NESS OF II MINDS IN UNISON (Gee Street)
U.K. hip-hop crews have long been dismissed as second-rate copies of their American cou-nterparts; recently acts like **Caveman, Dodge City Productions** and **Brother Like Outlaw** have stepped into the light with the growing popularity of acid jazz and funk. **BLO** combine the conscious new school vibe with a decidedly English, smooth jazz-funk feel that sets their flavour apart from the pack. Self-produced with a visit from **YD**'s **Femi Fem**, this American debut features lots of live instrumentation lending an org-anic cohesiveness that gives U.S. homeboys a view into the growing U.K. scene.

MC SERCH-RETURN OF THE PRODUCT (Chaos/Columbia)
MC Serch steps off hard on his solo return to wax coming out of the crash and burn of **Third Bass**, although the "baddest white boy to ever touch a mic" may have left a few things in the wreckage. Hardcore and mus-ically complex, Serch takes **...Product** to a new level but lyrically, it lacks the sense of humour that made Third Bass a unique force in hip-hop. Per haps the weight of stepping out of his former group's sha-dow was a bit much to handle; final analysis- an innovative and true-to-the-game, but so-mewhat uneven debut.

EPMD-BUSINESS NEVER PERSONAL (Chaos/Columbia)
Erick and **Parrish** come corr-ect once again to make doll-are as the hip-hop marketpl-ace finally catches up to the underground and new sch-ool becomes the flavour of the month. **Business...** is the same record the **Hit Squ-ad** have been pumping out of Strong Island since Day 1. They may flow about "Cross-over", but there ain't no sell-out here, just pure phat phunk. Their best yet...

INDIE/ALTERNATIVE

V/A-VOLUME MAGAZINE, #4 (Wor-ld's End/UK)
The fourth edition of this CD sized, full-color interview magazine/new and breakthrough artist sampler divides itself between fawning over British press darlings like **The Fall, Babes In Toyland, Throwing Muses,** and **Suede** and spotlig-hting "alternative" dance mu-sic's finest underrated or

unsigned new talent. Some musical highlights: **Ultramarine'** "Saratoga", a sublime slab of jazzy, **Eagles**-sampled (?) ambient acid; the Marley-meets-On-U-Sound roots reggae of **Bim Sherman**; "Shine", the swirly "wet-dreampop" debut of ex-pats **Flower Sermon; Dub Syndicate**'s echoey **Adrian Sherwood** splifflicated live dub; a new recording from **Spectrum** (ex-**Spacemen 3**'s **Sonic Boom**), "Soul Kiss"- a trancendant, otherworldly slice of organic knob-twiddling ambience; as well as tracks from **Aphex Twin Meat Beat Manifesto, Steroid Maximus,** and **PWEI**. Despite its stiff import price tag, **Volume** is a beautifully produced, graphically sharp, and musically upfront collection for followers of NME, Melody Maker, or the musically curious.

AUDIOAFTERBIRTH-COMMBINE (Emigre)

Imagine if **Trent Reznor** lived in Minneapolis instead of Cleveland, was less angry, more obscure, and **4AD** put out his record. Got it? Meet **P. Scott Makela** and Audio AfterBirth's debut, **Commbine**. Produced by an ex-Prince engineer and released by Emigre- the same label that gave us **Basehead**- this is not **Pretty Hate Machine**. Yes, it is aggressive, at times dark, and has a warped eccentric pop sensibility; but it lacks the accessible danceability that **NIN** has. An industrial record for the sedentary.

2 Bad Mice, from Page 5

"Not to say the paperwork doesn't get done though."

Responding to the charge of the commercialism running rampant through the U.K.'s rave scene, Rob Playford said this regarding his label: "At Moving Shadow, we make tracks strictly for the Underground and ourselves. We're certainly not making records for the money, that's for dead cert..."

In our hearts, not in the charts, Rob.

Romeo Romeo, from Page 6

Aggressive Groundbreaking Energy) concept. A uniquely NYC approach, R.A.G.E. is the application and integration of hard lyrics and vocals to thundering techno grooves, giving this so-called "faceless" music an identifiable image.

"I love techno but I like music with chorus and melody and vocals, but I think for techno to succeed here you have to make it human, someone creating this electronic music that people can identify with. It's like that song by **Mick Jagger**, "I Can't Get No Satisfaction", if you're going to tell me about that song, you're gonna sing the words. With techno, what are you going to sing, (sings "Belgian Hoover"-style track) you can't figure out what that is!"

"Americans relate to songs and artists. Take **Paula Abdul** for example, not that I like that kind of music," disclaims Romeo, "but she's up there, in videos, dancing, whatever. It's visual, people like visuals. I'm trying to bring that to techno."

TRiP MAGAZEEN
100 E. MLK BLVD.
SUITE #10
TAMPA, FLORIDA 33603
U.S.A.

POSTMASTER: DATED MATERIAL....PLEASE RUSH

06

THE BAY AREA'S FIRST UPFRONT DANCE CULTURE FANZINE!
FOCUS ON DETROIT
INNER CITY
PLUS 8
SCENE REPORT
KMS RECORDS GIVEAWAY
E-LUSTRIOUS IN ORLANDO
Record Reviews
TRiP

Eastern Bloc Comes To Orlando

In celebration of TRiP's FOCUS ON DETROIT, KMS Records and the Bay Area's First Upfront Dance Culture Fanzine have teamed up to giveaway 5 copies of their new double vinyl compilation,

JOURNEY THROUGH THE HARDCORE

The complilation lp featuring:

TRONIKHOUSE
TERRORIZE
BLAME
MANIX

THE HOUSE CREW
THE SORCERER
KISS THE SKY
& MORE

Just answer this easy trivia question: What member of the "Detroit Three" owns KMS Records?

Send the answers on a postcard to the address on the next page? Be sure to put your address, and where you got this copy of TRiP!!!

CONTENTS

FEET ff FIRST

VOL. I, #6/ December 1992

TRiP MAGAZEEN
100 E. MLK Boulevard
Suite #10
Tampa, Florida U.S.A.
(813) 238-0310
(813) 876-7473 FAX

EDITOR: Peter Wohelski
CONTRIBUTING EDITOR: Chris Milo

CONTRIBUTORS: DJ Three, DJ Ron-E. C, Annie P., Art Payne

ADVERTISING: Rates given on request-call or write for details.
BACK ISSUES: Back issues of TRiP are available for $1 postpaid.
SUBSCRIPTIONS: Available by sending a SASE to the above address.

It has been said that there would not be techno as we know it without Detroit. Countless artists, DJ's, producers, etc. have been influenced by innovators like **Juan Atkins, Derrick May, Kevin Saunderson** and their seminal dance tracks; it was even Juan Atkins that coined the term "techno" in an interview. We at **TRiP** feel that more people should learn about the roots of this music, as techno is not some new musical flavour of the month- it has a past, a present, and a future. We are its future. This issue has attempted to shed some light on what Detroit has, is, and will continue to contribute to the global techno nation.

Bay Area community radio station WMNF recently took the "Kenny K Wax Attack", the Bay Area's only true hip-hop radio show off the air. Kenny, a part-time member of **Digital Underground**, was replaced by a six-hour National Public Radio syndicated Black music program. For a station that claims to serve the Black community, WMNF just cancelled, as Chuck D. says, the only outlet for the Black CNN. To voice any complaints, write: **WMNF Radio, c/o Station Manager, 1210 E. MLK Blvd., Tampa, FL 33603.**

Respect and thanks is due to many peo ple this Holiday season. If you're not mentioned here it's because we ran out of room, not that we forgot... Shouts to: Matt E. Silver, Erin Norris, Kathy Gillis, Art Payne, Phil & Paul Hartnoll, Nicole @ Rising High, Damon Wild, Marcy Weber, Jared Hoffman, John Acquaviva, Mad Mike @ UR, DJ Icee, Todd Job, Glenn Boothe, Dr. Alex P., Albee Ragusa, Ishai Meron-RMF, and all who have contacted, read, or assisted **TRiP Magazeen in 1992. Joyeux Noel!**

....Flash from Detroit! **JEFF MILLS** has left **UNDERGROUND RESISTANCE.** Full details were not available, but **TRiP**'s Motor City sources report that Mills left just before the outfit's recent Australian tour. **UR** asked **ALAN OLDHAM,** longtime host of WDET-FM's **FAST FORWARD** techno mix show, to replace Mills. ...**RICK RUBIN**'s **DEF AMERICAN RECORDS** is the latest U.S. label to jump on the techno bandwagon, signing deals with Belgium's **PRAGA KHAN, MNO, LORDS OF ACID,** and **DIGITAL ORGASM** in addition to **KICKIN' RECORDS' MESSIAH**....Of the moment producer/remixers **FUTURE SOUND OF LONDON** now host their own show on London's 24-hour dance music station, **KISS-FM**; the duo also recently signed a megapound deal with **UNION CITY RECORDINGS**....Rumour has it that **MICKY FINN** is going to remix Gainesville's **AUDIO FM**....**HOUSE OF PAIN**'s next single, **"SHAMROCKS AND SHENANIGANS"** will be released as a joint venture between the group's label, **TOMMY BOY,** and Seattle indie **SUB POP**; Tommy Boy handling the 12" and CD5" and Sub Pop putting out a green vinyl 7"....**HoP** is also the first signing to **XL/UK**'s new hip-hop sublabel, **RUFFNESS**....Canadian industrialists **PRAYER TOWER** have signed to **THIRD MIND**.... **FRONT LINE ASSEMBLY** offshoot project **INTER-MIX** will release a new album of techno delights, **PHAZE TWO**, in Early 1993..... Is it true that **JOEY BELTRAM** has signed a deal with **ATLANTIC** ???; he's apparently been working on a remix of **"MY SOUND"** with **ROMEO ROMEO**....Planning to be in **BERLIN** in December?? The organizers of this Spring's **MAYDAY** event are doing one for Fall, to be held **DECEMBER 12** in a **7-8000** capacity warehouse. Only for the headstrong, the bill features **DJ CARL COX**, several techno outfits from Rotterdam playing live and a host of Berlin's top turntable terrorists....St. Petersburg's **CHANNEL ZERO** resident driver **DJ THOM NICHOLSON** is opening up a new clothing shop on 7th Avenue in Tampa's **YBOR CITY**. Called **ZULU GROOVE,** the shop will carry tons of fresh gear and should be open even as we speak....Rappers **LIVE SQUAD** plan to release a film short in conjunction with the release of their debut lp, **GAME OF SURVIVAL**. Out soon on Tommy Boy....Check out grunge rockers **MUDHONEY**'s hilarious techno piss-take on their new **PIECE OF MIND** lp. A total gas and a ½....The U.K.'s musician royalty collection agency, **PRS**, has targeted raves. Setting a tariff of 4% of the admission price, the agency has the power to prevent events from taking place if the license fee is not paid.

RAVE NEW WORLD
performing live
MOBY + THE prodigy
with
CYBERSONIK
USA
UK
+8 SOUND SYSTEM DJs
+8 RECORDS
RICHIE HAWTIN + J. ACQUAVIVA
SPECIAL GUEST DJ APPEARANCE BY MOBY
PSYCHECYBERADIANT LIGHTS BY SCOTTO
FRIDAY, JANUARY 29, 1993
THEE AREENA
501 N. ORLANDO AVE. (A1A)
COCOA BEACH, FLORIDA
INFO ☎ 407•784•5414
BUY TICKETS NOW THRU TICKETMASTER FLORIDA

Plus 8-True Techno Uproar-No Hardcore

Named for the high pitch that the label's founders were spinning records at, **Windsor, Canada's +8 Records** has emerged as one of the Detroit (Windsor is just across the river) techno scene's hardest and most collectible labels in three years of existence.

Co-founded by **John Acquaviva** and **Richie Hawtin**, +8 began after the pair met while in Detroit, John hanging out in the club Richie DJ'ed at. The pair eventually did a record in John's studio which was **"Elements Of Tone"** under the name **States Of Mind**, the label's first release. Acquaviva and Hawtin decided to put the record out themselves and start +8 to "do it how things should be done."

Releases like "Elements Of Tone" as well as **Cybersonic's "Technarchy"** (one of the first rave tracks), **F.U.S.E.'s "F.U.", Final Exposure's "Vortex"** (done with **Joey Beltram** and **Mundo Musique**), and **Speedy J's "Pullover"** have forged a distinct sound for the label that John Acquaviva says can't truly be labeled.

"It's not really a hardcore sound, there's lots of dimensions to us. We were sort of one of the people that started doing this sort of music; I mean, the whole name implied playing fast. Now labels like Rotterdam that have been influenced by us are doing it," explains John Acquaviva.

With this hard and fast streak running through the label's sound, one might ascertain that Acquaviva and Hawtin come from an industrial music background rather than house or hip-hop, like so many other techno label bosses. Only partly true, according to John, "I'd have to say that Richie came from a background like **Kraftwerk, New Order, Depeche Mode**, and definitely some of the **Wax Trax!** stuff. I'm a pretty poppy guy, really. Since I'm a little older, I grew up on things like **Gary Numan, Visage**, Depeche Mode, more of the synth-y, pop things of that time."

+8 is a label that cares deeply how it is percieved. John Acquaviva explained that respect is much more important to +8 than cashing in on techno's current popularity. "We make an effort to not capitalize (on our success), we want to stay underground in the sense that we try to be unique in one sense or another."

It is that desire for uniqueness and underground respect that made the label take a much-publicized "summer hiatus" and release things like **PLUS 8018** and **PLUS 8019**- condoms and a comic book respectively- instead of records. The comic book, drawn by WDET-FM DJ **Alan Oldham** (who did the artwork for Transmat's early releases and is now a member of Underground Resistance), takes the reader on a "graphic trip through a dystopic Detroit underground" with a unreleased flexi-disc soundtrack from F.U.S.E.

The reason behind the label's hiatus? "In the past year we've not been too keen on the way things were going in the outside world. I had had not much fun DJ'ing, the label had a few big hits (with Speedy J and F.U.S.E.) and we didn't want anyone to say that we capitalized on our successes. While everyone else came to the (New Music) Seminar in New York this year with all these new releases, we showed up with condoms and a comic book," recalls Acquaviva.

"We have no agenda to do volume (of releases at +8)... I'm not one to rush things and we basically stayed home (this summer) and worked on music. Instead of releasing all these remixes of "Something For Your Mind", **Jochem (Papp, aka Speedy J)** worked on his album and it's excellent. I mean, we all work out of our parents' homes and there's no pressure for volume. We want to do things with quality."

Besides the +8 imprint, Acquaviva and Hawtin also have a couple of sublabels to handle different genres of musical output, **Probe** and **Malego**. "We feel sort of uneasy about releasing lots of material on +8, again we try to make things on +8 special. Although there's no real set guideline, Probe is more for "clubby stuff", while +8 is for big projects.", defines John. The Malego label is primarily house.

"Probe actually came about in a backwards fashion. It started off as a joint project with **Hi-Bias** for New Music Seminar last year (1991), us doing "F.U." and they (Hi-Bias) did the other side, catalogued as PRO1," John explains. The F.U.S.E. track got a lot of attention and the label did a follow-up under the name **Circuit Breaker**. Many people thought +8 were being bootlegged, as the record had **'F.U.- +8'** etched in it. "Actually it was us just making fun of ourselves and not taking things too seriously." The label's pisstake got to the point where they actually had to name the label. "PRO actually meant promotional!" reveals Acquaviva.

The label's popularity in Europe demands that Acquaviva

FOCUS ON DETROIT

Detroit Scene Report-What's Up?!?

What Focus on Detroit would be complete without a full over view of what's going on in the Motor City? Much has been said in the past about Detroit's lack of a scene, despite the amount of music coming out of this city. **TRiP** asked **Art Payne**, Promotion Director for KMS Records and Streetsound scene columnist to give us the score...

CLUBS

Twenty 36- In Downtown Detroit's trendy "Woodward Strip", this tri-level club offers live acts on top, art gallery in the middle and DJ Alton Miller on the bottom.

The Vault- The new happening place for the Black "Dress to Impress" crowd with DJ Charles Hicks and crew in Downtown.

Club Inferno- Former site of the legendary **Music Institute**, this all-ages club plays "classic Bass, West Coast Techno, and an occasional 90's record" with live broadcast on WGPR (107.5 FM).

The Warehouse- Friday nights DJ Kim James and house DJ John Collins simulcast live on WJLB.

Industry- WHYT (96.3 FM) Hotmixers join house DJ John McConnel for a live simulcast and P.A.'s from national dance acts.

RADIO- Detroit radio is making a little progress with the support of the club simulcasts mentioned above. Another daring step has been the long overdue support of local music in Detroit.

RAVE REPORT

Detroit experienced its lar gest indoor rave to date at th he historic Majestic Theater 2 October, 1992. KMS Record brought together all Detroit' key techno promoters ar supporters like **RecordTime Panic, Voom, Unity,** and **RaveBo** along with DJ's like **Richi Rich** and **Juan Atkins** for one-night event. Featured liv were **Moby, Manix, Undergroun Resistance,** and **Blake Baxter** This event also had a secon room for garage and hous grooves. A follow-up even featuring **Altern 8, Inner City Cybersonik,** and **Carl Craig** i planned for 2 January 1993

LABELS

Underground Resistance (313-963-1025) is still kickin' after the Mills-Banks split with several new releases on **UR** as well as sublabels **Happy (House/Underground), Simply Soul** (funk/groove), and **Ghetto Tech** (techno/funk); **KMS** (313-259-1553) is also full of new vinyl with their new associated and sublabels **Transfusion, Vicious Music,** and **Serious Grooves**. Some new labels to check out- **Dow,** run by WHYT hotmixer Claude Young and **Black Nation**, Jay "Vice" Denham's label. Also to be recognized; **Aztonk** (run by Scott Kinchen, MK's brother), **430 West, Cyren America** (Santonio of Reese & Santonio's label), **Shockwave,** and **Undercurrent**.

uptempo tracks, slow melodic tracks, too."

The way that this then-futuristic electronic sound created by Saunderson and friends **Juan Atkins** and **Derrick May** has become dance music's most enduring influence, it's hard to fathom that this then-Eastern Michigan University student had to be persuaded to take his music hobby seriously, his mind set on a professional football career. "I would have played for anyone who would have drafted me," admits Kevin, "I'm still a big sports fan, while I was on tour in Australia, I went to what is their equivalent of the Super Bowl of rugby; I'm also a big Lions and Pistons fan."

Certainly the most prolific and visibly successful of the "Detroit Three", Kevin has been described by the other two as "extremely energetic" and a "go-getter". What has propelled him forward, beyond both Juan and Derrick? "I think I take chances more; I go on my first reaction most of the time, I'm a first reaction sort of person. As far as like the early tracks go, we just did them- not necessarily the right way sometimes. Derrick and Juan, on the other hand, have a certain standard about things, I think; they may only put out a certain type of record. I'm probably more versatile, I'll do a vocal record just as well as an underground record. My scope is broader,

Not only is Kevin Saunderson a techno ambassador, but he's a Detroit ambassador as well, playing up the excellent unknown talent in the Motor City, whether it's doing interviews, spinning at raves and parties, or utilizing this home-grown talent in some of his own projects like **Reese Project**. Saunderson describes the project as "me helping local Detroit talent. It's a thing that's more urban, more soulful, gospel-oriented, and show off the versatility of what Detroit has to offer. Hopefully someone will get a deal or get recognized; but it's my way of giving something back.

The Reese Project just recently released it's debut long player, **Faith, Hope, Clarity** after two very successful singles, **"Direct Me"** and **"Colour Of Love"**. Kevin also plans on taking the Reese Project on the road, doing P.A.'s and shows in both the U.K. and Holland this Winter.

In the meantime, the busy innovator will be spending the next couple of months doing remix work, overseeing his own **KMS** Records, before preparing for the next Inner City album. Shedding a little light on the subject, Saunderson said he wasn't quite sure what the next record would be like, although he was considering using real percussionists, and that it would have "a real African vibe."

Detroit innovator Saunderson, Inner

When one thinks about techno and its innovators, surely **Kraftwerk** comes to mind; Chicago acid house legends like **Phuture** and **Sleazy D**, too. When talk turns to Detroit, however, the conversation is not complete without the name **Kevin Saunderson**. As a prolific producer, remixer, label boss, DJ, ½ of the majestic **Inner City**, and creator of some of techno's seminal tracks, his impact has shaped the world of dance music immeasurably.

Born in New York City, Kevin Saunderson was privy to the musical diversity of the Big Apple, but it wasn't until his family moved to the tough, industrial city of Detroit that he was exposed to the influences that would make Detroit's seminal tracks like **"Rock To The Beat"** and **"Just Another Chance"** so unique. "When I moved to Detroit, there was this radio DJ, the 'Electrifying Mojo'. He was probably the first person I ever heard play all this really cutting edge music. I had never heard **Parliament/Funkadelic, Prince,** the **B-52's** or Kraftwerk until I moved to Detroit, and Mojo really inspired me to do something different, make a new sound and not be a standard R&B artist," explains Saunderson.

It is this pursuit of creating something different that is the driving force

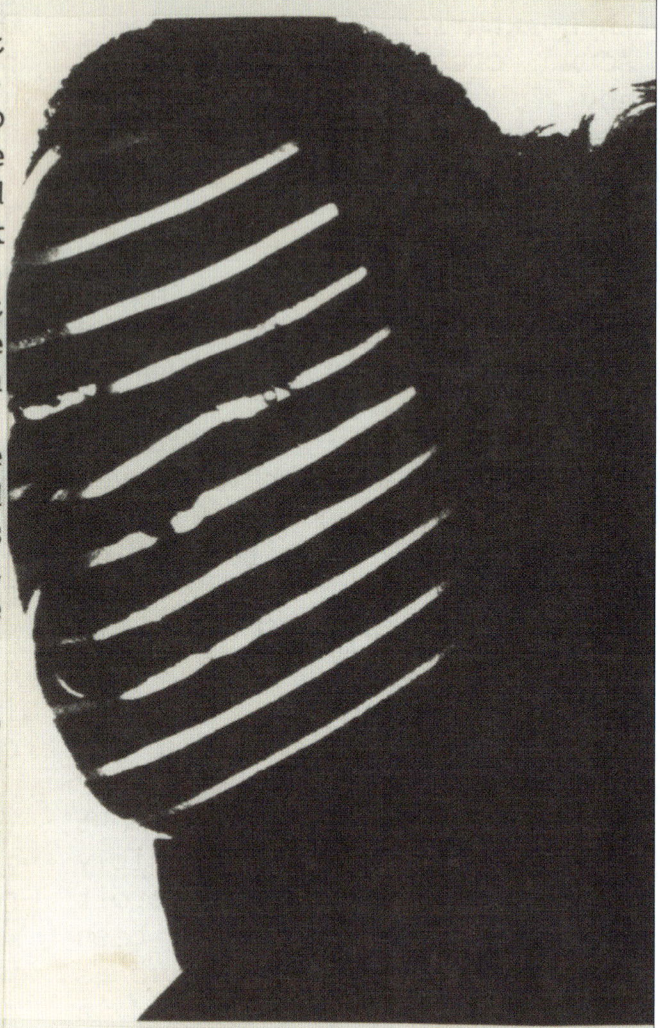

behind Inner City, the group that Kevin Saunderson is perhaps best known for. Fronted by vocalist **Paris Grey**, Inner City stormed onto the scene in 1989 with **Big Fun**, a debut that spawned two hit singles, **"Good Life"** and the title track, and altered the course of dance music forever.

The duo's record company, Virgin, anxious to repeat the success of Inner City's debut pressured Saunderson and Grey to put out another record as soon as the first died down. The result was 1990's **Fire**, an ill-recieved collection of

City get 'Praise' they deserve

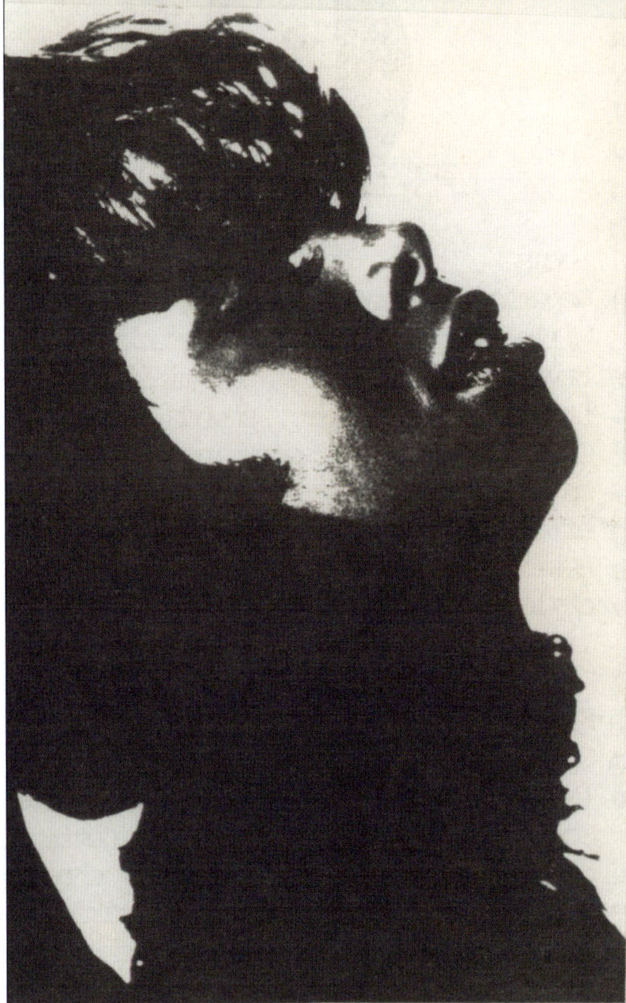

American R&B-flavoured tracks that Kevin admits "was not the record we should have done."

"It was a difficult situation, Inner City just sort of happened by mistake, and there was Virgin pushing us to put out the next record right away. We had no time to slow down and listen, it was all 'rush, rush, rush'," the man they call **"Master Reese"** says, almost resentfully.

In the meantime, the Rave movement sweeping throughout the U.K. and Europe incited Saunderson to observe the techno revolution that he helped to inspire by regularly DJ'ing at raves, something he hadn't really done since he was in college. Perhaps known for playing a lot of breakbeat records at the time, Saunderson says he has begun playing more "trancy stuff, not as much hardcore anymore; sort of trancy dub sounding things."

Witnessing the uniqueness of the U.K. Breakbeat House sound, however, Saunderson began to experiment on his own under the alias of **Tronik House**, a project that Kevin describes as "me having fun experimenting and making very creative tracks. It's a way to stay on the cutting edge."

At the same time, certain English tastemaker DJ's began playing **"Hallalujah"**, a track from **Fire** at their club nights, starting a great demand by U.K. clubbers and DJ's alike.

Virgin, readying itself for a new Inner City lp in the next year and feeling the time was ripe for a remix, approached hot-at-the-moment remixers **Leftfield** to the honors for the update. The always progressive Saunderson gave the duo the green light and off they went. Released on white label at the end of 1991, **"Hallalujah"** did very well and lent the group a much-needed shot of credibility. **continued Page 18**

TECHNO/HOUSE/GARAGE
12"/EP

THUNDERGROUND-"Thunderground"/"Chrome Roots" (Infonet/UK) Bandulu in disguise, this record is highly recommended. This label won't quit! Both tracks outstanding- minimal, driving, uptempo, dubby techno with "Thunderground" as the top pick with its smooth and bass infected breaks. Headstrong-must be played loud! **(CM)**

SPERMINATOR-"No Women Allowed" (Rotterdam/Holland) The pure techno equivalent of "Sesame's Treet"- wack concept and not very unifying. Well-respected tipsheet charts like **Brand-X** have been charting it, so give it a listen. We just can't find any depth. **(CM)**

PRODIGY-"Out Of Space" ep (XL/UK) Two remixes and a live track taken from the **Experience** lp **(see review later in this issue)** that are barely fair fodder for the underground. "Out Of Space" tests a bit of the acid while your kid brother or the clueless will dig the way too happy Uplifting Vibes Remix of "Ruff In The Jungle Bizness". Also included is the slice of live "Music Reach (1,2,3,4)".

ORBITAL-"Halcyon" (ffrr) The Brothers Hartnoll spend a rainy London afternoon knocking about with samples and out comes a freak pop song with underground cred. Using the "It's A Fine Day" sample, looped backwards, "Halcyon" is a hauntingly beautiful slab of dubby, melodic trance. "The Naked And The Dead" is a swirling, tribal chugger and its 11+ minute companion dub mix is all that and more with its massive driving pulse, buzzing synth, and bass-burning dub breaks.

H & M-"Tranquilizer" ep (Axis) This

RECORD REVIEWS

seems to confirm **Jeff Mills' separation from UR.** Now with Hood, Mills releases this three tracker. My fave, "Mutant Theory" is minimal hard trance with great sounds. "Sleep Chamber" is like something you'd find on a techno breaks record and is very effective for deep groove mixing. The B-side's other track, '88- acid, H & M style. Top for creative DJ's and deep listeners. **(D3)**

KAOTIC CHEMISTRY-"L.S.D." ep (Original & Remixes) & TONE DEF-"Projection" ep (Moving Shadow/UK) Ever since "Drum Scare", **Rob Playford & Co.** are getting deeper and deeper in dub- no cheeky samples or two note piano breakdowns here. Excellent "jungle" techno on all three with Tone Def being even deeper. "L.S.D."'s **Krome & Time** remix of "Illegal Subs" has a great intro but turns immediately into formula wackness. Considering the Moving Shadow's strong track record as of late, we hope the label's upcoming releases will keep Moving Shadow on a roll-no pun intended. **(CM)**

CHEZ DAMIER-"I Never Knew Love" (Serious Grooves) From KMS' new DJ's only spin-off label comes this smokin' soulful groover with the unmistakable vocals of Chez Damier. Check out the deep MK Club Mix with its hot breakdown and the AD Project from Toronto's bass and hi-hat chugging Change-up Mix.

CIRCUIT BREAKER-"Trac-K" (Probe) A

RECORD REVIEWS

limited edition, one-sided dub plate of hard Detroit minimal madness this stunner blazes along, sizzling hi hats searing. Much more tolerable on the ears compared to the last Circuit Breaker offering, Mr. Hawtin delivers a fierce chewn for the head strong.

DARKMAN/BI-FACE-"London Vs. Frank furt" ep (Sapho/UK) This split 12" celebrates two distinct styles of hardcore techno- breakbeat and trance- Darkman's London Side is a hard, dubby, ragga-flavoured slice of acid breakcore while Bi-Face's Frankfurt Side is a blinding pumper of hard ambient trance with a bleeping synth bassline. True to its vision, Sapho releases another gem for the DJ's with balls-Nice one!

BABY D-"Let Me Be Your Fantasy" (Production House/UK) This slightly ravey, live introed, piano driven, female vocal track rumbles along nicely, taking a swirly Peter Gabriel-sampled marimba breakdown smack into a synth-buzzing hardcore break. Part one of a two-part set, Production House gets top marks for one of the best vocal records I've heard in awhile.

GOLDEN GIRLS-"Kinetic" (R&S/Belgium) Licensed from Kudos Records and co produced by **Orbital**'s Paul Hartnoll this well-crafted trance biscuit pulses brilliantly, reminiscent of Felix, with a cool flute breakdown and subtle wiggling bassline. In mixes by both Frank De Wulf and Orbital. Massive.

LOVE REVOLUTION-"Love Evolution" ep (Network/UK) This upfront piano house bisquit has a slight **Inner City** feel throughout. Kevin Saunderson's wife Ann co-wrote two of the ep's three tracks and is guest vocalist on one, along with Reese Project's Rachel Kapp. It's nice to see more and more good true vocal records come out after a long absence. Worth checking out.

DISINTEGRATOR-"Lock On Target" (Industrial Strength) For their second release, NY's Disintegrator makes their debut on Lenny Dee's Industrial Strength label for this fourpack. The A-side is two tracks of marginal hard trance. The gems here are on the flip with the bass line burning, bongo beat, acid thumper, "Dark Black Ominous Clouds", which takes awhile to develop, but when it hits... "In The Sun" is a headstrong slab of devastating acid with its pounding 303 kick, crashing cymbals, and ethereal synth. Wicked.

FIX-"Flash"/"Dope Computer" (RMS) Strange Detroit techno-inspired electro funk at its best. One of the tracks on Kevin Saunderson's recent **Mixmag Live** tape, "Flash" funkily pumps along utilizing a cool little synth "solo" and backwards edits towards the end; "Dope Computer" comes in two mixes, one instrumental edit, one extended with old school rap and vocoder samples. Definitely for the adventurous, but a hell of a lot of fun.

EX 04-"Possessor"/"Seizure" (EX) "Possessor" is a massive chunk of brutal, synth-buzzing, percussive, acid breakcore in two mixes; also in two mixes, "Seizure" is a dark analogue turbo nosebleed stormer. One for the box of the more hardcore DJ's.

MOBY-"Next Is The E" (Instinct) The long-awaited release of this single comes in 4 mixes; the synth-buzzing, piano-driven I Feel It Mix, tribal Synthe Mix, the frantic Victory Mix, and a edit. Also included is the blinding ultra-hard-to-the-bone turbo headstrong Warp 10 nosebleeder, "Thousand". Buy or die, this is the shit! Go Moby!

SL2-"Way In My Brain" (Remix) (XL/UK) Another not so great 'ardcore track, and there have been some good ones lately. The remix is good, but that's it. Other cuts: "Drumbeats"- very typical and ravey; S.L.Electro is exactly what it says, Electro styled rave, nipping the old hip-hop track "Beat Boys" bassline; and "Aftershock", the standout track for the deep jungle tech-head.

LP/COMPILATIONS

PRODIGY-Experience (XL/Elektra) A very well produced and engineered selection of Techno/Rave from **Liam Howlett and Co.** Some of the stand outs are "Hyperspeed ("G-Force, Part 2")" with its rough beats and Early 80's cartoon sample; "Everybody Is In The Place-155 And Rising Mix"- the only groundbreaker on the album; and "Weather Experience", an 8½ minute slow introed to very good acid breakbeat climax track. The rest is typical Prodigy-good news for the fan, but not quite what the under ground hoped would be coming.

V/A-Techno Classics, Volume 2 (Rising High/UK) The second compilation of spot-on techno from the House That Caspar Built. All of your favorites are here, from the fierce and frantic Signs Of Chaos, Interface, and Audio Assault, the rumbly HHFD and Project One, to the in-from-leftfield experiments of Irresistable Force and

RECORD REVIEWS

Earth Leakage Trip, and the deep house feel of RHC. Essential for the true underground crew that knows the score.

ULTRAMARINE-Every Man And Woman Is A Star (Dali) Perhaps perceived as more of an indie band, per se, than a techno outfit, Ultramarine combine 70's folk sensibility with MIDI technology to create a slow ambient techno groove. Originally released on Rough Trade/UK **every man and woman is a star** is this Essex duo's U.S. debut. Ultramarine have mastered the art of effective sampling, drawing in listeners with familiar snippets of artists as diverse as **Kevin Ayers, Echo & The Bunnymen,** and the **Eagles.** A must have lp that shouldn't be missed at any cost. Massive.

APHEX TWIN-Selected Ambient Works 85-92 (R&S/Belgium) Richard James, aka The Aphex Twin reaches into the depths of his vast library of tracks and prepares a discriminating selection of ambient pieces dating from 1985 to the present. One of techno's current true innovators, the Twin enters the realm of avant garde composition with these pulsing, mesmerizing, swirling mind and body experiments. Deep, trancy, and almost cinematic in nature, this 13 track is a superb offering that must be experienced.

HIP-HOP/ACID JAZZ/R&B 12"

RECORD REVIEWS

PARIS-"The Days Of Old" (Sex Records) The Black Panther comes back with this smooth, saxophone-driven slow groove reminiscing about how it was back in the day. Released on what seems to be his own label amidst the controversy surrounding his second lp for Tommy Boy, this 12" is fair, but not what we've come to expect from the P-Dog.

D-INFLUENCE-"Good 4 We" (East/West) This London outfit blew up in the Spring of 1990 with a white label of the jazzy, soulful, funky, housey smash "I'm The One" (included here as a bonus track). Subsequently signed to **Acid Jazz** for a messy one single deal, the group took their act to major label pastures. Their first U.S. single, "Good 4 We" follows in the same mold as their breakthrough with its in the pocket groove and soulful, jazzy vibe. The U.K. Extended Mix is on the more soulful tip while the Dope Jazz Mix is the spot-on winner. Also check out the hip-hop injected remixes by **K-Cut** of **Main Source.**

LP/COMPILATION

PUBLIC ENEMY-Greatest Misses (DefJam/Chaos/Columbia) All respect due and all that, but I think P.E. may very well have fallen off. This dissapointing 'non-album' of mostly weak B-sides, fair remixes of past lp tracks, and a live cut from the group's January appearance on **BBC-TV** programme **The Word**, suffers froma serious lack of edge that hip-hop fans have come to expect from the mighty P.E. With crews like **Disposable Heroes** breathing down their necks, let's hope Chuck can rearrange his priorities and concentrate on music, not merchandising for 1993.

DON-E-Unbreakable (Island) Massive in the U.K. with hit singles like "So Fine" and "Love Makes The World Go Round", Brixton-born Brit-Soulie Don-E unlocks his groovy style of self-sufficient solo artistry with this debut. Chock-full of chewns that smack of yesteryear's classics, Unbreakable spreads a thick vibe of chunky jazz-funk, punchy songwriting, and soulful slow cuts from center to edge, reminding one of **Stevie Wonder, The Pasadenas,** and acid jazz sensation, **Omar.** If you're looking for a clean, classic-sounding record without a whole lot of pompous pretense, this one should do just lovely.

GRAND PUBA-Reel To Reel (Elektra) After the success of their debut album One For All, **Brand Nubian** frontman Grand Puba Maxwell busts out on the solo tip with a phunky joint of his own. Fronted by the mad success of the first single "360" and the boasting **BNH** track "Who Makes the Loot", Reel To Reel flows rammed and mellow, showcasing Puba's lyrical mastermind and deep record collection full of slammin' classics. This debut has a truckload of depth, however, it seems to be missing something intangible that would other wise make it shine above the rest.

NENAH CHERRY-Homebrew (Virgin) A worldwide sensation a while back with the massive "Buffalo Stance" and Raw Like Sushi lp, jazzman Don Cherry's daughter steps out of her family hiatus with the sensational Home brew. A star-studded sophomore effort with appearances and/or songwriting credits from Gang Starr, Lenny Kravitz, and R.E.M.'s Michael Stipe, this record not only shows great maturity but breaks new ground for this more-than-pop star. Despite the single "Money Love"'s radio-readiness, the remainder of Homebrew is a fresh blend of jazzy, hip-hop pop, intelligent, message-oriented funky jams and Massive Attack-inspired grooves. A record with street cred and pop sensibility that deserves to be noticed.

POSITIVE K-The Skills Dat Pay The Bills (Island) Wicked, fresh production, smooth lyrical flow, well-chosen samples, and appearances by Big Daddy Kane and Granddaddy I.U. mark this solid long player from this Brooklyn rapper. Deserves a peep.

PRINCE MARKIE DEE & THE SOUL CONVENTION-Free (Columbia) I know what you're thinking, "Wait a minute, I know that name..." Before you start to torture yourself, here's a hint: "Krush Groove"... Right! The Fat Boys' rapper! Now before you diss this and skip to the next review...seriously give this one a spin. If it's hip-hop you want- you're in, G; if you like a rootsy reggae backbeat- you're in, G. How about a smooth rap with soulful backing vocals? The Soul Convention singers take the lead on a few tracks like "Trilogy of Love" and "Trippin' Out" to give Free lots of depth and a true soul sound. Krush a groove on this one, you'll be "So Very Happy" **(DJ Ron-E C.)**

DEFINITION OF SOUND-The Lick (Charisma) The Lick, the second effort from Kevwon and The Don, slides into 50's surfin' and jangly hip-pop, slipping through well-proportioned mix tures of disco and Jackson 5-ish voc- als to the trendy but bassfully wonder ful dubby grooves on tracks like "What Are You Under". Incorporating all of London Town's hot-at-the-moment influences, Definition Of Sound forge a multi-cultural sound that is neither black nor white, just fresh and fun. **(AP)**

V/A-This Is Acid Jazz, Vol. II (Instinct) New York-based Instinct Records has scoured both sides of the Atlantic to find the funkiest grooves in the second series of compilations dedicated to this fresh musical hybrid. From the ultra cool of San Fransisco's **Vibes Alive**, the mesmerizing pulse of D.C.'s **Exodus Quartet**, London's **James Taylor Quartet**'s pure jazz appeal, and **2 Tuff**'s silky vocals, TIAJ, Volume II sheds a positive light on the many different musical stylings that encompass acid jazz.

THE REGULATORS-Get Ready For Hell (Demo) This full-length demo from Portland, OR is an engaging effort combining hardcore gangsta rap lyrical stylings and breakbeat techno samples. MC Death and Homicidal MC, the two rappers, throw down hard on each of the 10 tracks but some of the arrangements miss the target. For example, "Homicidal", the 130+ bpm turbo nosebleeder leading off Side 2 is just too fucking fast to be effective. On the other hand, tracks like "Apocalypse" and "Fear" are as good as they come; I can't help but feel like this could have been pared to say, six tracks, and had more impact. For info call 503.725.7055.

INDIE/ALTERNATIVE 7"/EP

FLOWER SERMON-"(Sugar) Lullaby" b/w "Flow" (Rough Trade/UK) The debut vinyl release from London's dreamy newcomers will melt you down into your armchair and entrance you with a bacchanalian orgy of organic technolog ical sensuality. "(Sugar) Lullaby" comes on like being in the back seat during a mad Morroccan cab ride while making love to your lover. The flip, "Flow", does just that. **(AP)**

NINE INCH NAILS-"Broken" ep (Nothing /TVT/Interscope) Finally after three years and many doubts that he would ever release another record, Head Nail **Trent Reznor** emerges from the depths of his own personal hell. A very angry, ugly collection recorded in secret, **"Broken"** picks up where **Pretty Hate Machine** left off with post-**Ministry** guitars along with Trent's venomous, image-encrusted lyrics adding to the ep's chaotic chemistry. Partially produced by **Flood** and including two hidden bonus tracks- **Adam Ant**'s "You're So Physical" and "Suck", Reznor's collaboration with **Pigface**- this ep is documentation of one man's downward spiral into major label domination, kicking and screaming all the way.

and Hawtin travel quite a bit as the **+8 Sound System.** In fact, at the time of this conversation with John Acquaviva, Richie Hawtin was in Europe. This extensive travelling has enlightened Acquaviva to the scope of influence that +8 has had on European ravers and labels. "I'm frankly embarrassed that we've influenced some of these people." disclaims John. "I don't really care for a lot of that (really hard) music, it's so angry and aggressive..."

Through the remainder of 1992 and into 1993, look for the Canadian-based label to release the second installment of the **From Our Minds To Yours** compilation, with limited edition pressings on way-cool glow-in-the-dark vinyl and custom record jackets and join both **The Prodigy** and **Moby** on a tour of the U.S. in a three country display of techno solidarity beginning in January.

continued from Page 11

After much buzzing about and anticipation, the group's third album was released. Entitled **Praise**, the album picks up where the debut left off three years ago with massive grooves, soulful vocals, and spiritual lyrics with a hardcore update. Kevin Saunderson explains, "Inner City is about doing something different, experimenting... We wanted to create a new sound and put forth a good, positive message. It's a record that's close to our hearts, me and Paris, and that's the way it came out. This is the true Inner City. It's a very versatile record, with some

THE ULTIMATE
rave
CONTINUES
ONLY FOR THE
HEADSTRONG II
featuring
ELECTROSET
"how does it feel?"
UTAH SAINTS
"something good"
ONLY FOR THE HEADSTRONG
The Ultimate Rave Compilation
also available
© 1992 FFRR
ffrr

SAINTS
UTAH
SAINTS
"SOMETHING GOOD"
A dynamic
collision of sounds that raves loud and wild.
The debut Album featuring "Something Good",
"What Can You Do For Me" and "I Want You"
© 1992 London Records, Inc.
LONDON

TRiP MAGAZEEN
100 E. Dr. M.L. KING Jr. BLVD.
SUiTE 10
TAMPA, FLORIDA 33603 U.S.A.

07

FLORIDA'S UPFRONT DANCE CULTURE MAGAZINE
NEW EXPANDED SIZE!!
TRiP
Feb. 1993
ORBITAL
ALTERN 8
ECSTACY
Chasing UFO's with
orb
Dr. Alex Paterson
108 GRAND*F.U.S.E.*SEQUENTIAL*BOOMSHANKA
NINE INCH NAILS*REDMAN*IRRESISTABLE FORCE*UTAH SAINTS
STEROID MAXIMUS*MAD COBRA*NAUGHTY BY NATURE

Hey, our first real letter! If you like the mag, have something to say, or just want to let **TRiP** know about what's going on in your part of the Global Techno Community, drop us a line to the address on the next page, and we'll print 'em! Your comments and ideas are welcome...

Hi All At **TRiP** Mag!!!

I'm a Techno/Rave Addict!! I have much cuts of Techno on CD, Tape, and Record. I've been to two raves, **Power Rave '92** and a X-mas rave at Metropol (a club in Pittsburgh). Both were kickin'.

Maybe you've heard of **Turbo Zen Records**? Ya, well that's where I got your 'zine.... It's slammin'.

Well to get to the point, I just dropped a not (sic) to you guyz in order to ask for a subscription to your lovley (sic) newsletter. So if you would be so kind as to put me on your mailing list, I would be quite thrilled. Thanks!

Peace, Chill Out, & Don't TECHNO For An Answer,

Rick Worth (aka STICKMAN)
Saltsburg, PA

CONTENTS

FEBRUARY 1993/ VOL. 2, #3

TRiP MAGAZEEN
100 E. Martin Luther King, Jr Blvd.
Suite #10
Tampa, Florida 33603 U.S.A.
EDITOR/PUBLISHER: Peter Wohelski
SENIOR EDITOR: Chris Milo
CONTRIBUTORS: Annie P., Kirk Field, DJ Three.
813.238.0310 Phone
813.876.7473 Fax

ADVERTISING: Rates given on request, call or write for details.

BACK ISSUES: Back issues of TRiP are available for $1.00 per issue postpaid/ U.S.A.; Overseas-write or call for info. Please specify issues or cover stars.

SUBSCRIPTIONS: TRiP accepts subscriptions, call or send SASE for information.

RETAIL STORES: If you'd like to carry TRiP Magazeen in your store, call for bulk rate information.

FEET *ff* FIRST

Sorry this issue is slightly late, but we've been running around Florida experiencing a "Rave New World", aka The Prodigy/Moby/Cybersonik Tour. Three dates, including Tampa, Cocoa Beach, and Gainesville respectively, each show above average in quality but due to their close proximity to each other, the magnitude of each event suffered and Central Florida's full underground potential was not reached.

All the shows had solid, energetic performances with Gainesville's crowd being probably the most refreshingly responsive-especially to the excellent range of House and pure techno from Plus 8 Sound System DJ's John Acquaviva and Richie Hawtin.

Cybersonik shed some light, Moby was as good as always, and The Prodigy actually sounded even better live than on vinyl. But after witnessing three of the U.K.'s top breakbeat acts within the past year (Two Bad Mice, Suburban Base Crew, and The Prodigy), we've come to the conclusion that U.K. dancers need to come to New York for a crash course with Crazy Legs and the Rock Steady Crew.

Two things we at **TRiP** would like to see change in the Florida scene as Spring rolls in... 1) Less fanatical practice of what the British music press says is or is not cool, and 2) The fact that "TV show or old hit sampled music" is the continual description of Techno, etc. by uneducated music journos. Although understandable considering it was novelty records that first caught the masses attention, this media faux pas is unacceptable because, with the odd exception, those records were merely a drop in the pan in the continual evolution of the underground and are no basis for defining anything

Hope you all like the new size of this issue, we sure do... Look for lots of cool new changes in the way **TRiP** looks in upcoming issues.

Shout outs go out to: Richie, John, & Dan from +8, Moby, Scotto @ NASA, Onions (NY), Flophouse Crew (SF), Rich Rosario, Halluci-Nation Records, Factor-E & PhD. (Atlanta), Chris w/ Smart-E's, Steve Mc Clure, Simon @ ROR, Charles

HYPE HYPE HYPE HYPE HYPE HYPE hype

....Not that it's any big surprise, but it seems like the **OTHER** Bay Area-**SAN FRANCISCO** has probably the States' best scene at the moment....With that in mind, now that **"RAVE"** has replaced **"GRUNGE"** as the mainstream media's musical buzzword, is it any surprise that San Francisco has replaced **SEATTLE** as the new hip city to live in?!?!....Cover stars **THE ORB** will be touring the U.S. in March; due to lack of promoter interest, there will be no Southeastern shows....New York's #1 MC, **ROMEO ROMEO** is currently on tour in Australia and Japan. Upon returning, he'll be finishing up his lp with **DJ CASANOVA**, which is being courted by a handful of major labels....With Detroit's **KMS RECORDS'** two new sublabel imprints- **SERIOUS GROOVES** for track and **TRANSFUSION** for techno- KMS will now focus on **"real" dance songs and artist development**. Parties interested in sending demos for potential signing and release on KMS and its associated labels are invited to send tapes and related materials to: **KMS RECORDS, c/o A&R DEPT., 1486 GRATIOT AVE., DETROIT, MI 48207**....Check out the Jan./Feb. issue of **OPTION** for possibly one of the best articles on rave culture to date, focusing in on what rave is really about- not what clothes to wear; a very insightful and positive portrait of the rave scene, unlike the one painted by **CBS-TV** newsmagazine **48 HOURS** during its January expose on the resurgence of LSD....Despite all the controversy surrounding his **SLEEPING WITH THE ENEMY** lp, prompting him to release the record on his own **SCARFACE** label, **PARIS** is still very much a Tommy Boy artist....Congrats go out to **ICE CUBE**, who married recently....**GANG STARR** have been busy lately, **GURU** working on a jazz/hip-hop lp with the likes of **BRANFORD MARSALIS, RONNY JORDAN,** and **COURTNEY PINE**, while **PREMIER** is producing the new **BDP**....Seminal Acid Jazz artists **YOUNG DISCIPLES** release their U.K. debut, **ROAD TO FREEDOM** domestically on **MERCURY**, out now....From **PORTLAND, OR** comes word of **TIDAL RAVE 3**, a three day party at Portland's **PARK AVENUE** club (doesn't every city have a club with this name? -Ed.). This event's 36 hours of "pure rave energy" drew over 500 of the Northwest's headstrong, featuring live techno in the area from **68,000** and DJ's **PASTA, BUDDY WEED, KRYS KILLS, NIKADEEMAS,** and **SPECIAL AGENT 086** on the decks.... **ROR, LTD.** is a new U.K. label. It's second release (see the review section), **"ALAS"** by **MINE THE RHYTHM** is a massive slab of deep acid breakcore madness. DJ's interested in being on the label's mailing list, send a letter of application including working credentials to **ROR LTD., 15 HANOVER SQ., LONDON, W1R 9AJ, U.K.**. Make sure you tell them you got the address in **TRiP**.

ed 12" by New York City act Crash reminds me of **Flesh For Lulu** meets **Jesus Jones**, sort of dancy, anthemic, guitar-driven synth-pop; the Club side's remix of the title track has a **Front Line Assembly**-lite meets techno treatment courtesy of **Communion** DJ **Tony Fletcher**. Not bad for the alternative dance-floor... Call 212.741.3198 for more information.

LP

STEROID MAXIMUS-Gondwanaland (Big Cat/UK) Possibly one of alternative music's truly innovative artist/producer/remixers, **J.G. Thirlwell** (aka **Foetus**) delivers yet another of his prolific Steroid Maximus projects. A maelstrom of sampling technology, **Gondwanaland** combines an eclectic cast of characters (including **Raymond Watts (Pig)**, **ex-Swan Roli Mosimann**, **Gumball's Don Fleming**, **and Voivod** skinsmasher **Away**) to collaborate on this collage of vintage bebop and big band jazz, tribal chants, Latin congas, Led Zeppelin drum solos, porn flicks, and more reconstructed by and with samplers into fresh compositions. Also included is a cover of "Powerhouse!", a Raymond Scott piece that appears in the **Ren And Stimpy Show**, originally released by Sympathy For The Record Industry as a 7" under the **Garage Monsters** pseudonym. This is a must for the strong of ear.

IS THE E EXPERIENCE REAL?

The Chinese sage Chuang Tsui once dreamt about becoming a butterfly and flying through a summer meadow filled with flowers. He awoke from the dream and asked, "Am I a man who dreamed he was a butterfly, or a butterfly who is now dreaming he is a man?" What is reality? Is it not what we make it?

"Cosmic Summer Love Affairs", as 60's drug guru Timothy Leary calls them, are relationships formed during an Ecstacy experience, but fall apart in the absence of E. Potential users of E should be aware that the empathy that Ecstacy can produce is no equal to genuine specific love. Things got so bad in the late 80's, that t-shirts and car stickers were printed saying, "Don't get married for six weeks after XTC."

ABUSE

Education starts with an E. Since MDMA has not undergone the usual trials required for a new drug, there is little hard information to report. Short term toxicity appears to be temporary and can be combated by sensible replenishment of minerals and vitamins (Magnesium tablets and Vitamin C are recommended "Sunday Morning" activities). What we are talking about here is the distinction between use and abuse, don't ever feel the need to compete with the E-head down the street who pops 'em like Smarties.

There is also truth in the old maxim that when you get high you can only come down. Don't expect to visit the moons of Neptune on Saturday night and not pay for your space travel a few days later. If you absolutely insist on taking Ecstacy (**or anything else, for that matter... Ed**), you owe it to yourself to find out as much as you can about it. And get street-wise, don't buy from a stranger and don't blame anyone else for your involvement. It's your life and your choice. Just say know.

SUGGESTED READING MATERIAL

Bruce Eisner-**Ecstacy, The MDMA Story**; Aldous Huxley-**The Doors Of Perception**; Timothy Leary-**Ecstatic Electricity**; Timothy Leary-**Greatest Hits: Collection of Essays**; Ralph Metzner-**Through The Gateway Of the Heart**

The Editor of **TRiP** would like to thank the author of the preceding story, **Kirk Field**, and **Mixmag** publisher **David Davies** for their permission and cooperation in reprinting this piece.

Hartnoll's breed DAT-free zone with Orbital

One of this Fall's more interesting tours was The Communion Tour, **a touring version of the popular Tuesday club night at New York's** Limelight. **Known for its successful fusion of a live venue and alternative dance club, Communion took its motto of** "spiritual technology all night long" **to 23 cities, presenting live three of dance music's more innovative acts, Meat Beat Manifesto, Ultramarine, and** Orbital.

Orbital is Paul and Phil Hartnoll. Though Londoners, the pair rose out of the Bleep Movement that came from Sheffield in 1990. The brothers found musical acceptance in the U.K. dance scene with **"Chime"**, a subtle, yet intense techno soundscape pumped with electro beats and mixed with dream-like elements that set them apart from the pack.

In a time where many P.A.'s are on DAT and the act is just miming along, Orbital firmly believes in the live techno experience, playing stuff that one will actually hear on the night, creating different warped-out mixes or working a single track for 30 minutes if the vibe is right. With influences derived from an industrial music background, the Hartnoll's were weaned on a diet of old **Cabaret Voltaire, Chakk, Hula, and early New Order**- all acts that are rooted in live performance. "It never occurred to me anyway, not to play live, because I used to play guitar and drums in bands and I always used to play live then," explains Paul Hartnoll.

"If people want to play their DAT's at parties, great. Sort of sidling up to the DJ and playing a few DAT's and a couple of records in between, that sort of thing, that's great," elaborates Paul, "But when people come along with two keyboards and couple of dancers that can't dance at all... It's not like watching a couple of professional dancers where you can go 'Wow, look at those moves'. It's usually a couple of their friends, raving away with a silly costume and somebody shouting 'Hardcore, you know the score'. It seems a bit pointless. Nine time out of ten they don't even do different versions for live, they're the same as the record. It seems really sad that these people can get 2-3,000 pounds for playing a bloody DAT!"

Unlike the breakneck 140-150 bpm's of a lot of the ravey, breakbeat based tracks in the U.K., Orbital have found themselves lumped into the rave scene despite the somewhat slower nature of their music. The Brothers' debut album and its preceding singles took on an approach full of layered melodies and interlocking rhythms, techno-y and almost cinematic in nature; a couple months later releasing the **Mutations** ep, a collection of guest remixes of lp tracks by Joey Beltram, Moby, Meat Beat Manifesto and others. Earlier this Fall, the **Radiccio** ep was released on the new London Records subsidiary, Internal. The ep was not necessarily a major change in sound but it was marked by **"Halcyon"**, a tribal, trancy, intelligent techno track with the **Opus III** vocal line looped backwards that made a major dent in the U.K. pop charts.

Paul Hartnoll explains its creation, "It just happened! I was messing around, and I had sat down to deliberately try and make a pop record one Sunday night, just being silly, not for any commercial gain or anything just for a bit of fun, really. It ended up that I didn't make a pop record- well, I did but I ignored it... We knew Kirsty (from Opus III) anyway and it just seemed funny. Right at the last minute, I turned (the loop) backwards, and said, 'Oh, that's nice.'" The track almost never made it out, as the sample's publishing company wanted 100% of "Halcyon"'s royalties, but with some legal work, ended up settling for 20%.

Orbital should be hard at work putting together the Hartnoll's second full-length release which should hopefully be out this summer.

Altern 8 scamming press with sound of Detroit

They've perpetrated numerous press scams like running for public office, creating a Vicks Vapo-Rub hysteria; they've exorcised the spirit of rock and roll at a rave with 20,000 in attendance officiated by an African Witch Doctor, and have enjoyed four Top Ten British Pop Chart hits. Yet, despite all the stunts and hype surrounding them, Stafford, England's **Altern 8** have been serious U.K. techno pioneers since 1990.

Forming Altern 8 as a side project of their other musical identity, **Nexus 21**, Mark Archer and Chris Peat met in a recording studio where Archer worked as an engineer. Peat, one of the area's better programmer/keyboardists, was recommended to Mark to help on a project he was working on; the rest is techno history.

Both influenced by the innovative music coming out of Detroit from U.S. labels like **KMS, Metroplex,** and **Transmat**, as well as Electro and Hip-Hop, the duo set out to create Nexus 21 with the vision of what Mark Archer describes as "Detroit-style Techno combined with a dancey beat." Emerging from the Acid exp- losion of '88, Nexus 21 released a couple of tracks and an album on Birmingham's **Network Rec- ords** that was heavily sampled and influenced by the "Detroit "Three".

As Acid House died out and the U.K. techno scene changed, labels like Sheffield's WARP and the Bleep movement from the North and the hardcore style of techno gradually evolved. Archer and Peat, excited by this different style of House decided to take on a side project that reflected this new musical energy. Christened **Alien 8**, but through a mistake the moniker turned into Altern 8; the duo decided to don radiation suits and masks to disguise themselves just in case the occasion arose that both Nexus 21 and Altern 8 were booked to P.A. at the same event.

Scams, hype, and comparisons aside, Altern 8 do take their music seriously, smelting hardcore techno elements with Detroit soundscapes and breakbeats that have won over a legion of both U.K. and U.S. ravers as well as cracking into the British Pop Charts. Tracks like "Infiltrate 202", "Activ-8", and "E-Vapor-8", with their trance-like melodies, sultry female vocals, and fiery backbeats have made notables like **Inner City's Kevin Saunderson** and the **Pet Shop Boys** stand up and take notice of Archer and Peat's pioneering approach, also having remixed tracks for **Cabaret Voltaire, Skin Up**, and re-rec- orded an updated version of **Evelyn "Champagne" King's "Shame"** that Peat and Archer describe as "brilliant" and "very clever".

1993 will see the return of Nexus 21 from two years of exile as the hardcore scene evolves away from rave-y style tracks and towards the longevity and credibility of the underground. Techno fans have not heard the last of Mark Archer and Chris Peat.

The Orb's Paterson plays Robin Hood to ban

LEEDS, ENGLAND- It's the day before his birthday and Dr. Alex Paterson is sitting backstage after soundcheck before tonight's gig in Leeds, fielding Trans-Atlantic questions from U.S. journos to promote the The Orb's dub-wise and intricate second album, **U.F.Orb**, due to be released in two weeks' time.

Alex Paterson's story is a complex one, filled with chance meetings, coincidence, friendships, and pure luck that even fairytales couldn't foresee. It may help to realize that Alex was born and lives in Battersea, an artistic and affluent section of South London with a very cosmic and magical quality, which possibly explains The Orb's spiritual essence. It's also home to Battersea Power Station, the ominous four smokestacked structure which Paterson describes as "a cosmic spacecraft" on Pink Floyd's **Animals** lp and the Orb's debut.

The story starts in 1979, when Alex's school chum and future Orbmate **Youth** gets a gig playing bass for legendary 80's alternative music stalwarts **Killing Joke**. Alex tagged along, finally nagging them enough to give him a job as a drum tech. It is here that the fairytale begins...

While on tour, the 19-year-old Paterson spends two days off his face on drugs, overlooking Germany's industrial Ruhr Valley and listening to Brian Eno's drifting, haunting ambient landmark, **Music For Films**. It is two days that will shape the life of young Alex forever, sowing the seeds of what is The Orb today.

In between stints with Killing Joke, Paterson spent time working in studios educating himself in the manipulation of funny noises and absorbing a ton of ambient music blagged from Killing Joke's record company-EG, home to the likes of Harold Budd, Penguin Cafe Orchestra, and Brian Eno. He also roadied for Brilliant, a band which featured Youth and KLF member-to-be **Jimmy Cauty** and managed by fellow KLF'er **Bill Drummond**.

When Killing Joke finally collapsed under the weight of their own mutual hatred, Alex found himself working as an A&R man for EG Records and Music, a position that Alex recalls "gave me a lot of freedom. As a publishing company, we weren't actively signing anything at the time, but it was license to find out what was going on in the music scene, but not have the pressure to sign anything."

Alex's "license" kept him in contact with Youth and Cauty, resulting in the creation of his own WAU! Mr Modo label and the first Orb release, the **"Kiss EP"**- an ep of mixes based around samples from New York's KISS-FM circa 1981. 1000 copies were pressed and it was deleted.

Alex and Jimmy also collaborated on The Orb's breakthrough single, "A Huge Ever-growing Pulsating Brain That Rules From The Centre of the Ultraworld", a take-off on the Minnie Riperton '70's hit "Loving You", championed by DJ's as the first post-rave house track. Shortly after, Cauty leaves to concentrate on KLF. It is Alex's direct influence on Cauty's **Space** lp and KLF's **Chill Out** that stand as prototypes and precursors to The Orb's ensuing full-length effort.

At the same time, Alex's DJ skills gained a big shot of cred when Land Of Oz club DJ **Paul Oakenfold** gave Paterson his own ambient room after Oakenfold heard Alex at a party. Combining House beats with ambient sounds and dub textures. Here at Land Of Oz, he met seminal experimental guitarist **Steve Hillage** after playing Hillage's ten year old "Rainbow

d of merry mates in ambient fairytale

Dome Musick" as Hillage and his wife **Miquette Giraudy** were, by chance, in attendance. The threesome hit it off as Hillage and Giraudy contributed to the Orb lp and Alex lent his talents to Hillage's **System 7** (known as 777 in the U.S.).

With new partner **Thrash** in tow, Alex released **Adventures Beyond The Ultraworld**, a double-length sojourn into time and space with a trippy, atmospheric, pulsating soundtrack including versions of "A Huge..." and possibly their most popular single, the Rickie Lee Jones interview-sampled "Little Fluffy Clouds". The album's dense weave of splifflicated flavours achieved a national Top 30 chart position and loads of critical acclaim that proclaimed The Orb as 'the missing link after Pink Floyd.' Paterson dismisses this comparison by saying, "We're nothing like Pink Floyd, Pink Floyd doesn't make dance tracks."

"It took two years for us to get where we are. I think we've proven that we can do these things and be popular as well as maintain credibility, using the U.K.'s strong club culture to our advantage," explains Paterson.

...Ultraworld achieved a national Top 30 chart position in the U.K. and garnered loads of critical acclaim, catapulting Alex and The Orb from "just something I did on Sunday afternoons" to a pop star (much to his chagrin) and in-demand-remixer. The Orb's remix credits read like a premier "Who's Who" in dance music- most notably Lisa Stansfield, BAD II, Depeche Mode, Front 242, Primal Scream and Art of Noise. Paterson would rather be working on his own material than remixing, yet finds that "it's a good chance to experiment on other people's records on their record company's money," but as far as any sort of approach to remixing, " we just do it, and see what comes about,

Alex and his band of shady mates return to the studio in the Spring of 1992 and in mid-Summer emerge with U.F.Orb, a gurgling, banghra-beated, dub-heavy affair drawing from Alex and Thrash's holidays in India as well as Alex's extensive dub record collection. Influenced by "heavy dubbers" King Tubby and the Revolutionaries, along with mellow-vibed things like Massive Attack, U.F.Orb is much more danceable but no less atmospheric than its predecessor, debuting at #1 on the U.K. album charts.

A group that is at no loss for a good laugh or a pisstake, in typical Orb humour, the lp's first single, "The Blue Room", clocks in at two seconds shy of 40 minutes- just long enough to be the longest single ever created and short enough to qualify for U.K. Gallup Poll singles status. The group was also asked to appear on Top Of The Pops, a show featuring U.K. pop acts miming to their latest single. Alex and Thrash take the underground approach and appear sitting on stage, flooded in laser light playing chess!

Shortly after their TOTP appearance, The Orb emerge for their third Peel Session as a four-piece punk band and record a riotous cover of The Stooges' "No Fun"! Alex recalls, "It was just something different and fun, it was just some old mates- Nick Burton, who was in a band called Westworld on drums, one of my best friends, Simon on bass, Thrash on guitar, and me singing. It was quite the riot..."

In the meantime, Alex, Thrash, and company plan to work on upcoming projects with dub pioneer Augustus Pablo as well as spending more time on their own adventures in dub, and touring the States beginning in March.

RECORD REVIEWS

TECHNO/HOUSE
12"/ep

ALAS-"Mine The Rhythm" (ROR, Ltd./UK) This second release from a fledgling London-based label is a refreshing slice of acidy breakbeat with a nice atmospheric pulsing synth breakdown early on. The Club Mix is the pick here with its manic breakbeat and rumbly bassburning acid lines, while the House Mix is more on the trancy tip with a pounding kick drum, wicked pulsing acid synths, and firing backwards flanged hi-hats. If you love the acid, search for this hard to find hottie.

108 GRAND-"Te Quiero" (Brute/UK) A relaxed chugging progressive house instrumental, this Pink Floyd sampled groover pumps along brilliantly in four forms; the Cheech side's short, but groovy Gypsy Mix, and the spacy, gradually-building Floyd-less Darren Emerson Underworld Mix; the Chong side's tribal Darren Emerson Strutt Remix and the slightly slower, deeper vibed, swirling synth-ed, episodic Acorn Arts Remix. Top chewn...

SUBWAY-"Launch Pad" ep (Rising High/UK) Hats off to Rising High- they do every style...not overdoing it and doing it well. This ep goes back to breakbeat for Rising High; any fan of Moving Shadow and the like will go nuts for it. Four strong tracks: ragga techno with some acid & a small touch of rave. **(CM)**

G-104-"Mind Missile" ep (Force, Inc./Germany) "Find your way into a brighter future", she says, then it's a full-on percussive workout in a more manic, in-your-face style than Infinite Wheel's "Lake Of Dreams"; works perfect slow or fast. Side 2 has a hardcore track, a rave track, and a cool acidy track with a time stretched (Thank You) "Mama Said..." L.L. Cool J. sample. **(CM)**

F.U.S.E.-"Dimensions"/"Into The Space" (+8) Now with the both already cool acid and Germany getting so much attention from the U.K. press, this could be the acid record to pull the trendy crowd who demand Felix or Rhythm Quest underground. Dare I say funky and smooth are the words for "Dimensions", while "Into The Space" is a elemental, rhythmatic slice of space music for the mood maker. **(CM)**

SEQUENTIAL-"Sequential" 12 ("the blue dot fax # label) This strange yellow promo label just unloaded a slew of essential German trance and hardcore tunes that are simply great. (Is this the POD label?) This 12" and its sister, "Sub-Sequence", both deliver some quality techno trance- each including an ambient mix to boot! Now available on Rising High with a remix, find and listen. **(CM)**

4 HERO-"Darkside" ep (Reinforced/UK) Reinforced have never been better; four tracks of some uniquely produced, deep and smooth breakbeat. "Journey From The Light" & "The Element" are the standouts with some of the coolest breakdowns in some time for this style of techno. If this and the Nebula II remixes are a sign, Reinforced should be slammin' for '93. **(CM)**

MEAT BEAT MANIFESTO-"Mindstream" (Mute) Jack Dangers, along with Renegade Soundwave, has the most sampled beats since the J.B.'s. MBM return with yet another contribution to the underground that better not be ignored; Orbital's mix is a slice of acidy trance which brilliantly builds and orchestrates to the point of hypnosis, then blip- the vocal track is punched in to great effect. Aphex Twin's mix is trademark in style, rough and beautiful at the same time, while Jack's Psychologically Speaking Mix is classic MBM. Nice to have a 12" with mixes that are different for a change- sack the attitude and play this record. **(CM)**

ORCA-"Dancing With Dolphins, Pt. 2" (Lucky Spin/ UK) Mega rave promoters Fantazia have created this label to further themselves. "The Power" is by far the best... spacy breakbeat with a haunting, almost digeridoo-ish synth, and a piano break- down that didn't suck. "Alive & Kickin'" is good piano rave- reminds me of early hours at Beecham Theatre. The flip has its moments, but is overall typical rave. Lucky Spin-1, Suburban Base-0. **(CM)**

BOOMSHANKA-"Do You Have The Power" (Cowboy/UK) Trademark noise-gated vocals and 1,2 bassline are not the selling point here, but the rude analog acid riff sets set this pulser off and running. Fierce! The writing side is more of a typical Cowboy record- not a bad characteristic- very atmospheric with a piano breakdown way down the line (deja vu). Recommended. **(CM)**

INNER SANCTUM-"Inner Sanctum" (Axis) Jeff Mills is on a mission, this time in a not over the-top well-produced prog- ressive house style. The Unseen Mix is our pick with its accent on tribal percussion but much too short compared to its sister mix with matching grainy, pulsing synth. The flip is "Transport"- a bit harder and techno-y. Very good and creating a buzz. **(CM)**

LP/COMPILATIONS

IRRESISTABLE FORCE-FLYING HIGH (Rising High/UK) After massive success with the Space Is The Place and Underground ep's the magical Mixmaster Morris has perhaps very well created the last word in defining ambient techno in Flying High. Similar to **KLF's Chill Out** lp and yet not unlike **The Orb**, the Irresistable Force has created a dense sonic tapestry that carries you to the land of post-rave spiritual bliss with its true techno(logy) vibe throughout. Deep, spacey, transcendent and atmospheric, there is no excuse or substitute for this LP. It is truly essential.

UTAH SAINTS-UTAH SAINTS (ffrr/London) Leeds duo Jez Willis and Tim Garbutt better known as **Utah Saints** drop their self-titled "guitar-stoked/

RECORD REVIEWS

techno-fueled attack" on our shores. Including the hits, "What Can You Do For Me?" and "Something Good", the record is, relatively speaking, on a wholly accessible level. But before one dismisses this as a load of commercial bollocks, first listen to the Saints' anarchistic approach to sampling, weaving such sources as **Slayer**, **Sylvester**, **Kate Bush**, **Simple Minds**, and **Crown Heights Affair** into a pleasantly danceable platter. There are several more upfront tracks on the latter half of the disc that should appease the techno snobs with their more underground nature. It should be understood, however, that **Utah Saints** is a record that takes techno to another level- out of the Underground for the unsuspecting public to grasp and be pulled back into.

V/A-BERLIN 1992: A TRESOR COMPILATION- THE TECHNO SOUND OF BERLIN (Nova Mute) Nova Mute, in association with Tresor Records/Germany, presents a musical survey of the DJ's and musicians that name for itself as one of the U.S.' most brutal techno outlets. This compilation highlights some of the best tracks released by this DJ Lenny Dee-run label: **Mescal-inium United, The Mover, Turbulence, Industrial High** (with **Rising High**'s **Caspar Pound** and **Marc Williams**), **English Muffin, Disintegrator**, and more. Topped off with sick graphics by Xelibrium, this is a great introduction to acid madness at its best.

HIP-HOP/ACID JAZZ/R&B 12"/ep

NAUGHTY BY NATURE- "Hip-Hop Hooray" (Tommy Boy) East Orange's hip-hop homies celebrate their true musical colours with this laid-back jam from their upcoming lp **19 Naughty III**. Setting the pace, Treach and crew show a lot of growth with this headnodder's mature lyrics, relaxed delivery, and smooth production. Also included is another lp teaser, a deeptoned, tense joint called "The Hood Comes First". Prepare for another blow-up in '93.

GROOVE GARDEN-"You're Not Coming Home" (Tommy Boy) The debut single by Tommy Boy's new Flavor Unit signing Groove Garden funks it up in an acid jazz vein with a breathy female vocal, laid-back drum groove, lazy piano and organ chording, and intermittent bassline. **De La Soul's Mase** turns in a stripped-down hip-hop radio mix, while Factor 3's Hard Beats mixes create a sensual, atmospheric groove, ala **Innocence** or **Massive Attack** in their dreaminess, starting with the beginning of **Tears For Fears' "Shout"**. Keep an eye on this one and the upcoming lp, it has the potential to be massive.

LP/COMPILATION

ICE CUBE-The Predator (Priority) "The Nigga You Love 'Ta Hate" is back for joint #3, **The Predator**. Debuting at #1 simultaneously on the Billboard Pop and R&B album charts, and employing the production skillz of some of the game's phat-at-the-moment producers- **DJ Pooh**, **Cypress Hill's DJ Muggs**, and **Sir Jinx-** resulting in 'Cube's deepest, ruffest, and most mature solo effort to date. The lp's first single, "Wicked", takes on a Das Efx-influenced ragga stylee, steppin' to the mic like a Ninja with the killer instinct. A must for the hardcore hip-hop lovers.

PARIS-Sleeping With The Enemy (Scarface) With a pent-up rage too hot for the majors to handle, Paris, the Black Panther drops his second effort

RECORD REVIEWS

after much delay and static. **Sleeping...** is a much improved effort from 1990's **Devil...** with its consistent production skills and menacing, tension-racked tracks. Whether he's taking out the President, cutting down some cops, or engaging in revolutionary tactics, Paris sleeps on no one here with no rest from beginning to end. Wicked and explosive.

REDMAN-Whut? Thee Album RAL/Chaos/Columbia) 1992 was definitely the year for the **Hit Squad**-between **EPMD**'s own shit, **Das Efx**, **K-Solo**, and now Jersey's **Redman-** Erick and Parrish are fully sporting the trunk of strictly underground funk. The prodigy called Redman steps to the mic with the best a debut MC can offer: rugged rhyme flow, tales rich in detail and metaphor, and a sense of humour, favoring 'fros, blunts, and the power of the funk. With production that burns smooth like a Phillies, **Whut?...** flows with the classic funk flavour, ensuring that the Hit Squad be making

RECORD REVIEWS

dollars for quite a while to come.

COMPTON'S MOST WANTED -Music To Drive By (Orpheus/Epic) Past releases by Compton's other niggas have been, at best, a marginal brand of gangsta' rap- poppin' gats, dissing the East Coast (i.e. **Tim Dog**-with **BDP** "South Bronx" samples), bangin' bitches, and boomin' bass. Not much has changed with this major label debut, but having bigger bank to drop on a better production budget, has given CMW more respect that has been long reserved for their more contoversial contemporaries. Worth a peep just to prove that CMW can drop a classy trunk of West Coast funk and not go soft.

REGGAE/WORLD MUSIC

MAD COBRA-Hard To Wet, Easy To Dry (Columbia) Star Dancehall DJ **Cobra** is the third in a series of reggae artists to be captured by major labels. With smooth but ruff production of Sly Dunbar and Steely & Clevie, Cobra's debut shouldn't alienate the dancehall massive while still catching the ears of the hardcore hip-hop head and giving fresh spice to a bland CHR radio palate. The album's positive highlights such as ragga-inflected slow jam crossovers "Flex" and the gangsta rap meets gun talk patois duet of "Dead End Street" (a duet with the **Geto Boys**) make the American public's introduction to dancehall culture a refreshing one.

SHABBA RANKS-X-Tra Naked (Epic) This release from our second favorite homegrown Jamaican export, X-Tra Naked exposes Shabba's sexy dancehall grooves with loads of special guests such as **Johnny Gill** ("Slow And Sexy"), **Queen Latifah ("What'cha Gonna Do"), and Chubb Rock** ("Two Breddrens"). However, tracks like "Rude Boy", and "Bedroom Bully" show our boy's true slackness towards the sex he would die a terrible death without. **(AP)**

V/A-BOGLE (Mango) Bogle is the hottest new dancehall dance craze to come out of Jamaica that is no uptown disco dance but pure ruffneck bizness. Named after a Trenchtown raggamuffin well-known for his dancing prowess and fashion style, the Bogle dance appeared towards the end of summer 1991. This "soundtrack" features true dancehall flavour with its ruffneck riddims and rhymes of slackness and gun talk from Jamdown's finest like **Buju Banton, Papa San** and newcomers such as **Little Lenny** and **Sasha**. For a authentic taste of the dancehall in its full flavour, **Bogle** is an essential entree.

INDIE/ALTERNATIVE 12"/ep

NINE INCH NAILS-"Fixed" ep (Nothing/TVT /Interscope) "Broken" marked Trent Reznor's return with brazen force and it was not a letdown. However, this limited remix ep retraces NIN's sound back to where it came from- technology! Excellent reworkings by Trent, Coil, and J.G. Thirlwell aka Foetus- the progressive remixer of the moment. These mixes are long, everchanging, and listenable as well as technically interesting. The guitars are still there, tweaked and manipulated around synths, tribal percussion & studio trickery. It'll be interesting to see what direction the album will take. (CM)

CRASH-"Man, Machine, and Human Dreams" The Radio side on this white label-

TRiP MAGAZEEN
100 EAST M.L. KING BLVD.
TAMPA, FLORIDA 33603
U.S.A.

POSTMASTER: PLEASE RUSH-DATED MATERIAL!!

08

Free In Florida! $1.50 Elsewhere
FLORIDA'S UPFRONT DANCE CULTURE MAGAZINE
TRiP
APRIL 1993
DOC MARTIN
MOBY-REVISITED
STEREO MC'S
YOUNG DISCIPLES*APACHE*KAM*D-INFLUENCE
RESISTANCE D*SANTONIO PROJECT*BIOTRANS*ANARCH-E

STEREO MC'S CONNECTED
INCLUDES
CONNECTED, STEP IT UP & DON'T LET UP
MAKE SURE YOU'RE CONNECTED...
ON GEE STREET COMPACT
DISCS AND CASSETTES.
ISLAND
GEE STREET
Gee Street™, Licensed to Island Records, Inc. ℗ © 1993 Island Records, Inc.

CONTENTS

FEET FIRST

FEBRUARY 1993/VOL. 2, #2

TRiP MAGAZEEN
100 Dr. M.L. King, Jr. Blvd. E.
Suite #10
Tampa, Florida 33603 U.S.A.
PHONE 813-238-0310/FAX 813-876-7473
EDITOR/PUBLISHER: Peter Wohelski
SENIOR EDITOR: Chris Milo
CONTRIBUTORS: DJ Grumpy C, DJ Three

ADVERTISING: Rates given on request, call or write for details.
BACK ISSUES: Back issues of TRiP are available for $1.00 per issue postpaid
SUBSCRIPTIONS: $10 yearly (8 issues)
RETAIL STORES: If you're interested in carrying TRiP Magazeen in your store, call for bulk rate information.

Wow, the past month and a 1/2 has been wild around the office! Actually we've spent most of our time on the road, eyeing the many events and parties going on lately.

Some of the highlights: Unity Promotions' Passion Valentine's Day eve after hours with Dave Cannalte and Kimball Collins driving into the daylight hours; Solaris,a poorly promoted event boasting a DJ line-up of Dom 'T' from London and Doc Martin along with P.A's from Baby Ford and Adamski. A handful of people showed, but those who did were treated to a wicked chunk of funk from Doc Martin, cool trance and acid from Baby Ford, and Dom 'T' with the house vibe on the decks. Miami's Winter Music Conference was next- many parties, several high points but Tony Humphries playing Jaydee at Warsaw totally blew the us all away; to Chicago for an Orb show that didn't happen- more about Chicago next issue- and back to Miami for Divine Playground, a "Lollapalooza with a smart bar"-type event with 808 State, Utah Saints, and an all-star DJ bill with Tim from Utah Saints, Keoki, Dimitry from Deee-Lite (with Kier in tow), and Germany's Sven Vath (who played a devastating after hours).

Shout outs go direct to: Santonio Echols, Doc Martin, DB @ Profile, Mika @ PLG, the +8 crew from WMC, Stephanie @ Moonshine, Jeff K. @ KDGE, Stace Bass, Dennis the Menace, Fred Strong, David Prince, Richard @ Zoe Magic, Heinz & Sven @ Eye-Q/Harthouse, Mark Fotiadis @ AAM, Amoebahead Prods.(RI)

On the hip-hop tip, it seems that the **HIT SQUAD**'s success in '92 has caused internal friction between **ERICK** and **PARRISH**. Spokesmen for the group declin ed specifics, but **EPMD** is no more....A strange phenomenon at house parties in **ROTTERDAM**, ravers chant "Jo-den, Jo-den" (Jews, Jews) at the climax of the event; sounds fascist to **HYPE!**, but apparently it's a football/soccer-specific thing associated with supporters of the **AJAX** football club but we just found an old **SKREWDRIVER** lp with "Hello to our friends in Rotterdam" in the liner notes....The major record labels recently cleaned out their dance music departments, dropping some top acts. Some of the casualties: **MASS ORDER**, **LI'L LOUIS** (Sony), **K-CREATIVE**, **OMAR** (Talk in' Loud/UK), **TEN CITY** (Atlantic), **INNOCENCE**, **DEFINITION OF SOUND**, **INNER CITY**, and **BOY GEORGE**'s **MORE PROTEIN RECORDS** (Virgin/EMI)....London's **MINISTRY OF SOUND** club recently launched **ACHTUNG!**, a Thursday night techno club with **DERRICK MAY** and **WESTBAM** spinning....Working together:**ICE CUBE** and **RED HOT CHILI PEPPERS**, **JAZZIE B** (Soul II Soul) and **JAMES BROWN**....The new lp from **A TRIBE CALLED QUEST** has been pushed back to late April/early May....Comics fans down with the Hip-hop tip might want to check out **BOOM**, a underground hip-hop comic from Toronto, ONT. For more info or dealer enquiries, write **DEAD LEVEL/BOOM, 1-211 DUNN AV., TORONTO, ONTARIO, CANADA M6K 2SS1**....Another casualty of the recession, groundbreaking World music organization **WOMAD** went bust recently.... Combining ethnic Indian rhythms and Punjabi slang with patois and Dancehall vibes, **APACHE INDIAN** is taking the British Reggae industry by storm with his "bhangramuffin" stylee....Congrats to the staff at **TOMMY BOY** for being named the **RAP IND EPENDENT LABEL OF THE YEAR** for the second straight year by **THE GAVIN REPORT**, an industry trade publication....Word comes from the East Coast tribe that an event called **RAVESTOCK** is tenatively scheduled to happen early this summer, more details as they come through the grapevine....Between 50 and 100,000 people participated in **HOUSE AGAINST HATE**, a fund-raising event opposing racism and supporting tolerance initiated by **JEROEN FLAMMAN** of **FIERCE RULING DIVA** and Dutch DJ Dano, along with clubs throughout The Netherlands, and select venues in Italy, and Switzerland. Coinciding with the dance marathon is the release of compilation of new tracks from **CHARLEY CASANOVA**, **HUMAN RESOURCE**, **SEQUENTIAL**, and Fierce Ruling Diva; all royalties going to benefit the **HAH** fund....Sadly, Tampa clubrunner/DJ **STEVE MC CLURE** is closing his Saturday underground night at **EVOLUTION** with a final blow out, **JUDGEMENT DAY**, Saturday, 10 April. However, Mc Clure is moving his popular night to Fridays at **DNA** beginning Friday, 16 April. For info, ring 813-971-3621 after 10 April..................................

Above: L-R, TRiP contributor DJ Three, Eye-Q/ Harthouse boss Heinz Roth, and your TRiP editor at 'Another World; Below: L-R, 'The Bunny', DJ Three, and Scotto (NASA/NYC) compare hair farming techniques at 'Rave New World'

Below: Top , L-R;unidentified crew member, 'The Bunny', DJ Grumpy C.Bottom, L-R: John Acquaviva (+8), DJ Three, Richie Hawtin (+8)

Above: Ishai Moran, RMF @ 'Rave New World' Below: DJ Sven Vath (Germany) searching for chewns at 'Divine Playground' afterhours

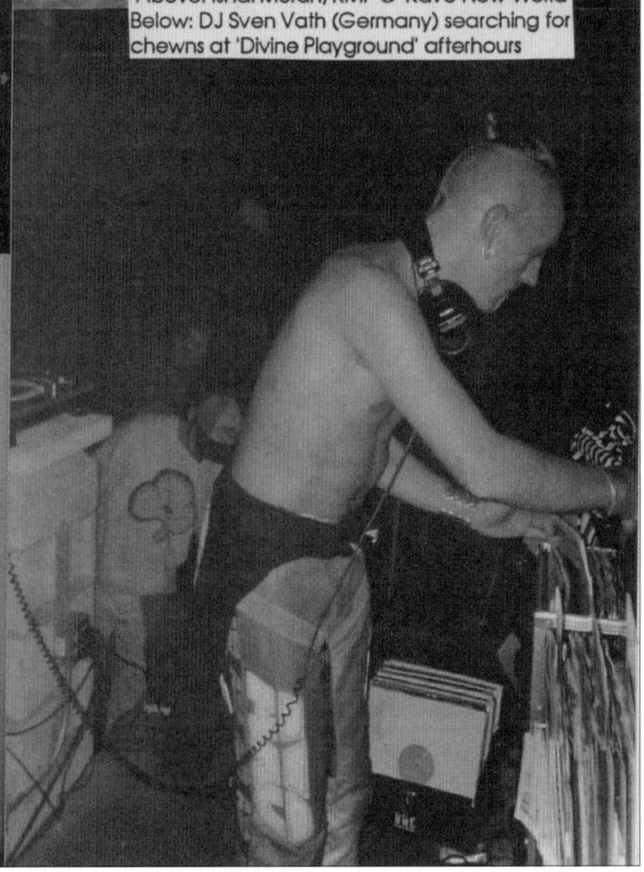

West Coast Scene Report

DJ Doc Martin blows in, kicks up the funk

L.A. DJ Doc Martin blew into town recently, kicking up a wicked cloud of funk before a handful of die-hards at SOLARIS. One of the L.A. scene's most- sought after DJ's, Doc is perhaps best known for his wide open musical taste and down-to-earth manner. TRiP was lucky enough to catch up with him and have a chat...

TRiP:We haven't heard much from you since MANIC (March '92) what have you been doing?

DM: It's been quite a mad year to say the least, I've been all over the U.S... Been in the studio a lot, I've been playing in New York, Chicago, D.C., Oregon, basically all over the U.S.

T:You said you've been doing some remix work?

DM:A kid named **ALY-US** from Strictly **Rhythm**, worked with a kid off E--**Legal** Records named **Herman** on his next single, Jon Hassell- who's worked with 808 State. Just a lot of independent stuff out of L.A., and on our own tracks.

T:What's the current state of the scene on the West Coast?

DM:The West Coast in general has been brilliant. L.A. has been less than brilliant. A lot of kids throwing parties that don't know what they're doing; they're just kids. I think new promoters should come up, but they should have some knowledge, not throw a party to have their name on the flyer. Portland is wic--ked, that's all I have to say about Portland; there's a kid from India who's doing things pro per. In Seattle, my man Rob is throwing some outrageous parties. But San Francisco-you don't even have to say a word- is the capitol. I've been playing up there more than L.A., to be honest.

T: Why San Francisco?

DM:When the promoters came in, they really had their shit together and came off on a spiritual vibe...they didn't try to commercialize it, they kept it very underground.

The State of The Scene- Moby Revisited

One year ago, techno and rave were new and fresh to many. "Alternative" music was no longer what it implied and scenes began sprouting nationally, wide-eyed with optimism and positivity.

Last March, TRiP interviewed Moby. Much has changed since then, so we thought we'd revisit with the face of U.S. Techno and briefly compare notes a year later.

On "Is Rave the unifying youth culture we thought it to be?"

"There are are a lot of people, like myself, that are attracted to this culture because it is sub versive, but I'm wondering if it's not just a lot of projection to label it subversive. A lot of the kids involved, they're not concerned whether its subversive or mainstream or not, they're there to party and have a good time. So I wonder if people like myself are trying to paint this scene in a way that it really isn't."

On "Rave vs. mainst ream media".

"...there's been so much attention, every major news program had their little thing on raving, and it generated all these expectations that I don't think the scene was able to live up to"

On "DJ's and music".

"I think that DJ's need to respond to things on a more genuine level, instead of saying, 'Oh gee, this record is from England and I read in <u>**Mixmag**</u> that it's a cool record, so therefore I'm going to play it.' They need to be saying, 'Do I love this record, do I want to play this record."

DJ DOC MARTIN, cont.

Even with 2000 people in the place it still has the feel of everyone knowing each other. Bigger is not better. It's like **RaveAmerica** on New Year's that did 18,000 people, you've got to stand back and go, "What the Hell?!?" Although lately we've been doing a series of after hours and we've been flying a lot of wicked, wicked DJ's from all over the world, they've been kinda coming through and doing their sets....

You play all styles of house music. Would you like to see more DJ's have this open-minded attitude to help edu--cate their crowd?

DM:I think each DJ should try to find their own sound, 'cause the only way you make your mark is if you're on the founding edge of something or if you come off a track no one plays. In California right now, L.A., pretty much a lot of people play the same stuff, but Oregon, Seattle, San Diego even, San Francisco- everyone's got their own little niche. I just think it's all about good music, there's so much good music out there, the crowd really needs to be educated, just because it's a techno song doesn't mean you have to buy it.

T:Your ideas on the current labeling and splintering trend in house music?

DM:I think the worst thing you can do is label music, it's so universal.

London's Stereo MC's break down musical

"I don't think we can be categorized, I think that we are just the result of all the music that we all have really liked," says DJ/remixer **Nick "The Head" Hallam** of U.K. charttoppers **Stereo MC's**.

Some may call it new groove funk, others hip-hop, and still others don't know what to call it, but it's phat anyway. Whatever it is, The Stereo's-rapper **Rob B.**, drummer **Owen If**, The Head, and vocalists **Cath Coffey**, **Andrea**, and **Verona**- stand poised to open one's ears and pump them full of funk and positivity with **Connected**, their first record in two years.

Coming onto the scene in 1989 with their debut album, **33-45-78**, a bridge between two cultures. It was a marg inal debut, but it laid the groundwork for the big things to come.

In 1990, with the release of their second effort, **Supernatural**, the band recieved serious critical acclaim and most importantly, serious props and respect from the American hip-hop community, joining forces with **Afrika Baby Bam** of **The Jungle Brothers** on a track.

A grassroots breakthrough in every sense, Supernatural spawned a **Billboard** Top 40 single in "Elevate My Mind" (the first U.K. rap single to ever chart so high), as well as "Lost In Music", a #1 dance chart smash.

This runaway success earned the Stereo's support slots on summer tours by fellow Britons **EMF** and the **Happy Mondays**, giving the band a captive audience in which to spread the spirit

of what the band is all about. With The Head on the decks, Owen playing live drums, and Rob pacing the boards and delivering the lyrical, the Stereo's opened many alternative fans eyes the summer of 1991.

"For starters, we've always been different, we've always had our own identity. We've been lucky, because when we go out (on the road), we're not getting put out as hip-hop. So fortunately, in trying to broaden people's horizons (by doing these types of tours) the response has been positive," explains The Head.

Originally a hip-hop crew, according to Nick, the group "still considers hip-hop to be the roots of what boundaries with charttopping Connected

we are, we've just developed our own sound. It's not something we've done deliberately, it's just happened like that. We just do what we feel; it's hard to explain ourselves."

This inadvertent freedom to bend musical boundaries has matured into a new album, **Connected**, an effort that breaks the band out of the hip-hop tag and into a livelier, funkier, more natural sounding groove. It's still the Stereo's you know and love, just more relaxed.

"When we sat down to work on the album, we started hearing parts in the songs that weren't possible to find on your record collection," explains The Head, "so we had musicians come into the studio and play the parts we wanted live, and then sampled them. It's given the album a more relaxed and more natural sounding feel I think, really."

This new approach has also changed the way the band does their live show. With the addition of three female vocalists and The Head turning in the 1200's on stage in favor of a sequencer and mixing desk. It's a change that has made the Stereo MC's "totally flexible. And with the three girls it gives people more to see and makes the show much more fun, y'know."

The Stereo MC's have always been about spreading a positive vibe with their lyrics and Rob B.'s rhymes on Connected are noe exception. "For example, we're talking about more different kinds of feelings, and I think Rob expresses them better now."

We're not about whacking you in the face with some political message- they (the lyrics) do say something- we want people to dance and have a good time first. If they want to get into the lyrics, they can take the record home later and get morose if they want."

Yet, the two-year break between Connected and Supernatural poses a minor challenge for the Stereo's in the U.S.- starting over from a roots level again, trying to regain a following that may have totally forgotten about the summer of 1991 and "Elevate My Mind".

If "Connected"'s MTV Buzz Clip airplay is any indication as to whether or not the Stereo MC's are up to the challenge, they won't be on the roots level for long.

RECORD REVIEWS

TECHNO/HOUSE 12"/EP

RESISTANCE D - "Human" ep (Harthouse/Germany) Harthouse, from the hart. Hardcore? No, hartcore! A new era (and hopefully a long one) of atmosphere and sound has crept into all styles of the underground (Are Florida DJ's listening?). Hard & beautiful is the equation for this German label and this ep is fabulous! "Connected Science" just builds and builds-a pure mental tr-ancer. "Morning Sunrise" grooves nicely, "Human" is simply fierce-the kick drum and melody are the shit. Hard to deny this track's urgency. (D3)

FRIENDS, LOVERS, & FAMILY-"Being" ep (Rising High/UK) Rising High continues to put out brilliant records. This 4-track ep is full of fast beats and bizarre noises, the best cut being "Heardoing Heroes". Very deep breakbeat techno. Excellent. (GC)

RABBIT IN THE MOON- "O.B.E." (Halluci-Nation) Groovier than "Fruit Of Love"...more atmospheric than most any dance track I can think of. Whatever man, this record is brilliant. unconventional arrangemen--ts, whispers, tribal percussion, and a wailing chorus that gives chills round out this uptempo groover. If your venue doesn't have boomin' sound, take it somewhere else and drop it, as it's a very aural track. Jump on this quick, it's gonna blow up! (CM)

GLITCH- "Trauma" ep (Industrial Strength) This release from Brooklyn's hardest label is just that- hard for hard's sake, manic nose-bleed pounding with not a whole lot of depth to speak of. There's potential here, but it misses the mark.

ANARCH-E-"Krazy Train" (Halluci-Nation) Alex Machine and DJ Punk Rock are back with the follow up to the "Punk Rock" ep with this galloping "Crazy Train"-sampled slice of top quality breakbeat with fierce acidy synths throughout and a cool Patsy Cline breakdown. Wicked.

PHUTURE ASSASSINS- "Roots & Phuture" (Rmxs)(Suburban Base/UK) Both "jungle" & "Progressive House" have been suffering lately... the former more than the latter. There are some gems, however, and this is one. Altern 8 lay out a very nice dark rmx with above average breakbeats & a sinister, yet minimal strings chorus. The 'Assassins handle the "Rephlections In Dub" rmx with some nice percussive breakdowns-congas & such-but the rest is pretty tame. A nice one for Sub Base. (D3)

HARDFLOOR-"Trancescript" (Harthouse/Germany) The follow-up to "Hardtrance Acperience", sort of. This record is actually a remix of "Hardtrance" with the parts played backwards and lots of other excit--ing things going on; it seems as if this record keeps building and building... Also included are N-Trance and Caspar Pound remixes. A great record that must be played very loud! (GC)

RECORD REVIEWS

CUSP-"Venusian Biosph--ere (Probe) The opening track from Plus 8's newest addition is a _very_ gradual pulsing groover that builds into a fierce but restrained galloping percussive acid workout sliding back down into ambience. Both tracks on the flip, "Drone Um Fut--urisma" and "Mars The Red Planet" are full-on driving acid trancers as only +8 can provide. Pure and essential.

PAUL MIX-"New Millen--ium" (Experimental) This strong first effort from St. Paul, MN studio head Paul Mix is a pump--ing piece of brilliant trancy house. With a re-mix by Damon Wild and Tommy Musto this is limited to 1000 copies on blue and white vinyl.

BIOTRANS-"Biotrans" ep (Stickman) Watch for this label from Toronto to deliver some quality underground house music. All four tracks on here smoke. The obvious hot one here is "Equinox", which has a _Twin Peaks_-esque synth line, great simple drums, and a groovy modest piano bit. "Terra Firma" is tribal house with a melodic chant and piano harmony, while "Celeste" is kind of a cliffhanger and heavy on acid and fin-ally, "Do It (Don't)" is in a league with Jay-dee. **(CM)**

ROBOT MAN-"Robot Man" ep (Definitive) Wow! There is a groove for almost everyone on this gem. All tracks and mixes are cool, but the Karl's Krispy Dub is the prize of this one with its wailing girl vocal sample and sexy bassline. Get it while you can, mates.

FUQ-"Hot Stuff" (ROR, Ltd./UK) A very nifty, yet '88 sounding track with a smooth disco-y vibe from this fledgling U.K. label that is kind of fun in a early morning kind of way. Check it out

LP/COMPILATIONS

BLACK DOG PRODUCTIONS- _**Bytes**_ **(WARP/UK)** With the underground's new--found interest in music that has depth for list--ening as well as dancing to. The second in WARP's _Artificial Intelligence_ series is _Bytes_, a col--lection from the mysterious Black Dog Productions Black Dog chews up the sound of Detroit and sp--its out a fresh mix of grooves deep, atmospheric, sometimes acidy, someti--mes ambient, and occasionally a bit jazzy for chilling out and definitely moving your body to.

VARIOUS ARTISTS- _**Speed Limit 140 BPM +**_ **(Moonshine Music)** Yet another compilation of up-front techno for the general public's consumption from this L.A.-based label-this time focusing on the U.K. hardcore breakbeat/"jungle" sound. Includes standout tracks from **NRG**, **Yolk**, **Kaotic Chemistry**, and **Urban Shakedown**.

MOONWATER- _**In Existence**_ **(Apollo-R&S/Belgium)** What it is about records like this that always jazz me up, I can't quite put a finger on. Maybe I'm old and don't dance as much as I used to? Nah, age is a state of mind. So is this record. Moody, atmospheric and emotional, with waves of sound flowing like water. Beautiful.

RECORD REVIEWS

VARIOUS ARTISTS- **__Amb--ient Compilation 2__** **(Fax/Germany)** Germany's Fax label has, in a per--iod of just a few months time, put out a slew of quality releases- all identified by a colored dot. This seamless and beatfree compilation br--eathes pure ambience from the speakers, taking you on a trip to a higher plane of the inner mind through its spiritual technology. As essential as Irresistible Force.

VARIOUS ARTISTS- **__Probe Volume One__** **(Probe)** In telligent techno has fi-nally hit the States and more and more DJ's and punters are opening their ears and playlists to the sounds of Detroit. This compilation from +8 off-shoot label, Probe, takes the best tracks from the label's first ten relea-ses. From the side with Hi-Bias (Texas Audio)that started it all to Circuit Breaker, Public Energy, Deko?, Spawn, and others, this is a more than sat--isfying compilation for those who are phuture phorward.

HIP-HOP/ACID JAZZ/R&B
12"/EP

ANOTHER LEVEL-"The Plan" ep (Square Biz Mae) A self-produced re-lease that smacks of a group with phat potential and is deserving of a wider audience. This th--ree track ep comes up more on the pop tip than I like, but these broth-ers can lay it down; "I Ain't Up (For No Games)" showcases some nice vo-cals, while "Paper Baggin It" hits as the requisite crew shout-out jam. "U & Me (Girl)" is the star here with some smart lyrical flow and pre-Pete Rock style production.

LIVE SQUAD-"Game Of Survival" (Tommy Boy) Strong and solid with no surprises, Live Squad comes ruff, rugged, and raw with this thick, full flavored gangsta funk joint straight from the ghetto.

LP/COMPILATIONS

STEREO MC'S-__Connected__ (Gee Street) Rebounding from a two year respite, tons of touring, and breakthrough success in America, the Stereo MC's burst back with __Connected__ Rob B and crew roll out a fuller, more natural sound on this one with the full-time addition of Cath Coffey and two other female vocalists and the use of live musicians in the studio, making for a stronger, more loose vibed effort. The lyrical is still subtle, a posi-tive word to make you think, but vastly matured. But true to the funk, the Stereo's are here to make you dance first and sing the message on the way home. __Connected__ should catch them the wreck they truly deserve.

YOUNG DISCIPLES-__Road To Freedom__ (Talkin' Loud) Released on import in 1991, this acid jazz classic sounds as fresh now as it did then. Gro--ovy, soulful, and full of swinging good vibes, __Road To Freedom__ took London's jazz scene and turned it upside down with Carleen Anderson's smooth voice, Marc's rare groove roots and Femi's hip-hop sen--sibility that has influ-enced many jazzy crews. A massive and most essen--tial record.

APACHE-__Apache Ain't Shit__ (Tommy Boy) '93 is

RECORD RH REVIEWS

the year of the Flavor Unit. With Naughty By Nature blowing up all over the place, Latifah set to drop some hardcore later this year, labelmate Apache stands to very well be the dark horse of the crew with this long player full of slammin' phat production by luminaries Large Professor, Mark The 45 King, ATCQ, and Apache himself. Standout tracks: "Tonto", "Do Fa Self", "A Fight", "Who Freaked Who" (with Nikki D), and "Woodchuck"

D-INFLUENCE-Good 4 We (East/West America) These former Acid Jazz signees finally release their long-awaited debut domestic. They've come a long way since the magic of their breakthrough, "I'm The One", and the magic remains. A bit more polished and R&B oriented than say the YD's or Galliano, uninitiated ears could compare D-Influence to BNH minus a bit of funk with their smooth rare groove meets Kool & The Gang/70's R&B ensemble vibe. Very cool and recommended highly.

KAM-Neva Again (Street Knowledge/ East-West) Straight of the hood with a trunk full of funk and down with Ice Cube and Da Lench Mob, this new face has that fresh off the street, pissed as hell intensity that 'Cube had with NWA but with Death Certificate's black conciousness. If you thought The Predator wasn't all that, check this.

INDIE/ALTERNATIVE/INDUSTRIAL/ EXPERIMENTAL

LP/COMPILATIONS

INTERMIX-Phaze Two (Third Mind) The World's Hardest Working Industrial Band makes a second foray into the realm of house music with their InterMix side project. Sort of for the uninitiated who don't know what techno is, Phase Two pales compared to the real deal with its recognizable samples and trademark FLA sounds. A nice listen, but know your roots.

BALANESCU QUARTET-Possessed (Mute) This string quartet brings to life chamber music versions of your favorite Kraftwerk toons and some gems from David Byrne and namesake Alexander Balanescu. A must for the Kraftwerk fan and challenging listen for the true music fan.

THE MOON SEVEN TIMES-The Moon Seven Times (Third Mind) Sounding sort of like Natalie Merchant doing a This Mortal Coil lp, this Urbana, IL based group's debut touches all the right places here- beautiful vocals and lyrics, shimmering guitar textures, atmospheric underproduction...a beautiful debut worth more than a listen.

VARIOUS ARTISTS-Manifestation (Axiom) Another collection of genre-stretching music from the roster of bassist Bill Laswell's label. From tribal funk and Bootsy-Meets-The-Avant Garde type experiments to dancehall dub, world beat workouts, and the left-field, odd-time signatured be-bop of Henry Threadgill, Manifestation provides an ear expanding look into this exciting label's adventurous New Music alternatives.

TRIP MAGAZEEN
100 DR. M.L. KING, JR. BLVD.
SUITE #10
TAMPA, FLORIDA 33603
U.S.A.
POSTMASTER: PLEASE RUSH...DATED MATERIAL!!

09

TRiP
FLORIDA'S UPFRONT DANCE CU AZINE
GAT DECOR
MARK NRG
808 STATE
UTAH SAINTS
TRiP FOTOFILE 2
The Man Like
SASHA
YOUNG AMERICAN PRIMITIVE*CODE 6*ENERGY 52*UP ABOVE THE WORLD
GURU*UTE*GROOVE GARDEN*WIRE*LE SHAUN
OHM*JOHN & JULIE*ACORN ARTS*DJ T-1000*ALTON M.*HAWKE

TRiP FOTOFILE 2

Top to bottom, left to right- Above: Foxy from NRG on the Chill Tour; @ Disney's Pleasure Island, Lto R-Ex's Damon Wild, D-Man, Dave Christophere (Halluci-Nation Records), DJ Three, Stace Bass (Unity Promotions); Trip 2001's Jask and Nick with Vortex/Brand X's DJ Moneypenny; ffrr's Danny Campbell @The Edge; Simon from Effective with Dave and Steve from Halluci-Nation

CONTENTS

FEET FIRST

MAY 1993/VOL. 2, #3

CONTENTS

TRIP MAGAZEEN
100 E. DR. M.L. KING, JR. BLVD.
SUITE 10
TAMPA, FLORIDA 33603 USA
PHONE: 813.238.0310
FAX: 813.876.7473
(When faxing, be sure to include a cover sheet)

EDITOR/PUBLISHER: Peter Wohelski
SENIOR EDITOR: Chris Milo
CONTRIBUTORS: DJ Grumpy C., DJ Three

SUPPORT THE UNDERGROUND!!!

ADVERTISING: Rates given upon request. Contact us for details.
BACK ISSUES: Back issues of **TRiP MAGAZEEN** are available for $1 postpaid per issue. Please specify issue # or cover stars.
SUBSCRIPTIONS: $10 Yearly (8 issues).
RETAIL STORES: If your store is interested in carrying **TRiP MAGAZEEN**contact us at **813.238.0310** for bulk rate information.

TRiP MAGAZEEN is published every six weeks and distributed to select outlets throughout Florida and the United States. We hope that our content will encourage awareness and positivity for the Global Underground. Nothing may be reprinted in any way without permission from the TRiP Posse. All rights reserved. All information is correct to the best of our knowledge at the time of print. Opinions expressed are not necessarily the views of the editors, but they could be....

I mentioned last issue that I went to Chicago recently. I grew up just outside the Windy City, so I know how bizarre the weather can be during March. Still, despite better judgment, my traveling companion and I scheduled our pilgrimage to the Birthplace of House in order to coincide with the Chicago date of **The Orb**'s tour. The tour was canceled, but "Fuck it," we said, "Let's go anyway!"

Aahh, home! **Phuture, Trax Records, Acid House, Michael Jordan, Wrigley Field,** and **deepdish pizza** all coursed through my mind on the flight to O'Hare. Expecting the weekend of my life, I could hardly wait to check out the state of the Chicago Underground. Sad to say, I was a little bit disappointed. In defense of my hometown, however, I will say that I was steered to the wrong places all weekend.

Shelter was tolerable, but the crowd were college kids on Techno and the music digressed into ravey sounding dated Belgian crap. Over it and unimpressed by the S&M performance art, we blazed and went to **KA-BOOM,** which sucked even worse. I think it was "Old Wave Night" or something. We called it quits, resolving to try again tomorrow.

The next night, I went for **CROBAR** while my companion, did **The Dome Room.** CROBAR was fun, with **DJ Mark Picchioti** playing a good set of acid, hard house, trance, and tribal tracks that sent me off. Unfortunately, my vibe came to an abrupt end when the gears switched to the Hip-Hop tip about 3:30. Way fucked up, having forgotten how to get to another club that was recommended (**RED DOG**), and tired of being told that I **looked** like I was from Florida (?), I took a cab home at 4:00. I heard however, that The Dome Room was **quite** a top night with **DJ Jeff Moyer** who worked tracks from **Hardfloor, Front Line Assembly,** and **Sunscreem** all into a nice groove. At least **someone** had a really good time...

Despite my complaints, I'm sure Chicago probably has a fair to good Underground, but I didn't get to see it very closely. A great music city, Chicago is not without some safe record stores and we hit them. **Gramaphone, Reckless, Wax Trax, Hot Wax, Dr. Wax...** not all are dance specialists, but highly recommended regardless. Also props to **UNTITLED,** a phat shop for some wicked gear.

If you're on line with the **Prodigy system,** you can give us a shout, say "Hi!", give feedback on TRiP, tell us what's going on in your scene, comment on a party, whatever, via E-mail. Our ID# is **HVPK67A.** Yeah, we know **Internet** is better but we're not paying for it, they are!!!! We plan on hooking up with Internet in the very near future, watch this space for info.

Shouts go out to the following:: **Damon Wild, DJ Money-penny, Jim Hopkins @ Zoe Magik, Simon & Lawrence @ Effective, Michael & Lee @ GTO/Dataflow, Brian & Matt @ Mute, Ken @ Caroline, DJ Thumper, Jennifer @ Industrial Strength, Karl Kowalski @ Definitive, Adam** (for guest listing me at CROBAR, even though you're too much of a wimp to meet me), **DJ Chris Fortier, Madhouse Crew (Atl.), Mike @ ExistDance, Danny G & Nicole @ Rising High, Charlie @ Brute, Ian & Wayne @ 33 Records/UK, Tom Terrell @ Verve, Rob Sherwood, Damon @ Chill....**

....**SONIC SOUL** is a new production crew based out of Baltimore, MD. These former members of **ATOMIC VIBE** have ventured out on their own dedicated to the advancement of the Underground with quality productions at raver's prices ($10 or less). Featuring the best in local talent as well as DJ's throughout the U.S., Sonic Soul aim to place emphasis on the music, giving DJ's the freedom to play for up to 2 hours. DJ's interested in playing a Sonic Soul event, send tape and working credentials to **SONIC SOUL, P.O. BOX 9511, BALTIMORE, MD 21237** or call **410-235-1131**...New York-based **SONIC RECORDS** presents the **LIMITED EDITION EP** series, bringing cutting edge sounds from the Underground to the U.S. Each release is limited to 2000 copies on vinyl and 2500 on CD, with new tracks scheduled every three weeks. The series' first releases are from **ENERGY ZONE** and **LAB WORKS**....**JOEY BELTRAM** comes out of his Smart-E's phase with some wicked new stuff from **CODE 6** to be released soon on **EXPERIMENTAL**....Hip-Hop legends **ULTRAMAGNETIC MC'S** are back making records after being dropped by Polygram at the end of '92, signing to **WILD PITCH/EMI**....The debut from San Francisco's **YOUNG AMERICAN PRIMITIVE**, long delayed by sample clearance difficulties, is due to be released May 25 on **ZOE MAGIK**....Rumour has it that **MOBY** has signed to **ELEKTRA** while **DANNY RAMPLING** seems to have scribbled his John Hancock for **DE/CONSTRUCTION**....L.A.-based **MOONSHINE MUSIC** has sewn up a licensing deal with **SVEN VATH's HARTHOUSE** label....**HYPE!**'s European sources tell us that The City Of Lights, **PARIS**, has been quite the hot spot lately. With Summer coming, it would be cool to spend a short break getting off our face in France!!! Over our Memorial Day Weekend, there's a **"LADIES OF TECHNO"** party with **DJ MONEYPENNY** (U.S.), **ELECTRIC INDIGO** (Austria), and others driving the wheels..This year's **NEW MUSIC SEMINAR** (July 20-24) has made a renewed commitment to dance music, increasing panels and events. The Seminar has moved from the Marriott Marquis to the Sheraton New York. Panels have been reduced in number with emphasis on making the topics more educational, interesting, or controversial. For more information, call **212-730-1703**....

Utah Saints...

Wavering between underground and 'stadium house'

Walking the fine line between underground credibility and commercial accessibility is often a double edged sword. As DJ's for Leeds' long-running **Mile High Club** as well as chart-topping band **Utah Saints**, this is a position that is nothing new to **Tim Garbutt** and **Jez Willis**.

The 'Saints exploded onto the scene about two years ago with **"What Can You Do For Me,"** an Annie Lennox sample-driven track with strong pop sensibility. Thinking that they'd press a few copies of the record and with the dosh they made, press more, the pair were more than surprised when the first 1000 white labels flew out of the shops. Leading to radio play and interest from the **ffrr label**. it was repressed commercially, the track leapt into the charts, peaking at #10.

With the amount of rave-oriented tracks flooding the U.K. charts at the time, many trainspotters began to scream sell-out. The band disagrees. Attests Jez Willis, "We didn't know why the record worked, we just knew Tim and I liked it.... If we really wanted to sell out, the easiest way for us to sell out would have been to put out several tracks that all sound the same in very quick succession." In a thick Northern accent, Tim explains, "In England, there was a nine month gap between "What Can You Do For Me" and "Something Good", and then another nine month gap and we're about to release our next single. So, in the meantime we've been a band, playing live, developing our sound and working in the studio."

As far as developing and expanding that sound, the band takes an approach to sampling that redefines the role of the musician, freeing him from the confines of conventional instrumentation. On their self-titled debut, Utah Saints mutated sources as diverse as **Motorhead, Slayer, Crown Heights Affair, Sylvester,** and most recognizably, **Kate Bush**. In taking them far out of context from their original source, that the band has created something that sets them apart in the sample-happy U.K. dance scene.

"The way me and Jez try to use samples, we never take samples from dance music unless it's seven, ten years old. We try and pull samples from different types of music like an Annie Lennox or Kate Bush or metal samples from Slayer," reveals Tim, "but if it's dance music, it's old disco... So many records at the moment just pull accapellas from a track from six months ago, resample it and put a dance track behind it,"

With sampling so prevalent in all sorts of dance music today, using technology to make music is not only an art form, but big business with tracks' original sources lining up to get paid. How does a sample-driven act like Utah Saints avoid paying through the nose for a sample clearance?

"When we sample somebody like an Annie Lennox or Kate Bush , we'll do the track first, finish it completely; not spend a whole lot of money, but take maybe two weeks to finish this one record, then we'll pass it over (to the sample's publisher) and try and get the sample cleared. If they say no, then we've just wasted two weeks in studio time and all we have to do is go back in and use a different sample if we can," says Tim, quite simply..

Besides Utah Saints, the duo are also in demand DJ's and largely successful clubrunners, having handled Leeds' longstanding Tuesday night Mile High Club. "It's like three clubs in one, really," replies Tim excitedly, " in one room, there's a friend of ours playing rare groove, in the Main room, Jez plays a mix of music-disco, soul, house, techno and in my room I play more house and techno, things like that."

Tim laughs, "I think it works because people come out to hear a whole bunch of different music," explains Jez. "It gets a little strange some times, I'll be finishing a record in my room, and then ten minutes later, you'll be in Jez' room and he'll start the same old record and he had no idea I just played it."

The Utah Saints have spent quite a bit of time this past year away from their club gig, opting to hit the road, touring extensively in both the U.K. and the U.S. with the **Shamen**. The band also headlined at the recent **Divine Playground** rave in March along with **Meat Beat Manifesto, 808 State** and a host of international DJ's that drew over 9000 r**ers to Miami's Bayfront Park.

The band also has a new single out in the U.K.,**"Believe In Me"**, while "What Can You Do..." has been remixed by **David Morales** in the U.S.

808 'not going for the green'. with new lp, Gorgeous

As soon as I sat down. I knew I was in trouble.....

A few days earlier, the **TRiP** staff had gone to Miami to cover the **Divine Playground** event and ran into **808 State** hanging about outside Bayfront Park, soaking some sun into their pale Mancunian skin. "Wicked label," **Darren Partington** blurted out as we walked by, referring to the **Transmat** logo on my shirt. We introduced ourselves and arranged to do an interview in a few days' time. I gave them a couple copies of the February issue and we went to sort out our accomodations.

"That was **really** stupid," contributor DJ Three tells me," you slagged their new record in that issue..." Sure enough, I **had** taken their new effort **Gorgeous** to task, claiming that they've "fallen the fuck off", and that the record paled in comparison to their groundbreaking tracks like **"Pacific State"**, **"Cubik"**, or the current underground standard.

What I found was that Mssrs. **Barker, Massey,** and Partington don't seem to care about what the underground thinks of them. They've made their mark in dance music history and they're more concerned with rising to the next level and making good cutting edge dance music.

"The way we see it, we expect people to grow with us, this is our sixth album, right. We're not a one-hit fucking wonder-we've been around for five years... In Europe, in Japan, and in England, the audience has grown with us album by album. This is the only country that doesn't understand this album, because America's two years behind England as far as dance music; so maybe in two years' time reviews like yours will be laughed at, people will say 'The **Gorgeous** album of 1993, might not have been what it was supposed to be'," Darren Partington explains.

Partington repudiates any claims that the group have compromised themselves for the green like is alleged by purists about **Altern 8** and **The Prodigy**, "We're not about making money on a scene or being trendy, we want to be one step further. In order to be one step further, you're not trendy. So in England, we're not a pop band, we're not a trendy band, we are what we are. We're not going to become a trendy band because of reviews like a lot of bands have; **Utah Saints, Jesus Jones**-this techno thing's taking off-**Sunscreem**-we need a piece of it."

Darren explains where the group is coming from, "In England, we don't have clubs that carried on until 6, 7 o' clock in the morning (? Ed.). We'd get sent home at 2:00. So we decided that, fuck else to do, we wanted to carry on dancing. We wanted to break down these barriers a little bit; these homophobic barriers, these racial barriers. The only way to do that is through this music. This is the purest subculture that's come along, you don't have to wear a certain uniform or think a certain way...."

808 State have just recently completed a version of the **Rolling Stones'** "Gimme Shelter" with **Robert Owens** to aid the U.K.'s homeless.

A conversation with Simon & Lawrence of Gat Decor

Hanson & Nelson make 'effective' Soul Sacrifice

As co-creators of one of 1992's biggest "progressive house" tracks, DJ's **Simon Hanson** and **Lawrence Nelson** made an indelible mark on the face of dance music with **"Passion"** under the name **Gat Decor**, an anagram for the London record shop they run.

A busy duo, the "Gat Decor Boys" still have the record shop, DJ regularly around London, run their own label, **Effective Records**, and are heavily in demand as remixers. **TRiP** caught up with them while in Tampa spinning at the opening of a new club and had a pint and a chat....

TRiP:How did the two of you meet and what sort of background do you have?

Lawrence: We met DJ'ing at a club called **Ah** (?) about three years ago and after about six months went to Ibiza DJ'ing, came back and opened up with Steve, Simon's brother and Simon started trading, selling records from their house. And then we started the record shop in Piccadilly, **TAG Records.** We started up the the shop and things just progressed from there. We did a club called **Naked Lunch.** From there we thought "Oh let's go into the studio" and Simon took another guy Simon, and we did some tracks and so on and the first track we did was **"Passion".**

T: Did you expect the track to be so massive?

Simon: No, to be quite honest, we weren't going to bring it out. We finished it and we were hemming and hawing, "No, no, we won't..." and Lawrence had a bit of spare money and we had 1000 copies pressed. We had them all delivered to the shop....

L: I was worried, there was 1000 copies just sitting in the shop and it looked like, a lot. But they went...

S: So we came out to America last year, and while we were away it went to #1, which was really great for us. And it went on to sell 42,000 copies in the U.K., I don't know what it's done worldwide. The coincidence here is that we've just signed a pair of Danish lads to our label called **Miro**, and we got a phonecall the other day and it's gone to #1.... What a coincidence, the second time we come back to America and we get our second #1!

T:Was there inspiration for "Passion"?

L: We just basically wanted to put together certain sounds that we liked that we weren't hearing in any records we liked at the time...

T: Has the success of the records significantly affected your lives?

S: Definitely, it's really laid the whole basis for the label. where usually it takes several releases to really establish yourself, the one track did it in one go. Now we've got six releases out, with about another two coming.

T: Tell me about Soul Sacrifice?

S: Well, we're not Gat Decor anymore, we won't bother you with the politics of that; we're now working under the name Soul Sacrifice which is with the singer **Elliot** of **Sly & Lovechild**, we're working with her now as well as under the name **Hanson & Nelson** depending the type of track we're working on.

L: Soul Sacrifice is more of a blues-housey...

S: .... sort of **Doors-type, Stranglers-type**, moody sort of house music.

L: You can see the influences, we use an organ keyboard... It's the first time we've done something with a proper type singer and recorded it. She's great to work with...

T: You two could be attributed to being instrumental in starting the "progressive house" movement in the U.K. What is the current state of that scene, is it alive or dead?

S: We never did use that term - progressive house is U.K.-produced house of which there's a lot of good stuff out there. It's given the U.K. an identity....

L: There's been furious debates with all sorts of people and yeah, it's definitely been good for the British music scene. But as far as strictly saying, "That is a 'progressive house' track", I mean, what is a progressive house record?

S:It's all House music at the end of the day.

T: Are you discouraged with the fact that there are labels to everything?

S: Yeah, because it got to the point where it wasn't trendy to be a 'progressive house' record so a lot of good stuff got missed.

T: Is it a fad or is this Britain's claim to fame as far as house music?

S: It's just the start, really, because it's British produced music and it'll get better and better. All England's ever done is import records from wherever and if they do well, they go back to that country and do well over there.

L: It's been a good move for us. Where in the past few years you can see DJ remixes, people like **Todd Terry, Tony Humphries, Derrick May** ruled things and you can definitely see this year and into next year British DJ remixes. You can see them coming through now- **Weatherall, Leftfield, Underworld, Boys' Own, Sure Is Pure**- giving British producers the chance to get to the same sort of level as a Todd Terry.

T: As DJ's, what sort of stuff are you playing at the moment?

S: A lot of techno and techno-oriented things, early acid... We both play sort of the same- I play sort of down, Lawrence plays it sort of up.

T: *Did* a track like Hardfloor do a lot to change things in the U.K.?

S: People were just waiting for a record to come out like that, I think a lot of DJ's were scared to play that acid house again, which it really is, I suppose.

Germany's Mark NRG comes to America

Frankfurt's **Mark NRG** came onto the scene about a year and a half ago on the **Overdrive** label making a name for himself with tracks like **"Celluloid"**. Influenced by electronic music like **Yello**, **Art Of Noise**, and **Kraftwerk** as well as industrial acts like **Nitzer Ebb**, Mark began doing music about four years ago, moving into techno because he found techno "more interesting because of the rhythm, it's so fast and so aggressive."

Mark also DJ's, having learned to DJ after learning the in's and out's of studios-he likes both. "When I play, it's lots of different music, I think it's very important to do that," he stressed, " go with the people and experiment by playing lots of different types of music. I play hardcore, but not all the time"

A special guest at a party on South Miami Beach during Winter Music Conference, Mark spun a searing set of acid trance and techno, but his current love is House and he plans to take his music in that direction. "I came from industrial music, now techno, but I think I will go into House music because in Germany, hardcore is overground and House music is the real underground at the moment and I like it!" He plans to start his own label to reflect this new direction, aptly called **House Music**. "I've got the first three releases at home, waiting to be released. It will be a mix between techno and house. Um...techno/house!"

Before jetting to Miami for WMC, Mark finished two releases both out now. On Overdrive, "Mark NRG Likes BK" is being shown on MTV Europe as the soundtrack for a British Knights commercial; the other, "Tribal Groovy Hartbeat" by Overboust is on Harthouse.

RECORD REVIEWS

TECHNO/HOUSE

12"/EP

IO BOGAERT- "Water" (XXP/ Belgium) I LOVE IT. A friend in Orlando told me it's the guy who did the **Technotronic** music.... Whatever, it's killer. A funky repeating tone, soothing bassline, thunder and rain with different tones and synths fading out the entire journey....that's just the Ambient Mix. All that plus a drum break and you've got a wicked track for the floor on the b-side. Excellent groovy trance. (D3)

SINGLE CELL ORCHESTRA- "The Liberated EP" (Zoe Magik) San Francisco labels keep churning out quality releases, track after track. "Heaven Knows" is a body-snatching acid trance driver that builds with two mixes; the original being a bit more edgy. The flip opens with "I Hear The DJ's Here", a slightly building, acid-tinged atmospheric progressive house track. Ambient DJ's will want to check the other two tracks, moody, dense, trancy, sub-100 bpm cruisers. **(PW)**

OHM-"Why Don't Ya" (Hubba Hubba/UK) Following-up to "Tribal Tone" with five mixes of this new track, not quite as accessible to any dancefloor as "...Tone". Underground techno/house with our favourite mixes of late, being Set of the Dancefloor inna tribal garage vibe and Breakdown Dub that is what it says. **(CM)**

RISING SUN-"Switch Of Love EP" (ESP/Holland) 5 Tracks of "intelligent" techno from....Japan??? Yes! And it's quite good. Logo side has two ambient based tracks that have a Detroit feel, while the info side more dancefloor. "Haze" and the title track are standouts; "Haze" with its odd, airy melody over a subtle breakbeat accented by a Miami 808 kik. "Switch Of Love" rolls in a more straight ahead trance style, uptempo and more melodic than say, **Paul Mix**. "Reconstruction" is uptempo, bassy, techno-house in a **Ricky Rouge** "Strange Love" style. **(D3)**

THE HYPNOTIST-"Pioneers Of The Warped Universe" (Rising High/UK) Back in the day a **Caspar Pound** b-side in the "builds and builds" league was a moody, moody piece called "Pioneers Of The Warped Groove". Well, it's back and better than ever in remixed form as "Pioneers Of The Warped Universe". Moonlighting as the theme song for U.K. rave promoters **Universe**, this is the lead track off of their compilation of the best current techno/hard trance tracks **Universal Techno Tribe.** **(CM)**

JOHN & JULIE- "Red Alert" (Dataflow/UK) Produced by GTO, this brutal hard acid pounder builds up to a cool oscillating synth breakdown before launching into an all out assault with siren screeches and distorted "Red Alert" sample. In three versions in varying degrees of hardness for the headstrong with #2 being the pick here. **(PW)**

ALTON M.-"I Like Havin' You" (Cyren America) This newie from Detroit is one of those male vocal records that just hits the spot. Hot, sweaty male crooning, reverbed keyboards, sizzling hi-hats, sexy deep bassline, cooing repeating female vocal ....tasty. **(PW)**

PEQUENA HABANA-"Pickin' Up Transmissions" (Zippy/UK) A **Murk** trip through **Azuli** in the U.K. A funky chunk o' house in 3 flavours: the "Why You Sweatin' Me?" vocaled Oscar G's Dub, the Groovin' Cuban Mix, which centers more on a "Scoo, Scoo, a-Scooby-doo" vocal- both with typical Murk percussion- and the third Ralph's Mission Control which is like **Strictly Rhythm** doing **"Voodoo Ray"**. Simple, funky, sexy, and working. **(D3)**

68000-"Expansion EP" (Pulse Soniq) From Portland, OR comes this three tracker... The title track isn't all that at its 142 bpm, but pitched down to -4 , it bounces quite nicely. The B-side pick, however, is the quite melodic tribal/trance tripper "Data Cloud 9". Nice one. **(PW)**

HAWKE- "3 Nudes In A Purple Garden" (Hardkiss Music) San Francisco....more and more incredible tracks all the time. 3 mixes of the title track, all packed with atmosphere; the 3 Moods In A Gurple Pardon a bit more on the funky tip while the 3 Nudes Having Sax On Acid is more straight up trance. The bonus gem is "Pacific Coastal Highway #1", funky acid with building strings and urgent piano. Very emotional, very good. **(D3)**

BONESBREAKS VOL. 7-"Progressive Vibe EP" (Groove World) **Frankie** continues his **Bonesbreaks** series with what he calls "progressive vibe"- quite different from what he was doing a couple of months ago. The six "songs' on this ep are very diverse, ranging from tribal to old school acid, to perhaps the best song here "Dreams On Plastic". Using an old **Beltram** drum loop and **Jaydee**'s "Plastic Dreams", **Bones** creates a definite floor filler. Not exactly very original, but it works. **(GC)**

UP ABOVE THE WORLD- 'Unleashed In The East" (ExistDance) "If I would know it was happening, if would know I was changing" opens this long, gradually building, sweeping trancer with a swirling acidline and a fierce,, transformed wail that trails into a lock groove of just the wail at the end of the record. A track that just begs for a climax that never quite comes. The flip, "Straight Up Caffeine" is an urgent slice of groovy, uplifting acid house that just pumps. Slammin' **(PW)**

REDSKINS-"Spread Out" / "Just Cool" (Kemen/UK) A top drum and bass program- nothing new in the mix here, just two fully urgent jungle tracks the way they should be done. No Stupid samples, Ragga to the bone. Ok, there is a third track that kicks for about 60 seconds until it's destroyed by rave stabs and the Minnie Mouse vocal bit. These days 2 out of 3 ain't bad, it's lucky! **(CM)**

DJ T-1000-"Liquid Metal Meltdown"/ "Hunter - Killer" (Generator) The second release on **Alan Oldham's** label does not dissapoint. The label side starts off with just an extremely irritating riff for about 3 minutes before the drums come in- definitely an attack on your brain. The logo side is similar to the first, just a little more tame. This 10" ends with presumably Alan declaring if you want to know what techno is than buy some records from Detroit. I agree. **(Nuff said. Ed.) (GC)**

REALITY STUDIO / NEBULA NINE- "Meta 1" (Lenny Dee RMX)/ "Hypnotic Trance" (UltraEthereal) A split 12" from Baltimore's **Reality**

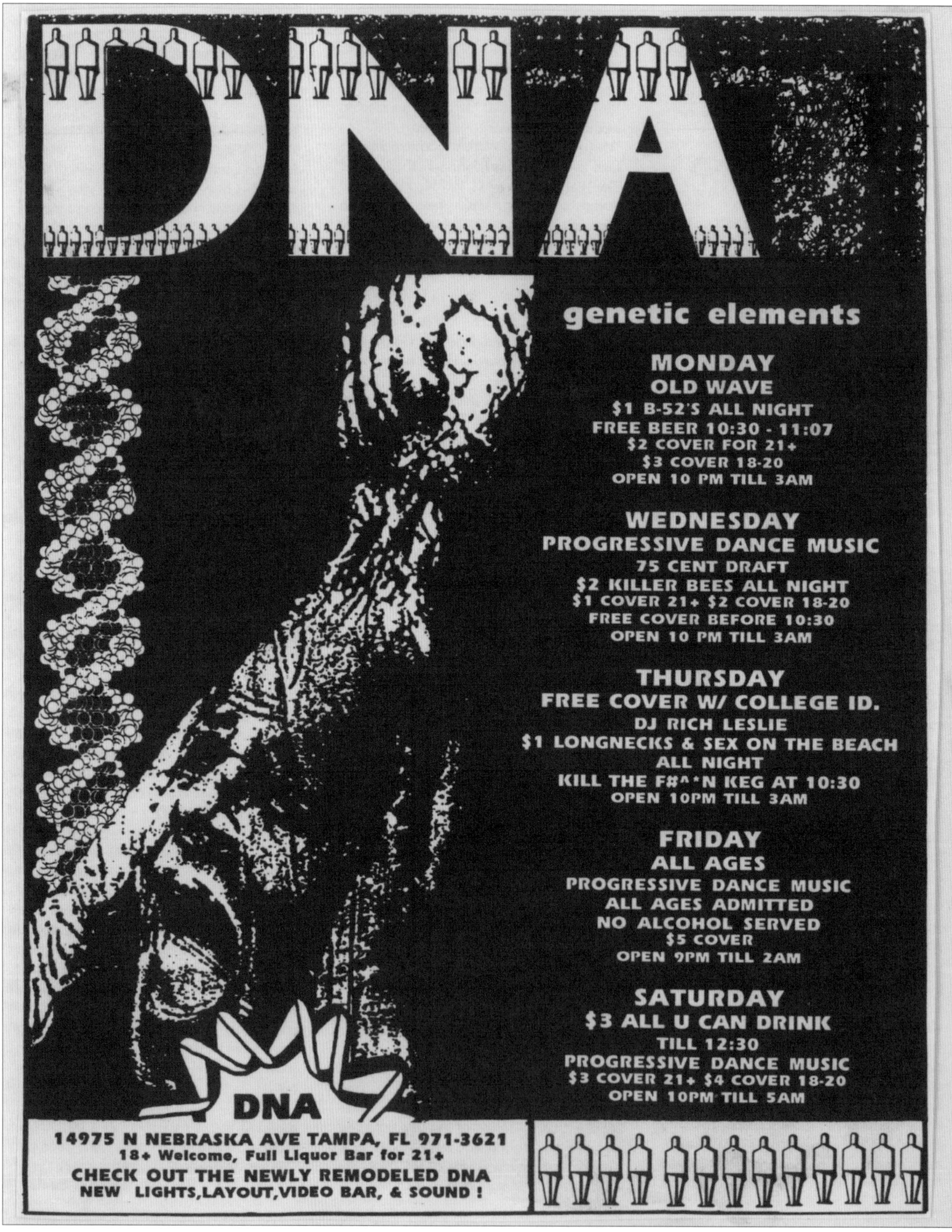
DNA
genetic elements
MONDAY
OLD WAVE
$1 B-52'S ALL NIGHT
FREE BEER 10:30 - 11:07
$2 COVER FOR 21+
$3 COVER 18-20
OPEN 10 PM TILL 3AM
WEDNESDAY
PROGRESSIVE DANCE MUSIC
75 CENT DRAFT
$2 KILLER BEES ALL NIGHT
$1 COVER 21+ $2 COVER 18-20
FREE COVER BEFORE 10:30
OPEN 10 PM TILL 3AM
THURSDAY
FREE COVER W/ COLLEGE ID.
DJ RICH LESLIE
$1 LONGNECKS & SEX ON THE BEACH
ALL NIGHT
KILL THE F#^*N KEG AT 10:30
OPEN 10PM TILL 3AM
FRIDAY
ALL AGES
PROGRESSIVE DANCE MUSIC
ALL AGES ADMITTED
NO ALCOHOL SERVED
$5 COVER
OPEN 9PM TILL 2AM
SATURDAY
$3 ALL U CAN DRINK
TILL 12:30
PROGRESSIVE DANCE MUSIC
$3 COVER 21+ $4 COVER 18-20
OPEN 10PM TILL 5AM
DNA
14975 N NEBRASKA AVE TAMPA, FL 971-3621
18+ Welcome, Full Liquor Bar for 21+
CHECK OUT THE NEWLY REMODELED DNA
NEW LIGHTS,LAYOUT,VIDEO BAR, & SOUND !

Studio and Denver's (?) **Nebula Nine** on the Baltimore-based Ultra Ethereal label; The Reality Studio's side is a hard tribal remix of "Meta 1" by **Lenny Dee** with pumping kik drum, tribal chants, and trademark hard stabs that seems tame by the Maniac's standards. This side also features a track with **Dan Nigrin of Glitch**, a tough percussive acid pounder with sizzling hi-hats and cranium crushing kik drum and noisy synths. The flip must have been designed to chill you out after that mayhem... Calm and soothing with a plucky synth bassline and light ambient synths washing over the top, "Hypnotic Trance" slowly builds. Both sides worth a listen. (PW)

BOOM OPERATORS-"Metamorphia" (MFS/Germany) Read the fine print and it's him again... **Cosmic Baby** with the juice behind "Metamorphia". A electronic guitar line and simple piano riff take turns complimenting each other in this funkified track that always turns in the right direction, not to mention the 2 minute intro that keeps you guessing the whole way. B-cut "The Block" is an invitation for your mind to put its guard down via a combo of thick and thin elements woven into a 4/4 trance groove. Soon to be a Florida hit! (D3)

TRANSFORMER 2 featuring ASLI-"Just Can't Get Enough" (Sonic) The follow-up to the massive "Pacific Symphony" and "Fruit Of Love" cruises along much the same lines, no major surprises over the four mixes but a nice track nonetheless. (PW)

FORMULA 7-"Mad Bones EP" (Quayside/UK) 4 tracks of semi-typical breaks- but go straight to "Dark Star" for a wicked breakbeat techno track. Some nice techno-y sounds, thick bass, and the flanged drum bit and strings breakdown ala "Mindstream" by Meat Beat Manifesto Pretty tough. (D3)

EQUINOX-"2 EP" (Vortex) **Damon Wild** and **DJ Repete** are back with the second phase of their **Equinox** project. This 4-tracker is simply brilliant! "Hard Drive" is just that- a brutal piece of percussive analogue acid madness. "Pollux" opens with a pounding kik, adding frantic hi-hats and a fierce wiggling acid line before reaching a crescendo. The b-side is more on the hard trance tip; "Surveyor-4" whirls in, gradually building, adding parts to the maelstrom, then breaking down before exploding and leaving you breathless while "Synod" is more hard and minimal. Again, absolutely brilliant! (PW)

ACORN ARTS- "Vanilla" / "Speed Controller" (X-Gate/UK) "Speed Controller" is typical progressive house fare, complete with "Bup, Bup, Bup, Bup-Bup" synth line and light tribal percussion. "Vanilla" is a very pleasant surprise, however. Uptempo, "hard-ish", tribal with a monotone synth and slight bell and vocal for occasional hypnotic melody. A really good trance track that just booms in a big space. (D3)

TRANCEPARENTS- "Child 1-4" (HOS/Switzerland) This record comes from the land of watches and cheese. No cheese here- the Swiss can make dance records, too. "Child 1" is the masterpiece here- a heavy acid line just keeps building and building and before you know it, it's over. Should have been longer. "Child.4" is ambient. Overall, very good. (GC)

ADVANCED WAVEFORM SYNTHETIX- "Fantasia" (EX) Written and produced by **Freddie Fresh** aka **The Modulator**. "Fantasia" is a chilled-out thumper in three forms, from ambient house to deep trance. "Suffering Souls" comes in two forms; a dark, acidic analogue galloper with manic bleeping and oscillating synths rolling over the top, while "Alex's Rhyme" is a blinding turbo nosebleed remix that starts with a distorted vocoder voice before charging in at a thundering pace. "Afterthought" is a backward masked piece of shout outs. A killer release from one of America's best underground labels. (PW)

ENERGY 52-"Cafe Del Mar" (Eye-Q/Germany) This new one from Germany is very hard to pass up **Cosmic Baby**'s mix begins with a powerful kick drum and evolves into a trance monster. Also included is a **Kid Paul** remix. Find this record. (GC)

CODE 6-4 Track EP (EX) I've been listening to this on a tape for a month and this clear vinyl gem means that **Joey Beltram's** back and with his best stuff since "Energy Flash". Melodic, atmospheric, and sort of funky, "Third Aura" trances nicely with a subdued breakbeat; "Last Voyage" has a sort of Detroit ala **Tronik House** kind of feel along with the

RECORD REVIEWS

track's sweeping synths. "AfterLife" is a moody ambient breakbeat trance vibe for the after hours while "Tempest" is a short, urgent "hard ambient" track. Welcome back, Joey. (PW)

PARADISE 3001-"Blue Highways" (ESP/Holland) The last one was good, this one's better. 4 tracks and one ambient bit with heavy bassline. All the tracks kick, produced by **Dr. Nuno** and one by **Jaydee** which is very subsonic. Other standouts are the acid house-styled "Mind & Motion" and the string inflected "Mellow Moebe". All nice, spacey, and moody for the after hours vibe. (CM)

SPICELAB-"Spirit Of Fear" (Harthouse/Germany) "Ant Attack" on side 2 is probably the best combination of extremely hardcore breakbeats with intense analogue keyboards. Magnificent. The other three songs are quite different. "Spirit Of Fear" is rather slow compared to the rest but is still quite tough. "S.Y.N.C." is very minimal and noisy, "Hyperspice" is similar to "Ant Attack" but more on the frantic side. (GC)

DJ ESP-"The Earthworm Sings EP" (EX) This dirt brown vinyl slab of is written and produced by Minneapolis DJ ESP. Hard but not brutal, "Wet Dirt" rumbles along with its manic buzzing synth line with gurgling acid just bubbling under the surface. "Sleeper" is a frantic minimal hard driving trancer, while "Hibernation" is more percussive with a cool repeating backward tape edit. (PW)

SEXTRAVAGANZA-"This Is Tribal America EP" (Tribal America) Severely overlooked by everyone here in the office last issue, this blinding tribal ep is quite a stormer.... five **Frederick Jorio** produced tracks on the house/tribal tip. The Hot side is more house-y, while the Hotter side is more tribal; all cuts are excellent. Don't repeat our mistake, this deserves your attention! (PW)

MINIMALISTIC SOURCE 4-"Girls On Top" (Fax/Germany) Yet another

RECORD REVIEWS

release on Germany's Fax Records. "Girls On Top" is an extremely hard driving trancer with a familiar acid sample speeded way up. A second mix of "Girls" is slightly different but not too much. "Edible Pumas" is also very familiar to "Girls" but has an extremely long intro before it explodes into acid and heavy beats. Wonderful. **(GC)**

V/A-"Guerilla Artists EP#2" (Guerilla/IRS) Already out as imports individually, this ep drops the best mixes from recent top releases by **Lemon Sol, Felix Da Housecat,** and **Tenth Chapter** for those who missed it as an import or need an extra copy. Props to Guerilla for their relatively timely domestic release of these gems. **(PW)**

V/A- "The Last Judgement, Part 1 EP" (Cold Rush/Germany) A various 4-tracker of hard acid trance from the depths of Frankfurt's underground. All tracks solid, trippy, and hard to the bone. Engineered by the Mover. **(PW)**

LIMELIGHT 4- "Momentum" (Fax/ Germany) Pete Namlook strikes again- seems Fax Records are a little easier to come by these days, but not much. 3 variations on a theme, "Momentum" is the pick for now time-tested hard trance in Fax style. The other 2 are a bit more common sounding harder than hard trance. There's not much of **Blade Runner** left to sample, Pete. **(CM)**

WILLIAM HENSEL- "Aftertaste" (ROR, Ltd./UK) A pretty synth washed ambient house piano pulser that flows nicely at either 33 or 45, although it drags and gets a bit too trippy when the main piano break comes in at 33 rpm. For the chillout room, either way. **(PW)**

SUBCULTURE- "TV Heaven" (Crib/ UK) 2nd release on Crib co-produced by Air Tattoo and buzzing real big in Florida right now. Head to the Spacey Mix for it's "I floated in the clouds" and "don't think I ever came down from that one" vocaled, percussive synth line accented groove topped with a boppy bassline tinted with occasional acid. Phantom signal Mix is in a more throbbing progressive house/trance styled bassline and synth, with a repeated sample style as well. Foundation-"Big Black Boot", Crib #003, is out any day now- they say third time's a charm...**(D3)**

FALLOUT- "Midnight Attraction" (ROR, Ltd/UK) This new label is still in the hit or miss stage with it's releases. Some are really spot on and others just miss the target. This rave stabbed, female vocaled, piano-y breakbeat, ragga MC'ed track with some acidy bits thrown in is a miss. **(PW)**

OVERBOUST-"Tribal Groovy Hart-beat" (Harthouse/UK) One of this issue's profiled artists, **Mark NRG,** co-composed and produced this bisquit on Frankfurt's Harthouse through the House of Rising High. Mellow but frantic, "Tribal Groovy Hartbeat" pumps along nicely while on the flip, "Tribal Interphase" is a driving acid trancer and "Lost In New York"'- a pounding hardcore thunderer with Mark singing a "New York, New York" breakdown into a punishing finish. "Start spreading the news...." **(PW)**

LP/COMPILATIONS

YOUNG AMERICAN PRIMITIVE- Young American Primitive LP (Zoe Magik) After delays for sample clearance, San Francisco's **Young American Primitive** releases his first lp, and it was worth the wait. Spiritual, magical, and uplifting, this debut whisks you on a current of tranceified energy filled with melodic, spacey ambient synths, deep tribal percussion, and sporadic slowed-up, groovin' breakbeats all linked by occasional sound bites. Massive to move to and a joy for listening, Y.A.P. has the potential to be America's next great face in the underground. **(PW)**

V/A-Rising High Techno Injection 2 (Instinct) Focusing on ambient and acid trance from the "House That Caspar Built", this second collection brings together tracks from the **Sapho** sub-label, licensed selections from German labels **Fax, Force, Inc.,** and **Pod,** as well as the Rising High stable. A fierce compilation accentuating Caspar's pure musical vision and excellent taste in licensing. **(PW)**

V/A-Excursions In Ambience (Caroline) Rich in atmosphere, the mating of ambient music and house beats has only begun to be explored. **The Orb** and **KLF's** groundbreaking adventures have generated a whole slew of sonic explorers, each taking a varied approach to this still new sub-genre. From the tribal flavor of **Future Sound Of London, Psychedelic Research Lab,** and **Tranquility Bass,** to the '70's pop sensibility of **Ultramarine,** and the minimalism of **Psychic Warriors Ov Gaia** and 777, Caroline has put together a fine array of tracks to soothe your spirit and move your body. **(PW)**

V/A-Transfusion (Sonic) With trance quickly becoming the leading edge of the underground, this tasty collection showcases the sonic spectrum of sounds from ambient to hardcore. Featuring tracks by **Orbital** and **Westbam,** Transfusion also highlights underground tracks from **Nighttripper, Odd Company,** and **Paradise 3000** as well as U.S. labels **ExistDance** and **UltraEthereal. (PW)**

HIP-HOP & ACID JAZZ

12"/EP

NAUGHTY BY NATURE-"It's On" (Tommy Boy) Donald Byrd sample driven, the Naughties strip this Kay Gee remixed jam way down. With the rhymes and beats mixed up, the track swings smoother, making for much phatter flavour than the LP version. **The Beatnuts** lay down a hazy, intoxicated remix, beefing up the downbeats and adding a Hammond organ for a touch of vintage jazz/funk. **(PW)**

V/A-"The British Underground EP" (Ruffness-XL/ UK) The British Hip-Hop scene suffers from a severe lack of identity and unity that keeps many wicked crews from getting the attention they deserve, often times struggling for years to finally get that coveted deal only to meet with apathy and poor promotion once signed. Props to **Richard Russell** and his **Ruffness** label for putting out this 4 track ep, showcasing some of the U.K.'s best hip-hop flavour. Personal faves **London Posse** contribute the dubby ode to buddha, "Pass The Rizla", as the **Lords Of Rap** throw down the Funkadelic- meets- Brixton- styled "MC Average". **The Brotherhood** kick "Put Up Or Shut Up", a rowdy, pint glass upside the head, jump around jam while **Twilight Firm** drop the psychotic trunk of ragga-funk, "Talking Outa My Head". Recommended for the heads looking for some new potent flavour. **(PW)**

HOUSE OF PAIN-"Who's The Man" (Tommy Boy) **Everlast & Co.** kick it with yet another chunky, raucous party joint from the soundtrack of the awful "Who's The Man" film. The flip is two remixes of "Put On Your Shit Kickers" which it makes it worthy of your flow. **(PW)**

GURU-"Loungin'" (Chrysalis) The lead single from the **Gang Starr** rhymer's star-studded solo project, **Jazzmatazz**, finds Keith collaborating with trumpeter **Donald Byrd** on this jazzy, cool vibed, 12". Pulling back on the rhyme reins a bit and preferring to let the horn blow, Guru intersperses the track with snippets of conversation between himself and Byrd. Among mixes from **Skatemaster Tate** (of L.A.'s **Stone Cold Boners**) and **Smash** (of N.Y.'s **Jazz Not Jazz**) and the requisite record company stuff, the pick here are the instrumental cuts for coolin' out and vibin'. Can't wait to hear the lp... **(PW)**

UTE-"One Time EP" (33/UK) This 11-piece group of transplanted Aussies from Luton produce this innovative, funky, vibey, and mellow three-tracker that will challenge the ears of house and acid jazz DJ's alike. "Give It" pairs a dissonant digeridoo bassline with a floating **Milesesque** trumpet and a laid-back, chugging rhythm section turning it into a driving be-bop journey. "To Me" takes the same bassline, adds congas, and an ambient synth line for a wicked, uplifting tribal vibe. The title track is an uptempo funk groover with rap from **Krazy Cool D-Zine.** A fresh slab o' wax for the mind and soul worth searching high and low for. **(PW)**

LE SHAUN-"Ready Or Not" (Tommy Boy) Straight outta Brooklyn, the Flavor Unit's "Black Widow Of Rap" hits hard with a tale of what happens to DJ's who dis her. A solid debut for a sister with an impressive list of credits, but this just whets my appetite for the new **Queen Latifah** LP. **(PW)**

LP/COMPILATIONS

UTE-Free to Be, Free To Breathe (33/UK) Released on a tiny independent U.K. label, this full-length from these Oz transplants pronounced 'Yoot' **(see singles review above, Ed.)** is probably one of the most exciting records in this genre I've peeped in a while. Organic, yet unafraid of technology, UTE straddles the boundaries between acid jazz and house, with an innovative, smooth, swinging, funky, and at times moody approach, adding fresh be-bop overtones and a touch of tasteful conscious rapping on some cuts. An album equally suited for the dancefloor as much as the listening room. Recommended cuts: for the jazz vibe- "Animation/Hypocrisy", "Six", The Third Way"; for the house groove- "Free To Be...", "Merci", For more info write, 33 Records, 33 Guildford St., Luton, Beds. LU1 2NQ, United Kingdom. **(PW)**

GROOVE GARDEN- Concrete Meadows (Tommy Boy) Jazz and Hip-Hop. **Gang Starr** and **Branford Marsalis** brought it to the underground, in '93 **Digable Planets** brought it to the mainstream, but Groove Garden's debut evokes more than just vivid images of smoky jazz cafes, Like an Afrocentric **DEEE-Lite,** rapper/poet **Amber Sunshower** adds a distinctly downtown, artsy, bohemian vibe with her eclectic, street smart rhymes- sometimes rapped, sometimes sing-sung- to **DJ Atsushi**'s sparse but thick and chewy funk flavour. Opening with "Kohaku", an abstract union of percussive chants, raps, and wordless vocal sounds, Concrete Meadows gets way out there at times- in a good way; but tracks like the whimsical "Yeah Said" and the soulful, sexy "You're Not Coming Home" bring it within reach of the not-so-left-of-center. Open your mind and let this flavour caress your aural palate. **(PW)**

P.M. DAWN- The Bliss Album...? (Vibrations of Love and Anger and the Ponderance of Life and Existence) (Gee Street) After the massive success of their briiliant debut and public altercations with **KRS-1** and **BDP** about fakin' the funk, P.M. Dawn return. It seems, however, that much of the innocence and spirituality that made Of The Heart... is gone in favor of showing the Hip-Hop community how hard they can be and that they're not sell-outs. Yet, when they get down to business, **Prince Be & Crew,** throw down a nice floaty pop track. **(PW)**

INDIE/ ALTERNATIVE/ INDUSTRIAL/ EXPERIMENTAL

WIRE-1985-1990: The A List (Mute) Boasting members of **The Cure, R.E.M., Sugar,** and **New Order** as among their biggest fans, **Wire** has indelibly and subliminally influenced the face of today's 'alternative' music with their ability to make pioneering, yet danceable and thought-provoking music. The A List is a compilation of "ultimate" Wire tracks recorded after their 5-year hiatus and breakup, specially selected by fans through a unique rating system. Opening with the shimmering grunge of "Ahead" to the sampler/sequencer experiments of "The Drill", this collection highlights this quartet's finest moments. **(PW)**

Available May 25th.
Young American Primitive
(Full Length Compact Disc) ZMCD-001
YOUNG AMERICAN PRIMITIVE
TASTI BOX
dg
daisy glow
SCO
SINGLE CELL ORCHESTRA
ZoëMagik RECORDS
S.F. 63 Fountain St, San Francisco, CA 94114 (415) 641-8023 Fax (415) 824-4246
N.Y. MCT, 333 W. 52nd St, New York, NY 10019, (212) 265-3740 Fax (212) 315-4601

415-751-6740
TWITCH REMIX SERVICE
VOLUME 11 AVAILABLE NOW
(Two Record Set)
DIRECKT two fatt guitars
MEAT BEAT MANIFESTO mindstream
HARRI skelph
CANTOR & MOSES cosmic dub
UP ABOVE THE WORLD unleashed in the east
HELICOPTER on ya way
SLAVE TO EXTERNAL disintegrate
CENTRAL FIRE central fire

TRiP MAGAZEEN

is

-A really small group of people who <u>truly</u> give a fuck.
-<u>Takin' no shorts</u> to become a bigger mag overnight.
-Not shoving heavily opinionated B.S. down your throat.
-Getting better all the time.
-Looking to expand, becoming the Southeast's Source for upfront dance culture information.

If you're an industry person, <u>send us your promos</u>! Techno, Tribal, Trance, Ambient, Breakbeat, Acid, House, Hip-Hop, Acid Jazz- if <u>you</u> *send* them <u>we</u> will *review*'em, our <u>DJ's</u> will *play* them.

<u>ADVERTISE!</u> TRiP has a circulation of 1500 copies and ravers throughout Florida and 8 other U.S. cities read this mag! Ad rates are very reasonable and are available upon request.

If you have a passion for this music, write about it! TRiP accepts writing contributions, letters, and scene reports from our readers.

Send your promos and contributions to:
TRiP Magazeen
100 E. Dr. M.L. King, Jr. Blvd.
Suite 10
Tampa, Florida 33603 U.S.A.

'cuz if the program's fuzzy, ya gotta knock da set upside the head...

TRIP MAGAZEEN
100 DR. M.L. KING, JR. BLVD.
SUITE #10
TAMPA, FLORIDA 33603
U.S.A.

POSTMASTER: PLEASE RUSH...DATED MATERIAL!!

10

SPECIAL NEW MUSIC SEMINAR ISSUE - SPECIAL NEW MUSIC SEMINAR ISSUE - FREE IN FLORIDA

TRIPS

FLORIDA'S UPFRONT DANCE CULTURE MAGAZINE

JULY 1993

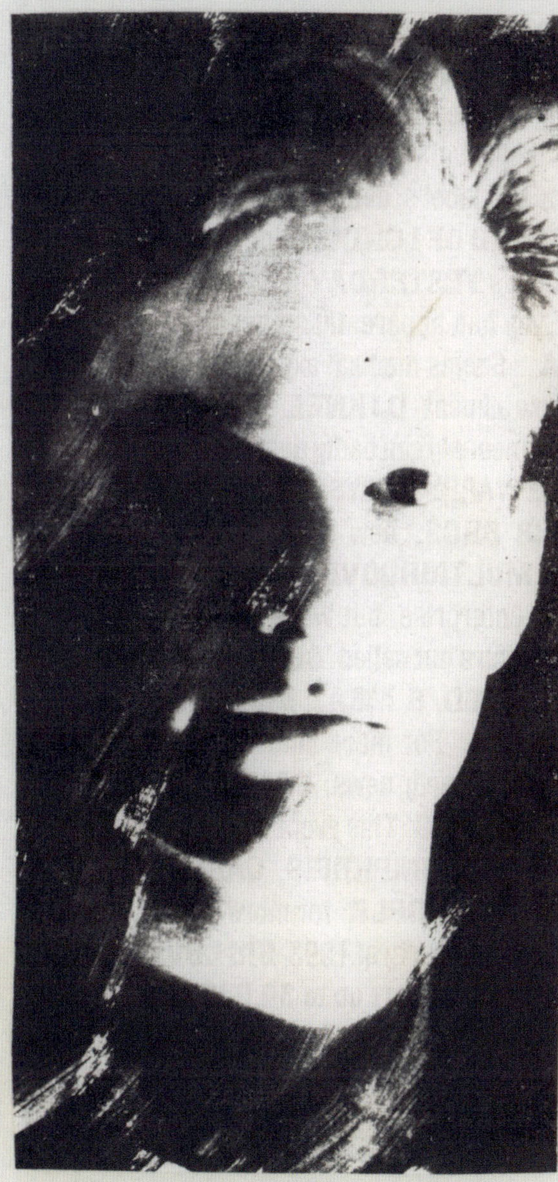

Greg Scanavino is the Young American Primitive...

You've heard the track. Its spiritual synths soaring, tribal percussion thundering with abandon, a melodic triumph of emotion. Released on a small independent label, San Francisco's Zoe Magik, the track exploded from the start, appearing on UK DJ Sasha's chart and debuting at #3 on Mixmag's Buzz Chart. Not bad for a unknown artist from California...

Born in Placerville, California, outside of San Francisco, this 24-year-old seems more like the weird kid next door rather than the next face in the American underground.

Like many kids with musical interest, Greg played pretty much self taught in garage bands through his college days. weaning himself on early 80's 'new wave'-Cocteau Twins, The Cure, New Order. surprisingly shallow, considering the depth of his music.

Often described as 'tribal' or 'trance', but after listening to his album, one can consider YAP's musings all that and more. Packed with soundscapes brimming with ambience, his debut eludes labels, offering music that reaches within the soul.

As part of the crop of artists creating the wave of quality music out of the San Francisco area, Young American Primitive is, at the moment, perhaps the most celebrated of the new 'sound of San Francisco'. But many others like the Hardkiss Family, Dub Tribe, Single Cell Orchestra, Ultraviolet Catastrophe, and others are also creating top tracks that have been making ears from across the big pond prick up and take notice.

This can only fare well for the state of perception towards the American House music scene.

HYPE HYPE HYPE HYPE HYPE HYPE hype

MLM PROMOTIONS presents **TRANCE-ATLANTIC**, a massive outdoor party just Southwest of Disney World in **ORLANDO, FL** from sunrise to sunset Saturday, **AUGUST 21**. Featuring live P.A.'s from the likes of **ALTERN 8, YOUNG AMERICAN PRIMITIVE, DREAM FREQUENCY, DIGITAL ORGASM,** and **FELIX** and DJ's such as **COLIN FAVOR, CARL COX, & KEOKI**, there will be a 10,000 square ft chillout area, 200K sound system, giant video screens, virtual reality machines, and other attractions. For more information, call **1-800-707-RAVE**....**MOONSHINE MUSIC** is putting out a series of DJ mix tapes. Called **JOURNEYS BY DJ**, the series' first release is from London's **BILLY NASTY.** DJ's interested in having their tape considered for the series should submit a tape to **MOONSHINE MUSIC, 6634 SUNSET BLVD., HOLLYWOOD, CA 90028.** Please include a complete track listing along with your name, address, & phone #....**ASTRALWERKS** is the name of a new dance imprint from **CAROLINE RECORDS** dedicated to the progressive side of dance music- trance, tribal, ambient, progressive house and acid jazz; the label's debut release is **TALES OF EPHIDRENA** by **ANDROGYNOUS AMORPHOUS**, a **FUTURE SOUND OF LONDON** side-project....**HYPE!** sources recently spotted German deckmaster **SVEN VATH** in Miami's **YESTERDAY & TODAY RECORDS** purchasing a copy of his own **ACCIDENTS IN PARADISE** LP. Sven had apparently stopped in Miami after shooting a video for a track from **ACCIDENTS...**, **L'ESPERANCA**.... Seems medical experts are being asked to diagnose **UTAH SAINTS** frontman **JEZ WILLIS**' bad knee as a new ailment- **DJ KNEE.** Apparently spinning records, twisting around to look for new selections and dancing simultaneously can badly damage the knee joints; thanks for the tip, Doc....**WAX TRAX/TVT** have arranged to license WARP's **ARTIFICIAL INTELLIGENCE** series for domestic release....Debut signings to **GIANT/WARNER BROS.**' new **MEDICINE** dance label, **FIERCE RULING DIVA**, were recently arrested while DJ'ing at **MULTIGROOVE**, a weekly club night in **AMSTERDAM**. **FRD** were charged with taking part in an illegal enterprise, but were relesed an charges dropped the next day....**IN DEFENSE OF ANIMALS** has a cool brochure out called **'BEYOND THE BEATS'** with statements from members of **SKINNY PUPPY, CONSOLIDATED, & MEAT BEAT MANIFESTO** outlining courses of action for ending institutionalized abuse of animals. For more information, write, **816 FRANCISCO BLVD., SAN RAFAEL, CA 94901**....In Trans-Atlantic party news: **DANCE EUROPE** is a weekender taking place **SEPTEMBER 24,25,26** at **EURODISNEY** in **PARIS**. This event promises two rooms of music featuring names like **SASHA, WEATHERALL, GARNIER, HUMPHRIES, OAKENFOLD** and others, along with P.A.'s from **INNER CITY, REESE PROJECT**, and **M-PEOPLE**. for more info, phone **011 44 071 494 1153**....The **UNIVERSE** crew announce their largest and last party of 1993, **BIG LOVE,** AUGUST 13, in Wiltshire. Dispensing with peripheral attractions, this party will transport up to **30,000** partiers back to the old school, creating a vibe where the music and atmosphere come first. On two stages and an adjoining ambient arena, DJ's include **MICKEY FINN, MIXMASTER MORRIS, COLIN FAVOR, FRANKIE KNUCKLES, LENNY DEE,** and others; P.A.'s from **APHEX TWIN, RISING HIGH COLLECTIVE**, and the **PRODIGY**....

FEET FIRST

Welcome once again to **TRiP Magazeen**! Whether you're a regular reader of us or peeping between our pages for the first time, we hope you dig this very full, although, um...thin issue. It's been a **difficult** summer for us here, but next issue we'll be back, phatter than ever with all kinds of reviews, news, and features on **GTO, Mixmaster Morris, Jaydee, Future Sound Of London, The Source**, and a **NMS** recap.

If you're a **NMS delegate**, welcome to New York from all of us here, we hope you find TRiP to be an exciting, informative, and unbiased source of upfront information! Be sure to say **"Hi"** to our **Contributing Editor DJ Three**- he'll be covering the Seminar as well as playing at a handfull of parties during Seminar week. Check our boy out; we're not just saying that because he works here, but because he's one of Florida's best!

So what goes on down here you might ask? The summer has been busy with many events and parties throughout Florida. Just a few of the acts/DJ's that have been or will be in Florida recently: Love Decade, Felix, Sasha, DJ Hell, Cosmic Baby, Keoki, Sven Vath, Colin Favor, Carl Cox, Young American Primitive. The scene here is pretty strong, although lacking in unity at times between the different areas of the State.

Shouts go out to the following: **Caspar, Morris, Pypee & the Crew @ Rising High, Greg Scanavino, Brian & Reese @ Astral Werks, Future Sound Of London, Robert Leiner, Robin Albers, DJ Moneypenny, Catherine @ R & S, Dave Mirsky & the Crew @ MARZ...**

DJ CHARTS

MICHAEL & LEE
GTO/DATAFLOW
LONDON, U.K.

English Muffin-Blood of An...
Bulletproofed Split-Distortion Bastard
Undergr' Nation/Rot'dm-I'm The Master
Ongaku 02
Spectral Emotions-Chap. 1,2,3
John + Julie-Red Alert
Progressive Attack-Secrets Of Love
Charly Lownoise/Mental Theo-Verrotted
Vapour Space-Gravitational Arch..10
Tellurians-My Name Doesn't Matter

DJ JETSTREAM
DEFINITIVE RECORDS
DETROIT, U.S.A.

Jagga-Finite
Wll-Charged Latinos-Latin Prayer
Jopan-Bisca
Blunted Dummies-House For All
Liberator-Stand Above Me
Fluke-Electric Guitar
Fortran 5-Time to Dream
Sublime-Transamerican
Mother-All Funked Up

ALTERNATIVE RECORDS
TAMPA, FLORIDA
TOP 10 SALES- 10 JULY 93

Underworld-Rez
God Within-Raincry
Dig The New Breed-4321
Soul Sacrifice feat. Sly-Soul Sacrifice
Humate-Love Stimulation
Digman (X-Gate Promo)
2 Bad Mice (Movin' Shadow White)
Scientist-New Style
Visions Of Shiva-How Much Can You
Sven Vath-L'Esperanca

DJ CHARTS

DJ T-1000
UNDERGROUND RESISTANCE
DETROIT, U.S.A.

Passarani/Monteduro-Dreaming Detroit
Robert Armani-Planet A ep
Niko-Mindflux
Marco Zaffarani-M25
X-313-Cybernator
Drexciys-Seaquake/Like Water
Rich Lee-Rock so Hard
DBX-Phreak Trax
Vapour Space-Gravitational Arch..10
Underground Resistance-Acid Rain2

DJ NIKADEEMUS
DJ'S IN SYNC!
PORTLAND, OR

Urban Primitivism-Fuck
Anal Snax-Barbaque
Subject V. Mills (ULR RMX)
War-Rotterdam Is Shit
Hardsequencer-Amiga
Sigmoid 909-Speeding Overload
Alici-Sound Of Roar
Zekt-Senseless
DJ Hell-Spring Aus Den Walken
Joey Beltram-Code 6 ep

GARY & BRIAN
FUTURE SOUND OF LONDON
TOP 10 ALL TIME TRACKS

Morton Sobotnik-Silver Apples Of The Moon
Fredric Chopin-Piano Music Etudes
Aphex Twin-Analogue Bubblebath Vol.I
A Certain Ratio-Flight
Cocteau Twins-Lazy Calm
Anything by African Head Charge
Psychick Warriors Ov Gaia-Linkage
Klaus Schulze-Picture Music (@ 45rpm)
A Clockwerk Orange Soundtrack
Tangerine Dream-Illuminations

TRiP MAGAZEEN
100 E. Dr. MLK, Jr. Blvd. Suite 10
Tampa, Florida, 33603 USA
FON: 813-238-0310
FAX: 813-876-7473
(When faxing, please use a cover sheet)

EDITOR/PUBLISHER-Peter Woholski
SENIOR EDITOR-Chris Milo
CONTRIBUTORS-DJ Grumpy C, DJ Three
SUPPORT THE UNDERGROUND!!!!
ADVERTISING-Rates given upon request.
SUBSCRIPTIONS/BACK ISSUES-$1 each, $10yearly
RETAIL STORES-If you're interested in carrying TRiP in your store, contact us @ 813-238-0310.

RECORD REVIEWS

TECHNO/HOUSE 12"/EP

RISING HIGH COLLECTIVE-"Fever Called Love" (Hardfloor RMX) (Rising High/UK) Happy, happy! Joy, joy! One of my favorite all time classic tracks gets the **Hardfloor** acid treatment and only refines its perfection. A spot on reworking that does not dissapoint.

GOD WITHIN-"Raincry" (Hardkiss Music) The Hardkiss family does it again! The Spiritual Thirst Mix is a soaring, string-synth washed track with a subdued chugging breakbeat whilethe flip's Submerged Mix is more atmospheric with its percolating bassline, light percussion and crashing cymbals leading to the track's main theme and a wall of gently swirling synths. Beautiful and essential.

RAY LOVE-"Symphony Of Love" ep (EX) This latest from Ray Love sets a new mark in pushing the envelope of house music. "Spirit Of Love" is a pulsing ambient house groover with a nice melodic synthline running smack into a fully orchestrated symphonic break and flowing back to ambience. On the back side, "The Solution" is a slow building atmospheric acid trancer that graduates to a steady thumping groove while "Tranquility" is perfect for chilling out while keeping the energy flowing. Top notch.

TRIBAL MASS-"Deception" (Euphonic) Deep and groovy is a good way to describe the second release from this Florida-based label. The Original Mix is, yes- deep and groovy with its echoing organ riff and a cooing female vocal. A nice late night mix. Odell's Lush Groove Mix opens with an almost "Papua New Guinea" esque intro before a bass-style break beat drops in that sends Florida's East Coast crazy and a driving synth line. A nice mix, but too choppy for my taste. A good second release from a label that has yet to hit the ground running.

2 IN MOTION-"The Edge Of..." (ROR, Ltd/UK) This record borders on the bizarre. The Club Mix is an oscillating, fierce acid driven breakbeat trancer with a thunderous kik drum breakdown. A track that reminds me of the **Spiritual Combat** record on R&S a year ago. The flip's House Mix is more on the acid house vibe.

D.O.P.-"Dance Your Socks Off" ep (Guerilla) The **Two Kevin's** are back with this 4-tracker dedicated to U.K. DJ **Alistair Cooke** who passed recently in a car wreck. An ep that offers a chewn for everybody, "Hear I Go" is a groovy bongo driven slice of U.K. House and "Non Stop" is a bouncy chunk of disco-y funk , ala **TC 1993**. The other two tracks reflect a little more techno-oriented side of D.O.P., similar to their **Chameleon Project** work.

GROOVE COMMITTEE-"You Need Someone" (Tribal America) The up-and-coming king of New York Garage, Victor Simonelli, produced this smooth vibed track; garage doesn't get much better than this. In five forms including dubs, accapellas, and a swinging demo version.

VEGGI GROOVES-"Jeep Warehouse Beats, Vol. I" (Super Doppler Communications) Similar to the 'Sounds Of Silence' ep's that Florida DJ's are scurrying for this six-track ep from Denver deserves serious props for some pretty wicked grooves. Opening with a hip-hop style break , Veggi Grooves progressively moves deeper into late night vibe territory; if you're looking for some new grooves, this is worth checking out.

LP/COMPILATIONS

ORBITAL-Orbital (Internal/UK) The Hartnoll Brothers return, picking up where they left off with their debut. Also self-titled, this second effort reflects the changes that the underground has made over the past year and a half. Deeper, trancier, richer in texture, and emotionally stirring, this album is one can only get better with the test of time.

ANDROGYNOUS AMORPHOUS-Tales Of Ephidrena (Astral Werks) This **Future Sound Of London** side-project is reminiscent of FSOL's wonderfull **Accelerator** LP, full of triball percussion, dub basslines, Flamenco guitar textures, and atmosphere all strung together with short environmental soundscapes. A wonderful debut release for this new label. A must for the fan of so-called "armchair techno".

HIP-HOP/ACID JAZZ

PROFESSOR X-Puss 'N Boots (The Struggle Continues) (Polydor) Brooklyn's **X-Clan** is the 'music & politics' wing of Black conciousness organization **Blackwatch**. Stepping out of the shadow of X-Clan, leader Professor X comes forth with his first solo project. An afrocentric eye opener to the reality of black life and society's subliminal mixed messages. Full of depth in all ways- production, lyrical content- Puss 'N Boots is often difficult to digest in one dose. A pretty cool record with a lot to say, however taking several spins to comprehend fully.

V/A-Tampa Sucks (Spoinky Pop) A well-packaged collection of talent from the Tampa Bay area's much maligned music scene. Focusing primarily on the indie/rock genre, the album's compilers had the open ears to include tracks from the area's budding hip-hop community. Brandon's **Outside N** drops "Criticall Condition"- science with a Consolidated flavor; **Dirty Blond** flexes some serolus promise with "Kickin Up Dust"; while A&R types should pay attention to **Tap, Ghost, & Phobia's** "Executioner", a phat-flavored, urgent headnodder- these guys are ready to bust out with madd skillz .

11

Free In Florida! $1.50 Elsewhere
V11.0
FLORIDA'S UPFRONT DANCE CULTURE MAGAZINE
NEW MUSIC SEMINAR RECAP
RISING HIGH'S CASPAR POUND
MIXMASTER MORRIS
FUTURE SOUND OF LONDON
HARDKISS MUSIC
HARDFLOOR
JAYDEE
GTO
RABBIT IN THE MOON*SILENCE*DAISY GLOW*2 BAD MICE
LAZER WORSHIPPERS*DELTA LADY*FUCKIN' HOSTILE*REALITY STUDIO
SLAM*SPACETIME CONTINUUM*TCX-2*AUDIO F.M.*MOBY

UNDER THE
WATER
STIRS THE SOUL
OF THE
UNDERGROUND
BLUE
UND
ER
GRO
UND
VOLUME ONE
FEATURING
TRIBALISTIC
INTERAMBIENT
HARD CORE
TRACKS BY
NEBULA NINE GLITCH
MONSOON
REALITY STUDIO
DISINTEGRATOR
JIMMY CRASH JOSH WINK
LENNY DEE
DAMON WILD REPETE
AVAILABLE FROM
ULTRA-ETHEREAL RECORDS
1400 ALICEANNA
BALTIMORE, MD 21231
410-522-1001

CONTENTS

TRiP Magazeen
V. 11.0/September 1993

NEWS

FEATURES

CHARTS/REVIEWS

FEET FIRST

Thanks for waiting! With so much happening the last two months it's been a task for the few of us that make up **TRiP Magazeen** to get this one out. Each issue is getting a little bigger and a little better. As always, your letters/input, etc. are encouraged. We get more out of state mail than local, how about it Florida?

The latter half of this summer saw many great parties here in Florida and of course, a few not so great ones. The bulk of the sour parties are almost exclusive to two groups: 1) Promoters who bite off more than they can chew or 2) First time or out-of-town promoters who don't have a well-rounded, if any, understanding of Florida's scene- past, present, or future. You as a partygoer ultimately choose where you go and have little control whether a party delivers its promises or how many people show up.

Advice we can give, based on previous exp-erience, is choose parties whith DJ's you feel make an effort to play quality parties, giving you some assurance that with your good attitude the night could be a lot of fun. A good attitude is the key here. Walking into a party and immediately trying to spot everything you dislike is not our idea of a good time.

As '93 begins to wind down, more home-grown music is beginning to be noticed by the rest of the world with such labels as **Euphonic, Halluci-Nation,** and of course, **Murk,** paving the way. Coupled with Florida's unique scene and responsive dancefloors, 1994 could be a magical year. TRiP believes in the concept of the concious party and encourages all of you to pursue your creative endeavors- no matter what genre- with all you've got. Your only obstacle is yourself. Read on....

Shouts to: Alan Oldham & Mad Mike @ UR, Dom @ Deltra, Hardkiss Family, Damon & Moneypenny @ EX, Jeff K. @ KDGE, Onionz, DJ Chris Fortier, Renaat @ R&S, Marcy @ MCT, John & Richie @+8 (Congrats, John!), Ishai Meron-RMFx2, Aquarhythms massive, Halluci-Nation crew, DJ Taylor, Spacetime Continuum/SF, Laurent Garnier, and all the people at NMS that we met, partied, and schmoozed with...

TRiP Magazeen
100 Dr. MLK, Jr. Blvd. E.
Suite 10
Tampa, Florida 33603 U.S.A.
FON: 813.238.0310 **FAX:** 813.876.7473
(When faxing, please use a cover sheet)
EDITOR/PUBLISHER: Peter Wohelski
SENIOR EDITOR: Chris Milo

CONTRIBUTORS: DJ Crystar, DJ Grumpy C., DJ Jask, DJ Orion, DJ Three

SUPPORT THE UNDERGROUND!

ADVERTISING: Rates given upon request. **SUBSCRIPTIONS/BACK ISSUES** $1 each, $10 yearly **RETAIL STORES:** If you're interested in carrying TRiP in your store, contact us @ 813.238.0310 for bulk rate infromation

TRiP Magazeen is published approximately every six weeks and distributed to select outlets throughout Florida and the United States. We hope that our content will encourage awareness and positivity for the Global Underground.

DATELINE DETROIT: Looks like **UNDERGROUND RESISTANCE** are coming out of hiding to play their first live shows since last December. **MAD MIKE & CO.** will hit Australia, Denmark, and "some places I can't say because I don't want to jinx them," says newest member **DJ T-1000**. T-1000 will also be doing some solo shows in Frankfurt with **PCP** (Planet Core Productions)....**GYROSCOPE**, a new imprint launched by **CAROLINE RECORDS** specializing in ambient music, has released its first two titles, **NEROLI**, by ambient pioneer **BRIAN ENO** and **THE FAMILIAR**, a collaboration between **ROGER ENO** and **KATE ST. JOHN** (ex-Dream Academy)....The much-talked about **UNIVERSE** party originally scheduled to go off at the end of July in **SAN FRANCISCO** is now slated to happen **18 SEPTEMBER**. With three arenas, Universe plans to deliver the best of the West Coast (**THE HARDKISS FAMILY, JENO, GARTH,** and **MICHAEL COOK**), Europe (**LAURENT GARNIER, CARL COX, SASHA, ANDY WEATHERALL**, and live appearances from **APHEX TWIN** and **ORBITAL**), and a disco tent featuring **GEORGE CLINTON**. Also planned is live shamanic recitation from **TERRENCE MC KENNA**, and a tribal drum circle coordinated by **THE BEAST** (aka the **GRATEFUL DEAD'S MICKEY HART**)....**AMP** is a new, exclusively alternative and underground dance record pool based in the Tampa Bay area, servicing DJ's in the Southeastern U.S. Initially limited to 30 members, AMP stresses a strong line of communication between its members and minimal shipping distances to recieve product because of the pool's regional proximity. Could this finally be a record pool that is worth the true progressive or underground DJ's time (and money)??? DJ's and labels interested in more information, call **813.659.0671**....**ORBITAL** will be touring the States later this Fall. Expect support acts for the Hartnoll Brothers' "MIDI Circus-like" tour to be finalized in upcoming weeks....**FFRR** has quite an ambitious schedule of Underground releases coming out this Fall, including tracks/LP's from **U96, VAPOUR SPACE, ONE DOVE,** and **CALIFORNIA DREAMING**, a compilation of tracks from West Coast labels including **ZOE MAGIK, HARDKISS MUSIC,** and **C-LEVEL RECORDINGS**....After two wicked ep's on **LORD MICHAEL'S VORTEX** label, **EQUINOX** has broken up; the team of **DAMON WILD** and **DJ REPETE** citing "creative difference" for the split. Meanwhile, Repete has a new label, **12 GAUGE**, distributed through **NORTHCOTT**....Cocoa Beach's **MARZ** club is closing. The club is going out with an explosive final weekend of guests to blow things out September 11 with WARP Recording Artists **RHYTHM INVENTION**. No confirmation as to the rumours that the club will reopen or is being remodeled....Is a deal between **COWBOY/UK** and **SONY MUSIC/US** in the works?!?....From the Birthplace of House comes word of a new label called **ORGANICO**. The label's first release is the **"THEME FROM CLOSE ENCOUNTERS"** with remixes from San Francisco's **DUB TRIBE** and Chicago DJ **DERRICK CARTER**. DJ's interested in getting on the label's mailing list, send a list of your working credentials to **ORGANICO, 858 ARMITAGE AVE., #197, CHICAGO, IL 60614**....The **KALIEDO LIGHT K2ON** is a new video lighting system developed by **KALIEDOVISION** that creates dynamic live sound to light graphic effects synchronized to the music. Operated via computer, the system is comprehensively controlled, allowing the operator to select colours, graphic sequences, strobe, freeze frame, as well as input and effects levels. Perfect for massive video walls or small ambient room set-ups, the system is distributed by **PACE SYSTEMS**. For more information, call **M. LAURA MURPHY** at **504.837.4224**....The crew at **INDUSTRIAL STRENGTH** are starting a third new label, **BASTARD LOUD**, to help keep up the pace of release schedule at **IS**. Expect the new label's first release later this month....**INSTINCT/SONIC RECORDS** have recently signed some new acts of the ambient variety- **HUMAN MESH DANCE, O'MICRON,** and **EVOLVE NOW**. The label will also be giving **THE IRRESISTIBLE FORCE**'s **FLYING HIGH** LP a long overdue domestic release later this month. **HARDFLOOR**'s new classic **"HARDTRANCE ACPERIENCE"** has been released through **MOONSHINE MUSIC** along with mixes of **"TRANCESCRIPT"** and the previously unreleased **"ACPERIENCE 2"** with the full-length **TB RECUSCITATION** to hit domestic shelves soon....**MOONSHINE** has also released the **UNIVERSE** compilation album that was released in the U.K. through **RISING HIGH** with tracks by **THE HYPNOTIST, LAURENT GARNIER, ILLUMINATE, DAVE ANGEL, SUBURBAN HELL, SVEN VATH, SEQUENTIAL,** and other top trance bisquits....London's **ULTRAMARINE** follow-up their smashing debut **EVERY MAN AND WOMAN IS A STAR** with **UNITED KINGDOMS**, to be released on **SIRE/GIANT RECORDS** October 12. The duo of **IAN COOPER** and **PAUL HAMMOND** will also be touring the U.S. with **BJORK**....

U2 ZOOROPA
ZOOROPA:
The new album from U2.
Ten songs recorded March through May of this year in Dublin. Includes "NUMB" and "LEMON"
Produced by Flood, Brian Eno and The Edge.
ISLAND
© 1993 Island Records, Inc.

HARDFLOOR GIVING ACID RESUCITATION WITH TB 303

Oliver Bondizio and **Ramon Zenker** are Germany's **Hardfloor**. The Dusseldorf-based duo's debut track **"Hardtrance Acperience"** is a now classic TB 303 symphony of epic proportions.

Released on Sven Vath's **Harthouse** label, the gradually building track has almost singlehandedly spawned an acid revival, going back to the days of '88, thanks to the licensing of "Acperience" to the Harthouse/UK imprint through London's **Rising High**. Oliver and Ramon agree, however, that acid never really died- it was merely underground, long a staple of the clubs in Europe.

"I was very surprised because I thought nobody would understand a record that goes 8 minutes, building step by step every 32 bars before a break, and coming again. It was a track that came from the heart- we were very surprised, especially in the U.K." admits Ramon.

The success of the track has catapulted Hardfloor to underground stardom with many wanting the **"Hardfloor Treatment"** for remixes- having lent their touch to tracks by **Robert Armani** for **DJAX** and a mix of **Rising High Collective's "Fever Called Love".** As to their approach, Ramon explains, "We want to keep the original, we don't want to make a new song. We like to give the song new elements- Hardfloor elements! Our kind of arrangement that builds up slowly, breaks, and comes again."

Oliver and Ramon recently visited New York during **New Music Seminar**, performing at a **Harthouse America/Moonshine Music** party at **The Shelter** and meeting up with longtime NY techno scene cornerstones **Damon Wild** and Brooklyn's **Adam X**.

Hardfloor is one of the new breed of acts eschewing the "rave style" of performing, opting to play completely live. It's Oliver's rationale that there is no reason not to play live. "(It takes) not much time to make a track. If you create the track in one day - to play live it's not very hard. It's very minimalistic; you need a drum machine, a sequencer, maybe some effects, and a 303 machine, that's it!"

Hardfloor's Robert Armani and RHC remixes are out now, along with their full length album **<u>TB Recuscitation</u>**. Dedicated to the inventor of the Roland TB 303, the album will soon be released domestically on Harthouse America through Moonshine Music.

HOLLAND·S JAYDEE MAKING•GROOVY HOUSE FOR GROOVY PEOPLE•

"It was very strange, it was a warm summer night in August and I was sitting outside with a friend of mine and it just hit me. I said to my friend, "Let's go make a track," and we went into my home studio and ten hours later there it was," tells Dutch DJ/Artist **Robin "Jaydee" Albers** about the making of his #1 club smash, "**Plastic Dreams**".

Before "Plastic Dreams", the Utrecht-based Albers spent a great deal of time as a DJ, doing a show on the national radio network for eleven years, playing in clubs, and as the organizer of the **DMC Mixing Championships** in Holland from 1985 to 1990. Jaydee is also known as one of the first DJ's in Holland to introduce beat mixing techniques to Dutch club DJ's.

After massive response from European and american DJ's alike, "Plastic Dreams" was recently licensed to **Epic** in the U.S. by Belgium's **R&S Records**. A flavourful track with an unmistakeably groovy organ riff it crosses over to many different genres of music. A fact that Jaydee didn't intend to create, a bit ashamedly.

"Black people like it very much, white people like it very much, yellow people like it very much. People who are of hardcore house like it, people who like mellow groove house, they like it. It was not my goal to make a record that was so wide- I didn't want to make a crossover," explains Albers.

Ironic then, that this record almost never saw the light of day, almost being rejected from a compilation CD being released by the distributor of Jaydee's own **First Impressions** label because of length. After consenting to an edit, the track was released on the CD, a copy of which landed in the hands of R&S Records head **Renaat Van De Papeliere** through remixer **Frank De Wulf**. Renaat licensed the full-length to R&S and the rest is history.

Jaydee recently came to the States to play a series of live shows at New York's **Limelight, Palladium,** and **Shelter** clubs. He found Shelter to be an enlightening, yet nerve-wracking experience. "Shelter was great... I I had heard to be careful because if they don't like it they shout at you and turn their backs. I was very nervous. It was surprising how good the reaction was."

Expect a full length LP of "House music for groovy people" from Jaydee this Fall on R&S.

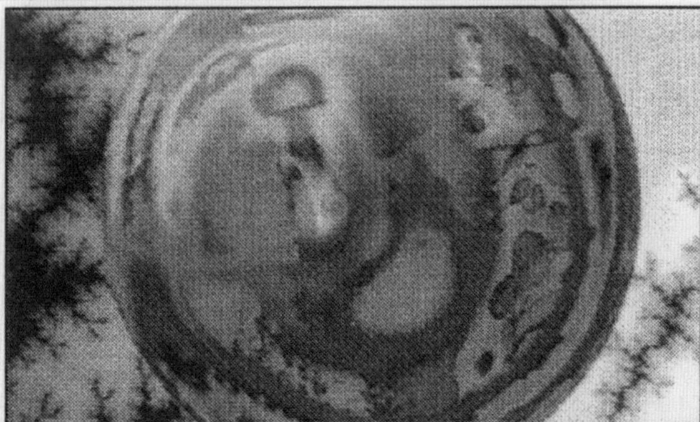

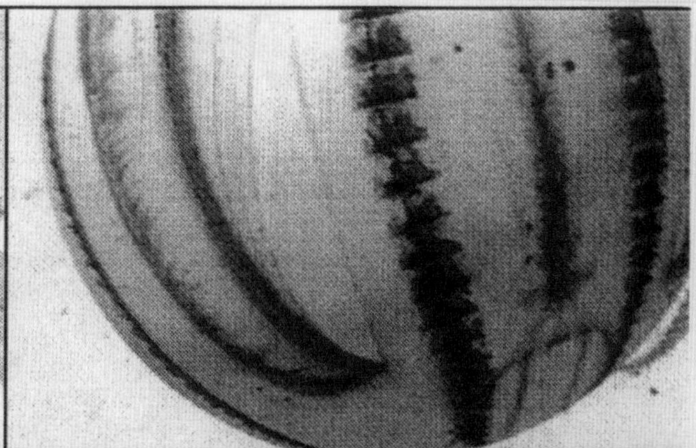

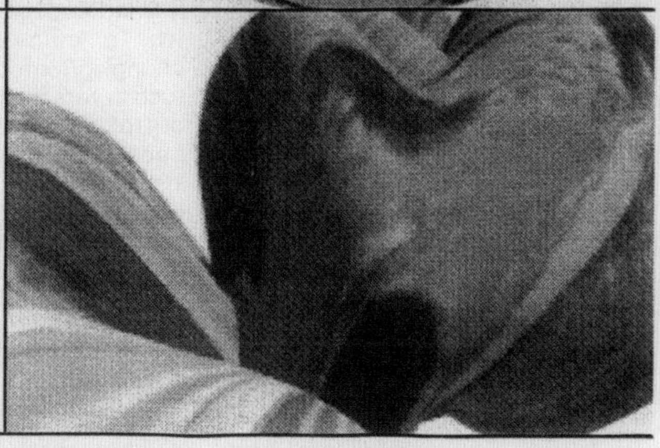

Invading psychotic headspace with FSoL

England's groundbreaking Future Sound Of London came into prominence with **"Papua New Guinea"**, a dubby **Meat Beat Manifesto** and **Dead Can Dance** sampled masterpiece. Prior to then, **Brian Dougans** and **Garry Cockbain** had been bumming around the dance music world releasing tracks under various names, one being the '88 classic **"Stakker Humanoid"**. Last year, after a full-length FSOL album, **Accelerator**, and a slew of remixes, the pair signed to Virgin/ UK for a hefty sum, gaining their own label, **Earth Beat**,in the process. Responsible for some of the most progressive dance-oriented music to come out of the U.K., FSoL recently released a collection of some pre-EB tracks titled **Tales Of Ephidrena** under the guise of **Amorphous Androgynous**. FSoL just finished work on their second album and TRiP caught up with Garry Cockbain not long after the completion of this still-untitled work for a chat...

TRiP: Most people are familiar with you through Future Sound Of London, although you've been going music for quite awhile under different names. How did FSOL come about?

Garry/FSOL: I guess through making a living... (Laughs) Most of the stuff we've done since **"Stakker Humanoid"** is earning a living. To a certain degree we were experimenting with a lot of different names and listening to a lot of different styles... Generally running around like headless chickens, really. (All that) was really important in coming up with a track (**"Papua New Guinea"**) which you couldn't really pin it down to a particular genre, especially in this country.

T: Is Jumpin' & Pumpin' your own label?

FSOL: No, it was a label we worked for, but we basically took it over in becoming chief A&R men and deciding what came out and when. After all these years, having your own label was very much a dance thing to do. It was something I never totally wanted to do because we spend purely 100% of our time doing artistic things. We've got a lot of business to do in a normal day anyway, running your own label is a mighty thing to do.

T: Is Accelerator ever going to be released in the U.S.?

FSoL: Maybe, I believe you've got a problem over there with samples. I think people are scared of this sort of music over in the States...

T: It's viewed as disposable...

FSoL: I think we have to completely de-learn everything that we've learned through what ostensibly was a innovative and life changing form of music. It was such a remarkable, isolationary osrt of sound. Now I think it's become a very, very tired format in this country. There's thousands of people earning a goos living out of it and its become a matter of sustaining those livings rather than the music. It's much more to do with the fact that dance music can no longer be outside the test of time element of music. The age of putting out a thousand white labels andmaking a couple thousand bucks is not particularly apt anymore. Our approach to music is to leave tracks on the shelf and if they last, then let's release them.

T: How do you feel about the term "armchair techno"?

FSoL: We prefer to term our music **"Psychotic Headspace"**... It's kind of a very deep, evocative soundscape and it doesn't root itself in any particular form of techno, much more in a deep-rooted listening music that evokes times and places and feelings. It can be quite harsh but it can be quite beautifull-it's not a Zippy, Hippie type ambientwhich I feel is rooted in the past.

T: It's refreshing to have albums being released with a continuity instea of a colection of tracks...

FSoL: Well, yeah. I think that if somebody can release10 tracks with spaces in between them and make a great album, then they're a fucking genius! Whenever we get 10 tracks for an album and put them next to each other they sound like tacks; we have to start repairing them by joining them together to make it a seamless flow. It's half the process, but at the same time we're very critical of what we do. The new FSoL album is the most seamless piece of music we've ever written... The way that the tracks join is a very non-linear piece. But I think the album format isthe next format to be bastardized. We've ssen the 12" completely taken the piss out of over the last couple of years. Albums were always not supposed to sell in this form of music and ourselves and other people have proven that to be wrong, proven that you can sell depth without having ostensible singles.

The next step is audio visual music. The whole idea behind FSoL is to present a broadcast system, really. ...Not to be a typical band

Technoheads GTO consolidate U.K. techno scene with Dataflow

Shrouded by the pseudonyms of their many different projects, **Michael Wells** and **Lee Newman** have almost anonymously made their impact on the dance music world. Perhaps known to many as the industrial experimentalists **Greater Than One** which released a handful of singles, two albums and an ep for Chicago's semina l **Wax Trax**! label. The pair have also inflicted dancefloor mayhem under the recurring guises of **John + Julie, Signs Of Chaos, Church of Extacy,** and **GTO**.

Making the transition from noise terrorists to dance producers was not as easy as it may have seemed. "We did 'Pure' (the first single under the GTO name in 1990) because so many people were saying 'I like the track but I can't dance to it.' It (the transition) was quite hard, but we started going out to clubs and getting interested in dance music. It's strange that the industrial thing dropped off at the same time and dance music picked up," reminisces Michael.

This transition, however, has not made the duo traditional dance artists. "There's still the edge of experimentation. Ususally we start off making tracks with sounds or different ideas, or a title, the same way we did with Greater Than One. Nothing we do is song-based...," says Wells.

Lee and Michael have released their tracks on several different U.K. labels- **WARP, Rising High, React, XL,** and **Nova Mute**. Clearly dance music industry veterans, the two realize at times dance music is an industry, but as artists, have seen the business end get in the way of the music. This has prompted them to start their own label, **Dataflow**. "Basically, we feel we know our music better than anyone else and to have an A&R person tell you how to do your record or mix it or gear it for a certain market is a bit much really," reasons Michael. For now Dataflow is only releasing the pair's own tracks, but they look to release other artist's tracks in the future.

Their main project at the moment is GTO. Signed to Nova Mute, they've released a single, **"Love Is Everywhere"** to positive review with an album to be released this Fall. Doing a full-length dance LP is much different than the industrial soundscapes of the Greater Than One albums, one which Michael Wells says is difficult. "It's quite a hard task. We like having our music out as soon to the date that we'v e recorded it....recording a (dance) album is another one of those music industry problems."

In between work on the GTO lp and the Dataflow label, Lee and Michael also run the **Dataflow Technochart**, a free tipsheet of DJ chart returns worldwide. (Lee also writes the **"Technohead"** column for **DJ Magazine**) "We started the chart because it's very difficult in Europe, the U.K. especially, because this music's still underground. This was a way to get consolidated and get people together and be part of one scene. It seems to be working!"

Lee and Michael currently have out two "Technohead" projects- an ep called "The Passion" and a compilation album- both on React/UK, a Signs Of Chaos ep on Dataflow, and hopefully a GTO LP this Fall.

Getting horizontal-a conversation with Mixmaster Morris

Mixmaster Morris , aka the Irresistible Force, is easily one of the Underground's most influential DJ's, playing chillout rooms worldwide. A longtime face in the London acid house scene, Morris sported an impressive list of credentials including a pirate radio show, some Psychic TV gigs, and The Shamen's Synergy tour before coming to the attention of Caspar Pound and Rising High, releasing two ep's, "Space Is The Place" and "Underground", and an album, Flying High. Chillout techno in its purest form, Flying High won rave reviews and quickly established the label as the U.K.'s premier label for ambient music. TRiP is excited beyond belief in bringing you this exclusive interview with Mixmaster Morris.

TRiP: How did you get involved in ambient music as opposed to other types of dance music?

Morris: Several things. Firstly was seeing (techno) all going wrong, long before it did. When techno and House music started, people did it for love and not the money, nobody told you how to do it, you did it your own way. Nowadays if you do something different, DJ's will tell you how to do your own job. The great thing about a chillout room is that so far no one tells me what to do. It's a way of going into a room where you can play all night and have complete freedom to use what technology you want and play what music you want. At that point, I was going out, playing live sets, playing live techno at raves- it's so rare over here, there's just lots of miming acts... It got so you go across the country to play for 10-15 minutes. You think, "What's the point," so you move in the chill room. I was doing 4-5 hours live and you learn a lot more playing for 5 hours than playing for 10 minutes. When I first started doing the rooms, I found that I didn't have enough music to do it all night, so I went and got a lot more ambient music. Then I found I only had enough music to do one night, so it was getting boring because I had a residency, so I started getting more and more, and there still wasn't enough music. So I started making records; it's like the first House DJ's- you make the record that doesn't exist because you want to play it!

T: Did you start out as a DJ first or playing music first?

MM: I've been from one to the other so many times, it's difficult to remember which came first. I started out as a musician first. Really everything I do dates back to when I got into sampling, which was about '84. I was convinced it was going to change the world. I'm still flying the flag of sampling, which I'm fairly being scapegoated. It's not sampling's fault people make boring records, it's people.

T: I read you did some shows with Psychic TV?

MM: I did a few, it was '88 or something like that. Just when they were trying to introduce acid house and they were still pulling an audience of Goths. They'd hear a drum machine and all press themselves up against the back wall.

T: How did you get involved with The Shamen?

MM: I met up with them in '89, when I knew they were going to do a new kind of live show. I did a support gig with them and that led to me joining their crew full-time and going on the road with them for 2 years. We did about 120 gigs together all over Europe. They were very influential gigs because it was the first time that a rock band crossed over and took a touring club on the road. The press is full of things about MIDI Circus...people are all dating it all back to Synergy.

T: When you play live, in addition to turntables, how much equipment do you usually bring?

MM: Everything I've got... I'm doing less and less of that taking the whole bit out- computers, samplers, mixers, the decks, tape loops, shit...a serious headache. Nowadays, I've got a CD mixing console, so I tend to go out with that and a box of CD's and records. I can blow more people's minds with just records than anybody's seen with the live set. I can do more places and do more things... At the moment my #1 priority is to play as much ambient music to as many people as possible and to see proper ambient rooms at raves. In Germany, of course there's now a big ambient scene. In England, it's just breaking its head above ground. The music's popular, but DJ's are all kind of fighting against it. Let's just say no big rave has had a chillout room until the Universe party last May.

T: How big was the room they set up for that party?

MM: At Universe, the chill out room was about 1000 people sitting in the chill all night, really into it. Now I want to go further and do all ambient- we, me and Aphex (Twin) did a party last week in London called Telepathic Fish that was all ambient for 18 hours, the two of us. No techno at all, people knew that, and there were 300 people getting down, getting horizontal, and getting out of their heads. We think it's time to lie down and be counted.

T: You just completed an album with Pete Namlook?

MM: It's called Dreamfish, on a new label called FAX Global. It'll be on Rising High, too.

T: You've been doing a lot of stuff with the Aphex Twin, it seems?

MM: I haven't been doing live stuff for quite awhile, but we're doing ambient rooms together. It's a good combination because people think I play the weirdest music they've ever heard and Richard comes on and plays something even weirder. then when I come back on, everyone is so pleased to hear it again. He's the ideal foil because his idea of ambient is mush more industrial than mine, I think.

T: Are you at all wary about how the press are going to take to the whole ambient movement?

MM: They know there's got to be a change and a lot of them are into it. Surprisingly, we've had a lot of support from KISS-FM...

T: What do you think of those who call ambient music "really nice new age" or "hip easy listening"?

MM: Well, at the moment ambient music is up for grabs. Everyone is using it to deacribe whatever they're doing, and a lot are using it to describe weak House music. I just want to make sure (the term) goes down as being, the phrase I've been using is 'radically beautiful'. It has to be progressive and experiemental, it has to have the leftfield angle that's dropped out of techno. You make some leftfield techno, fine- there's a market for it, but DJ's won't play it. My attitude is that Alex (Patterson) has proved everybody wrong after 30 years of saying you can't make experiemental music and get it in the charts.

T: What have you been working on lately and what can we expect from you in the future?

MM: Of course the Namlook album and a new Irresistible Force album late in the year. Other than that a lot of DJ'ing and remixes...Barbarella, Transform, an indie band called Bang Bang Machine that people have been going mad for.

T: What about the German scene, people like Dr. Atmo and Dr. Motte?

Pound aiming at Global Techno with Rising High

Founded by **Caspar Pound** with the royalties earned from his days as an original member of **Homeboy, Hippie, and A Funki Dred,** London's **Rising High** has become one of the U.K.'s leading dance labels. From the hardcore jungle of fellow HHFD member Marc Williams' **Project One** to the dark trance vibe of Caspar's own **The Hypnotist**, the **Irresistible Force**'s pure ambience to the licensing of top quality tracks worldwide, the "hardcore crew" called Rising High has one aim in sight- techno on a global level. The label recently hooked up with the **Universe** party organization in co-oridinating **World Techno Tribe**, a companion compilation of choice global techno for Universe's **Tribal Gathering** this past May which drew over 30,000 people to join the best DJ's and acts techno has to offer. **The Darkman** himself took time out to chat with **TRiP Senior Editor Chris Milo** about the label's effect on the U.K. music scene, breakbeats and racism, and the label itself.

TRiP: It seems you, knowingly or not, have had a really big effect on the British music scene by licensing the Hardfloor track.
Caspar: I was putting out German stuff for a long time and its a bit like hammering against a brick wall over here. I think that it started to give way and the Hardfloor just sort of came at the right time and went bang- strainght into the trendy clubs, the garage clubs, the hard clubs, the techno clubs and sort of everyone really. These people never used to like our stuff at all, it was very distant and they sort of look down on the smaller, techno-y labels.
T: How did the label get involved with Universe?
C: That was a very special one, Universe, it wasn't like any old party. It was a big change, apart from being the biggest party ever. There was a big change of direction, it was the first time in this country that it hasn't been completely jungly, hardcore-dominated, rave and Vicks, rush your bollocks off kind of thing. So of course, we wanted to be associated.
T: Were you an integral part of that, did they contact you?
C: Well, yeah, we're a better lot to do that kind of shit, so we sat down and compiled the album together snd the techno tent was sort of the tent of the event. There were as many people there as were in the jungle tent, and for England, that's incredible, really. And the funny thing was, they were playing techno in the jungle tent, they were playing techno in the garage tent, (Mixmaster) Morris was playing techno in the ambient tent... (laughs)
T: We keep hearing that the younger kids don't want to har new music, just jungle.
C: Well you have to look very carefully for good records, but I'd be silly to ignore the ideas that come out of some of those young kids in London, 'cause they're fucking crazy, but no one notices them because they get lost in the crap white labels. Serious producers could do well to listen to what some of those guys are doing.
T: Do you attribute the stagnant behavior in the jungle scen to the DJ's?
C: I don't think there's a stagnation in the jungle scene, I think it's a victim of racism. It's purely disliked because of the Black element, it's bullshit. I defend the jungle scene to the death- it's young, hard,

and exciting. No one talks to the jungle people about it. They talk to garage DJ's and fucking techno snobs about it. I'm a techno snob but I don't ignore it; you take techno and in London, Black techno is very fucking relevant. There's also little racist ways to say in things- like rave flyers- like "No Ruffnecks". That's what Blacks call themselves in London. But they say 'ruffnecks' just means troublemakers- but when they say that they mean no East London, North London jungle crowd. It's pure racism, no more no less.
T: The label has been releasing more licensed tracks as opposed to when Rising High first started. Why?
C: Not somuch 'licensed' tracks, I don't chase around looking for hits- I'm not into being that kind of label. I like working with friends, people I've known for years since The Hypnotist first went over to Germany. these are all longtime people who are starting to come into their own.
T: Your new track is "Pioneers Of The Universe"- basically a remix of 'Warped Groove'?
C: Yeah, it's a lovely track...I scare myself with that record. It's a big strain to make Hypnotist records- there's a lot of dark vibes in the studio; it's very intense between myself and the person I work with.
T: Are you still working with Marc Williams?
C: The same kind of thing- a lot of shit went down at Rising High at Christmas. There were a lot of changes with some people on one side of the fence and some on the other. We left a few people behind, basically.
T: Is Homeboy, Hippie & A Funki Dred now defunct?
C: No, Marc and I are still very, very cool, but that was a business thing. We're about to start on some new stuff.
T: The Dominatrix project with you, Plavka, and Lenny Dee?
C: That's one of my favorite projects, good fun.
T: The Sapho label?
C: Sapho is named after my daughter, she's 3- you're the first people I've ever told that to. Sapho is like Rising High's daughter. **Pypee** runs Sapho...it's basically what Pypee likes really, we talk together and sort it out.
T: It's seems like the label is a small, close knit crew?
C: Yeah, it's small, but it's huge. It's Global, it's everybody, but there's a sort of a hardcore crew. At the moment it's me, **Plavka, Pypee, Morris,** and **Nicole** and **Michael**, who take care of business.

TRiP FOTOFILE: NMS RECAP '93 TRiP FOTOFILE: NMS RECAP '93 TRiP FOTOFILE: NMS

by DJ Three
There was a lot of skepticism this year for those in the Techno/House Nation planning to attend NMS, seemingly due to the lack of interest in dance music. Needless to say, a few panels came about, but more importantly a lot seemed to get accomplished simply be walking about the lobby. I'll also add that for the Seminar in general, the noticeable effort to work out some of it's rough spots seemed to make a change for the better.

A Cloudy Recap of 'New Music Nights'
After stopping by **Vicki DMC's** surreal birthday get together at **Tavern On The Green** (just imagine older couples dancing to **"Strings Of Life"** under hundreds of tree lanterns???), it was off to the **Tribal America** party where in 2 small, very packed floors with **Guy Ornadel,** Florida's **Dave Cannalte** and upstairs, U.K. Super DJ **Grahme Park,** among others pumped housified tunes. Unfortunately it was impossible to get upstairs when Park went on because of all the people lined all the way down the staircase. The remainder of the night was spent at **NASA** for the **Harthouse** party. Here we caught very good, **very live** performances by **Arpegiators, Spicelab,** and **Hardfloor,** as well as **Sven Vath** playing between sets. Not soon forgotten will be Paris DJ **Laurent Garnier's** set. Aside from the 15 or so people watching, the dance floor also was blown away by his technical mix of emotional trance and techno, not to mention he's nice guy, too.

The next night had us off to **Matt E. Silver's "Hardcore To Heaven"** party at the **Ritz** with 4 rooms of madness. The main room was **HARDCORE....** Gabbercore... It even started off with a death metal band followed by the likes of **Lenny Dee, Fierce Ruling Diva, Digital Boy, Adam X** and more. The "Heaven" room had **DJ Ronald** (Basic Beat/ Holland), Laurent Garnier, **Steve Loria** (L.A.), and myself. Also an ambient room with **Soul Slinger** and more, and lastly the Detroit Room (which I didn't find 'til it was too late) with **Juan Atkins, Kevin Saunderson, Eddie Fowlkes, and Blake Baxter.**

Taxi cabs shuttled us back and forth from here to the **URB** party (Hello Raymond & Co.) located in an interesting drag bar. here we had hip-hop upstairs with Japan's deckwizard **DJ Honda** & Co. and House/ Techno downstairs with **Doc Martin,** Steve Loria, **Young American Primitive,** and **Moby** as M.C. giving stand-up comedy his best shot- it was a good one too, I must mention that several drag queens had the men at this casual affair fooled longer than you can imagine!

The **Hardkiss** party was a major highlight of NMS nights. Held at a great location, **Scott & Robbie Hardkiss, Jon Williams** (Mixmag DJ os the Month), along with the Northeast's afterhours man, **Onionz** provided the soundtrack for this intimate party. The music and vibe were curiously parallell to an above average night in Centrall Florida and the partying was getting crazy. So crazy we continued on to **Save The Robots** with Sven Vath's German crew. only to lose complete track of time and anything else while losing "it" to **Keoki** and **Doc Martin.** We heard the British House Nite with **M-People,** Grahme Park, and more was great as well.

From top, L to R Clockwise: DJ Three, Steve Loria & Doc martin (L.A.), and Dave Cannalte (Orlando) at Vicki DMC's party @ Tavern On The Green; Marc (Jam &) Spoon; Hardkiss party flyer; Sorted's Josh Wink and the quiet guy from Spooky; DJ Laurent Garnier (Paris)

RECAP '93 TRiP FOTOFILE: NMS RECAP '93 TRiP FOTOFILE: NMS RECAP '93 TRiP

From Top Left, Clockwise: NE afterhours man, DJ Onionz; Harthouse party flyer; Zach (Ind-X), Karl (Definitive), and Three; Germany's Sven Vath; NASA anniversary flyer; Lady Miss Kier (Deee-Lite) and Heather (B.U.G.) at the B.U.G. party

The **NASA One Year Anniversary** party was very nice. I always hear about the kiddie crowd and such, but frankly the crowd was brilliant- all smiles, friendly and not at all annoying. Unfortunately, the building NASA is held in was shut down the next week. Good luck to both NASA and The Shelter, 2 of the most popular nights in Manhattan.

Closing night took us to a warehouse in Brooklyn for **Nova Mute**'s party, which due to what we think were events in the city, had no one there. Really unfortunate because the location and line-up were very cool. This brings us to our big last minute surprise.... After a tedious journey, **Dave Christophere (Halluci-Nation), Richie Hawtin (+8), Karl f rom Definitive, Zach (Ind-X)**, travel pal Jaime, and myself arrived beneath a huge Golden Gate-like span bridge in of all places, the Bronx. Here we found a great sound system, a DJ wearing an Indian headdress, and over 150 kids enjoying a beautiful Underground vibe to smooth, pulsating trance and acid. One of several free parties that **Frankie Bones & Crew** have been throwing called **Back To Basics**, we were all very happy we made the effort to get there. **(X-tra thanks to Heather from Under One Sky for helping us continue that memorable night well into Sunday morning!)**

That was it for NMS... I then hit the road for a mid-week tour of Baltimore & D.C. and their scene which didn't allow me to see much (feel free to write us a bit if you live there). Stop by **Modern Music** if you're in Baltimore for club/rave info... Back to New York to play **Caffiene**, a Long Island club where Onionz and resident **Micro** showed me the NY Underground...Long Island style. If you go to New York and you're from Florida, check into what's happening at Caffiene. With guests from San Francisco's **Jeno** to +8's Richie Hawtin, something is usually happening there. Lastly I checked out a party on the Lower East Side called **B.U.G.**- put on by yet another **Heather**, who was kind enough to invite me to play. This night had 3 rooms, nice people, film loops, etc., and DJ's like Moby, **On-E (NASA), Johnathan Kadish (Net), Joeski (BUG)**, and others I didn't catch. A lot of fun.

As you can probably gather from this, even if you don't have business to do, Seminar is a good time to go to New York- no matter what type of music you're into.

Time to sleep....check the photos!

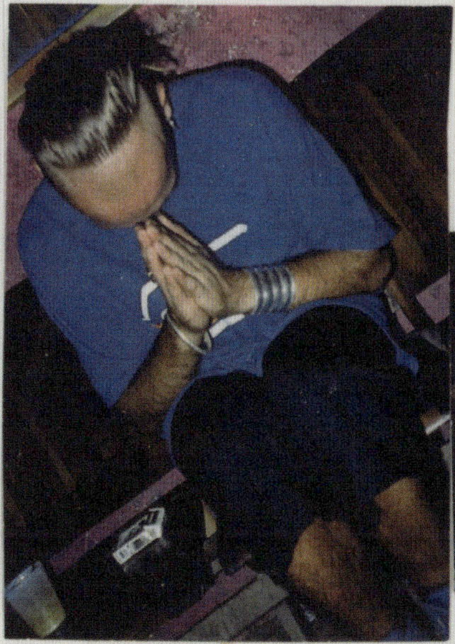

From top left, Clockwise: Nova Mute party flyer; +8's Richie Hawtin and Adam X (Direct Drive) at Back to Basics in the Bronx; Back To Basics, Sunday A. M.; L.I.'s Caffiene; Moby DJ'ing at the B.U.G. party

NEW TRANSMISSIONS FROM PLANET DETROIT
Now
X-313 "WORLD SONIK DOMINATION" EP
OUT
Passarani & Monteduro "Roma Meets Detroit" EP
TXC-2 "20 Hours To Paradise" EP
Level A and DJ T-1000 "Nikita" 12"
Still Available
Generator The New Power source
313.862.5468 VOX. • 313.963.0213 FAX
Distributed by Submerge
R
r
Hello La,
ROR, its the new. We promise V.F.M. records.
Money ready; as we want to come into your house.
YOWZA
TRiP
FLORIDA'S UPFRONT DANCE CULTURE MAGAZINE
Florida's Upfront Dance Culture Magazine!
The Most Up-To-The-Moment
News, Reviews, DJ Charts, & Interviews
JOIN THE TRiP POSSE-
SUBSCRIBE!
Get the Southeast's unbiased source for dance culture information delivered from the Underground -
direct to your house -eight times a year!
The first 15 subscribers will recieve a FREE Chillout/Ambient mix tape by TRIP DJ's Grumpy C. & Orion!
Name
Address
City/State/Zip
8 issues, $10; checks/m.o. only, payable to Peter Wohelsk
TRiP Magazeen 100 E. MLK Blvd. #10, Tampa, FL 33603

Label Profile:

hardkiss music

Longtime advocates of the San Francisco scene, the **Hardkiss Family** collective has been throwing parties, DJ'ing, and most recently, releasing some of the Underground's most spiritual tracks (**Ultraviolet Catastrophe, Hawke,** and the latest release, **God Within**) on their own **Hardkiss Music** label. A busy bunch of guys, **TRiP** tired to pin them down for a phone interview, to no avail...but **Scott Hardkiss** called and suggested a fax interview. Here's a brief and slightly irreverent look into the mind's eyeof one of the Underground's most sought after domestic labels...

TRiP: Who is the Hardkiss Family and how long have you been together?
Hardkiss: Hardkiss has been around, in one form or another, since approximately 2 A.M., September 7th, 1988. Since that moment we've been off out heads, putting on raves, DJ'ing, puttingout music, and making public (and private) nuisances of ourselves. The current line-up includes **Gavin Hardkiss**, who records as Hawke, **Graham Seaman,** who handles bookings for the DJ's and talent, and the mystical Hardkiss DJ's: **Scott Hardkiss** (God Within), **Robbie Hardkiss** (Little Wing), & **Jon Williams** (High Adventure). Each of us performs a variety of functions including feeding the horses, borrowing money, sifting through the trash, buying drugs, and yes, giving interviews.
T: What made you decide to start the label?
H: There was no choice, our work was laid out clearly before us.
T: Does the label have a motto?
H: "Love, Love, Love."
T: How would you describe the "Hardkiss Sound"- i.e. do you feel the label has a specific sound?
H: One might describe the current Hardkiss sound as a modern fusion of tough, funky African rhythms with subtle European melodies and sounds. It's an on-going experiment of spirituality through technology- beautiful, forward-thinking, surrealistic soundtracks for sex and prayer...
T: What do you think sets you apart from the other music coming out of the West coast at the moment?
H: Intense emotion, stylistic diversity, and pretty colour sleeves.
T: With so much of the dance music press focused upon San Francisco, what do you think is making U.S. created music different from the U.K. and Europe?
H: America invents it, Europe turns around and sells it back to us.
T: What are your long and short term plans for the label?
H: We want to encourage everyone to try their hands at making this music--engineers and technology make it accessible to all of us, including non-musicians. Then, we want to support all the talented young Americans who have started to make underground dance and ambient music. People need to take pride in their own cities, their own scenes, not just become style-slaves to some pre-packaged British fashion. For example, one of themost talented artists in the country is living amongst you in Tampa-- **David Christophere**, the **Rabbit In the Moon**. We need to support these people.
T: Where do you project the music going in the future?
H: Not too far off, music will be unleashed which will be so fucking psychedelic, that even people who hear it completely sober in broad daylight will be completely transfixed, staring off into the pure warm haze with unfixed eyes and a beautiful knowing half smile.
T: Anything else TRiP readers should know?
H: The second coming is near, it's **not** what you expected....

FUTURE SOUND OF LONDON, cont.

but not be faceless either. I think the time to be faceless is kind of over to a certain degree. I don't think that you have to be embarrassed about being in an electronic band and trying to P.A. it or put on in a typical fashion.

T: Another way you've brought your music 'full-circle' is through radio- you've done some shows on KISS-FM...

FSoL: We basically put on a three-hour show that was one huge mix...mixing up Tangerine Dream but spinning beats underneath it so that it actually had beats, mixing into ambience- you'd have to hear it. The whole idea is basically the proliferation of expression in electronic music really coming to the fore and radio is one of the growth areas for us. I think the range of expression is unending, really.

T: Do you DJ or are you asked to do ambient rooms?

FSoL: I think with everything- DJ'ing, remixing- we're hitting a strange time at the moment...It's all gotten rather cushy and people like ourselves are always **anti** any things being cushy. We've kind of gone against that; we've been taking a bit of a slagging in that field but we're crossing over to a new field which is an older, an in-depth listening crowd who are against the norm, too.

T: What about live gigs?

FSoL: I don't think we're at that stage where we'll do anything live for awhile, to be quite honest until we've formatted a way to conveying something of depth. I don't want to be two guys behind a bank of technology.

T: Tell me about Amorphous Androgynous?

FSoL: We've had the studio rebuilt and I guess our sound has changed to a certain degree. **(Tales Of Ephidrena)** represents the old studio, which I kind of really like now- it seems we've lost an aspect of it. It's two way really; to represent the old studio, giving it a different name and to see what we could come up with in the new one. I personally wasn't happy with it as a life changing album. I'm a great believer in music being life changing, it always has been for me. I think very little of our music changes my life, but tha't perhaps because I'm so dead to it after awhile. So in a way some of those tracks are quite old and we've become dead to them, so ti seemed fitting to put them out under a name and at the same time research not going through any mediums at all. Doing no advertising at all; we've actually signed quite a big deal here in the U.K. with Virgin; and the idea was to completely undermarket some-thing- and Amorphous seemed to fit it quite nicely in that we put it out completely without any club promotion, any mixes, any singles, and sort of researching word of mouth and point of sale. We're quite business-oriented, you see. We take an acute interest in business and the way that our music is being percieved.

T: What is EBv?

FSoL: It's our record company. We feel record companies can no longer be record companies if they cannot provide all different forms of expression for their artists. Right down to retail you have a problem if you want to express yourself in a number of formats, shops don't like it. We argue the reverse at EBv **(Earth Beat Visions)**, you'll have shelf you'll have a video, a film, a piece of music, CD-I in the future, if it ever gets off it's arse, books- all means of expression, means of communication and they'll all be on one shelf. We've confined EBv to being a very, very word-of-mouth, P.O. Box thing because retail won't understand it at the moment, even though certain components will be.

To contact EBv, write:

EBv
P.O. Box 1871
London W10 5ZL
United Kingdom

Mixmaster Morris, cont.

MM: Atmo,- a very good friend. We tried to bring Atmo over for Universe, but because he's Iranian, he wasn't alowed into England because of the racist government we have over here. Atmo is the DJ at the XS club in Frankfurt-still the only proper ambient club in Europe. Two nights a week is all ambient and everybody lies on the ground... Dr. Motte is planning a free ambient festival in Berlin the day after Love Parade. Things like that will break this music to that crowd. I think Amsterdam will emerge as an ambient centre, just like it emerged as one of the early techno centres and it would seem obvious that San Francisco would get on the vibe also.

Flying High will be released domestically on Instinct Records later this month.

DJ CHARTS

DJ Moneypenny
"The Transmission"
WBAI-FM/NYC

Loopzone-404 ep
Zolex-More Mystery
Kosmik Experience-Voyager In Trance
Tranceparents-Child 6
Lazer Worshippers-The Golden Gates
Neuromancer-Journey Into Cyberspace
RabbitIn The Moon-Outerbody Experience RMXS
Electric Indigo-No Headroom
Joey Beltram-Evil AD ep
Nico-Frontiers

Jeff K.
Edge Club 94
KDGE-FM/Dallas TX

Underworld-Cowgirl
God Within-Raincry
Country & Western-Positive Energy
Club Deluxe-Funky Rhythm
D:Ream-Unforgiven
RuPaul-A Shade Shady
N-Joi-Boom Bass
Sure Is Pure-One Drop Of Rain
The Good Men-Give It Up
The Beloved-Outer Space Girl

Chris Fortier
Marz/Various SE One-Offs
Cocoa Beach, FL

Nu Tribe-Nu Tribe
Delta Lady-Anything You Want
P.O.B.-The Essence
Slam-Positive Education
Edge Records #9-Spirit
Rabbit In The Moon-Outer Body Experience RMXS
Freaky Chakra-Halucifuge
Moby-Move
Jonny L.-Ooh I Like It
Power Fun ep

dj charts

DJ CHARTS

Damon Wild
Experimental Records
New York, NY

S.D.L.-Volume 3
Joey Beltram-Evil AD ep
Acid Revenge ep
Electric Indigo-No Headroom
Unknown Structure-Monotrax Vol. 2
Hardfloor-TB Recusitation LP
Apollo Ambient Collection
Lazer Worshippers Theme (EX20)
BioDreams ep (EX 17)
Nico-Frontiers

Scott Hardkiss
Hardkiss Music
San Francisco, CA

Freaky Chakra-Halucifuge
Rabbit In The Moon-OuterBody Experience RMXS
Slave To Eternal-Slave To Eternal
Young American Primitive LP
Amorphous Androgynous-Tales Of Ephidrena
Sueno Latino-Sueno Latino
Spacetime Continuum-Florescent
Reload LP

DJ Nikadeemas
DJ's In Sync!
Portland,OR

Cold Blooded Split-Vol. 2
Frankfurt Trax, Vol. 4
Fuckin' Hostile-Fuckin' Hostile
Color Climax Corp.-Lust Probe
Sanchez Fernando-101% Acid
Tumor-Tumult
Polygone-Polygone
Disintigrator-Machines
Joey Beltram-Evil AD ep
Men From Del Bosca-Magnetica

dj charts

DJ CHARTS

Mixmaster Morris
Irresistible Force
London, U.K.

YMO-Hi-Tech Hippies
Matteo Silva-Ad Infinitum
Harvey Bainbridge-The Voyage
Irrestistible Force-Lotus Position
Chill Out Or Die
Rubik-Deep Thought
Syn 4-Yugoslavia
Heavenly Music Corp.-In The Garden Of Eden
Voyager-Arrival
Astralasia-Univeria Zekt Mix II

Taylor
Various One-Off & Weekly Events
Los Angeles, CA

Hope-Treefrog
Voices Of Kwana-YaYe
Vinx-Nervous Buildup
Vernon's Wonderland
D:Rream-Unforgiven
New Order-World
Spooky-Land Of Oz RMX
Delta Lady-Anything You Want
Moby-Move
Ritmo-Rivals-(Analogue City Rmxs)

Jay Patrick Ahern
Aquarhythms
Dublin, Ireland

Punjabi MC-Souled Out
William Orbit-Water From A Vine Leaf LP
New London School of Electronics
Psychedelic Research Lab-Terenah
V/A-Narcosis LP
Transglobal Underground-I, Voyager RMX
Dave Angel-New Orchestrations
Lark-Tetra
Ujang Sur Yana-Sabilulungan
Detune-Opaque

dj charts

RABBIT IN THE MOON-"Phases of An Outer Body Experience" (White) Atmospheric, emotional, and totally groovy, this was a massive Florida hit in its original form. Now remixed this record is poised to explode on an unsuspecting global underground with three mixes you shouldn't be without... Newcomers **Electronic Dream Plant** give the track a straight-up hard trance treatment, losing none of the original's emotion, where on the same side is the Burning Spaer Mix by TRiP contributor **DJ Three.** An apocalyptic, thundering (literally!) bass monster, this mix takes you on a rhythmic journey to sonic Nirvana with acid, tribal percussion, plucked string synths, and slow, looping breakbeats building to the main theme of the original-beautiful! The Rabbit's own remix is a trancer with a thumping intro before plunging headlong into driving hi-hats, an extended piano break, and a gurgling acid line. Also included is a way too short ambient mix and the original for those who missed it the first time around. **(PW)**

FREAKY CHAKRA-"Halucifuge" (Exist Dance) This latest hottie from L.A.'s Exist Dance is a deep trancer in three forms; the atmosphere-laden Blind Dive Remix where the High Lonesome sound System instructs one on how to open the door to a higher conciousness, the 300 Mic's minimal ambient trance, and the pumping, acid-tinged, guitar-sampled Freaky chicken Peck. And wait! There's a bonus track... Chunky, funky, and way groovy beyond belief describes "Trancendental Funk Bump", a Fat Albert, Superfly, and Shaft themed stomper with a syncopated back-beat vibe. Ultra recommended. **(PW)**

BIOTRANS 2 ep (Stickman) Ah, yes. Just what I've been waiting for-they're back...Oliver Barkovic and Marc Pompeo, also known as the Biotrans. They come forth with a fantastic new ep. 4 tracks of deep, experimentall house-all good, especially "Manna". This track goes deep inside your soul to uplift you to higher grounds of massive enlightenment with it's reversed "Paul Revere" breakbeat overpelled by cool bass, symbolic synth lines and strings of passion, plus a lot more. "Overmind" has acid lines that builds and builds. "Freedom 1" and "Yesu" keeps you in a deep state of House that you'll never forget. The Stickmen do it again! **(Jask)**

OBX-"Eternal Prayer" (Ascension/UK) This Rising High sublabel's first release is a **MLO** produced track by **Darkman & Marshall.** This falls into the midtempo hardtrance category with a **Caspar Pound** remix on the flip. Caspar's mix is where to go- skilled 303, subtle breakbeats here and there, sublime spoken word and a real thumpy kick drum. **(CM)**

POB-"The Essence" (Seismic/UK) Excellent sounds and arrangement. Uptempo, tribal and acidic with wonderful melodies and changes. The writing side is the pick, a record not to be missed- deep, urgent, and leving a smile on your face, all at one time. More like this, please. **(D3)**

2 BAD MICE- "Underworld" ep RMXS (Moving Shadow/UK) Long awaited follow-up to "Bombscare". Not quite sure what to expect, but was surprised to find out that **Rob & Co.** had not sold out. This 4-tracker is very minimal drum and bass with atmospheric keyboard lines and few samples. The remix comes on 10" square vinyl with 2 Bad Mice and **DJ Hype** mixes. The 2 Bad Mice mix of "Tribal Revival" is hardly tribal at all, but still is good when played loud. It strays a little too far from the original, but it is a remix. The DJ Hype remix is another story. Totally uninspiring and very formula-actually pretty lame and not what I expected at all. Although this is billed as the new style (breakbeats and weird noises, totally for the head) and it will probably open people's eyes to a different scene, people like **Holy Ghost, Inc** and **Friends, Lovers, and Family** have been doing this for a couple of years now. Anyways, very quality return for the mouse. **(GC)**

DAISY GLOW-"Daisin' The Glow" ep (Zoe Magik) San Francisco keeps churning them out- this one's a bouncy, piano-driven garage groover of the deep-vibed variety. Alter ego's **Tasti Box** also aontribute a punchy horn-oriented edit. The flip reworks two previous DG tracks- **Ian** and **Justin** from **C-Level** give the "Theme From Daisy Glow" a 'progressive trance' treatment as labelmates **Single Cell Orchestra** turn in a slower but dark and chunky remix of "Sunday In The Park" with lots of atmosphere. **(PW)**

BABYLON TIMEWARP-"Durban Poison" RMXS (Subliminal/UK) The first Babylon Timewarp showed what the definition of hardcore breakbeat was about. This time they move on in creating a hard, monstrous breakbeat track ("I Come In Peace", plus they spice up "Durban Poison" with some dope remixes. This new track is wicked and gets much props- simply bad ass, pulsating drums, bass to make the Earth shake and yes, no cheesy, speeded-up Mickey Mouse samples. One of the few taking jungle to the next level. Check it! **(Jask)**

UNDERGROUND RESISTANCE-"Galaxy 2 Galaxy" ep (UR) Mad Mike is back, this time with a double back excursion through the outer reaches of Detroit. Seek now and play often! **(PW)**

LITTLE GREEN MEN-"Close Encounters Of The Third Kind" (Organico) This debut release from the people who bring you Reactor Magazine takes the trippiest movie theme from our youth and gives it a reworking for the Techno Generation. The original is a percussion-ladentrance bisquit with tribal chants instead of the theme's familiar synth tones. Labelmates Dub Tribe's brilliant Dub Encounter mix gets atmospheric and dubby with a gentle but deep kick drum, cascading synths, and sublte use of "those tones". Chicago DJ Derrick Carter's Acid Encounter mix is a wicked acid-laced deep trancer that invades your mind and body, gradually building to a

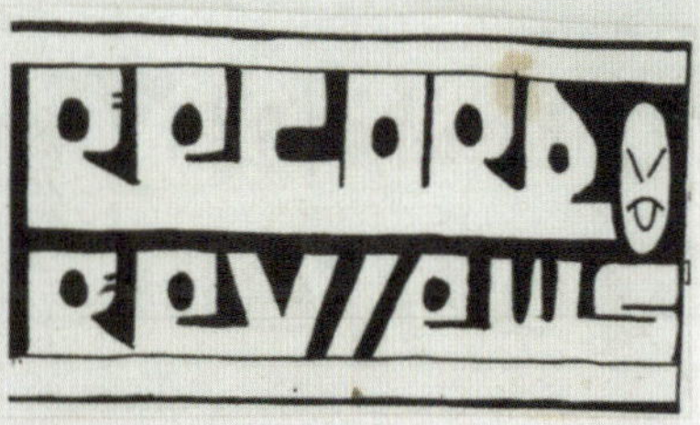

minimal breakdown before kicking in and searching the heavens for extra terrestrials. With this depth, I hungrily await more Organico vinyl . **(PW)**

LAZER WORSHIPPERS-"...Theme" (Experimental) I've always loved tracks Damon Wild and Tim Taylor. Lazer Worshippers was originally a B-side by N2O with ambient synth, whale sounds, and an Egyptian Lover drum track **(Hey! Give me my record back....Ed.)**. Now as the Lazer Worshippers theme, it's a 10-minute masterpiece with a way funky new drum track. The B-side boasts an Ambient Mix and a wicked 4-5 minute introed deep trance track with excellent, tribalish background atmosphere. Another great 'experiemental' record. **(D3)**

DELTA LADY-"Anything You Want" (Hard Hands/UK) Hard Hands come back with great, heavy, drummy progressive trance in 2 forms. The Delta Dub Charge begins fairly typical but is elevated to a new level twice through two excellent breakdowns that will definitely add life to your floor. The other mix chugs with a stabby synth verse, heavy percussion and a good vocal also taken to the next level with wicked breakdowns and bridges tha must be heard in a club to get the full effect, especially the bass! Another great track from the consistent Hard Hands label. **(D3)**

DREXCIYA 2-"Bubble Metropolis" ep (UR) A 6-track ep ranging from experimental to just plain strange. One of the tracks has narration that reminds me of the 20,000 Leagues Under The Sea ride at Disney. Not for closed minds- there's definitely something in the water in Detroit. **(GC)**

TODD TERRY-"Unreleased Project Pt. 4" (White) One man, one sound that continues to amaze me. "Todd Almighty" since Day One has been producing tracks that stand out above the rest. Definitely one of my early influences. This time he rises one level beyond in creating 5 very distinctive house tracks that do the job. Todd Terry- apioneer exploring new depths and succeeding in them. Get this one. **(Jask)**

LEVEL A & DJ T-1000-"Nikita" (Generator) Direct from Detroit and limited to 500 copies, this double-A sided deep trance track gradually seeps into your subconcious with wafting synths, a percussive bass line, hand claps, and hi-hats before the kick drum jumps in and pushes you to the point of after hours ecstacy. Solid and subtle **(PW)**

WINX-"Nervous Build" (Sorted) The debut release from Nervous' new techno sublabel is 4 tracks of deep mid-tempo house with very cool acid lines by Philly's Josh wink. The standout here is "Nervous Build" and yes, this cut lives up to its name by building up to a hard driving acid groove with some cool tribal sounds. All four are slammin' for any style set you desire. **(Jask)**

FUCKIN' HOSTILE-"Fuckin' Hostile" (Industrial Strength) The label says industrial strength and I should know by now that **Lenny Dee** doesn't fuck around. Led by a Pantera sample, this is bonecrushing, turbo-powered, hardcore of the most extreme. My favorite is thedisitegrator remix- minimal brutality at its best. Only for the headstrong from the Maniac Psycho to you. **(PW)**

JABARI featuring ROB BROWN-"Bring Back The Love" (TOMA) On the garage house tip with soothing vocals to sooth your soul. 4 very good mixes one this 12", but the Deep Mix is the shit! Slammin' house from the heart, most definitely. **(Jask)**

RIOT SQUAD-"Nonshlentustokken"/ PSYODOMY-"Black Mantra" (12 Gauge) The brainchild of DJ Repete, this label's debut release has two distinct sides. Riot Squad's brutal parody of our favorite (?) Rotterdam track seems to take a stab at the Limelight/Vortex camp. The real gem and the reason to own this is "Black Mantra", a dark, pulsating cool-as-fuck hard trancer produced by Damon Wild. A must for this track alone. **(PW)**

RADIATION-"Meltdown" (DirectDrive) 2 mixes of the same track, one by Richie Hawtin and one by Jimmy Crash. Richie's South Of Detroit Dub is minimal driving acid that is very long and hypnotic. Extremely well done and defintiely the standout. **(GC)**

EPIPHANY ep (Sapho/UK) Just when you thought everything was going as good as it could be, Friends, Lovers, and Family come along and fuck everything up. This ep is typical FLF: incredible breakbeats, tingly atmospherics, and weirdness, except for one thing. A very intense female vocalist named Victoria Taylor-Roberts... "Suffer Your Reality" is fast with a full vocal (not Minnie Mouse samples) that will give you chills. Also included is "Vast", a mid-tempo trancer, again with vocals; "SAW F.M.", a very slow grooving breakbeat track. FLF doesn't need Bill Cosby to tell you how dark they are; it doesn't get any better than this. Respect. **(GC)**

ROBERT ARMANI-"Circus Bells" (Hardfloor RMXS) (D-JAX/Holland) Yeah, you know it, "hardfloor remixes are in the house of Robert Armani. On the D-JAX label, Robert Armani's "Circus Bells" gets acidnated the the Hardfloor guys which turns this track into a massive acid builder that will keep you jumping. Fucking dope! **(Jask)**

EDGE #9-"Diversion" ep (Edge/UK) Not a Structure ep this time. 5 tracks, the main track, "Spirit" is uptempo British trance complimented with subtle breakbeats and GTO "Elevation" stabs. Side 2 has "File 57" which is exceptional British hardcore; "TPT 303", a horn laden, midtempo acid track; "Dare", the horns continue in a downtempo, jazzy fashion, complimented by piano and string chords, and lastly; "Codes"- a short ambient bit, which I liken to circa Blade Runner **Vangelis** **(CM)**

NAGACHIAN ep (Frankfurt Beat/Ger)

This is actually the alias of **Ramin** of "Brain Ticket" and Afrotrance fame. "Flash" is the logo side- it just doesn't cut it with the way novel Flash Gordon sample. The writing side, however, delivers 2 excellent German trance peices delicately produced with elements of breakbeats, 303, familiar Ramin synth sounds, and tribal percussion. A lighter sound similar to recent **MFS** releases for Ramin **(CM)**

MATT WOOD-" What Am I Gonna Do With You ?" (Tribal America) Seems Louis Balo Guzman took this Barry white classic and transformed it into three solid tracks, two of which can be played in one night and no one would fucking know. This 12" offers a hypnotic swirl and happens to be a long, strong House mix with an interesting accapella break that's DJ friendly. A must have! **(DJ Crystar)**

AUDIO FOR MOVEMENT-"Epiphany"/ "Hymn Of Praise" (Euphonic) One year after their funky techno trance debut, Florida's own Audio FM return in a more progressive house/groove style. "Hymn Of Praise" in its original form is very predictible progressive house, similar in style to a Limbo record, except for it's down tempo. The Govver's Delight Mix is a very nice ambient dance version, perfect for lounging music. "Epihany" is the best track for the clubs. A lush piano anthem inro into funky percussion, hands-in-the-air synths, and grooving progressive/trance bridges. It should bring back good memories for many, especially here in Florida. **(CM)**

JEEK-"Ragga" (Tribal America) five very interesting dub track. the first two are stale, sounding too much like **Masters At Work.** Skip those and go straight for the tribal mixes. On the flip side, this 12" offers something for everyone; the Original House Vocal mix (with no vocals) has over seven minutes of pure underground XTC. Check out the jungle beats- tribal at its best. **(DJ Crystar)**

PHUTURE SCOPE-"Plastic" (Emotive) We subscribe to the opinion tha this is **DJ Pierre**'s wild Pitch Mix of "Plastic Dreams", but you don't have to. This marks a change in the Wild Pitch mixes. Different keyboard arrangement, heavy bass, and breakbeats. If you like Pierre or midtempo, funky, heavy trance, check it out. Side 2 has a track by **Jaydee** and a vocal deep house track by David Chang. **(D3)**

MOBY-"Move" (Elektra) Moby's major label debut is simply brilliant. different, but very Moby, there's something here for all and there's no excuse not to have this. **(PW)**

SLAM-"Positive Education" (Soma/UK) Merke & Co. are back and we are very impressed. There have been too many poor trance techno records coming via the U.K.. this record is the real deal. "Positive Education" is an undeniable electronic groover. Side 2 is called "intensities In-Ten-Cities" and ahving heard it ona big system, I'm hooked. Nice ambient intro into a steady, washy, 909 groove with subtle guitar and piano. Comparable in style to **C.J. Bolland**'s "Mantra", this is my favorite Soma record ever. **(D3)**

RABBIT IN THE MOON-"Orisha" (Hallucin-Nation) That crazy Rabbit's follow-up to "O.B.E." only serves to confirm that this is one of America's more interesting underground musicmakers. "Orisha" 's Original mix is a dreamy, galloping commerciall trancer with escalating swirling synths, light percussion, and intermittent samples that narrate your journey. The Mad On A Dub mix bears little resemblance to the original, save for the main theme. Opening with a solo piano intro and adding a marimba before leaping inot a chugging drum track and a vaguely familiar vocall sample that will send your dancefloor off! Dubasex is an atmospheric, pan piped deep-vibed bass boomer for the afterhours. **(PW)**

ELECTRIC INDIGO-"No Headroom"/ 'Skyway" (Experimental) There's a 303 on the label, that means this is gonna be some seroius acid. Needle to vinyl, this does not dissapoint, Austria's DJ Electric Indigo delivers two fierce hard trance monsters that just do your head in. Most tasty & delicious. **(PW)**

Record Reviews

PSYCHEDELIC RESEARCH LAB-"Terenah" (Gyroscopic) Originally appearing on Caroline's Excursions In Ambience compilation, this track resurfaces in four remixed versions as the second release on the Emotive-distributed Gyroscopic label. The label side is more atmospheric with Spy's Sub Mix- a soothing, subtle groover with a wam female vocal and kick drum to ease the crowd into cool out mode- and the Sleepwalker Mix, a gradually building beatfree sonic trancer. On the back are two tribalesque house tracks- one up, one down- using pieces of the original theme to revamp the different mixes but losing the track's original ethnicity and atmosphere. chillout DJ's should stick to the label side **(DJ*)**

COOL SUMMER CUTS ep (Overdrive/ Germany) A very differnt release for Overdrive, not quite as hard as other releases, but very good nonetheless. Both sides contain the same song, which is not a good sign, but the quality makes up for it. Starting out with a long hypnotic intro, this grows into an upbeat melodic trance cut. Very similar in fell to Eye-Q and MFS releases. **(GC)**

THE ADVENTURES OF DANIEL LITE-"I Want Your Love" (Tribal America) A bit late, ain't we? With most house tracks heading in a different direction, Mr. Frankie Foncett decided to stay in the overused but still good **"Maurice Joshua & E. Smoove"** kind of groove. too bad, as the only thing that saves this 12" is the **Mood II Swing** mixes. Two and a half for trying, three and a half for the 'Swing mixes. **(DJ Crystar)**

OR- "Future Eternity" (Drone) A weird and diverse, but poorly produced four-tracker from Miami. Some breakbeat, some hardcore, some acid breaks, and a strange atmospheric track. There's lots of potential with some cool ideas, butnone cohesive enough to make a go of it. **(PW)**

Record Reviews

CHARLIE CASSANOVA-"House Of Fun" ep (Basic Beat/ Holland) The so-called Ambassador Of Techno goes for the House vibe on the A-side of this ep. "Can You Have It" has a buzzing synth, bouncy pianos, and a chugging drum track with repeating "You can haveit, if you want it" female vocals. The flip's "Trance Dancer" is decent pulsing uptempo trance house fare. Not a stormer by any means, but a solid ep nonetheless. **(PW)**

DEEP CONTEST-Ripost ep (FNAC/France) A quality 3-track ep on Laurent Garnier's FNAC label from Ludovic and DJ Deep. Very straight-forward trance; "Sexual Behavior" is best here, twisting and turning for nine minutes. Keep it up, guys. **(GC)**

DOME PATROL-"The Cutting Edge" (XL/UK) New on XL, this 12" takes "The Cutter" from Echo & The Bunnymen in two mixes, one breakbeat, the other an acidic mix by Damon Wild. **(GC)**

SPACETIME CONTINUUM-" Flurescence" ep (Reflective) You've heard about the cool, hologram labeled ambient record by now, so get with it! Ambient treasures from San Francisco, 4 tracks to choose, all very lush, all very good. **(CM)** Ditto, ditto, ditto! **(DJ*)**

LIQUID CITY-"Feelin' Free" (Tribal America) Creative Creative Noise Productions have served up a delightful blend of rhythms in this 12" sure to keep the floor jammed. From the Masters & Servants Mix with its low end bass kick and "jump up", "I will" samples, this record serves its purpose. Very well put together! **(DJ Crystar)**

TCX-2-"20 Hours To Paradise" (Generator) Level A and DJ T-1000 return form the sublime techno experience of TCX-1 to bring you a sequel. "Love You More" is an uplifting instrumental happy house joint outta Detroit that keeps your butt shakin'. "The Real Camille" goes for the deep house stomper to great effect with its organ and synth workout. The B-side opens tribal to the bone. "Our Man In Kenya" is a 909 meets kalimba duet that makes you want to travel to the Bush and let inhibitions run wild. Mellow and sexy, "Intuitions" finishes up on the jazz tip with a laid back drum groove, soaring flute, and sensual pulsing organ-riffs, that is. a really nice, multi-faceted ep for listening, dancing and ? **(PW)**

LP/COMPILATIONS

PETE NAMLOOK & DR. ATMO-Silence (Rising High/UK) The chillout is just now being acknowledged as being just as important to a good party as an energy-filled dancefloor. The door is only now opening for ambient scenes worldwide to truly thrive with the popularity of artists and DJ's like Aphex Twin, Mixmaster Morris, and The Orb's alex Patterson. One of the scenes's cornerstones is Frankfurt's XS club where their ambient only nights bring people queing up to get horizontal and hear the cosmic sounds of Dr. Atmo. With Silence, Atmo- along with FAX Records guru Pete Namlook- creates the celestial sound of the planets orbiting through space. already a classic and groundbreaking peice of ambient work prerequisite for any sunday morning session. **(DJ*)**

DRUM CLUB-Everything Is Now (Butterfly/UK) Lol Hammond and Charlie Hall-London's Drum Club- have brought true techno back to the Capital's club scene with their handful of singles on Guerilla, the rammed and pulsing Thursday Drum Club nights at Soundshaft and now a full-length LP on Youth's Butterfly imprint. Full of emotional energy and power as well as subtle beauty, Everything Is Now ventures into the outer reaches, manouvering easily between tribal, trance, and ambient textures. With a bit of mellow acid and a warm friendly late night groove that washes over you like a Spring rain, this is a brilliant record with something for DJ's and clubbers alike. It won't leave my turntable **(DJ*)**

MOBY-Ambient (Instinct) With Moby already having released his major label debut this is sort of a let down. Compiled here is what seems like some noodling around in the studio and unfinished ideas released to capitalize on Moby's popularity. The LP opens with a series of demo quality tracks which are nice but subpar with what we would expect from Moby- not quite lush and melancholy enough. The remainder of the Lp is short, underdeveloped ideas for tracks; some are really top and one wishes they were longer or more complete. Others are sort of a viewing a=of the artist at work, one feels almost guilty for listening as if you're eavesdropping on the artistic process. Perhaps in the future there will be another ambient project released on his own terms and then I won't feel as guilty. **(PW)**

REALITY STUDIO-Chaos Theory (Ultra-Ethereal) Combining deep tribal beats, ethnic chants, and hard acid elements, Baltimore's Reality Studio open a different door to the Underground. where other acts use tribal rhythms within a more vibey frame, Chaos Theory adopts a different approach, laying the groundwork of World Beat grooves and adding thecno elements to drive the tracks. There's some really interseting things going on here and I'd like to see how this act develops. Also included is the Lenny Dee remixed version of "Metamorph", "Meta 1", reviewd here a few issues back. **(PW)**

SYSTEM 7 (Big Life/UK) The first System 7 record marked the recording comeback of Steve Hillage, whose work with 70's avant garde progressive rock act Gong and subsequent solo work like Rainbow Dome Musick left seminal impressions on ambient artists like The Orb's Alex Paterson. On System 7, Hillage collaborated with such talents as Derrick may, Paul Oakenfold, Youth, Steve Waddington (of The Beloved), ex-Simple Minds' Mick McNeil, Sunsonic's Andy Falconer, as well as Paterson and Thrash to make a solid but slightly candy coated effort. This time Hillage and wife Miquette Giraudy retain only the necessary ingredients by cutting things to the core, while shaking the tag of being an Orb side-project as well. Orbmates Alex, Thrash, and Youth- along with cohorts Louis Keogh and Tony Thorpe, appear only in production and mixing capacities on less than half the tracks. Much deeper, more atmospheric, and harder than before, V2.0 of System 7 journeys deep into the underground, tapping into upliftin melodic hard trance, pumping groovy acid house, and buoyant ambient tracks- all with Hiilage's signature guitar synthesizer textures. A wonderful record that earns its own underground credibility with one listen **(DJ*)**

V/A-DIGITAL ODYSSEY (Moonshine Music) This latest compilation from Moonshine highlights the deeper, vocal side of House music. Featuring top tracks from Masters At Work, Transform, Crunch, and others, this'll keep you groovin' and singin' until your feet hurt and your voice is raspy. as susual another strong entry into the Moonshine back catalogue. **(PW)**

BRIAN ENO-Neroli-Thinking Music Part IV (Gyroscope) Many of Brian Eno's early ambient works like On Land and Music For Airports have the ability to give the listener a sense of place. His latest work, Neroli- inspired by the orange blossom dirivitve oil used in aromatherapy- transports one to an orange grove. Through some recent study Eno attempted to map the relationship between smells. Deeming it impossible, he gave up but drew a similarity between that and the ability to notate electronic instruments in modern recording production. Coming to the conclusion that if scents and music have this indescribable quality, then the next step was for him to use scent names to describe and title his music. Relaxing, tranquil, and extremely minimal in nature, Neroli is a nearly hour long continuous piece of music exploring texture, tone, and space drifting into time itself. With DJ's and critics alike citing his early experiments as a seminal influence on ambient house, everything Brian eno does in this genre may not be brilliant to some, but is perhaps a veiw into the future of music that deserves full attention **(DJ*)**

FUSE-Dimension Intrusion/SPEEDY J.-Ginger (+8/WARP) Warp's Artificiall Intelligence series has made the U.K. indie music press elite change thei collective minds about what techno truly is. Of course, in their own high and mighty manner, they've coined a phrase, "armchair techno" , that they can build up or tear down when they feel good and ready to. Funny thing though, this music has been made for years and no bullshit NME or Melody Maker journo looking down their pointy nose at it will make it go away or go out of fashion in the Underground. In fashion or not, Detroit's +8 Records has been steadily churning out top quality tracks for over three years now; the label's influence has been strongly defined by these two releases licensed by the sheffield-based label for the AI series. Richie Hawtin's FUSE (Future Underground Sound Experiements) is a combination of some previously released tracks, but mostly new pieces in an ambient direction, including a re-recorded version of the limited edition "Dimensions". with these newer tracks, Hawtin masters the art of Detroit fueled chillout grooves- minimal synth textures, gentle but insistant hi-hats, and gradually building subtle acid lines. Jochem "Speedy J." Paap's Ginger pushes the envelope as well with its Rotterdam via Detroit blend of pulsing ambient house that glides through your psyche yet makes your body want to move. Both most excellent and essential. **(DJ*)**

LIGHTS IN A FAT CITY-Somewhere/ TRANCE MISSION-S/T (City Of Tribes) Trance states are induced by rhythm, regardless of whether they're technology driven or acoustic instruments and voices. Perhaps one of the most mind-altering sounds is the one of the digeridoo, an instrument indigenous to the australian Aborigines. A long tube capable of creatin haunting, swirling, oscillating tones, the digeridoo has come to be recognized through the work of notably, the Aphex Twin, as well as more commmercial artists. With a sprinkling of conventional instruments and technology, These two albums released on Zoe Magik's tribal/ world music sister label, City Of Tribes couple the indigenous music of australia and the digeridoo to ambient dance music without compromising the native music's original content. Sad then , that these albums almost never saw the light of day.. Lights In A Fat City's master tapes were turned over to digeridoo player Stephen Kent by the group's origianl label after the label went out of business. Kent's new project Trancemission was signed to City Of Tribes and both albums were released for us to enjoy. Somewhere is closer to its tribal and indigenous roots, while the other roams, experimenting within the framework. Tracks like "Bo Diddgely" at times remind me of things I might have heard coming out of New York's Knitting Factory; others are pure chillout amblence. Perhaps leftfield for some, but this is magic to me. **(DJ*)**

RABBIT IN THE MOON
ORISHA
The New Release • Out Now
HALLUCI~NATION
ONE NATION UNDERGROUND
INVISIBLE
HAL 004
PHONE 813 • 239 • 3622 FAX

MAD HOUSE INVITES YOU TO DEEPSKATE I
AN ALL NIGHT UNDERGROUND EVENT
SATURDAY, SEPTEMBER 25
- 1993
12:15am till 6:30 am
(just after midnight) (sun. morn.)
✱ Area to dance ✱ Area to rollerskate ✱ Skate rental FREE with admission
$7 at the door ✱ All Ages
Early Arrival Is Appreciated
DJ' spinning Disco & Skate tunes from the past along with the House & Techno of the future.
DJ's
THREE (Tampa) • STEVE McCLURE (Halluci-nation)
ANDY HUGHES (Marz) • GRUMPY "C" (Tampa)
- Special Guests & Live Overdubs
Event location:
UNITED SKATES OF AMERICA, INC.
5121 N. Armenia • Tampa, FL
INFO TEL
(813)969-0270
ARMENIA
HOWARD (ONE WAY)
HILLSBOROUGH
275
I-4
1 BLOCK S. OF HILLSBOROUGH ON ARMENIA
E
S
N
W
Intelligent Lighting & Projections by
SPY VS SPY
Plus: Direct from XANADU "The Bunny"
special thanks to:
SMART BAR BY
DANCING WARRIORS PRODUCTIONS
HALLUCI-NATION
ONE NATION UNDERGROUND INVISIBLE
jester emotion
amp
Record Source
record store
Liquid Culture

12

Free In Florida! $1.50 Elsewhere
TRIP
V12.0
FLORIDA'S UPFRONT DANCE CULTURE MAGAZINE
APHEX TWIN
TERENCE MC KENNA
ORBITAL
ULTRAMARINE
VAPOUR SPACE
EXPERIMENTAL
FUTURE SOUND OF LONDON*PINK ELLN & ATOM HEART*LEFTFIELD & LYDON
THE SOURCE*DERRICK CARTER*BJORK*DANCE FEVER*GROOVE CORE
PLASTIKMAN*LISA CARBON*EARTHRISE*GLOBAL CUTS*B.T.

MUSIC FOR A TECHNOLOGICALLY ADVANCED SOCIETY
HUMAN MESH DANCE
HYALINE
HUMAN MESH DANCE "HYALINE" (EX-261)
POST TECHNO AMBIENT AND TRANCE. FEATURED ARTIST ON CHILLOUT (EX257)
"technohead"
CHURCH OF EXTACY
CHURCH OF EXTACY "TECHNOHEAD" (SNC-2027)
HARD AND TWISTED FROM THE BRAINS BEHIND GTO. FULL LENGTH DEBUT!
PROTOTYPE 909
ACID TECHNOLOGY
PROTOTYPE 909 "ACID TECHNOLOGY" (SNC-2028)
A TRANCY, KRAFTWERKIAN BLEND OF PURE ACID AND SPACEY TEXTURES. FEATURES TAYLOR 808 FROM HUMAN MESH DANCE
evolve NOW
the dream EP
EVOLVE NOW "THE DREAM EP" (EX-262)
AMBIENT BREAKBEAT FROM NORTH CAROLINA'S JAMIE RUDOLPH. FEATURED ARTIST ON CHILLOUT (EX257)
Lisa carbon & friends EXPERI-MENTAL POST TECHNO SWING
LISA CARBON AND FRIENDS (SNC-2025)
WARPED ACIDIC JAZZ FROM GERMANY'S POD COMMUNICATION LABEL.
OMICRON
OMICRON "SYMBOLIS" (EX-263)
5 TRACKS THAT RANGE FROM AMBIENT TO HARD TRANCE. FEATURED ARTIST ON CHILLOUT (EX257)
instinct
26 W. 17TH ST. #502 NY, NY 10011 CSERVE RAVENET ON ROCKNET: 72170,1753. SEND US A S.A.S.E. FOR A FREE CATALOG.
LOOK FOR EVOLVE NOW AND OMICRON IN THE SINGLES SECTION

CONTENTS

TRiP Magazeen
V.12.0/November 1993

NEWS

FEATURES

MUSIC

FEET FIRST

As 1993 draws quickly to a close, we here at **TRiP** have been reminiscing about a few of the magic moments that have made this year memorable from a Florida perspective. Here's a brief look at our favorite moments this year: **Cybersonik/ + 8 Sound System**-Rave New World, Gainesville (Detroit 101 with John, Richie, & Dan); **Doc Martin, Dom T, Baby Ford**-Solaris, Orlando (a crap party with 25 people, but great music); **Tony Humphries**-WMC @ Warsaw, Miami (witnessing "Plastic Dreams"'true 'crossover' potential); **Sven Vath**-Divine Playground after hours-Soundshock, Miami (simply spellbinding); closing night of **Evolution**-Tampa (Tampa Posse coming together with **Moneypenny, Guy DMC**, and **Gat Decor** in the house); **Cosmic Baby**-Infonet 3, Orlando (what a live show should be-live); closing night of **Marz**-Cocoa Beach; **Madskate**-Tampa (a great vibe, tunes from the old school to new, rollerskates-how much more fun can you ask for?); **Discovery 2** @ Vibe, Tampa. If you were there, you know how great they were. If you weren't, you missed a good party and hopefully you caught the next one. If you're reading this from another state or country, let us know of some of the parties that made your scene memorable this year and we'll print them in the next issue!

In 1994, we'll be bigger and better- more pages, better quality, deeper penetration into the Florida market in addition to the States, and greater involvement in the Florida scene. A few of these changes have already begun to take shape. With this issue, **TRiP** is now available through **Deltra Record Distribution** as well as direct, making it easier to get the Southeast's Upfront Dance Music Info Source. TRiP has also begun **OSCILLATE**, Florida's (and perhaps the Southeast's) first intelligent techno/ambient/chillout club night.

On the second and fourth Sundays of each month, **OSCILLATE** provides a perfect end to the weekend by turning on your brain and relaxing your mind. TRiP contributors **DJ Orion** and **Grumpy C.** serve up a blend of galactic melodies, tender accapellas, softly cushioned beats, Detroit-fueled chillout grooves and wicked visuals for getting horizontal. Call us @ 813.238.0310 for more info... Also, the two have teamed up for a 90 minute mix tape that is available for **$8** or **$12** postpaid with a new subscription to TRiP.

....continued on Page 22

TRiP Magazeen
100 Dr. Martin Luther King, Jr. Blvd, Ste. #5
Tampa, Florida 33603 U.S.A.
FON: 813.238.0310 FAX: 813.876.7473
(When faxing, please use a cover sheet to our attention)
EDITOR/PUBLISHER: Peter Wohelski
SENIOR EDITOR: Chris Milo
ASSISTANT EDITOR: Wayne Consiglio
EXECUTIVE ASSISTANT: Jackie Rosquete
CONTRIBUTORS: DJ Grumpy C., DJ Jask, DJ Orion, DJ Three

SUPPORT THE UNDERGROUND!

ADVERTISING: Rates given upon request. **SUBSCRIPTIONS/BACK ISSUES:** $10 yearly, $1.50 each, postpaid. **RETAILERS:** Contact **Deltra Record Distribution** (310.202.8554) **OR** our offices for distribution info. **TRiP Magazeen is published every eight weeks and is distributed throughout the United States. We hope our content will encourage awareness and positivity for the Global Underground.**

HYPE!HYPE!HYPE!HYPE!HYPE!HYPE!HYPE!HYPE!HYPE!HYPE!HYPE!

After much legal wrangling with their former label, **BIG LIFE**, **THE ORB** has signed with **ISLAND RECORDS**. Back in the U.K. after a much too brief U.S. tour, **DR. ALEX & CO.** have released a quadruple vinyl live album (**LIVE ORB '93/EVIL BRO 39'**)including some new tracks out now on import, with a domestic release slated in January; in the works is a collaboration with guitarist **ROBERT FRIPP** and **THOMAS FEHLMANN**....In other Orb-related news, the group's **WAU! MR. MODO** label has been renamed **INTER MODO** and has inked a licensing deal with **R&S**....Word has it that **DERRICK MAY** has come out of recording retirement to do a brand new **RHYTHIM IS RHYTHIM** lp....**ASTRALWERKS** and **R&S** are teaming up for a U.S. tour in December with a live performance from **CAPRICORN** ("20 Hz") and DJ's **ABRAXAS** (Fierce Ruling Diva) and **REESE** (Limelight, NYC) working the 1200's to promote the two labels' licensing of the **GLOBAL CUTS** compilation in the States.....Speaking of licensing, **POW WOW TRANCE** has licensed former **UNDERGROUND RESISTANCE** member **JEFF MILLS'** solo lp **WAVEFORM TRANSMISSION** and his conceptual **X-103-ATLANTIS** lp from Berlin's **TRESOR** label along with a collection of works from **JUAN ATKINS** and an album from **EDDIE "FLASHIN'" FOWLKES & 3MB**; **INSTINCT** has licensed for U.S. release the two latest efforts from electronic music pioneers **CABARET VOLTAIRE**-**PLASTICITY** and **INTERNATIONAL LANGUAGE** with a third lp, currently in production, to be released in February 1994....**NEW 'ZINES: MINDFOOD** is a 'zine based in London dedicated to the ambient side of techno. Run by the **OPEN MIND** collective who throw the **TELEPATHIC FISH** ambient tea parties, Mindfood is a upfront guide to ambient happenings, releases, and personalities. For info contact Open Mind, **102 GROVE VALE, LONDON SE22 8DR**; The **E. 909 ST. MAG** is the latest tip sheet effort from Florida garage DJ, **CHANG**. Published with the intent to educate the Southeast on deep, soul-stirring, God-fearing, four-to-the-floor U.S. House, the mag features charts, reviews and an interview with Orlando-based visual whiz-kids **FACTORY VISUALS.** Write E. 909 St. Mag c/o **4304 B HARGRAVE ST, ORLANDO, FL 32803....**The Los Angeles date of **NASA** 's **SEE THE LIGHT** tour featuring **ORBITAL, APHEX TWIN, MOBY**, and in an adjoining ambient room, **VAPOUR SPACE** was cancelled ten minutes before doors opened by the L.A. Fire Marshall for fire code violations....Is there truth to the rumours that **TRANSMAT** is leaving Detroit to set up shop in London?!?!....Cocoa Beach's **MARZ** club has re-opened with resident DJ **ANDY HUGHES** ....**BLACK DOG** have apparently sacked the manager of their **GPR** label recently, leaving the imprint's immediate future in limbo....The **SHAMEN** are working on their follow-up to **BOSS DRUM**, due out this Spring....**RABBIT IN THE MOON**'s "O.B.E.", a Florida and NMS '93 hit, heavily sought after on white label, is due to come out through **HARDKISS MUSIC** with remixes by **ELECTRONIC DREAM PLANT** and TRiP contributor **DJ THREE**, with Hardkiss remixes to follow in early 1994....**R.I.P.: UNIVERSE....**Paris Super DJ **LAURENT GARNIER** made his first trip to Florida with 2 appearances over Thanksgiving week @ Simon's in Gainesville and at The Edge in Ft. Lauderdale....**WORKING TOGETHER: ANDREW WEATHERALL** and **ICE-T**, **DR. ATMO** and **SPACETIME CONTINUUM, STEVE HILLAGE** and **CHARLATANS UK....UR** go back on the offensive this month, this time spreading the word of world techno domination to Japan and Scotland. This tour of duty will be the last for **DJ T-1000**, who is taking leave from the front line to plan strategy from UR's Detroit HQ and handle day-to-day operations of his own label, **GENERATOR**. T-1000 will, however, continue to do solo DJ missions into enemy territory at an underground party near you....Chicago-based label **ORGANICO** have announced that they will not be releasing the album from U.K. party organizers **SPIRAL TRIBE** as was previously planned. It seems the collective's legal hassles have forced the group deep underground, prompting **BIG LIFE**, their home label, to sever their recording contract....

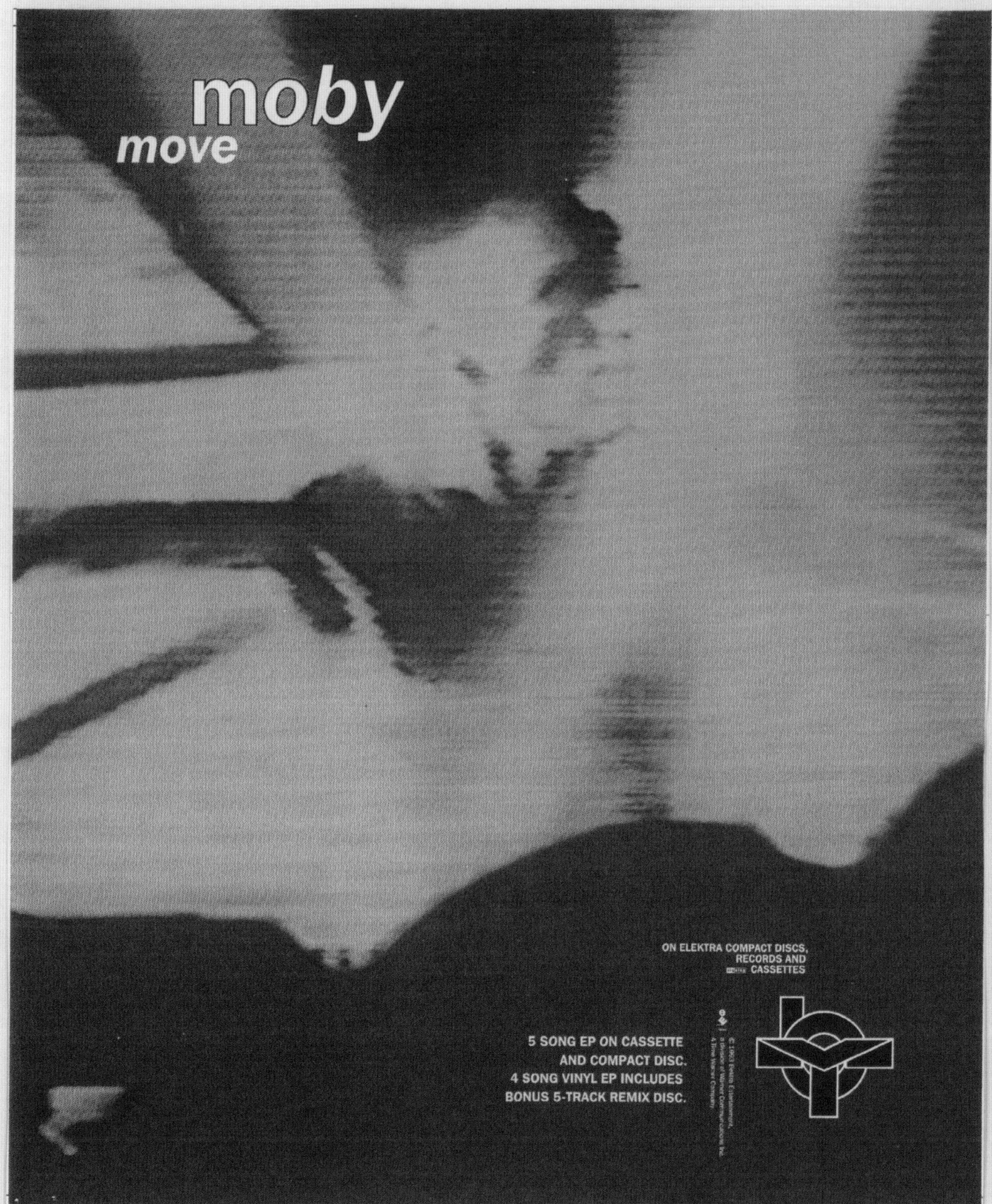

moby
move
ON ELEKTRA COMPACT DISCS,
RECORDS AND
CASSETTES
5 SONG EP ON CASSETTE
AND COMPACT DISC.
4 SONG VINYL EP INCLUDES
BONUS 5-TRACK REMIX DISC.

Brits Ultramarine return home for United Kingdoms jazz, folk roots

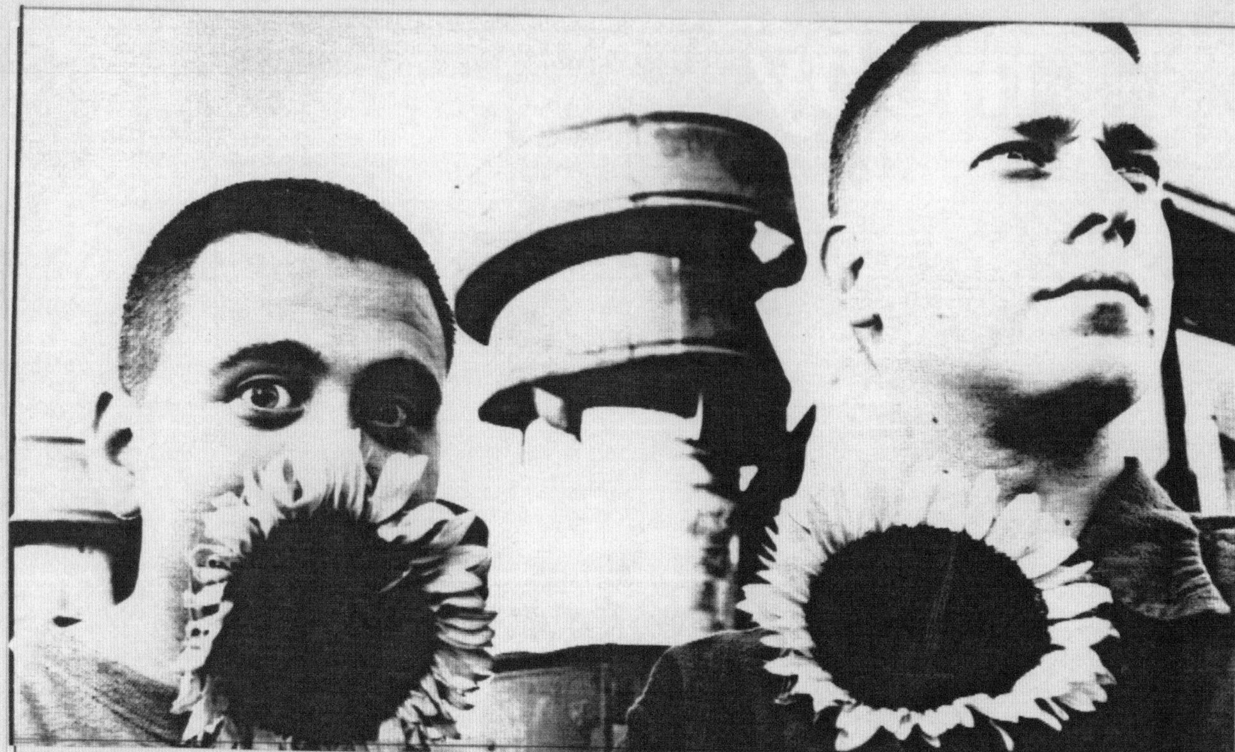

Fusing the elements of '60's & '70's folk, new school hip-hop, jazz, and '90's minimal electronic technology, Britain's **Ultramarine** have carved themselves a niche somewhere between indie-pop sensibility and ambient techno surrealism.

The band's debut lp, **Every Man and Woman Is A Star**, was a pristine mesh of warm acoustic textures, jazzy hip-hop beats, and subtle 303 acid blurps accompanying the listener on a imaginary trek across America.

Every Man... garnered enough critical praise that now defunct super indie Rough Trade picked up the LP from the tiny Braniak club label for wider release, in turn giving it a U.S. release through Elektra.

Press clips from across the Atlantic were positive enough to put the band on last year's **Communion** tour, a touring version of the popular Manhattan club night, opening for fellow Brits **Orbital** and **Meat Beat Manifesto**.

Having never before been to the States' and facing American audiences, Ultramarine's nucleus **Paul Hammond** and **Ian Cooper** found the Communion tour to be a really positive experience, being able to expose their music to a new audience by playing under little pressure.

"We really enjoyed that tour, things really couldn't have been better for us and we had a really good time. We just did a tour of England and it was pretty grim compared to that tour," admits Ian.

Upon returning from their actual trek across America, the duo signed with Warner Bros., and set out into the countryside of their homeland to work on their second record, to be titled **United Kingdoms.**

Similar in tone to Every Man..., United Kingdoms uses clarinets, flutes, and saxophones to accent the band's organic influences and jazzier side, although not a conscious move says Paul Hammond.

"I think this is the same kind of record-just more organized. A lot of (the first LP) came together in mixing, it was very random and it worked."

"The actual composition was a lot easier than we thought. If you think about it, the composition of the last record would have been really two years from the beginning of work on this one. It was a bit of a daunting task; we signed to Warners and this was our first major label release, so we did feel a bit of pressure."

Not denying their folk influences, Ultramarine also enlisted the talents of their favorite singer, **Robert Wyatt**, of British folk/rock act **Soft Machine**, on several tracks of United Kingdoms.

"On one level, it was a big dream come true, you know. He's our favorite singer, we thought about working with him, but it's one of those things you don't think would actually happen," explains Paul.

"Seeing him behind the glass, singing away at your own music, it's quite moving," continues Ian, "plus the way he worked, he was very professional and quick..."

The band has spent most of the past few months on the road touring having played toured Europe and the U.K., recently doing a date with **Black Dog** and **Spooky** for the now-institutional monthly **Mega Dog** parties in London.

"We're very happy to be asked to do those kinds of things because it's quite a mixed audience and we're happy to play for people who are open-minded about the stuff they listen to."

The band just completed a mini-tour of the U.S. with **Bjork** and are looking to return to the States early in the new year.

Obscure Vapour Space meteorically shoots to fame

Less than one year ago, **Mark Gage** was just another electronic musician creating music out of his apartment. Since then, the Rochester, New York native has released two acclaimed singles through Canada's **Plus 8 Records**- one on the **Probe** sublabel under the name of **Cusp**, the other on **Plus 8**, the massive and gorgeous **"Gravitational Arch Of Ten"** as his current nom de vinyl and name of his studio, **Vapour Space**. In a short span of time, Gage has gone from relative obscurity to becoming the first American artist signed to the **ffrr** label, fielding interview questions, and preparing to leave for his first major tour, doing the ambient room on **NASA's See the Light Tour** with **Orbital, Moby,** and **Aphex Twin.**

TRiP interrupted Mark Gage as he prepared a tape to be played in the ambient room the day before leaving to go on tour.

TRiP: What are you putting on this tape?
Mark Gage: I'm just using a lot of old, classic electronic stuff, weird stuff, bizarre stuff; **Barry Adamson, Sakamoto, Jarre, Eno,** whatever... Lots of old Mute stuff- **Frank Tovey and Boyd Rice, Duet Emmo,** and all of that. It's all pretty classic stuff as far as I'm concerned, it's still viable in the scheme of what's going on today. I have so many friends who are 18-24 that are doing electronic music now and they have no idea who half of these people are. I have the privilage of being older, I'm 31, and have lived through a lot of it, so I'm more aware.
T: How did you get involved with John (Acquaviva) and Richie (Hawtin) at Plus 8?
MG: Primarily through demo stuff-about a year and a half ago I sent John a demo of some stuff which I really can honestly say that it wasn't some of the better material I've ever done. My production style is, at that stage, what really sold me to John. They made no promises to me at that point, just 'Keep working' kind of thing and get back ahold of us. Which was really the way to do it because it just inspired me to work harder. John's real good about instilling that kind of a feeling in most people. I couldn't ask for any better people to be hooked up with; John has hooked me up with remix jobs with R&S...
T: Have you done or are about to do remix work?
MG: Most of the things have all been done now, it's just a matter of when they get released. Everything's going to be cropping up in the next three months, I'm really, really lucky because it's going to be pretty intense; I have a lot of stuff happening at one time and everyone's going to wonder, "Where did this guy come from!" I did remixes for Renaat at R&S for a band called Orsoncarta (sp?), Claudja Barry on Radikal, Overdance mixes for a band called Automatic, I also did a FUSE re-edit for Richie which is on the new "Train-tracs" CD single... In the last eight months I've done so much, you're going to be seeing it all in the next six months... You probably got a copy of the ep; the full-length album will be out in January and that's already finished.
T: You've had a meteoric rise to prominence...
MG: But the funny thing is, I've been doing this for ten years it's just that I've never offered any of my material for anyone to listen to. If you have the Plus 8 12" of Vapour Space, the b-side is a track from '83 and one from '87. Those are no lies that are taken straight off analog cassette tapes... It's very overwhelming, my publicist called me today and said the <u>New York Times</u> Music Editor is way into what I'm doing and wants to do a story on me... We went with the ffrr deal because of the capacity of the deal they were offering, plus they gave me complete and total freedom. The album **(Themes From Vapour Space)** went right through when they heard it... I did it in thirds, 1/3 at home, 1/3 with John in Canada, and 1/3 at a friend's facility in Rochester; the tracks vary from '83 to '93.
T: Tell us about the "Magnetic Gravity Arc Suite"?
MG: It's all remixes done different people and myself... The first six minutes are the original mix. After that comes a mix by **Coleman Horn** (C/Sphere) & **Fred Giannelli** (Psychic TV) from **Telepathic.** Then the mix after that would be half of **John Acquaviva**'s, the latter half. After John's is Fred Giannelli's mix- he did one on his own, that's at 120 bpm. Then there's an interlude where the tempo switches from 120 to 135 and into a mix of mine. After that's the other half of John Acquaviva's mix and it ends up the last six minutes are **Mark Ryan** from **Hi-Bias** and **Toronto Underground Records. Look for Vapour Space's debut lp in January 1994.**

Orbital blinded by See The Light Tour

"The theory of the moebius is that time becomes a loop." -Orbital

And time does become a loop... It was this same time last year when brothers **Phil and Paul Hartnoll**, aka **Orbital**, came to tour these shores with mates **Ultramanrine** and **Meat Beat Manifesto** on the **Communion** tour. When we met up with the brothers, they were ready, following the tour to return to the studio to work on their second album, but with no definite clue as to where it would take them musically.

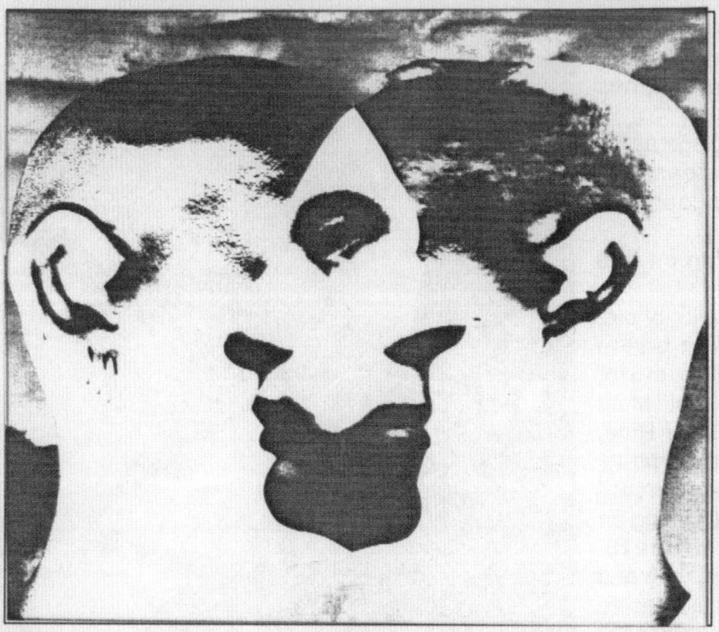

So here they are (or just Phil, actually) a year later and they're preparing to come back to the States as the headliner on a U.S. version of the 'MIDI Circus' tour in support of the new album, also entitled Orbital, and affectionately known to fans as 'the brown one.'

Taking 4 months to complete (hey, you've got to stop for Christmas!), the album has a more linear feel to it, perhaps due to the Hartnoll's whatever goes attitude towards the studio.

"It's more organic, as we just go into the studio and start something and not know what it's going to end up like until it's done really. It evolved as we were doing it.", explains Phil.

Wanting a full collection of new tracks, while their record company wanted their hit single **"Halcyon"** on Orbital found the brothers having to devise a happy medium by re-working the track-coming up with a more delicate piece than the original.

"They wanted the single on the lp; we did a show last New Year's Eve in London and (**Kirsty Hawkshaw** of **Opus III**, who sang the original vocal) came on and started jamming with her voice- it was brilliant. so when it came time to do the LP, we just rang her up and said, "Oh, come in and have a sing-song over the top of this." We just DAT'ed it and took some choice bits, just for a bit of variation, you know, because we're a bit conscious about putting singles on our LP's"

Also included is "Remind", a re-adaptation of the pair's storming remix of MeatBeat Manifesto's "Mindstream" which Phil and Paul liked so much, they took to playing it in their live gigs.

"Once we got into the studio it was something we wanted to get out of our system onto vinyl and do it like we did live and not having to worry about Jack's vocals. We knew a lot of DJ's would mix his vocals out and it's one of the rare remixes we've done that we've really enjoyed and stolen it back."

One of their other remixes that they've taken to playing out is "Kinetic", a track under the pseudonym of the **Golden Girls.** "Originally it started as a friend of ours who lived around the corner did a track and he asked us to remix it-he's our mate, really-so we got all together and did a remix. It went out on this really small label in London and **Renaat** from **R&S** heard and wanted to release it. Since the small label was really dodgy and messing this third person around so much we didn't take any notice of it and signed it right over to R&S. Renaat wanted our remix, not really the original track, so I thought, "let's make up a new name." I chose the Golden Girls because there were three of us and I really like that programme," Phil says sheepishly. "Ever since then, it seems like everyone's had a go at that track, **Frank DeWulf, Paul Morley**-everytime I see that record there's a new remix of some kind on it."

Since the import release of Orbital, the Hartnoll brothers have been busy as expected being on the road with MIDI Circus, the traveling "techno-Lollapalooza" that made its way around the U.K. this past summer featuring **Aphex Twin, Spooky, Drum Club**, and other acts, including Orbital, which inspired their recent tour in the U.S.

"Everything I expected (MIDI Circus) to be, it was and it went well. I think everyone who went to the shows had a good time, which was my main concern. but it did quite a lot of good as far as saying, "you can do this live, you don't have to mime toi this music."

In addition to touring, the duo have done some remixes for an English 'crustie' band and for **Guerilla Records** (**Abfahrt**'s "Come Into My Life", out now), as well as vying for the soundtrack on a English film project called **"Shopping."**

"We've been dying to get our hands on a piece of film scoring, and we finally got a chance. We've been heavily influenced by a lot of soundtracks, what with our Dad constantly listening to them when we were younger. We love it-the whole cinema thing, it'd be lovely to do it."

Orbital recently finished their "MIDI Circus"-like excursion across the U.S. Organized by New York's **NASA** club, the **See The Light Tour** hit 15 cities, spreading our House Nation's techno gospel according to the Hartnoll's, along with **Aphex Twin, Moby,** and in an adjoining ambient room set-up, **Vapour Space.**

Excursions In Ambience
§ the second orbit §
EXCURSIONS IN AMBIENCE
The Second Orbit
[ASW 6105]
Further explorations of spirituality through technology featuring Material, The Grid, W.F.O. and Locust and special remixes by The Orb.
SPACE TIME CONTINUUM with TERENCE MCKENNA Alien Dreamtime
[ASW 6107] Terence McKenna speaks of the psychedelic experience, the evolution of man and the end of history.
Space Time Continuum charts the peaks and valleys of a dazzling ambient-house trip.
Together, they propel the forward escape into hyperspace.
A live performance recording.
SPACE TIME CONTINUUM WITH TERENCE MCKENNA
ALIEN DREAMTIME
GLOBAL CUTS VOLUME 1
[ASW 6109] Probing the Tribal-House tip and featuring club hits by X-tactic, Capricorn and Remy & Sven.
GLOBAL CUTS
GLOBAL CUTS
SPAWNING THE SWEAT
X-Tactic / Capricorn 12"
Space Time Continuum w/ Terence McKenna-"Speaking In Tongues" 12"
W.F.O.-"No-One In the World"
Autocreation-"Dark Smile" 12"
ASTRALWERKS
For mail order information contact P.O. Box 2759 New York, New York 10116-2759
© 1993 Caroline Records, Inc.

Losing sleep and making noise with the prolific Aphex Twin

From the time he was thirteen, **Richard D. James**, aka **The Aphex Twin, Polygon Window, Joyrex, Diceman, Blue Calx,** etc., has been cranking out countless tracks and creating new and unmatched innovative sounds with his reconstructed and rebuilt gear. Making his mark with the ominous 155 bpm **"Digeridoo"**, the Cornwall-born James has easily since become one of techno's most prolific artists. Ranging from sensitively ambient to brutally hard and all points in between, his unique and thought-provoking style has made him an in demand remixer, putting in time for tracks by a Who's Who of Indie music, including **Meat Beat Manifesto, Saint Etienne, Curve, Seefeel,** and **Jesus Jones. TRiP** caught up with the Twin, about a week before embarking on **NASA's See The Light** tour along with **Orbital, Moby,** and **Vapour Space.** We're delighted to bring you, our valued reader, this opportunity to see some of the man behind the pseudonyms, Richard James.

T: Just for the record, give us the general lowdown on how you got started...

AT: Well, I've always been totally into making noise, basically, since I was really little. The first thing I can remember doing is pissing around with piano strings, 'round back of the piano, shit like that. I always really wanted to make electronic music, mainly because it just involved using myself and no other band members. With electronics, you're able to set things going and basically take the place of anyone else. The idea of phoning people up and getting them out of bed to go into the studio to do tracks is like the worst for me. I started doing lots and lots of experimental stuff with tapes when I was about 11, just using crude bits of equipment that I picked up in junk shops and stuff like that. Then I bought a synthesizer and I thought it was really shit and started pissing about with it. It only cost like 40 pounds or something like that; I was really interested in electronics as well, so I started dabbling, doing basic changes to keyboards, making them sound a bit better. As my knowledge of electronics sort of grew and grew, I was able to construct more complex things until I got to the stage where I was building and designing all my own gear, which I use exclusively.

T: You mentioned being into noise, were you into early industrial music, things like Throbbing Gristle or were you oblivious to it?

AT: I didn't know anything about it until a few years ago. I've been totally stupid regarding other people's music. I've always wanted to make music and I've had to do it to stay sane basically, since about 14 onwards. Listening to other music wasn't- and still isn't- a part of making music for me. I've got so many ideas it's as if I don't need to be inspired by anyone.

T: You seem to be pretty prolific, are you perpetually in the studio?

AT: If I wasn't so busy, I would be. I've had to give up sleep recently, just so I could get stuff done. It sounds funny, and I laugh at it, but it's got a more serious side to it, because I think I'd actually go mad if I didn't write tracks. I've never been into sleeping much anyway, since I've been quite young. I've always seen it as a waste of life and if I could stop sleeping, it'd be the equivalent of getting an extra 20 years of my life! I get like an hour a night, which is cool 'cause now I've got more stuff to do.

T: Is it true that a lot of what you've put out recently are actually tracks over a year old?

AT: Older than that probably... I'll tell you, the stuff that's come out recently is all from the same period, sort of the "Digeridoo" period, which is about 4 years old. That's where I created stuff which is most suitable to be put on vinyl; it sort of goes with what people are making. But the stuff I've put out on vinyl is only a very small part of what I actually do. It's not really an insight at all into what I actually make. It's just the stuff that's closely assimilated to the stuff that's coming out in the rest of the world...

T: So what you're saying is that what you release is a concious decision as to what is going on in the rest of the world?

AT: Yeah...the first records were sort of record company decisions, and I had sort of been going along with that sort of theory. I mean, I don't care what records come out or what anyone thinks of the stuff, but the thing is I want more time to make music- which means I don't want to get a job, which means I've got to get some money to live on, which means I've got to sell records. Selling records means, up to this point so far, putting out records that people can relate to. But the actual fact is, I couldn't give a shit whether they can relate to them or not.

T: If you were going to play me a track you did, say, yesterday- what would it sound like?

AT: I know the tracks I did yesterday and they weren't in 4/4 time, I did one track which had like 9 syncopated rhythms on top of each other- it was pretty complex. If it was on record, I just know DJ's would never play it. Most people have closed minds and I'm willing to experiment. I lost a DJ'ing job like 8 times when I was first starting out because I used to get

for playing all the music that I wanted to play.
T: We know you make your own gear. Is there any new music technology that you're interested in, using, or taking apart to alter?
AT: I keep a very, very close ear to the ground with technological developments. To tell you the truth, there's nothing that I think's worthy of replacing the stuff I already use. There's little bits and bobs, little gizmos, where I think, "Yeah, this is cool...", but most of the sound-producing type equipment to me is fucking shit. Something I'd really like to do, and it's a bit far-sighted, but there's bits of gear that I've got in my mind that I'd love to make, which I couldn't because it'd be too complicated. I've got designs of equipment that I'd love to take to Roland and say "If you want a fucking decent bit of gear, make this, you Japanese sicko..." We've got some interest from Roland to do some drum sounds for a drum machine and half of me was like, "Fuck off, I'm not letting anyone have my sounds!", but then the other half thought it'd be cool to be immortalized in a drum machine forever.
T: What other music do you listen to outside of techno and house music?
AT: I like things like **Terry Riley** and **Stockhausen**; quite mental, avant-garde sort of stuff. The usual names, **Steve Reich**... minimalism- I really like the ideas behind it. The triple ambient lp that will be out in January is very much sort of based on minimalism, I suppose.
T: And how old are the tracks that are going to be on that record? ***continued on Page 23***

RICHARD D. JAMES: A SELECTED DISCOGRAPHY

Aphex Twin ep (Mighty Force/UK)/Sept. 1991
AFX/Analogue Bubblebath (Mighty Force/UK)/Sept. 1991
Analogue Bubblebath, Vol. 2 (Rabbit City/UK)/Dec. 1991
Didgeridoo ep (R&S/Belgium)/January 1992
"Metapharstic" (Mayday Compilation)/May 1992
Zylem Tube ep (R&S/Belgium)/June 1992
Joyrex J4 & J5 ep (Rephlex/UK)/July 1992
Mescalinium United-"We Have Arrived" RMX (PCP/Germany)/July 1992
Diceman-"Polygon Window" (Artificial Intelligence compilation) (Warp/UK)/August 1992
Bluecalx (Philosophy Of Sound and Machine compilation) (ART-Rephlex/UK)/October 1992
Selected Ambient Works 1982-1992 (R&S/Belgium)/November 1992
Meat Beat Manifesto-"Mindstream" RMX (PIAS/Belgium)/January 1993
Analogue Bubblebath, Vol. 3 (Rephlex/UK)/January 1993
Polygon Window-Surfing On Sine Waves (Warp/UK)/January 1993
Seefeel-"Time To Find Me" RMXS (Too Pure/UK)/Summer 1993
Vertebral Ridge ep/Madreporic Plate RMX ep (Warp/UK)/

Carrying on about Re-evolution, True Hallucinations, and Alien

"Terence Mc Kenna is the most important-- and the most entertaining--visionary scholar in America. To be uninformed of his ethnobotanical discoveries is to be oblivious to the central thrust of human conciousness , which is not to survive with the dung beetles, but to soar with the Gods." -Tom Robbins

Whatever you want to call him- radical philosopher, ethnobotanist, author, technoshaman- **Terence McKenna** has become, perhaps accidentally, the rave generation's spiritual voice.

In his books, Archaic Revival, Food Of The Gods, and True Hallucination, McKenna explores shamanism and what he calls "the ethnopharmacology of spiritual transformation." Through his many speaking engagements, occasional "spoken word" appearances at raves, and a collaboration with the **Shamen**, Terence's ideas and theories have captured widespread attention.

Earlier this year, McKenna participated in an underground party combining his theoretical "raps" with the ambient textures of San Francisco's **Spacetime Continuum** and didgeridooiste **Stephen Kent**. Recorded for posterity, New York-based dance imprint **Astral Werks** has released the performance as a full-length LP entitled **Alien Dreamtime.** showcasing the work of both McKenna and Spacetime. A longform video is also available.

TRiP recently spoke with Mc Kenna from his Occidental, California home; a joy to listen to with his unmistakeable tone of voice, we chatted not so much about his theories, but about what Terence McKenna is like, computers, television, rave culture, and his meteoric rise to cultural icon...

TRiP: How did you get into this line of work?

Terrence McKenna: Well, I guess probably what sealed it for me was that I happened to go to Berkeley to the University the Fall of 1965, so that was just the center of the LSD culture, the anti-war movement, all these counter cultural things. I had earlier been aware of the psychedelic experience from reading Aldous Huxley, but once I actually had it, it just seemed to me the most interesting phenomena around, so I've more or less pursued it ever since on many levels: chemical, historical, botanical, anthropological...

T: What are your thoughts on the use of psychedelics in underground dance culture and the culture in general?

McKenna: I think it's a process of seeing the movement self-educated. I mean, I think the new wave of interest in these things came from MDMA, but I think it's moved beyond that now because the realization has been made that shamanism and traditional activities with these things connected up to a very rich set of cultural values. So it isn't like you're advocating something radically new and untried, you're actually advocating a return to a very old cultural path. I think that House culture can learn a lot from the mistakes of the Sixties, mainly to avoid media co-option, to avoid a direct political confrontation, such as the the anti-war movement and to move more gradually but more deeply and permanently into people's lives and the lives of the culture.

T: Through musical artists like the Shamen and now Spacetime Continuum, your words have reached a lot of people who have never heard of you or never experienced what you have to say. How did you get involved with those two particular artists?

McKenna: A lecture of mine was sponsored in London by **Frazer Clarke** of Evolution Magazine. **Colin Angus** came to that talk and was just simply interested in what I said. He is a university educated microbiologist, so it was familiar territory for him; we got together and talked and that was the taped conversation that became "Re-evolution." on **Boss Drum.** As far as Spacetime, I think the Shamen thing brought me to their attention. I'm working with other groups as well; I have a CD coming out in England- **Coil** has sampled me, the **Orb** has sampled me...

T: How do you feel about that?

McKenna: Oh, I'm all for it. I think collage is the great artistic breakthrough, authentic, original breakthrough of the 20th Century. It begins with Dada and multimedia is just going to make this part of the culture, the idea of owning ideas is a very peculiar, capitalistic conception. I think artists should be supported for their work, but I certainly think that the culture is for all of us to sample and reassemble in whatever way we want.

T: Do you do a lot of parties like Alien Dreamtime?

McKenna: I don't do too many raves. I do maybe a couple a year here and a couple when I'm in London...

Dreamtime with technoshaman Terence McKenna

I'm actually a hermit, I don't know how I got into this high-profile, razzle-dazzle stuff. I want people to know about psychedelics and I'm willing to actually interrupt my own love of solitude to go talk to them about it. I just think it's very bizarre that this central experience of the self is secret, legislated against, and condemned. I associate it with the last gasp of Calvinism and that it's some effort to stand between people and the experience of their own body; it's the same impulse that makes drugs illegal, frowns on rock'n roll, frowns on dance. It's a fear of the unconcious, the power-obsessed do not like people carrying on- but people like to carry on. I'd like to turn them on to the concept that through psychedelics they can actually bring a spiritual dimension back into their lives that isn't in the hands of the churches or Madison Avenue.

T: How do you spend your time?

McKenna: I try to write a lot. I spend far too much time answering fan mail, I don't have an assistant... This is not, at this point in time, a money-making operation. When I'm at home I spend a lot of time on the telephone, writing letters, and working on different projects. I spend a lot of time on the road and that's pretty much talks, workshops, book promotions, that type of thing. I have three, four books in print and next Spring there'll be a fifth one. When that book comes out basically my whole rap will be available to people and at that point I'd sort of like to step away from this public stuff. We need to turn this scene into a studio band!

T: Why do you think that you as compared to a say, Timothy Leary, have been chosen as a iconic figure by this culture?

McKenna: Well, Leary certainly had a run for his money and dominated this issue in the 60's and early 70's. He's a friend of mine, I like him very much, but I think he's interested in other things these days. I think probably the reason I became the icon of the psychedelic position is because nobody else wanted it. I didn't have to elbow anybody to standup and say everybody should look to this. People have been very fearful for their careers and their freedom... You can't get any academic to take a public position because they're feeding at the trough of NIH grants and big science. It was basically a position that was vacant and I've been doing this since 1983. In a way I'm dissapointed that I haven't spawned any imitators. There's lots of room in this field; I like the hemp people, I'm glad to see all that coming forward... The argument is basically though, that it's a very useful thing and you can make a lot of money on it. They're not confronting directly how great it is to be loaded- but still, they're softening up the mainstream to har new positions, but people speaking up for the psychedelic experience, you just don't hear about it.

T: It's very funny how the government actually percieve this stuff. I mean they actually believe that this is more harmful than something so much more damaging such as crack cocaine...

McKenna: Or alcohol and tobacco... It's a very skewed thing. I wrote a book called <u>Food Of The Gods</u> that was about drugs- all kinds of drugs, not just psychedelics- morphine, tobacco, sugar, television, all these things we discussed as drugs...

T: Television <u>IS</u> a drug, isn't it?

McKenna: The average person watches 6 hours a day, the average person... So that means millions and millions of people a day are being warehoused in their apartments- they're afraid to go out on the street because of crime, they don't have any money to spend- watching television. It's a freaky drug because it's the only drug where the dealer controls the experience. You blood pools in your ass, you stare at the screen because it's small, there's all these measurable physiological changes. If people were smoking something that did that to them, the entire society would be hysterical. Something about the fact that it's delivered electronically makes us relate to it as utterly harmless and the cultural consequences of this are not yet fully in view.

T: Computers are such a big part of our society. What are your thoughts on this medium?

McKenna: Essentially what's happening is that the unconscious of the Human Race, which has always before been held in libraries, is being downloaded into this globally-distributed coral reef of silicone and its accelerating creativity fantastically. It's a catalyst for creativity exactly the way psychedelic drugs are. I'm a McLuhanist and the main point that McLuhan was concerned to make was that technologies shape culture in ways that the culture is never aware of until the change has already happened. What tremendous democratization of information is occuring under the influence of

continued on Page 23

Label Profile:

In less than two years, New York's **Experimental Records** has almost immediately become one of the most consistent and well-respected domestic imprints around. As part of the **Northcott Productions** family of labels, **EX** originally began as an outlet to market tracks that couldn't be labeled or weren't right for the licensees of it's (now) import sister label- **Atmosphere**.

Named by **Tim Taylor** and Northcott head **Silvio Tancredi**, the first slew of releases came out mysteriously, with plain black labels and very little or no information about the track, save a artist and a track listing- if that. The first record was by **Alex Alot**, a pounding, analog synth driven track with samples taken from **Ministry** and **Art Of Noise**, followed by EX's biggest record to date, Tim Taylor's **"The Horn Track"**, a powerful classic breakbeat stormer that was licensed by the **ffrr** label.

From ethnocentric breakbeats and pounding analog madness to deep trance and ambient techno, Experimental avoids the pigeonholing of a specific sound by choosing tracks that label director **Damon Wild** says he "...hates to categorize; we like to keep it scientific and different."

"Each record has a different focus and we try to appeal to different territories, "The Horn Track" was one of our biggest records and it was #1 in London, the **Modulator** (EX6) record was big in France, "Timmy's Trance" was a hit in France. They all do well in different areas, we don't just gear ourselves to specific territory, and we can broaden ourselves all around," says Damon.

EXPERIMENTAL RECORDS DISCOGRAPHY (so far...)

EX1 ALEX ALOT-"Jacob Your God"
EX2: EGYPTIAN EMPIRE-"The Horn Track"
EX3-TIM TAYLOR/DAMON WILD-"N2O"
EX4: POSSESSOR-"Possessor"
EX5: AURABORA-"E-Strings"/"Magic Kingdom"
EX6: MODULATOR-"Modulator"/"Timmy's Trance"
EX7: EX BREAKS
EX8: DR. JEKEL & MR. HYDE-"303 System"
EX9: FREDDIE FRESH-'Comatone' ep
EX10: RAY LOVE-"Arabian Warfare"
EX11: MODULATOR-'Painkiller' ep
EX12: PAUL MIX-"New Millenium"
EX13: ADVANCED WAVEFORM SYNTHESIS
EX14: DJ ESP-"The Earthworm Sings"
EX15: JOEY BELTRAM-'Code 6' ep
EX16:DAMON WILD/RAY LOVE-"Symphonies Of Love"
EX17: BIODREAMS ep
EX18:ELECTRIC INDIGO-"No Headroom"/"Skyway"
EX19: LAZER WORSHIPPERS ep
EX20: RISING SONS-"Afghan Acid"
EX21:THE EARTHWORM SINGS-"Natural Glow"
EX22: DIFFUSION-"Even Moaning"
EX23: NIGHTVISIONS ep

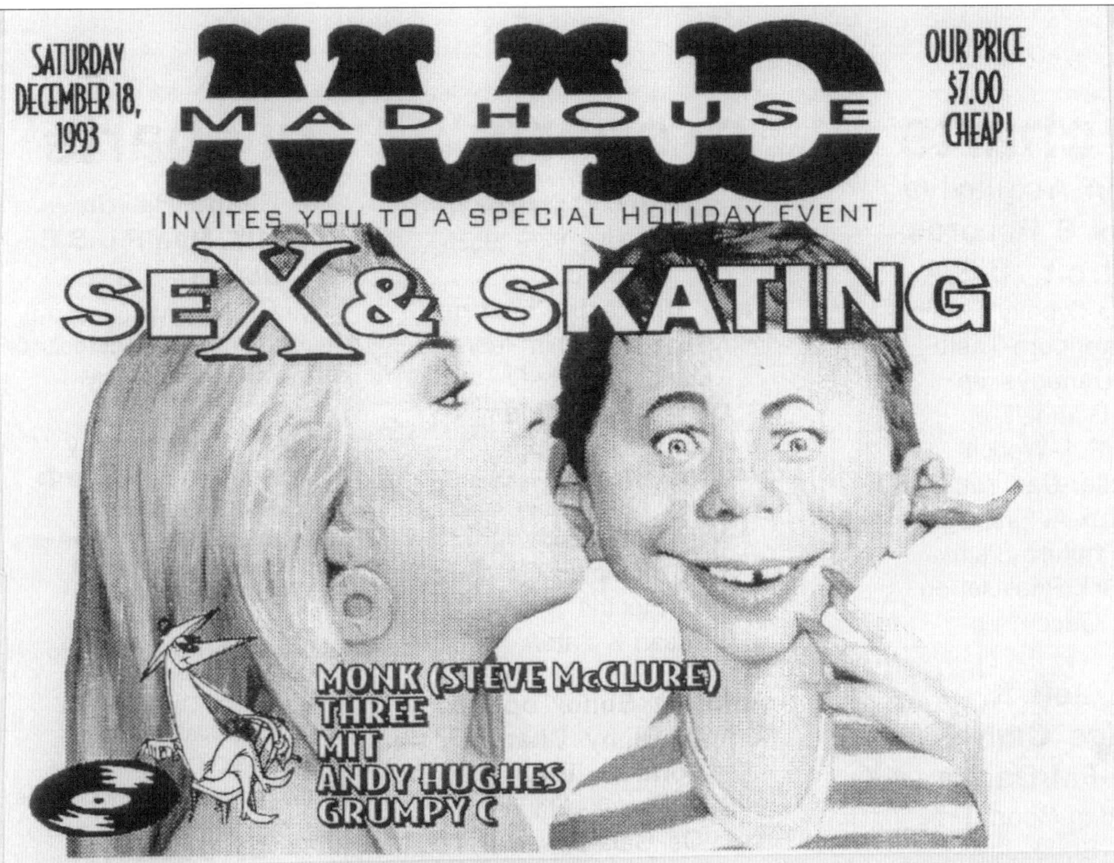
SATURDAY
DECEMBER 18,
1993
MAD
MADHOUSE
OUR PRICE
$7.00
CHEAP!
INVITES YOU TO A SPECIAL HOLIDAY EVENT
SEX & SKATING
MONK (STEVE McCLURE)
THREE
MIT
ANDY HUGHES
GRUMPY C

MAD HOUSE
INVITES YOU TO SEX & SKATING
AN ALL NIGHT UNDERGROUND EVENT
THIS IS DEEPSKATE #2. FOR THOSE OF YOU WHO MISSED SEEING YOUR FRIENDS BUST THEIR ASS LAST TIME, COME PARTY WITH US THIS TIME.
SATURDAY, DECEMBER 18, 1993
12:15am till 6:30 am
(just after midnight) (sun. morn)
PRIZES & CONTESTS/HOLIDAY FUN
AREA TO DANCE • AREA TO ROLLERSKATE
SKATE RENTAL FREE WITH ADMISSION
◆$7 at the door ◆ All Ages
◆Early Arrival Is Appreciated
DJ' spinning Disco & Skate tunes from the past along with the House & Techno of the future.
MAD DJ's
• MONK (STEVE McCLURE, Halluci-nation)
• THREE(Tampa) • ANDY HUGHES(Marz/Vibe)
• MIT(Tallahassee) • GRUMPY "C"(Tampa) & Friends
Event location:
UNITED SKATES OF AMERICA, INC.
5121 N. Armenia • Tampa, FL
MADHOUSE INFO
(813)323-0146
ARMENIA
HOWARD (ONE WAY)
HILLSBOROUGH
275
I-4
1 BLOCK S. OF HILLSBOROUGH ON ARMENIA
E
S N
W
FIRST CLASS
US POSTAGE
PAID
TAMPA, FL
PERMIT #1878
Birds DO IT, Bees DO IT, Come Watch
"The Bunny" DO IT
Intelligent Lighting & Projections by
SPY VS SPY
special thanks to:
jester emotion
SMART BAR BY
DANCING WARRIORS PRODUCTIONS
THE BLUE FUNK YBOR CITY
the drop shop
VINYL FRONTIER
HALLUCI-NATION
ONE NATION UNDERGROUND INVISIBLE
amp
Record Source
Liquid Culture
props
MOVE
the alternative record store

dj charts

John Acquaviva
Plus 8 Records
Detroit, U.S,A.

Fluke-Groovy Feelin'
Capricorn-Taste
Deneuve ep
Giannelli ep
P.J.-Work It
Veinmelter-Can You Feel It
Sysex-At First Light
Phuture-Slam
Chuck Phulasol ep
Oricom ep

Jeff K.
Edge Club 94
KDGE-FM/Dallas, TX

Luvdup-Good Time
Staxx-Joy
The Daou-Give Myself To You
Bjork-Big Time Sensuality
Dub Tribe-Mother Earth
The Other Two-Selfish
INXS/Ray Charles-Please (You Got That)
B.T.-Embracing The Future
RuPaul-Little Drummer Boy
YMO/808 State-Light In The Darkness

Andy Hughes
Marz (Cocoa Bch)/Vibe (Tpa)
Cocoa Beach, FL

All Boxed In-Happen
Bedrock feat. Kyo-For What You
Rabbit In The Moon-O.B.E. RMX
Ritmo Rivals-Americano Slide
Ralphie Rosario-You Used To Hold
Xen Mantra-Hollow Vibe
Delta Lady-Anything You Want
Berra-June Project
Power Fun-I Want
Vinyl Blair-Scratch 'N' Sniff

dj charts

Laurent Garnier
10 Tracks I Like Very Much Indeed
Wake Up/Paris, France

Rhythim Is Rhythim-Icon
Dark Comedy-Q
Dune-Desert Storm
Inner City-Ahnongay
X-313-World Sonic Domination
Essence Of Nature-Blue Orchid
Mazdaratti-Foxhunt
DJ Skull-Stomping Grounds
DBX-Electric Shock
Scan X-Satori

Ambient Soho/Top 10
compiled by Chantal
London, U.K.

Sun Electric-Kitchen
Banco De Gaia-Desert Wind
Chronological Harmonizations
Higher Intelligence Agency LP
Chapterhouse-Global Communication RMX
Astralasia-Pitched Up...LP
V/A-Feed Your Head
Pete Namlook-Definitive Collection
UVX-Elevate
Seefeel-Quique LP

DJ Chang
E. 909 St. Mag/Various
Orlando, FL

Rhythm Masters-Spanish Ritual
Oscar G.-Crib ep
Myakka-Escape From NY ep
Colourblind-Nothing Better
The Angel-Spirit Of Love
Creative Force-It's So Good
The Klubb Kidz-Come On
Georgie Porgie-All Because Of Me
Cro & Company-Just A Kiss
Simply Black-Give 'Em Love

dj charts

Richie Hawtin
Plastik Man/F.U.S.E.
Detroit, U.S.A.

4 New Plastik Man acetates
6 Rephlex White labels out soon on various size vinyl

DJ Moneypenny
Experimental Records
New York, NY

Pressure Generator-P.G. Ominous
Rising Sons-Cathedral
Sun Electric-Pitcheon
Evolve Now-Rhombus
Black Sun-The Classic Trip
Nightvision-Nuclear Sun
?-001-Daybreak
Infidus-Death By Stereo
X-313-Cybernator
Galaxy 2 Galaxy-Journey/Dragons

DJ Oddessy
Vagabond/Bloom/BBC
Philadelphia, PA

4 Hero-Golden Age RMXS
Dave Angel-Royal Techno ep
House Of Gypsies-Sume Sigh Say
Warped Kore-The Power
M Beat-Surrender
Funky Tribalist-T.B.A.
Caucasian Boy-Northern Lights
Bokaye'-A-Uo'-E
PJ-Work It
3 Alarm Project-The Alarm ep

Trevor Lamont
Zenith Productions
Wilmington, DE

Ricky Rouge-Strangelove RMX
Vinyl Blair-Scratch N' Sniff
Pancake-See The Stars
J.C./Jam Experience-(Love) The Deep Beat
Slam-Positive Education
Laurent Garnier-Wake Up
Mindwarp-One
Soundcraft-The Wibbler
P. Sample Proj.-Here What I'm Sayin'
Anthony Acid-Doe, Doe, Doe

TRiPmag CHARTS

Underground Dance Music Chart (in no particular order) Compiled by DJ Three

Nightvisions (EX 23)
Feedback-I'm For Real ep
Bandulu-Downward Glance
Balil-Island
Dub Tribe-Mother Earth
Underworld-Dogman Go Woof
Rhythim Is Rhythim-Icon
Laurent Garnier-Planet House
Vinyl Blair-Trancespotter
Future Sound of Hardcore-Euphoria

TRiP House Chart Compiled by DJ Jask

Creative Force-It's So Good
P.J.-Luv Will Make It Right
Robert Aaron-Sax In The Ozone
DJ Joe T.-Play With Voice
Smooth Touch-House Of Love
The Plan-Release It
Juicy Fruit-Liferaft
The Messenger-Main Vibe
Politix Of Dancin'-Release
Platinum Crew-Getting Me Hot

TRiP Ambient Chart Compiled by DJ Orion & Grumpy

Billie Ray Martin-4 Ambient Tales
Sun Electric-Kitchen LP
Morgan Fisher-Humtone #4
Astralasia-Univeria Zekt
Orange-Quarter ep
Future Sound of London-Cascade
Alien Community-Interdimensional Communication
Chapterhouse-Global Communications RMXS
Bjork-Anchor Song (Black Dog RMX)
Inky Blacknuss-Blacknuss

RECORD REVIEWS 12"/ep

APHEX TWIN- "On" ep (WARP/ UK) The prolific Richard James re-emerges in his Aphex Twin guise, his first on the Sheffield-based Warp label. This double purchase double pack contains four new tracks on the first disc- "On", "73-yips", "D-scape", and "Xepha"- ranging from hypnotic and ambient or melodic and lush on one end to percussive or hard experimental workouts on the other, all with that trademark Aphex distorted kick drum. The second disc sports three remixes of "On"; one each from **Reload** (with original "Twin", Tom Middleton), **u-ziq** (pronounced music), and **28** and a remix of "D-scape". Reminscent of "X-Tal" from **Selected Ambient Works** but faster, with a fragile piano melody instead of synths in its original form, "On"'s remixes reconstruct the track from a simple reworking to unintelligible beatfree ambience. More brilliant experimental techno from the Aphex Twin. **(DJ*)**

FUTURE SOUND OF LONDON- "Cascade" (Virgin/UK) After the interesting release under the pseudonym **Amorphous Androgynous, FSOL** return as themselves taking their fusion of experimental soundscapes and very danceable percussion to the next level. "Cascade" is a 36 minute theme divided into six parts. Part One is probably the best for the dancefloor with its combination of emotional melody and ambience with irresistible drum tracks. Parts 2-6 each focus on different elements to each extreme. Tech-heads will recognize the clever sample of the classic blue label by **The Source.** We're anxiously awaiting the full LP due in January. In the meantime, play this very loud. **(D3)**

THE SOURCE-"The Source Experience" (R&S/Belgium) Robert Leiner follows his "Organized Noise" ep with five tracks of more experiemental music. A couple of tracks are a lot harder than most of "Organized Noise", but are still really good. Long and trancy while still having a rough edge, the best is the title track. A required purchase. **(GC)**

DERRICK CARTER-"Sound Patrol ep" (Organico) We first heard Chicago DJ/Producer/Remixer **Derrick Carter** from some friends this past Spring after hearing his **Cajmere** track, "Wet Dream", with it's "I ain't fucked all week" refrain. Six months, a slew of DJ gigs worldwide, and a charttopping remix later, this former **Symbols & Instruments** member gets his own thig and out pops this ep. With a pumping kick drum and a slight tribal house feel, "The Griffin's Song" dances melodically with a mellow keyboard line and 303 sequence, while "Do Things Dance" serves it up chunky and funky with a sample nabbed from **Die Warzau**'s "Strike To The Body". Flip the vinyl over, and Derrick carjacks you to Detroit with the experimental "Storm Watch", closing out with a syncopated, piano house groover, "Lachesis Vs. Atropos". A great ep of inspired tracks with a lot of character and diversity from one of the underground's best, yet underrated producers. **(PW)**

P.J.-"Work It" ep (Stickman) Once again Paul Jacobs is back and does not dissapoint. Four fresh flavourish tracks-all good. "Luv Will Make It Right" is on a very cool jazz tip with organ sounds straight from the soul. The vocal sample may be old, but it's good and well used. "Work It", the second track is a tribaldelic hopuse cut that will stomp any floor-believe dat! On the jazz side, "All Over Jazz" and "P.J.'s Groove" are two slammin' acid jazz tracks with a hip-hop appeal to them. Old school? Try "P.J.'s Groove", you'll definitely reminisce on the beats... If you like House and jazz the way I do, get this! **(Jask)**

INNER CITY-"Ahnongay" 10" (Six by 6/UK) This is the shit. Hard house beats with cool percussion and keyboard lines like only **Kevin Saunderson** can do. Reminiscent of his **Tronikhouse** work, it also has a weird Bob Dylan-like vocal sample. One of the best records out. Excellent. **(GC)**

DJ EFX-"The Essence Of Sound"

(Pound America) Debut release from Pound America, the newest member of the San Fran-based 3rd Floor family. Four DJ EFX produced tracks-two jazz/hip-hop and two breakbeat fueled garage tracks. More releases are soon to come and by the looks of things, should be ones to watch for. **(CM)**

NAOMI-"State of Mind" (RMXS) (Basic Beat/Holland) "State Of Mind" comes in four mixes, one breakbeat oriented and three house mixes. Cool organ riff and a funky, groovy feel. **(GC)**

FULL MOON ENTERTAINMENT VS. LEMON 8-"Outta Sight" (Basic Beat/Holland) Thumping melodic house with good changes and lots of organ. **(GC)**

DUB TRIBE-"Mother Earth" (Organico)/"Trip Ta Funk" (Ultra-Ethereal) These two 12"'s offer a look at two distinct sides of San Francisco's incredible Dub Tribe. "Mother Earth" displays the group's spiritual side with a groovy tribal breakbeat, subtle trancy synths, and some acid to help spread the message to reclaim our planet with peace, love, understanding, unity, and respect as only the West Coast can do in three mixes. "Trip Ta Funk" shows Dub Tribe in full-on party mode with a funky house joint that reminds one of **Nu Yorican Soul** in flavour. **(PW)**

B.T.-"Embracing The Future" (Music Now) Out of the Washington, D.C. record shop, Music Now step out in a big way with two very West Coast sounding tracks that are probably best described as progressive trance. Both "Embracing The Future" and "Deeper Sunshine" combine elements of melodic trance/ambience with funky tribal breaks and anthem styled climaxes. A very big buzz on this one- check it out. **(D3)**

VIRTUOSO SYNTHESIS-"EOS"/ "Syssex" (Wax Brothers) Yet another slab of vinyl from Florida, this one the debut from **DJ Todd** of **Simon's Innermind** club in **Gainesville** on presumably their own label, Wax Brothers(?). "Syssex" is electro progressive house with some interesting vocal samples...some ethnic, some soulful and gated, then some bass to accent the beats, all topped off by an uplifting house style piano. "EOS" is on the funky tribal tip with lots of layers of percussion phasing into progressive style synth arrangements. **(D3)**

JUICY FRUIT-"Liferaft" (Definitive) Get ready 2 B saved from the waves! "Liferaft" will keep your head out of dangerous waters and make you inhale the deep freshness of the Detroit house vibe. Very funky in a way, but nonetheless, this is deeep! The **John Acquaviva** mix is so good with its **Scritti Politti** sample to compliment the fat taste; but hold your horses, that's not all. This track also gets the **Stickmen** treatment, and my oh my, they do it again. House to the bone! A splendid work of art. Mad props to the Definitive crew, they just keep getting better and better. **(Jask)**

GROOVE CORE featuring NICOLE-"You Know" (Dub) An excellent newcomer debut from Miami's Mitch Dupre'. Very deep penatrating house with superb vocals by Nicole. Four mixes ranging from deep sleep to damaging dubness with cool trancy sounds. DJ's on the dubby garage tip will dig this one. **(Jask)**

meandJACK-"Viva House" (Jack001/UK) Excellent British styled old school techno on this one-sided 12". An ambient synth intro gives way to midtempo breakbeats and electro elements, then...<u>massive, long</u> sweeps of deafening bass, a big horn breakdown, followed by more beats and bass round it off. Wicked track. **(D3)**

JUNO REACTOR-"Laughing Gas" (NovaMute/UK) A track and a remix from the group's forthcoming NovaMute album, <u>**Transmissions**</u>, this is an oscillating, acid-grooved slice of good commercial trance with a cool rolling bassline. **Youth**'s On The Other Side Mix is more atmospheric, moody, and minimal as it swirls around your head. **(PW)**

BLUE-"4 of 7" (Sabres Of Paradise/UK) Four tracks of real typical **Sabres Of Paradise** material. All four are rather long, dubby, chunky, and full of percussion. No new ground is being broken but they are digging deeper than most people. **(GC)**

DATACLOUD-"Dreaming Of Phobos" (Probe) Five track ep from **Plus 8** subsidiary. "Birth of Gaspra" is exceptionally good with a droning pulse and well done acid line although there are no drums. "2020202" is a frantic acid workout that moves along rather quickly. **(GC)**

CREATIVE FORCE-"It's So Good (Suburban) Another hottie stright out of London from House Producer of the Moment, **Victor Simonelli.** Very, very, oh so good is the word for this slammin' house track that is so undeniable with it's soothing vocals, courtesy of George Eliezer; and if that's not enough, this also has a **Tommy Musto** club mix to compliment this well-produced record. Oh, and one more thing- there's a previously unreleased accapella version on the b-side. Only time will tell how many people will sample this smooth vocal. **(Jask)**

LEFTFIELD & LYDON-"Open Up" (Hard Hands/UK) Yep, Leftfield with **Johnny "Rotten" Lydon**...and it totally works! The track is a heavy, urgent groove with a most effective full vocal from Mr. Lydon. An instrumental is included which is more trademark Leftfield-with extra tribal percussion taking the place of the vocal. Give the vocal side a shot! I haven't seen it get a negative response yet... Even further out are the **Sabres of Paradise** and **Dust Brothers** remixes (on a separate 12"). The Sabres' I Hate Pink Floyd Mix, a reference to a t-shirt Lydon wore during a **Sex Pistols** TV performance) is straight up dub, while the Dust Brothers' is not quite as hip-hop as previous work but still executed in a heavy percussive trance style. **(D3)**

POLITIX OF DANCIN'-"Release" (Strictly Rhythm) DJ Digit and **DJ EFX** are at it again with the West Coast flavour of House to spice up your dance floor. This time they bring you a stomping track with four mixes, two of which are tribalistic versions by DJ EFX. Now on the Digit side there are the 3rd Floor mixes that are my pick and the ones to play, Strictly bumpin' house with vocals that are just simply bad-ass- best vocals I've heard in awhile. This is my favorit Strictly Rhythm record at the moment, definitely House for the body, mind, and soul. A must. **(Jask)**

DEATH BEFORE DISCO/SCUBA DEVILS-"Ministry"/"Celestial Symphony" (NovaMute/UK) From Belfast's **Sugarsweet** club comes this split 12" from **DJ David Holmes**. "Ministry" is a pulsating, hi-hat driven acid builder like **"Rez" Goes To Ireland** that rises to an anthemic synth climax before journeying further into the depths of analog bliss. Holmes teams up with his **Dub Federation** mates on the flip, a uplifting progressive trance bounder. **(PW)**

FUSE-"Train Tracs" (WARP/Wax Trax!/TVT) Remixed from the **Dimension Intrusion** LP, "Train Tracs" comes in a variety of mixes; on the import is the original, the harder "Train Abuse", and the long, dreamy, mostly ambient "Kaboose." The domestic CD single **(why NO vinyl!?!)** contains still more mixes, plus a mix by **Mark Gage** (Vapour Space) that is wonderful. Essential no matter what. **(GC)**

STASIS/NURON 12" (Likemind/UK) A split 12" of traditional pure electronic music. Very Detroit sounding. Scrumptious minimal techno from **B12** and friends. **(GC)**

?-"Daybreak"/"Drums Of Freedom" (001 White) Sent in the latest mailout from Northcott this 12" is a mystery- although we have our theories. "Daybreak" is a slice of uplifting acid trance in two forms, one straight up, the other drummy and percussive. The flipside is a boomy, deep tribal techno biscuit with an indecipherable slowed down voice in the breakdown. A killer on a big system. **(PW)**

KREEM featuring JENNIFER WILLIAMS-"Now Is The Time" (KMS) A well-produced deep house track by the man called **Kevin Saunderson**. The vocals here are simply full-on phat; don't know what this **Jennifer Williams** looks like, but this girl can sing! Four mixes-all good. My pick is the club vocal- simply penetrating house with a good vibe, but disco/ house DJ's should check out **Terrence Parker**'s Seven Grand Disco Dub Mix. Don't forget your bell bottoms and platforms. **(Jask)**

CHUCK PHULASOL (Definitive)

Four tracks full of Funk,
Full of Soul,
Full of Disco,
Full of Hip-hop,
Full of Tribal,
Full of Spunk,
Phul-on funky.
Nuff said. **(Jask)**

T.P.M.-"Boogaloo" (Stickman) One track, five different mixes by 'The People Movers'. Check out **Nick Holder**'s Underground Mix and **David 'Las Americas' Alvarado**'s Lord Sadat's Mix- both are definite floor movers. This is deep house taken beyond another level by the Stickmen. Much props. **(Jask)**

RIOT SQUAD II-"Nonshlentustokken" (DJ Gizmo RMX) (12 Gauge) It's baaaack! Prepare to die. **(PW & Jask)**

INKY BLACKNUSS-"Blacknuss" (Sabrettes/UK) Alex Knight of **Fat Cat Records** releases a rather experimental techno platter that was probably too weird for Sabres Of Paradise. The Andience Mix is ambient with a style all of its own. The rest is pretty well out there. There needs to be more records like this. **(GC)**

ELECTRO MUSIC UNION-ep (Metatone/UK) First release from a new UK label. A four-track ep with a mostly warm electronic feel. "Vapourous Vacation" is the highlight, an excursion into house/techno and ambience. Hopefully the rest of the releases are as good. **(GC)**

PINK ELLN & ATOM HEART-"Elektronikka" (Rising High/UK) Two twenty-three minute excursions in techno, each very experimental and full of aural hypnosis. Said to be recorded live, "Electronikka" is seamlessly split into two parts the first is mainly synth and drums all merging, creating very atmospheric, tone-like percussion. Part 2 is more straight ahead in its percussion, mixed with ambient electronic sounds. "Electronique" begins with a long ambient intro eventually being joined by a kick drum and hi-hat patterns. It's difficult to paint a picture with words for this type of record. How about, "It's really cool." **(D3)**

BJORK-"One Day" (One Little Indian/UK) This 10" comes with **Sabres Of Paradise** mixes: one at 105bpm that has a really cool kick drum and the other at 52.5bpm that is extremely dubby. Both have Bjork's unique vocalizing and Andrew Weatherall's weirdness. **(GC)**

BJORK-"Anchor Song"/"Come to Me" (One Little Indian/UK) Another remix 10", this time 'bitten by **Black Dog**'. A very different interpretation of the Icelandic princess' work. **(GC)**

DANCE FEVER-"Out On the Dancefloor" (Definitive) Dance Fever goes funky on us this time... Karl's Motion Mix is very disco-y with all that funk and spunk feeling. My favourite mix, the Piled Witch Mix, is just wicked. Made up of just a hard kick, flanging hi-hats, a deep distorting bassline, and some cool tribal sounds. The other side features features a strictly West Coast style, tribal house in effect mix from **Las Americas** and a deep circus type of house mix by **John Acquaviva.** Not what I expected, but I like it. **(Jask)**

LaTRECE-"I Want To Thank You"

(Area 10) A deep soulful house track produced by **MK** on his long dormant Area 10 label with three mixes to choose from for your listening and dancing pleasure. Definitely not a record to pass up, if you are into deep house. MK does it again! **(Jask)**

JIDE MAX PROJECT-"Culture Groove" (MicMac) Yes, this is the label that brought you **Two Without Hats** back in the days; remember "The Breeze" and "Try Yazz"? This cool release from Mic Mac-**no lie**- is two deep house tracks from **Jide "Pb" Max.** "Without You" has a very San Fransisco-y tribal mix to it but the Shelter Mix is my favorite. This will take you be\ack to the earlier house days with it's smooth seducing organ sound. Welcome back, Mic Mac! **(Jask)**

FIRES OF ORK-S/T (Apollo/Belgium) Pete Namlook and **Geir Jenssen** (Biosphere) team up for a rather upbeat record for Apollo, but still deeply ambient. This moody house song has yet **another** Blade Runner sample. Experimental chillout with the accent on **mental. (GC)**

KEN ISHII-2X12" White label (R&S-Apollo/Belgium) Ken Ishii follows up his excellent "Garden On The Palm" ep with six tracks of pulsing techno-3 on R&S that are experimental and 3 on Apollo, the Apollo 12" being more accessible despite its ambience. **(GC)**

BILLIE RAY MARTIN-"4 Ambient Tales" (Apollo/Belgium) Mrs. Martin continues her rather cool collaborations by hooking up with **The Grid** for four extremely ambient songs. Mostly accapella with very minimal instrumentation, sparse steel guitar and synth washes provide the backdrop for Billie Ray's soul-tinged vocals. All four songs are rather short with radio edits and instrumentals spread out over 2 pieces of vinyl. **(GC)**

DAMON WILD-"Nightvision" ep (EX) Another analog masterpiece from Damon Wild and his Experimental label. "Nuclear Sun" is the hardtrance soundtrack to the next Ridley Scott sci-fi thriller with its mood altering 303 and forceful bassline. Only clocking in at 5:40, this could only be improved by being longer-so buy two! "Melatonin" is more uplifting with lush synths and an atmospheric break. **(PW)**

ANTHONY ACID-"Phony Alibis" (Atlas) With that kind of name, I thought this record would be all 303 acid, but I was wrong. The b-sides are the prize here, "Doe, Doe, Doe" and "Tribal Souls". Both have very cool tribal sounds and wicked synth lines...Quite appealing. **(Jask)**

LP/COMPILATIONS

SABRES OF PARADISE-Sabresonic (WARP/UK) Full length debut from **Andy & Co.** (although it may seem like some of their remixes might be long enough to be an album). Seven tracks on the vinyl plus an extra beatless version of "Smokebelch" on the CD. This LP ranges from the subtle ambience of "Clock Factory" to the slow dub of "RSD", to the thumping trance of "Smokebelch". Overall **Sabresonic** is great, very satisfying. You can be sure there is lots of percussion and reggae-inflected tracks. In the liner notes they "would definitely not like to thank God", but I'm sure they thank Jah for the basslines. **(GC)**

3 PHASE- Schlangenfarm (NovaMute) Germany has certainly dominated the Underground press this year with its smooth pulsing, emotional trance sound. Overshadowed by their counterparts in Frankfurt, Berliners have recently had a turn in the spotlight with much attention on labels like **MFS** and artists such as **Cosmic Baby.** Steadily producing quality music for years is the Tresor label and acts like 3 Phase. Perhaps best known for "Der Klang Der Familie", 3 Phase's first full-length LP, **Schlangenfarm,** is an intelligent blend of slow atmospheric trance, acid house, and classic Detroit-fueled grooves. A post-modernist '90's soundtrack that is equally brilliant in the Lazy Boy, behind the wheel, or on the dancefloor. **(DJ*)**

V/A-Excursions In Ambience: The Second Orbit (Astral Werks) Picking up where the first edition of this series left off, **The Second Orbit** further probes this rapidly expanding genre of music with a guided tour through The Orb's **Wau! Mr. Modo** (now InterModo) label compiled by Mr. Modo himself. Looking to the future as well as the past, the compilation features tracks either remixed by Dr. Lx & Thrash **(The Grid, Maurizio, Material)**, only on limited edition 12" released by Wau! **(Megatonk)**, or previously unreleased **(WFO, Schizophrenia, Locust, & Autocreation)**, highlighting the small label's commitment to ambient excellence. An essential second chapter to Astral Werks' guide to spirituality in technology. **(DJ*)**

THE ORB-Live Orb '93/Evil Bro 39' (InterModo-Island/UK) Recorded live at shows in Copenhagen, the Glastonbury Festival, and Tokyo, Dr. Lx and Crew close out the year and celebrate a new deal with Island with this quadruple record set documenting the live Orb experience. With the cover art spoofing Pink Floyd's **Animals** with a stuffed sheep hovering over yet another power station, all your Orb favorites are here-along with two new tracks "Plateau" and "Valley"-totally redone in a deep(er), splifflicated dub that flows into your subconcious mind like a thick, resinated haze. Completely essential. **(DJ*)**

V/A-Transmitting From Heaven (Exist Dance) L.A.'s enigmatic **Exist Dance,** in a relatively short span of time, has positioned themselves to be the next West Coast label to garner world-wide recognition. This compilation gathers most of the label's releases (many now out-of-print and a bonus track). Recorded in **Heaven** (their home studio), **Tom Chasteen** and **Mike Kandel** have turned out an array of aural treats ranging from the atmospheric, ethnically laced breakbeats of **Tranquility Bass, Eden Transmission and Up Above The World's** tasty acid flavoured trance experiments, to the multiple flavors of the High Lone-

some Sound System. Fresh and unique, **Transmitting...** shows why this label is next to blow up- their tracks' timeless quality. **(DJ*)**

V/A-California Dreaming (ffrr) The crew at **ffrr** saw it fit to compile some of the more outstanding tracks that have come from California, spawning the **"West Coast Sound"** tag. Included are tracks from now-established labels like **Zoe Magik, Exist Dance, Hardkiss, TCX/N-Fusion, C-Level, and Trip 'N Spin.** Definitely worth picking up. **(CM)**

V/A-Global Cuts (Astral Werks) Concieved as a vehicle for tribal house inventors and **Wonka Beats** founders **Remy Unger** and **Sven Van Hees**, this **R&S** sublabel has quickly established itself as a home for these two Dutchmen's powerful tribal percussion and progressive house workouts as well as other artists that are just left-of-centre. Opening with the massive first release, **"Piano Power"**, this compilation briefly goes through the label's catalogue from Unger and Van Hees' **X-Statik** and **Soul Searchers** pseudonyms and the driving marching percussion of **Capricorn**'s "20Hz", to Detroit's **Eddie "Flashin'" Fowlkes** and London's **Fabi Paras**. Each track is uniquely primal, pumping, and uplifting as only Global Cuts can provide. Highly recommended. **(PW)**

LISA CARBON & FRIENDS-S/T (Sonic) The sleeve says "experimental post-techno swing-file under warped acid". Think 808's and analogue synths meet swingin' jazz and groovin' funk. Warped indeed, but wicked. Listen with an open mind. **(DJ*)**

CABARET VOLTAIRE-Plasticity/ International Language (Instinct) Marking two years since their last domestic release, electronic innovators Cabaret Voltaire continue their re-definition and reinterpretation of the genre they helped to inspire with **Plasticity** and **International Language**. Not unlike 1991's bleep-influenced **Colours**, the Cabs explore the realm of both deep trance and ambient soundscapes on the first two parts of this trilogy. Combining elements of House, Dub, and ambience with organic and synthesized sounds, smooth beats, and catchy hooks, both releases ooze of warm electronic vibes and simple elegance. With the final part of this trilogy due in February, these releases do no deserve to be slept on despite their long-standing import status. **(PW)**

AIR-You (Rising High) Originally released on Germany's **FAX** label, this **Pete Namlook** creation can be described in one word- beautiful. Not as ultra ambient as his other releases, **You** is more atmospheric with lush chords and lots of feeling. Still extremely chilled out, but more of a complete album with a beginning, middle, and end. Excellent. **(GC)**

DIVINATION-Ambient Dub, Vol. 1 (Subharmonic) From a mysterious New York label comes this relatively ignored, but very cool ambient gem. A marriage of pure atmosphere, dub basslines, and beats, **Bill Laswell** and friends explore the ambient environment with this eight track experiment in chillout grooves. Between mind-altering ambience to lush rhythm-oriented trance excursions, Ambient Dub, Vol. 1 is definitely a collection of music to wrap your head around. **(DJ*)**

HEAVENLY MUSIC CORPORATION-In a Garden Of Eden (Silent) Named after a track from a Brian Eno/Robert Fripp collaboration, the **Heavenly Music Corporation** takes you on a trip to a far away place where your body is only excess baggage, only your mind and soul are needed. Once spiritually transported through "Cloud Structure Silence" **In A Garden Of Eden** proceeds to relax your mind, cleansing your soul of its negative energies, and massaging you with its almost beatfree ambience. Upon your "Reentry", all parts-body, mind, and soul are reconnected, realigned, and rejuvinated. **(DJ*)**

ONE DOVE-Morning Dove White (ffrr) Imagine Sunscreem's **Lucia Holm** and Primal Scream's **Bobby Gillespie** getting together with super DJ/producer **Andy Weatherall**, locking themselves in a studio for a week with their record collections, a baleful of primo skunk and coming out of the haze with an album inspired by all their favorite records rolled into 8 tracks. OK, now that's **One Dove**-sweet femalevocals, celestial melodies, processed guitars, rumbly dub basslines, and production, along with strong <u>songs</u>. Despite their Glaswegian roots and choice of producer comparing them to the Primals, the group's talent and Weatherall's top notch production sets **Morning Dove White** as one of the most enjoyable Club/Indie hybrid LP's of 1993. Ambient/chillout DJ's will find many of the tracks useful while the rest may have to settle for the remix double pack with mixes by Weatherall, **Slam,** and **Hardkiss Music. (PW)**

V/A-Blue Underground (Ultra-Ethereal) Last year at this time, the (North)East Coast scene was playing harder, faster, more acidy tracks while DJ's in Florida were into breakbeats and the U.K. progressive house sound. A year later and the two scenes, although miles apart seem to have more in common musically than ever. **Blue Underground** documents the best of the East Coast scene by bringing together tracks from **X-Crash** (Bklyn), **Josh Wink** (Philly), **Damon Wild & DJ Repete** (NYC), **Lenny Dee, Glitch** (Balto), **Koenig Cylinders/Disintegrator** (L.I.), and other lesser known, but no less talented American artists in an exploration into the harder, deeper side as well as things atmospheric, tribal, and trancy. A well-concieved compilation. **(PW)**

V/A-NovaMute, Version 1.1 (NovaMute) Born following the demise of the **Rhythm King** label, Mute Records' in-house dance imprinthas quickly gained credibility by releasing top tracks from artists- established or not- worldwide. Originally to be a U.K.-only label, **NovaMute** forged a U.S. distribution deal, givng the underground a domestic outlet for this worldwide flavour. **Version 1.1** displays this planetary tastefulness from London to Berlin to Detroit and back, compiling the best of the label's U.K. releases and teasers from some upcoming full-length projects. Whether you like it hard and acidy, deep and groovy, ambient, experimental, or all of the above, this compilation puts it al together in one wicked double CD package. **(PW)**

PLASTIKMAN- Sheet One (NovaMute) **Richie Hawtin** returns as a new alter ego for this full-length album of experimental ambient techno. Smooth and sleek in its minimal simplicity, this **IS** the future-now. Also check out the import 12" with **"Spastik"** and **"Gak"** remixes. **(DJ*)**

EARTHRISE-Deeper Than Space (Silent) A somewhat hit-or-miss 5-track LP from California ambient artist Adam Douglas, aka Earthrise. I prefer the more drifting, spacey cuts here as opposed to the dubby, Orb-like tracks. Very nice guide to better ambient listening in the liner notes. Respect. **(DJ*)**

V/A-Chill Out (Instinct) Ever since the **KLF** and the **Orb** brought the genre of ambient electronic music to the post-rave generation, it has become techno's most exciting and rapidly growing movements. From total beatfree ambience to bubbling, cushioned beats, and subtle pulsing trance, **Chill Out** has represented this music's global influence by featuring artists as diverse geographically as well as musically. Not just a compilation, this collection assembles as primer which documents the ambient genre's innovators as well as the future. Feed your head and let the technology guide your spirit. **(DJ*)**

HUMAN MESH DANCE-Hyaline/ O'MICRON-Symbolis/EVOLVE NOW-The Dream (Instinct)/PROTOTYPE 909-Acid Technology (Sonic) Looking back two years ago, many people were wondering whether Americans could make electronic music on the same level as the Europeans. With the acknowledgement and respect given to American artists such as **Moby, Young American Primitive, Vapour Space** and the **Hardkiss Family,** it is now more than apparently obvious we can. Instinct now presents the debut of their newest crop of American musicmakers, first exposed on their Chill Out compilation. Probing into ambient territories, **Human Mesh Dance** molds organic textures and dense electronics into mind-nourishing and body-soothing soundscapes; **O'Micron** explores the realm of atmospheric, emotional, German-style hardtrance; recorded live to DAT in a weekend, NYC's **Prototype 909**'s debut is a smooth, deep and hardtrance experience into analogue acid of the most hypnotic variety. Nice experimental hardcore.; Perhaps the surprise of the foursome is the moody, breakbeat-driven trance of **Evolve Now**. Combining haunting melodies with chugging breaks, this classically-trained, Aphex Twin/LFO influenced Romantic composer creates a very unique and special ep of spiritual, dramatic breakbeat moods. A must regardless of your inclination towards breakbeats. **(PW)**

V/A-Trance Odyssey (MicMac) We have to admit we were a bit skeptical when this came into the office, but we flipped it over and saw who were all involved- **Keoki, High Lonesome Sound System, Freddy Fresh, Tetsu Inoue, Joey Beltram**.... potential! Boy were we wrong! Spanning the range of styles from sweet, melodic trance and building acid pulsers to jumpy house-fueled groovers and journeys into atmosphere, this could very well be one of the most overlooked CD compilations of the year. Try this! **(PW)**

V/A-Cream Of Tomato (Moonshine) London's **Tomato** (pronounced "Toh-mah-toh") **Records** was created two years ago by a pair of frustrated Virgin A&R types. Fusing disco, funk, and American house with a swinging London attitude, the label has created quite the stir in progressive house circles with tracks from **Pascal's Bongo Massive, Infinite Wheel,** and **Nature Boy** (all included here). As always, Moonshine Music assembles the pick of the harvest, bringing this groovin' label's crop to our market. **(PW)**

V/A-From Here To Tranquility (Silent) If there was to be a center of the ambient music scene in the United States it would have to be San Francisco. With all the music coming out the Bay Area with such an atmospheric quality and labels like Silent releasing so much ambient music it just has to be. **From Here To Tranquility** is a 10 track compilation showcasing ambient artists from San Francisco, including **Spacetime Continuum, Heavenly Music Corporation,** and **Psychic TV.** A very big must-have for ambient explorers and open ears. **(DJ*)**

MULTIMEDIA/VIDEO

Alien Dreamtime (City Of Tribes) A companion to **Spacetime Continuum**'s **Alien Dreamtime** CD out on **Astral Werks,** this longform video documents the live ambient improvisation of Spacetime and "raps" from noted author, ethnobotanist, radical sociophilosopher, and technoshaman **Terence McKenna** at a party in San Francisco this past February. More than a performance "documentary", **Alien Dreamtime** intersplices live footage from the event with the actual computer-generated visuals used at the show by **Rose X Media**. Deeper than just your average post-party chillout video, this is a multimedia education into the spiritual-ity of this culture which more people in this scene should learn about. For more information or to order, write City Of Tribes @ 63 Fountain St , S.F., CA 94114, or call 1.800.767.4748 **(PW)**

Feet First- continued from page 3

Some last bits before we bid you adieu for the holidays: you may have noticed that we moved. Not far, just upstairs, but please note we are now in **Suite 5**. Your mail is important to us, so insure it gets to us by adjusting your files now. We apologize for our severe tardiness this issue, it's hard at times to get all of us together to work on this thing, this has been one of those times. Thanks, we'll make it up to you right away in '94 with a new issue just after the new year. Peace! The **TRiP** Staff!

McKenna, continued from Page 13

of computers. The people who are professionals and are paid to predict how this technology will impact upon us have been wrong every time. I can remember when PC's were introduced in the late '70's, everyone said, "This will be the death of literacy.", and in fact, PC's created the greatest boom in publishing since the printing press. So they don't understand the effect of these technologies. Multimedia is setting the stage for virtual multimedia interaction and this is part of a very important cultural trend, which is the trend towards the dematerialization of reality. In other words, capitalism cannot save itself if it insists on dealing product made out of matter. Capitalism's only hope is to go virtual and deal in objects made of light and surfaces. This can only be done in a kind of cyberspace that becomes more and more explicit. The success of television in warehousing millions of people and taking them out of the loop of political decision-making is certainly is being read as a green light for the development of ever more immersive technology. Now these technologies will be used by the establishment to pacify people, control people, so forth and so on. But if the thing develops correctly, the amount of information and potential search power that will go into the hands of the individual will impower anarchistic ideas and attitudes far more than it will impower scenarios of control. The PC itself was never intended for civilian use. The original chip was developed as a guidance system for a Sparrow missile in the middle 70's and it did not make Navy design specs. So they spent several millions of dollars developing this thing and they were going to junk it because it couldn't control a missile. and somebody dragged it out of the wastebasket and said, "You know, you could put a keyboard and a screen on this thing and you could sell people a little tiny machine."

T: It seems like your only constraint is how fast your machine is, how much memory you've got, and how big your hard drive is as to what you can accomplish these days...

McKenna: And your imagination... If people get their hands on this technology, it doesn't matter if you're a black woman in some ghetto, or a poor rural person in Minnesota, but you have a vision, you can intimate that vision with that machine. So I think that it's for creativity and anarchy and democratic values and diversity and all that, an enormous boost. And it's a drug, it's another drug. They don't want to face this because they make so much money out of all these drugs. TV is an enormous moneymaking enterprise and so are computational machines.

Terence McKenna has a Mac IIci w/CD-ROM.

Essential Phuture Reading:

A Quick Guide To The Works Of Terence McKenna

With brother, Dennis:

The Invisible Landscape

Psilocybin: The Magic Mushroom Grower's Guide

By himself:

The Archaic Revival

Food Of The Gods

True Hallucinations

Aphex Twin, continued from Page 11

AT: There are some quite new tracks on there, but a lot of them are two, three years old and have been digitally mastered and stuff. It's quite clean it sounds a lot different compared to some of the other stuff.

T: I understand you've been DJ'ing some ambient rooms and such as of late...

AT: Yeah, I do some small parties and stuff for friends... **Mixmaster Morris** and I make a really good team DJ'ing; I sort of classify him as liking the more uplifting, 'nice' music. I really like that stuff as well, but I just prefer the darker side, more disturbing ambient music.

T:What is the lowdown on your recording situation?

AT: The deal hasn't been signed yet, but the deal is with Warp, which is U.K. and Europe, exclusively as Aphex Twin and Polygon Window, which won't be used; Rephlex is for all the other names I may use for the U.K. and Europe, and Sire is exclusive for everything, but only in America.

T: Is there going to be an Aphex Twin release in America soon?

AT: In the U.K., it's a 4-track single and a 4-track remix of the single, which'll have 2 remixes I've done and 2 remixes by two other artists. **(the Vertebral Ridge and Madreporic Plate ep's)** In America, both those records will come out on Sire, but they'll both be missing a track because of a chart thing over there.

T: Rephlex is your own label that you run with your friend Grant...

AT: We've been working really, really hard with some good demos, but we only like to put out the stuff we really, really like and think is fucking excellent. We didn't want to turn Rephlex into some avant-garde label like **Nonesuch**, so we've got people like **Kosmik Kommando** who do more "conventional" techno, which we think will make a good compliment to the label. Grant's like the busiest man in the world, with his girlfriend and a couple friends, it's a lot of work.

T: What do you like as far as current techno goes?

AT: My favorites are usually older things and there's not much that comes out these days which I think, "Yeah, this is fucking good." I like a lot of things by **Pete Namlook**, the **Air** lp, bits and bobs like that; **Dr. Atmo** and his album **(Silence)**, people like that I sort of favor at the moment. I'd say my favorite artists at the moment are some of the people we have releases coming from on Rephlex.

T: What about your live show?

AT: I don't think I've ever done a bad show anywhere. Any bad show I didn't really enjoy. I don't care, usually, if crowds hate it or love it, because I'm a bit of a selfish person, really, and I only do gigs because I like to hear my stuff loud.

Expect domestic release of the Aphex Twin's 'On' ep just after the first of the new year...

NOVAMUTE
NovaMute : Version 1.1
3PHASE
SCHLANGENFARM
plastikman
sheet one
JUNO REACTOR
NOVAMUTE
Version 1.1:
Double length CD featuring previously unreleased full length and 12" mixes from 3 Phase, Spirit Feel and Plastikman (Richie Hawtin)
3 PHASE
Schlangenfarm
A seductive brew of classic Detroit techno and cutting edge trance...
PLASTIKMAN
Sheet One
More cerebral madness from Plus 8 techno/acid guru, Richie Hawtin
JUNO REACTOR
Transmissions
Ben Watkins confronts us with the phuture of high energy trance; finally music as modern as it is timeless...
Also available on NovaMute:
Tresor II Berlin-Detroit "A Techno Alliance", Probe-"Mission USA",
Berlin 1992 A Tresor Compilation-"The Techno Sound Of Berlin", GTO-"Love Is Everywhere E.P."
© 1993 NovaMute. Manufactured for and distributed by Tommy Boy Music Inc.

13

Free In Florida! $1.50 Elsewhere
TRIP
V13.0
FLORIDA'S UPFRONT DANCE CULTURE MAGAZINE
A TRiP EXCLUSIVE!!!!
A GUY CALLED GERALD
CABARET VOLTAIRE
THOMAS HECKMANN
ONE DOVE
SYSTEM 7
JBL

DJ MIX TAPES

YOUR FAVORITE INTERNATIONAL DJ'S LIVE IN THE MIX ON 90 MINUTE CrO2 CASSETTES UNAVAILABLE ANY-WHERE ELSE!!!

-OVER 130 CASSETTES OF ALL STYLES AVAILABLE-

Jungle/Breakbeat- Techno- Trance- Garage- House- Gabber- Classics

Just A Few Worldwide Deckmasters Available To Choose From:

Grooverider Derrick May David Morales
Carl Cox Sven Vath Slipmatt Lenny Dee
Tony Humphries Laurent Garnier Joey Beltram
Moby Sasha Roger S. DJ Hype
Paul Van Dyk Dave Angel John Digweed
DJ Disciple Andy Weatherall Juan Atkins
Todd Terry Paul Oakenfold Fabi Paras
Frankie Knuckles Justin Robertson
Cirillo Jumpin' Jack Frost Fabio
Bobby Kondors DJ Pierre Danny Rampling
Pete Heller Orde Miekle (Slam) Larry Levan
Masters At Work

To Order:

Send list of tapes wanted with Personal Check or Money Order (in U.S. Funds only) for $12 + $2 postage & handling to

Harlem International
30 1/2 Maple Street
Suite G-6
Potsdam, NY 13676 U.S.A.

Please make out checks & money orders to **Mike Calvin** Additional tapes available; send $1 for complete list.

TRiP Mag V.13.0/Page 2

TRiP Magazeen

V.13.0/January 1994

CONTENTS

NEWS

FEATURES

MUSIC

ABOUT THE ISSUE

This issue was created on a Macintosh Powerbook 160 with a whopping 12 MB of RAM on board with Aldus Pagemaker 5.0 and Adobe Photoshop. (Thanks, Hacker Boy!) Scans were made via a Apple One Scanner. Output was made on a Apple Laserwriter Pro 630 in 600 dpi mode and then pasted together by hand with loving detail. Hey, we're getting better at this DTP stuff!!!

SHOUTS OUT TO:

Mixmaster Morris, Billie & Jonah @ Reflective, Alan Oldham, Sean @ Matrix, Joost de Lyser, Pete Namlook, Andrea the House Frau, Laurent Garnier, Sioux & the Crew @ Formula, DJ Reade, Drum Club, Steve Hillage, Chantal & the Open Mind/Telepathic Fish Collective, The Cyberbetty Hussy-Hating Society (Tampa Chapter), Ben Watkins, Zach @ Ind-X, DJ Chang (nuff respect to the E. 909 St. Crew!), DJ Andy Hughes, Aquarhythms massive/Dublin, Brian Walters, David G.

FEET FIRST

1994. A New Year, a time to forget the past and look to the future. January is a month to reflect on the positive things that happened in the 12 months prior and how to enhance them, not dwelling on the negative occurances of last year and moving ahead. That's what those resolutions one makes at New Year's are for, to set a game plan for the future.

We're pretty lucky to have one of the best scenes in the States right here in Florida. Good DJ talent with a wide variety of styles, responsive dance floors, some strong labels like the recently relocated **Bottom Line** (a belated welcome!) , **Vibe**, and of course, **Murk** in addition to some rapidly growing and promising imprints like Tampa's own **Halluci-Nation** and **Torpedo**- what more could a partygoer ask for?

This is definitely the year to make our scene shine in the spotlight and really come into its own. As a willing participant in the underground here, it's your responsibility to support the people-DJ's, promoters, mags, shops, etc. -that make an effort to ensure a quality night out and try to keep the underground vibe prospering and moving towards the next level, not stagnating or backwards.

Last issue we included in the mag a copy of a flyer sent to us by our friends at Chicago's **Organico** label that they found in San Francisco. Sort of a manifesto for preserving the underground integrity of the House Nation, it may not be totally relevant to every scene, but it gives you the partygoer, something to think about as we move into the future. If you didn't see it and you want one, write us and we'll send you a copy... See you next time...

TRiP Magazeen
100 East M.L. King Blvd.
Suite #5
Tampa, Florida 33603
U.S.A.
FON: 813.238.0310
FAX: 813.876.7473
(Please use a cover sheet to our attention when faxing)

EDITOR/PUBLISHER: Peter Wohelski
SENIOR EDITOR: Chris Milo
ASSISTANT EDITOR: Wayne Consiglio
EXECUTIVE ASSISTANT: Jackie Rosquete
CONTRIBUTORS: J. P. Ahern, Mike Bagley, DJ Grumpy C. DJ Jask, DJ Orion, DJ Three

TRiP Magazeen is published every 8 weeks and is distributed throughout the United States. We hope our content will encourage awareness and positivity in the Global Underground.

HYPE!HYPE!HYPE!HYPE!HYPE!HYPE!HYPE!HYPE!HYPE!HYPE!HYPE!HYPE!

....The Phone Company is splitting the Area Codes to **DETROIT**. South Detroit remains 313, while North Detroit will become something else. I guess **RECORD TIME** will have to get a 313 extension because if you're not calling 313, you're not calling Detroit in our book. Just kidding,.,,The founders of L.A.-based **MOONSHINE MUSIC** have split, turning the label into two separate companies. Founder **STEVE LEVY** retains the Moonshine name, while co-founder **RICARDO VINAS' PLANET EARTH RECORDINGS** will house the former Moonshine back catalog and maintain the label's U.S. licensing deals with various European imprints, including **HARTHOUSE**....Look for **ASTRALWERKS** to release the long-awaited second album by **FUTURE SOUND OF LONDON, LIFEFORMS**, in early 1994 along with albums from **TRANSFORMER 2** and the domestic release of **QUIQUE**, the debut from U.K. ambient/indie act **SEEFEEL**.....That new **FSOL** lp will have collaborations with Cocteau Twin **LIZ FRASER** and guitarist **ROBERT FRIPP....DEEP SPACE TIME** is a clothing company specializing in holographic clothing. Founded in London a few years back, these British ex-pats are now based in San Francisco. Seen on the backs of **SPACE TIME CONTINUUM, MIXMASTER MORRIS**, and **BONO** of **U2**, their collection of gear includes jeans, vests, jackets, hats, and velvet/lycra separates made of a patented holographic fabric. To order or for wholesale information, call 415.863.8681 or fax 415.863.2448....As we went to press, we came across a really great piece on the recent **AMBIENT WEEKEND** in Amsterdam with performances by Mixmaster Morris, **PETE NAMLOOK, BIOSPHERE, HIGHER INTELLIGENCE AGENCY, CHRIS & COSEY, DAVID MORLEY,** and others in **THE FACE**. Pick it up if there's still some copies aroundin your favorite magazine shop....**HYPE!** sources say to expect a follow-up to last year's massive **DIVINE PLAYGROUND** party in Miami this March. Last year saw Germany's **SVEN VATH**, along with U.S. DJ's **KEOKI** (Limelight/NYC), **DIMITRI** (DEEE-LITE), several of Florida's top spinners, and live performances from **UTAH SAINTS, 808 STATE**, and **MEAT BEAT MANIFESTO** draw over 9,000 people to Miami's Bayfront Park....Speaking of Miami, **WINTER MUSIC CONFERENCE** is right around the corner, March 1-5 at the Fontainebleu Hilton Resort and Spa on Miami Beach. We went for the first time last year and had a blast soaking up some sun and catching all the great talent down to spin and perform. Some of the best parties of last year were at this conference- so don't miss out! Call 305.563.4444 for more information....**WAX TRAX!** has just released the latest installment of **WARP**'s Artificial Intelligence series by **AUTECHRE** domestically through **TVT**. Catch Autechre live, along with **DJ LEWIS (THE ORB)** atMiami's **WARSAW** during WMC....Next on tap in this series are albums from **KENNY LARKIN** and the just released VIRTUAL STATE by **CABARET VOLTAIRE's RICHARD KIRK. Call TVT at 212.979.6410 and tell them that you want them to license the Kenny Larkin and Richard Kirk albums domestically....** Is it true that the **MURK BOYS** are going to produce the next **MADONNA** album? Maybe it'll give the Material Girl back some underground cred that she's been sorely lacking lately....Ambient artists of the moment, **GLOBAL COMMUNICATIONS** have signed to **DEDICATED**, home to indie shoegazers **CHAPTERHOUSE, SPACEMEN 3, SPIRITUALIZED**, and the **CRANES**. The duo is also known as RELOAD....The often-sampled but never imitated **RENEGADE SOUNDWAVE** returns after a long hiatus with a self-titled new single on **MUTE** with **LEFTFIELD** remixes....San Francisco-based **REFLECTIVE RECORDS** follow-up to Spacetime Continuum's **FLURESCENCE** ep is a full-length CD compilation from Pete Namlook's **FAX** label entitled **AMBIENTO**. Look for more Fax releases on this label in 1994....**UR's ALAN OLDHAM** has started **GENERATOR COMICS**, a side project to his Generator Records. In case you didn't know, Alan did the label art for all the original **TRANSMAT** releases and currently draws for **DJAX UP-BEATS**....

by Jay Patrick Ahern

Frankfurt-born and now Mainz-based cosmic adventurer Thomas Heckmann is known for being the first German artist to make a true Detroit influenced acid record. Influenced by early 70's electronic music, '60's psychedelia, '80's synth-pop, and seminal Detroit, Heckmann currently makes stunning acid workouts on several labels including **Force, Inc., Lab Works, D-JAX Up Beats** and his own **Trope**. TRiP's man across the water, J.P. Ahern, tracked the man down and performed Rorchach Testing and here is the result...

TRiP: What motivates you to make music and what aliases do you work under?

THOMAS HECKMANN: Sex, drugs, and money! No, I'm only joking... AGE, Skydiver, Parrot Torture, Drax, Spectral Emotions, Purple Plejade.

T: I understand you are a curator of an analogue museum... What is your finest specimen?

TH: The Mellotron. It's an original from '67 from the BBC!

T: Do you reckon analogue sounds are still largely unexplored or do you find yourself working withsample-based sounds as well?

TH: Most of the stuff is produced by analogue machines 'cause I'm too lazy to sample or arrange-sometimes- but I've got a Casio FZ 20M sampler which is like an analogue synth in its possibilities! There's still more than a 303.

T: OK, word association game, tell us the first thing that enters your mind on the following...Frankfurt...

TH: (empty silence)

T: Mainz TH: Nice city to live in.

T: Psychic experience TH: I've had a lot, but I won't tell you.

T: 120-124 bpm TH: Italo-disco

T: Save the vinyl TH: I'm saving it.

T: Derrick May TH: Most selfish person, but has done good stuff.

T: San Francisco TH: My girlfriend is there at the moment and there is not much love on Haight Street!

T: Berlin TH: It's dead.

T: Mandatory military service TH: Useless, I did social work instead.

T: Solitude TH: Dark pattern of my life...

T: Simple beauty TH: I like basic beauty that is pure and natural.

T: Trope TH: What's that?

T: Germany vs. Detroit- who are the innovators?

TH: I don't think there's a versus, but we learned a lot from Detroit, but anyway, we, I took it a little further 'cause I mixed it with my influence... Without being arrogant, I was the first German artist to release a real Detroit-oriented acid record- remember AGE/Trope?

T: "Section 2" was, in my opinion, a very special track, perhaps a sign of things to come?

TH: "Section 2" was, I think, successful 'cause it had the energy of the moment in it and was very positive although it was a hard track. That's maybe my way beside the others! Wait for Drax Three!

T: Define exploration.

TH: Buying new instruments and finding a fuckin' cheap modular system from Moog or ARP!!

T: Define tranquility.

TH: What I really need after touring!

TRiP Mag V.13.0/Page 5

by Mike Bagley

Since their inception, Sheffield's **Cabaret Voltaire** have indelibly influenced the face of modern electronic dance music with their innovative audio and visual efforts. Beginning with their early Dadaist tapeloop experiments and film and video soundtrack work, to their more 'commercial' industrial breakthroughs and excursions into pop, **Stephen Mallinder** and **Richard Kirk** have had a career filled with ups and downs, but always full of inspiration. After a bad relationship with a major record label (EMI) in the late '80's, the Cabs have chosen to stay underground the past few years, opting to go the indie route, redefining and reinterpreting the genre they were instrumental in creating through their own **Plastex** label and other side projects such as **Sweet Exorcist** and **Sandoz**. The duo's latest releases- Plasticity and International Language- parts one and two of a three part trilogy, have recently been released domestically through New York-based **Instinct Records**. The third installment is due this Spring, also on Instinct. The Cabs' Richard Kirk took some time out from behind the desk at Western Works to chat with **TRiP** about the past, present, and future of the Sheffield innovators.

TRiP: Hello Richard...it's been about 14 years that you've been together, right?

Richard Kirk: Umm, quite a long time; we were working for a few years before we actually put anything out on vinyl.

T: Your early releases were great- Voice Of America and The Crackdown are classics; I hear the upcoming release kind of gets back to the band's beginning stages.

RK: Basically, we've gone off in a new direction in what we're doing-sort of going back to the original ideas that inspired us. After International Language, it seemed obvious that the third lp would follow in that tradition. As usual we rethink and move on to something else. There's no big mystery behind it.

T: So the whole idea process of these three releases started with Plasticity and kept building?

RK: We've been sort of working on and off on some of these tracks for two years. International Language was completed and mixed in two weeks, but we had been collecting the sounds over a long period.

T: Well, the past three years has seen the band go from industrial to House, Sweet Exorcist and the Bleep movement, and now techno/ambient rhythms. How has the transition been from a musician's standpoint?

RK: It's just been one long learning process. each time you get a new piece of equipment or get inspired by a new way of working, it just kind of leads on to the next thing. A lot of it has to do with technology. I don't think we could make the records we're making now without the use of computers, not in a formulized and disciplined way.

T: You had difficulties to put it lightly, with EMI, do you think they expected too much from Cabaret Voltaire?

RK: I think they thought we could be another Pet Shop Boys or something! It just didn't work out because we dabbled with commercial pop, and although I'm proud of the music we made during that time, I'm much happier with the direction we've taken within the past three years.

T: How do you get the fans of your earlier work to pick up on the new sound?

RK: That's difficult. It's unfortunate if people can't move with the times, because we try to keep changing. That's the reason we've carried on making music for so long and I don't think it's fair for people to expect us to stay in one place. Otherwise, we would have packed it in a long time ago.

T: Let's talk about Plasticity, especially the first single

"Low Cool." Were those gangs sampled during the L.A. disturbances?

RK: It was done before. As usual we had first and then I found this video on Samoan gangs which fit into the context of what we were doing. It was ironic that we were working on this as things were going on in L.A..

T: You're very famous for your use of found dialogue. Are you still going out and recording whatever comes your way?

RK: Strangely enough, with the new album we're finishing off, we went out into the streets and recorded a few things which will find their way into the mix.

T: What about the advertised video for <u>Plasticity</u>?

RK: It's an unfortunate situation. The company that was going to put the video out went under, so we never got enough money to finish it off. There's about two hours of video material sitting on the shelves. We used some of it during live performances last year, but when the deal fell through, it remained untouched.

T: Speaking of live performances, I caught the New Music Seminar show two years ago in New York. Will you ever play the States again?

RK: There's a possibility that next year ('94) we may play some dates.

T: Will the live shows be as intense as they once were, or will we see some sort of an Orb-type of presentation?

RK: It will still be very much in-your-face. The last dates of our last tour in England were pretty much a "traditional" Cabaret Voltaire experience....I don't think it will be too laid back.

T: You've got some solo records, <u>Black Jesus Voice</u> and <u>Ugly Spirit</u>- can we expect more?

RK: There's one project I did called **Sandoz**; there's a CD called **<u>Digital Lifeforms</u>** that came out in May. I've just recorded a solo lp for Warp Records that will be released in February.

T: Any more work as Sweet Exorcist?

RK: Sweet Exorcist is myself and a guy named Parrot from Sheffield... Yeah, probably..

T: So what's in your CD player these days?

RK: All sorts of things. A lot of techno and ambient, quite a bit of House, and a lot of ethnic and African stuff.

T: After the MARRS record ("Pump Up The Volume") came out, you said that "it was so damn good, I wish we had done it..."

RK: I can't remember if it was Mal or me?

T: I'm pretty sure it was you...

RK: Yeah, it was a good record...

Motown. '70's funk. Marc Bolan. Punk rock. 4AD ambience. Pop, and lots of it-from '60's surf and mid-1970's AM Radio to '80's indie. Top it all off with a huge dollop of dub and you get **One Dove.**

Longtime members of the Glasgow underground, One Dove (Vocalist Dot Allison, keyboardist IanCarmichael, and Jim Mc Kinven), frustrated with the scene banded together, capturing the attentions of first **Slam** and then DJ/Producer **Andrew Weatherall** with the fusion of their melting pot of influences, prompting them both to put One Dove singles out on their labels **Soma** and **Boy's Own**, respectively. Their Weatherall-produced debut, Morning Dove White, has drawn comparisons to fellow Glaswegians **Primal Scream**, as it similarly bridges the gap between the underground dance scene and indie sensibility with its strong emphasis on songs without losing a step of dancefloor accessibility. Now released domestically, the group is now bringing their sounds to an American audience.

TRiP: Basic question: how did you all get together?

Jim McKinven: It was born out of frustration because at the time when we came together, Glasgow had such a poor scene musically, nobody was doing anything and we were 3 of about 10 people who wanted to do something strange and new. So it was quite natural that we gravitated to each other, we went to the same clubs, wanted to do the same thing. So we got together, me and Dot-we worked in the same bar- and we knew Ian throught the studio he owned and we just started from there.

T: You used to be in (early 80's new wave group) *Altered Images*, right? ("Happy Birthday")

JM: That's my grisly past...

T: One Dove sits between a lot of categories of music. What do you consider yourselves- indie, underground?

JM: I think we have a foot in both camps. I think we have a foot in both indie culture and dance culture and we're one of the few bands who can embrace the two sides and find both sides actually embrace us. People like **Primal Scream, Ultramarine,** we may actually be on the verge of doing something new, **Underworld**, too...

T: It's one way to expand a fan base...

JM: Not only that, but if the indie kids are coming to you and you can show them that club culture is great, maybe they'll check out some clubs and club kids will see that they're missing stuff by not coming to check out bands. We wouldn't deny either side-we come from classic pop and club culture-for sake of the other.

T: That probably comes from your past in Altered Images, right?

JM: Not only that, but more so your record collection that tells what you're going to sound like. We're really diverse, we listen to stuff like **Dusty Springfield**, classic **Beach Boys**, all the way through to **Massive Attack, Underworld**, and early '70's reggae.

T: With those sort of influences, I guess it was pretty natural to have someone like Andrew Weatherall produce your record?

JM: It's funny how natural that was, because people said there's not a lucky bump in any of them- and maybe that was the luck. You see, after we met him, it was so obvious that we work together because he comes from the same pop resources we've got- to make classic pop and break boundaries and always be challenging in what you do. He's also got the same taste in his record collection, only about 10 times the size.

T: How do you feel about all the comparisons to Primal Scream?

JM: I'm actually quite flattered to tell you the truth because I'd rather be lumped in with them than **Take That! (Ed: the U.K. New Kids On the Block)** You see, Andy has this vision of classic pop and the Primals were sort of the rock side and we're the dance side.

T: What was he like to work with in the studio?

JM: He 's MIDI, sort of a MIDI DJ. Which is good because Andy's not the slightest bit technical, he's more from the old school producers, sitting in the back, coming up with the ideas.

Dot Allison: I think he's a bit of a technophobe...

T: Dot, you were a biochemist, or studying to be one?

DA: I was, I left and never ever looked back. I got qualification because I didn't know what i wanted to do, but I always wanted to do music.

T: There's a strong emphasis on songwriting with One Dove which is **continued on Page 21**

ONE DOVE's RECORD COLLECTION:
A SHORT CROSS-SECTION

Prince Far I-Dubwise
The Clash-Black Market Clash
Renegade Soundwave-In Dub
Bobbie Gentry-Ode To Billie Joe
Just about everything on 4AD
Tom Waits-Swordfishtrombones
T. Rex-The Slider
Jacques Brel-Is Alive And Well And Living In Paris
George Clinton-Atomic Dog
U-Roy-The Great Psalms
Sly & The Family Stone-Dance To The Music
Dub Syndicate-Echomania
Al Green-Greatest Hits
Beach Boys-Pet Sounds
The Chiffons-Greatest Hits
Dusty Springfield-Dusty In Memphis
Burt Bacharach-This Guy's In Love With You
Augustus Pablo-King Tubby Meets The Rockers Uptown
Depeche Mode-Violator
Orange Juice-1st album

From his groundbreaking work as an original member of **808 State** to his solo project and signing to what was then CBS in the late 80's to his more recent forays into British hardcore or jungle and deep house Gerald Simpson, aka **A Guy Called Gerald,** has made top quality music. Simpson sort of dissapeared around the start of the 90's before resurfacing with some new tracks under several pseudonyms on his own **Juice Box** label. Having recently released a collection of older tracks circa 1991 called **28 Gun Bad Boy**,(Ed. see review section) Gerald sat down for his first interview in years with contributor **DJ Three** to discuss his past, present, and future in an exclusive to Florida's Upfront Dance Culture Magazine.

DJ THREE: Did you ever get things sorted out with 808 State, or are you still not on good terms with them?

GERALD: Yeah, oh yeah, we got it sorted out and everything. The people that were starting all the trouble in the first place, they're not even working with 808 State anymore. Everything's cool, I might even start a little project with them. I'm in the position now where I'm in control of everything I do, so I know a bit more about the business now than I did then.

D3: So Ricky Rouge is really you, right?

GS: Yeah, but don't tell anyone... The reason we did it that way was because on one of the ep's I put a jungle style on one side with a bit more funky on the other and I got slagged off in a few English magazines, like Dom Phillips or someone, really slagged it off. So I decided any genre of music that I do-and I do quite a few different styles now- I'm going to put it out under a different name. I've got some techno stuff coming out, sort of like Detroit-style, under the name Inertia. Have you heard the lp **Panic In Detroit**? That track, "Satisfaction?"

D3: That's you?!? Speaking of Detroit, do you still have a relationship with Derrick?

GS: Yeah, he's living in Amsterdam or something like that now. I phone him up sometimes. I'm going to try to put some tracks out on his label, not Transmat, but Fragile. There's so much going on, I wouldn't mind putting a lot of energy into more like the jungly kind of thing. But it's really gone now, it's not even jungle anymore....

D3: I prefer to call it British hardcore now because it's the only type of dance music that is U.K. originated, created, and supported.

G: You know the Reinforced label? They're doing a film documentary on the scene. A lot of people still think it's Rave, but if you listen to it, it's totally in a class of it's own. We're going to try and put that thing through on this documentary.

D3: There's no scene for it, what scene there was for it down here just sort of phased out. It's just so hard to find good records, distributors won't bring as many over as there's so many and so many are crap. Is there still an underground breakbeat scene over there? I've heard many tapes from some of the big, so-called rave DJ's over there and I haven't been very impressed.

GS: My favorite DJ is Fabio, he's really diverse... Whatever style I seem to like, he can play it. As far as **the scene goes, it's sort of like find your favorite DJ and follow him around, basically.**

D3: What's an average day in the life consist of for you?

GS: It starts out by going into the studio and working on a track from 10 o'clock in the morning until about 7. After that, we get into edit mode and start editing.

D3: You've got quite an extensive library of old stuff to sample from because you've got very original samples and very original production...

GS: I've got a really, really big library. Most of the stuff is on DAT because I don't have enough room to have it all on discs and things, although I've found a new storage device, the Sony Mini-disc. It's much smaller.

D3: Do you do your own vocals on a lot of tracks?

GS: On the Ricky Rouge stuff, yeah.

D3: The media has pretty much ignored you since your 'encounter' with Dom Phillips and you've stayed pretty underground. Do you live in Manchester...

GS: Well, I work in Manchester, but I come down to London to play because the clubs in Manchester are not really happening. I like the jungle and garage scenes mostly like Paradise for jungle and for garage, Ministry Of Sound...

D3: Where's the best scene for breakbeats in London, North or South?

GS: I'd say North. There's a lot going on up there.

Most of the clubs that I go to are in North London, sometimes I'll jump in a car with Fabio or Randall and half of the clubs that they go, I have no idea where they are. There's this one roller rink place that's really good.

D3: Would you say that the jungle scene is much smaller that the media would have you believe compared to say, the Rave scene?

GS: It's probably a lot more intimate, everyone sort of knows everyone. Just like the DJ mix thing going on there, like Grooverider, Fabio, Randall will all have a different mix of a track, everyone's got their own personal mix. Everyone's so personalized, sort of influenced by the West Indies and the dub plate sort of thing **(In the early days of reggae and dub, often times producers would make personalized mixes of new tracks for sound system DJ's. These acetate-like records were single-sided and pressed directly from the mastering lathe plates, thus the name dub plates-Ed.)**, plus the American hip-hop thing, that's a big influence. The two of them gel together, and we add a European feel to it all.

D3: Would you say there's more of a hip-hop attitude as far as ego involved or is it more of an 'techno' attitude of peace and unity?

GS: It depends. At a club I go to, the Paradise club, you get a mixture of both with the ragga toughness and everything.

Born as a re-entry into recording for guitarist **Steve Hillage**, an ambient pioneer with his work with '70's avant-progressive rock group **Gong** and subsequent solo work, **System 7** has finally stepped out from behind the misconception that the project was just another side project for Hillage's collaborator, **Dr. Alex Patterson.**

After quietly leaving recording in 1980, Hillage turned to computers and record production to occupy his time, producing acts as diverse as **It Bites, Cock Robin, Real Life**, and **Simple Minds**. In fact, Hillage fundamentally considers himself a producer- "It pays the rent," he says, having recently completed projects by French/Arab singer **Rachid Taha, Blink, the Charlatans UK**, and a few film scores.

System 7 grew out of this desire to produce. Influenced by house music, Hillage was inspired to return to recording himself, but was against a solo album. "It provided me with a new area where I could work as an artist and a producer, but in a different way. I thought, 'If I'm going to start working again, I want to do something different," Hillage explains, "I was more into a collaborative thing. Once the project got going, we met people who expressed an interest in doing some things, did some tracks, and it crystallized into an album."

One of the people he met was Alex Patterson, an A&R man and DJ. "He was working at EG Records (home of **Brian Eno** & **Killing Joke**), and I was producing a band called Dub Chapter for EG. I met him there and I heard some things he was playing in the office; I went down to his ambient night at Heaven, a club in London-this is in 1989, when the Orb was just starting. I found he was playing one of my records that we had done in 1979 called **Rainbow Dome Music**. We got on very well and started working together. The first thing we did was the first System 7 12" ("Sunburst") and then some stuff on the first Orb album. It was all done about the same time," reveals Hillage, dispelling the misconception that System 7 is an Orb side project.

Steve explains it pretty succinctly, "We were inspired to get involved in House music, we met Alex, who was getting involved in his own personal musical quest, and it all formulated into 2 separate projects."

The first System 7 album was largely collaborative, featuring contributions from Patterson, **Youth, Derrick May, Paul Oakenfold**, longtime partner **Miquette Giraudy,** and ex-Simple Minds' keyboardist **Mick McNeil.** Although not apparent to many, Mick McNeil was an obvious choice for Hillage, having previously produced the Scottish band in 1981. "There was this instrumental track on the album I produced with them called **"Themes For Great Cities"** which became a big acid house favorite in '88. It was played by people like **Andy Weatherall**, and **A Corporation Of One** remade it and mixed it with a track from **Queen** called **"It's The Real Life."** So I thought, 'I made this track with Mick in 1981, and it's become a House classic, let's make another track together.'"

It did well in the U.K., so when it came time to license the album in the United States, the band had a small problem-their name. It was

continued on Page 21

by Wayne Consiglio

French DJ/remixer/producer **Laurent Garnier** has quickly burst into the Global spotlight within the past year with his dazzling technical mixes, Detroit-fueled tracks on his own **FNAC** imprint, as well as his distinctive remixes for **Resistance D, Energy 52,** and others. After cutting his teeth at Manchester's **Hacienda** in 1987, Laurent returned to France, DJ'ing at all the first acid house parties in Paris. After returning to the Hacienda for a year in 1988, he has been an in demand DJ throughout Europe as well as at his own club in Paris, **Wake Up**. Now looking to establish his name in the U.S., Garnier recently made a tour of the States, playing two dates in Florida. A very warm soul with a burning passion for the underground and the music he plays, **TRiP** woke him up after a long night to do this get-to-know type profile that hopefully will inspire some to...**WAKE UP!!!!**

TRiP: Very few people know who you are, so tell us a bit about yourself for the record.

Laurent Garnier:I'm 28. I'm French. I lived in France until I was 18. when I was 18, I moved to England. I started DJ'ing in '87 at the **Hacienda**. I was doing every Wednesday night there as a regular spot. I was playing with **Mike Pickering.** It was more like a party night than the rest of the nights there, It was more like mixing a lot of music together; Hi-NRG mixed with House, mixed with Hip-hop, mixed with disco. I did that for a year. Then I went into the Army because (in France) the Army is compulsory- that was in '88. When I was in the Army, I was at the same time going home every night, so I was DJ'ing 5 nights a week working at all the Acid House parties in Paris. The complete beginning of House for a lot of countries in Europe-not for England- especially for France. It was only a small gay scene that was going to the Acid House parties; so it was Wednesday nights in the Locomotive club and there was a Tuesday night that was successful at the Palace called Pyramid. That was run by English people and **Colin Favor** was flying in every week and playing with me. Friday nights I had a night called The Jungle at the Rex Club that was really, really cool. I did that for a year and then I went back to the Hacienda to do a regular spot there on Saturday nights. In '89 I came back to Paris and started DJ'ing full time. From then on, I've just gone at it full force. I mean I've played everywhere-lots of countries...

T: I see here that you're booked solid through the end of March at practically everywhere.

LG: Actually, now I'm booked through May; it's not everyday, but basically every Wednesday, Thursday, Friday, Saturday 'til May. It's a lot of countries-I mean I'm going to some weird countries like Israel and Greece- and that's really good. I'm really pleased....

T: Doing all the traveling that you do, is it hard to keep up with buying records?

LG: Traveling around and buying- it's the only way to keep up with music traveling as much as I do. If you lock yourself up in one country or in one area, you're dead because you're only listening to what the people where you're from are listening to. I mean, I just spoke to my manager in Paris an hour ago and he said to me, "I'm so glad you went away because people get used to you every week." I run a club on Thursdays called Wake Up! People get you every week for the last 3 years and last night everybody sort of found out that you weren't there, and they all came up and said, "Where's fucking Laurent? Why's the music like this?" and stuff like that and they all got pissed off. But if they get me every week, they get bored of it. So it's good that I travel and I get once a year I'm not there and they'll go, "Fuck!" I'm learning a lot in this country. I'm learning that the music they're listening to is progressive or whatever. I think they're going to lock themselves into their own narrow-minded music or whatever. Traveling is the only key to learning so much about music. I mean, I come here (USA), I buy records. I go to Italy, I buy records. I go to Spain, I buy records. I go to fuckin' Germany and I buy records. I just take the best from and do my own thing, you know?

T: So you own a record store?

LG: Yeah, I own a record store and I sell everything from **Masters At Work** to **Rotterdam Gabber**. A real wide range of music... I'll sell everything from **Industrial Strength** to **Strictly Rhythm**- and I sell a lot of everything. The kids got their own ideas, I never try to influence a kid. I mean, if a kid comes in and buys 200 Gabber records, I'll say to him, "Do you really like this music?" But until he gets about 50 or 60, I'm not going to say anything. If he buys 60 records, I'll figure that the kid must love it and I want to know why. I'll ask him, "Where do you come from, why do you like this music?" And it's all the same. The Gabber kids come from a heavy metal background, you know, stuff like that. They're not dance oriented kids. It's very interesting how heavy metal is crossing over with dance music and there you have Gabber. It's just interesting to meet these kids and get to know them.

T: I remember back in '88-'89, when I was really into the Manchester scene- *New Order, Stone Roses, 808 State, Happy Mondays, A Guy Called Gerald, The Hacienda*- I would see your name on flyers for the Hacienda and whatnot. But the first time I saw your name on a record was the *Inner City* remix you did. What had you done before that, if anything?

LG: I did a couple things before, but you don't really have to know that. I mean, my first project was called **French Connection** on **Eastern Bloc Records**. One side was a New Beat/Belgian track and the other was a beautiful garage and an LFO/technoish track. That was 4 or 5 years ago. After that, I started working for **FNAC**, then was the first Laurent Garnier 'French Connection' ep, a remix of that, then the remix of Inner City and at the same time I had **"Stronger by Design."** Then **Choice** and **Alaska**, then **"Wake Up"** on **Warp**. And my new one **(Planet House ep)** is coming out next week- that's it. I've remixed a lot of people. My future remixes should be the new **Cosmic Baby**; a 4-track remix ep coming out in January of my stuff remixed by **Jeff Mills (ex-UR), Paul Van**

Dyk, Sven Vath, and **Deepside**. It's going well, production is cool, and I'm getting more on as a producer. It's going slowly because it's not my main job. I mean, I'm still learning in the studio. I want to concentrate more on my music.

T: Which do you prefer- DJ'ing or producing?

LG: I travel so much, I've got the record shop, the club, the radio show; I haven't got a lot of time for producing. I'm going to have to make myself some time. I want to do some tracks and not listen to them for like 3 weeks and then come back to them. I love music. I know exactly what i like and that's the kind of music I want to produce and that takes time. So what I'm going to try to do is go to different places for a week or two straight and then take a week or two off and go into the studio. I mean, I say that now, but who knows...

T: If I'm not mistaken, this is only your second trip to America along with this year's New Music Seminar. You're not as popular here as you are in Europe. Also the type of music you like and play while you DJ is played by hardly anyone in this country....

LG: Yeah, the Techno scene in America is very small, but it will kick off. Last night (at the Edge in Ft. Lauderdale) the kids didn't know hardly any of the records that I played. Some of them left because they didn't know the records, but a lot stayed because it was different. That is like France 4 years ago. It's small, but it will get bigger and keep getting stronger. Hopefully more of the kids here(in Florida) will become a little more open-minded and realize that there's different music than just the progressive house that mostly all the DJ's here play. France is the same because there were very few DJ's and they all played the same. Then some hardcore DJ's came and all the kids said, "Fuck, I like this because it's different, so I'm going to listen to this and listen to these DJ's." Then **Derrick May** came and he opened more eyes still. That's what makes the scene strong. I see Saturday, you've got **CJ Bolland**

continued on page 23

dj charts

DJ DIGIT
3rd Floor Productions
San Francisco, CA

Luvdup-Goodtime
Masters At Work-When You Touch Me RMX
Aretha Franklin-Deeper Love
DJ Duke-Blow Your Whistle
Romanthony-Make This Love
Funky Disco-It's A Funky Groove
Bjork-Big Time Sensuality
Jimi Polo-Do You Wanna Know
House Of Nice-Free
Mr. Ragoo-Make Me Feel

DJ EFX
3rd Floor Productions
San Francisco, CA

Romanthony-Make This Love
Judy Cheeks-So In Love
Smooth Touch-House Of Love
Guantanamo-You Got to Feel It
Slamm Project-Northside
Luvdup-Goodtime
Lovestation-Best Of My Love
Mr. Ragoo-Make Me Feel
Prince Of House-Get It Started

DAVID G.
Torpedo Records
Tampa, FL

Soundman-The Factory
Romanthony-Testify
The Daou-Give My Love
Discipline-Reachin'
Full Swing-Choices
Pascal's Bongo Massive-Pere Cochon
The Plan-Release It
Tribal Jazz-Volume 1
Linn Lockamie-Love So Strong
Romanthony-Make This Love

dj charts

THOMAS HECKMANN
Top 10 of 1993
Exit 100/Drax/AGE
Mainz, Germany

And Also The Trees-The Klaxon
Pet Shop Boys-Very
Beavis & Butthead
Aural Expansion
u-ziq LP
Suicide (1st LP)
St. Etienne-So Tough
Cranes-Forever
Dead Can Dance-Into The Labyrinth
Spectral Emotions-Chapter 3

DJ LOUIS
Mary's House-WVUM 90.5 FM
Miami, FL

Havanna-Condensed
Circle City-Moments Of Inertia
MASI-Apache Stress
Perks Of Living Society-H.A.L.F.
Probe-Rapid R
Flavour-No Matter What You Do
Hanson/Nelson-Move In Motion
NY Connection-Want It
Loni Clark-U
Lost Tribes- Gimme A Smile

DJ READE
Nova Mute Records
New York, NY

Beautyon-Your Ignorance
Cristal Palace-Mind Manipulation
Juno Reactor-Transmissions
Luke Slater-Star Travel
Dance 2 Trance-We Came/ Peace
Lotus Take One ep
Plastikman-Plasticine
Trans 4 M-Amma(Moon Mix)
DJ Reade-Ascension ep
Anything by Atom Heart

dj charts

JOOST de LYSER
Surreal Sound
The Netherlands

Q-Moog-Forbidden State
?-AR 9060
DJ Funk-Move Your Body
Clementine-Relative To Me
Tim Harper-Star Trekkien
Mark Bernard-Load
69-Sound On Sound
Basement Trax-One Track Mind
Drexiya 3-Aquatic Beta Particles
Vapour Space-John's Anti Gravity

JAY PATRICK AHERN
10 Plastique Tasties of 1993
Aquarhythms
Dublin, Ireland

Kenny Larkin-Tedra
Dave Angel-Family ep
Orange-Quarter ep
Chronological Harmonizations
Balil-Parasight
Marvo Genetic-New World Basics
Stasis-Point Of No Return
Joey Beltram-Code 6 ep
Born Under A Rhyming Planet
V/A-California Dreaming

AMBIENT SOHO/TOP 10
compiled by Chantal
London, U.K.

Autechre-Incanabula
Beaumont Hannant-Tastes & Textures, Vol. 2
Robert Leiner-Dream Or Reality
Tuu-One Thousand Years
Slowdive-In Mind (Reload/ Bandulu RMXS)
Balil-Parasight
V/A-After 6 AM
Plastikman-Sheet One
V/A-Tonteraege Fur Synapsen Massage 01-02
Seefeel-i-o1

TRIPmag CHARTS

UNDERGROUND DANCE MUSIC CHART
10 URGENT GROOVES
COMPILED BY DJ THREE

Digital Sects ep
Rabbit In The Moon-Phases
Red Planet IV-Base Station 303
Avalon-Harlequin
4Boy 1Girl Action-Hawaiian Death Stomp
Cybordelics-Peter Pan
Fabio Paras-Shiva Shante LP
3 Phase-Rota
Jaya- I
Aloof-Agent O

TRiP HOUSE CHART
COMPILED BY DJ JASK

Wave-Thoughts Of You
House 2 House-Do for Me
The Soundman-The Factory
Full Swing-Choices
4th Measure Men-4 You RMXS
Masters At Work-When You Touch Me RMXS
Sabrina Johnston-Peace RMXS
Loni Clark-U
Cast of Thousands-The Sun Will Shine
DSK-Feel So Free (Murk RMX)

TRiP/OSCILLATE AMBIENT CHART
COMPILED BY DJ ORION & DJ GRUMPY C.

Vapour Space-Themes From... Air II
Metal Masters-Spectrum (Dopple J Mix)
Namlook/Inoue-Shades Of Orion
Coldcut-Autumn Leaves (Irresistible Force Mix)
Divination-Ambient Dub Vol. II
Cybertrax-Drifting
Gilgamesh-Delta Rain Dream
Modesty-Eternity's Fool
Terre Thaemlitz-Tranquilizer

RECORD REVIEWS 12"/EP

4 BOY 1GIRL ACTION-"The Hawaiian Death Stomp" (EPI/UK) New one from **David Holmes** and **Kris Needs** with Jagz and Burns at the controls. The writing side opens up with crowd noise and a sample about fucking with the future and that's pretty much what it does. With typical David Holmes percussion, an exceptionally good acid line, and some guitar noises (more like feedback than crap UK Disko Party Funk riffs), this record gets the job done. The label side is the same except it's slowed down to a crawl to really fuck your mind up with deep, deep dub. Another excellent record from an incredible producer and DJ. **(GC)**

4th MEASURE MEN-"4 You" RMXS (Area 10) Finally, a record worth bringing back!! With some dope new mixes, a bonus track, and a limited blue vinyl pressing, get a grip and get it quick- **MK** is at the helm, so get ready to sweat. The "4 You" remix is ALL that, keeping all the sensuous original sounds intact and fully equipped on the deep tip. The bonus track, "Given" is a flowing four-on-the-floor cut with sexy horns, disco-y synths, and nightcrawling basslines. All in all, the whole record is phat, so good luck trying to find this hot gem on cool blue wax. **(Jask)**

69-"Sound On Sound" ep (Planet E-R&S/Belgium) Carl Craig as 69 is back with this supposedly super limited ep full of some real true to form experi**mental** techno from Detroit. This is a total futuristic electronic sound, techno with hints of garage and acid house influence and minimal tweaks of each sound. If you're into some deep or avant garde sounds, try to get this. **(CM)**

DIGITAL SECTS ep (Matrix) This new label from Detroit hits the bullseye big on its second release from four top producers, **Kenny Larkin, DJ T-1000, Claude Young,** and **Sean Deason.** Kenny Larkin shows why he is going to be the man in '94 with "Aurora", a luscious track with a swingy string synth intro, percussive hi-hats and deadly bass that grooves along into a steady pulsing kick before repeating. S.I.N.'s "Kindred Souls" is on the moody tip with atmospheric synths slowly building up a slow, syncopated drum break. "The Menacer" pumps out some funky tribalesque experimental Detroit from DJ T-1000 with some cool acid blurps and a hi-hat breakdown, while Sergio's "Disko Gruv" takes discoey house to task, giving it's chunky fatt guitar riffs a fresh Motor City lube job. This ep is a must! If you can locate a copy, buy it at all costs! **(PW)**

JAM & SPOON-"Right Is The Night"/ "Follow Me" (Dance Pool/Germany) "Last week I witnessed one of the most astonishing DJ sets I've ever experienced in Britain. A set to compare with the first you ever heard or any from Weatherall, Holmes, and Emerson throughout 1993. It came from Laurent Garnier. The man behind French label FNAC Records and supplier of the most essential acid-techno moments last year.

The European have energy, attitude, and an air of exuberance that puts most of our home-grown talent to shame. Think Garnier, Dag, Hardkiss and Mark Spoon. Even the one British DJ who compares to these names, Underworld's Darren Emerson, who was stunning tonight, was given an education by Garnier's wizardry.

Garnier was unbelieveable, halting tracks midway for a split second before jolting them back with the full weight of his elbow. It was downright hard, the pace quickening whenever the crowd looked jaded, until he unleashed last year's most intense, Slam's "Positive Education."

Then at 5:20 am, he provided us with the most memorable 10 minutes you could ever hope to experience- that moment we hope for every time we go out. Jam & Spoon's "Follow Me". If you don't know, it features an unprecedented two minute breakdown-beatless but overloaded with the sound of an angry bumble bee trapped in an empty beer glass. It's outrageous. Some have chosen to mix this in with beats (Daley, Perry, and McMillan) but failure to play it in full means the most extraordinary release in years is destroyed. After two minutes it kicks back in. Working the expectant crowd into a frenzy, it finally comes, with the most testing rate of BPM's on the scale. Orgasmic. Check with the Drum Club's Charlie Hall, this scribe was in tears.

The greatest track, the greatest DJ, fuck, the greatest club, and yes, the greatest moment I've ever , ever witnessed in a club." (Reprinted from Melody Maker) **Shit, I just thought it was cool when I played it at Simon's in Gainesville. (DJ Three)**

THE PLAN-"Release It" (Torpedo) a splendid new debut out of Tampa from **DJ David G.** Real dubby house tracks at it's best with horns, phat beats and very deep basslines. All mixes are very pleasing but check out "Majestic", it's a cool out cut with nice propelling strings and soothing bass tones. A very nice record to mix with and if smooth dubs are what you seek, you better get this. For promos contact David G. @ 813.229.6985. **(Jask)**

BALIL-"Parasight" ep (Rising High/UK) Created by **Black Dog,** this 4-track ep is simply excellent. More on the techno side than the jazzy freaky weird stuff that Black Dog usually do, all 4 tracks are great. My favorite is "Rosary Pilots" with its great 303 line and electro beats. "Avidya" is also a standout on the abient side of things. **(GC)**

ALOOF-"Agent O" (Flaw/UK) Not on cowboy, doing a cub night called **Flaw**, and debuting their lates on a label of the same name, the Aloof strike back with an excellent track with heavy bassline, kick, and tribal drums all woven with a brilliant violin lick. Go straight to the Life's A gas Mix as the Full Rant Mix is not. I always felt The Aloof were beyond the short-lived and never developed tag of progressive house and with producers and labels like **Slam, Sabres, Warp, Kris Needs, David Holmes,** and **Underworld** 1994 looks very good for Britain and its place in techno. **(CM)**

AVALON-"Harlequin" (Ind-X) A guy named Zach returns from his not-so-well-known but excellent **Halogen** ep with Avalon. 3 tracks: "Harlequin" is a wonderful trance record with bells, pulses of bass, acidy synth, and some smooth chords. Imagine a Qat dub by **Sasha** without the progressive riffs; "Deus Ex Machina", a deep ambient techno bit, and "Steps of Odessa"- uptempo techno/trance. A good record! **(D3)**

DISCIPLINE with BOBBY PRUITT-"Reaching" (Miami Soul) Another floor driving house cut on the gospel tip, produced by **Ralph Falcon** of Murk. But, surprise! This is not just another gospel house track. Mr. Falcon throws Bobby Pruitt's soaring vocals in your face, escalating so high even Michael Jordan couldn't fly that high! Backed by dark, heavy basslines, shellacking hi-hats, and a slow-riding beat, you can't resist. With several mixes, there's no excuse not to reach for this! **(Jask)**

UP ABOVE THE WORLD-"Trying To Reach You" (Exist Dance) Yet another pulsing atmospheric acid-funk trance excursion from Heaven. A wicked funk workout bassline and 303 propels this track with it's self-titled spoken word sample and accompanying dialogue while the flip adds Middle Eastern elements to the mix. A good record, but a dissapointing follow-up to "Freaky Chakra" **(PW)**

TRIP TA FUNK-"Here I Come Baby" (Ultra Ethereal) Back again, **Dub Tribe**'s alter ego hit the mark in the funky breaks house category with "Here I Come Baby"- similar beats as "Mother Earth", house stabs now known as the 'Robin S.' sound, and title sample topped with a nice saxophone. The flip is an acidy funk type track, ala Bonesbreaks style, also with saxophone. **(CM)**

SABRINA JOHNSTON-"Peace" RMXS (EastWest/Germany) I've always heard that deep house and garage is the true underground thing in Germany. Well, now finally I get a taste of it on this slammin' double packin' promo remixed by their #1 House DJ, **Boris Dlugosch.** If you liked the original "Peace", you'll like this even much better. Sabrina's vocals are perpetuated into a level never taken before. with a touch of organ, fine horns, and some nice beats, this promises to be a hit again with several mixes to choose from! **(Jask)**

APHROHEAD-"In The Dark We Live" RMXS (Bush/UK) Created by **Felix Da Housecat** and remixed by **Dave Clarke**, this is one record not to be missed. Dave Clarke's 312 Mix uses a pounding kick drum slowly adding percussion and a wicked acid line although still fairly slow, with Felix's ramblings over the top. Very fine. The 313 Mix again uses a pounding kick, but this time it's much faster and is more Housecat style while the Unreleased Mix is a typical DJ Pierre/ Housecat house track with high-pitched stabs and pitched down vocal samples. Very good. **(GC)**

ESSENCE OF NATURE-"Blue Orchid"/ CYBORDELICS-"Fairy Tales" ep/ ARPEGGIATORS-"Elements" ep (Harthouse/Germany))/METAL MASTERS-"Spectrum" (Harthouse/UK) OK, the green series from Harthouse wasn't so hot, but if the first three yellows are any indication-things are looking real good. To the point: Essence of Nature- "Blue Lotus" is fast but don't let it stop you, pitch it down if it's a big deal, beacuse it's great! By the way, Sven and Ralf did it. Cybordelics: "Peter Pan" is one of the best trance grooves in awhile, a sonic hypnotic intro sliding into a great melody to make you smile. Arpeggiators: 4 tracks of electronic hardtrance, all of which are pretty fast and very good. And an extra treat-Harthouse/UK via Rising High deliver the UK debut of Metal Masters' "Spectrum", the sceond and highly memorable Harthouse release which was heavily talked about but sure didn't seem to get played much. The original is here along with an excellent mix by **Caspar Pound**, who makes the track accessible to almost any floor, especially with the added bassline. A cool electro-ish mix is also included by **Double J** aka **Mike Edwards** of **Jesus Jones**, but that's another story... Check out these records! **(D3)**

SPASMS-"Recreation" (D-Jax Up Beats/Holland) This red vinyl slab serves up some more excellent bangin' acid from Djax. 4 tracks, the writing side has screechy synths, killer acid blurps, and percussive elements drive this monster until almost the end where it breaks down. The other cut on this side is very minimal and spacey with tinkly synths, hi-hats, subtle acid, and a insistant kick drum. The flip side is more of the same and just as good. Choice. **(PW)**

CIRCLE CITY-"Moments Of Inertia" (Warp/UK) Warp, a label that rarely misses, has been on a roll. The original mix is where it's at, a fairly heavy, electronic/analoguish track in a league with the label's previous smash Resoraz, but not a copy. This one is more an over-the-top sound likely to work in most clubs. Incentive to give this one a try will be the Rhythm Invention remix, which to me just doesn't have the original's energy. The Kleptomaniacs Meets Circle City is likened to L.A.'s Exist Dance label in style. **(D3)**

TEMPLE OF ACID-"Temple Of Acid" (Aura/UK) The Hypnotist takes his remix of "Kerosene", rearranges it, makes it faster, and adds about 8 minutes to it. Intense acid and a breakbeat halfway through add to the excitement. The B-side's Vortex Mix is a squiggly little acid track with a housey keyboard line that is quite effective. **(GC)**

MAZDARATTI-"Foxhunt"/"Sleeps with The Foxes"/"Elephantine" (Telepathic) Fred does the business with hard techno tracks that are just incredible. "Foxhunt" is quite mad with a subtle resmeblance to Vapour Space is style but harder still. "Sleeps With the Foxes" is an elemental mix of "Foxhunt". "Elephantine" is another stormer with a keyboard line that sounds like an elephant blowing its trunk and a drum track quite similar to **Prince's "Erotic City"** or some other funky electro thing. **(GC)**

LOXODROME-"Loxodrome" ep (Jumpin' & Pumpin'/UK) Nice return to the clubs for Jumpin' & Pumpin'. Four tracks of uptempo trance/ techno slightly on the older style British acid tip. The stand out for clubs would have to be "Heavy Ride" with its pulsing synth line and late coming freestyle-like beats. "Society Red" takes you back a bit- in a "Pacific"-vein, but not a soundalike. A tactful use of **Juan Atkins'** "Clear" is utilized in the ambient-ish "Avenue T"- T standing for techno. A sign of things to come for Jumpin' & Pumpin'? Hope so. **(CM)**

GHETTO TRAX (Accelerate) 4 more old school hard house tracks from **Dan Bell.** Shuffling beats and bleepy noises describe all four tracks here, with each being different and able to stand on their own. **(GC)**

EXIT 100-"Circuits" RMX (Force, Inc./ Germany) The German master of Acid, **Thomas Heckmann** revives his Exit 100 acid classic, "Circuits"- sweeping synths, frantic 303 lines, relentless kick...strong. The flip contains two new tracks, "Revolution" and "Electrocute", a pair of decent straight-up German hard acid trancers. **(PW)**

RED PLANET VI-"The Long Winter Of Mars" (Red Planet) Mad Mike...is good. Just plain good techno trax with yet another fully smokin' 808 acid track, "Base Station 303" as well as excellent techno from tribal to acid. A double pack that Mixmag had in its Buzz Chart before Mike himself even had it mastered! Good, good, good. **(D3)**

SMC UNITY-"Move 'N Groove" (Mercury/Germany) A smokin' debut from a young trio out of Germany. A track with a very silky feeling to it- sexy vocals, oscillating organs, and building basslines- "Move 'N Groove" is dope; also check the remix plus the bonus cut on the acid jazz vibe, "This World's for You" is a slow rhythmic soul slinging track with cool breaks- very D-Influence-y. Overall, some good deep house. **(Jask)**

S.I.N.-"Doomsday" (Matrix) A solid Detroit acid trancer, this should be called "Boomsday" with its big, boomy kickdrum reverberating throughout; gurgly acid and driving hi-hats with synth stabs also accompany the package. Sounds good on a big system... On the flip side, "Trancefour" opens with a housey piano line, handclaps, and a spooky synth that goes on forever before a bassline and kick break in-a track that doesn't seem to go anywhere. "Past, Present, Future" is a groovy slice of four-on-the-floor Detroit techno/ house, combining elements from- you got it- past, present, and future. Nice stuff. **(PW)**

DENEUVE-"Clairvoyance"/ "Refingered" (Telepathic) Fred follows up the brilliant Mazdaratti record with 2 more great songs, this time going for a more mellow approach. "Clairvoyance" is dreamy, uptempo acid house with excellent chords and a groovy bassline. "Refingered" is fairly fast but not hard, like a more straight forward mix of "Clairvoyance" but almost totally different. **(GC)**

GIANNELLI-"Salacious"/"Eloquence" (Telepathic) Still more goodies from Telepathic-"Salacious" is an upbeat acid tune with a quite housey rhythm track, while "Eloquence" is a late night deep house gem with wonderful sounds. This is the kind of record you'd hear if you were, well, nevermind. **(GC)**

BIODREAMS-"Return To Paradise" ep (Experimental) On the writing side, a long ambient intro guides you down the path into "Synthetic 9", a very dramatic slice of experimental ambient hardtrance. On the label side, "Snake Charmer" is my pick, a deep, sensual, slow atmospheric groover with tribal percussion, subtle acid, and a wicked sub-bass breakdown while the other cut is more uptempo acid. **(DJ*)**

TERRACE-"Midiology" (GPR/UK) More melancholy techno from Steffan Robbers. 4 tracks with two being mixes of the title track. The best is "On The Freeway", an intensely sad song probably written on the way home from a funeral or something. Steffan must be a really sad person, but then again if he wasn't, he wouldn't make such beautiful music. **(GC)**

BACK TO THE RHYTHM featuring ALVA McGILL-"What Can You Do For Me" (House-N-Effect) Pumpin' straight out of Chicago comes a deep vocal house track with a garagey feeling. One of Chicago's finest, **Rick Lenoir** of Four On The Floor is on the production tip, so you know it's gotta be smokin'! Four mixes to choose from, all outrageously superb. The vocal mix stays true to the game delivering pure sweetness from the soul. The two dub mixes are also pleasing, but check out the Underground Mix-strictly smooth with a touch of 303 acid lines uniting with driving beats, a cool organ riff, and tasty bass. Definitely a label to watch for in '94. **(Jask)**

GILGAMESH-"Trescore" (Fragile/ Transmat) This latest gem from Transmat is a gradual building sonic trancer licensed from Trigger which, once at full steam, gallops into nothing. The B-side, "Delta Rain Dream", begins as a buzzing miasma of swirling synths before a melody emerges, spinning, tweaking, evolving. A track that takes experimental ambience to a new level. Brilliant and outstanding. **(DJ*)**

HEMISPHERE-"Hemisphere" (FAX/ Germany) Pete Namlook teams up this time with **Steve Stoll** aka **Datacloud**, and the result is a s great as you would have guessed. The 4 songs on this CD are completely atmospheric and full of energy. More great material from the most prolific producer to date. **(GC)**

FULL SWING-"Choices" (Strictly Rhythm) With that name you gotta know who's gotta be behind this blazing house stomper. Yep, you guessed it, **John Ciafone** of **Mood II Swing...** John's on the solo swing on this one and really does a top notch job on the production. "Choices" is full-on funkness with pumpin' percussion, cool breaks, and stylistic vocals by **Lee Smith, Jr.** Known for his hip-hop background, John fuses the dopest beats and breaks with House on the B-side to generate a fresh track, "Fierce Dancin'", with phat horns hovering all over the place. One word, fierce! Househeads, get with the program and make this record your 'Choice'! Schwing! **(Jask)**

COLDCUT-"Autumn Leaves" (Irresistible Force RMX) (Arista/UK) Forget the Nellee Hooper and Well Hung Progressive House mixes and go straight to the Irresistible Force Mix. Put together by our man **Mixmaster Morris** and **Laurence Elliott-Potter** (of **Friends, Lovers, & Family**), the production is very typical of Morris- uplifting synths and sweet melodies subtly building to a single boomy kick drum thump, with a warm as sunshine sample of the vocal line sliding in towards the end. Nice and effective. **(DJ *)**

JEFF MILLS-"Berlin"/"Late Night" (DJ Pierre Mixes) (Pow Wow) Jeff Mills gets the Wild Pitch treatment on two tracks from his Waveform Transmissions LP. A trademark DJ Pierre reconstruction of these two hard techno numbers, the one big problem is that it sounds like whoever mastered the final mix must have been outside when it was done because it's pressed so shitty it's unreal **(GC)**

HOUSE 2 HOUSE-"Do For Me"(Strictly Rhythm) A very sweet harmonizing vocal track on the house tip. "Do For Me" comes with two most excellent mixes and an accapella. strong vibrant vocals layered with symbolic strings, breezy synthlines, tender bass, and easy flowin' beats. The B-side consists of another track, "I Really Do". Now if this doesn't move ya butt, I don't know what will. this is House at it's best. **(Jask)**

SLOWDIVE-"In Mind" (Reload/ Bandulu RMXS) (Creation/UK) Yet another indie shoegazer band attempts to revive their failing career by getting the ambient remix treatment. I don't know what the original track of this sounds like, but I really could care less. Reload and Bandulu turn in wonderful reconstructions here; Reload's is atmospheric with slow, heavy, reverberating beats while Bandulu's is a hallucinogenic fusion of spacey synth washes and manipulated vocals with dubby polyrhythmical beats over the top. Blinding, just fucking blinding. **(DJ*)**

ROBERT LEINER-"Dream Or Reality" (Apollo/Belgium) Under his given name, **The Source** puts out an excellent ambient record on Apollo in three mixes. The original mix is pure ambience with a pulsing kick drum to let you know that you're listening to a record and not just lying outside, looking up at the stars. The Into The Dream Mix is my favorite with its 'Something's happening to me. Something wonderful." sample and the melody from Electrotete's "I Love You". If this is any indication of what the album has in store, we're in for a surprise. **(GC)**

TERRE THAEMLITZ-"Tranquilizer" (Comatonse) A unknown New York based producer has made simply one of the coolest pure ambient records out at the moment. Opening with gentle waves of synths, "Tranquilizer" pauses for a moment before resuming, adding some light percussion and the most devastating subsonic bassline before returning to tranquil silence. Look for more works by Thaemlitz on the upcoming Plug In + Turn On compilation on Instinct Records this Spring. **(DJ*)**

LP/COMPILATIONS

PSYCHIC TV-Peak Hour (T.P.O.Y./UK) To review this, I'm going to ignore most anything anyone knows or thinks about PTV and say this: Peak Hour has something for funky breaks people, techno people, ambient people, and progressive trance people and it's all very well done. San Francisco has done Genesis and Family well. If you can find it, get it. **(CM)**

UNDERWORLD-DubNoBassWithMy HeadMan (Junior Boys'Own/UK) An album for the Bjork crowd for sure. If indie dance critics though it's genre had no future, Underworld is here to kill them all. The 12"'s are it as far as techno, outside of a couple of album tracks-namely "Surfboy". Honestly though, the album is very cool; vocals, dance, rock, techno-this is going to be huge in time, no doubt. **(Ed: Remember these geezers who recorded for Sire circa 1987, sans Darren Emerson?!?! Just watch the major labels start to feed...) (CM)**

V/A-Extra Sensual Perception, Vol.2-The Trance Groove (Sonic) A top compilation of recent choice tracks from this excellent Dutch label including **Nico, Cosmic Baby, Rising Sun** (aka Ken Ishii), **Ghetto Brothers** (Blake Baxter & Orlando Voorn), **Beyond** (Giis Vroom), and others. Worth checking out if you like good trance with depth. **(PW)**

V/A-DJ Culture: The Stress Compilation (Moonshine Music) The debut release from the newly re-organized Moonshine Music is this collection of progressive party funk classics from the **Stress** label mixed by U.K. pin-up DJ and Florida favorite **Sasha** as well as former Mixmag editor turned Stress A&R man **Dave Seaman**. Tracks here should be very familiar to most partygoers here in Florida-what more could you ask for, a CD full of favorite tracks mixed by one of Florida's favorites. If you're into the party funk- you need to own this! **(PW)**

TRANSFORMER 2-Transformations (Astral Werks) The debut full-length from Belgium's **Transformer 2** is a nice, easy-flowing collection of commercial trance/house. Included are all the singles dancefloors worldwide have come to know and love- "Fruit Of Love", "Pacific Symphony", "Just Can't Get Enough", but the album does nothing to break new ground. Not bad, but not amazing, either. If you've got the 12's, save your $. **(PW)**

V/A-Juan Atkins Presents Magic Tracks: Deep Detroit, Vol. 2/EDDIE "FLASHIN'" FOWLKES & 3MB-The Birth Of Technosoul (Pow Wow Trance) It's nice to see a domestic label outside of Detroit take an interest in exposing the vital music coming out of Detroit to a unwitting American audience. First **Jeff Mills**, now **Juan Atkins** and **Eddie "Flashin'" Fowlkes** get the treatment by the New York-based Pow Wow Trance imprint. Deep Detroit, Vol. 2 highlights a new generation of Detroit techno artists influenced and produced by the innovator, "Magic" Juan Atkins. Featuring tracks by Eddie Fowlkes, **Drexciya**, and Juan under the guise of **Infiniti**, Vol. 2 only serves to further display the wealth of talent that goes virtually unnoticed in the States. Much has been said over the years about the Detroit/Berlin connection, as many Detroit techno producers have moved to Berlin, finding a much more receptive climate to their music. Eddie Fowlkes, an innovator along the same token as the Detroit Three, has been even less acknowledged as an innovator. One of the pioneers of the 'technosoul' sound, Fowlkes teams up with Berliners **3MB** on this lp recorded in both Detroit and Berlin. Respect again to Pow Wow for this dedication to true techno. **(PW)**

JUNO REACTOR-Transmissions (Nova Mute) Originally concieved by principal member **Ben Watkins** as an ambient project to accompany an art installation, Juno Reactor's debut album seeks to help redefine techno as a legitimate musical genre. Absorbing the globe's multi-cultural influences and cross-pollinating through modern technology with elements of acid, ambience, and techno beats, Transmissions succeeds in at least, if nothing else, pushing the envelope a bit further than most. From ambience and deep acid builders to nice commercial trance this is a solid and engaging effort from beginning to end. Recommended. **(PW)**

SECT-Telekinetic (Third Mind) From the Pacific Northwest, more specifically, **Vancouver**-Home to **Skinny Puppy** and **FrontLine Assembly**-comes this bastion of techno. Ah, just kidding. If you listen to tons of the old S'Pup and FLA records (among others), you'll hear loads of wicked analogue sounds-303, 808, Juno 7- so it's only a progression of time that somebody would eventually make a record like this. Unlike Front Line's **Inter-Mix** project, which seemed to interpret techno rather than create it, Sect have great sincerity for the Underground and it shows. Could be the next place to spawn a strong scene... Check this out. **(PW)**

VAPOURSPACE-Themes From... (ffrr) "Gravitational Arch Of 10", Vapourspace's debut single on Canada's Plus 8 took the underground by storm earlier this year, appearing on Mixmag's Buzz Chart and numerous DJ returns worldwide. Not bad for only the second release from the nom de vinyl of Rochester, New York's Mark Gage. Now with an album deal with the ffrr label, the first for an American artist, Vapourspace comes out of the bedroom and into the album format with Themes... Divided into four distinct elements-Earth, Air, Fire, & Water- the album explores not just 'techno', but the world of electronic music as a whole, utilizing acidic and ambient textures to create beat-driven and beatfree soundscapes to propel you on an outerworld journey of aural bliss. One of the best full-lengths to come out in this very young year that will be at the top of many 'Best of '94' charts at year's end. We have only one complaint- with 12 tracks on the lp, why are none of them indexed on the CD? Great for an uninterrupted listening experience, but not terribly DJ friendly. **(DJ*)**

MATERIAL-Hallucination Engine (Axiom) Uncle Bill Laswell and his loosely assembled band of rotating musical explorers known as Material return with the ambient fusion of Hallucination Engine. Experimenting with ambience in an organic form, Material has joined multi-cultural elements such as traditional

Eastern musics, jazz, and dub reggae with funky breakbeats, spoken word, and hip-hop, pulling them at random out of a hat and melding them together to create an new fusion. Thoughtprovoking but not always on the mark, Hallucination Engine changes the standard perception of what ambience is-ambience is anything you make it-there are no rules. **(PW)**

DIVINATION-Ambient Dub, Vol. II (Subharmonic) Bill Laswell's new label has quickly followed up the excellent **Ambient Dub, Vol. 1** with a second installment subtitled **Dead Slow**. Enlisting fellow bassman **Jah Wobble, Mick Harris** of Lull (also Painkiller, Scorn, and ex-Napalm Death), and Material member **Jeff Bova** to expose a dark side of dub, Dead Slow is a collection that I think would make **The Orb, Jah Shaka,** and **Pete Namlook** proud. On the mag's Ambient Chart for a reason-check it out and see for yourself why. **(DJ*)**

AMBIENTO: A Fax Compilation (Reflective) San Francisco-based **Reflective Records** follow up **Spacetime Continuum's** Flurecence ep with this CD collection of material from Frankfurt's **Fax** label. Run by **Pete Namlook**, the label has pumped out over 100 limited releases within it's first year, all colour-coded for artist and genre of music. **Ambiento** highlights just six never before available domestically solo compositions (**Air, Hearts Of Space** and Namlook) and collaborations between Namlook and **Dr. Atmo (Escape)**, Spacetime's **Jonah Sharp (Alien Community)**, and **Coeur Atomique**. If you've never heard or been able to find Fax releases in the States, this is your best bet at the domestic price point. Choice stuff. **(DJ *)**

MARVIN WILSON-Guide (ROR, Ltd/UK) The hit-and-miss ROR label take an excursion into the ambient arena with this album by house producer **Marvin Wilson**. As one might expect, **Guide** explores ambience from the eyes of a house producer- happy, uplifting tracks; nothing too particularly out there or trippy, good keyboard sounds, subtle beats...pretty nice stuff, but a little obvious and too new age-y sounding for me. **(DJ*)**

LUKE KOYLE-Structured Ambience In The Powers Of 10 (Gyroscope) Wow, what a headtrip this one is... Opening with a long interlude of deeply chilled ambience, this intensely vivid album from Canadian film composer Luke Koyle shifts gear into a pleasantly unexpected free jazz mode that just took me by surprise. Over 47 minutes, Koyle fully explores the composition's avenues and possibilities, flowing between ambience, free jazz, and other live instrumentation and surprises to create a completely cerebral, but not overtly heady selection. For those looking for something a bit different in their chill session, this is most recommended. **(DJ*)**

SHAMEN-Different Drum (One Little Indian/UK) An import-only release, the Shamen have assembled a collection of remixes from the charttopping **Boss Drum** lp. Perhaps more accurately termed a 'pop/club/ambient update', **Different Drum** brings together all the mixes done for the singles off the lp and some previously unreleased mixes done for this collection. The pop types will dig the first side of the two discs, with **Beatmasters** mixes of each single, but the best mixes turn up on sides two and three with ambient and House retakes by **Mixmaster Morris, Mark Mc Guire, Future Sound Of London, Richie Hawtin,** and **Maurice Joshua.** A cool collection of mixes for the fan of either the group or the remixers involved, or even a DJ wanting to freshen up some favorites before the new Shamen lp comes out this Spring. **(PW)**

AUTECHRE-Incanabula (Warp/Wax Trax!/TVT) First appearing on Warp's **Artificial Intelligence** compilation, England's **Autechre** (pronounced 'Aw-tech-er') has quickly become the talk of the 'intelligent techno' crowd, outselling indie acts Smashing Pumpkins and The Breeders upon Incanabula's release in England. Now unleashed on the domestic market by Wax Trax!/TVT, Rob Brown and Sean Booth turn their influences of acid house, old school electro, Miami bass, and Detroit techno into an innovative and flowing release that builds with a sense of tension that leaves you thinking as well as chilling. Incunabula is an acquired taste, but after the first few listens, it gets inside your mind and it won't let go... **(DJ*)**

LARAAJI-Flow Goes the Universe (Gyroscope) Ever since Brian Eno produced his **"The Dance #3"**, Laraaji has been known as a pre-new age ambient explorer. This is no exception. Mostly consisting of beatfree tracks, the album also features some very interesting ethnocentric percussion cuts featuring zither and mbira perfect for mixing over things or as feature pieces, and a very out of place vocal cut, "Laughing In Tongues". Co-produced by **Michael Brook** (whose **Sleeps With The Fishes** is a classic) and with some assistance from Roger Eno, **Flow Goes The Universe** is a step into the next level of ambience and out of the New Age tag for Laraaji. **(PW)**

NAMLOOK/INOUE-Shades Of Orion (Fax Global/Germany) AIR-Air II (Fax/Germany) The prolific **Pete Namlook** enters 1994 with these two CD releases, **Shades Of Orion**and **Air II**, a follow up to the first Air lp. Shades Of Orion, a collaboration between Namlook and **Tetsu Inoue**, is the most recent release on the **Fax Global** label; four tracks of classic Namlook ambience, both with and without beats. Subtitled 'travelling without moving', Air II picks up where the first left off, taking the listener on 11 'trips' in one short hour. Organic, yet other worldly, this album smoothly drifts through your subconcious' orbit, beats and live percussion occasionally propelling you to the next destination. A very sensuous follow up-play them back to back. **(DJ*)**

System 7, continued from Page 11

not because of a copywrite infringement with Apple Computer's new Macintosh operating system of the same name as had been reported, but due to another band in the States having the rights to System 7. Known now in the U.S. as **777**, Hillage says that the group found it kind of neat that Apple decided to name their operating system after them.

The second System 7 lp, 777, takes a more stripped down and focused approach than it's predecessor. 'Leaner and meaner' is what Hillage and crew prefer to refer to it, cutting the collaborations to the bare minimum, working with just **DJ Lewis (Bandulu, the Orb)**, and **Alex** and **Thrash**. The result is a deeper, more atmpspheric and trancy sound accented by smooth beats and Hillage's signature guitar stylings. This 'leaner and meaner' approach was not entirely intentional, says Hillage, as it just sort of turned out like that during the writing process, but wanted to work on the project by themselves. "We were learning on the first record and we've become experts by the second," jokes Steve.

During this time Hillage and Miquette Giraudy, who are the core of System 7, have taken on some live gigs, participating in this last summer's MIDI Circus tour. Playing live with System 7 is a activity which Steve Hillage finds challenging.

"**Underworld** and ourselves are the only two techno bands (on MIDI Circus) that use guitars and it's nice because some sounds people think are keyboards, which really surprised and intrigued people. The guitar is just as viable an instrument in this music as anything other piece of technology."

System 7 will begin recording their third album at the end of February, after Steve and Miquette return from an extended holiday in Bali. How the record will sound remains to be seen, but the 42 year old Hillage would say "that it will be influenced by what we are into at the moment- right now that happens to be harder stuff, really hard beats with intensely spacy sounds."

"Some of the stuff I've been into lately that I like is Underworld, Darren Emerson's project, **3 Phase**- I really like that track they did about a year ago, **"Der Klang Der Familie"**, that's a prime example of a hard track that's really elegant- "Trancespotter" by **Vinyl Blair, Orbital...** The new stuff will be as we say 'deeper and wider with a side order of harder!'"

As far as guest collaborators go, the third album may contain contributions from **Derrick May** (Hillage may reciprocate by going some work on the long-awaited Rhythim Is Rhythim lp), Orbital, and **Laurent Garnier** ("Miquette met up with him last week in Paris and we may do some stuff.").

So what does this ambient innovator think about the rising awareness of ambient music in the underground?

"We've had quite a few people ring us up asking us to do **'Rainbow Dome Music II'**, but we don't consider what we do now to be ambient. We're into rhythmic dance music with a sort of elevating spacy approach. Compared to The Orb, we aim for music that you can play on a big system at a major dance event, not just chillout rooms. We like big systems, big bass drums, with a certain spaciousness. The primary goal is to make music that people can listen to and enjoy in a big dance setting as well as at home."

"(System 7) is almost like a hobby for us, we do it because we really enjoy it, we meet loads of interesting people, and it's great to work with interesting people and sell quite a few records to boot!"

One Dove continued from Page 8

that is very apparent in your influences. How did you incorporated that in One Dove?

DA: I just think we value a good song. We enjoy people that write good grooves, but I think if we want to write classic pop, which is what we want to do, and hopefully make music that people can set memories to and have moments in time that that music will take them back to, I think that we have to have a really strong song in order to do that.

JM: A song's just like a foundation that you can put any sound on you want. If you've got a great chord sequence and melody, that's just a foundation to do anything you want. People think that songs respect you, but they don't actually free you and if you've got a strong song you can do anything with it you have a chance to go into the studio and do anything you want or go anywhere with it. You can make it a hard rocker, ambient- anything. We've never gone into the studio without a song first.

T: So now the scene in Glasgow is really good we understand. I've heard that some new licensing has really messed up a good thing for the city.

JM: It's really, really good. When the club scene took off in Glasgow everybody just went for it, embracing it with open arms. A bunch of councilors blamed some of the violence on the club scene. So they banned people from entering clubs after 12 am and cut the licensing hours from 4 am to 2 am and there's police at every club to ensure that is enforced. These councilors really hate seeing people enjoy themselves, so they take it out on the kids.

T: That's awful considering that Glasgow won that City Of Culture award a few years back...is anything being done about it?

JM: There was no violence in the clubs, violence doesn't happen in the clubs, but in the streets. All they did was make sure more people were on the streets. I thought everybody would just go home, but it hasn't worked that way, people are finding ways around it. No matter how many laws you pass, you can't stop people from enjoying themselves. It's really polarized everybody and given them all a common enemy because it hurts indie as well as club culture.

TRIP FOTOFILE:

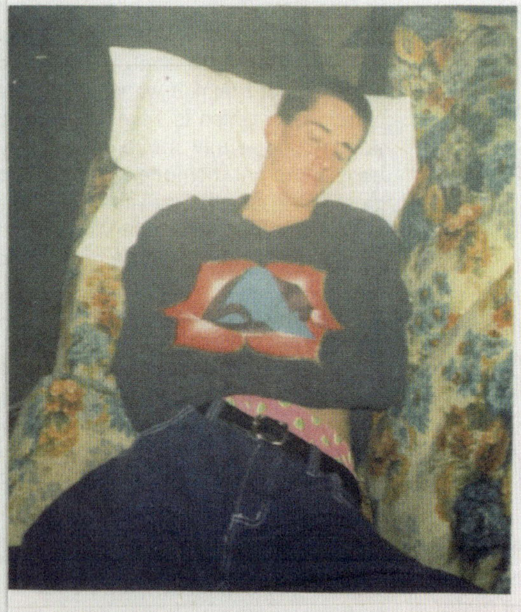

From left to right, clockwise: Godfather of Techno, **"Magic" Juan Atkins** finishing a mix at Artificial Intelligence (Miami); **Keoki (NYC)**, sans glasses chilling out at Artificial Intelligence; Germany's **Cosmic Baby** during his video shoot New Year's Day in Orlando; **DJ Icee** and TRiP's **DJ Three** at Emerald City (Ft. Lauderdale) Thanksgiving Day; Tampa crew enjoying Sunrise in Miami at Artificial Intelligence; Fully chilled at TRiP's **Oscillate** ambient club night.

Laurent Garnier, continued from Page 13 playing **(Ed.- referring to the Artificial Intelligence event in Miami in November. CJ Bolland never showed though, 'flight delay' the reason given by the promoters)**. The kids are going to be wiped out. Mr. Bolland plays hard as fuck. I'm not mad about it but a lot of people love it. And I respect that very much. He produces beautiful music, but he plays music much harder when he DJ's, which is usually the case. And **Juan Atkins**, too. He plays some fucking weird shit. Very weird shit, some of the weirdest shit I've heard in my life. But I think it will be good for the kids; even if he clears the dancefloor. If he clears it, it's because they'll recognize it aas different and that's good. I don't see anything bad from a DJ clearing a dancefloor. It doesn't mean shit- it just means that the kids understand that it's different. Then they'll start to realize, "Well, that's good and that still sucks." That's the good thing about it. Even if you clear a large portion of the dance floor, you're still working towards something.

T: As you know, there aren't many people around Florida who take chances while they DJ...

LG: That's their own problem. I've got no respect for people like that. I mean, if they're a DJ to pick up the women, then they should get the fuck out now! I think if a DJ is really into what he plays and plays what he loves then that's OK no matter what kind of music it is. But a problem I see here is that people aren't playing what they love, they're just playing for the crowd. I mean, you have to play for the crowd, but you also have to play what you like and show your personality. Music is so wide-ranged that you can't close yourself off to one type of music. Like, "Ooh, I'm a progressive house DJ and I won't play anything over 135 bpm." That's pathetic. If you don't take risks or chances, who else is going to do it? I hope that after last night people will go out and pay more attention to domestic records. I went to that shop in Orlando and the guy was **really** trying to sell me all this boring, white, progressive garbage and I looked at him and I said, "I don't want this shit..." And he said, "This isn't shit, this is good!" I said, "Show me domestics- **Transmat, Underground Resistance, +8...**" and he looked at me like I was a fucking alien! He said, "You buy American records?" I said, "Yeah- and on top of that, I play them!" He was looking at me like I was buying this totally experimental new music. This music's been around for years. It's what music is all about. This is real music. I found my **Choice** ep23 on **Transmat** in the bargain bin- I was embarrassed. Not because it was my record, but you don't put fucking Transmat in the bargain bin. No fucking way. He should be ashamed. That should never happen, no matter what. It's crazy.

T: What do you think of the shorter sets more popular in the U.S., because you're accustomed to playing for 6-7 hours?

LG: I flew here in 12 hours and all I got was a fucking hour and ten minutes. What the fuck is that?!? How are people going to remember me? I only came over here because I wanted to get known here and see what's happening. For sure the next time I come here, if I don't play for 3 hours it's not even worth it. How can I show people what I'm like in an hour and ten minutes? Maybe a lot of kids went home and said, "That guy only likes techno, that's all he played." No, I don't just like techno; I like garage, house, some breakbeat. I wanted to tell those kids what I'm all about.

T: What do you think of other producers. Who are some of your favorites?

LG: Mad Mike of UR. I went when I was in Detroit this week to his house and I spoke to Mike for about 3 hours. He's so intelligent, so into his shit. I'll tell you, I thought Derrick May was the best producer, but he hasn't done fuck all for years. Now I think Mad Mike is far in front of everybody. He's *definitely* the best producer worldwide in my mind. He's the man- he's the fucking man... He produces awesome garage, awesome house, awesome techno. No one can fucking touch him. Derrick has more feeling than him, but Mike's the shit at the moment. Big respect to the **Detroit Posse**- make sure you write that...

"spiraling vortexes, flowing from nowhere into your reptilian stem...mesmerizing, eroticizing..."
- Mondo 2000
ALIEN DREAMTIME™
60 minutes of true video hallucinations
featuring
Terence McKenna, Rose•X,
Space Time Continuum
and Stephen Kent
To Order Direct: 1-800-767-4748
Catalog Number COTVT-001-3
City of Tribes Communications
63 Fountain Street, San Francisco, CA 94114 (415) 641-8023

14

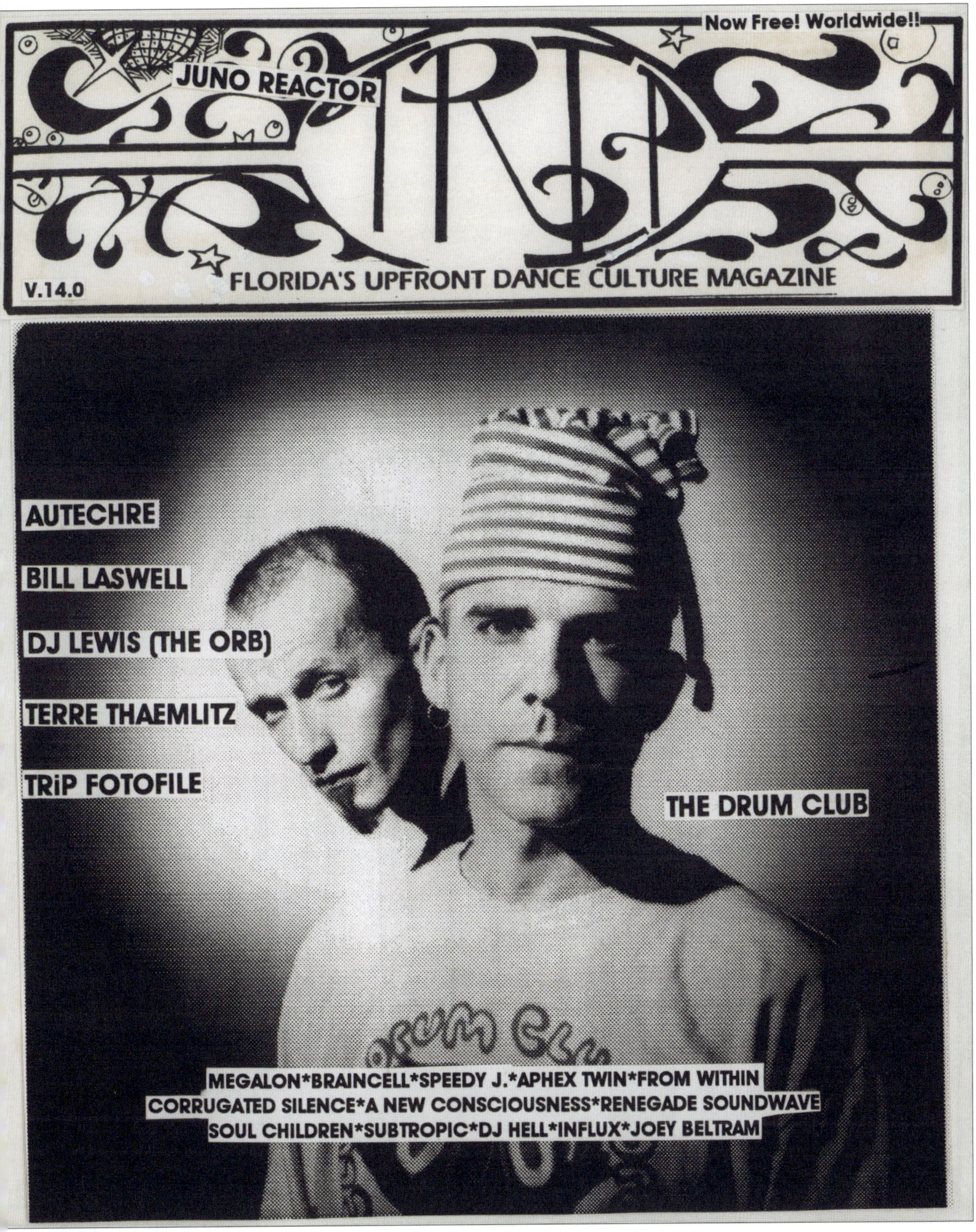
Now Free! Worldwide!!
JUNO REACTOR
TRiP
FLORIDA'S UPFRONT DANCE CULTURE MAGAZINE
V.14.0
AUTECHRE
BILL LASWELL
DJ LEWIS (THE ORB)
TERRE THAEMLITZ
TRiP FOTOFILE
THE DRUM CLUB
MEGALON*BRAINCELL*SPEEDY J.*APHEX TWIN*FROM WITHIN
CORRUGATED SILENCE*A NEW CONSCIOUSNESS*RENEGADE SOUNDWAVE
SOUL CHILDREN*SUBTROPIC*DJ HELL*INFLUX*JOEY BELTRAM

DIGITAL DREAMING
instinct RECORDS
PLUG IN + TURN ON
DOUBLE CD SET
PLUG IN + TURN ON
DOUBLE CD SPOTLIGHTING THE INSTINCT ARTISTS AND THE NEW ELECTRONIC UNDERGROUND. FEATURES EXCLUSIVE TRACKS FROM CABARET VOLTAIRE, THE DRUM CLUB, HUMAN MESH DANCE, GTO and TERRE THAEMLITZ.
EX-267
RISING HIGH
TRANCE INJECTION
RISING HIGH TRANCE INUJECTION
DOUBLE CD FEATURING THE LATEST TRANCE, AMBIENT AND INTELLIGENT DANCE FROM RISING HIGH RECORDS. INCLUDES DREAMFISH, RD.1, THE IRRESISTIBLE FORCE, AND MORE...
EX-265
kickin hardcore
KICKIN HARDCORE LEADERS
THE FIERCEST, DEEPEST, HARDCORE JUNGLE BREAKBEAT FROM THE UK STREETS. INCLUDES TANGO + RATTY, THE JUNGLE HOUSE CREW AND NOISE FACTORY.
KX-4105
TECHNOSONIC
volume 4
A JOURNEY INTO TRANCE
TECHNOSONIC VOL. 4
VOLUME 4 IN THE BEST SELLING SERIES OF UNDERGROUND TECHNO FROM ANTLER SUBWAY RECORDS. FEATURES ADAMSKI + TRANSFORMER 2, GRAYLOCK AND OLIVER ADAMS.
SNC-2030
26 W. 17TH ST #502 NY, NY 10011 / CSERVE RAVENET ON ROCKNET: 72170,1753 / SEND A S.A.S.E. FOR A FREE CATALOG / FOR DISTRIBUTOR INFO CALL 212.727.1360

TRiP Magazeen

V.14.0/April 1994

-NEWS-

-FEATURES-

-MUSIC & STUFF-

-THE COVER-

Holding cred with both the trendies and the travellers, London's **Drum Club** scored big in '93 with their popular Thursday night Drum Club, a brilliant debut lp, **Everything Is Now**. and last summer's acclaimed **MIDI Circus** tour. Now poised to release their second effort, **Drums Are Dangerous**, **Lol** and **Charlie** have taken a more danceable approach this time out. See what the lp has in store for your ears in this exclusive chat with **TRiP**.

-ABOUT THE ISSUE-

This issue was created using Aldus Pagemaker 5.0 and Adobe Photoshop on a Power Macintosh 8100 with 16 MB of RAM. Scans were made using an Apple One Scanner and output was done on a Hewlett Packard Laserjet 4M... Yeah, and then we woke up!! Oh, if you only knew!

SHOUTS OUT TO:

Charles @ Anarchic, Meredith Chinn, DB, Josh Wink, John & Carla, Dan Bell, Hardkiss Family, Sean & Rob Autechre, Hilary @ HOS, Tobias @ Superstition, Ian @ C-Level, Sean Deason, Terre Thaemlitz, DJ Hell, Jason Bentley, Raymond @ URB, Dave @ Silent, Oliver Lieb, DJ Lewis (The Orb), Ken, Louis, and all @ 'Mary's House'/WVUM-FM, Bruce, Jayson, & Drew, Ishai, Aquarhythms massive, Carol @ Moonquake, Michael & Tina @ Planet Dog & Megadog, Seefeel, the Stickmen (next issue... promise!!!), Jonah & Billie (thanks for the lovely t-shirt!), Katrien @ R&S, LuLu @ PlinkPlonk

FEET FIRST

Our bodies have fully recovered and the dust has finally settled from the **Winter Music Conference** in Miami at the beginning of March. As with most conferences, panels are a waste of time and the real action takes place at the bar.

So what were we able to suss out from our short working vacation? 1) The L.A. contingent partied harder than anyone else present. 2)House still rules the Miami underground. 3)South Florida's almost terminal techno scene (for lack of a better phrase) is showing signs of a renewed prognosis.

Two years ago the focal point of Florida's then infant 'rave' scene, South Florida fell prey to poor promoters, parties that don't promise what they advertise, inadequate sound, Hurricane Andrew, etc., etc., leaving partygoers deeply discouraged and dissapointed.

Just recently it seems that there has been a new spirit emanating from the area with a strong committment to doing parties right and rejuvinating the scene in South Florida. They're called the **Lollipop Guild**. By no means do they deserve all the credit, but their desire to educate and rebuild the scene should be a looked at by other promoters in the scene down there. Based out of Ft. Lauderdale's **The Edge** club , they were responsible for the **Emerald City** party, which drew over 1200 people to hear France's **Laurent Garnier, Keoki, DB**, and a host of top Florida DJ's last November. They've since been sowing seeds with a weekend late-night club and the occasional after hours.

continued on Page 26

TRiP Magazeen
100 East M.L. King Blvd.
Suite #5
Tampa, Florida 33603
U.S.A.
FON: 813.238.0310
FAX: 813.876.7473
(Please use a cover sheet if you fax)

EDITOR/PUBLISHER:
Peter Wohelski
SENIOR EDITOR: Wayne Consiglio
EDITOR-AT-LARGE: Chris Milo
EXECUTIVE ASSISTANT:
Jackie Rosquete
CONTRIBUTORS:
Jay Patrick Ahern, DJ Grumpy, DJ Jask, DJ Orion, DJ Three, Matt(y) Dillon, Terre Thaemlitz

SUPPORT THE UNDERGROUND!!!
ADVERTISING: Rates available upon request.
SUBSCRIPTIONS: $10 yearly for six issues, postpaid.
RETAILERS: Contact DELTRA RECORD DISTRIBUTION (310).222.8554 or our offices for info.
TRiP Magazeen is published every eight weeks and is distributed throughout the United States.
We hope our content will encourage awareness and positivity in the Global underground.
Opinions expressed are not necessarily those of the editors.

HYPE!HYPE!HYPE!HYPE!HYPE!HYPE!HYPE!HYPE!HYPE!HYPE!HYPE!HYPE!HYPE!HYPE!HYPE!

In a surprise move, Northcott's **DAMON WILD** has left the **EXPERIMENTAL** label to open his own label and studio. Assuming his position as A&R director at the label is **DJ MONEYPENNY**, moving up from promotions. A long time supporter of **TRiP**, we wish Damon the best in his new venture....Word has it that **KEN ISHII** has started his own label called **DUB RESTAURANT**....French label **FNAC** has folded. Expect a new imprint from French DJ/Producer **LAURENT GARNIER** and partner **ERIC MORAND** soon....Originally limited to 2500 copies on England's **MIGHTY FORCE RECORDS**, the **APHEX TWIN**'s **'ANALOGUE BUBBLE BATH'** has been re-released domestically through **TVT**....**HARTHOUSE AMERICA** aka L.A.'s **PLANET EARTH RECORDINGS** has released **SPICELAB**'s **LOST IN SPICE** lp, **HARDFLOOR**'s **"INTO THE NATURE"**, and the Florida trance classic **"HUMAN"** ep by **RESISTANCE D.** in the States, with albums from **VERNON** ("Wonderer") and **FRANKFURT/TOKYO CONNECTION** to follow soon....The next release on Harthouse ambient sublabel **RECYCLE OR DIE** is **#9 DREAM** by **WALTER DAHN & HELMUT ZERLETT**, due out in May....**C.R.A.S.H.** (Communication Ritual & Audio Sensory Happening) is a new Wednesday club night in Tampa. With two separate rooms, the night promises to serve up an 'eclectic mix of alternative and underground sounds for a progressive subculture'. With DJ's **STEVE McCLURE** and **RICH LESLIE** hosting the main room, film loops and visuals by **HALLUCI-NATION MAGIC** and a rotating music policy of different sounds each week in the back Opium Den, this promises to be one of the best nights out here. C.R.A.S.H. is located in the Masquerade, 1902 East 7th Avenue, Tampa. For more information, ring **813.247.7065**....**PETE NAMLOOK**'s **FAX RECORDS** has added two new sublabels. **YESTERDAY + TOMORROW** is dedicated to connecting the classical side of ambient and the ambient side of classical to show that ambient is not only a music born out of techno culture, but a sound which was there from the beginning of time. **AMBIENT WORLD** is a label created for the finest ambient music. With 2/3 of the profit given to the artist, the label offers the possiblility for an ambient artist to live, even from small quantities, and do his own music without restriction or discussion....**MOONSHINE MUSIC** has released Volume 4 in the popular **SPEED LIMIT 140 + BPM** breakbeat/jungle compilation series along with **UNITED STATE OF AMBIENCE**, a compilation of American ambient artists including **YOUNG AMERICAN PRIMITIVE, DUB TRIBE, HAWKE,** and **LUNA SOL**-an ambient project by **RABBIT IN THE MOON.** Moonshine has also signed Limelight DJ **KEOKI**....San Francisco's **HARDKISS MUSIC** is starting a home listening/ambient label called **SOFTKISS**....Seems the U.K. is waking up to the sounds of Detroit as **DERRICK MAY** begins a new monthly residency at Manchester's **HACIENDA**....Fellow 'zine publisher **HEATHER HEART** and boyfriend **ADAM X** release their first ep "Analogistic Warrior", underthe name of **X-HEART** on **DAVE CLARKE's MAGNETIC NORTH** label. Heather publishes Brooklyn-based 'zine **UNDER ONE SKY**....Props go out to U.K. journo **SIMON REYNOLDS** and the posse at **VIBE** Magazine, whose recent piece on the London jungle scene is the best we've ever read from a 'major' music publication....Based in Halifax, Nova Scotia, **COGNITION AUDIOWORKS** is a new label specializing in electronic and experimental music. **RHYTHMIC DISSONANCE**, a 14-track sampler of Halifax-based talent is the label's first release, due 4 April 1994....Spacetime Continuum's **JONAH SHARP** has been working on various club and party ventures with **MIXMASTER MORRIS** and **ROBERT LEINER** (aka The Source)....**C-LEVEL RECORDINGS**, whose **"ELEMENTS OF TRANCE"** ep was recently licensed by Belgium's **R&S**, has started a new sublabel called **CITY OF ANGELS**. For mailing list inquiries, send a list of working credentials to 8391 Beverly Blvd., Ste. 184, Los Angeles, CA 90068....**VISIBLE RECORDS** is a new label out of San Francisco. The label's second release is 'Odyssey Nine', an ep of progressive trance from **JOEY BELTRAM**. For more information on the label, to submit tracks, or DJ inquiries, call 415-292-4079....Look for two exciting projects to be coming soon on **ASTRALWERKS**; the first is a mixed cd of tracks from **ROBIN "JAYDEE" ALBERS**' ("Plastic Dreams") **FIRST IMPRESSIONS** label, the second is an ambient collection compiled by the designer of the **ANARCHIC ADJUSTMENT** line of gear, **CHARLES UZZELL-EDWARDS**. Charles is an ambient DJ/composer whose collaboration with Pete Namlook, **A NEW CONSCIOUSNESS**, was recently released on Fax....The U.K.'s Grateful Dead, **OZRIC TENTACLES** is touring the U.S. in April. The Ozrics are perhaps better known to the underground by their techno offshoot, **EAT STATIC**....The long-awaited collaboration between Cocteau Twin **LIZ FRASER** and **FUTURE SOUND OF LONDON** will never be released. Apparently the Cocteau's management doesn't want her voice on the material. Word to Cocteau manager **RAYMOND COFFER**: Give us a big break, mate. Loosen up and let the woman sing on the bloody record, maybe it'll revive interest in their crap new record....Fresh from their U.S. tour, **AUTECHRE**, and indie/ambient heads **SEEFEEL** both have ep's coming out on **REPHLEX** soon...**THE SANDALS' "Feet"** is getting the **HARDKISS FAMILY** remix treatment for an upcoming U.S. release....**ORBITAL** release their Peel Sessions and all the remixes of "Lush" together domestically on the **'DIVERSIONS'** ep, out now on **FFRR**....

S.I.N. • KENNY LARKIN • CLAUDE YOUNG
DJ T-1000 • FREQ • SEAN DEASON
MATRIX
DETROIT
TECHNO
GETS INTELLIGENT
CONTACT: MATRIX RECORDS
C/O SEAN DEASON
2030 GRAND RIVER # 202
DETROIT, MI 48226
phone/fax 313.964.5425

Autechre: attracting 'artificial intelligence'

Inspired by the austere and bleak surroundings of their hometown, Rochdale, located high above the hills outside of Manchester, **Autechre** (pronounced 'Aw-teh-ker') have turned their troubled small town experience into a liquid technological dreamscape fueled by Detroit, old electro, hip-hop, and Miami Bass.

Unhappy with their treatment by another record label, **Sean Booth** and **Rob Brown** sent a tape to Sheffield's Warp label, capturing the attention of Rob from Warp with a track only added as an afterthought, **"The Egg"**. Preserved along with **"Crystel"** on Warp's Artificial Intelligence compilation, these two tracks served as the impetus to start the label's acclaimed 'electronic listening music' series.

Picking up where these seminal singles left off, their debut album, **Incanabula**, outsold such indie acts as Smashing Pumpkins, The Breeders, and Bjork upon its release.

TRiP caught up with Sean and Rob from Autechre just before they embarked on a whirlwind tour of the U.S. along with **DJ Lewis** (The Orb).

TRiP: I understand that the two of you started out making cut-up tapes on Rob's recordable Walkman?

Sean Booth: Yeah, when I was really young, I used to cut up bits of tape, things from television, and cut them up and make weird soundtracks and stuff. I then got into electro and made pause-button mixes with the tape deck. Then I got in touch with Rob, who was doing turntable mixes-we met through a mutual friend when we used to do graffiti.

T: You're from a small town, what is it about these little English towns that spawns all this great music?

S: You can't say, really, because you live there. We don't know any different;you'd have to be an outsider, really.

T: What sort of influences do the two of you have?

Rob Brown: Just everything we hear, really. I think people are influenced by everything they hear; we listened to a lot of electro, some industrial like **Coil, Nine Inch Nails**, a lot of decent music, really.

T: I think I read someplace where you mentioned you both were into Miami bass- Luke Skyywalker and all of that sort of stuff...

S: Yeah, very much so. We were really young then. It was the sounds more than anything, that's what attracted us to it- just that unique sounds, all those smart bass drums and everything...

T: What is the Autechre live show like? is it a different experience than on vinyl?

R: Yeah, it's harder. Apart from a chill-out room or an ambient set-up, we can't really get people dancing with the sort of stuff off the album. It's a bit too complex, maybe. The stuff that we do live is generally our harder edge, that never made it to the Incanabula album. All the stuff that will be coming out in the future will be harder than on Incanabula.

S: It's the fact also that you're in a club full of people, you can't really resist the sensation to make them all jump around. You want to something a bit heavy; I mean, if you've got a club full of people and you do a nice, mellow set, unless they're all off their heads, they won't appreciate it. They're going to appreciate that more if they're at home, so we try to make the set a bit more energetic, just from a personal standpoint.

T: Have you done ambient set-ups in the past?

S: We do mellow stuff live. The set comprises of some hard stuff, some really deep dubby stuff, and some mellow stuff, so when we get into the club, we just sort of decide exactly what we're going to do depending on what the crowd is into.

T: What are some of your favorite records, ones that made you think, "Wow, I want to make music like that!"

R&S: "Music Madness" by Mantronix, "Clear" by Cybotron, there's a really long list. It's weird because we don't sound like any of those records. We have this idea of what we really like, so when a tune comes up, and you just think, "Yeah, that's exactly it."

T: You've been able to create a well-rounded mix of all of your influences without wearing them on your sleeve, and in the process come out with something totally original.

S: We didn't do that on purpose, it's just that with the album we used to spend a couple of months working on each track. We didn't have much equipment and the result was something we had been listening to for two months and we were really into it. The newer stuff is a little bit more instant, and it's a lot moodier. If you're used to our style, you'll be into the new stuff, but if you haven't heard Incanabula, don't buy the new album when it comes out.

T: What does Incanabula mean?

S: It's in the dictionary **(Ed. Interviewer now feels very stupid),** but if you don't know what it means, we'll tell you. It means the early stages of something, it's Latin.

T: The story seems to go that you were on another label and were getting jerked around, how did you hook up with Warp?

R: We phoned them up and I said "We're in a lot of shit, can you help us out, we need an outlet for our music." and no one else was prepared to take it, because it was a little bit out there for people. Warp seemed to be the only guys doing what everyone else termed as weird stuff. Sean phoned up Steve Beckett, had bit of a moan about the general state of the music in England, and they were in the same sort of frame of mind, so he said to send a tape along. It so happened that a lot people were sending that sort of stuff in, and that started the whole Artificial Intelligence series off.

T: What do you think of all the press that the series and underground dance music in general, has gotten in the U.K. music press like NME and Melody Maker?

S: We're a bit wary of the press sort of hyping it too much, but it's too late for that because they've already done it. We're just going to see it through, because the press are going to get tired of it and start calling it, but we'll still be there in ten years making the same decent music. It's not going to change the way we percieve what we do. We're only making music for ourselves and if the press want to write about it and say it's great then it's their fault. If other people like it, that's when we get a bit of satisfaction, but seeing a decent press review means nothing.

DJ Lewis Keogh (The Orb/Bandulu)

T: How did you get involved with Alex Paterson?

Lewis: I know Alex's girlfriend, Lisa, from going to **Shoom** about six years ago. She used to make me tapes of Alex mixing records into unreleased Orb stuff and I listened to that and thought if that's what he likes the I can serve him up with stuff which he's going to like even more. I done Lisa a tape when they were going on holiday to Morocco, knowing full well that it would be played within earshot of Alex. He heard it and asked who it was, and he got me a job in Switzerland doing a gig and that was it.

T: What is your role in an Orb show? I know you like to open the night.

L: What I really like to do is do it from the doors because then you can play stuff like **B12, Black Dog,** and the more ambient Detroit stuff because compared to an actual Orb show, it's got quite a few drums in it as The Orb's pretty ambient. If I play after the Orb's done their set, everyone goes mad. All it needs is just the drum machine sounds in there, because they've been standing around, chilling out for the ambient stuff. The first place a lot of those tunes were heard, Reload, Black Dog, B12, and danced to them. I've read interviews with Black Dog and B12 and they think that their music has never been played to a large crowd that's danced to them.

T: What about Bandulu?

continued on Page 26

Laswell 'Rockit'-ing the Hallucination Engine

by DJ Grumpy

Pick up any of the most influential records of the last 20 years and chances are you'll find **Bill Laswell**'s name on it somewhere. Bassist, producer, remixer, you name it, Laswell has worked with **everybody**. From pop to hip-hop, jazz to P-Funk, and beyond, the man is always stretching the boundaries, fusing together different musical genres, and creating totally fresh new sounds for other artists or his own projects like the long-standing loose musical collective called **Material**.

After having trouble finding homes to release many of his projects, Laswell started his own label, **Axiom**, to put out his own work and the works of other like-minded artists.

Always looking into the future, Laswell has just recently begun a new sublabel called **Subharmonic**, showcasing 'music of the extreme', both metal and ambient with two volumes of ambient work entitled **Divination** and an album from Laswell's metal side project, **Praxis**.

Our man DJ Grumpy battled a case of nerves and a less than talkative studio-worn Laswell, to shed light on this multi-talented musical influence.

TRiP: So what are you working on right now?

Bill Laswell: I'm working with this Haitian group, **Voodoo 151**. I'm mixing that right now for about a week; that's what I'm doing right now. I really don't like to talk too much about things before they come out.

T: So you've been staying busy...

BL: Yeah. I'd say I've been making music consistently for the past ten years, so I've pretty much been busy.

T: I really like the Divination 1 & 2 projects. Do You plan to do more of that sort of style?

BL: Thank you... Yes, I really enjoyed doing those projects and I'd definitely like to develop that more.

T: The new Material album, Hallucination Engine, has a track ("Mantra") that The Orb did a remix on. Do you have any plans to work with them again?

BL: Nothing's scheduled, but I would definitely like to.

T: Are you familiar with Pete Namlook? Your Divination stuff is similar to things he does.

BL: Yes, I spoke with him the other day, and we're trying to plan a record for March. He's very talented.

T: How did you get into the more ambient side of making music?

BL: In a way I was always doing that, from the beginning. In the early 80's I worked a lot with (Brian) **Eno** and with a lot of different psychedelic bands. There was no specific area to work in with that kind of music, but over the last couple of years it has opened up and there's more of an interest. It evolved kind of naturally. I've been incorporating that for a long time and lately, it's been a bit more trendy. There's a lot of interest in the genre, so you could actually do more in this area, but I've sort of been there the whole time.

T: Is there anyone left that you haven't worked with that you'd like to?

BL: No, not really. I've been talking for years with **Ornette Coleman** to try to set up a project. And we're closing in on finally doing one. but there's not a lot of people, really. I've been pretty lucky.

T: Because you have a very wide range of style, do you have any specific influences?

BL: There's probably a million of them and you sort of forget them as you go along...

T: What would you be your favorite project that you've done?

BL: Any that I've finished. There's been quite a lot of them.

T: What do you plan to do in the future? Do you plan to do more stuff like Divination?

BL: I'm trying to develop a lot of things in that area and also some techno and hardcore techno. That's more of an experiment for me. And just continuing to work with musicians... There's a lot of spoken word records coming out on Axiom and a project with **William Burroughs** and **Ornette Coleman**. My schedule is pretty full.

T: Do you have any desire to do soundtrack work?

BL: No, I haven't in the past. I've always thought of it as background music for something that wasn't too impressive to begin with. I haven't really tried...there is a possiblility of that now. For the last 10 years I've said the only things I won't do are remixing and soundtracks, but for the last 2 years that's all I've wanted to do...

Bill Laswell's Top 10 Ambient Tracks

1. Miles Davis-In A Silent Way
2. Autechre-Incanabula LP
3. Lull-Dreamt About Dreaming
4. Brian Eno-On Land LP
5. Pete Namlook-The Definitive Ambient Collection, Volume 2
6. Aphex Twin-Selected Ambient Works, Volume 2
7. Naked City-Absinthe
8. Material-'Mantra' (Orb Remix)
9. Pete Namlook-"The Dutch Side Of The Milky Way"
10. Funkadelic-"Maggot Brain"

Comparing passports and aural oddities with Juno Reactor

In the thick of the English music scene for most of the last decade, **Ben Watkins** has seen musical trends come and go as part of bands like **Empty Quarter, Sunsonic, Flowerpot Men,** and **Psychoslaphead**.

Recording under pseudonyms such as **Electro-tete, Jungle High**, and now **Juno Reactor** (with cohorts **Stef Holweck, Jans Waldenbeck**, and **Mike Macguire**), Watkins has assimilated his global travels and cross-cultural influences into **Transmissions,** Juno Reactor's debut album, thus satisfying both his wanderlust and addiction to technology.

TRiP spoke with Ben Watkins from his London flat shortly after the release of Transmissions.

TRiP: How did you come up with the name Juno Reactor?

Ben Watkins: It all started off two, two and a half years ago as an art project where my girlfriend, who's a sculptor, built this enormous, concrete structure that was seventy foot long and looks a bit like a dinosaur's tail with lots of lumps in it. She did this exhibition in this massive empty warehouse, her and this other girl. It was really beautiful and it took a long time to do. So, for the opening I wrote a piece of music for it that was about an hour long and we got in a 4000 watt P.A. system and blasted it through that. That's going to come out through the Orb's label in about two months time. **Alex Paterson** came down and he did some overdubs for it. Anyway, this sculpture was called the **Juno Reactor**, named after the female goddess. It all just started from there; we did this other art exhibition where we got hold of a 30 foot Bloodhound surface to air missile and drove it around London with an armoured personnel carrier in front and behind. We drove it past the House of Parliament, down Whitehall, around Trafalgar Square, up Piccadilly, and into this art galllery called the Deer Armour, which is sort of shaped like a silo. We had to take the missile apart, take it in, put it back together and make it upright, and we played the Juno Reactor soundtrack as well. It was really heavy-I loved it, but some people found it a bit too much. That's generally how it came about.

T: I knew there was an Orb connection...I know about the Electrotete stuff. Didn't you do a record on Wau! Mr. Modo a few years back?

BW: Yeah (hesitantly). I did the **Apollo XI** track with Alex. I try to forget about that, actually. I didn't like that very much. When we were doing it, I sort of half liked it. We spent a day on it, it never really- we didn't get out the best ideas we could have. I've got loads of copies...

T: How did you hook up with Alex?

BW: I've known **Youth** and Alex for about 10 years. So I started doing ambient stuff in '83 with Youth on this project called the **Empty Quarter** and just got into the whole electronic thing then through bands like **Kraftwerk, DAF**, that early to mid-80's crowd. I loved DAF. I thought they were absolutely amazing, and they really got me off on that sort of sequenced mode and the fact that you could get rid of the drummer and bass part of the band and stopped a lot of the hassle and made it much easier to go out live. When I heard **Yello** with their sort of three dimensional sound imagery, that really made me think again.

T: As far as the end of the 80's, were you more into the 'industrial' stuff or the more 'acid house' sound that was emerging in England then?

BW: I think I was pretty much into the acid type of things rather than industrial because I felt that the industrial thing for me happened in the early 80's. I had this band called the **Flowerpot Men** and we were very **DAF, Suicide**-orientated- very hard and pretty mean. Actually at that time I think I kind of went into a bubble with **Sunsonic**; we had gotten a studio and we just sort of pissed around in there and learned how to use everything and pretty much ignored everything that was going on at that point and got into our own thing. We went to some of the sunrise parties and things, but not really.

T: Electrotete, Jungle High, are names of some of your more current works. Now that Juno Reactor has seemed to take off, what's the status of the other projects?

BW: I think what we're going to try to do is that all the projects like **Johann**, who I work with in Jungle High, and **Steffan**,who's my partner in Electrotete, is to put everything under Juno Reactor...the other stuff is all very similar that it's easier to package it all together under one name.

T: You do a lot of traveling...where have you been lately?

BW: Well, I haven't been away that much lately, I've been stuck in here, but **Mike** is off in India at the moment... Part of the problem with

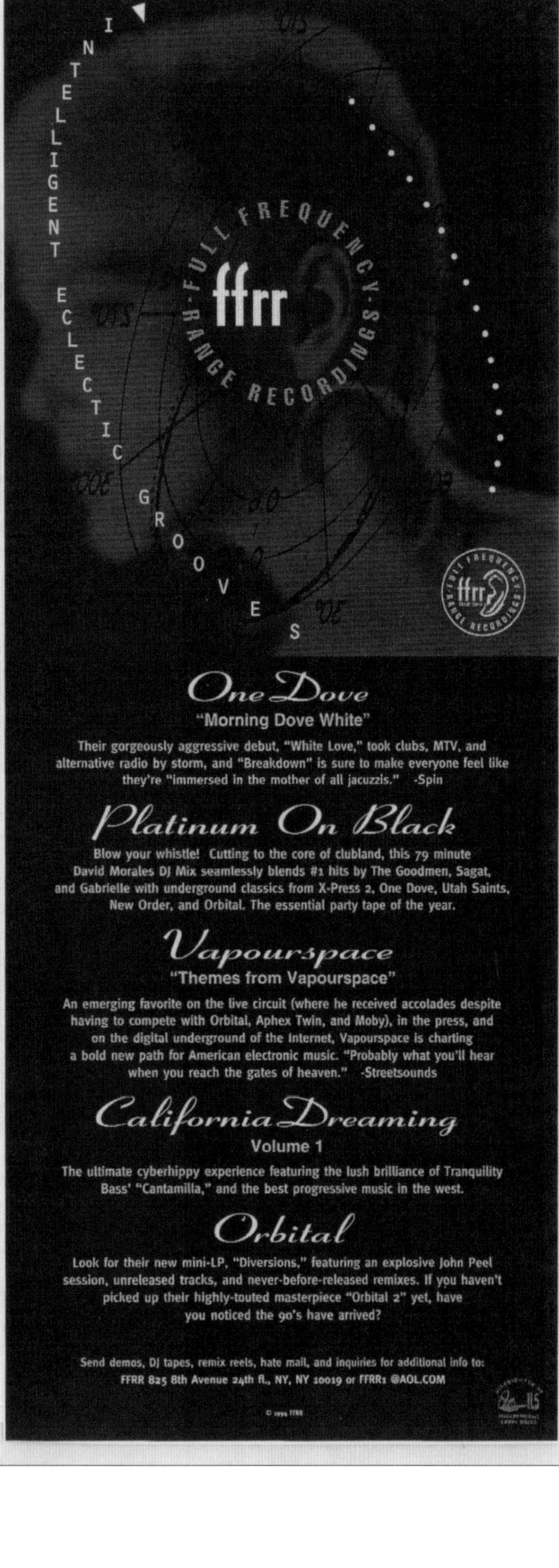

exist dance

"We try to make music that will make your eyes want to roll back in your head."

- Exist Dance co-founder Mike Kandel

And for the past three years, the L.A.-based Exist Dance label have been collectively rolling eyes back in the heads of clued-up DJ's worldwide with over ten releases. The label has emerged virtually unrecognized in the underground, overshadowed by its San Franciscan counterparts and with very little press hype.

'Transmitting' from Heaven, their studio, former CalArts students **Mike Kandel** and **Tom Chasteen** have parlayed their influences of early industrial, hip-hop, acid house, and world music into a Mac and poured out tracks by such highly sought after and heavily anticipated monikers as **Tranquility Bass, Eden Transmission, Up Above The World**, and others, with remixes done under the guise of the **High Lonesome Sound System**.

From trance to tribal, ambient to ethnic, hardcore breaks to chunky acid funk, each Exist Dance release has a distinct flavor, packed with obscure ethnic textures and deep emotions that build an intense mood over a track. At times hard and primal, other times soothing and subtle, but always mysterious and seductive; it's this special quality that has placed their records on the turntables and in the charts of DJ's as diverse as **Justin Robertson** and **Keoki**, **Sven Vath** and **Doc Martin**.

1993, and so far in 1994 has seen Exist Dance undertake some remix work, collaborate with Keoki, release a compilation, take on for the first time outside talent with the addition of **Freaky Chakra** and **Tylervision** to the stable already residing in Heaven, re-release the Tranquility Bass singles remixed with a new track. A busy year for a label with a so-called 'sleeper' status. With more to follow, we're sure. **(Editor's Note: As we went to press, we were informed that Exist Dance has moved to Washington State where they will "make use of global technology by faxing and phoning business dealings and enjoy better herb in the studio")**

EXIST DANCE DISCOGRAPHY

Merge-"You Move Me" 4/91
Tranquility Bass-"They Came In Peace" 6/91
High Lonesome Sound System-"Champion Sound" 7/91
High Lonesome Sound System-"We're Go" 10/91
Eden Transmission-"I'm So High" 1/92
Odyssey 2000-"The Odyssey" 3/92
Voodoo Transmission-"Voodoo Fire" 6/92
High Lonesome Sound System-"Waiting For The Lights" 8/92
Up Above The World-"Straight Up Caffeine" 1/93
Tranquility Bass-'Mya Yadana" (Excursions In Ambience compilation) (Caroline Records) 4/93
Freaky Chakra-"Halucifuge" 7/93
High Lonesome Sound System w/ Keoki-"We Are One" (Trance Odyssey compilation) (Adrenalin Records) 9/93
Michael Kandel-"5/18/93" (Chill Out compilation) (Instinct Records) 9/93
'Transmitting From Heaven' compilation 10/93
Up Above The World-"Trying to Reach You" 12/93
Tranquility Bass-Broadcast Standard Series, Vol. 1 3/94

LABEL WHORS GO TO THE MALL.
THE REST GO UNDERGROUND!
WORLD UNDER GROUND
★Specializing in all types of House Music
★Direct U.K. imports as well as domestic and out of print house and dance
★We pay top dollar for your 12's and C.D.'s
★Listen before you by
★Mail order, and weekly fax list
★New and used Techno, Alternative, Hip Hop, and Disco 12's and C.D.'s
★Legal herbal blends and smoking accessories
★Club gear by Gat, Tip, Qambiant, Tribal, Stupid, Pervert, Dog Eat Dog, Tasty, Thump, Kickwaer, Label Whore, John Doe, Anarchic, and hemp ware by Hempstead
★Fimo beads and jewelry
★Art by Scrambel Campbel
Tune in and turn on to a different world.
WORLD UNDERGROUND
Peace thru Music
927 S. HOWARD AVE., TAMPA, FL 33606, 813-251-1307

KLAUS SCHULZE
72 - 93
the essential
Founding member of Tangerine Dream and legendary force in the ambient-electronic movement, The Essential is a double CD retrospective, compiled and remastered by Schulze himself. Find out why Europe is calling Schulze 'the Father of Trance'.
21 years in 141 minutes.
Carol 1896
Mail Order Info: Semi - Automatic, PO Box 2759, New York, NY 10116
© 1994 Caroline Records Inc.
CAROLINE

John C. Lilly
E.C.C.O.
The words and wisdom of John C. Lilly set to ambient music by P.B.C., Spice Barons, and the Heavenly Music Corporation
JOHN C LILLY
E.C.C.O
Unidentified Floating Ambience
SpiceBarons, Patternclear, Satellite IV and more define the undefinable on this ambient compilation.
From Here to Tranquility Vol. 2
Volume 2 of the series includes Pelican Daughters, Legion of Green Men, Lotus, Trancendental Anarchists, Single Cell Orchestra, Patternclear, Cirrus Minor, 68000, Tylervision, Robert Rich, Air
the silent (r)evolution has begun
Dealer, wholesale mail order inquiries welcome.
From Here to Tranquility Vol. 2 distributed exclusively through Caroline Records 212.989.2929
SILENT
101 TOWNSEND ST • SUITE 206
SAN FRANCISCO, CA 94107
415.957.1320
FAX 415.957.0779

Drum Club warn of 'dangerous' new lp

Lol Hammond and **Charlie Hall**, otherwise known as **The Drum Club**, perhaps stand poised to turn the U.K. music scene upside down. Their debut album Everything Is Now, after a couple of successful singles on the **Guerilla** label, was an inspired musical journey which unfolded into a warm, friendly collection of tribal beats, organic ambient sounds, and techno futurism.

The Drum Club, their aptly-named Thursday night club night, has become one of the most popular nights out in the Capital, attracting a crowd of London trendies and traveller partiers alike for a mix of tribal, techno and trance, progressive house, and ambient vibes.

During the final stages of recording their upcoming lp, Drums Are Dangerous, the two ex-punks had a spot of tea and a chat with **TRiP** about where their last album went, where their new album is going, and all points in between.

TRiP: Let's start with the basics: how did you and Charlie come to meet?

Lol Hammond: Well, we met through the London club scene and Charlie's a DJ, I'm a musician and I'd just done this track called "Made In Two Minutes", a bit of a rave anthem and he wanted to remix it. He couldn't play, so I went into the studio with him to help and we got along really well. That was about two years ago and we took it from there. We used to be involved with Spiral Tribe and we did the first two singles with Spiral Tribe; we were doing both at the same time, doing the big parties with them and doing both the club and act, the Drum Club.

T: So you were involved with the whole Castlemorton party?

LH: Yeah, we were there, rockin'! It was amazing, amazing...I did loads of interviews...that was when the traveler party scene came to public attention. We were even doing interviews with CBS News in America, actually. It's gotten so difficult to have a party, the police and establishment have cracked down so much, so we just had to concentrate on music, really. Most of my friends involved in that have all gone abroad they're all doing it in countries like France and Spain where it's still a bit more relaxed and they haven't gotten wise to it yet, which is what they've done in (the U.K.).

T: I understand the authorities have really cracked down on the big party organizers...

LH: Oh, definitely. It's gotten impossible, you get a sound system together and they come over and take it away from you. We lost a lot of money, money we didn't have.

T: So about Drum Club, I really enjoyed the first record, Everything Is Now...

LH: Yeah, we're trying to sort out an American deal actually, we want to make sure we go to the right people. Sorry, I'm very tired at the moment, we're working on the new album this very minute and doing a remix for our friend who used to sing for **N-Joi, Saffron**. She's also singing on the new album, two tracks...

T: What's the new lp going to be like?

LH: More clubby... **Maxine Harvey** who did the re-vocal for the remix of **"Sound System"** and did all the **KLF** stuff, she's working with us again; she's done two, Saffron's doing two, and the rest of the tracks are all samples and instrumentals. The album's going to be called Drums Are Dangerous, it's a real step up from the first album; although we love the first album, it's a real bedroom cheap sort of album. We've expanded the Drum Club sound, but I think the first album's got a lot of charm and ambience. It is quite ambient, isn't it? Quite strange because I've been listening to more ambient stuff than ever, but we seem to have picked up, the songs are faster and gotten more clubby. I love ambient music, but it's weird how things turn out. Some people make a more kicking album, then make an ambient one and we seem to have gone the other way 'round. I'd love to do an ambient album, I've even got the title: **Where's The Fucking Drums?!?**

T: Last summer, you were part of the MIDI Circus tour...

LH: I came up with the name, MIDI Circus, I got the cue from Lollapalooza, you know. I thought there should be a techno version. Our friend, **Emma** from **Lush** was on the tour two years ago and she kept sending me postcards and telling me all about it.

T: Besides her playing on the first album, the two bands did a project together didn't you?

LH: It was a very limited tune because the record companies, **Big Life** and **4AD**, were pissed off. It's wicked, it's changing hands for like 20-30 quid already, it was done between Emma and **Miki** and me and Charlie. It's such a shame that one of the best things we've ever done and it's limited to 1500 copies. It sold out in one day.

T: You seem to like that sort of collaborative spirit.

LH: I like working with people that they don't expect you to work with. Eno used to do that and I think it's quite interesting. We're going to do a project with **Robert Owens**, something real housey, which is not what people expect and I love doing that. Like Saffron, she comes from a club/pop background and people are shocked that she's working with us, but it always seems to work.

T: It seems that you have a lot of musical influences that are open-minded as well.

LH: Besides techno, which I listen to 90% of the time, I like the **Cocteau Twins** a lot. I love her voice, she'd be the ultimate voice on a trance track.

T: Charlie, as the DJ half of Drum Club, what sort of style do you play when DJ'ing?

Charlie Hall: I probably tend to play deeper or harder stuff than we make. Basically, our music is a combination of **Lol**'s melodies and my beats; I've always been into melodic, funky techno and obviously loads of stuff on that tribal tip.

T: How long have the two of you been doing your club night?

CH: We started it in March of '92 and initially we wanted to get the sort of music that we like,especially deep European techno, stuff that's got a little more drum and bass rather than the Detroit, pure techno. We were working with Spiral Tribe, the vibe was great but the music was starting to get a bit insane, a little bit too fast. We wanted to hear something in between and there just wasn't anywhere. When we started the club, we advertised it as a techno club and no one would come because in '92, techno was associated with breakbeat music, quite erroneously. We were running for about six months and nobody came, but all the DJ's- **Andy Weatherall, Darren Emerson, Phil Perry, Fabio Paras**- they came and played for almost nothing because they believed we were doing it right.

T: So did it just one day just explode and the place was packed?

CH: Not quite, but it did turn one week. I really don't know whether it was anything to do with it, but it coincided almost to the week with the release of our first single on Guerilla. We get about 600 people in there every week now.

T: Is it a mixed crowd; indie and techno kids as well as trendies?

CH: We get a lot of the free party/festival people, loads of students come down, and a lot of people who are really into the music. It's sociable, but people are there to listen to the music rather than socialize. Not so much of the trendy crowd, you get some people who look trendy, but really listen to the music. Mostly people just take their shirts off and go for it.

T: I understand that the two of you come from the old punk movement. What do you think about all the old punks like Weatherall, Alex Paterson, Kris Needs, etc., dominating the U.K. dance music scene?

CH: I think that it's the most immediate form of music. Punk was sort of a shout, an exclamation; you couldn't sit down and listen to punk music. It was mood music, you went out and and you went for it. I think the old punks like that about techno, it's very immediate. When I was a punk, I was 17 and too young to really get involved and nothing came around and really interested me until the dance thing.

CHARLIE HALL'S TOP 10 TUNES OF 1993

Drum Club-"Sound System"
OBX-"Eternal Prayer"
Exquisite Corpse-"Inner Rhythm"
Pressure Of Speech-"X-Beats" (Drum Club Remix)
The Source-"The Source Experience"
Underworld-"Dog Man Go Woof"
Greylock-"Acceleration by Trance"
Plastikman-"Krakpot"
Perry & Rhodan-"The Beat Just Goes Straight On & On"
Psychick Warriors Ov Gaia-"Rhythms, Vol. 1"

World Sonik Domination: Alan Oldham gives the full 411 on the

If you've been into Detroit at any time over the last few years, you've probably been touched by the work of or at least been familiarized with the name **Alan Oldham**. Whether it was spinning the tapes of what was to become the first techno records on his ***Fast Forward*** radio show, doing the label art for the first releases on **Transmat**, DJ'ing at countless clubs and parties, or making his own tracks, Alan has been involved with the Global Underground from Detroit since virtually Day One.

Tapped by **Mad Mike** almost a year and a half ago on the eve of an Australian tour to replace **Jeff Mills** in **Underground Resistance**, Alan also runs his own label, **Generator Records**, travels DJ'ing under the name **DJ T-1000**, and still draws a lot of label art for **D-Jax Up Beats**.

A wealth of information and insight on Detroit and the Global Underground, **TRiP** Editor **Peter Wohelski** spent the better part of a recent afternoon picking the brain of Mr. Oldham on the mystique of Area Code 313, his artistic endeavors- both vinyl and pencil oriented, and Detroit's past, present, and future. Read and enjoy...

TRiP: How did you get involved in the Detroit scene?

Alan Oldham: Well... (laughs) Back in the mid-80's, when I was in college I got a radio show on our local **NPR** (National Public Radio) affiliate (WDET-FM) called *Fast Forward*; that was 1986.

T: You did the show for a long time before you quit...

AO: Yeah, I did the show for six years. When *Fast Forward* first came on the air, that was when **Derrick, Kevin**, and **Juan** came out with their first record. It was the same year. In fact, the night of my first broadcast, I went over to Derrick May's house, his old house, and he gave me a whole gang of stuff to play on the air, which turned out to be the very first techno records, you know, **"Nude Photo", "When We Used To Play"** by **Blake Baxter**, the very first **Model 500** stuff- **"Off To Battle"** and **"Electric Entourage"**, and all that. The very first **Inter City**, not **Inner City**, record which was **Suburban Knight**... I did that for six years and then I got the call to be in Underground Resistance when Jeff Mills quit. I took his spot on stage and I've been doing it ever since.

T: Was Fast Forward just a dance music show?

AO: The original plan for Fast Forward was supposed to be what is now termed as World Beat. It was not so much 'World Beat' as it was old **Isley Brothers** and **George Clinton**, mixed with jazz fusion- which was still kinda in at that point in time- **Weather Report, Lenny White, Mahavishnu Orchestra**, stuff like that. Then later on, as techno began to build, that turned out to be all I was playing. And later I was juxtaposing techno and the then-nascent Chicago house into **Cabaret Voltaire**; I was into **Skinny Puppy, Severed Heads, Front 242**, all that kind of stuff. I was juxtaposing all that electronic music together... In '88, that's when Derrick and those guys were at the peak of their powers with the acid house explosion (in the U.K.). I was introducing Detroit to a lot of that stuff and they didn't even know about it. Detroit is pretty liberal in terms of music, if you put it out there for people to get, then they'll get into it. Problem is there's no sustained basis anymore, so people kind of go back to their old ways.

T: What was it like to be at the beginning of all this? Did you have any notions as to what sort of impact these tapes Derrick gave you would have?

AO: No. It began a little later on, like a couple months after that incident, that's when **Neil Rushton** (now head of Network Records and Kevin Saunderson's manager) started coming to America and started to hang out with Derrick and those guys and that's when the first 'techno' album came out. That's when I knew it was like a big international deal. A lot of us, man, we're from Detroit-we're isolated, you know. I mean, nobody's got money to be traveling and then all of a sudden, all of these Brits are swooping down on us trying to exploit this music and it was a very exciting time. I'm glad to have been at the forefront of that...

T: Did you know Derrick just from doing your artwork?

AO: I knew Derrick since we were kids; Derrick used to live around the block from me in our old neighborhood, which I don't live too far from now. He used to live around the block and play, ride bikes, and do all the things that kids do. I didn't run into him again until years later and he was just doing **Transmat** and I was struggling. At that point I wanted to be a cartoonist, I really wanted to draw for Marvel and DC and shit... He saw some of my art and he liked it and said, "Why don't you draw me some shit?" And that's how I started doing that. So I drew some stuff for **"Nude Photo"**...I did a lot of stuff for Derrick. Unfortunately, see, he never told me that my artwork was helping him sell records and he was like, "Yeah, this is real good. Here's your money." But then when I finally took a trip to Europe, years later, I saw people just drooling over the shit, it's crazy...

T: Was there any sort of direction as to what you draw for the labels, or do you just go for it?

AO: He used to give me all the information that he wanted on the

313 mystique, UR, Generator Records, and the Fantastic Four

record and I just drew from there. I still do. Like the stuff I do for D-jax, whatever comes into my head, I just draw it. (**Saskia from D-jax**) would just call me up and say, "I need five labels." So I'd do whatever. Then she'd fax me back and tell me what she liked and I'd do more of it. It's not a structured thing at all.

T: Obviously, your style lends the label a certain identity...

AO: I only do artwork for D-jax now. It's really cool that I got that opportunity to work with her...

T: How did you get involved with Underground Resistance? I know you joined when Jeff quit, Mike must have liked what you were doing before that; were you doing tracks prior to that?

AO: I did one ep before that, for D-jax. I recorded under the name of Signal-To-Noise Ratio, this was back in '90. That's the only thing I did before I got in UR. Coincidently, that's when I started doing the label art for her as well. I was doing the show and I had one ep on D-jax and that's basically when Mike came into my life and told me, "Jeff quit, we need someone to go to Australia." They had a big Australian tour; everything was booked, tickets were bought, venues were booked- everything was ready to happen... Mike was desperate, and he called me up. We went to Australia, we rocked 'em, it was over... At that point was when I became part of Underground. On the plane back, Mike was asking me about doing a label for **Submerge** (UR's in-house distribution company) because he had just had the idea for Submerge. That's when I decided to do **Generator**. That trip was very fateful to me, it was pretty much my turning point in life. It's as profound as all that. I was sitting around, eating fuckin' Cocoa Puffs and Banks calls and says he needs someone to go to Australia with him. I'm like, "Cool." I said, "So when you leavin'?". He says, "Tomorrow." "O.K.," I had my shit packed up and I was out.

T: How long was that tour?

continued on Page 25

-Generator Records Discography-

GEN001: TCH-1 ep

GEN002: DJ T-1000-"Liquid Metal Meltdown" 10"

GEN003: TCH-2-"20 Hours To Paradise" ep

GEN003.5: Level A & DJ T-1000-"Nikita" 12"

GEN004: X-313-"World Sonik Domination" ep

GEN005: Passarani & Monteduro-"Roma Meets Detroit" ep

GEN006: T-SHIRTS

GEN007: Hardsignal-"Aeolus 14 Umbra" 12"

GEN008.5: Freq-"Plastique" 12"

GEN009: DJ ESP-"Transporter" 2X12"

Terre Thaemlitz: Ambient Technics & Psychic Ability

by Jay Patrick Ahern

From out of nowhere, New York-based DJ **Terre Thaemlitz**, to those in the know, has perhaps become the brightest new talent in the blossoming genre of ambient music. *"Raw Through A Straw"/"Tranquilizer"*, Thaemlitz' first single on his own **Comatonse** label, was brought to our attention by U.K. ambient DJ **Mixmaster Morris** who called it 'the best American ambient record out.' Now signed to Instinct Records with two tracks on the label's new **Plug In + Turn On** compilation and a full-length album release to follow, we turned Terre over to contributor Jay Patrick Ahern for analysis.

TRiP: How did you get involved in music, particularly ambient music?

TT: Well, my first smart move in the music field was crying relentlessly when my parents tried to start me on the Suzuki method of violin playing at the age of 2...

I think you're really asking me about my entry into the current scene, though. I came to New York in 1986, when the fat NY club sound was really coming together and I lived in the Lower East Side, which was the heart of the NY/NJ deep house scene. By '89 I started spinning at benefits for different organizations such as ACT-UP/NY, as well as spinning on the Midtown drag circuit. I like to work a vibe more than a beat, so I ended up being considered a jazz DJ. Then I began working on my own tracks and allowing interests in experimental noise and electronic music to play a larger role. I used to call it atmospheric house, and my tracks started getting play off cassette in ambient rooms. **Electric Lounge Machine** (now the **Departure Lounge**), which was NY's first and only ambient club, were playing my tracks and then took me in as a DJ there. It was more about creating "ambience" than spinning contemporary ambient tracks. I had just set up my own label, **Comatonse Recordings**, when **Instinct** heard me DJ, checked out my own tracks and signed me to a multiple record deal.

T: Define your 'ambient.'

TT: Conceptually: Non-spiritual realism. If you get an emotional high from it, attribute it to people coming together rather than some alienating concept of contacting a cosmic essence. Formally: I still like the traditional definition of ambient as an all-encompassing sound including the incidental sounds of the environment you play it in, etc. I think the role of contemporary ambient within the club scene has revised this definition by turning the listener's focus toward a shared, calming social experience, rather than an overwhelming awareness of one's isolation within a world of chaotic sound.

T: Has Europe been an influence or are you purely an American phenomena?

TT: Both European and Japanese techno-pop had a large impact on me while growing up. But I think my experience with the music was specifically American. In particular, having grown up in more rural areas of the Midwest, the electronic music I listened to was very alienating to those around me-yet it was basically party music. I had a pretty rough time out there socially, so I think I was attracted to techno-pop's promise of the ultimate cyber party...even though I was typically alone and blasting it out of a beat up 1960 Ford, barreling down a dirt road.

T: Do you find that NY ambient artists are more influenced by the deep house scene?

TT: There's a large group of us in NY who have been involved in deep house and came to ambient through an extension of mellow and jazzy vibes. It's almost considered the new 'quiet storm' music. It's a little more soulful and down-to-earth approach, rather than the spiritual-technology outlook that prevails on the rave circuit. I think it's making this a great time to be in NY because it's bringing various scenes together. I think that during times like these, before people have strong preconceptions about a musical genre, that the most interesting tracks are produced.

T: Melody or mesmerization? Explain.

TT: Personally I tend to favor mesmerization over melody because I think melody can be too literal, particularly in ambient.

T: Is California dreaming towards a more commercialized scene?

TT: I think each city and region has a different approach toward sound which has to work locally. Stylistically I think a lot (but not all) of Californian ambient lacks edge and gets too milky for me, which I associate with commercialism. But that's somethiing I've heard in most club music out of California, so I think there's something in the West Coast experience which is generating a sound I find hard to get into.

T: How do you feel about 'majors' getting involved with the U.S. underground?

TT: Major labels are always dipping into the underground well. I think it can work both ways if the Underground keeps its head, although the multi-billion dollar corporations will always come out on top. We know the major labels operate through formulas. They break the music down into consumable styles and do market research on it, then feed it to the herds, fattening them up for the next purchase. It's beyond Orwellian. Unfortunately, in many places in the U.S., there is little or no access to independently produced tracks. In this way major label visibility is important.

T: Thought for the day?

TT: For today and everyday: Always practice safer sex! And sterilize your needles with bleach and water if you shoot up!

TRiP Fotofile--TRiP Fotofile--TRiP Fotofile

From Left to Right: Dominic Fordyce (Deltra Record Distribution), Robbie Hardkiss (SF), Justin King (C-Level), and Gavin Hardkiss (SF) throw down at the Autechre showduring WMC; LaTrece, MCT's Marcy Weber, and Mark 'MK' Kinchen lounging at the Fountainbleau bar; Chillin' in the ambient back courtyard at the WMC wrap-up after hours at The Edge, Ft. Lauderdale; *oscillate*'s DJ Orion and Jay Patrick Ahern (Aquarhythms/ Dublin, Ireland) in the ambient mix at WVUM-FM; Gavin Hardkiss and *oscillate* DJ Grumpy enjoying the morning sun, WMC after hours; Josh Kay (Soul Odyssey) at Deep, Ft. Lauderdale; DJ Icee (Orlando) at Deep; TRiP's Jackie Rosquete and friends relaxing in the Opium Den at C.R.A.S.H., Tampa; ambient tribal techno act Lovecraft live at a recent party at Club Unity, Lakeland.

dj charts

DJ TAYLOR
Various Clubs & One-offs
Los Angeles, CA

Yothu Yindi -'Timeless Land'
Rabbit In The Moon-'Phases/O.B.E.'
Womack & Womack-'House/Secret'
Jean Michel Jarre'-'Wooloomooloo'
Cosmic Baby-'Loops Of Infinity'
Havanna-'Disorder'
Quivver - 'Saxy Lady'
Alana Din - 'Angel'
D:Ream-'UR The Best Thing' (Perfecto Mix)
Nico-'Moonfrog'

SANDRA COLLINS
Various Clubs & One Offs
Los Angeles, CA

Rabbit In The Moon-'Phases/O.B.E.'
Yothu Yindi-'Timeless Land'
Sonic Infusion-'Unfuture'
Circle City-'Moments Of Inertia'
Cygnus X-'Positron'/'Superstring'
Nico-'Moonfrog'
Sublime-'T.G.V.'
Buzz & Noe-'Alone'
Paragliders-Paraglide
Quivver-'Saxy Lady'

THE DJ KOLECTIV
Innervision, Megadog, Liberator
London, U.K.

Acid Junkies-"Cocaino"
Reefa-"Inner Fantasy" (RMX)
Plastikman-"Krakpot"
Speedy J-"Pepper"
Megalon-"Darkness' (Shaded In)
Ege Bam Yasi-"Ex Ovo Omnia"
Rabbit In The Moon-"Phases/O.B.E."
Mindwarp-"Too"
Megalon-"Darkness" (Shaded Out)
Fabio Paras-"Birth Of Shiva Shanti" (RMX)

dj charts

DJ HELL
Worldwide
Munich, Germany

Planetary Assault Systems-'Planetary Funk, Vol. II'
DJ Funk-'Street Trax 1'
Hell-'Gefeert + Geferdert'
Dave Clarke-'Red 1 (Of 3)'
Love The Machines-'L T M 2'
Fly By Wire-'Last Voyage'
Robert Hood-'Minimal Nation'
I.O.-'Decay' ep
Air Liquide-'Mandra Gora'
N.Y.C.-'The Dub'

TERRE THAEMLITZ
Fonky Classics To Chill To
Comatonse Recordings/Instinct Records
New York, NY

O'Donel Levy-Time Has Changed LP
Kool & The Gang-Light Of Worlds LP
Curtis Mayfield-'Give Me Your Love'
Gwen McCrae-'Feel So Good'
Roy Ayers Ubiquity-'..Loves The Sunshine'
Marvin Gaye-'After The Dance' (Inst.)
William DeVaughn-'Be Thankful...'
Timmy Thomas-Why Can't We Live... LP
Sylvester-Here Is My Love
Earth, Wind, & Fire-'Mom'

BRIAN WALTERS
Mental
New York, NY

Acid Junkies-'303 vs. 101'
Ultrahigh-'In The City'
Speed Jack-'Storm'
Route 66-'Bunker 012'
Subsonic 808-'Blue Label Vol.2'
Hexagone-'Burning Trash Floor'
Fortress-'Birdman'
Joseph & His Cousin-'Milchglas'
Affie Yuseff-'White Walls'
Microset Morning-'Elle dort'

dj charts

DJ T-1000
Generator Records
Detroit, U.S.A.

Modular Man-'Mod One'
Underground Resistance-'Cyberwolf'
Freq-Plastique
DJ ESP-Bad Acid
Clementine-'Cosmopolitan/Cosmos'
Jeff Mills-'Cycle 30' ep
Electric Indigo-'5% Tribe'
All Dan Bell tracks on Accelerate
Exposure-'Acrid Abeyance'
Mind Design-'Inner Space'

JOSH WINK
Winking Productions
Philadelphia, PA

V/A-A Deeper Shade Of Techno
Minimal Nation-"Museum"
Hardtraxx, Inc.-"Bun Kun"
Techno Grooves #9-"Expiration For All"
?-"Lonely Winter"
It's Thinking-"Down In A Bubble"
Winx-"How's The Music"
Starjuice-"3 Base"
Kinesthesia-"Kobal"
Shockwave-"War Drums"

CHARLES AMBIENTO
Anarchic Adjustment
San Francisco, CA

Namlook/Hawtin-From Within
Klaus Schulze-The Dome Event
FFWD (Orb & Robert Fripp)
Aphex Twin-Selected Ambient Works, Vol. 2
Chapterhouse-Blood Music RMXS
A New Consciousness LP
Bernard Cribbins-Hornby Railways
Aural Expansion ep
Anarchic Ambient Compilation
Dark Horse & Mr. Ambiento-"Dogs, Cats,& Birds"

TRiPmag CHARTS

UNDERGROUND DANCE MUSIC CHART

COMPILED BY DJ THREE

Lazonby (Brainiak White Label)
2001-"Crystal"
Baby Ford-"Monolens"
Baruka-"Play It Loud"
Transglobal Underground (Kris Needs RMX)
Conemelt-"Wallop"
Aloof-"Mind"
Velocity-"Lust" (Rabbit In The Moon RMX)
Kenny Larkin-"Q" (RMX)
Innersphere-"Let's Go To Work"

TRiP HOUSE CHART

COMPILED BY DJ JASK

DJ Duke presents Black Rhythms, Vol. 3-"Turn it Up (Say Yeah)"
Las Americas-"Look, Listen, Love"
Barbara Tucker-"Beautiful People"
River Ocean feat. India-"Tribal EP"
Van Helden-"Egyptian Magician"
Chicago Trackwerk Vol.2
Hidden Agenda-"Story Of My Life"
Phuture-"Spirit"
Todd Terry-Unreleased Project Pt. 5
Jazz-N-Groove-"A Better Way"

OSCILLATE AMBIENT CHART

COMPILED BY DJ ORION & DJ GRUMPY

Tranquility Bass-Broadcast Standard Series, Vol.1
From Within-From Within LP
Quad-Quadraville EP
Terre Thaemlitz-"Hovering Glows"
Kenny Larkin-Azimuth LP
Aphex Twin-SelectedAmbient Works, Vol.2
James v. Sabres Of Paradise-"Jam J"
Influx-Unique LP
Johnny Favorite-Exploding Plastic Ambient Mix
Global Technological Innovations: Unreleased, Vol. 1

RECORD REVIEWS 12"/EP

MEGALON-"Darkness" (Plink Plonk test/ UK) Another goodie from **Plink Plonk**. This one takes you on a minimalistic journey into the depths of your mind, and along the way you'll probably be dancing. True underground music from a label that doesn't get enough credit; but they probably don't mind, since the music speaks for itself. **(G)**

SOUL CHILDREN-"Soul Searching" (Bomb) L.A. DJ **David Alvarado** follows his two smash **Las Americas** records with a four tracker on his own label that is more on the old school tip, making it a bit more accessible to any DJ, not just House. A funky breaks track "The Gate", a wicked funky acid houser, "The Son", and the pulsing chords tribal groover "Eternal" are all tops. Check it. **(D3)**

SPICELAB-"Spice Is A Full-time Occupation" (Harthouse/Germany) Oliver Lieb creates three more terrific German trance tracks. You would think that someone who has released as much stuff over the past couple of months as Oliver has, his capacity to keep writing good material would diminish. Not true. This EP is wonderful. Each track is great. My favorite is "Pigs In Spice" but the masses will be sweating to "...Fulltime Occupation." Keep an eye out for a full-length **Ambush** LP, **LSG** remixes by **Mark (Vapourspace) Gage**, and in his spare time did an ambient CD with **Dr. Atmo** for **Fax**, **Music For Films**. **(G)**

FREQ-"Freq" EP (Matrix) This six track ep is full of many different textures: deep, moody, dark, hard, minimal, acidy, pulsating. With one eye looking to the past and the other firmly fixed on the future, this is the new breed of Detroit. Pay attention to this label and others like it, know the future. **(PW)**

BRAINCELL-"Braincell 2" (Harthouse/ Germany) Three straight ahead acid tracks that are quite hard and minimal. The best is the **Hardfloor**-styled "Forbidden Forest". **(G)**

LAZONBY (Brainiak/UK white label) Think Vapour Space, "O.B.E.", "Strings Of Life"... Every now and then (but never often enough) I stumble upon a track like this: celestial voices, chimes, tribal percussion guide you through the four minute intro, then into a hypnotic trance groove with a stomping kick. The other side boasts smooth production with electro styled percussion and breaks beneath a melodic groove not far from the feeling **"Pacific"** used to give me. One of the best from the U.K. in some time. **(D3)**

CAPPIO BROS.-"Caffiene 4 Daze" (Stickmen) This is one record you won't sleep on. **The Stickmen**, at it again with the help of the coffee addicted **John Acquaviva**, deliver some old school acid house and very, very Chicago-ish pounding 909 drums with 303 mayhem. Not your cup of tea? Try the Maxwell's House Mix- definitely good to the last drop! Four freshly brewed mixes that might keep you up for 4 daze! **(Jask)**

TRANQUILITY BASS-'Broadcast Standard Series, Vol. 1' (Exist Dance) After renewed interest in their Tranquility Bass moniker from appearances on various compilation CD's, the crew at Exist Dance have assembled all three Tranquility Bass tracks- either long out-of-print or unavailable on vinyl- in remixed form on one vinyl platter. Opening with the version of "Cantamilla", a smooth and dreamy string-introed, Latin jazz inflected breakbeat groover from the California Dreaming compilation and a chunkier "Mya Yadana", complete with a strengthened breakbeat compared to the original. The flip's mix of "Cantamilla' turns the track into a swinging acid jazzier version, closing with the spaced out ambient Sea of Tranquility Mix of "We Came In Peace", a trippy version of what Voyager is playing to alien lifeforms throughout the galaxies. **(Orion)**

SHAPE CHANGER-"Crystal Dreams, Vol. 1" 2X12" (Experimental) The latest from NY label Experimental, **EX27** is a six track EP on two records, ranging from the beautifully dark "String Of Love" to the harsh acid of "Filter Mirror". Overall, this is highly recommended. **(G)**

BARBARA TUCKER-"Beautiful People" (Positiva/UK) Maybe the House anthem of the year. So much hype went into this record way before it was released, and justifiably so, because the people at Strictly knew it was slammin'! No one can doubt a track when you've got **"Little" Louie Vega** on the production and the beautiful voice of Barbara Tucker together. Definitely a positive song with a positive message for all the people in the world. That's what it's about! That's what's missin'! Be sure to ccheck out the import only Commission Mix; "Little" Louie does it again! **(Jask)**

THE ALOOF-"Mind" (Flaw/UK) The Aloof quickly follow-up "Agent O" with an even harder British styled acid track recorded at **Sabresonic Studios**, giving it a sound and feel similar to **David Holmes'** "Johnny Favourite". Oncce again, one side is an avant garde vocal excursion, but I prefer the more mad instrumental. Either way, "Mind" is sonic and wild loud. **(D3)**

AURASFERE-"Greenhouse Effect" EP (Experimental) Yet more quality trance from Experimental with four tracks on two discs. Each one is excellent; extremely long pulsating intros to basically each track. Completely hypnotizing, the beat just creeps up on you, as it seems like it's been there the whole time. **(G)**

CYGNUS X-"Superstring" (Eye-Q/Germany) A collaboration for **Sven Vath** cohorts **A.C. Boutsen** and **Ralf Hildenbeutel**, this two tracker is on the positive trance vibe. "Positron," at 134, is perhaps a little more of the obvious choice with its chugging hi-hats, thumping kick, and uplifting organ line. However, "Superstring" shouldn't be overlooked because of its sprightly 150 tempo. A solid, if not terribly memorable, ep nonetheless. **(PW)**

CORRUGATED SILENCE-"Sleepless Nite" (Holistic/UK) A one-sided wonder you'll either find amazing or tedious. I find it amazing. Yet another beautiful celestial female vocal intro into a rolling bass wave that never goes away. Tribal drums from **Rabbit In The Moon**'s "O.B.E." give way to a pulsing trance groove augmented by a (gasp!) guitar solo! The record is just plain different- just before a heavily gated outro, a breakbeat peeps in, making it sound like you mixing in another track. Fucking wild. **(D3)**

BASEMENT TRAX-"Volume 1" (Basement Trax) This take off on the infamous **Trax** label is brought to you via those nice men at Plus 8. Produced by the mysterious **'Jack Master'**, we get kick-ass acid house. "Bang The Box", with its sonic innuendos will be the main floor attraction- and make use of that 'bang' accapella. "One Trac Mind" is pretty mental, while "Manic Dancer" is definitely the trance inducing groover. Drop at the right time and watch 'em go! **(D3)**

DJ DUKE presents BLACK RHYTHMS, VOL. 3-"Turn It Up (Say Yeah)" (Power Music Trax) **Duke** delivers a hardfloor tribal house stomper on us this time. The man is hot and just keeps on pumpin' out tracks that fill dancefloors everywhere. Very limited and on red vinyl, so get yours before it's too late. **(Jask)**

UVX-"Ultraviolet Explorer" (Magick Eye/UK) Another goodie from the always weird Magick Eye label. Three tracks on this ep; one is an experimental slow dub reggae number, another is a quite cool acid track with neat panning noises and a clock chiming, while the third track is a decent trancer that isn't quite as loud as the others. **(G)**

DIE SCHIESZE featuring Michael Whitehead-"Emotion" (Dub) Another stomping vocal track produced by a fresh new up-and-coming producer, **Mitch Dupre**. "Emotion" comes with four mixes ranging from deep garage, to tribal, and Hi-NRG. Strong, slammin' vocals by **Michael Whitehead** really takes this track into higher grounds. A nice follow-up to the last Dub release. **(Jask)**

PROGRESSION-"Reach (Further)" (X-Press 2 RMXS) (Sorted) NY DJ **Micro** follows up his first **Sorted** label release with remixes from **X-Press 2** and himself and **Vicious Vic**. Micro's mix is the pick; an obvious floor filler with balls ala heavy kick, nice break, and an energy building breakdown. X-Press 2 smooths things out a bit while keeping the funky breaks on one mix and deliver a more tribalesque House mix on the next. A good release for Sorted. **(CM)**

ROBOT MAN-"Doo Da Doo" (Plastikman RMX) (Definitive) A single A-sided slab with a Plastikman remix of this '93 House stormer. Not as out there as Plastikman as it is a kick ass acid house reworking with 'plastik' touches here and there. It <u>will</u> do da doo... **(CM)**

BRAINCHILD, VOL. 2-"Singularity" (Eye-Q/Germany) Solo project from **A.C. Boutsen** does not dissapoint. Two mixes of the same track continue in the familiar **Eye-Q** style: a pounding beat with lush atmospheric keyboard lines. Very good hard trance. **(G)**

SEAN DEASON-"Sean Deason" EP (Matrix) A four tracker by **Sean Deason** is release #3 from this wicked young label from Detroit; "Pump" is an effective Chicago style jack track complete with **Mr.Lee** sample; "Feel It" is more of a stomper with a hard kick drum, driving hi-hats, and "ooh, yeah" crowd sample. On the b-side, "Hindenberg" is a textbook uptempo deep Detroit track which builds up gradually, adding and subtracting elements of the mix before breaking down to the immortal radio broadcast of the Hindenberg Disaster. Rounding things out is "Prozac", a lazy, hazy sort of track. **(PW)**

SOUND CROWD-"The Public Image" EP (Red/Ireland) From the cold deep depths of Ireland's (!) House underground comes a handful of pretty good tracks ranging from acid house to some upfront hardfloor garage. The standout here is "Touched By The Hand Of Todd", meaning **Todd Terry**. In fact, the whole record is dedicated to the samplemaster and he deserves it. Four clovers for this record, not bad for the Irish! **(Jask)**

ASCENDANCE-"Out There" EP (C-Level Recordings) Four tracks by one **Paul Grogan**, each in collaboration with one of the **C-Level** stable- **Ian Rich, Justin King**, etc. All four are progressive house in the 125 BPM range, if labels like **Stress, DeConstruction, Cowboy** and the like are your forte, then don't miss this one. **(CM)**

LAS AMERICAS-"Look, Listen, Love"/ "Do It" (Definitive) Full on deep, groovalicious tribal tracks from West Coast man **David Alvarado**. "Look, Listen, Love" pounds through your inner consciousness to release massive sweatiness, and to top it off it gets the **Robot Man** treatment. Electro-propelled, oscillating House to the core. The **Chuck Phulasol** remix of "Do It" is quite the disco treat as well. Much props to the Definitive crew... **(Jask)**

JOEY BELTRAM presents...-"Odyssey Nine" (Visible) Beltram has beenn doing all sorts of things. Some good, some not, with recent standouts being **Code 6** and his ep on Trax. Odyssey Nine is a three tracker; "Drums Of Orbit" is a hard tribaal acid house bit with some synth on top, the lackluster "Vamp", but "606 Bonus" is some fucked up old school Chicago type drum style. **(CM)**

? 002-"Heaven & Earth" (NCP) The second installment in the 'mystery artist' series done by Northcott. Again no writing credits... The best side is the '?' side with its icy keyboard sounds over mellow atmosphere- it's definitely a winner. Just as good, if not slightly better than the first. **(G)**

SPEEDY J.-"Pepper"/"Beam Me Up" (BMU/Holland) First off, let me say that Speedy's album <u>**Ginger**</u> has been kept a secret way too long. No DJ who plays progressive house OR techno would not find a favorite track to play. The album version of "Pepper" is a progressive/trance DJ's best bet, however, this remix strays a bit too far in an uneventful fashion. The super disco "Beam Me Up" gets a good reworking by the **Pegasus** label crew though, not your average funky guitar bit, this track just goes and goes. **(CM)**

TESTE-"Regions"/"Praecox" (Probe) The **Teste** boys are back with more way out experimental techno and ambient mayhem after a few hits of acid and a couple releases on their own **Switch** label (**Perceptrons, Plasmalamp**). Totally tripped out and for the head, these two tracks take you into a completely different realm. For the chillout DJ's with balls. **(Orion)**

DJ GOOD GROOVE-"Drummatic Tales" EP (Disko B/Germany) This 12" comes on cool white vinyl. The music is very minimal with basically just simple drum patterns and squiggly acid lines. Something for the DJ craving monotonous repetitive sounds that are good for mixing. Nothing new but worth a listen anyway. **(G)**

ROBOSTICKMEN-"Feel Free" (Stickman) A collaboration between Definitive's **Richard Michaels** and the Stickmen. No let down here, another good Stickman record has been born. **"Feel Free"** is hardhitting, slow-sticking, rambunctious raw grooves that flow into one masterpiece. The track's other mixes by **Robotman** and **Derrick Carter** are also deep. Don't miss this deeper than deep slab of vinyl if you like the deep, hard stuff. It's just so deeeeeep! **(Jask)**

SUBTROPIC-"Throb" (Reflective) A new 12" from San Francisco's Reflective label. This is an EP that doesn't really fit into a category, but several different styles-ambient, dub, tribal, and minimal techno-melted into one new kind of sound sometimes all in one track. Quite a different listeninng experience. **(G)**

ACID SCOUT-"Acid Scout" EP (Disko B/ Germany) For the most part, this blue vinyl slab is fairly mediocre fast German techno on the minimal tip. After further probing with the turntable's stylus, I hit the gem. A slice of slow, **King Tubby** meets **Kraftwerk**, deep-inhaling, techno-dub, complete with echo chamber drums, thundering bass, and percussion sounds that pan all sorts of crazy ways. **(Orion)**

PATRICK PULSINGER-"Dogmatic Sequences" EP (Disko B/Germany) Old school German-style acid techno with very raw production. Pretty standard compared to what's causing a buzz these days. "Agom Drag" is a stand out; very dark and dreary. Not as good as some other Disko B stuff. **(CM)**

JAZZ-N-GROOVE-"Freedom" (SubUrban) Prepare to be free, because this record has the key to unlock your freedom. An almost uplifting feel good track with **Mystery Marquis** on vocals, this is very comparable to a **Victor Simonelli** and **Tommy Musto** style with 'freedom' chants complimented by a jazzy piano riff. One of my favorites at the moment. **(Jask)**

TERMINATOR BENELUX-"Red Alert" EP (HOS/UK) Two cuts, two mixes each. "Red Alert" is standard trance techno with annoying vocal samples, so hit mix two which does the business with its electronic blurts and oscillating hard bassline. "The Plague" is a contrast of synth riffs and modern electronic sounds. Now that the word 'trance' has been taken away from its rightful place as an adjective and is being used as a label for for music, that is the signal for an abundance of "good enough" records. **(CM)**

OMEGAMAN-"2 Saxxy"/"Happy Organ" (Definitive) No stoppin the bum rush, Definitive pumps out another worth the dosh release produced by **Robotman**, the 'Robocop Of House.' "2 Saxxy" takes you on a venture thru deep hummified organs, uniting with some funkifies sax riffs that hover over phat bass to a flowing phat beat. "Happy Organ" is on the trance tip with wicked, wicked, wicked basslines, out of this universe. I just wish it was pressed better. **(Jask)**

RISING SONS-"Afghan Acid" (RMX) (Experimental) Damon Wild and **Tim Taylor** return with a remix of one of the best tracks of '93. Nice and hard with lots of acid, but sorry, this remix just doesn't get the job done like the original. Two other tracks included are rather good; two out of three ain't bad. **(G)**

LIL' LOUIS-"I'm Hot For You" (SPG Music) It seems that **Lil' Louis** has got the **'Stickman Fever'** cause he had the Stickmen remix the shit out of this jam. The No Offense Mix has a very Murky feel to it. With a deep grungy bassline, slow slippin' kick, and 'hot for you' samples, this is just too damn sexy. Don't pass up the Rhythm Method Tribal Mix and the Phoenix Mix- both are full-on tribal stompers that have the power to make any dancefloor crazy. **(Jask)**

FULL MOON SCIENTIST-"Old Man River's Crying" (Hard Hands/UK) Home of progressive dub masters **Leftfield, Hard Hands** take the art of dub to a new depths on this one. One side explores the vocal side of dub with a slightly out of the norm 10 minute make vocal track with echoey piano, percussion, guitars, and bassline, breaking down into sweet beatfree ambience for the track's remaining 4 1/2 minutes. The other side is a driving percussive stormer for the dancefloor while the second track is a chunk of manic, left-of-center ambient dub. Wicked. **(Orion)**

YAKOTA-"Panicwaves" (Harthouse/Germany) The writing side is a very **Cosmic Baby/Eye-Q** type track that leaves me a little uninspired. However, the logo side is the shit. Very uptempo hard acid track with an extremely cool keyboard line. **(G)**

UTE-"It's A Soul Thing" (33/UK) Strictly slow but funky groove-dwelling acid jazz tracks to just chill out to. Nice flavorful Hip-hop beats, phat basslines, a cool sax, tastee organ riffs and a kick ass piano, you can't go wrong. This four tracker takes you for one of the phattest rides of your life; top notch acid jazz from Leeds! **(Jask)**

LP/COMPILATIONS

APHEX TWIN-Selected Ambient Works, Volume 2 (Warp/UK) Works, Vol. 1 was not so much ambient music as it was ambient dance music. What we are presented here with Volume 2 is more related to what the term was originally coined in reference to electronic music. The most obvious and easily digested comparison is **Brian Eno's Music For Airports**, both in packaging (icons instead of song titles) and musical content (very minimal, sometimes disturbing, other times beautiful). After reading a review of this that stated all the tracks left you "waiting for something that never happens", this affirms that a contemporary sound of ambient has come to light and happily, in our opinion, this is far from it. **(D3)**

V/A-UNITED STATE OF AMBIENCE (Moonshine Music) A friend of mine was telling me the other day about a track he heard that had a 'cool ambient beat.' His statement really bothered me. I felt the same way about this collection. Ambient is defined in the dictionary as 'an encompassing atmosphere', while **Eno** defined ambient in a musical context as background music that should seep through one's subconscious. With that in mind, virtually none of the tracks featured here are truly ambient, but more like 'ambient with beats' or 'ambient dance music.' 'Ambient' is now used to describe (often inacccurately) lots of music that doesn't necessarily have a category; not to be nit picky and say that this particular genre of music cannot have a broader interpretation of its definition, but I had hoped that Moonshine, as an American label making a conscious effort to educate people as to the music of the underground would present a more accurate context of what this music is. The liner notes refer to layered electronic music and indiginous tonal color while implying a sense of tribalism. And the compilation is that, albeit heavy on the tribal percussion, as opposed to layered electronics and and tonal colors. Particulars aside, credit is due to Moonshine for taking the chance on this very strong, although slightly mislabeled, collection of American artists including **Dub Tribe, Luna Sol** (the two artists with the two most truly ambient tracks), **Hawke, Elements Of Ambience**, and others. **(Orion)**

HARUOMI HOSONO-Medicine Compilation From The Quiet Lodge (Tristar/Sony) This is **Hosono**'s first solo project to be distributed in the U.S., making it his first official appearance on the U.S. music scene since **Yellow Magic Orchestra**. It's about time! Medicine Compilation is a collaborative effort between Hosono and various performers from the Japanese pop and club scenes. Fitting snugly into the contemporary ambient genre, the album touches on numerous elements from Hosono's prolific solo career, ranging from his 'non-standard' ambient sound experiments ("Deira") to cyber folk pop ("Honey Moon") to farty acid rhythms ("Medicine Mix") to ethno-fuck ("Mabui Dance"). My personal favorite was "Sand Storm Edit," which features an elecctro-acoustic guitar solo over desert winds guaranteed to quiet any gathering. Overall this is one of Hosono's stronger albums, and for those unfamiliar with his work it serves as a good place to start. **(TT)**

ROBERT FRIPP & BRIAN ENO-The Essential Fripp & Eno (Caroline) **Robert Fripp** and **Brian Eno** are undoubtedly two of the most extraordinary musical pioneers in contemporary music. From 1973-1978 together they recorded two albums, **No Pussyfooting** (an experiment in guitar drones and electronic treatments) and **Evening Star** (an ambient landmark). A third album, incorporating 'sampled' sounds and pre-dating that technology, **Healthy Colours I-IV**, was never completed. Digitally remastered, this compilation touches on all three, including the full Healthy Colours sessions. An essential purchase for new ambient explorers researchig their roots. **(PW)**

KLAUS SCHULZE-The Essential: '72-'93 (Caroline) As a founding memeber of **Tangerine Dream, Ash-Ra Temple**, in addition to his own solo works, **Klaus Schulze** laid many of the foundations for today's techno and industrial scenes. Sampled by the likes of **William Orbit, Future Sound Of London**, and **The Orb**, Schulze is currently referred to as the "Father Of Trance" by the electronicc dance world's European cognoscente. The Essential is a double CD collection spanning Schulze's career from his early work with sequencers and analog synths to his later, more pre-New Age excursions and recent concert length sampler and computer pieces. A great leaping off point for (re) discovering this innovator of the ambient genre. Look for this coming to a chill room near you. **(Orion)**

V/A-PARASOLS, VOL. I (Plink Plonk/UK) This three record compilationhas some of the finest minimal, experimental, deep, and emotional House music released in the past year and a half. Although **Plink Plonk**'s definition of House is not exactly the one you hear the most about, they have built their own sound around creativity and a desire for something more. All of the artists use pseudonyms in order for each to get a fair listen, something that few people do because if you have a big name, you can sell anything. This is where the future of House begins-in the hands of people who care and want to do something different. Buy this or you will be missing out on the future. **(G)**

V/A-RISING HIGH TRANCE INJECTION (Instinct)/V/A-SECRET LIFE OF TRANCE (Planet Earth) A dilemma. Two Americcan labels have released essentially the same compilation. Assemble the two and you have in essence, **Secret Life Of Trance, Vol. 2**, an import released by London's Rising High. So which one does the consumer choose? **Planet Earth**'s is one CD of more choice dancefloor trance cuts such as **Hardfloor**'s reworking of **RHC**'s "Fever Called Love", **OBX**-"Eternal Prayer", as well as more intelligent tracks from **Balil** and **New London School Of Electronics**. **Instinct**'s version is two CD's offering a few of the same tracks while including more lesser known trance plus a selection of intelligent and ambient pieces like **Dreamfish, Irresistible Force**, and **Cybertrax**. Which do you buy? Both. Throw them in your five disc changer and program the two together into one wicked old Rising High megamix tape. **(PW)**

V/A-12x12 (Stickman) It was last year about this time when I met these two guys from

from Toronto, Paul and Greg, at Winter Music Conference. They had just started a new label, **Stickman**, and kindly laid on me their first two releases to review here. I fully remember them telling me to stay in touch and let them know what I thought of these records, good or bad, so they could make better records. I brought them home and the shit exploded off the turntable, they were so good. Twelve months later, these two have piled up 12 releases and a truckload of major props- even clocking a record on Strictly! This compilation refreshes your memory of all the dope-ass Stickman shit in the past year and teases you with a new track. If you know,slap this in the disc player and reminisce. If you don't, time to go to class and get schooled. **(PW)**

SPICELAB-Lost In Spice (Harthouse America/Planet Earth) The full-length debut from **Oliver Lieb's Spicelab** project. There are four tracks here that are at least ten minutes plus; that length of time is needed to convey the wide spectrum of musical input and emotion that make up each track. It's not uncommon to find tracks that are hard and intense while still having a strong melody and soothing mellow breakdowns. Unafraid like other techno snobs to use speeded up breakbeats to add extra punch to a track, Spicelab's **Lost In Spice** is wonderful for both club use and home listening although some may find it too hard to sleep to. **(G)**

V/A-SPEED LIMIT 140 BPM+, VOL. 4 (Moonshine) Moonshine continues its breakbeat compilation series with another good collection. Although this does feature such great tracks as **Metalheads**' "St. Angel" and **DJ Crystl**'s "Crystlize", nearly all the tracks suffer from the **"What Can We Do With Mantronix' "King Of The Beats" Break That Hasn't Been Done Six Million Times Already?" Syndrome**. This is what has turned many people away from the breakbeat/hardcore scene: the excessive overuse of the same break over and over and over again. A track might be incredibly good and then 'that beat' comes in and the needle gets picked up immediately. All the tracks featured here are quite good and some are even creative and original. A step in the right direction and overall, a good collection. **(G)**

V/A-UNDERTONES, VOL. I (One Movement/Australia) A way cool jazz and hip-hop compilation on Australia's **One Movement** label featuring worldwide talent like **Urban Poets, Banana, UTE**, and others. Full of phat swingin' grooves of many flavors, this is the perfect choice when your sittin' around, kickin' it. A definite must to find here in the States for acid jazz aficianados. **(Matty)**

RENEGADE SOUNDWAVE-Howyadoin' (Mute/Elektra) Finally, after what seemed like a five year absence, **Renegade** return with a full-length LP. I'm sure everyone has heard the self-titled first single, "Renegade Soundwave," and if not you should own it. Now. Anyway, the LP is not exactly what I expected; actually, I'm a little dissapointed. There are a couple of really cool songs like "Howyadoin'," with it's rockin' guitar and slammin' beat, but there are a few disspointments like "John Holmes." Any song named after a porn star should rule, no matter who does it, and this one really doesn't refer to Mr. Holmes or his conquests. A couple of the instrumental songs aren't too bad, but they should have **Gary Asquith**'s trademark vocals on them. What makes up for any shortcomings is "Blast 'Em Out"; excellent scratching by Turntable Terrorist, a stolen beat from the **Beasties**' "Looking Down A Barrel Of A Gun," and good lyrics. There should be ten tracks like this on the LP. Overall, it's decent, but after such an extended absence Gary should have something cooler to say than "Renegade Soundwave" over and over... **(G)**

V/A-KICKIN' HARDCORE LEADERS (Instinct) A compilation of twelve previously released ruff and rugged breakbeat tracks from London's **Kickin'** label. Including tracks from **Ruff Rider, Twin Bass, Tango & Ratty** and especially **"Roughneck Business"** by **Ellis D. and Swan E.,** this is a great collection of now oldies for the breakbeat and jungle crew. **(Matty)**

V/A-ETHNOTECHNO: SONIC ANTHROPOLOGY, VOL. I (Wax Trax!/TVT) As the name implies, this compilation is a collection of both previously released and specially commissioned tracks fusing indiginous music from around the world with digital technology. Enlisting the likes of **Juno Reactor, Sabres Of Paradise, Ken Ishii**, Cabaret Voltaire's **Richard Kirk**, and others to escort you on a futuristicc ethnomusicological study, exploring these global people's unique and exotic musics, always ending up with something fully integrated with today's state of the art. **(PW)**

INFLUX-Unique (Sapho/UK) James Bernard graces us with an almost perfect LP. One of the most unrecognized producers of today James has been steadily releasing records for about a year now under the guises of **Cybertrax** and **Influx**. This LP has a style all its own, hence the title **Unique**. Bernard combines wonderful melodies and intense rhythms together to come up with a sound all his own. Each track is incredible, some being remixes from previously released EP's. Not afraid to take chances at all, the music world could definitely use more producers like James Bernard- or maybe one is enough. Hopefully this LP will bring him the attention he truly deserves in the underground. **(G)**

DJ HELL-Gefeert Und Gefedert (Disko B/Germany) The title of this double vinyl LP from Munich's **DJ Hell** has something to do with the feathers it's packaged in. Sorry, we flunked German. Anyway, over the seven tracks, minimal and Detroit-influenced are the names of the game here with Hell effectively displaying some different styles within that framework. Included are some faster acid-laced hard trance numbers, a couple of smooth pulsating deep house tracks (one with a very cool funk bassline leaping out of the minimalness), an experimental piece that is harsh, whispering, and white noice-like in nature, and a Moroderesque reworking of **Throbbing Gristle**'s "Hot On The Heels Of Love". Also featured is a reconstruction of "My Definition Of House Music", which was released in original form on R&S. The rework is pretty unintelligible and it's good and minimal, but my inner ear cries out to hear that **David Byrne** sample from **The Forest** that made the original so catchy. An LP that really grows on you as you delve into it. For those looking for something different. **(PW)**

V/A-PLUG IN + TURN ON (Instinct) Within the past year or so, dance music has seemed to come back down to Earth. Artists are becoming less and less faceless while adding an individual personality to what's already on vinyl. **Plug In + Turn On** is a compilation that spotlights this concept with a well-concieved mix of leading edge artists and rising new talent. Divided over two discs, one 'trance', one ambient, the tracks by the more established acts (**Cabaret Voltaire, Drum Club, GTO**) are choice and serve as reference points for the listener, but the real highlights are the ones from artists like **Terre Thaemlitz, Mothering Noise, Mysteries Of Science** (a side project from **Dominic Woosey** of **United Frequencies of Trance** fame), and the new tracks from **Human Mesh Dance** and **Evolve Now**. Full of fresh, creative ideas, these new talents highlighted here offer a prime view into the future that deserves continued listening and attention. Let's meet here a year from now and check to see how timeless this collection sounds. **(PW)**

PETE NAMLOOK-Ambient, The Definitive Collection 2: The Artists' Cut (Ambient World/Germany) The first release on **Pete Namlook**'s new **Fax** subsidiary **Ambient World**, is the answer to the release of a similar compilation by a well-known U.K. label without permission. 2/3 of the profit from this and subsequent releases on this label will go to the artists involved. Including tracks from **Escape** and **Silence** (w/ **Dr. Atmo**), **Sequential** (w/ **Tetsu Inoue**), **Hearts Of Space** and **Minimalistic Source** (w/**Pascal F.E.O.S.**), and his **Dreamfish** project with **Mixmaster Morris**, The Artists' Cut shows off some of Namlook's finer works, both solo and in collaboration. **(PW)**

V/A-BARRAMUNDI (Astralwerks) Subtitled 'an intoduction to a cooler world,' this debut collection from the new ambient imprint of Belgium's **Antler/Subway Records** takes it's name from an Australian fresh water fish. Opening with a track from the label's latest signing, **Jaydee** (yes, that Jaydee), **Barramundi** wastes no time time plunging fathoms deep with "Think 4 A While", a cool seven-minute plus beatfree current, flowing through an underwater landscape. The rest of the compilation is filled with various flavours of ambience from sort of a behind the scenes crew of the late 80's EBM and New Beat movements that are quite good. The picks: Jaydee, the Orb/Orbital/Irresistible Force influenced **MLF Gaia**, and **Transformer 2**'s (!) Prophet 5 driven "Prophesy" **(Orion)**

BARK PSYCHOSIS-Hex (Caroline) The newest strain in the growing genre of ambient music is indie ambient. Influenced by dance music culture as much as the lush sounds and textures of **A.R. Kane, Spacemen 3/Spiritualized, Durutti Column, David Sylvian**, **'Spirit Of Eden'** period **Talk Talk**, and the **4AD** label, these futurists are taking the broken wreckage of indie and reviving it with various bits of dub, techno consciousness, avant-garde composition, or self-indulgent bliss. One of the latter is London's **Bark Psychosis**. Their debut **Hex**, simply reminds one of all the glorious chilled out moments listening to all the people previously mentioned for the first time, rolled into a 70+ minute trip. Brilliant and perhaps more geared towards the home chillout session rather than the ambient room, save the pure texture of "Pendulum Man", this is a grand debut. Take notice. **(PW)**

JOHN C. LILLY-E.C.C.O. (Silent) **John Lilly** is a psychedelic explorer whose LSD experiments were the loose basis of the film ***Altered States***. **E.C.C.O.** is an acronym for Earth Coincidence Control Office, which according to Lilly is 'an invisible force, entity, or organization of higher dimensions that controls what we think are coincidental events in everyday life situations.' The music here captures the essence of Lilly's work using raw tape recordings from his experiments. Given the remix treatment by **P.B.C., Heavenly Music Corporation**, and **Space Barons**, the material here is prime mixing for under-the-influence excursions deep into the chill. **(Orion)**

V/A-INTELLINET: THE STORY SO FAR (Intellinet) **Intellinet** is the distribution company set up by John and Richie at Plus 8. A compilation of tracks from most of the label's releases in megamix form by **Vapourspace's Mark Gage**, this is divided into two 38-minute parts: 'For The Head' and 'For The Feet.' 'Head' contains tracks from **+8, Probe, Telepathic**, and **Accelerate** while 'Feet' is more of the hard house and disco funk stuff from the **Definitive, Stickman**, and **Malego** labels. An excellent representation of these labels, this is an essential purchase for the compilation buying public, mixed quite well by Mr. Gage. **(G)**

V/A-FROM HERE TO TRANQUILITY, VOL 2 (Silent) The second in Silent's ambient series focuses on the work from artists around the world, noting that this music is truly a global movement. Out of the eleven tracks selected here, a little less than half are truly outstanding as tracks on their own compard to the volume of really good ambient being released worldwide. Much better for listening end to end than for ambient DJ's. Highlights: **Pelican Daughters, Single Cell Orchestra, Tylervision,** and **Air**. **(PW)**

ESCAPE-S/T (Fax/Germany) A two CD album from **Pete Namlook** and **Dr. Atmo**. The Escape project is in essence, about 'travelling in space' and its risks and advantages. The first disc is a collection of four dance and four ambient oriented tracks that were previolsy released on vinyl and are long out-of-print. The other disc is a brand new ambient piece "The Futurescape", consisting of several parts examining space travel from the perspective of the child, the adult, the expert, and the astronaut. A complete juorney easily broken into pieces for DJ's. Was that a **Cocteau Twins** sample I heard, Pete? **(Orion)**

THE WHOLE TRAFFIC-S/T (Fax Sublabel/Germany) A collaboration between **Dr. Atmo** and the **Basalt Boys**, **The Whole Traffic**, as the name implies is an album of 'car-oriented' ambient music. Mostly with beats, this fresh and innovative sounding release is druglike, designed to be listened to while traveling at certain speeds with each track. Most effective when listened to repeatedly, this is one step forward to the next level. (Note: Non-metric friendly people will have to do some math or get a friend who is metric to calculate the KPH speeds to MPH) **(Orion)**

FROM WITHIN/A NEW CONSCIOUSNESS (Fax World/Germany) Two separate collaborations between **Namlook** and +8's **Richie Hawtin** and Anarchic Adjustment design head **Charles Uzzell-Edwards**. **From Within** is Namlook Goes To Detroit, with Pete's synth washes and Richie's analog toys over the top. Brilliant. **A New Consiousness** is more like Charles' album with Pete producing. With and without beats, the album takes an environmental approach using creative recording techniques and unconventional objects as instruments. Creative and refreshing to listen to. **(Orion)**

Alan Oldham, continued from Page 15

AO: We were there almost a month. We played Melbourne, Sydney, and Adelaide. Adelaide is the best city in Australia for techno, bar none.

T: What makes you say that?

AO: They just have a beautiful scene. It's a small town, they're mental for techno, every venue plays a form or genre of techno or house. They don't even really have a live music scene, it's all DJ's.

T: Are you still doing live gigs with UR?

AO: Well, UR's not touring that much anymore. we just did Tokyo. I planned to quit, but we're not doing that much live shit anyway. But whenever we do a show now, it's just me and Mike. Mike is very selective as to where we play.

T: What's the story with Generator, then?

AO: I have a partner who's outside of everything, he was doing production and co-production on all the early Generator stuff. We had some tracks that were sitting around... The concept's all mine, but Mike came up with the initial money to get started. We did the first release and we paid Mike Banks back and we've been on our own ever since. (Submerge) crunches the numbers and I create. It's a great setup.

T: Where is the label going?

AO: Gen is going really international at the moment. We've got these guys from Tokyo that are doing an ep for us, we're talking to **Electric Indigo** from Berlin, we've got the new **Marco Passarani & Mateo Monteduro** who did two separate ep's for us, **DJ ESP** from Minneapolis did a double 12", **Sean Deason** is with us for a 12" which should be out imminently.

T: The label's first couple releases had a 10", a limited edition double A side, a single sided release. Are you going to do more things like that in the future?

AO: The new Freq record is double A sided, I want to do another 10" this year. We did GEN002, my record on 10" and it was smokin'. In fact, I credit it as starting all this 10" fever that's out there now because there were none before we did it. We're just trying to break new ground. That's what it's all about, man. A lot of these labels like Harthouse and cats like that are trying so hard to be major labels themselves and the whole idea of this is to break new ground.

T: Before you joined UR, were you DJ'ing regularly?

AO: I went through my tour of duty here in Detroit. I played clubs, I played Top 40 clubs, all kinds different types of clubs. In fact, I learned to DJ in the clubs because I didn't get my own turntables until way later, so I basically learned on the job. I paid my fuckin' dues, man. I went through the wringer, I get a little success now, and I really think that it's time.

T: Is the scene in Detroit as bad as everyone always says it is? We've heard conflicting reports, what's your opinion?

AO: Yes, it is. It's hard to say. I came up through it, it's very strange and it's just not cool. It's very, very tired. It's happening for some people, but from my point of view, man, the scene is gone. All the cool kids leave Detroit.

T: Everyone making this music in Detroit is Black. From your perspective, do you see a lot of racial things going on with the politics of the music?

AO: When it comes to techno, there's a real dichotomy there because, on the one hand, it's been taken out of black folks' hands. The heyday of that is over.

T: I guess that was when Neil Rushton came to Detroit?

AO: There's the dichotomy. It doesn't seem like Rushton took it out of our hands, per se, the colonization of acid house and the co-option of the early Chicago and Detroit theme. I really don't see this as being the focal point of that, because these Europeans gave these brothers here a standard of living that that they had never known up to that point. Before that, people were like if you weren't making R&B or in a band, you were stupid. The whole underlying thing, in my view, is that studios were throwing away 909's and 303's and black kids were buying the shit for cheap and making house music out of it. Now you can't find a 909 because everyone's trying to go back to that sound, but the white kids who had money who were making their own or working in studios at the time, they were throwing all that old analog shit away. I don't see that as being the colonization- when I look at in America how techno music has turned, it's the ascension of **Moby**. It's really two things, I can't put it all on Moby. It was a couple of years back, maybe '90-91, when the majors were trying to package rave in the States. You had **Quadraphonia**, **T-99**, fuckin' **Sir Mix-A-Lot** had a techno mix of "Baby Got Back", and the majors were trying to push that rave sound. That's when the major record companies got ahold of this kind of music and then Moby was pretty much chosen to be the avatar of this music...white guy, unassuming, non-threatening Christian, da da-da da-da, he plays this fuckin' ecstacy music but doesn't do it himself, let's make him into this. That to me is the hallmark. Personally, I like Moby, he's a really nice guy. That's what I see as being the focal point here in the States, that's when a lot of kids got into the music. I feel when it gets to a major label stage, when it gets to a stage where there can be some real money made, it becomes white. Just like everything else in America. The higher up you go, the whiter it gets. The music wasn't squashed because it was an African-American art form, I just feel it was squashed because they couldn't put it in a box like they put reggae, jazz, and other indigenous African-American art forms in a box. This music is so amorphous, it changes so much so fast, that major label politics are antithesis to this kind of music. So I don't feel that it was squashed racially, but then again, if there's any real money to be made, i.e. Moby, there's the ones who are going to make it. On the other hand, illustrating it as the dichotomy that it is, if white kids hadn't gotten into techno and if it remained black-i.e. the Music Institute crowd- I wouldn't have the career that I have, a lot of people wouldn't have the careers that they have, they wouldn't be selling the that records they do, and they wouldn't be touring, and I'm very thankful for that.

T: Having said that, how do feel about the States? You've played in different countries, would you rather be here or somewhere else more appreciative of your work?

AO: In my younger days, I was like, "I'm going to move to Holland." As I get older, I see more and more that America is still the place to be. Racial politics aside, if you know how to play the game, you can get paid. That's what America's all about, and the older I get I believe that fundamentally. I think that Europe is cool to go and visit. It's a very beautiful place to be, but for people like us it's not cool for people to go over and stay. It's hard because a lot of our livelihood as techno artists depends on our mystique to the European audience. when you go over there and you stay over there and start showin' your ass and

Continued on Page 26

Feet First, continued from Page 3
party, bringing in some of the best and most diverse DJ talent from out-of-town to work the decks with resident **Bruce Wilcox**.

During Winter Music Conference, we saw first hand the sewn seeds begin to bud as the Guild hosted a slew of international and regional talent for a conference wrap-up after hours. Featuring two rooms of music with **Josh Wink** (Philly), **John Acquaviva** (+8 Records), **Steve McClure** (Halluci-Nation Records), **DJ Three** (TRiP), **Chris Harshman** (Simon's, Gainesville) inside the club while ambient, intelligent techno, and chillout grooves were the order outside, courtesy of **Jay Patrick Ahern** (Aquarhythms, Dublin), **Ken Coleman** ('Mary's House'/WVUM-FM, Miami), **Oscillate** DJ's **Grumpy, Orion,** and **Matty**, with **Robbie Hardkiss** (S.F.) playing some strange, fun, and funky tracks to close out this truly trancendent morning at about 11:00.

The Lollipop Guild just had another large scale event, this time with Germany's **Paul Van Dyk, John Debo** (Boston), and a full selection of Florida talent which drew 1500 people on 31 March.

Commercial radio is still ignoring the underground, but college stations like **WVUM-FM** are leading the way with 'Mary's House'. Hosted by 'VUM music director **Mary Koma**, this 10-1 Friday night mix show is the only place to hear underground sounds on the airwaves in South Florida. Resident **DJ Louis** opens the show with a upfront selection of deep house and progressive trance, while Ken Coleman closes out the evening with an hour of ambient grooves, reserving the middle spot for local and out-of-town guests.

The South Florida scene still has a way to go before it builds itself back up to the enthusiasm of the area's early days. Support for an **Autechre** show with a sharp DJ line-up during the conference was dismal as only a couple hundred people showed, but those who were in attendance were going for it. Nonetheless, we're encouraged to see things in South Florida are looking brighter and will only get better with proper care and nurturing from the promoters and partygoers down there.

(Thanks to Scott Lawrence for background information used in this column)

DJ Lewis, continued from Page 7
L: I'm like the non-musician out of the four of us. I mean we're all DJ's, we're all record collectors, but they all play musical instruments and I don't. I don't like to blur the lines between being a musician and being a DJ. That's what's wrong with House music really. DJ's think they're musicians, and they're not. They're just DJ's that go into the studio and make a record that sounds like a record. I prefer people that use the equipment as it was intended.

T: So with Bandulu are you sort of a 'sample collector'?

L: Yeah, I give them samples to use. On a lot of our early stuff, because we didn't have a lot of equipment, we sampled a lot, but not a lot of people noticed. Reviews used to say 'minimal samples'... (Laughs)

T: So what's going on with Bandulu at the moment?

L: Sort of heavy digital reggae, but not like ragga beats. We've been doing a lot of stuff like 'Phaze In Version', three or four tunes in that very reggae, but techno-y sort of set.

Juno Reactor, continued from Page 9
JunoReactor is that Steffan lives in France, Mike lives in India, Jens lives in Amsterdam, Johann lives in Germany and half the year he's in India as well. A lot of the time our sampling really happens from, say, television. I think everyone in Juno Reactor really likes traveling and sort of eating up the essence of the music that's happening in that particular area, so it's not so much sampling the music from different countries but more like taking the feeling you get when you hear the music that's played there.

T: It must be hard to get you all together to work, so do you send tapes to each other, or how do you work?

BW: What happens is that Steffan will come over for a month and we'll work then, and Mike will be here and I'll work with him then, then Jens will come over and I'll work with him... Now the album's out and we've done two gigs-we did a gig in Denmark and a gig in Paris and they both sold out, so we're sort aiming to go live from about April until the end of the summer.

T: Any plans to come to the U.S.?

BW: Yeah, I think so. What we're hoping to try and do is link up with some people like radio stations or something and put on special events in certain areas like what is going on in Europe with parties in quite weird locations but putting on a really good event.

T: You just finished a stint on tour with The Orb in Europe. How did that go?

BW: Excellent. Essentially what was happening was like ambient rooming it; for me it was really good because I'm not a DJ- Mike and Jens take over that but I thought I'd do it because I thought anyone could be an ambient DJ. It was really good because it gave me a different mentality toward listening to records and it gave me two weeks of just listening to music rather than writing it.

T: Do you spend a lot of time in the studio?

BW: Yeah, maybe 12 hours a day. All of that time is generally writing, maybe an hour a day I'll be listening to other music. When I go home I'll listen to music, but it's a completely different listen. It's almost like everything's in competition, listening to other people's ideas, seeing where they're going, and evaluating. When you're DJ'ing, you're just like "Shit, this is really good." and being surprised, so that's what I really like about it.

Look for a new 12" from Juno Reactor with remixes of "The Heavens" and "High Energy Protons" by Mark Gage out soon.

Alan Oldham, continued from Page 26
takin' your shoes off, putting your feet on the desk, they don't want to see that. They want to see 'DJ T-1000'. They want to see you come in, rock the fuckin' crowd, get the crowd all worked up into a frenzy, and then book. You stay about a week, soak up some flavor, and then go home and put out some records. A lot of the cats I know that get souped up by goin' over there and staying are fucked up. You see, in Detroit, none of these people can front- because we know each other. We go over to Europe and we're these mythic Detroit figures, but we have to go home to renew that. I feel that way.

T: Kind of like Green Lantern having to recharge his power ring, huh?

AO: Perfect...

T: Final comments?

AO: In the words of Juan Atkins, which I sampled on one of my records: Know what techno is. Buy shit from Detroit, then you will know.

C.R.A.S.H.
COMMUNICATION RITUAL – AUDIO SENSORY HAPPENING
C.R.A.S.H. every wednesday
...AN ECLECTIC MIX OF ALTERNATIVE & UNDERGROUND SOUNDS FOR A PROGRESSIVE SUBCULTURE.
The C.R.A.S.H. Team has completely re-modeled the club visually featuring two separate rooms:
In the Main Room:
Steve McClure
plus
Richard Leslie
In the Opium Den (in the back room)
Three
plus
Guests
film loops & visuals:
Halluci-Nation Magic
LOCATION:
Masquerade
(813) 247-7065 • 1902 E. 7th Avenue, Ybor City
Open 10pm - 3am+ / 18+ Welcome, 21+ to Drink / Full Liquor & Smart Bars

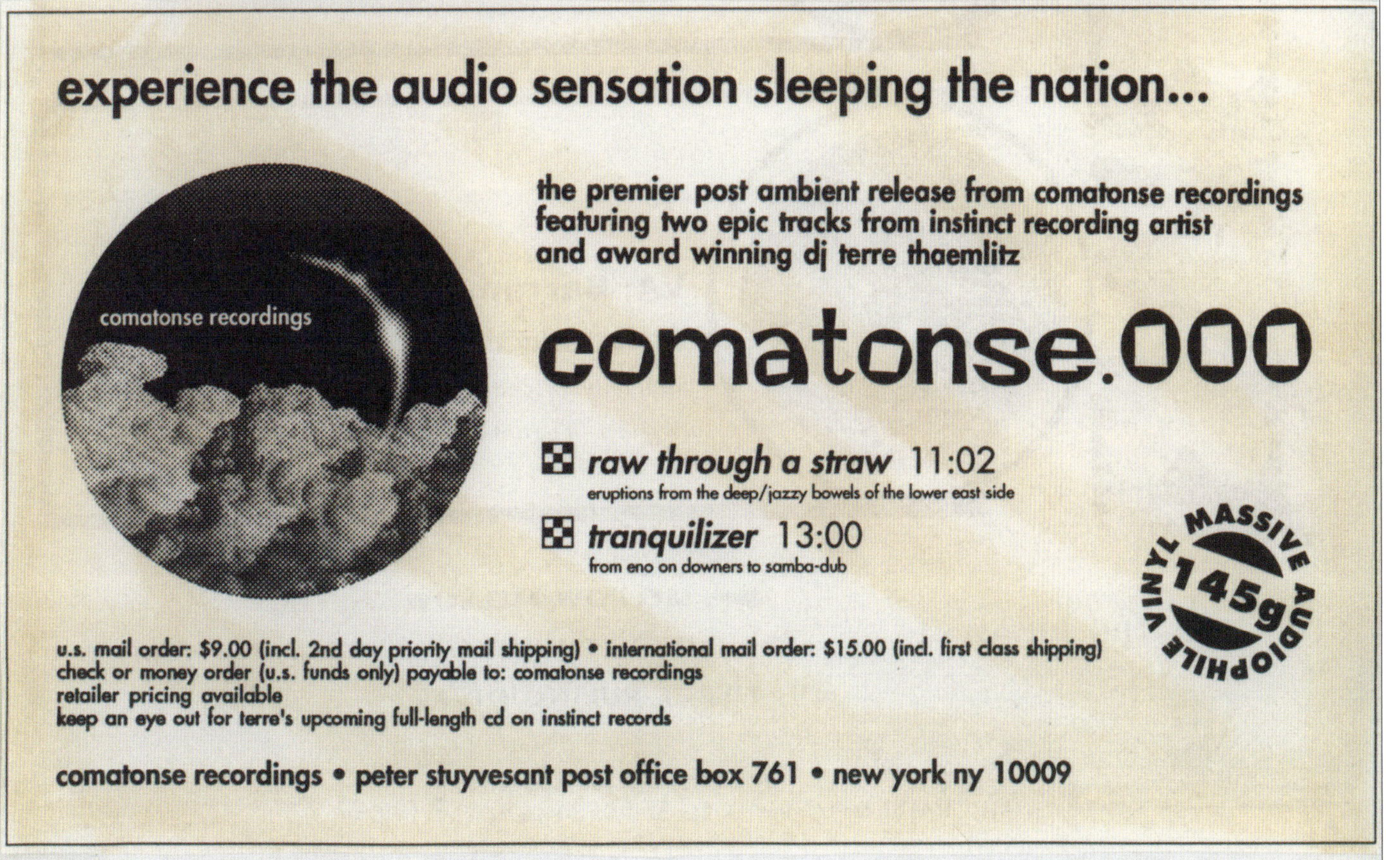
experience the audio sensation sleeping the nation...
the premier post ambient release from comatonse recordings featuring two epic tracks from instinct recording artist and award winning dj terre thaemlitz
comatonse recordings
comatonse.000
raw through a straw 11:02
eruptions from the deep/jazzy bowels of the lower east side
tranquilizer 13:00
from eno on downers to samba-dub
MASSIVE AUDIOPHILE VINYL 145g
u.s. mail order: $9.00 (incl. 2nd day priority mail shipping) • international mail order: $15.00 (incl. first class shipping)
check or money order (u.s. funds only) payable to: comatonse recordings
retailer pricing available
keep an eye out for terre's upcoming full-length cd on instinct records
comatonse recordings • peter stuyvesant post office box 761 • new york ny 10009

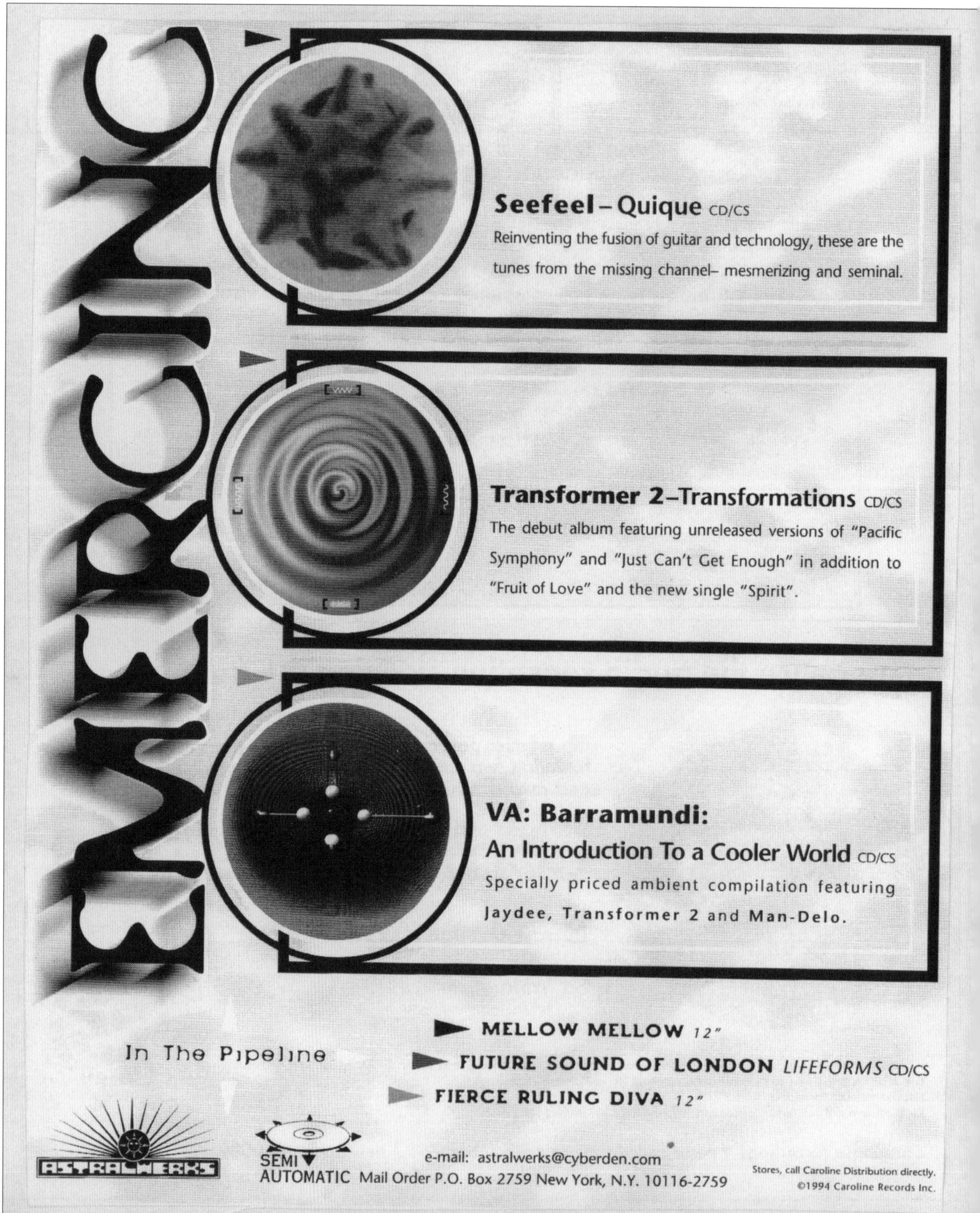
EMERGING
Seefeel – Quique CD/CS
Reinventing the fusion of guitar and technology, these are the tunes from the missing channel– mesmerizing and seminal.
Transformer 2–Transformations CD/CS
The debut album featuring unreleased versions of "Pacific Symphony" and "Just Can't Get Enough" in addition to "Fruit of Love" and the new single "Spirit".
VA: Barramundi:
An Introduction To a Cooler World CD/CS
Specially priced ambient compilation featuring Jaydee, Transformer 2 and Man-Delo.
In The Pipeline
MELLOW MELLOW 12"
FUTURE SOUND OF LONDON LIFEFORMS CD/CS
FIERCE RULING DIVA 12"
ASTRALWERKS
SEMI AUTOMATIC
e-mail: astralwerks@cyberden.com
Mail Order P.O. Box 2759 New York, N.Y. 10116-2759
Stores, call Caroline Distribution directly.
©1994 Caroline Records Inc.

15

Free! Worldwide!
TRIP
V.15.0
FLORIDA'S UPFRONT DANCE CULTURE MAGAZINE
BIOSPHERE
OLIVER LIEB
BLACK DOG PRODUCTIONS
SEEFEEL
DJ HELL
MATRIX RECORDS
WIN FREE +8 GEAR!
DUBTRIBE
DKO*INFLUX*MANTRAC*PHENIX*AMBUSH*CYPHER 7*L.S.G.
GLOBAL COMMUNICATIONS*SINGLE CELL ORCHESTRA
ROBERT MUSSO*TWO SANDWICHES SHORT OF A LUNCHBOX

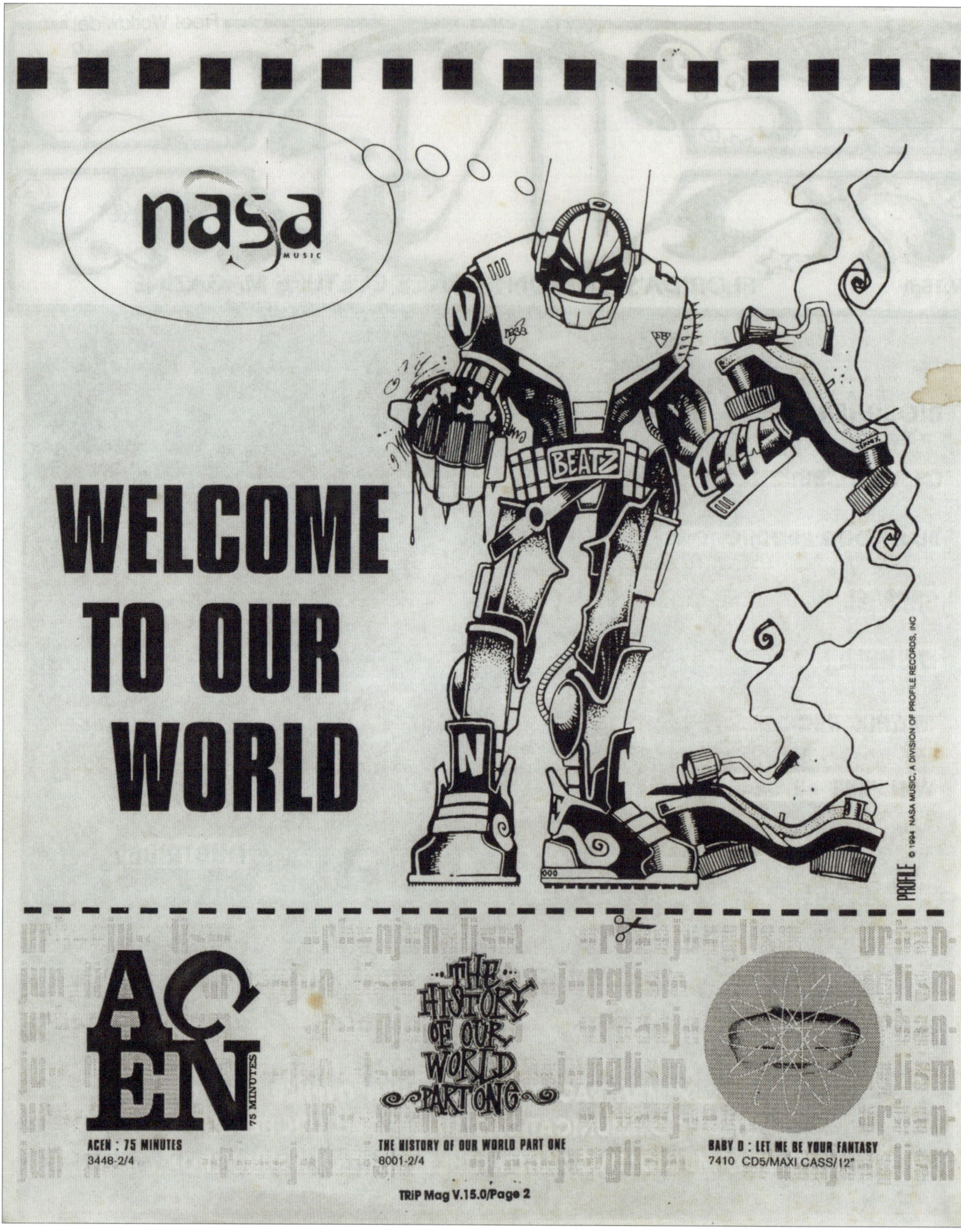
nasa
MUSIC
WELCOME TO OUR WORLD
BEATZ
© 1994 NASA MUSIC, A DIVISION OF PROFILE RECORDS, INC
PROFILE
ACEN
75 MINUTES
THE HISTORY OF OUR WORLD PART ONE
ACEN : 75 MINUTES
3448-2/4
THE HISTORY OF OUR WORLD PART ONE
8001-2/4
BABY D : LET ME BE YOUR FANTASY
7410 CD5/MAXI CASS/12"
TRiP Mag V.15.0/Page 2

TRiP Magazeen

V.15.0/June 1994

-THE COVER-

Beginning with now-legendary jam session parties in their backyard, San Francisco's **Dubtribe Sound System** spread a message of peace, respect, and higher conciousness through their music in their fully live performances and captured on vinyl tracks. An appeal to save our planet, their first 12" **'Mother Earth'**, has catapulted the duo into dancefloor notoriety worldwide. With a new 12" out on Organico and a full-length LP on tap, **Sunshine & Moonbeam** talk about Dubtribe's origins and the messages they try to convey to every partygoer.

-ABOUT THE ISSUE-

This issue was created using Aldus Pagemaker 5.0 and Adobe Photoshop on a Power Macintosh 8100 with 40 MB of RAM. Scans were made on a Hewlett Packard IIcx and output on a HP 4M Plus... The dream continues!

SHOUTS OUT TO:

Katrien and Marcos & R&S, Gary Cobain, Geir Jenssen, Tina @ Planet Dog, Magick Eye, Irdial Discs, Ian @ Dragonfly, Pete & Charlie @ Fax, DB, Lol Hammond, Youth, Tony Marcus @ Mixmag for the mention, Joost @ Surreal Sound, Mark Riva, LuLu @ Plink Plonk, Mike & Tyler @ Exist Dance, Dubtribe, Alan @ Generator, John @ +8 for the gear, Sensory Collective /Ft.L, Eric Lee @ Journees for the shirt, Aquarhythms, DJ Taylor, Kurt @ Drop Bass Network, Ruth @ Underground Source, Rupert@PostCont.

FEET FIRST

Sometimes this column is the most difficult thing to write in this mag. You get caught in the grey area between wanting to impart something really deep and profound but without coming off like a twit. Or be stupid, trendy, and gossipy like some other mags. There's even the temptation to get on a soapbox and preach about various topics-drugs, music policies, scene politics, dodgy promoters, etc., etc. But we don't.

We try to point out all the positive things about our scene and encourage those who are doing things in such manner to continue, hopefully sparking others to think about their actions-as an individual and as a part of a collective scene. As they say, it only takes one person to spoil it for everyone else.

So what's the point of all this, you say? Well, the way we see it, there's been a lot of disrespectful attitudes going around the Florida scene lately. If you're a partygoer here, you know what we're referring to. Maybe you're experiencing similar things in your part of the Global Underground if you're reading this from outside of Florida? You may agree that some or all of these things hinder others' right to a good party.

We don't want to get into a big lecture, point fingers, or right the scene's wrongs. At this point, all we can say is this...think about what you do. Respect yourself-body, mind, and soul. Respect the people and space around you, regardless of whether it's inside or outside the party. Be responsible for yourself (and to an extent, the people you came with).

CORRECTION: Last issue in the **HYPE!** column we wrote that **City Of Angels** was a sublabel of L.A. based **C-Level**. It is not. It is, however, co-run by C-Level partner **Justin King**. In his review of the **Escape** LP, DJ Orion suggested that there was a Cocteau Twins sample used. **Fax's Pete Namlook** called to point out that it was not and that he doesn't sample other ambient or techno artists. Ever. We stand corrected.

TRIP Magazeen
100 East M.L. King Blvd.
Suite #5
Tampa, Florida 33603
U.S.A.
FON: 813.238.0310
FAX: 813.876-7473
(please use a cover sheet if you fax)
E-MAIL: oscillate@aol.com.

EDITOR/PUBLISHER:
Peter Wohelski
SENIOR EDITOR: Wayne Consiglio
EDITOR-AT-LARGE: Chris Milo
EXECUTIVE ASSISTANT:
Jackie Rosquete
CONTRIBUTORS:
Jay Patrick Ahern, Joost De Lyser, DJ Grumpy, DJ Jask, DJ Orion, DJ Sprinkles, DJ Three, Andrew Duke, Ian Rich, Robert Shea, Terre Thaemlitz

SUPPORT THE UNDERGROUND!!
ADVERTISING: Rates available upon request.
SUBSCRIPTIONS: $10 yearly for six issues
RETAILERS: Contact DELTRA RECORD DIST. (310) 202-8554, RECORD TIME DIST. (313) 773-7373, or TRIP direct for info.
TRIP Magazeen is published every eight weeks and is distributed throughout the United States and into Europe. We hope our content will encourage awareness and positivity in the Global Underground. Opinions expressed are not necessarily those of the editors.

HYPE! HYPE! HYPE! HYPE! HYPE! HYPE! HYPE! HYPE! HYPE! HYPE! HYPE! HYPE! HYPE! HYPE! HYPE! HYPE! HYPE! HYPE!

FUTURE SOUND OF LONDON, inspired by their radio show appearances, played a 'live' gig this past May via an ISDN digital phone link broadcasting over **BBC RADIO ONE** to several million Europeans from their own studio, prompting some festival promoters to inquire about appearing. They've completed a 10 minute pilot for **YAGE**, the accompanying film to their new Lifeforms LP, directed by their visual consultant **BUGGY G. RIPHEAD**....**C-LEVEL's IAN RICH** has been quite the busy bloke lately. He's started two new labels: **SMOG**, which will focus on what Rich calls "across the board dance music, kind of like Cleveland City, having an emphasis on putting out good tracks," and its techno offshoot, **QUAKE**. He's also finishing up tracks on a full-length LP for his **ELEMENTS OF AMBIENCE** side-project. For DJ inquiries on Smog or Quake, call **1+213-368-6664**....**PLINK PLONK** is setting up three new labels this summer: **RICOCHET** (very deep house), **LOW-VOLTAGE**, (smooth Detroit-influenced tracks) and **E.A.R. (ELECTRO AUDIO RESPONSE**, harder European trance and techno (a gabba-free zone))....**BOY MEETS GIRL, LTD.** is a U.K.-based merchandising company handling merchandise for U.K. labels **LIMBO, ACID JAZZ, HOOJ CHOONS**, and others in the U.S. For more information or merchandising inquiries, call **1+818-760-2777**....Sounds like this year's **MONTREUX JAZZ FESTIVAL** will be quite the event with scheduled performances from **AMBUSH, EARTH NATION** and a improvised live ambient performance by **RALF HILDENBEUTEL, DOMINIC WOOSEY**, and **STEVIE BE-ZET**....Look for **ORBITAL** and guests ex-Shamen sidemen **PRESSURE OF SPEECH** to tour the States later this Fall....**MIXMASTER MORRIS** has left the **RISING HIGH** label after three years. Sources cite disputes over support for the new **IRRESISTIBLE FORCE** album and the label's lawsuit with **PETE NAMLOOK** as reason for the split....**BILL LASWELL** has been busy as usual, working on ambient projects with **SPACETIME CONTINUUM**'s **JONAH SHARP** and **TETSU INOUE** and traveling to Frankfurt later this summer to work on the follow-up to his collaboration with Pete Namlook, **PSYCHONAVIGATION**....**JONAH** from **SPACETIME** is finishing work on a new LP. Look for his **REFLECTIVE** label to release work from Heidelburg's **DEEP SPACE NETWORK** later this year....Detroit-based **GENERATOR** will be releasing **WORLD SONIK DOMINATION**, a compilation of the A-sides from the label's first year and some new tracks through **KICKIN'/UK.** Generator will also be rereleasing the long out of print **SIGNAL TO NOISE RATIO** ep originally released on D-Jax Up-Beats along with a 2X12" by Minneapolis' **DJ ESP** and a limited edition, promo-only X-313 7".... Famous New York club night **N.A.S.A.** have made the transition to record label. A sublabel of **PROFILE** (where N.A.S.A. co-founder DB does A&R), the label's debut launch will be a 'History of U.K. Breakbeats' compilation CD, digitally mixed together like a mix tape....**NEW MUSIC SEMINAR, NEW YORK CITY, JULY 19-24, 1994.** See you all there....**GLOBAL MEDITATION** is a collection of spiritual, ritual, and meditative traditional music from around the world. A four CD box set, each disc focuses on different elements of the music- vocals, harmonies, rhythms, etc. The set is available through **ELLIPSIS ARTS**. For a free catalog or to order, call **1+800.788.6670**....Run by U.K. cyber-hippy spokesman **FRASER CLARK** and his **EVOLUTION** posse, London's metaphysical ambient/intelligent techno club **MEGATRIPOLIS** comes to the U.S. this summer, hosting a free megarave during this year's **WORLD UNITY FESTIVAL** at the Arizona's Grand Canyon, August 21-28, 1994. For more information, call Gabe @ **1+212-927-6384**. The 'zippies' will also be making tour stops in New York, Boulder, Denver, the Rainbow Gathering in Wyoming, San Francisco, and Santa Cruz.....Ambient DJ/artist and former Anarchic Adjustment designer **CHARLES UZZELL-EDWARDS** has formed a new clothing company called **ENVIRONMENT**. His new project with Pete Namlook is called **CREATE**, out now on Fax....Out soon on Hardkiss: "Phoenix", the new **GOD WITHIN**; with remixes by **RABBIT IN THE MOON** and **DUST BROTHERS**.....**PUBLIC SPACE** is a new ambient after hours club in L.A. dedicated to the 'new-edge sounds of ambient and electronic music.' The promoters envision the club as a space where musicians, writers, and visual artists can collaborate in a spontaneous manner. For more information, ring **1+310.822.7847**....Now settled into their log cabin in Washington State, the **EXIST DANCE** crew have a new release in the pipeline direct from Heaven called **CAP'M STARGAZER vs. COMMANDER MINDFUCK**....

instinct 1994 records
TRANCEFUSION 2
snc-2031
Trancefusion 2 continues with a collection of trance from around the globe. Features YOUNG AMERICAN PRIMITIVE, SABRES OF PARADISE, ORBITAL and PROTOTYPE 909's new single "Love Sky."
chillout
PHASE TWO
CHILLOUT PHASE 2
ex-268
The long awaited follow-up to the critically acclaimed ambient collection. This double CD set includes tracks from APHEX TWIN, SAD WORLD, CABARET VOLTAIRE and many more.
CABARET VOLTAIRE "THE CONVERSATION"
ex-273
BRAND NEW CABARET VOLTAIRE. The double CD conclusion to the Cab's trilogy is a masterpiece of bubbling trance and haunting ambient textures.
emit0094
EMIT 0094
ex-280
Blissful organic ambient from the UK's Time Recording. Features BAD DATA, COCO, STEEL & LOVEBOMB, and MIASMA in one of the most chilled out compilations of the year.
instinct
26 WEST 17th St. #502 NEW YORK, NY 10011
CSERVE RAVENET ON ROCKNET: 72170,1753
FOR A FREE CATALOG SEND US A S.A.S.E.

TECHNO AND TANNING: TIPS BY MUNICH'S DJ HELL

With his work as an A&R man at Frankfurt's Logic Records tracks and remixes on labels like R&S and Disko B, as well as a stint at Berlin'sfamous Hardwax record shop, Munich-born **DJ Hell** could be considered one of Germany's most respected long-standing DJ's. Influenced by everything from early punk and New Wave to Hip-hop, funk, and soul to techno pioneers like **Cabaret Voltaire** and **D.A.F.**, Hell draws from these diverse sources in his own tracks to the tracks he picks behind the decks. Overshadowed by his fellow countrymen like **Sven Vath** in the States, Hell recently visited the U.S., stopping in Miami during Winter Music Conference to play a few gigs and soak up some Florida sun. **TRiP** spoke to him just after the Conference, where he gave us the scoop on his new album and general beachfront etiquette...

TRiP: You're from Munich, do you still live there?

DJ Hell: I was born in Munich in the countryside and moved to Frankfurt in 1992 and worked for Logic Records as an A&R manager. Then I moved to New York for a couple of months, '92 I think, and I worked at Limelight with **Jeff Mills** and did the Future Shock parties with **Repete** and **Damon Wild**. Then I returned to Berlin and worked at the **Hardwax** record shop. I've now moved back to Munich to build my own studio and started producing my own stuff and I now have an LP ready.

T: A full-length album?

H: Yeah, it's a double 12" on Disko B. Seven new tracks of completely different styles- jazz-house to kind of ambient, kind of jazzy, kind of acid music... All my influences really. The name of the record is <u>Tar & Feathers</u>, the promo copies have feathers on the cover. It looks really strange!

T: It sounds like you have lots of influences?

H: Yeah, really everything. I started DJ'ing as Punk came up in '78-'79-then I used to play for free drinks, Cokes. Then I fell in love with the New Wave stuff and that evolved into playing a lot of rap music from the States because some friends from New York were sending me tapes of Red Alert and Chuck Chillout. I think all that comes out in the new album.

T: I find it very interesting that so many old punks have such an influence on the dance underground today...

H: A lot of people are into electronic dance music, but in different ways; **Alex Patterson** from The Orb, **Youth** was in Killing Joke. I spoke with **Dave Clarke** from Magnetic North recently, who's doing a lot of really good funk stuff at the moment, and he's got a lot of the same influences like Ultravox and the Damned. I really like his remixes on **Bush.**

T: You've been known more for playing really hard when you DJ, but I noticed when I heard you play the other night that it was very minimal...

H: I'm more into this minimalistic style- minimalistic, hypnotic, acid darkness kind of feeling. I had a problem in Holland at this party called Hellraiser; they booked me because of my name, thinking I must be one of the hardest DJ's in Germany. I played my hardest stuff, but it still wasn't hard enough for them. The fastest I play now is 160 bpm; I understand the music and I think it's a lot of fun to jump around and have a good party, but for me as a DJ, no.

T: The first track that you did is probably one of my favorites, "My Definition Of House Music' on R&S- I love that string sample. Where is that from?

H: It's from a play called <u>The Forest</u> and I sampled it from the soundtrack David Byrne did for it. That was my first track, on R&S, but now I'm on a Munich label called Disko B. and they've been really grea t so far.

T: Where are your some of your favorite places to play?

H: In Europe? There's one club in Berlin called Electroid it's really small- maybe 50 people and it's packed. That's one of the best for me at the moment. There's a club in Cologne, the Warehouse, and in there's a lot of small clubs in the countryside, not in the big cities. Switzerland, Austria...

T: What are things like in Europe now? Is it still very hard?

H: No, just different. On the big rave scene there is a lot of commercial music, always the same labels-**Harthouse, Superstition, Bonza i**- time after time. I think things have changed in just the last month, the kids are sick of hearing the same music all the time and I think there's a new scene coming up, an avant garde scene with different kind of music. Perhaps its more intelligent, although I don't like to use the term intelligent because it has nothing to do with intelligence, more minimalistic and more experimental.

T: What do you do when you're not DJ'ing or in the studio?

H: Believe it or not, I do a lot of sports. I like (soccer) a lot and play squash, but I'm usually working in the studio and I hang out with friends in Munich.

Hell's LP, Gefeert and Gefedert, is out now on Disko B.

Black Dog Productions: The Speed Of Thought

by Joost De Lyser

Probably the most interesting of the 'new' British techno artists are London-based **Black Dog Productions.** Sometimes hiding behind aliases (such as **Balil, Plaid, Repeat** (with **Mark Broom**), and **i.a.o.**), **Ken Downie, Ed Handley,** and **Andy Turner** were responsible for some of the most innovative dance records of 1993 and now 1994.

TRiP: Where are you from?
Ken Downie: Totnes, Devon, the birthplace of the programmable computer.
Ed Handley: Originally Cambridge, just by the science park.
Andy Turner: Windsor, England.

T: What is your musical background?
K: Very strange.
E: I grew up on electro and hip-hop.
A: Classical, ska, electro, and anything I've heard.

T: How did you meet each other and Wayne (from GPR)?
K: Ed replied to an advert I'd put in 'Music Technology' and he brought Andy along a month or two later. After nearly calling oursselves **The Cheeba Smarties,** Black Dog Productions was born. We met Wayne, from GPR, after we'd had our third EP release, he was tipped off by a DJ friend of ours, Mark Broom. He liked what he heard and we managed to negotiate a non-exclsive one year licensing deal together.
E: Doing solo bits up to 1988 and then the ad in MT, I knew Andy from way back as a DJ.
A: I met Ed in the early hip-hop days, Ed introduced me to Ken.

T: What does 'The Black Dog' mean? Why do you use this name?
K: It's a primal archetype that has been around for as long as humanity itself. My personal reason for using it is that it refers to 'Apust,' an Egyptian God called 'Opener Of Ways,' who appeared to me in a dream in early 1987. It seemed like the perfect choice. Since starting the band, we've also seen that the name functions on many different levels than the one we first investigated. There's even a town in England called Black Dog.

T: Who is the philosopher of you guys?
K: I'd say we all are, we just philosophize about different things.
E: I steer clear, too young really, but would listen to Sheikh Al-Alawi.

T: Who is your favorite movie director, and movie?
K: Ridley Scott, ***Brazil***, and anything with Jacques Tati in it.
E: Yeah, much the same. Ridley Scott is the one with both budget and guts, but the best ideas still come from young directors.
A: Mike Leigh, ***Life Is Sweet*** (at the moment).

T: Who designs your artwork?
K: Most of the ideas and origination are done in house, here at **Black Dog Towers,** then we have to try and explain what we want to our long-suffering friend Richie B., who tries to recreate what we explain to him. We also know a brilliant cartoonist called Tim Frost, who can draw a very good dog portrait when asked nicely.

T: What is your favorite musical instrument, and why?
K: The veena, because it's incredibly ancient and cuts across everything.
E: The 303, even though we don't use it much... It is so overused by others. It is one of the only instruments that you can turn on and get usable sounds right away. Just that and drums.
A: The triangle, a much underrated musical innovation.

T: How would you describe your music?
–Music.

T: You run a BBS (bulletin board system)? Tell us about it.
– It's a global ccommunication center that can be accessed by anyone with a modem, 24 hours a day. The number is (011) +44 (0)81-983-3472.

T: Your favorite record of all time?
K: 'All Mod Cons,' by The Jam and **"Sergeant Pepper,"** by the Beatles.
E: I can't pin down an all-time favorite, maybe "It Is What It Is" for purity.
A: The bloke who stuffed marshmallows up his nose.

T: What do you think House music will sound like in the future?
K: Like us and **Irdial** (Discs).
E: Unlike House music now.
A: What is House music?

T: In Holland, labels like B12, Irdial, GPR, etc. are being hyped. People are buying records just for the label, not the music. What do you think of that?
K: Yes, I've noticed that over here. I suppose there will be elitists in any scene. People shouldn't be sheep and buy what magazines and DJ's tell them to. They have a mind they should exercise before parting with their money. But...I like all those labels you mentioned, and would probably buy all their reccords if I had the money.
E: You can't tell people what music to buy; ultimately, it's a personal decision, however much hype is there.
A: We've always tried to avoid hype. This seems the best way of getting it.

(Reprinted by permission from Surreal Sound 'zine, Holland. For more information on Surreal Sound, fax (011) +31 1 1792000)

Frankfurt rising star Oliver Lieb hits supernova with mulitple guises

Working overtime. That's got to be the simplest way to describe Frankfurt's **Oliver Lieb.** In the past year and a half, the 24-year-old has pumped out over twelve pieces of work on six different labels under various guises including **Spicelab**, **Ambush**, and **L.S.G**... And that hasn't even covered collaborations with **Pascal F.E.O.S.** (Resistance D.), **Torsten Stenzel** (Humate), and ambient DJ **Dr. Atmo**. Oh, and did we forget to mention that the guy does live shows throughout Europe? Perhaps one of the most amazing things about Lieb's prolific output is that the quality of his work has remained high with not a bad track in the bunch.

Beginning his musical education in the early 80's, young Oliver Lieb bought a bass guitar, giving it up after a few years of lessons for a keyboard and home experimentation.

By 1989, Lieb had created enough material to attract European attention, releasing "System" by **Force Legato**, an industrial techno track on the Abfahrt/ZYX label in Germany, selling over 40,000 copies and prompting a remix in 1990. Lieb recorded for the label for two years under several different projects.

DJ Jorg, a partner in Delerium Records, met Lieb in a club in 1992 and suggested doing a project together. The result within a few short months was **Psilocybin**. Each of the three releases were completely different than its predecessor and well as progresssively harder.

Prior to that project with Delerium, Lieb had linked up with

Sven Vath's **Harthouse** label and was working on the first **Spicelab** EP. A new trance fusion of acid, ambience and house elements, whetting the appetites of DJ's everywhere for the next EP.

The follow-up, ***Quicksand*** EP, a wildly popular and heavily charted release in both the U.S. and Europe was of a more schizophrenic quality, displaying Lieb's experiments with different styles and rhythms. A third EP, ***The Spirit Of Fear*** followed shortly.

The Spicelab LP, **Lost In Spice**, released late last year was recorded in a week and a half with the concept of creating an album that one could listen to at home. The five tracks suck you into its cosmic landscape, forcing the listener to draw their own interpretation of the album.

Another project, **Ambush**, also surfaced. Focusing on harder, more acidy, and tribal tracks, Oliver has released two EP's with a full length Ambush LP to follow this Summer.

Although preferring to work solo, Lieb's several recent collaborations have also garnered great critical attention.

With strong studio accompaniment like Resistance D.'s Pascal F.E.O.S., and Dr. Atmo (with whom Lieb reinterpreted the **Koyanisquatsi** soundtrack), these tracks have showcased not only the German's good taste in working partners but diversity in styles-from breakbeat-driven trance to beatfree ambience.

Spicelab's Lost In Spice is now available domestically through Harthouse America/Planet Earth Recordings. Expect the L.A. based label to also release the full-length Ambush LP. Lieb recently made his American live debut at Circa '94 in Los Angeles.

-A SELECTED OLIVER LIEB DISCOGRAPHY-

FORCE LEGATO-"System" (Abfahrt/Germany) 1989

PSILOCYBIN-Part 1 & 2 (Zyx/Germany) 1991

SPICELAB-Quicksand EP (Harthouse/Germany) 1992

SPICELAB-Spirit Of Fear EP (Harthouse/Germany) 1993

SPICELAB-*Lost In Spice* LP (Harthouse/Germany) 1993

SPICELAB-"Spice Is A Fulltime Occupation" (Harthouse/Germany) 1994

AMBUSH-Ambush EP (Harthouse/Germany) 1993

AMBUSH-The Remixes (Harthouse/Germany) 1994

MINDSPACE-Mindspace EP (No Respect/Germany) 1993

LSG-LSG EP (Superstition/Germany) 1993

OLIVER LIEB-*Constellation* LP (Recycle Or Die/Germany) 1993

-W/PASCAL F.E.O.S.-

INFINITE AURA-"Infinite Aura" (Eye-Q/Germany) 1993

AZID FORCE-Azid Force EP (Superstition/Germany) 1993

-W/DR. ATMO-

JAVA-"Cosmos" (Eye-Q/Germany) 1994

MUSIC FOR FILMS- *'Koyanisquatsi'* LP (Fax Sublabel/Germany) 1994

-W/TORSTEN STENZEL (HUMATE)-

PARAGLIDERS-Paragliders EP (Superstition/Germany) 1993

REMIXES

SVEN VATH-"Ritual Of Life" (Eye-Q/Germany) 1992

Blurring the border between indie and ambience

Seefeel

In the wake of indie rock's slow death in the U.K. new bands thatobscure the defined lines between indie rock culture and dance culture have emerged out of the aftermath, fusing guitars and new technology. Not too far off in feel from late 80's groups like **A.R. Kane** or **Spacemen 3** nor far removed from ambient either, these bands have been tagged indie/ambient by the trend-hungry British music press. Formed in December of 1992, London's **Seefeel** is probably of the highest profile in this new hybrid, touring with the likes of **Aphex Twin** (a longtime friend and "Time To Find Me" remixer), **Autechre**, and the **Cocteau Twins**.

Initially signed to the **Too Pure** label (the same people who brought you Stereolab and P.J. Harvey) on the strength of their demos, Seefeel's first single sold 500 copies to start, while their debut album **Quique** (pronounced 'Keek", named after a Roland 808 drum machine sound) sold 10,000.

Recently in New York to promote the release of Quique in the U.S., **TRiP** spoke with **Sarah Peacock** and **Justin Fletcher** about the indie/ambient tag, remixing, and what their music is really about.

TRiP: The British music press have found a new label, Indie/ambient. Does Seefeel come from an indie background or are you more rooted in dance music culture?

Sarah Peacock: I think they're all quite different, really.

Justin Fletcher: We all listen to different genres of music. I think we're all influenced by 'indie music', The Smiths, Cocteau Twins, that sort of thing. But then again, Darren listens to people like Thomas Kohner and German atmosphericstuff, he likes film soundtracks. Mark's sort of more techno minded... I'm into everything, I grew up with blues and then into dub reggae, indie... I used to hate disco music, high energy music made me cringe.

T: Do you consider Seefeel to be an indie/ambient band?

SP: I think it's something that can be leveled at us, definitely. Just the fact that on stage we're a bit like a rock band, we'll be playing to tapes and all the songs will be exactly as you hear them on the record, only with a bit of a live edge to them. It's not something we're always very happy with because it's a very superficial thing, indie/ambient, and it seems quite cynical when you put it like that; whereas we try to be totally honest and just instinctive about what we're doing.

T: Where does the band dirive their sound, there's a lot of different elements that are floating around?

SP: I think initially it was us getting into technology through guitar effects and influences like My Bloody Valentine, Cocteau Twins, then getting into samplers and gathering more technology, sequencers; with all that technology your capacity you've got for writing songs is more to do with dance music structuring than songs. It opens up a whole new avenue...

T: Seefeel is a band that is really validating the guitar in this sort of music, where does your approach to the instrument come from?

SP: I think it's the basis for the whole sound. There's no keyboards

on any of the records. All the sequences are samples of looped guitars. We hope we're doing it in a very non-rock cliched manner.

T: Where do you think Seefeel fits between the two genres?
JF: We're not an ambient act. We just do music we enjoy. I'd call ourselves 'Slambient'; our live show is quite harsh and in-your-face, not really mellow at all.
SP: It's pretty loud and in-your-face and we like to do a lot of things with our engineer like dubbing off the mixing desk or manipulating the bass so it's bowel shaking...

T: Have you done more mellow, ambient room type set-ups?
SP: There is another side of Seefeel that we've developed for the live thing, a live mixing set that Mark and Darren do with just the basic tracks coming off that ADAT and them doing all the effects live on the mixing desk.
JF: It's really chillout room stuff, very dub-influenced. I sort of prefer the four piece, but that's because I'm not doing anything! (Laughs)

T: Straddling the fence between indie and dance culture, do you go out to clubs often? Are there any clubs or DJ's that you like particularly?
SP: There's a club that's just started by a friend of ours called **Quirky.** The DJ's there are **Kevin Hector** and **Tara Patterson** who are the other members of **Autocreation** with our sound engineer, **Locust**. Aphex Twin is totally mad when he DJ's, all sorts of ambient drones. If you're in the wrong frame of mind it'll totally freak you out; **DJ Lewis** (Keogh, Bandulu/The Orb) is really brilliant, **Weatherall**... There's some really good ambient DJ's as well, **Mixmaster Morris, Tony Morley, Alex Patterson**...

T: I understand that you're venturing into remix work?
SP: Yeah, Mark's done a remix for Autechre ("Basscadet")...**Beaumont Hannant** also did one.
JF: We haven't really been asked, but we're into it.
SP: I had a bit of a go at one with this band we played with, sort of a goth-ish, Nick Cave sort of band, but I don't really think they liked it. It's really fun to do; I'd love to do it, so if anyone's got any offers... It's something that's easier done individually than as a band. Mark was really keen to do the Autechre remix, so we let him get on with it even though we might have liked to have a look in.

T: Anything new coming out soon, outside of the Autechre remix?
JF: We do have a new ep on Warp that's basically four new tracks, almost. It's quite different, stripped down, more minimal than anything we've done before. It's called **'Starethrough'**. We're also doing something for Richard James' label, **Rephlex**. I'm not sure when that's going to come out, but it's almost finished, maybe early Summer.

Seefeel's Quique LP is available domestically through Astralwerks with their first two import EP's, *"More Like Space"* and *"Pure, Impure"*, combined on one CD for domestic release entitled Polyfusia due July 22nd. The *"Starethrough"* EP is out now on Warp. Mark Clifford and Darren Seymour of Seefeel will be in New York during New Music Seminar doing a series of live mixing sets.

NORWAY'S BIOSPHERE TURNS FROZEN SURROUNDINGS INTO ICY AMBIENCE

Imagine for a moment, the Arctic Circle after an evening snowstorm. An eerie calm sweeps over the settling snow drifts as stars in the icy sky reflect off of them, crystal-like. The tranquil beauty of the moment is frozen forever as you travel by car into the inky darkness.

Now, put that mood to music and you have but one facet of the music of Norway's **Biosphere**.

By the age of 17, **Geir Jenssen** had discovered the world of electronic music, scanning the radio waves for strange, synthesized sounds in his hometown of Tromso, Norway. Jenssen went on to form **Bel Canto**, a 4AD-esque act with a distinctly icy quality, a product of their frigid surroundings. Geir did two albums with Bel Canto before going solo, first with **Bleep**-releasing an LP *North Pole By Submarine*- and now Biosphere. Signed to R&S Records' ambient label, **Apollo**, Biosphere has released two albums, *Microgravity* and *Patashnik*.

TRiP's DJ Orion recently spoke with Geir Jenssen from his home in Tromso about Arctic living, film soundtracks, astronomy, and radio as a medium for the ambient genre.

TRiP: Where is Tromso located?

Geir Jenssen: It's North of the Arctic Circle. It's as far North as Anchorage, Alaska.

T: You were a memeber of Bel Canto. Coming from a sound like that, you must have a wide variety of influences...

G: Yes. Everything from acid techno to Brian Eno and Dead Can Dance.

T: Certainly, Norway's a cold place. Your music is very moody and even icy. Do you think you would have the same sound in your music if you lived elsewhere?

G: No, because when we did the first Bel Canto album we went to Brussels and it changed. We started to make more electronic body music. I just had to go back to Tromso because I didn't want to sound like **Front 242**.

T: You use a minimal sort of studio setup. Do you subscribe to the theory of 'less is more' or is it a financial matter?

G: I think it's a combination. (Laughs) It's very nice to have the equipment in the living room, so I can work whenever I want. I can wake up after sleeping and continue, I also don't have to take the bus to the studio. An author has his typewriter or his PC or whatever and I have the same feeling, that you don't need a lot if you can express yourself on what you have. I'm going to buy a bit more expensive equipment now, but I also like that it, in a way, has to be minimalistic because you don't have memory enough (in the gear) to add more parts. I think it's worked so far.

T: On *Micrograviity* as well as on *Patashnik*, you've used a lot of film samples. Would you like to do soundtrack work in the future?
G: Yeah, I did a short movie, 20 minutes long this Spring. I also was working on a project supported by the government where I was allowed to use a camera and mix the images I found with music. I was doing it with a friend; he was doing the shooting while I was the director. It was very fun to work with pictures and music from a script.

T: Are there any directors you'd like to score for?
G: Of course, I'd like to work with **Stanley Kubrick** if he was going to make ***'2020'*** or something...**Jim Jarmusch**...

T: Maybe you could reinterpret the soundtrack for *2001* and release it as part of the Music For Films series on Fax? Speaking of Pete Namlook, you've worked with him in the past on the Fires Of Ork project, tell us about that.
G: It was fun because I was listening to a lot of Fax stuff and I have my own mail order company, a very small one, I import techno records and ambient and I was thinking maybe I should call him to see if it was possible to get records directly from Fax. I didn't, but suddenly I had this letter from him that said he really liked my first album and he would like to work with me. He works very differently from me because he has a lot of equipment, everything. He also works very fast and he's very talented with sounds.

T: I noticed you did something with Marcos Salon on the latest Outlander ep ("Vision"). Are you working on any other collaborations at the moment?
G: (Surprised) Are you sure? I was working with him two years ago. I was recording some new Biosphere tracks in Antwerp and we did some tracks. I don't think we liked them then.
T: How did you get involved with R&S?
G: You've heard of Mental Overdrive? It's a guy called Per Martinssen, he's also from Tromso. He released 3 ep's on R&S. My album was first released on a small Norwegian label and Per took it to Renaat. He had only listened to the album for about 15 seconds when he knew he wanted it and he called me. So, thanks to Per... The plan was to release it on Crammed/SSR, but I don't know what happened. I just had to sell it to somebody to pay my rent.

T: Unbeknownst to you, a wise decision to make, selling it to Renaat, huh?
G: I think so, too. (Laughs) It was my favorite label at the moment when he called.

T: How does *Micrograviity* sound to you now? Does it sound dated at all?
G: I don't think it sounds dated; that was my goal, I didn't want to use cliches. I was thinking if Crammed was going to release it, it would be a year before it was out and if I had used a lot of stupid samples everyone else had used, it would have sounded very dated. I tried to make it very timeless and I think it worked.

T: Define ambient music as it pertains to Biosphere.
G: Brian Eno called his music 'ambient'; it was to be like 'wallpaper', it should be in the background. You shouldn't listen to it, but be more as background music. I want my ambient music to be more like an abstract picture than wallpaper. It should be so good that it attracts the listener, you have to look at that picture, you can't just use it as background music. It should inspire the listener.

T: On "The Shield", you sampled a satellite dish that takes pictures of the Northern Lights?
G: That's the project I was telling you about that was funded by the government. The project was that I had to find a location in Tromso and sample sounds and take pictures and make something out of it. The dish sends out radio waves and they are returned by the Northern Lights. The samples are more from the machinery; the radio waves also disturb the FM radio band and I sampled the noises the waves make.

T: I understand you are a big astronomer... Tell us about that.
G: Five years ago, I started to be very interested in astronomy, but at the moment I'm not that interested in it because a lot of the things that they are interested in are not that important for us. For example, if they found out that the 'Big Bang' happened not 15 billion years ago, but 15.2, it's not that important. They're not answering the big questions, 'why do we have intelligence in the universe'. I've never even stargazed, it's more of a mental thing, imagining traveling in space...

T: You recently completed a U.K. tour. What is the Biosphere experience live?
G: I think it's quite good. At first I didn't want to play live because I was imagining myself just standing there - boring. In working with a friend who's very good with video, lights, and lasers, I think it works very well. It's very massive in a way, a big video screen with very abstract computer images...images from the project I told you about, we even bought some film from NASA.

T: Tell us about the Melkweg Ambient Weekend in Amsterdam which you were a part of. *(For those who don't know, the* ***Melkweg*** *-Milky Way in Dutch-* ***Ambient Weekend*** *was an ambient festival in Amsterdam held last Halloween weekend including performance artists, and live sets from* ***Higher Intelligence Agency, Chris & Cosey, David Morley, Pete Namlook, and Biosphere*** *and dj's* ***Mixmaster Morris, Ambient Daan, Joost Van Bellen*** *and others)*
G: It was very relaxed, there were mattresses on the floor. I'll be playing the second festival the first week of June.

T: Have you ventured into DJ'ing at all or do you strictly make music?
G: I'm DJ'ing a little bit on the local radio station every week for one hour. I have my own show.

T: Radio is a very effective medium to expose this music to people.
G: It's great when people are calling and saying, "Where did you get this music? I've never heard anything like that before!". It's the same thing that happened to me in the early 80's. I heard a radio program with early 80's electronic music and for me it was something completely new and interesting. I think without that radio program, I wouldn't have been making music myself.

Both Biosphere LP's *Micrograviity* and *Patashnik* are available through Apollo

Dubtribe Soundsystem: Spreading the

Beginning with now-legendary jam session parties in their backyard, San Francisco's **Dubtribe Sound System** are spreading a message of peace, respect, and higher conciousness through their music. Inspired by their fully live performances, their first 12" **'Mother Earth'**, a dubby progressive house appeal to save our planet has catapulted the duo into dancefloor notoriety worldwide. With a second 12"-**"Sunshine's Theme"**- out now on **Organico** with a full-length LP on tap, plus tracks from their **Trip Ta Funk** alter ego on **Ultra-Ethereal**, both **Sunshine** & **Moonbeam** talk to **TRiP** before hitting the road for yet another cross-country tourabout Dubtribe's origins and the messages they try to convey to every partygoer.

---Moonbeam first...

TRiP: Who is the Dubtribe Sound System? When you go on the road, is it just you and Sunshine, is it a whole core of you?

Moonbeam: Well, it's mainly just Sunshine and I and then we have a third member who's pretty much been steadily traveling with us. He's really great, he does the technical and soundstuff that's really invaluable. That's all at the moment.

T: How did you and Sunshine meet and start all of this?

M: Many years ago, they were doing a weird sort of acid jazz, hip-hop, electronic music sort of thing and I auditioned when it was in that realm. There were like twelve people in the band at the time and it was kind of unfocused, we were trying to do everything-all these different types of music-and perform in dance clubs. It was good for what it was, but it was kind of out of hand and unfocused.

T: As I understand the story, Dubtribe started out doing these tapes and people wanted to book you as DJ's, not realizing that this was a live act...

M: They were a bit confused. They'd say, "What do you mean?", when you tell them you perform live, and then you tell them and they still don't get that either. Unfortunately, bands who do (play live) have a bad reputation, they don't typically work in a dance environment. We didn't like that; it was weird in the beginning, because nobody even knew we were playing. We'd play for a couple of hours and then we'd be done and we'd all look at each other, and go, "Okay, let's go home now."

T: I understand that your live tapes make the rounds like Grateful Dead tapes do...

M: That's what we've been told. That's how we got our first tour, this DJ, **Onionz**, in New York. He heard our tape and he told everybody on the East Coast that our tape was great and he loved us and that they should book us; we've yet to meet the man. It's pretty phenomenal, we'd make like 100 tapes, tops. Everybody's heard it and everybody knows the songs, it's weird.

T: How many tours have you done? Are you out on the road much of the time?

M: We've done eight cross-country tours and up and down the West Coast, I can't even count anymore. We haven't been to the East Coast since last November.

T: Dubtribe is very much about a spreading a message through your music and a certain sense of a conscious party. What's your philosophy?

M: I've been going out for a long time and, for me, the House Movement is something that I saw earlier as just that- a movement we've seen that kind of fizzling out, people saying they're burned out, 'I don't want to go out anymore, I'd rather go to acid jazz clubs", and stuff like that. Somewhere along the line somebody lost the point and I believed in people coming together and dancing and getting to know each other and have sort of a haven for people of like mind to gather.

T: You've done a series of flyers that you distribute at gigs out-lining some things to think about as an active part of the scene.

M: That's what I think a party is, a place where you learn about things and taking it out with you into the world and believing that and living that, not learning about it and having a good time for one night, and "Oh, yeah, we're all together and it's great..." Hopefully, a party is place to nurture that kind of a feeling. We deal with a lot of education in that respect, teaching people that that's what it's all about; you just don't go out, take four E's and freak out and not remember what happened. There's so much more; if you're going to do that- cool, but you should be educated as to what you're doing and respect yourself and the people you're around. It's really difficult to remember that and to want to teach people because it's not like there's not a whole lot of a reward in it.

T: Dubtribe is a melting pot of music- progressive house, acid house, party funk, ambient; are there a lot of ideas and influences struggling for a voice here?

M: I think it's a way to explore other areas of music we were interested in. Dubtribe can do it all, but it's hard to broaden that scope and still be Dubtribe. We want to do it all and it just seems like we want to get so much material out and that doing it under different names and with different people was a good idea.

T: To our knowledge, the first real recorded work you'd done was the remix of 'Close Encounters' on the first Organico release. Do you plan to do more remixing in the future?

M: Yeah, Sunshine is getting known quite extensively for his remixing skills. He's been doing some work with a lot of people, producing them. helping them get their stuff out and remixing them as he goes. Mostly local people that we've met, mainly DJ's from San Francisco.

T: It's pretty obvious that you would sign with a label like Organico which has such a culture-conscious philosophy as well. How did you hook up with them?

vibe of positivity for the House Nation

M: A guy here named Perry who owns a clothing store and he's good friends with Matt (Adell of Organico). He sent Matt a tape and Matt came out and saw us; we were having one of our Dubtribe parties at our house and he loved it. A lot of labels had been pursuing us prior to them and I'm glad we waited, it's really been worth it.

T: There's a Dubtribe album waiting in the wings, right? Is it live?

M: Yeah, it should be out soon. It's all live, we did it last winter; we're pretty happy with it and it covers a lot of material we did over the past year and a half.

T: There's some other singles coming out as well, aren't there?

M: Yes, there's another 12" called "Deep Dub" and an ambient album as well. And tons more where that came from! (Laughs)

T: Do you still throw Dubtribe parties?

M: Yeah, but we've been away so much and we're DJ'ing as well now. So we definitely keep busy.

T: What's the scene in San Francisco like at the moment?

M: It's coming around again and really going back underground, smaller parties are what's really going on here. There's no more really big raves of the old standard like Organic; basically it's in a state of change at the moment. I think it's definitely lifting up again and people are having more interest in the underground.

T: Where's the music going? We've heard deep, funky house rules things...

M: It's hard to say, it would be good if there was an event with all different styles, but as long as DJ's keep trying different things and bringing all different elements together in the music. Hopefully, more and more people we know will make their own music-I think that's probably the best way to keep the evolution going.

---Now enter Sunshine...

T: Who is Trip Ta Funk?

Sunshine: Trip Ta Funk is just me by myself, Dubtribe is a collective of many of us at different times and that's the sound system that plays live. That's really what we are, we're Dubtribe Sound System. We just produced an album for a woman named Terra, an album called Terra Deva, and that'll be out on Ultra-Ethereal. There's Sunshine remix EP's off that and a Moonbeam remix, too, an ambient mix.

T: I was asking Moonbeam about the messages you try to convey through your music. What is your side to the Dubtribe message?

S: As someone struggling to transcend the genre, what's up with me is very important to tell someone like you...we've been working really hard on our remixes and our tracks and things we produce to transcend the genre because there's a lot of people out there right now saying that they've got 'it' and if you want 'it' that you've got to be like them; a big fantasyland, sort of retroactive thing, and frankly, being retroactive is never revolutionary. I think really our goal is to try and make other people think for themselves. There's nothing we're doing that is really phenomenal or outstanding- what it is, is that we just did it.

I wonder where people's heads are at? Ambience is on the rise, reggae is on the rise, dub is on the rise... Do you know what dub reggae really is, do you know what it's about, do you know where it came from? Why can't we amalgamate everything together? Isn't that what house music is all about?

It's not about having a phat record, I don't even think DJ's know how to DJ anymore because of phat records. Records like "Funk Machine" ruined House music for everyone because it's not what a DJ can do, it's what a DJ can buy. DJ'ing is what you put together, create something new, and on that level you're able to take it to a whole other dimension.

It isn't the record, it isn't the DJ, it isn't the audience- it's everyone together, a symbiotic relationship that demands participation, consciousness, attention, and a willingness to go. If you haven't got that, you might as well go lock yourself up in a closet someplace, it's not worth it. Stay home and watch MTV... I think that the House scene, the rave scene, the acid jazz scene, the ambient movement- I mean, the whole trip- we've scarcely scratched the surface on evolution, on progress, on change before it became a catch phrase, before it became a trendy sort of status thing... At that point, what's the use-you may as well be on MTV. I think that we take what we say and what we do, maybe a little too seriously; I mean, "Mother Earth"- we believe that...

T: Well, considering the state of our world and where it's going, somebody's got to step up and slap a few people in the face and say, "Wake up!"

S: It's getting to that, isn't it? It isn't what you think, it isn't what you believe, it's what you do- and that's what you are...I don't think I'll be happy until the conservatives are all naked and with long hair and the hippies have all go crewcuts and work everyday. I think what we need is to push the limits in every direction, it doesn't mean having no boundaries, it just means to explore, move on, and stop being on automatic pilot. The best question in the world is "Who the hell are you?" Everyone would rather line up with their baseball hat and a backpack and "I'm a raver!," or slick their hair back, get wraparound shades and "I'm an acid jazzer," or shave your head, get a reflective coat and be an ambient type. It's not about that, we watched that come and go with punk rock. The 60's are not back, the 60's are long gone and worth it. Yes, I have long hair and I drive a van with yin/yang stickers on it, but that doesn't mean I'm a hippie, nor do I look to the 60's for any inspiration at all. Frankly, what they did didn't work. By the time the ***Mod Squad*** hit TV, you'd think these people would've woken up and said, "Uh-oh! It's like nowadays, you look around and

continued on Page 16

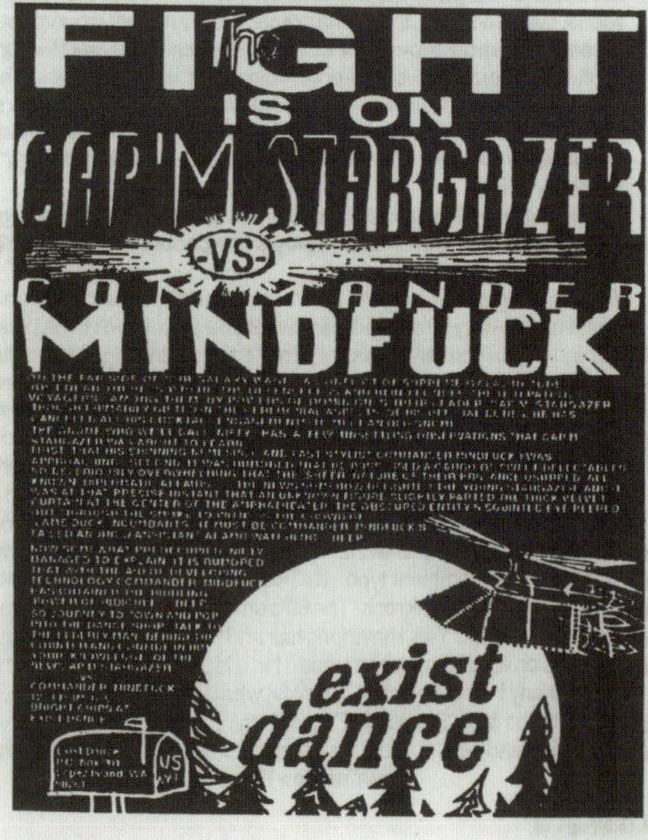

(Dubtribe Sound System, continued from Page 15)

it's long hair and love beads...everyone's trying to make a buck. I think we've got to acknowledge that there's someplace to go from here and we need to go and we need to go there together.

Everyone asks, "Where's the rave scene going?" Well, the rave scene's dead, friend, haven't you heard? There's so much more than that, and there's no reason why you can't stop in the middle of what you're doing and throw in an ambient jam.

T: People need to open their ears and minds more, test the boundaries and realize that this music came not solely from the U.K., but originated and is rooted in places like Chicago and Detroit...

S: Yeah, Bobby Kondors, Robert Armani, Robert Owens...they had it... But the reality of it is, those people had a sense of urgency. You're talking about the gay community and in the mid-to-late '80's, there was an epidemic and there was a massive number of people dying in front of everyone's eyes. Hence, there was an immediate call for unity, brotherhood, and love. And on that level, the sad thing is, it was too late, wasn't it? Isn't that the way it is?

There's so much we can learn from what happened back then, but the sad thing is, is that I play a record by the Voices on Nu Groove now, and they're talking about the music, and holding on, and rising up and brothers and sisters getting together, and it clears the floor because it's too slow or it's not techno...

T: So what happened to the scene along the way?

S: I think somebody saw somebody else making a lot of money and so they all jumped on the bandwagon and said, "Rave, rave, rave." Next thing you know, you couldn't get 15 people to come to a warehouse. Soon as that starts to happen, it's time to shut your doors and move along. It's like our Dubtribe parties, we started getting 20-30 people and by the time we were getting 300 people, we said it was time to change tack and we changed the idea entirely. That's the only way to go is to keep it cool, keep it real- keep the message trancending and transpiring and moving in and out among people.

Granted, a lot of people tell us when we explain to them what i just told you, "Well, you can't preach to the converted forever. You guys could be massive, it's time to take your message to everyone." But frankly, everyone isn't ready for it. There's no demand for what we're doing on an MTV level or on a Warner Bros. level. They may be saying, "We'll sign you up and we'll all get rich." Well, that's nice, but that's not really what we're into, that's not what we're looking for. I look to the people who really invented the San Francisco sound...people like **Garth** and **Jeno**, **Ernie Munson**...those DJ's blow my mind today...**Tomas**, **Markie Mark**, people that got off the boat and came here- we didn't know what was going on. The **Hardkisses** still lived in Baltimore; they just started making this magical music that blew everyone's mind.

To tell you the truth, we were playing acid jazz in '89 and we were into that, and parties like **Wicked** and **Come Unity** started in San Francisco and that music just lifted us and changed us. We thought "My God, something is really happening," and it was so exciting and we wanted to do it ourselves. If anything, that's the message you share with people is that you can, that it's easy and that you should do it too. With a little love in your heart and a couple hundred bucks for white labels, you got it, man. There's nothing in your way but yourself.

Matrix: The Future Sound Of Detroit

by Jay Patrick Ahern

Beginning as a Detroit Techno oriented newsletter more than two years ago, the name Matrix has blossomed into one of the newest and hottest labels from the Motor City since the emergence of **Underground Resistance** and **Plus 8**. Headed by **Sean Deason**, a graphic artist by day and an up and coming young producer under the names of **SIN**, **X-313**, and **FREQ** by night, Matrix made a big splash with <u>**Digital Sects**</u>, a mini compilation combining the talent of the likes of **Kenny Larkin**, **Claude Young**, **Alan Oldham**, and Sean himself. U.K. contributor **Jay Patrick Ahern** talked to Sean and traced the evolution of Matrix, his production abilities, and the future sound of Detroit.

TRiP: Tell us about the Matrix newsletter and its metamorphosis from news letter to label; what inspired your involvement with techno?

Sean Deason: I can't tell you how many people still ask about that little newsletter from more than two years ago. **Matrix** was a one page, three issue newsletter **Dan Bell** and I started when he first moved here from Toronto. It was sort of an insiders report on the Detroit techno scene with interviews, DJ charts, record reviews and a label by label breakdown on who was doing what where.

I'd been into electronic dance music since about 1980 thanks to **Mojo**, who I used to listen to on the radio every night almost religiously. A funny thing about the Detroit scene, we were all little kids listening to the same radio show at the same time throughout the city, and we've gathered together in our adult years, drawn together by this shared experience, which has changed us forever. A lot of people heard the show but few actually absorbed or understood the message it sent to our minds and souls.

After **Cybersonik** got big, Dan was too busy to do the newsletter, so I took over all of the responsibilities of producing it. Then my career as a graphic designer took off and I became too busy to do a good job at covering the scene and I gave it up. But the name Matrix wouldn't die. So a year and a half later I decided to use the name for a label. I asked Dan if it would be okay if I took the name and he was fine with the idea.

T: How did you get involved as a member of X-313?

SD: X-313 is a project I did with **Alan Oldham** and his former partner **'Level A'**. I'd been DJ'ing for awhile as DJ-313 and doing graphic design under the studio name of 313Grafix, so the name was sort of a natural progression. Alan and I have been friends for about 10 years now and when he started Generator Records, he wanted to bring me into it. So I went into the studio one day, pressed a couple of buttons and X-313 was born. It's funny, until it came out six months later, I'd forgotten about it. Next thing I know it's huge! To this day it's their biggest record ever.

T: Is house a love supreme in Detroit and will it merge or conquer Detroit techno?

SD: House music is just a diversion right now. people are laying low while the debris from rave settles. The way things are now, there are only about six 'techno' labels in town. Everyone else has gone underground to regroup or have switched to house or garage. It's up to labels like **Matrix**, **Generator**, **Art Of Dance**, etc., to carry the torch now. We have to represent our city in the world market, to show who the innovators are. Kenny Larkin is one of the best techno artists this city has right now. He's a madman in the studio! I'm always impressed when I'm in the studio with him. He's been a tremendous inspiration and influence to me and my music. I can always tell which songs I've done directly after coming back from visiting Kenny because they're always so dramatic. That's what he inspired in me, a sense of drama. Look for some upcoming projects from he and I working together in the future...

T: Who is Dan Bell?

SD: In my early days Dan Bell was my greatest supporter. He gave me the 'MIDI Crash Course' which taught me all I needed to know to begin my techno career. He hooked me up with Richie Hawtin who brought me into his studio and taught me programming. Richie used to leave me in his studio for hours on end just to play around with his stuff in hopes of having me on as a +8 artist. Nothing came of my sessions with him but I learned a lot. Dan Bell is the techno "artist." His new stuff is so minimal yet so brilliant, it defies all ideas of what techno is. Everything he does is an instant classic! I remember my first studio effort was when Dan and Kenny Larkin used to share a loft. I (with the help of Kenny) did this really bare track, it had only four sounds in it, tops. Dan came in while we were finishing it up and he did his mix down on it. Man! He stripped it down even further! When he was done, it was just drums and bass line and much slower. And it was awesome!

T: If Grand River Avenue is the axis of the techno universe, where is the center, who lives there, and how many refugees show up on your doorstep per annum?

SD: The techno universe has an ever-shifting center. No one person or group of people can claim its center at any given time. The vibe has passed from one person to another, increased and passed back again. Sometimes it'll be evenly dispersed, others concentrated in one area. Right now 2030 Grand River is techno's sanctuary. Any and every visiting techno refugee invariably shows up here during their visit to Detroit.

T: Tell us about FREQ...

SD: Freq is my latest and favorite project. It's the closest I've come to putting my soul on wax. There's six songs on this first EP and I have enough Freq tracks for the next three EP's. When I do Freq there is no preset style or sound to shoot for. It sort of creates itself.

T: What is minimalism?

SD: Minimalism is a place I passed by quite often on my way to other destinations. I think one day I'll stop there for a visit.

dj charts

ANDREW DUKE
Cognition Audioworks
Halifax, NS

Mazdaratti-Precognition
Pharmakol-Critical Mass EP
Resistance D.-Ztrings Of Life
Myxd Barrys-Getting Into the Swing
Mogual-Best Before End EP
The Inca & DJ Stef-Music Scan EP
Schotoma-UV Index EP
Quick Reverse-Limiter
Ryman-Themroe
Odyssee Of Noises-Firedance

LEE NEWMAN/MICHAEL WELLS
G.T.O. DJ Team
London, U.K.

Dialectum-Pitchfall
Johnny Violent-Johnny Is A Bastard
G.T.O.-Data-Trax, Vol. 1
Fourtrezz-Da Hardattack
Disciples Of Annihilation-2X12"
Carnaval Of Sound-Honey Bee
Motion 1-House On Fire
The Gatecrasher-Part 2
B.C. Kid-Wild & Wonderful EP
Huubl-Deflection/Why My

JACQUELYN CHRISTIE
Flipside
New York, U.S.A.

K.O.T.-K.O.T.'s Anthem
Esser-Forces
Jamiroquai-Emergency On Planet Earth
Angel Moraes-I Like The Way You...
Umosia-Feeling High
Dub Tribe-Sunshine's Theme
51 Days-Paper Moon
Hardhead-New York Express
Sun Sun Sun-Curious
Ricardo Marrero-My Friend

dj charts

JONAH SHARP
Spacetime Continuum
San Francisco, CA

u-ziq-PHI*1700(u/v)
Drexiya 4-Aquapac
Velocette-MicrocosmiK ep
Model 500-Sonic Sunset
Carl Craig-Quadrant Dub
Mass Observation-Scanner
Vulva-Mini Space Vulvette
Seefeel-Starethrough ep
Beaumont Hannant-Tastes /Textures Vol. 3
Chapterhouse-Blood Music RMXS

DJ KELLY D.
The Sensory Collective
Fort Lauderdale, FL

UFN Experience-Vol.1 Dark Entry
Felix Da Housecat-Thee Morning After
Aquastep-Toast
Union Jack-2 Full Moons & A Trout
The Resonant Interval-Memory
Afrotrance, Vol. 5
Cygnus-X-Superstring RMXS
Superstition All Stars, Vol. 1
Velocity-Lust (Rabbit In The Moon RMX)
Mantrac-In 'r' ep

DJ TAYLOR
Lost City, Sketchpad, Various
Los Angeles, CA

Essa 3-Revolve
Hysterix-Talk To Me
Underworld-Dark & Long 2
Lex Loofah
Renegade Soundwave (Leftfield Mix)
Eat Static-Implant
Peppermint Lounge-Lemon Project
Sourmash-Pilgrimage To Paradise
Inca-Synchronous
Jam & Spoon-Find Me

dj charts

DB
N.A.S.A.
New York, U.S.A.

Nicolia-Ready To Flow
History Of Our World, Pt 1
Piece Of Mind-Piece Of Mind
808 State-Bombadin
XL-Fluxland (Live RMX)
he Step-Yeah You (Roberts RMX)
Dave Clarke Presents Red 2
James V. Sabres-Jam J
Dust Bros ep
Moby-Hymn

BRENDAN NELSON
Megatripolis/Ambient Soho
London, U.K.

Galaxy 2 Galaxy-Journey...Dragons
Edger Froese-Maroubra Bay
Aedena Cycle-The Travellers Dream
Ralf Hildenbeutel-Inner Peace
Alien Signal-Dawn Of A New Era
Carl Craig-Dreamland
Robert Schroder-Timeless
As One-Dance Of The Uighurs
he Martian-Search Your Feelings
Global Communications-Sublime Harmony

CHRIS FORTIER
Reunion, Lift
Orlando, FL

Powercircle-It's So Good
Morigan-Landing Crew
Johnny Vicious-A Little Bit Higher
Solitaire Gee-Teazer
Bhasmantan-Wicked
Aria-My World Is Empty
All Things Nice-Aural Drive
Hoof-The Foot Club
Groove Island-Music
European Associated-Spanish West

dj charts

CHARLES UZZELL-EDWARDS
Fax +49-69/450464 (U.S.)
San Francisco, CA

TB 303 Sampling CD
Orb-Pomme Fritz
Robert Musso-Transonic
Nine L-Houston, We Have A Problem
Velocette-Microcosmik EP
Likemind-Fugue/Neuron
As One-Isatai
Virtualizer-Sex Technology
Orb & Fripp-F.F.W.D.
Create-Macro

DJ PEZ
Various One-Offs
Ft. Lauderdale, FL

Resistance D.-Ztrings Of Life
Autechre-Basscadet RMXS
Hardfloor-Funalogue
B12-Tribeca
Gorn-e.l.la
Union Jack-Two Full Moons & A Trout
DHSS-Hutchburn
Namlook 4
Gate/Sol LP
Risiing High Collective-Liquid

DJ T-1000
Generator Records
Detroit, U.S.A.

X-313-Interferon
DJ ESP-Transporter 2X12"
Hardfloor-Confuss
Hexagone-Burning Trash Floor
DJ Plank-Attitude
Acrid Abeyance-Bon Appetit
St.Germain-The Black Man
V/A-World Sonik Domination
Model 500-Sonic Sunset
DJ T-1000-Sonik Reducer

TRiP MAG Charts UNDERGROUND DANCE MUSIC CHART

compiled by **DJ THREE**

Rabbit In The Moon-"Deeper"
Underworld-"Dark & Long"
Secret Cinema (Speedy J. RMX)
Jaydee-"Music Is So Special"
Future Sound Of London-"Lifeform Ends"
Innersphere-"Internal Aftershock"
Harmonya-No War
Winc-"Thoughts Of A Tranced Love"
Perfect Sync-"Body Slam"
Piece-"Free Your Soul"

TRiP HOUSE CHART

compiled by **DJ JASK**

The Klubb Kidz-"Don't Want To Hurt You"
Joi Cardwell-"Trouble"
Wizard Of Wax-"Gonna Set You Free"
Face 2-"The EP"
Freedom-"Closer"
Hardhead-"New York Express"
Red Light-"Thankful" (Victor Simonelli RMXS)
Sole Fusion-"Basstone"
Aaron Smith feat. D'Bora-"Going 'Round"
Beat People-"What Must I Do"

OASiS AMBIENT CHART

compiled by **ORION, GRUMPY, & MATTY**

Single Cell Orchestra-Angelic Science EP
Beaumont Hannant-Texturology 1&2
Cypher 7-Decoder LP
Mouse On Mars-Vulvaland LP
Two Sandwiches Short Of A Lunchbox
Cabaret Voltaire-The Conversation
#9 Dream-Rhythm and Irrelevance
Gone-"Smoking Gun"
Wagon Christ-Phat.Lab Nightmare
Bandulu-Presence

RECORD REVIEWS 12"/EP

INFLUX-'TB Rage' EP (Sapho/UK) James Bernard aka **Influx**, aka **Cybertrax** unleashes three more fine examples of disturbing acid. The standout is side A, it is long and full of very good acid and cool breakdowns. James Bernard shows us why he's still one of the best American producers today. For the acid connoisseurs. **(G)**

MANTRAC-'In 'R" EP (Plink Plonk/UK) Mantrac follows up the ultra-cool 'Coaster' ep with a six track double pack extravaganza. All tracks have the necessary ingredients to make a quality underground dance record. Original programming, fresh ideas, and of course, capable songwriting. The best tracks here are the deeply emotional "Rize," the shuffling, almost repetitive "Runaround," and it's extremely chilled ambient version, "Reminisce." Yet another excellent record from Plink Plonk. **(G)**

INCARNATE-'Convolution' EP (Post Contemporary/Canada) I've been after this one for awhile. The Vertical side opens with a track that reminds me of something from From Within- phased 4/4 drumbeat with twittering synth and fluttering synth underneath, breaking down to fluttering synth and bassline before building back up and slipping into trippy beatfree ambience. The Horizontal side is similar in tone. Both sides have short experimental interludes. It was worth the search. **(Orion)**

DIFFUSION-"DCB Phase"/"Firewater" (Experimental) Two track EP from Experimental; "DCB Phase", brooding acid trancer with a pumping kick, multiple squiggly 303 lines, and a humming tone in the background that breaks down to drums and 303 and "Firewater", a more uplifting track with acoustic guitar and cooing vocal sample running alongside subtle acid. **(PW)**

FREQ-"Plastique" (Generator) Limited to 500, this double A-sided release is a moody, emotional look into the analog mind of one Sean Deason. This track is intense: deep basslines, passionate 303, hi-hats and handclaps building and releasing tension, kick drum propelling you higher, faster, leveling off, easing back and then evenly cruising to the finish. Almost better than sex... Towel, please. **(PW)**

GLOBAL COMMUNICATION-"9:25" (Dedicated/UK) Emotional and organic, this one-sided LP teaser literally whispers into your consciousness as spacy synths sweep cloudlike overhead. With gentle, warm melodies punctuated by an undeniably groovy breakbeat and a jazzy guitar riff, 9:25 passes by like a bright Spring day. A sweet tease in anticipation of the full-length, 76:14. **(Orion)**

JUAN TRIP-'Masterpiece Trilogy' (F Communication/France) 'Louis' Cry' is probably the strangest record I've heard in quite a long time. The Original Mix is a quite catchy 'house' track with completely out of place and extremely annoying (but still cool) high pitched squeals tha sound very scary. Laurent Garnier's version is a little less frightening. Mr. Garnier uses an elaborate intro to highlight the very catchy riff and then the almost irresistibly undeniable rhythm track comes in... By the way, there's also an eleven minute track that's just as weird on the A side. **(G)**

TWO SANDWICHES SHORT OF A LUNCHBOX-"Too Good To Be Strange" (Apollo/Belgium) David Morley and Andie from Inky Blacknuss collaborate here on this weird 3-tracker of ambience with and without beats. Subtle syncopated beats drive through the logo side, "Too Good To Be Strange," alongside twangy analog synth sounds, bleepy bits, and creaky sounds effects in the background. Very cool. The info side, "Too Strange To Be Good," is beatfree and bizarre, while "Nearly There" pulsates, blurps, beeps, and drones on. An excellent and creative collaboration I'd like to see more of. **(Orion)**

DKO-'Carol In Heat' EP (Sapho/UK) If all records were as cool as B1 on this new Sapho white label, then there'd be a lot of cool records. B1 is extremely dark and hard acid that is out of control. The atmospheric/ambient breakdown will probably bring goosebumps to your arms. There are also three other acid tracks that are very, very good also-dark trippy acid stuff. Wicked, bangin' acid from these mysterious American producers. **(G)**

A TO-BE-NAMED COLUMN...by DJ THREE

Editor's Note: One of the highlights of TRiP's publication process is your dear editor hounding Editor-At-Large and Florida favorite, DJ Three, to finish his review assignment on time. In light of increasing demands on Three's time, we've decided to help lighten his load by giving him a space in which to turn you on to essential vinyl. Look for a full blown debut of this to-be-named column next issue.)

Lots of funky breaks tracks released this time around and as with any style, just a few stand outs; first and foremost being **Dust Brothers-My Mercury Mouth EP (Junior Boys' Own/UK).** With an overabundance of material, they hit the mark again with 2 hip-acid-house (?) tracks and a downtempo dub trip. Take note that the track labeled "Dust-Up Beats" comes in 2 forms on 2 separate 12"! The only way to distinguish them is by reading the inner seam. If it says **JBO-20 B1**, your track will be what sounds like a remix of "Chemical Beats." If it says B2, you've got a new track which peaks and peaks with signature Dust Brothers style. Happy hunting!...**DJ Icee** quickly pumps out another 4 tracks of "Energy Trax" entitled **Encyclopedia Funktanica**-British old school at its best with all the best breaks...If you haven't already, check out the **C2R** ep on Knight Life Recordsfor more of that 'Energy Trax' style from Orlando...Now out West to San Fran where **Twitch Records** follows Ultraviolet Catastrophe with **Central Fire.** 3 cuts; "This Is A Shout Out" has funky breaks and acid with title vocal sampled throughout and hip-hop ("Let The Rhythm Hit 'Em") breakdowns. "This Is A Dub" removes the vocal and concentrates on beats and acid which we like. Each mix a collaboration between one named **Courtney Neilson & DJ Spun**. "Central Fire" is 2 parts edited to 1 track and is the standout. Part 1 is on a funk tip with guitar riffs and subtle spacey elements, Part 2 takes over with wicked percussion from the San Fran classic "Hip-Hop Salsa" by Bad Boy Orchestra as the spacey elements get bigger and more familiar. Find it....**Zoe Magick** also return with **Essa 3-"Revolve"**- analog trance madness not far from Gipsy's latest, one mix a bit funky with the mad synth. Now stepping to more Techno/Trance sounds...Do your best to track down **Erik Van de Brock (Shiver 003)**. 5 tracks of electro-acid from Germany that would make Arthur Baker proud. "Subsonic Sound-scape" is causing major damage on Florida sound systems and "Ursa Major 7" & "Oiled Love" also do the business. If you dug **UR003**, this is the one....Robin "Jaydee" Albers has proven to be a consistent producer since his smash "Plastic Dreams." Under the guise of **Greylock** he's released 2 which did not live up to media hype, but the 3rd entitled **"The Movement"** is very nice. "Momentum Instrumental" is excellent pumping trance with a sweeping analog-sounding synth breakdown, also "Windjammer" with its astonishing percussion, grooving melodic intro, and trancy bassline. Percussion seems to be the word for **Jaydee** with the first follow-up under his name on R&S called "Music Is So Special." Very impressive-in 4 mixes, each very different. Dance Mix is the main- tribal percussion and subtle hypnotic oscillating keys build and build keeping things very involved. Let The Drums Speak Mix does just that; an abundance of tribal sounds into a breakbeatish groove, that's topped off finally with a 4/4 stomp. This is a very good record....**Underworld-"Dark & Long, Part 1 &2" (Junior Boys' Own/UK).** Two 12's here as they continue to gear their singles to underground techno instead of the indie vocal sound of their LP. 4 mixes in all, if you play trance, you should not be without them as they are excellent. Period. **Oliver Leib** gets his **Paragliders -"Paraglide"** track given the **Rising High** remix treatment. If Union Jack's "Two Full Moons..." moved you, go directly to Humate's interpretation of "Paraglide"-

moving,urgent Eurotrance to say the least....Seems most of my favorite British trance records are being made by the same people: **Simon Berry** (POB, Union Jack), **Craig Walsh** (Soundscape, Cause), and **David Hedger** (Innersphere, Mojo Risin'). David Hedger as **Innersphere** has just released "Infernal Aftershock", if you thought the last one had wicked acidy synth spurts, wait'll this hits a big sound system! Side 2 is "Vernal Equinox," like Carl Craig on Exist Dance...**Exploding Plastic Inevitable** has just released Hedger's 1st 12" under his own name with 4 tracks, 1 being a psychedelic sitar thing. The other tracks more out there trance than Innersphere, although the writing side boasts some very butt-moving percussion that I think some people will dig. **Billy Nasty** has a white label on Morgan King's **OM** label which is a pulsating bassed, airplane-like swooping synthed, pounding drummed trancer on one side whilst the other is almost a little too stabby in its synth arrangement....On the House tip, **Eightball**'s on a roll, following African Dreams' success with Mack Vibe....The dub feels at home with a **Murk** record in your set and the new **Funky Green Dogs** "High Up" is what they coin as 'classic Murk' now. The words deep and accessible rarely merge in harmony in the mounds of house and techno that come out, but Murk have got it down to a science....**Emotive** do very good by releasing domestically my favorite **Felix Da Housecat** ever-Aphrohead-"In The Dark We Live (Thee Lite)." Carl Craig's **Paperclip People-"Throw"** may be the wildest house cut so far this year...once in it's 12 minutes, my floor got packed, cleared-one guy booed-then it got packed and cheered at the end (?!?). Go figure-it's not as accessible as Murk, but if your floor is into house, give it a spin.

SINGLE CELL ORCHESTRA-'Angelic Science' EP (Reflective) Miguel Angelo Fierro aka Single Cell Orchestra returns with his first EP since 'Liberated,' released on Zoe Magick in early 1993. Angelic Science is a collection of six ambient and experimental tracks ranging from dark beatfree excursions, stripped down noise treatments, harsh acid trance workouts, and bizarre beat-oriented works. A engaging and original EP from an American with both a gentle touch and strength of ear. Most recommended. **(Orion)**

BEAT PEOPLE-"What Must I Do?" (Geeman Wax) The O.G. (Oscar G. from Murk) is at it again! One of my favorite records at the moment. **(Jask)**

ASTRALASIA/SUNS OF ARQA-"Sul-E-Stomp" (RMXS) (Magick Eye/UK) Don't know who's mix is who here on this white label, but the stamped side at 45 rpm is an Traditional Irish Jig/trance stomper...got that!?! The first set of synths are kind of hands-in-the-air ravey, but as the track continues it slips into a smoother trance feel. The white side at 33 is a drifting atmospheric trancer ala "Stella," but not quite as infectious. Nice. **(PW)**

PHENIX-"Guaguanco" (Unclassified?) The ? label finally has a name and true to its name, knocks out a fucking blinding and bizarre Tito Puente On Acid Afro-Cuban percussion stormer! Agogo bells, congas, a uplifting vocal chant, thumping kick, and a crazy timbale solo in the middle- this is the record to set the crowd on fire!! The Chant de Nanigo mix is a chant and percussion 'accapella', while the B-side serves it up less ethnic and more trancy. Hard, hot, sweaty and full of tasty spices! **(PW)**

SANDALS-"Feet" (RMXS) (ffrr) The Sandals' smash is given the once over by Slam, the Dust Brothers, Next School, and the Hardkiss Family on this domestic release. If you're not familiar with the import, the Dust Brothers' mix is true to form in the Dust Bros. style; Slam's take reminds me of 'Energy Flash' in a way, with it's flaring hi-hats, hand claps, and squiggly acid. The Next School mix is a chunky slice of cut-up, sample flavored, funky grooves, breaking down to a slow party funk guitar riff. Good stuff- love the frog! The Hardkiss' Fungus Mix is 70's funk-inflected with pumping kick drum and wah-wah guitar. Not bad, but not what I hoped for. A little too relaxed and spliffed for my taste. **(PW)**

GENETIX-"DNA" (Millenium/UK) Oliver Leib continues his extremely prolific output with a very strong 12" that departs a little from his harder stuff as Spicelab. DNA V.2.0 is a smooth acid track with catchy keyboard parts that make this record a very integral part of any acid/techno/hard trance set but is slow enough to be played with anything. **(G)**

THE KLUBB KIDZ-"Don't Want To Hurt You" (DJ Exclusive) Pure power pumpin' House perpetuated by sweet vocals, damaging basslines, and deep raw beats. Side B is a different story - get ready for hardcore massive breakbeats from the mind of DJ Duke. Simply vicious. **(Jask)**

X-CRASH-'Descension' EP (Drop Bass Network) Extremely noisy Brooklyn hardcore from Adam and Jimmy. Staying true to the Brooklyn underground, this 4-tracker is pounding and extremely annoying. If these guys get any scarier, they'll have to make a Children Of The Corn 3 with all of those Midwest and Brooklyn nutters as the killers and Woody McBride as Malachi. Truly twisted stuff from Milwaukee via Brooklyn. **(G)**

ODYSSEE OF NOISES-"Firedance" (Eye-Q/Germany) Ralf Hildenbeutel solo with a very basic German trance monster. No matter how formulated Eye-Q records might sound, they are all good. This one is no different. Pounding rhythms and spine tingling keyboard that can't be refused. although there is a harder mix and a slower mix, "The Sunrise" is still the one. **(G)**

GLIDE-"Jelly" (Buffalo/UK) The rest of this is a throwaway, but the gem here is the Throne Of Feedback Mix. Atmospheric synth washes open into dubby, tuned down timbales, and a echoey processed guitar by Will Seargent (Echo & The Bunnymen?!?), slide blissfully into pulsating ambience. Not mindblowing, but a really pretty piece that should not go unnoticed. **(Orion)**

LECTROLUV featuring ALVAUGHN JACKSON-"Struck By Luv" (Eightball) A record I knew I didn't even have to listen to before I bought it! Not because of Eightball, but the man behind the production, a mucho talented Fred Jorio droppin' the mad skills... Alvaughn Jackson really turns it out on the vocals and Junior Vasquez' Factory Mix is no disappointment, but check out my favorite, the Dope Dub. **(Jask)**

PSYANCE-"The Answer" (+8) Ron Allen returns to Plus 8 after a very long absence with 3 exceptional Detroit techno cuts. On the A side, "The Answer" is a very back to basics Detroit track with emotion-filled stabs, metallic percussion, and a repeated vocal of 'Give Us The Answer." The two on the flip are also sublime chords with thumping beats. My favorite is the 8th Dimension. Welcome back, Ron! **(G)**

DUBTRIBE-"Sunshine's Theme" (Organico) "Sunshine's Theme," the follow-up to the massive "Mother Earth" comes in four forms, all diverse but similar. The Original Mix is a sweet, melodic 120 bpm groover with nice prodding female whispers and flown in female vocal from Moonbeam, leading up to Sunshine's scene soliloquy. Sunshine's Remix is a very effective slice of smooth dub with pulsing synth washes and echoey vocals gliding over bongos and a slow breakbeat.S'nice... The Dubstylee Mix is more on the progressive party funk tip while things end up with the more uptempo 1/2 Tab Acid Mix. Similar to the remix but up and more insistent with more hand percussion, subtle 303 acid line, and whirling synths over the top. **(PW)**

ORFEUS-"Jungle Trance" (DJ Exclusive) Trance and jungle house colliding into one phatt jam of powerful rhythms of ungodly nature, not to mention hypnotic tribal percussion on the loose. Go straight to the 'Compression Dub' and DJ Duke's mix and play, play, play... You won't be disappointed. **(Jask)**

MAZDARATTI-"Precognition" (Telepathic) Fred Giannelli returns with some help from Mark Gage. This is one of the best tracks this year, a very hard acid stomper even though it's not fast at all. The arrangement and keyboard parts are amazing. The flip side is an edit. For maximum results pitch it up to +8. Incredible. **(G)**

MARTIN BOND-'Liquid Echoes' EP (Visible) Yet another colored vinyl slab from the Visible crew... Opening with "Essence," a slow, meditative techno number featuring a piano loop and blippy treated vocal snippets; "Cosmic Voices," experimental deep house with atmospheric yodeling and string bassline - like a less old-school and more minimal "Raincry" of sorts. The B-side is two mixes of "Essence," one by Mark G! (Darwin Chamber) and a second by Seofon which is more dreamy and breakbeat house-y. **(PW)**

GREEN NUNS-"Whirling Dervish" (Triumph) The a-side of this white label is rather good, a slowly building intro transforms into a midtempo acid track with a distorted 303 that works really well. This track is extremely well done and very effective. The 2 songs on the b-side are either different versions without the 303 or just sound like it. Worth searching for. **(G)**

AMEBA-"Duble Trouble" (Triumph) Another one of those throwaways with a bright little gem on the inner grooves. This time a slow dub headnodder with pulsing synths, 303, blippy sound effects, and breathy flutes that doubletimes with a chugging breakbeat halfway through before slipping back into the haze. For the ambient dub selectors. **(Orion)**

HALLUCINOGEN-"Alpha Centauri"/ "LSD" (Dragonfly/UK) Latest release on Youth's Dragonfly label. Two high quality trance workouts here- "LSD" is straight-up with LSD samples included, while "Alpha Centauri" is the stronger of the two with a very creative 303 and exceptional amounts of "trance." **(G)**

THE HOUSE featuring ANGEL WILLIAMS-"My Luv" (Dub) Dupre' and Crew are at it again giving us strong vocal house from way deep in Miami. If you like Murk stuff, you'll like this-check it out! **(Jask)**

VULVA-'Mini Space Vulvette' EP (Reflective) 5 track ep from San Francisco's Reflective label. Each track seems to have been transmitted from another galaxy, all 5 having a very surreal, space-like quality to them. Gently pulsing beats and weird synth washes guide you through this collection of intergalactic blips and bleeps. A quite exciting and original 12". **(G)**

IN SYNC/PLUTO-'InS/2' (Irdial Discs/UK) From one of the Underground's coolest, most interesting, and uncompromising labels comes this nifty 3-tracker that we missed and thought you should know about, because you probably missed it too. Seemingly a split 12" (or at least a co-production) from Irdial's InSync and Pluto (of Plink Plonk notoriety), the single track side, "Subway Route," is a sublime slice of mellow, jazzy after hours techno. Too pure, wicked. The two track side; "Suttee's Comet" feels similar to the flip with it's atmospheric intro before adding some grooving midtempo deep Detroit house elements, while "Ratcatcher" is faster, thumpier, and more uplifting and intense but with a big smile. An incredible track. If you're looking to the phuture, search for this **(PW)**

VELOCETTE-'Microcosmik' EP (Reflective) 4 more experimental ambient tracks from Reflective; two tracks are very chilled while one is a noisy techno thing that's pretty good. The last one is a long intro into somewhat of a beat. **(G)**

DERRICK CARTER'S SOUND PATROL-'The Music' EP (Organico) This fine piece of wax works was produced by Chicago's Derrick Carter. Blastin' with all sorts o' experimental styles of deep acidified house, some on the trancy tip. But that's all right, Derrick came through this time: my favorite cut, "The Eternal Insomnia of Living." Old ass Chicago acid house feel in effect!! If you want to know more, you're just gonna have to purchase this. Phatt ass shit... **(Jask)**

SNEAKY CASH (White) An interesting white label with two mixes to choose from. One is filled with tweaky 303 acid lines, the other is more garage-y and you'll love the mood it creates. Although it's simple and sounds like a couple of kids messin' around, it has a certain charm and is worth checking out. **(IR)**

AARON SMITH featuring D'BORA-"Going 'Round" (RMXS) (Vibe/Chicago) Hot, hot, hot! I mean steaming! Maurice Joshua, Georgie Porgie, and MK on the remixes, what more could you ask for?!? **(Jask)**

LSG-"Fragile" (RMXS) (Superstition/Germany) This remix EP contains 3 mixes by Mark Gage (Vapourspace) and one by Pascal F.E.O.S. (Resistance D.). Two of Mark Gage's mixes sound like a Vapourspace track and one is a very ambient version that is very nice. Pascal's mix is much harder and doesn't leave you much time to catch your breath along the way. **(G)**

INDIKA-"Baltic" (NovaMute) New to the NovaMute label is the UK trio Indika with their "Baltic" 2-track. The title track is twenty minutes of dark tribal trance with a subversive acid line buried in the mix. Indika manage to hold your attention through the duration by the use of subtle builds and varied breaks, though the obvious nick of the percussive clang of Polygon Window's "Quoth" could have been avoided. The other track, "Bloc," is quite different. sounding a bit too Harthouse-like and lacking a logical flow, it ain't really my cuppa tea. Still, two thumbs up for the epic A-side. **(AD)**

HARDFLOOR-'Funalogue' EP (Harthouse/Germany) Oliver and Ramon continue to destroy our bodies with their unmistakeable style of dancefloor mayhem. This five track mini-album is a non-stop assault on our feet because you can't help but dance! The best is 'Funalogue' with the incomparable Hardfloor arrangement. Their songs are very similar to something Michael Jackson would do; not in content or style, but because you remember every single detail of each song. **(Where are you going with this, Grumpy? Ed.)** Anyway, there's also a slow (107 bpm), funky acid cut to keep these guys on the edge. **(G)**

DISSIDENTEN-"Jungle Book, Part II" (Eye-Q Germany) Dissidenten provides two mixes of "Jungle Book, Part II," a shiny bit of Eye-Q trance. The Mantra Trance Mix is built around a Liz Fraser sample from the Garlands period. Fraser's chanting works well paired with surging tribal percussion that rises and falls precisely where needed. The faster Be-Zet Mix drops the tribal elements and replaces them with quivering strings, bubbling and gurgling acid, and bland, basic percussion. A man speaking of spacy ideas and things trance-like becomes more dominant, while Fraser's vocals are used as an afterthought. Love the tough tribal version, hate the safe trance take. **(AD)**

69-'Lite Music' EP/"Jam The Box" (RMXS) (R&S/Belgium) Carl Craig's 69 project continues on R&S with a four-track EP, 'Lite Music' and 'Jam The Box' remixes. 'Lite Music' is one of the cooler 12" released so far this year. From the almost industrial "Jam The Box" to the beautiful "Desire" and the hard breakbeats of "My Machines," it takes a strong stomach to listen to this as it's not exactly 'lite music,' but it's still very good. The 'Jam The Box' remixes come separately and are also essential. The Heavyweight and Medium mixes are very similar with the only difference being the arrangement, both are more dancefloor friendly than the mega-hard Lite Mix. This track should be one of the biggest of the year. **(G)**

SHABANG-'Trouble' EP (Stickman/Canada) A most powerful, phatt vocal house track featuring Michelle Weeks laying down her gifted voice. Lots of mixes to choose from on this gem from the Stickmen! Mad respect to Mitch Moses on the production tip... **(Jask)**

PAPERCLIP PEOPLE-"Remake Uno" (Planet E/Open/UK) Carl Craig takes the e2e4 sample from 'Sueno Latino' and uses it to create a beautiful and wonderful early morning epic. The domestic contains 2 versions basically the same and the import on Ministry Of Sound's Open label has an extra song. "Throw" is a 14-minute house throbber. This is an essential purchase. **(G)**

SOLE FUSION-"Basstone" (Strictly Rhythm) "Little" Louie on the hard tribal tip...from start to finish, good percussion and nice synth lines from the Master At Work. **(Jask)**

TECHNOVA-"Tantra"/"Tantra" (RMXS) (Sabres Of Paradise/UK) The Original Mix is a Middle Eastern dub breakbeat extravaganza. The Innersphere remixes on the original 12" is similar to the regular version, just with a little more four-on-the-floor element. The remix 12" has Innersphere mixes that are very minimal and quite effective on a loud system. **(G)**

SAD-D & SOMA-'Drogue' EP (Hardbeat) This second release on this Florida label is three tracks of strong German/Harthouse/Eye-Q influenced trance. The fourth track, "Afrique" is a simple piece of ambience with sporadic pounding kick drum sections that ruin the track's flow. Very well produced and arranged, let's hope it doesn't get lost in the shuffle with other similar imports. **(PW)**

V/A-'X-Sight Trax' EP (X-Sight) Four tracks here, one each produced by Keoki, James Christian, Nico, and Rhythm Method. The Keoki-produced Nylon Twins' "Pinocchio" is a groovy slice of thumpy disco-y house with a butt-shaking bassline and "I'm real" samples. James Christian's "Jungle MPH" is a chunky tribal houser, complete with bongos, wails, and synth stabs. Under the guise of Darkstar, Nico turns in "Keep Movin'," a smooth deep house pulser, and Rhythm Method contributes "Beat On The Drum," a percussion-flavored tribalesque track. **(PW)**

LP/Compilations

EAT STATIC-Implant (Planet Dog/UK) If Dubtribe is the U.S. techno scene's answer to the Grateful Dead, then Bath-based Eat Static is the U.K.'s. An offshoot of the Ozric Tentacles, the Statics should be familiar to most due to Sasha's Qat remixes last year. Implant displays a very funky approach to the dancefloor: groovy midtempo trance techno with fat acid blurps and blops, spoken word samples, with the occasional funky breakbeat thrown in, plus some very engaging ambient and chillout groove tracks. If you played "Mother Earth" and you're looking fothing different, pass on that new Stress record for one week and check this out. **(PW)**

AMBUSH-The Ambush (Harthouse/Germany) Super-producer Oliver Leib must live in the studio and take lots of vitamins. Not only does the guy release tons and tons of work, but it's all excellent or at worst, above average. With this outing, the full-length realization of his Ambush project, Leib fuses ethnically influenced percussion with the sounds of techno. Now this isn't new, you may say, as gobs of people, including Leib's boss, Sven Vath, has executed the same fusion to stellar results. Instead of the obvious approach of combining indigenous sounds and rhythms with technology, Leib uniquely links slanted and unconventional sounds with these ethnic elements in innovative Leib fashion. All textures are explored here, from light percussion and chant driven ambience with beats, tribal drum and synth safaris, and drum circle and drum machine ensemble celebrations. This is Oliver Leib's vision of modern tribalism and yet another successful production from the Frankfurt workaholic. Incredible.**(PW)**

V/A-ARTIFICIAL INTELLIGENCE II (Warp/UK) Pay very careful attention to the liner notes-a series of Internet entries regarding the A.I. series- and then read the editorial by artist/writer David Toop. Now you may or may not understand why Warp is (supposedly) ending the A.I. concept. AI 2 consists of tracks by previous A.I. artists or already established artists with the exception of Darren Fitton and Mark Franklin. A great collection of songs from now-charted territory. Thanks to Warp for making an interesting chapter of electronic music accessible to so many. **(CM)**

A MISSION INTO DRUMS (Eye-Q/Germany) Recycle Or Die is an overshadowed CD only ambient sister label to the much more visible and dancefloor oriented Harthouse and Eye-Q imprints. In it's short existance, ROD has released to date six albums by members of the Eye-Q Brain Trust (as they call it), including Stevie Be-Zet, Oliver Leib, and Ralf Hildenbeutel. A Mission Into Drums is a collection of six (four on vinyl) tracks released on the ROD label, reinterpreted with beats by their producers, Be-Zet, Leib, and Hildenbeutel each choosing two of their favorite tracks. The result is some uplifting meditative trance and chilled out ambience with beats. This is compulsory listening and hopefully will inspire those moved to search out the beatfree companions to these tracks for the full effect. Highlights: Leib's "Dimension X" and "Subsonic Interferences" from Constellation, "Maya & Aliens" from Stevie Be-Zet's Archaic Modulation, and Ralf Hildenbeutel's "The Journey". **(Orion)**

TERRA DEVA-San Francisco House Culture featuring Terra Deva (Ultra-Ėthereal) The underground musical melting pot known as San Francisco is captured on this second collection in a series by Blatimore-based Ultra-Ethereal. Featuring performances from vocalist Terra Deva, ragga star Lawrence D., and the Dubtribe Sound System, the tracks range from smooth acid jazz/house and funky breaks driven acid workouts to ethno-ambience and 70's hard funk bumpers. The standouts are "Explore Acid," "Dubtribe," and ""Explore Ambience"**(PW)**

#9 DREAM-Rhythm And Irrelevance(Recycle Or Die/Germany) The long awaited sixth release from Recycle Or Die is by Helmut Zerlett (who was co-responsible for rod004, Baked Beans) and painter/musician Walter Dahn. Rhythm and Irrelevance is a realization of the composers concept to bring the spirit and energy of the early German electronic avant garde together with the technological innovations of the '90's. Densely textured and rich in modulation, the album unfolds gently, seeming dark and somber at first but with each session displaying new elements. Close your eyes, take a deep breath, sit back, and listen with an open mind, and you will hear. **(Orion)**

ASTRALASIA-Whatever Happened To Utopia? (Magick Eye/UK) The third LP from Astralasia continues the adventures into the realm of ambience, picking up where the acclaimed Pitched Up At The Edge Of Reality left off. Swirling melodies, sweeping synths, bits of acid, chunks of dub, and subtly cushioned beats and ethnic elements assist in propelling you on this astrally navigated journey into a new dimension. Full of depth, this full-length is highly recommended for the chillroom and beyond. **(Orion)**

LEO ANIBALDI-The Virtual Language (PowWow Trance) Licensed from ACV, the domestic release of this album from 21-year-old Italian exiled DJ/producer Leo Anibaldi is a concept album of sonic terrorscapes, dark, experimental acid tracks, and monster techno anthems. This is just an insight into the career of this quickly rising techno talent. Be one of the ones who know , get in on the ground floor with this. **(PW)**

FUTURE SOUND OF LONDON-Lifeforms (Astralwerks) By now, after countless interviews explaining themselves and even more reviews in other publications, what more can be said-pro or con- about Future Sound Of London and their new album? Well, here's another review... FSOL have taken what the Orb have done one step further in releasing an album of experimental electronic music on a major label and selling millions. Every reason I've heard in regaards to what people feel is lacking on Lifeforms seems to be something FSOL have made an effort to achieve. They've seen house culture approach rock-n-roll and/or major label mentality in production and distribution...even in performance (in House Culture's case, the lack there of) and consequently released a big middle finger of an album. They took their circumstance after their first chapter of success on a path that most would never dare-the unbeaten path- and regardless of yours or my opinion of the music, they did it with success. Lifeforms is as much an FSOL record, if not more so, than anything prior. An uncommon balance of porous, grainy sounds in harmony with perfect, polished sounds with artful hints of influence. I also like the fact that they use their samplers as instruments, rather than record and playback devices. "Cascade" was an excellent single. While some claimed it was 'too out there,' who could deny the beats on a dancefloor? Hopefully "Lifeform" with Liz Fraser will be released and if not "Lifeform Ends" would be an excellent 12" as well as "Omnipresence." FSOL have never really fit into the "structure" of techno and house, so more power to them as there wasn't supposed to be structure here in thhe first place. **(CM)**

CABARET VOLTAIRE-The Conversation (Instinct) Cabaret Voltaire complete the final piece of the trilogy started with 1992's Plasticity and 1993's International Language with the double CD collection The Conversation. As everyone praises Future Sound Of London as the contemporary ambient genre's new innovators, the true innovators of post-ambient electronic music, Cabaret Voltaire, sneak in unnoticed and without fanfare to take Lifeforms' depth and liquidity one step even further into the next dimension with this third piece of the puzzle. Much warmer and and more organic than FSOL, Cabaret Voltaire make the true masterpiece of 1994... Essential. **(Orion)**

ROBERT MUSSO-Transonic (Fax Sublabel/Germany) Simple, but complex, dense, yet clear meditative ambience with beats, trance, and future world music from Bill Laswell collaborator Robert Musso. Except for Laswell's bass playing, all other sounds here are loops, samples, and found sounds treated for the final effect. Hypnotic, sonic, and genre transcendent. **(PW)**

FLOPPY SOUNDS-Downtime(Wave Music) DJ/producer/engineer Francois

Kevorkian is the man behind this Wave Music label. The man's innovative work on projects by artists as diverse and innovative in their own right-Depeche Mode, Kraftwerk, U2, and King Crimson among others- has carried over to the label's debut and the debut from New York 'studio hacks' Floppy Sounds. Not easily definable, Downtime dabbles into ambience, into dub, into chillout grooves in a decidedly left-of-center experimental manner that is both accessible and mildly disturbing. An album that takes a couple listens to really embrace and get your head around. **(PW)**

THOMAS FEHLMANN-Flow (R&S/Belgium) Thomas Fehlmann is perhaps one of the underground's most underrecognized, yet often collaborated artists. Working alongside the new breed of innovators in his homebase of Berlin, Fehlmann was instrumental in bringing over the innovators from Detroit (Atkins, Baxter, Fowlkes, UR), produced some of the most classic house music on the planet (Marathon), collaborated with Sun Electric, KLF, and of course, The Orb, plus his influential Palais Schaumburg project in the early 80's with Holger Hiller and his first solo project, Ready Made. Now is the time for Thomas Fehlmann to become a name in his own right. The Flow EP is a direct result of Fehlmann entertaining himself in the studio without the confines and restrictions of the 12-inch format or the dancefloor. The outcome is six tracks, ranging from hard grooving digifunk and swinging hi-tech jazz to funky electro-influenced chillout grooves and big, booming densely layered listening techno. Everything here is dancefloor-friendly, but perhaps better suited to the chillout room or home listening session. Worth checking out despite the steep import price. **(Orion)**

ORB-Pomme Fritz (InterModo-Island/UK) Pomme Fritz, The Orb's 'Little Album' as it's being called, is the debut of what could be called The Orb: The Next Generation. Things have changed on the Starship Orb, only slightly, but enough to notice. Thomas Fehlmann, of Sun Electric fame and long-time Orb collaborator, is now aboard the Starship full time and his input is just enough to change the sound subtly. The dub influences are not gone completely, instead replaced for a more experimental electronic sound, and a big dose of Alex and Thrash's sense of humor. In fact, one may even think Alex went off the deep end. Now don't worry, Pomme Fritz is still The Orb we all know and love, just a new side in the evolution of our favorite ambient explorers. Open your mind and your ears and let it suck you in. **(PW)**

CREATE (Fax World/Germany) This second collaboration between Pete Namlook and San Francisco-based artist Charles Uzzell-Edwards is a continuation of sorts on A New Consciousness, which was released late last year on Fax World. This hour plus piece, "Macro," takes some time to get where you're going, but once you arrive-lush sweeping synths, precious melodies, percussion pillows, and environmental elements keep you there. Recorded in Charlie's tiny studio in the Upper Haight section of San Fran, the Namlook says the album has a certain Frisco feel to it. I've never been there, so I don't know. But I want to find out. **(Orion)**

BANCO DE GAIA-Maya (Planet Dog/UK) I have written about Planet Dog Records many times now, enough (I hope) that you should have become a fellow fan, enthused and enthralled at every new release as I am, needing only to be told that there is a new record out in order to gain motivation enough to find it. If this is not the case, then I give you one last chance, and it comes in the form of Banco De Gaia's first full length album. It contains some of the most glorious ethno-trance grooves I have ever heard! Banco De Gaia have developed a style that is simply beautiful, heart-meltingly lovely and dubby music, equally suitable for dancefloors or chillfloors or cloudfloors. Highly recommended for cerebral massages of pan-cultural bliss, full of fluttering, soaring singing visions and voices, with many influences, most of them from across the world. Many people have been making ethno-ish ambient-ish music for some time now, but I really think Banco De Gaia are one of the best. **(RS)**

2350 BROADWAY 2 (Fax World/Germany) The second 2350 Broadway collaboration between New York's Tetsu Inoue and Pete Namlook is a double CD inspired by Winter 1994 in New York. Close your eyes and experience the heart of a large city after a snowfall-environmental beatfree best heard than listened to. **(Orion)**

V/A-CHILLOUT PHASE TWO (Instinct) This double CD set continues in the same encyclopedic vein as Instinct's first Chill Out compilation, combining numerous facets of the contemporary ambient genre that you usually don't find all in one spot. The tracks range from the synth and string washes of Sad World's "Apadana" to the electro-experimentation of Prototype 909's "Understand." There are plenty of classics here, such as Air Liquide's "Sun Progress," (the groovy inner track from the blue vinyl) and a mix of Irresistible Force's "Space Is The Place." There's also recent stuff from big cheeses such as the Aphex Twin ("Blue Calx"), Dominic Woosey as Mysteries Of Science, the Drum Club, and Cabaret Voltaire. But hey, you don't have to be a music mogul to be fierce! Human Mesh Dance definitely pulled it off with "Wet Moon," which will be DJ-accessible on a limited edition vinyl double album out this summer with hand-picked tracks by Instinct comrades Omicron, Mysteries Of Science, and Terre Thaemlitz. **(DJS)**

ROBERT ARMANI-Trancematik: The Best of Robert Armani (PowWow Trance) A collection of choice tracks from the 'King Of Minimalism,' Chicago DJ/producer Robert Armani. Now this is techno--pulsating, driving, sensual, otherworldly, emotional, sexual, even primal. This is a essential purchase, full stop, as all the classics are here: "Muzik Man," "Ambulance Two," "Circus Bells," etc. **(PW)**

PETER KUHLMAN/ALBAN GERHARDT-Wandering Soul (Yesterday & Tomorrow/Germany) The second release on this Fax sublabel dedicated to 'connecting the classical side of ambient and the ambient side of classical' is a collaboration between Fax's Peter Kuhlman (his real name) and German cellist Alban Gerhardt. This is what Peter Kuhlman likes to call 'classical-ambient chamber music.' And that it is. As with Passion, Y+T's first release, this accomplishes the label's mission: to draw a correlation between the beauty of classical music and the beauty of contemporary ambient, perhaps establishing the ambient artist as a serious artist in his own right, not as some studio hack behind a wall of technology. In my opinion, it offers a refreshing respite from the (overtly) electronic onslaught and takes the genre out of the chillout room and into the recital hall. **(Orion)**

DEATH CUBE K-Dreamatorium/CYPHER 7-Decoder/AZONIC-Halo(Strata) The first three releases on Bill Laswell's Subharmonic sublabel, Strata, are all black and mysterious. Actually, each release is enclosed in a fully black jewel case, presumably to allow the music, not the packaging, to speak for itself. The label's debut, a cryptic anagram for Laswell guitar god Buckethead, is five tracks of dark, disturbing treated guitar and bass experiments. Totally fucking mental. The second release, by Azonic (Andy Hawkins), is described as violent ambience. I say it's Steve Vai on bad acid. Fuck that, Steve Vai wishes he could do something this cool-dissonant, resonant, demented, and even more totally mental than the first. The third, Cypher 7 is a collaboration between studio hired guns Jeff Bova and Alex Haas. This release is perhaps the most 'accessible' of the trio reviewed here, the duo exploring the worlds of ambient dub ("Dead Drop"), pulsating beatfree textures ("Piece Of Blue Sky"), environmental experimentation ("Dream Spiral"), and minimalism. All three are excellent, depending on your frame of mind and reference. In short, a mixing record, some really scary noise, and a brilliant ambient collaboration. Check them all out. **(Orion)**

ADHAM SHAIKH-Realignment(Modulation Elektronik/Canada) A four track album from this Vancouver, B.C. based producer. All four tracks are on the average of about 17 minutes long spanning smooth melodic trance, deep, densely layered ambience and points in between and beyond. Haunting, meditative, introspective, Realignment takes you into the inner realm of consciousness, offering a spiritually inspiring musical journey. **(Orion)**

NAMLOOK III/NAMLOOK IV/NAMLOOK V (Fax/Germany) Three solo Namlook recordings: The first, titled "Aliens In My Suitcase" is a minimalistic approach to ambient. Using only a 606 and an early suitcase synth, Pete wrote these during the Summer of '93. This is music you can feel- no melodies were used, just pure subharmonic tones. The second, recorded live in San Francisco is a completely improvised performance dedicated to various pieces of equipment that were either missing, broken, had minds of their own, or had to be coerced to cooperate during the recording. An incredible mix of analogue technology! The third is recorded live at Namlook's first U.K. show at Wembley Arena 10 April 1994. **(PW)**

TOURNESOL-Kokotsu(Apollo/Belgium) Tommy Gee and Thomas Lynge, better known as Danish duo Tournesol, mysteriously crept iinto the underground consciousness with an eponymously titled double pack on R&S that drew trainspotters attention, by both it's colorful sleeve and the music inside. Influenced by the likes of Pink Floyd, Eno, 808 State, Weather Report, and Jimi Hendrix, the pair look to further establish their name in the field of experimental dance music. Kokotsu, their full length debut, fully looks to the future, fusing electronic and acoustic sounds into abstract dance, listening techno and pure ambience, turning what the mind only daydreams and ponders in sleep into reality. Original and to-be-timeless. Highlights: "Henka," "Draagmad Ultramarine," "Cathedral," "Holy Cow." **(Orion)**

AMBIENT OTAKU (Fax Sublabel/Germany) The solo debut of Japanese-born, New York-based Tetsu Inoue. Mostly chilled, the album is on the environmental and minimal side of ambience. If you like his 2350 Broadway collaboration with Namlook, you will enjoy this musical treat. **(Orion)**

MO BOMA-Myths Of The Near Future, Part 1 (Extreme) As ambient music becomes more and more popular, I find myself searching for music off-the-beaten track on labels unaffected by dance publication hype. Extreme is one of those labels. It just puts out interesting music- ethnic, noise, experimental, indigenous, jazz, whatever. Mo Boma is a collaboration between German composer and multi-instrumentalist Carsten Tiedemann and Icelandic bassist Skuli Sverrisson who has worked with guitarist Allan Holdsworth and jazz artists Full Circle). This second release between the two is the first in a trilogy of releases that meld world instrumentation with jazz, freeform rock, ambient, and funk causing a coherent and passionate trans-cultural and trans-technological improvisational environment. Top notch listening and some choice tracks for the chill room as well, I wouldn't mind hooking them up with some of ambient's more avant garde producers. **(PW)**

MUSIC FOR FILMS: KOYAANISQATSI (Fax Sublabel/Germany) The prolific Oliver Lieb is at it again with this re-interpretation of Godfrey Reggio's Koyaanisqatsi in a collaboration with Dr. Atmo. Synchronized to the film beginning when the film's title dissapears from the screen, the ambient piece gathers multiple sequenced lines that build up to a complex structure of movements. Lieb and Atmo have created a masterpiece for pure listening, with or without film accompaniment. **(Orion)**

YOKOTA-The Frankfurt/Tokyo Connection (Harthouse America) The Frankfurt/Tokyo connection is a highly recommended full-length release from Susumu Yokota. Clocking in at over 72 minutes total, many albums of this length suffer in certain areas. Over the course of eleven tracks, most of them around 140 bpm, Yokota delves into a myriad of trance styles, exploring many possibilities without overreaching or including any filler cuts. Acid and trance particulars are juxtaposed with traces of breakbeat, tribal percussion, tricky rhythms, and tasteful, moody strings. That Yokota covers so many bases and does well with them all is quite a feat. No aggressive acid, no anthemic trance, just the best bits of both and music that forces you to pay attention and listen. **(AD)**

SILENCE 2 (Ambient World/Germany) Rereleased on the Ambient World label, this is the second part to the successful collaboration between Pete Namlook and DJ Dr. Atmo. Ambience with classical elements and a philosphical approach to themes. Classic and essential. **(Orion)**

UZECT PLAUSH-More Beautiful Human Life! (Apollo/Belgium) As ambient music turns more towards experimental electronic music for inspiration, labels will turn to recognize the contributions of long-time underground electronic pioneers. Uzect Plaush is Paul Schutze, an Australian-born electronic composer who resides in London. Besides releasing 5 solo albums of which this is his sixth, Schutze has also worked as a sound designer and on over 23 TV, film, and animation features, shorts, and documentaries. More Beautiful Human Life! reflects a new and separate stream of work for Schutze as his truly avant garde approach reaches a new audience with this release on Apollo. A release for the adventurous of ear. **(PW)**

V/A-EMIT0094 (Instinct) Contemporary ambient on the soulful side- this CD is the shit! All of the tracks have a very loose touch to them, most use common jazz/funk instrument sounds such as piano, conga and jazz percussion, organ, electric bass, etcc., to lesser and greater degrees. The compilation opens with Coco, Steel, & Lovebomb's "Harlem," which is a warped revisiting of early urban soundscape tracks by Earth, Wind, & Fire and Kool & The Gang. The mood is set. "Sweat" by Voodoo Warriors Of Love brings in a little more contemporary ambient feel, but doesn't let loose of the free groove. None of the tracks do- they just take you deeper and mellower, resting you up for the final beat ddrops in Woob's "Void, Part One." This is destined for many an afternoon of repeat play in my CD player, highly recommended for anyone looking for smoove contemporary ambient without that sharp cyber edge. **(TT)**

V/A-ONE A.D. (Waveform) As the American wing of Beyond, the U.K. label that brought us the Ambient dub compilations over the past few years, Waveform look to bring the best of these seminal collections to the U.S underground on one CD. Remixed and remastered, One A.D. highlights tracks from then undiscovered acts such as Banco de Gaia, Higher Intelligence Agency, A Positive Life, and Original Rockers. A smart sample introduction to the genre. **(PW)**

V/A-EXCURSIONS IN AMBIENCE-THE THIRD DIMENSION (Astralwerks) Previous versions of Astralwerks' Excursions In Ambience series has focused solely on the world of electronic music. This third installment brings together some of the ambient genres most prominent names (Spacetime Continuum, Air, Aphex Twin, Future Sound Of London), while exposing a few little known artists (Grain and Divination), and widening the scope by including artists of a indie rock background (Seefeel, Sonic Boom, Nirvana producer/engineer Steve Fisk). While many will say that this third excursion is perhaps the most commercial of the series, The Third Dimension does a great job at opening people's eyes to the fact that there are no rules to ambience. **(PW)**

V/A-HISTORY OF OUR WORLD (NASA/ Profile) In the year or so since rave's demise, we've seen the uniquely U.K. form of music called 'jungle' fall out of vogue with DJ's and partygoers not only in the U.K., but here in the States. Labels that were at the forefront of jungle or hardcore then like Moving Shadow, Reinforced, Production House, and of course, Suburban Base, are again at the head of the pack, having reinvented the genre with a darker, more underground attitude. With this renewed lease on life, the genre has recently seen a spurt of popularity, both over there and here in the U.S., although it's popularity will probably never approach the height it once had. Mixed like a DJ tape by New York DJ DB, this compilation is an in depth and seamless look at the genre's past and almost present history. Included here are some of the best hands-in-the-air favorites as well as other slices of seminal ruffness. **(PW)**

RESISTANCE D.-<u>Ztringz Of Life</u> (Harthouse/Germany) This full- length debut from Pascal and Maik contains 8 beautiful songs that have to be felt as well as listened to. The LP's standout is definitely the electro remix of their 'hit' "Cosmic Love" The only thing missing is the masterpiece, "Human," still, this LP is a must have. **(G)**

INTER STELLAR GROOVE POWER
FUTURE SOUND OF LONDON
Excursions In Ambience
§ The Third Dimension §
FUTURE SOUND OF LONDON
LIFEFORMS
"Music for the complexity, chaos and strangeness of living now. Soundscapes that change what we hear and how we listen to it."
-The Sunday Times
ASTRALWERKS
EXCURSIONS IN AMBIENCE
THE THIRD DIMENSION
The dazzling new chapter in the exploration of spirituality through technology. Featuring new and unreleased tracks from Future Sound Of London, Spacetime Continuum, Seefeel and Aphex Twin.
TECHNO
MANCER
IV
THE HARD EDITION
Howze O' Dy-No-Mite
TECHNOMANCER IV
THE HARD EDITION
Over 70 minutes of mutherf**kin hardcore and acid. Gut wrenching electronic dance music. Not for the weak of heart. Featuring Zolex, Daedalus Project, and Trancesetters.
HOWZE O' DY-NO-MITE
60 plus minutes of sonic progressive-dance bliss. Featuring Mellow Mellows' "One 4 Love" and an earful of Jaydee's new label First Impressions. The first in a new series of DJ-mixed CD releases. [oh yeah, it's also available on cassette, you eediot!]
SEMI AUTOMATIC
Mail Order P.O. Box 2759 NY NY 10116-2759
E:mail: astralwerks@cyberden.com
Stores, call Caroline Distribution directly.
©1994 Caroline Records Inc.

16

Free! Worldwide!
TRiP Magazeen
Florida's Underground Dance Music Magazine
V.16.0/New Music Seminar Recap Issue
Future Sound Of London
Global Communication
Kenny Larkin
Ralf Hildenbeutel
Paul van Dyk
Tetsu Inoue
Youth
Stickmen
Plink Plonk Competition
Germany's Cosmic Baby

From the prolific minds behind
Front Line Assembly,
Semantic Spaces is a musical odyssey
through strange lands and alternate realities.
Delerium
SEMANTIC SPACES
brainbox
PRIMORDIA
A sensual trip
through shifting
aural landscapes
NETTWERK
Nettwerk Productions, Box 330 - 1755 Robson St., Vancouver, BC, Canada, V6G 3B7 Tel: 604-654-2929 • FAX: 604-654-1993
E.mail: Nettwerk@mindlink.bc.ca Nettwerk BBS: 604-731-7007
Tour Dates: DATES@Nettwerk.wimsey.com Connect FAQ: INFO@Nettwerk.wimsey.com
Nettwerk News: NEWS@Nettwerk.wimsey.com The Catalog: CATALOG@Nettwerk.wimsey.com
World Wide Web URL: http://www.wimsey.com/nettwerk/
Mailing List ("Subscribe" in message): Nettlist-Request@Nettwerk.wimsey.com

TRiP Magazeen

V.16.0/September 1994

-NEWS-

-FEATURES-

-MUSIC & STUFF-

-THE COVER-

A classically-trained piano prodigy who entered the Nuremburg Conservatory of Music at the age of 7, Berlin-based **Cosmic Baby** discovered synthesizers and electronic music in 1980 and from there, the only way was up.

His debut album on MFS, ***Stellar Supreme*** and his energetic live show took Cosmic throughout Europe and to Australia and the U.S., earning Cosmic **Best Live Performer** in dance music publications worldwide..

On the eve of the U.S. release of his first album for Logic, Cosmic Baby spoke candidly with TRiP Editor **Peter Wohelski** about the adjustment to techno star and the emotions behind *Thinking About Myself.*

-ABOUT THE ISSUE-

This issue was created using Aldus Pagemaker 5.0 and Adobe Photoshop on a Power Macintosh 8100 with 40 MB of RAM. Scans were made on a Hewlett Packard IIcx and output on a HP 4M Plus... The dream continues!

SHOUTS OUT TO:

Mark & Tom, Morris & Russell, Tetsu, Felice @ Girlie Action, Wendy K., Cosmic, Carlos SoulSlinger, Dan DC and the Base 10 crew, Manabu & Danny @ Sublime, Instinct Ambient posse, LuLu @ Plink Plonk for the gear, Megadog/Planet Dog, Jeff & Leslie, Brent @ Extreme, Michael @ Nettwerk, Dan Curtin, Tamara Palmer, Kenny Larkin, Steve McClure @ Halluci-Nation, Ray & Todd @ URB

FEET FIRST

A couple of months back, I recieved a mysterious sheet of fax 'terrorism' detailing the sorry state of the scene in the Northeast, New York in particular, specifically, Manhattan. I read it several times thinking I perhaps missed the point, but I had to disagree. Until recently.

The TRiP staff went to New York in July for New Music Seminar to schmooze, booze, abuse, shop, play a few gigs, soak up the NY vibe, and hear some of the World's best talent assembled for this yearly gathering of global (dance) music people.

In retrospect, here are some impressions from a techno scene in trauma... 1) The House scene in New York is fantastic. Always has been. Always will be. One must go to Sound Factory on a Saturday night once before you die. Underground parties in Manhattan seem to make the mistake of trying to recreate the Sound Factory with what the fax calls 'turncoat techno DJ's.' and failing. 2) For a city that holds so much techno talent, there's very little support for the DJ's and artists (and the record labels) by the promoters and partygoers. Many are people who want to see their scene at home flourish, but in wanting to participate, end up getting worked by the promoters and treated with apathy by the partygoers. 3) Manhattan promoters have to be the world's most ruthless, backbiting, scumsucking leeches in the world. I thought that parties are supposed to be for the enjoyment and enlightenment of the the people who support the scene, but often I saw a great disregard for the people who attend and more attention to how much money is being made. In one way or another, poor spaces with little or no ventilation, air conditioning, or fans, and in-fighting between promoters

continued on Page 36

TRiP Magazeen
100 East M.L. King Blvd.
Suite #5
Tampa, Florida 33603
U.S.A.
FON: 813.238.0310
FAX: 813.876-7473
(please use a cover sheet if you fax)
E-MAIL: oscillate@aol.com.

EDITOR/PUBLISHER:
Peter Wohelski
SENIOR EDITOR: Wayne Consiglio
EDITOR-AT-LARGE: DJ Three
EXECUTIVE ASSISTANT: Jackie Rosquete
CONTRIBUTORS:
Caped Crusader, T. Confucious, Joost de Lyser, DJ Grumpy, DJ Jeffee, DJ Orion,, Andrew Duke, Ian Rich, Terre Thaemlitz

SUPPORT THE UNDERGROUND!!
ADVERTISING: Rates available upon request.
SUBSCRIPTIONS: $15 yearly for six issues
RETAILERS: Contact DELTRA RECORD DIST. (310) 202-8554, RECORD TIME DIST. (313) 773-7373, or TRiP direct for info.
TRiP Magazeen is published every eight weeks and is distributed throughout the United States and into Europe. We hope our content will encourage awareness and positivity in the Global Underground. Opinions expressed are not necessarily those of the editors.

HYPE! HYPE! HYPE! HYPE! HYPE! HYPE! HYPE! HYPE! HYPE! HYPE! HYPE! HYPE! HYPE! HYPE! HYPE! HYPE!

The **UNIVERSE** party organization returns! Universe, in association with **FRANKFURT BEAT**, has assembled the cream of DJ's and live acts from around the globe to assemble at Munich's Old International Airport on October 1st, 1994 for Universe's **TRIBAL GATHERING '94. COSMIC BABY, C.J. BOLLAND, SPICELAB, DAVE ANGEL, DAVE CLARKE, LAURENT GARNIER, JEFF MILLS, RICHIE HAWTIN, DAG, PAUL VAN DYK, FABI PARAS, ALEX PATTERSON,** and **MIXMASTER MORRIS** are among the top talent confirmed so far....Reported last issue as NASA Music, **PROFILE** has launched **SM:)E (SMILE) COMMUNICATIONS**, a new cutting edge dance label that looks to 'communicate positive feeling through technology.' The label plans to work interactively with all communication formats available to bridge the gap between technology and music. Early releases include projects from **AIR LIQUIDE, 2 BAD MICE**, and **PETER VRIENDS**, plus an interactive **'DJ-ROM'**....Dutch 'zine **SURREAL SOUND** is starting an agency for underground (read: 'intelligent' techno, ambient, experimental electronic dance) artists worldwide who are looking to get their music out. Fully artist driven, the agency will solicit tracks to labels looking for new artists, allowing the artist to choose the label that offers the best deal, charging the label, not the artist, a small amount or percentage. For more information, contact **011+31 1179 1396**....**SEEFEEL** have signed an American deal with **EAST/WEST RECORDS**....A 20-year-old **RICHIE (PLASTIKMAN) HAWTIN** fan recently spent 5 1/2 days in jail after Texas police stopped him for speeding. Upon search of his car, the authorities arrested him for 'possession of a controlled substance,' believing that the perforated artwork for Plastikman's **SHEET ONE** lp may contain 'controlled substances.' This charge is a 2nd Degree Felony/Schedule 1, punishable by 2-20 years in jail with up to a $10,000 fine....**R.I.P.: AAHZ**. Florida's perhaps most well-known club night has ended as Orlando's revered **BEACHAM THEATRE** has been sold, leaving resident DJ's **KIMBALL COLLINS** and **DAVE CANNALTE** temporarily homeless. May the basslines rest in peace....San Francisco's **FREAKY CHAKRA** has signed to **ASTRALWERKS**....**FUTURE SOUND OF LONDON** plan to resume their **3-D HEADSPACE TOUR** of 55 U.S. college radio stations again this fall; rumor has it that FSOL are working on a New Year's Eve event, complete with full visuals, to be available on ISDN satellite worldwide....**RABBIT IN THE MOON-"DEEPER"** out soon on **HALLUCI-NATION**....Florida hardcore/jungle DJ **AK 1200** has signed to **SUBURBAN BASE**....**INSTINCT AMBIENT** has licensed several collections from Pete Namlook's **FAX** label. Instinct will be releasing a Fax compilation as well as 2 CD sets of **ALIEN COMMUNITY** (PN & Jonah Sharp), **SILENCE** (PN & Dr. Atmo), **SAD WORLD** (Dr. Atmo & Ramin), and **AIR** in the coming months....instinct Ambient artist **TERRE THAEMLITZ** has completed remixes for **MATERIAL** and the **GOLDEN PALOMINOS**....**MOONSHINE MUSIC** has recently expanded into distribution, signing deals with **DMC AMERICA, CITY OF ANGELS**, and three other to-be-named labels over the next six months....The coolest promo item at the moment-**PLANET E** paddleballs. Wish we had one.....From the Far East, **SUBLIME RECORDS** is a new label that seeks to become a vehicle for the new consciousness of the ambient, electronic dance, and intelligent techno movement by recognizing artists as shamans, or guides, aspiring to reveal the underlying mechanisms and inter-dependencies which our society has forgotten. The label is currently releasing its first group of recordings from Japanese and International artists such as **KEN ISHII, SUSUMU YOKOTA,** and **DAN CURTIN**. For more information or distribution inquiries, ring **Deep Distribution at 1+216.382.3101**....**THRASH** from The Orb has done a dub remix of **KILLING JOKE'S "REQUIEM"**....**EXPERIMENTAL** is gearing up for their 30th release, a limited-edition package by **MAGENTA** with a magenta colored 12" disc of hard trance and a blue vinyl 7" of pure ambience. Also on the ambient tip, the label will be releasing a CD compilation of ambient concepts from various EX artists.....**INTERAX GLOBAL NETWORK** is a loose collective of worldwide party promoters that have united to bring together their events from around the globe by linking them via Internet and Interactive Video Network (IVN) satellite uplink. The organization is attempting the first international uplink event October 14-16, 1994, with events in New Zealand, Australia, British Columbia, California, and New Hampshire joining the two mother events in Texas, and Georgia. For more info, call **1+404.881.6362**....Dallas-based **SPACE RECORDS** returns after over a year hiatus with its third release, **SEDONA-"PULSATION"**, the brainchild of DJ's **RELOAD** and **DALE CHARLES**....Chicago DJ **MARK FARINA** is apparently tutoring World Super Middleweight Boxing Champion **NIGEL BENN** on the finer points of working the wheels of steel. Benn is apparently quite the mellow House and Garage DJ, having worked for guest spots at London's **MINISTRY OF SOUND**....Planet Dog artists **EAT STATIC** and **BANCO DE GAIA** will be making their U.S. debuts at New York's Limelight, Wednesday, September 21 as part of a bill with **ST.ETIENNE**. Planet Dog/Megadog honcho **MICHAEL DOG** will also be DJ'ing as well....**DUB SHACK** is a mail order tape network for Jungle enthusiasts bringing the sound of London to the States. For a catalog, write **P.O. BOX 8106, WILMETTE, IL 60091**....The recently completed **SYSTEM 7** lp features collaborations with **DERRICK MAY, LAURENT GARNIER, DJ LEWIS (BANDULU)**, and **YOUTH**....In celebration of the fifth volume of R&S Records' compilation series **IN ORDER TO DANCE**, which coincides with the 10th Anniversary of the label, a string of events under the banner of **R&S REPUBLICA** will be taking place in the label's home base of Gent. Between September 5th and the 11th, a 24-hour radio station will broadcast techno and ambient music presented by **KENNY LARKIN, DERRICK MAY, JUAN ATKINS, "MAD" MIKE BANKS** (Underground Resistance), **JOHN PEEL, KEN ISHII, GEIR JENSSEN** (Biosphere), **FRANK DE WULF, SVEN VAN HEES, SUN ELECTRIC, COLIN DALE** (KISS-FM, London), **PAUL SCHUTZE** (Uzect Plaush), **MARK VAN HOEN** (Locust), and label head **RENAAT VANDEPAPELIERE** among others. Also during the week, Gent's Museum of Contemporary Art will be presented with the first limited edition copy of In Order To Dance 5, a plexiglas, battery-powered light box, an ambient dinner party will be held at Electric Island with food, drinks, and live entertainment by **DAVID MORLEY, MIXMASTER MORRIS**, and others. The official In Order To Dance Party, **A GOOD NIGHT OUT** will round out the week with Juan Atkins, Mixmaster Morris, Colin Dale, **STEVE COP, KING KONG** (Mantra Club, Copenhagen), and Renaat Vandepapeliere DJ'ing and **SPEED JACK** live....

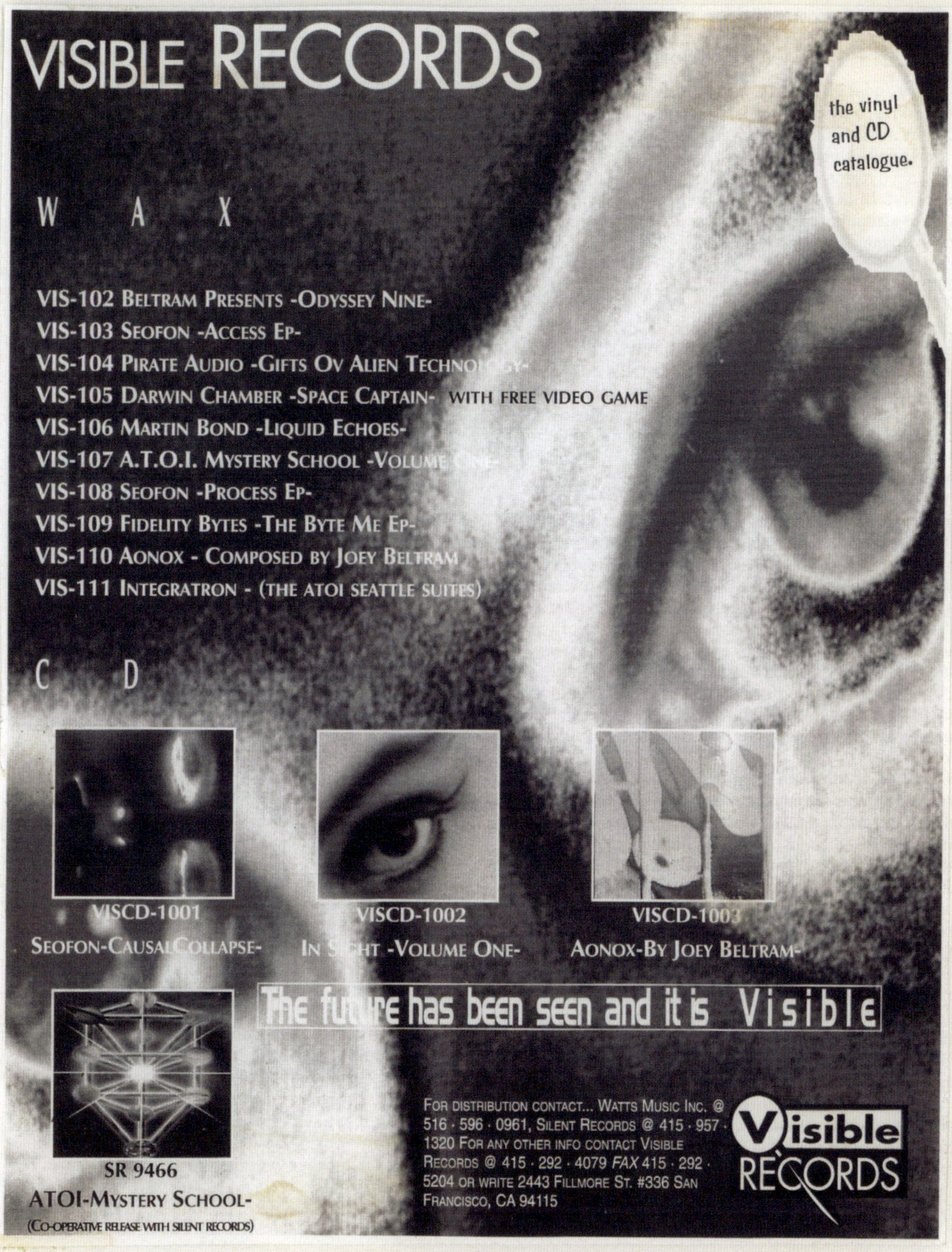
VISIBLE RECORDS
the vinyl and CD catalogue.
W A X
VIS-102 Beltram Presents -Odyssey Nine-
VIS-103 Seofon -Access Ep-
VIS-104 Pirate Audio -Gifts Ov Alien Technology-
VIS-105 Darwin Chamber -Space Captain- with free video game
VIS-106 Martin Bond -Liquid Echoes-
VIS-107 A.T.O.I. Mystery School -Volume One-
VIS-108 Seofon -Process Ep-
VIS-109 Fidelity Bytes -The Byte Me Ep-
VIS-110 Aonox - Composed by Joey Beltram
VIS-111 Integratron - (the atoi seattle suites)
C D
VISCD-1001
Seofon-CausalCollapse-
VISCD-1002
In Sight -Volume One-
VISCD-1003
Aonox-By Joey Beltram-
The future has been seen and it is Visible
SR 9466
ATOI-Mystery School-
(Co-operative release with Silent Records)
For distribution contact... Watts Music Inc. @ 516 · 596 · 0961, Silent Records @ 415 · 957 · 1320 For any other info contact Visible Records @ 415 · 292 · 4079 FAX 415 · 292 · 5204 or write 2443 Fillmore St. #336 San Francisco, CA 94115
Visible RECORDS

Kenny Larkin: Perfecting techno(logy) through the Art Of Dance

by Joost de Lyser & Peter Wohelski

Kenny Larkin is easily one of the best techno artists in this new breed of Detroit producers. Starting out on the **Plus 8** label where he released a few singles before leaving for the **Buzz** label in 1992. This last Spring, Larkin released ***Azimuth***, a full-length LP of Detroit-influenced high-tech jazz, space funk, and melodic techno on Sheffield's **Warp** label that garnered great acclaim for this member of Detroit's new generation of innovators.

TRiP: When did you first become interested in (making) music and what kind of music was this?

Kenny Larkin: I have been interested in music my whole life. Everything from classical to jazz and everything in between. I have always had an ear for music. Since I was little I was able to listen to a record and peck the piano the melodies I heard in the songs.

I formally never took any lessons, but I started fooling around with music in 1985, when I bought a little tiny Casio keyboard and tried to duplicate house music, which was very easy to do.

T: What was your first contact with techno music?

KL: I got into House music in 1985 through **Terrence Parker**. We went to high school together and he was a DJ. He had this weird music that hardly nobody in our school got into, except for the few who picked up on the spiritual vibe the music provided with its repetitive, hypnotic nature. I went to the Air Force in 1986 with House music as my way of life, musically and in 1988, I got out and came home to an entirely different scene happening in Detroit. There was another type of music emerging, or that had already emerged while I was away, and I immediately took to it. **Derrick May** had a mix show on Detroit's main Black radio station and even though I didn't know him at the time or his music, I knew that the music that he mixed was the kind of music I wanted to do. The music that he played, I later found out was from Detroit.

T: How did you meet John and Richie from Plus 8, and did you ever regret leaving their label just before their big success?

KL: I met Richie in a club in 1989 where he just started DJ'ing at, and he too, wanted to make some music. So I bought my first real synthesizer, a Yamaha DX-7, and we talked about starting our own label. Richie met John shortly after and they got together and formed Plus 8. I left Plus 8 because they were not taking care of business properly with me. There was a Plus 8 World Tour in September of 1991 that featured all the arttists on the label playing live all over Europe. I was told by John thaat there was no interest in Kenny Larkin in Europe, so they kicked me off the tour. Meanwhile, I had friends in Europe sending me flyers and possters with my name on them saying that I was playing live. That is what made me leave Plus 8. I have absolutely no regret of leaving Plus 8...their music ahs changed a lot during the last few years and their style has become quite hard, whereas I have, I feel become more refined.

T: How did you come to release tracks on Buzz?

KL: I hooked up with Buzz after the New Music Seminar of 1992. When they heard the tracks, they loved it and decided to license it for Europe. Derrick May loved the tracks also and I licensed it to him for America... I think "War Of The Worlds" was my best 12" ever, and and so did other people. I thought putting it on Transmat would give it the recognition it deserved.

T: After your dealings with Plus 8, you started your own publishing and intended to start your own label. Do you think it's important for artists to have more say in what happens to their music?

KL: I definitely think, if you are able, that you should control your own music and do the best you can for yourself. Even though the label may push your project, they still won't give it the attention that you will.

T: European techno fans (used to) have a very idealistic view

about the original techno producers from Detroit, yet most of the originators are selling out: signing to 'big' labels, doing two remixes a week or DJ'ing at big commercial parties, playing music other than techno. As a result, a lot of people in Europe are very dissapointed in them. Where do you stand on this?

KL: I know of no one from Detroit selling ut by signing to major labels. Kevin Saunderson is the only person that is with majors and I think he is doing what he does best. I think a lot of people doing this music, or any music has to go look into the future and decide where they would like to go with their music. If that is ultimately with major labels and remixing, fine, they have fulfilled their dreams. Why should we condemn that? The problem lies where in the process of changing that dream, they compromise who they are and what their music is about, and what their music is.

T: Interesting sounds have been coming from Detroit every

year and are always new and innovative. How do you explain this self-innovating aspect of (Detroit) techno music?

KL: Personally, I feel that the sounds do play a big role in the music, but it is how the sound is used that is more important. That is what keeps Detroit on the edge.

T: What have you been doing since Azimuth came out?

KL: I just took a short hiatus, chilled out and regrouped because (the album) took a lot out of me. This album I just finished for R&S took three times as much as the first one did. I took a break, bought some new gear; it seems like everytime I finish a big project, I buy new stuff and it knocks the studio down for a few weeks.

T: I understand you're going to start Art Of Dance officially?

KL: As a matter of fact, I'm starting on the first single right now, a Dark Comedy track. I don't know if I'm going to dive into the pool and keep coming out with tracks, but I'm definitely going to put this next track out (on Art Of Dance). I don't know if I want to dedicate the time, I don't think I have the patience to run the business side of it. It's draining enough to do the music...

T: What's the new LP for R&S sound like?

KL: The new album is twice as good as the first one. Easily. It's still the same groove, nothing's changed...it's a continuation of the first album, a lot of the tracks are more emotional. There's a few more clubby tracks on it...there's like 16 tracks.

T: What happened to the Laurent Garnier remixes for *Azimuth*?

KL: Laurent did do a mix and he sent it to me and I didn't like it. So, Laurent pretty much didn't call me after that. I haven't talked to Laurent in seven, eight months...I called him 20, 30 times, left messages on his machine... He still hasn't called me back. It's too bad because we were really cool when we started hanging out and all that, we did some DJ tours together.

T: Do you DJ a lot?

KL: Yeah, as a matter of fact I'm going to Scotland in September to play live and then to Munich in November to DJ. I haven't done anything for a couple of months because I wanted to take time off.

T: Are you signed to R&S now?

KL: No. This is just a straight-up licensing deal.

T: You did a show during Seminar, do you play live often?

KL: That was the second live show I'd done since '91. I wasn't into playing live, really, and I didn't know I liked it so much. I want to do it some more, not too much more, get around so people can see me and see my face. People say, "I thought you were a white guy?" "No, straight-up, brother!"

T: Are you still contemplating doing an ambient album?

KL: Oh yeah! I would even start working on that after this Dark Comedy project. Oh, no, I'm straight up serious, I wasn't passing air...I'd put that on Art Of Dance. It wouldn't be a classic ambien album, what I would do is make a lot of the voicings jazz-oriented, like "Tedra," it wouldn't be a straight-up electronic, mechanical, quantized, all that kind of shit. I really get into that kind of stuff right now.

T: Is there going to be a Dark Comedy album?

KL: Yeah. In fact, this project that I do, that tracks are going to be on the album. I'm essentially doing the single first, then I'm working on the album. I'm also going to put "War Of The Worlds" on the album, too.

Portions of this were reprinted from Surreal Sound 'zine, Holland. For more info on Surreal Sound, fax (011)+3111792000

TETSU INOUE: AMBIENCE IN A NEW YORK STATE OF MIND

One of the best yet unrecognized talents in the ambient and experimental electronic music genre is Japanese-born, New York-based **Tetsu Inoue**. Interested in electronic music since his teens, he is known most notably for his collaborations with **Pete Namlook** on Fax, however he has worked with the likes of **Atom Heart** and **Station Rose** among others. Recently **TRiP's DJ Orion** got better acquainted with Tetsu and talked about Fax, his upcoming works-solo and in collaboration, and the current state of ambience.

TRiP: Did you grow up in Japan and how long have you been here in the U.S.?

Tetsu Inoue: I was born there and I've been in the States for seven years.

T: How long have you been interested in electronic music and what sorts of influences do you have?

TI: Since I was in high school or something...I was definitely interested in **(Haruomi) Hosono** and **YMO**, I grew up with that, **Tomita**, and Japanese ethnic music.

T: Were you a listener or did you go buy a keyboard right away and decide to start making music?

TI: First, I started playing guitar and I got sort of frustrated playing guitar because there's not much sound you can make.

T: What was your first synthesizer?

TI: I bought a Pro 1...I still use it.

T: What is your studio like? Big, small...

TI: It's medium sized. I don't use a computer, although I plan to use one in the future. I'm mostly doing live recording, live sort of sequencing, I even do parts live. Other people just sequence everything and when they want to mix the DAT, they just sit. I don't do that.

T: You've done other stuff besides chillout stuff, more dancefloor things as well...like on Gyroscopic, some pretty hard acid stuff.

TI: That was a long time ago-I've always been interested in ambient music but at that time, nobody wanted to release ambient music. It was really difficult. In a way, it's sort of the same approach as deep chillout stuff, very dry and in front of your face, the harder stuff can make you relax too.

T: Is ambient music is your main focus now?

TI: I like to do a lot of ambient music, but I also like electronic music...I've planned a tour with **Atom Heart**; Atom Heart's main project is **Lasagane Benthaus** and I'm involved in that project. Beginning of September until the end of September we're going to tour from Sweden to Spain...strictly beat oriented stuff.

T: How did you get involved with Pete Namlook and Fax?

TI: First of all, in 1989, I was collaborating with **Station Rose** ("Public Brain Session") and we toured. The concept was a 'public brain session'- frequencies that put you in a certain state of mind. We played with frequencies on stage and had visual things, like a mind machine. This was sort of at the same time as acid house, but instead of playing acid house I wanted a pure, electronic sound. But I decided to quit and I went to India for a year and I came back... Uwe and I produced Station Rose together-Uwe is Atom Heart-Uwe and Olaf run the POD Communications label. That's how I met Peter. Peter was a POD Communications artist, too. His first ambient release was on POD, **Sequential**. I met Peter in New York, I didn't know him from before in Germany. We started playing together and we both liked ambient. Peter was so frustrated and I was also frustrated.

T: Did you do any beat-oriented stuff on Fax?

TI: Datacide (with Atom Heart), the vinyl was more beat-oriented, sort of acid-ambient. Ambient music has so many different directions, I believe, it's the fun part of it.

T: That's a positive and a negative about the genre right now because you're seeing experimental artists like Paul Schutze getting recognized but you're also seeing music that doesn't have a category being

continued on Page 37

INTRODUCING
FAX-USA
FAX COMPILATION
AIR 1 & 2
SILENCE 1 & 2
SAD WORLD 1 & 2
ALIEN COMMUNITY 1 & 2
coming this fall...
all double CDs
the drum club cabaret voltaire
deep space network prototype 909
woob sub dub human mesh dance
terre thaemlitz omicron evolve now
adham shaikh mysteries of science seti
PLUG IN & TURN ON X.2 DOUBLE CD
cabaret voltaire
deep space network
sub dub
the drum club
mysteries of science
PLUG IN & TURN ON X.2
2 CDs : 2 hrs. 28mins. 3 secs.
INSTINCT RECORDS 26 W. 17th St. #502 NY, NY 10011
compuserve: 72170,1753
send a SASE for a free mailorder catalog
instinct

A LOOK INSIDE THE EYE-Q BRAINTRUST-RALF HILDENBEUTEL

by Andrew Duke/Photo by Gaby Gerster

Germany's **Ralf Hildenbeutel** (pronounced "Hill-den-BOY-tull") has only been seriously involved in the music field since 1990, yet in that time he has managed to lend his talents to many diverse areas. Hildenbeutel, 25, began his reccording career with soundtracks and then moved on to become involved with electronic dance music. As well as his solo material under his own name and as **Odyssee of Noises**, he has worked with **Sven Vath** on **Barbarella**, on Vath's solo project, ***Accident In Paradise***, and collaborated with **Stevie Be-Zet** and **A.C. Boutsen** on the **Zyon** album. Plus there are the many remixing/production duties he has undertaken with a myriad of Eye-Q/Harthouse labelmates.

His latest release is something quite different. Together with guitarist **Markus Demi**, he has formed **Earth Nation**, a band-oriented project as opposed to the usual studio-only outfit that is often found in techno circles. **"Alienated,"** was released in May on the Eye-Q label with ***Thoughts In Past Future***, the full-length release, following in June. Those familiar with Hildenbeutel's work will easily appreciate the lush textures, pristine production, and overall depth of this new material. *Thoughts In Past Future* melds together ambient atmospherics, tribal rhythms, and trance elements, and the usual Hildenbeutel sound, but adds guitar in various applications, and even employs vocalists in more conventional song-based structures on a few cuts.

TRiP contributor Andrew Duke spent his dime to have a look inside the man behind the Eye-Q Braintrust, Ralf Hildenbeutel.

TRiP: What was the goal you had with mind working with Markus Demi on the Earth Nation project?

Ralf Hildenbeutel: The main idea was to try and put conventional instruments together with electronic music. We used a lot of guitars, but in a different way than is usual. We sampled the guitar, edited it, and put it into the playback and didn't just play it over a finished track. This was actually the main idea, so that's how we started and we just let it go.

T: How would you describe the Earth Nation material? Would you say it is similar to the work you have done with Sven Vath on *Accident In Paradise*?

RH: It's hard to describe. It's like electronic music that's very percussive. *Accident* was not song-structured, it was more based on instrumental music. We even used some vocalists (on *Thoughts In Past Future*). It's not a dance album, and it's not just an ambient album because we did use a lot of beats.

T: How are you promoting the Earth Nation release?

RH: We're going to put a band together and our next step is to perform this live with a real bandd like a drummer, bass player, guitars, and keyboards. We'll try to perform this music on a stage but not in the conventional electronic way (with everything coming from a sequencer). This is mostly all going to be played (live) and this is the next step. First, we are going to play at the Montreux Jazz Festival and then we'll see about some gigs in the U.K. We'll just see what happens...

T What is your connection with Markus Demi?

RH: He was in Los Angeles for seven years at G.I.T. and he's actually a conventional guitar player. He came back to Germany, and I knew him from years ago in Frankfurt. We just had this idea that we could do this together because he's very open not only to guitar music and rock but he's also open to new music and this electronic stuff...

T: You started piano lessons at the ageof nine, and then you got into electronic music when you were fourteen. You've now only been doing dance music for three or four years. Tell me about your early work.

RH: The Zyon lp was first, around 3 years ago, and was done with Stevie Be-Zet and A.C. Boutsen. This was the first dance music project. After Zyon I did *Barbarella* together with Sven Vath, then the *Accident In Paradise* album, and the the Hildenbeutel solo project on **Recycle Or Die**. (***Looking Beyond***) was an ambient instrumental album, very minimalistic. Two tracks used percussion and some

rhythmic elements, but mainly it's without any beats.

T: Sven Vath describes the Harthouse/Eye-Q label as a big family andd your philosophy is that you don't just make records, but that you have a vision and it's a whole way of life.

RH: The most important thing is the music itself and to make no compromises. It is like a family, and our vision is to always try and find new ways (to make music). In the Euro Top 20 you have to have a rapper and a singer and we don't do this because the music is the most important thing to us, not just sales.

T: Describe your recording set-up.

RH: We use a 48 track analog board and we arrange keyboard sequences on computer. We use the tape machine for when we have vocals, but normally we just do everything straight to the board. We master it straight from sequencing so we don't use tapes. It's kind of digital, but in an analog way. we don't havve very old stuff; we like analog sounds, but we've got a lot of Roland stuff and Korg; we do have some analog stuff, so it's kind of a mix.

T: You started working on the new Sven Vath album in early May of this year. What are your plans for the follow-up to *Accident In Paradise.*

RH: The title is going to be ***The Harlequin, The Robot, And The Belly-dancer*** and each character will have a face. The three characters will be described (with two or three tracks for each character). The last album was more ambient and this album will be more of a mix. (In total), we will probably work three or four months on it.

T: Does it bother you that Sven Vath recieves all the attantion for the *Accident In Paradise* release and the material recorded under his name even though you are responsible for all of the programming and production? Do you feel you deserve more recognition or are you content to relatively anonymous when working with him?
RH: No. The best way to describe (our relationship) is in the classical sense of producer and artist. He's not the singer or something, but he is the artist and I'm the man in the background. It was always clear that (*Accident In Paradise*) was his album even though we did the music and everything together, and I programmed. I don't do the work (he does. He is) always touring and promoting his own record, so it's very clear and no problem at all.

T: What kinds of music do you listen to when you're not busy recording your own material?
RH: I started with classical, and I'm still a big classical fan, so at home I often listen to classical music or **Keith Jarrett** or stuff like that. There are so many different types and styles of good music everywhere so I don't only listen to electronic music or House music at home...stuff like **Peter Gabriel** or **Sting**. I like stuff like this very much. Sometimes I do listen to House or electronic music, or Indian music, so it's very mixed. (At a club) I like trance, hard trance, some acid stuff. It's easier to say what I don't like. I'm not very into the breakbeat stuff and, of course, I'm not very into gabber. It's not my taste at all. I also like to hear House music, depending on the situation. In some clubs you can hear House and it's great, if there's a good atmosphere...ata rave hard trance is the best for me. I don't watch labels, I just hear the music and I like it.

T: What do you see for the future of electronic music in general and for your own music?
RH: I think it's going to open up and we're going to see many more different styles. Like a tree, it's going to split (and move in different directions). Ambient will (change) into something different (as will) electronic, Euro, dance music, and techno; hardcore will be more hardcore and harder. We'll see many different things. I don't think about (the future of my music,) I just let it go. All I want is to go further and not back. Try to find new ways, check out new things, and just see what happens.

Sven Vath's LP, The Harlequin, The Robot, and The Bellydancer, is out now on Eye-Q Records.

Created as a contrast to their better known and acclaimed techno project, **Reload**, Somerset natives **Tom Middleton** and **Mark Pritchard** explore what they deem "the lighter side of human nature" with **Global Communication.**

Meeting in a club where Mark was DJ'ing early Detroit techno, Middleton (the other 'twin' in **Aphex Twin**) and Pritchard formed their own label, **Evolution**, releasing singles under the names Reload, **Rebus, E621, Link, Mystic Institute**, and Global Communication, capturing attention with a Global remix of a MI track entitled **"Obsilon Minos."**

In the meantime, Reload had signed to **Infonet**, and released the magnificent ***A Collection Of Short Stories***, a dark and detached piece of electronics to massive acclaim.

A chance meeting with **Andy Sherriff** of **Chapterhouse** who expressed his interest in the burgeoning ambient scene struck up an interest in Global remixing the group's *Blood Music* album. Accepting the task, Tom and Mark took the pieces of the tracks that they liked and reinterpreted the LP into ***Pentamerous Metamorphosis***, five tracks of the most tender, emotionally stirring ambient music of recent memory, prompting other indie bands like Slowdive to solicit their remix services.

Signing to **Dedicated**, home to not only Chapterhouse and the Cranes, but Spacemen 3 and offshoot Spiritualized, Global Communication has released their own full-length debut, **76:14**. Using numbers to identify the album's tracks, forcing the listener to use their imagination in interpreting the album without any pre-defined notions, 76:14 is a self-contained universe of sonic bliss, taking the ambient genre to an new level of harmony between man and machine.

After an aborted interview in New York City, and several attempts to coordinate upon their return to the U.K., **TRIP** finally caught up with both Mark and Tom, hard at work in the studio working on some remix projects. They took time out between twiddling knobs to share insights and here's the conversation...

TRiP: So how did you and Tom meet?

Mark Pritchard: Well, we met at a club here at home where I was DJ'ing at. I was playing a lot of the early Detroit techno and stuff like that. We met and found we had similar interests and decided to have a go at working together on music.

T: What sort of musical background do you have?

MP: I was into more heavy, guitar-type stuff earlier on, but out where we live, in the West country, there's not a lot of people that you can find to put together a band, really. Electronic music is so much more conducive to working by yourself. Eventually I bought a keyboard and started working by myself.

T: You've used many different names for different projects; what distinguishes one from another?

MP: Reload is a bit darker, electronic, while Global Communication is much lighter. E621 is a bit funkier, and the Link stuff is more for the dancefloor, clubbier type stuff.

T: How do you decide what is going to be, say, a Reload track and what will be Global Communications, etc.?

MP: It's not something that we plan out, really. We just sort of do it and decide as we're working or when we've finished.

T: When will there be another Reload album?

MP: Oh, probably not for awhile. We're working on some remixes for some people and then we're starting up our **Evolution** label again with a compilation of tracks from all the releases. We've also gotten some things from other artists that we're going to remix and release on the label. Global also has a remix ep coming out soon that we have to finish. I think Dedicated also wants us to put out another EP after the first of the year, so I don't know. Probably in the summer of next year, there'll be a new Reload LP. It depends on if we do this EP, but it's up to us, really.

T: I understand that you've put out some jungle records? What were those released on?

MP: Yeah, I think jungle's really brilliant! I did two of them on **Recoil,** which is actually a sublabel of Evolution. There's so much really excellent music coming out of the jungle scene at the moment...some of it's hard to find here where we live. I've gotten these tapesthat have some of the most wicked tracks on them, and it's stuff that the DJ's have dub plates of, you know, like 10 copies and it's stuff that the label won't release for six months or so. Or it won't ever get a release at all. So it's hard to find out what the tracks are.

T: The two of you went to Russia earlier this year(along with Aphex Twin, Autechre, Alex Patterson, and others). Besides getting quite ill, how was the experience, and how are you feeling now?

MP: I was glad to have gone and been able to see some of Russia, the whole tour was quite a mess, with people not getting paid...it was a quite weird situation. I'm feeling better now and I'm just taking it easy and letting things take their course.

T: So I guess your first visit to America was much more rewarding than the trip to Russia?

MP: Yeah, America was amazing. It was quite overwhelming actually.

T: How did the Chapterhouse remix come about?

MP: Tom and Andy from Chapterhouse met through this girl who I think is Andy's girlfriend. He told Tom how much he liked our Obsilon Mi-nos track and asked if we wanted to do something like that to their album which was about to come out. We sat down with them and listened to the album and took the sounds in the background that we liked and reworked it.

T: It's a very moving emotional piece of music. I had heard that it even moved the band to tears when they heard it...

MP: When we played it back for them, there was one track from their album that was very special to one of them and was particularly emotional. And when they heard our reinterpretation we just sort of sat in silence for a while and it looked like they were a bit moved.

Enter Tom Middleton...

T: I get the impression that Reload is more Mark's project with you and Global Communication is your project with Mark. What is Global Communication and what is the difference between Global and Reload?

Tom Middleton: The main difference is, it's basically like a yin and yang thing. If you think about human beings, there's two different major aspects to human beings and that is like a dark side and a light side. Good and bad, white and black, that kind of thing. Global Communication is like the lighter side of human nature, the sort of more uplifting and positive emotions. Reload is more dark and sinister, things people don't like to think about.

T: On the album, 76:14, you used numbers so signify the tracks rather than worded titles. Why?

TM: Yeah, it's called 76:14 because we basically did away with a name for the album and names for the tracks because names tend topredefine what something's going to be about and the whole concept of the album is something to let the listeners use their imagination. They can make up their own names for the tracks. They listen to the music and sort of generate their own images in their head, conjure up things. We're translating our emotions and feelings into the music and telling little stories with the tracks.

T: What have you been working on lately?

TM: We're working on a remix for **Jon Anderson**, the singer from Yes, **Future Sound Of London** and us have been asked to to mixes. We recently did a remix for **The Grid**...also some work for some Japanese artists that we've worked outto put out here on our Evolution label. Also a mix for the **Golden Palominos**, but I don't really know what's goin on with that.

T: Whatever happened to the Primal Scream reinterpretation that was talked about in the press?

TM: We had talked about it, but we really couldn't get out head around the tracks that they sent us to listen to, so we told them no.

T: The LP's hardly out, but you have a remix ep coming out soon?

TM: Yes, with mixes by **The Grid, Michael Brook, Spritualized,** and **The Orb.**

T: What was working with the Orb like?

TM: It was mad. We spent a couple days in the studio just before we came to America, with Alex, Thrash, and Thomas Fehlman sort of outlining what we wanted to do, smoking a lot, and generally having a big laugh. We came over, leaving them to finish it up how they wanted. We're still waiting to hear the final tape, but it'd be great to someday put out the entire session, who knows...

T: When you came over for New Music Seminar, the two of you DJ'ed at a few parties. Do you get asked to DJ often at home?

TM: Not often, but we're getting asked to do it more and more, mostly ambient rooms, but we'd really like to play to the dancefloor as well.

Global Communication's remix of The Grid's "Rollercoaster" is out only on CD single. Look for the remix ep of tracks from 76:14 with personalizations from The Grid, Spiritualized Michael Brook and The Orb later this fall.

Lifeforms: re-invading FSOL's 3-D Headspace

Last year at this time, **TRiP** spoke with **Garry Cobain** of **Future Sound Of London**. Cobain and partner **Brian Dougans** had just released under the guise of **Amorphous Androgynous**, ***Tales Of Ephidrena***- a seamless collection of tracks compiled from their old studio. Excited by the completion of the second FSOL album, Dougans talked about the contents of the upcoming album and the concepts and ideas that the duo had dreamed up to revolutionize the underground as we know it.

One year later, on the eve of the release of this second album, ***Lifeforms***, a swirling miasma of layered sounds, samples, beats, chaos, and ambience, Cobain and **DJ Orion** resumed their conversation. All we can say is, what a difference a year makes...

TRiP: Last time, you had just finished Lifeforms, and you talked about how it was the most seamless piece of music you'd ever written. Now after having heard it, I'd say that it has the potential to change the way people percieve contemporary electronic/ambient music. Your thoughts?

Garry Cobain: I think whenever people around us make something important we kind of run away from it. Everybody around us was going "Great track! Whoo, yeah! Great bass!", and this kind of shit, you know? With all the crap dance music that was going on we just went, "Right. Tracks and bass, let's not do any tracks or any bass., let's not do any drums." That"s why ambience came back for us< it was just running away from the people that were making all those elements mechanisms by which to sell music. A certain beat would get to a certain crowd which would sell a certain thing. We just *hate* that whole crowd...

T: There's a few collaborations on Lifeforms- Toni Halliday from Curve, Robert Fripp...how did those come about?

GC: (In the case of Robert Fripp,) we've got a DAT of his, it wasn't a direct collaboration. He's very organized and that's very hard for chaos merchants like ourselves, we like to keep things open and we never commit to having anyone come down to the studio. Robert finds that quite difficult to deal with, so we basically have 3 hours of guitar from him on DAT, and we dip into those whenever we feel like it.

T: What happened with the collaboration with Liz Fraser of the Cocteau Twins?

GC: That took about a year and a half to pull off. I had written her a letter, which was lost, and then (Stephen Mallinder of Cabaret Voltaire) put in a good word, fnally I was given her home number by somebody who said she'd like to talk. After two phone conversations, we finally got into the studio. It was a pretty odd day, It was caught in the worst sort of industry red tape, apparently Polygram wants Virgin to give them the rights to a Peter Gabriel and Meat Loaf duet. It was such a completely debilitating experience. It's been settled now and it will be released.

T: Tell us about the film that you're working on forthe album, Yage?
GC: It's going to be a feature film that we're going to try to get on IMAX theatres worldwide. We've just now gotten our hands on the technology, several Silicon Graphics workstations and Macs to really complete the project. It will be unlike anything anyone in the computer graphics field has ever seen.

T: Are you directing with Buggy G. Riphead (FSOL's visual 'consultant') or are you going the concept and he's bringing it to life?
GC: I'm not much as far as trying to actually do all of the graphics work. We'e come up with the concept and told Buggy what we want to do and he conveys that to some people that we have working on that end of the production.

T: Last year when we talked, I asked you about live shows and you said that you hadn't come up with a 'live' concept at that point. I understand that you're doing some live gigs via phoneline from your studio. Elaborate on that...
GC: The phoneline is quite an interesting extension of what we've been about for the last couple of years, we've done quite a few radio programs. We've been quite frustrated in the way that the rock press over here has tried to encourage electronic musicians to go out on the road and try and emulate the rock set-up and have been really supportive of anyone who's tried to do that. I've seen all the gigs that they've written about and they're basically lying. It's quite sad; they've mostly been very boring and we never wanted to do that. With the advent of ISDN, we now have the chance to do the kind of live performance that throws up some of other questions in the hypocrisy surrounding that.

T: What is ISDN?
GC: It's a digital phonelink that means you can literally broadcast full frequency sound down the phoneline. So we're doing it through (BBC) Radio One. We're broadcasting live from the studio for two hours and basically doing a Future Sound of London 'gig' and broadcasting on Radio One across this country and Europe. We'll be hitting close to a miilion people live and playing to a cowshed. We've been asked to do an festival, where we'd do a live gig from the studio and broadcast it live through their PA...

T: What is the status of the EBv label?
GC: EBv is still going through a period of change, really. (FSOL) have gone through some changes, the periods of fighting that we would go through in order to complete our music is no longer the case. We just work on separate media if there's ever an argument. We're very creative in our business and we've made alot of steps on the business side of EBv; we have worldwide distribution of audio-visual products. Now we have the setup to be able to get our films released and play around the world, which is a very big step in what we intend to do.

T: How does the upcoming Amorphous Androgynous lp differ from *Tales of Ephidrena* and for that matter, *Lifeforms*?
GC: I don't see Amorphous Androgynous as a separate project (from FSOL), I think it's a natural progression. In fact, we just got rather tired setting ourselves up as Future Sound Of London. The next album will be just a continuance of the way we're working, which is a non-linear listening experience. We're trying to get that more and more sophisticated. The one away from *Lifeforms* now is to get where you have a different kind of linearality but there are certain dynamics, like getting into really, really hard sections out of the ambience, and getting into a more variety of instruments like trumpets. Almost getting into some conventional instruments and really doing the treatment on them and putting conventional equipment through the machines.

T: How does that relate to the Amorphous Androgynous concept?
GC: To a certain degree, we sacrificed that album to Virgin. We said, "Take this and give it to all your territories around the world," because we were having a lot of misunderstanding about what we wanted to try and do (with FSOL). We gave them certain guidelines, I think they learned a hell of a lot because they found that it actually sold more than people that they were putting serious budgets behind.

T: What are your thoughts on the state of contemporary ambient music? It seems people would rather have chillout rooms for the body, rather than for the head...
GC: That's a fairly major point, one that can confuse my mind very rapidly. I find it very hard, I've actually found now that the music is no longer from my community, my community of acquaintances and friends. It's difficult to play them stuff, now I just move onto the next subject, because no one knows what to say, really.

T: It's my fear that the genre will be absorbed as just another type of dance music. I like the fact that the medium is danceable, but I really discourage the notion that ambient music is dance music.
GC: We term our music 3-D Headspace... I think ambient music is rooted in depth of production and listening. It can involve beats, but as long as they're beats that can be programmed such that they are intricate and turn your head about. We're actually getting into a new kind of beat, after a period on Lifeforms where it was almost like the ultimate thing we could do was not take part in a mechanism which has come about in England that is repulsive, and that's dance music. Our extreme statement was to put bass in the mix, but don't put basslines, and don't give drumbeats.

T: Were you involved in the compilation of the Brief History of Ambient series on Virgin?
GC: One thing about the current ambient scene is that it casts this rather convenient eye which just ignores the history of music. People are more sophisticated as far as the range of music and the depth, we're constantly trying to update and deepen our music and those two releases put (the release of Lifeforms) back a bit because they had quite an impact because somehow it established a framework for the history of music again and the current scene was ignoring it.
"Lifeforms, Part 1-7" with Elizabeth Fraser is now available through Astralwerks. *Environments*, the upcoming Amorphous Androgynous LP is due to be released sometime in early 1995.

Thinking About Myself: An inspection of

A classically-trained piano prodigy who entered the prestigious Nuremburg Conservatory of Music at the tender age of 7, Berlin-based **Cosmic Baby** discovered the world of synthesizers and electronic music in 1980 through the music of **Tangerine Dream** and **Kraftwerk** and from there there was no stopping this emerging talent.

After moving to Berlin to continue his studies, Cosmic met up with the people who will be instrumental in launching the European techno scene: **Westbam**, **Tanith**, and **Kid Paul**.

From there, the only way was up. In addition to releasing his own material, fusing his classical techniques with analog electronics, Cosmic has collaborated with Kid Paul (Energy 52), **DJ Jonzon** (Futurhythm, Veinmelter), and perhaps most memorably with **DJ Paul van Dyk** as **Visions Of Shiva**.

His debut album on MFS, ***Stellar Supreme*** and his energetic live show took Cosmic throughout Europe and to Australia and the U.S. (stopping over in Florida for Infonet 3), earning Cosmic **Best Live Performer** honors in various dance music publications worldwide.

Despite these extreme highs, Cosmic has also had his lows, coming to grips with his career and uncomfortable status as a rising 'techno star,' documenting them on his first album for a new label, **Logic**, called **Thinking About Myself**.

On the eve of the album's release in the U.S., Cosmic Baby spoke candidly with TRiP Editor **Peter Wohelski** about the adjustment from musician to so-called techno star and the emotions behind *Thinking About Myself* and where Cosmic goes from here.

TRiP: When we saw you last it was New Year's Day 1994 and you were in Orlando. Catch us up, what have you been doing since then?

Cosmic Baby: From Orlando I went to London to see the staff at Logic UK and did my first club gig at Club UK. It was the opening party. It's the club in London where people go to listen to the more European techno and trance, it was packed. Paterson was playing, Cox was playing, Dave Angel was playing, DJ Dag from Germany. it was a really cool night. After London, I went back to Berlin and worked on the score for a ballet **(Futura)**. It's a company of six dancers **(Pyro Space Ballet)** and they worked for two years to bring out a very altered futuristic dance piece. It's the same in music as it is in dance, there are really tight, sharp little categories and it was interesting to collaborate with them because they were into creating something very new that crosses borders, and in the end, hopefully gets rid of the borders. The premiere was in April. I did "Fantasia" remixes which come out in Europe in September. Then I went to Australia for six weeks and played in four cities and had some time to relax, went to the Great Barrier Reef... I'm not only interested in going to cities to play there and then leave, but the music to me is a privilage to be able to meet people and experience different things.

T: Your gig at Infonet 3 in Orlando last summer was truly instrumental in bringing the idea of live techno to the Florida scene, you even wrote the liner notes for the new album while you were here. Florida must be a special place for you now?

CB: It's the area in America, to me, where I love to be and play, and hang around people.

T: After your last visit to Florida, there were a lot of press photos of you wearing Sea World t-shirts. With dolphins as part of your logo, what were your impressions of the park?

CB: Mixed impressions. On one hand, I was very happy to see dolphins for the first time, and on the other hand I was very depressed because they were put in jail. I spoke to some insiders and they said most of the dolphins living there die after one year and they just get another one and give it the same name as the one that died. When I wore the shirts and gave interviews, I always said that I wanted to

TRIP Mag V.16.0/Page16

introspection with Germany's Cosmic Baby

tell people that Sea World is not as great as you might think it is.

T: What do dolphins symbolize to you?
CB: Basically, I dreamt about them when I was young, 3, 4, 5 years. Then I saw Flipper and I started reading books about them in connection with extraterrestrial intelligence and UFO's. They have a different intelligence than (humans), they live within the eco-system and are creative and harmonious, without being destructive. That's the basic idea behind its symbolism, along with the yin & yang.

T: Let's talk about music. You're one of the few artists in this music that is still using a true piano sound...
CB: Now I'm on the edge, if you would have asked me eight years ago, I come from a classical background, but now, I'm into electronics and I love electronics. Now I think electronics are great and give you lots of new possibilities that allow you to be creative in a very short period of time. You don't need a lot of people around you, or money. For me as a musician, the longer I play with electronics, the more I have the desire to make and share music with people and maybe two years down the road make a record with a real grand piano and violins, instead of sampling them. If I can meet some people that I think can work with me and do something very special, then I will try to do some acoustic stuff and integrate it.

T: Ambient artists like Pete Namlook are already integrating electronic music with classical acoustic instruments. Do you think this is a way to take this music out of the club and into the recital hall?
CB: I think Pete Namlook is one of the most gifted German modern musicians I know. Sometimes the ambient room is thought of as the dustbin, a room where people who have had too much E and can't move any more go in and let them listen to some weird music without drums. I think ambient music is brilliant and is an important part of a party.

T: Why did you leave MFS for Logic?
CB: At a certain point, I had to look behind the wonderful techno paradise and there was a point where I realized I can't do this alone anymore. Three years ago, there was a telephone and a fax machine and I recieved 200-300 calls a day, "Do you want to play here? Do you want to make this record here?" I realized that to stay the person I am, that means to be alone or spend time with my girlfriend or spend 8 days in a row working on music and nothing else, I had to find somebody who can help me, and give me advice. I met a guy and we talked about our vision and he helped me to realize that techno music is not a paradise where everyone is a friend to everyone. In the case of MFS, MFS is a so-called independent label, but in truth, Mark and Torsten are really, really nice guys, very inspired, but are just the scouts and the person behind the label had very different intentions by letting them deal with people like **Paul van Dyk, Mijk Van Dijk**, or myself. (Mark and Torsten) just want to release good music, but the contracts were made by very different people. With Logic, I have a very free contract, different from anyone else on the label. It's not money, but the control. To be independent to me means to have control and freedom about the music you want to make.

T: It seems that in the past year, you've had a lot of wonderful experiences but you've also experienced some very difficult, depressing moments-the full spectrum of emotions. It's these emotions, high and low, which make up the album, isn't it?
CB: Of course. That's it. Each period of the hard and fantastic year 1993. That's life; I'm happy that more and more people know me, but which is more important, the development of my career is going and going. Every month, I'm on a new level because I have the privilage to meet so many people and see different parts of the world. Music is still such a organic, major part of my life, there shouldn't be a division between the public Cosmic Baby and the private Cosmic Baby. I want to be just me.

YOUTH

From his days as bassist with '80's U.K. aggro-rockers **Killing Joke** through to his then co-pilot status with **The Orb**, remixing, , production work with acts like popsters **Crowded House**, and his own Butterfly label and it's Dragonfly subsidiary, **Youth**'s name has been synonomous with diversity and musical experimentation. Recently reunited with Killing Joke for a new album, ***Pandemonium***, Youth spoke with **TRiP** on his involvement and Killing Joke's influence in dance music, his Dragonfly and Butterfly labels, and new projects.

TRiP: After leaving Killing Joke, how did you become involved in dance music?

Youth: We were always involved in dance music with Killing Joke. But I was trying to do something completely different. I wanted some fresh challenges and dance music, to me, was the one that I culturally felt most emphatic about.

T: In many ways, Killing Joke has had an effect on not only the rock generation, but in techno, as well.

Y: A lot of journalists have mentioned the band's influence on (rock), but I've pointed out that it's been just as apparent with techno culture. It means as much to me when people like **Sven Vath** give Killing Joke namechecks; **Moby, Andrew Weatherall**, are all big Killing Joke fans.

T: Where do your influences lie these days?

Y: I'm listening to a lot of dub again. Quite a lot of early Chicago acid music-909's and 303's are really getting me going again. I'm really interested in a lot of the stuff on my **Dragonfly** label. We've just finished a new album of stuff and the feedback we're getting from all these international DJ's is fantastic...

T: Are you doing more outside production work, as opposed to your own stuff these days?

Y: I'm doing many things simultaneously at the moment, which I really enjoy. Last year, I really focused on production. This year, I'm focusing on Killing Joke, but I'm also doing some mixing...recently **Steve Reich** and I'm working with (Orb main mixer) **Greg Hunter...**

T: Do you still DJ at all?

Y: Yeah, some this year, mainly doing dub and chillout sets. I really enjoy doing that type of set because I've got a little more flexiblility in how diverse of a set you do. I also like playing some of the Dragonfly more full-on stuff, I generally play off DAT. I've played in New Zealand, Egypt, Sinai, Goa- it's a buzz because very few people have heard music like that coming off DAT with a 15K rig set up outside...

Look for an album of dub mixes from *Pandemonium* and a collection of dubbed-up Killing Joke classics later this year.

PAUL VAN DYK

Only having been DJ'ing since 1991, Berlin-based **Paul van Dyk** has quickly rose among the most sought-after DJ's in the world. Perhaps best known for his collaboration with **Cosmic Baby, Visions Of Shiva**, and his remix of **Humate**'s **"Love Stimulation,"** van Dyk recently made the transition to solo producer, releasing the **Green Valley** ep on Germany's **MFS** label. In Los Angeles for business and to play a party, this rapidly-rising Florida favorite shed some light on "Who is Paul van Dyk and and what is he about?"

TRiP: Where are you originally from? Paul van Dyk: I was born in East Germany and then we kind of escaped to West Germany. I lived for a year in Hamburg and I grew up in Berlin.

T: How did you get into the music?

PvD: I started listening intensely about 8 or 9; not just listening to radio, but finding out who the artists were and how they did (the music). I know everything about my idols like **New Order.** Later, I went to clubs and found it interesting what you could do with two turntables and two records. I practiced at home for about two years before I played out.

T: How long have you been DJ'ing publicly? Do you have a regular resident spot at any clubs in Germany?

PvD: My first time in public was in March of '91. (The club) it's in Berlin, called the **Dub Mission** club, I play there twice a month, the rest of the time I travel.

T: How was the move from DJ'ing to remixing and production?

PvD: It wasn't planned. It started with **Cosmic Baby** and I becoming good friends, he tought me all the first things to (making music). Soon I started doing remixes that were successful, like **Humate** and **Dance 2 Trance.** Cosmic and I decided to do a record together and we did the first two **Visions Of Shiva** records...

T: How do you go about approaching a track for remixing?

PvD: When you listen to the remixes that I've done, they're totally different from the original. What I usually do is pick up the really strong sounds, then I build my own track around it, thinking about what they tried to translate, and keep that feeling.

T: What other remix projects are you working on now?

PvD: I did an ambient track for Effective Force, I did a mix which is a bit more trippy and weird for my music, some more Nervous stuff. I don't want to do remixes for dance projects because tracks I really like, I don't have to remix because they're perfect. For me, it's more exciting to do something like I did with Inspiral Carpets or New Order.

A second ep and a full-length lp from Paul van Dyk is set to be released on MFS later this Fall. Hear him in Gainesville at Simon's September 17th.

ambient
CHILLOUT PHASE TWO • EMIT 0094 • DEEP SPACE NETWORK
"BIG ROOMS" • WOOB • OMICRON "ACROCOSM" • SETI •
TERRE THAEMLITZ "TRANQUILIZER" • MYSTERIES OF SCIENCE
deep space network
woob
omicron
chillout
seti
instinct
instinct records 26 w. 17th st. #502 NY, NY 10011 • send a SASE for a free mailorder catalog
THE ABOVE CDs CAN BE ORDERED DIRECT BY SENDING $12 FOR EACH TITLE ($15 FOR CHILLOUT PHASE 2 (double CD))

TRiP FOTOFILE: GERMANY

T.Confucious of Rabbit In The Moon recently went to Germany to attend Berlin's legendary Love Parade. A massive event attracting over 20,000 people from across Europe to hear a prime selection of both German and worldwide talent over three days. Here are a few of the many moments he was able to steal on film.

From L to R, Clockwise: Sun electric live at Love Parade; A fierce ruling diva at the Love Parade party; Spacetime Continuum's Jonah Sharp; Richie (Plastikman) Hawtin and his brother, Matthew live?; the mass of humanity that is Love Parade.

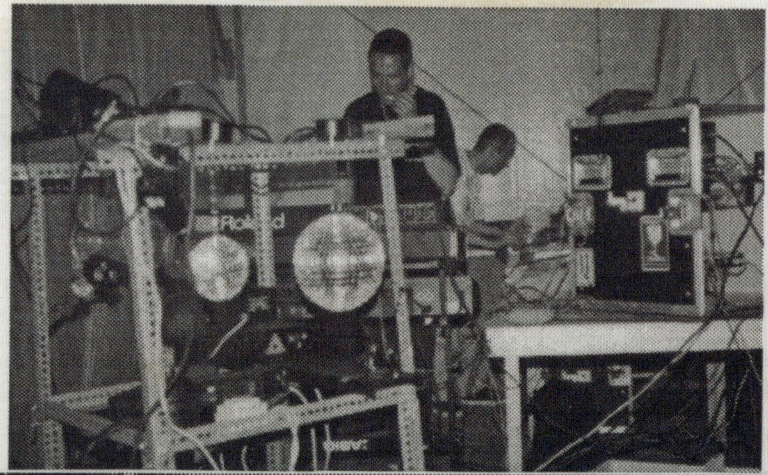

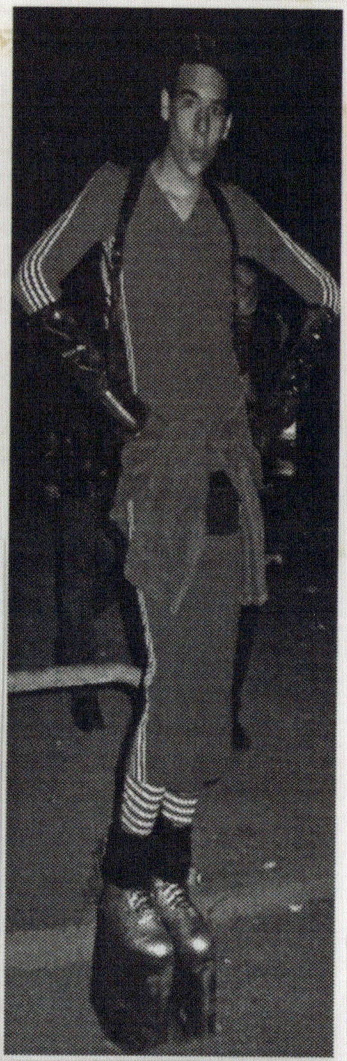

TRiP FOTOFILE: NEW YORK CITY

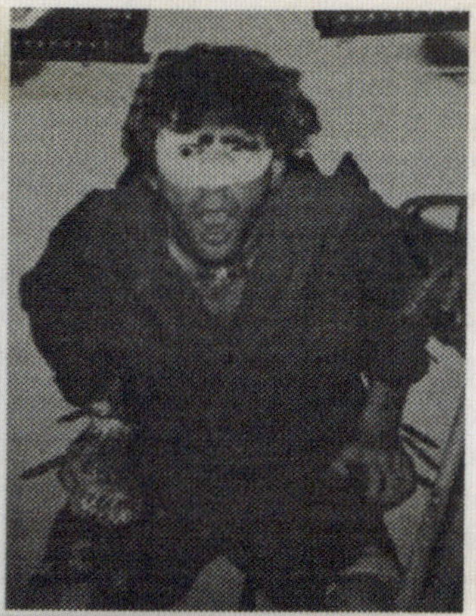

Moments from New Music Seminar from the eyes of the TRiP staff: From L to R, clockwise: Mixmaster Morris in the chill at the ambient only event at The Cooler; Scott Hardkiss in disguise (?) at the Hardkiss Masquerade Ball hours before being broken up by NYPD Blue; Ovum Recordings' Josh Wink; Vinyl Junkies...Mark and Tom of Reload/Global Communication foraging for Strictly Rhythm records at the Eightball shop; Rising High's Caspar Pound with girlfriend, Plavka (Rising High Collective), and a very happy bottle; In the spirit of things...two of the TRiP contingent incognito at the Hardkiss Masquerade Ball.

TRiP FOTOFILE: LOS ANGELES

TRiP Editor-At-Large DJ Three recently went to L.A. to play Public Universe, a two venue event, one dance, one ambient, sponsored by Astralwerks Recordings and L.A.'s Green House Record Pool. Featuring Scott and Robbie Hardkiss from San Francisco, Three and others in the dance venue with 'brother' Gavin and Exist Dance's Mike (Commander Mindfuck) Kandel among the guests responsible for altering minds in the ambient venue. Some picture postcards from behind the eye of our man, Three. From Left to Right, clockwise: Getting down at the dance arena; Mike Kandel of Exist Dance, Getting Down, Part 2; Gavin Hardkiss; letting it all hang out in the ambient venue.

by DJ Jask

Deriving their name from a stag party they were at in which the guy who got to fuck the stripper was known as 'the stickman,' the Toronto via Detroit-based **Stickman** label, in little over a year and a half, has turned the House music world on their collective ear with the unique sound of tracks from **P.J., Biotrans, The Captain, Cappio Bros.,** and of course, **The Stickmen.**

Both as a label and as artists, The Stickmen aka **Greg Zwarich** and **Paul Mintsoulas,** have been tapped for their stylistic diversity, doing remixwork for various artists, even releasing a record on Strictly Rhythm - "Da Real Shit"- with more to follow.

TRiP's Head of the House, **DJ Jask** hooked up with the Stickmen via the fax machine to discuss House music in Canada, European travel, and the finer points of coffee drinking, both hot and over ice.

TRiP: We know where you got the name, so tell us how you got together?

Stickmen: We met in high school where we started DJ'ing together, doing parties and that sort of thing. This was back in '84... Then Greg went away for university and met **John Acquaviva**, before Plus 8 even started. We didn't DJ much in university, but we kept in touch with music via other DJ friends.

T: What made you decide to start the label?

S: After John and Richie started Plus 8, we sort of helped here and there and realized, "Hey, Let's start our own label!" We started buying as much gear as we could afford. Within one year, we had an okay studio and finally released our first record, **STIK001**, "Summer of '87," "D-Talks," "Just Be For The Dawn"... That was January '93. It did pretty good, so we were glad and we got rid of the initial 1000 that we pressed.

T: How would you describe your sound and what do you think sets you apart from other music coming out of New York, Chicago, and Miami?

S: We like most dance music (House, Garage, Techno, etc.) harder tracks as well as vocal house-y stuff. So we would have to say that we go in different directions every release as well as mixing harder sounds with vocals. We don't want to be House guys or techno guys...you know what we mean. New York is New York, and Chicago is Chicago and Toronto is Toronto. We want to have our own sound just like they do.

T: How is the House scene in Canada?

S: **Toronto** and **Montreal** are the biggest scenes for House (in Canada) right now. Especially Toronto. But we think too many DJ's try to be New York DJ's and not have their own style.

T: How did you hook up with P.J., Paul Jacobs? He's really been producing some great tracks on the jazzy tip.

S: Paul Jacobs- we met him by a fluke. We had an ad in a paper because we were selling our old (Akai) S-900 sampler. He came over and bought it. We talked to him and he said he was doing some House/Dance music. He brought a tape over the next day and the rest is history.

T: Do you DJ? What about live gigs?

S: We DJ when we can. No live P.A.'s yet.

T: How did that project on Strictly come about and will there be more projects on other labels in the future?

S: When we were in New York, we stopped by Strictly to say "Hello" and introduce ourselves to them. We kept in touch with **Bari G.** and **George Morel** and when we recorded "The Real Shit," our release schedule was backed up, but we wanted that track out. So we sent it down to Bari and George and they put it out. We hope to more projects (remixes and tracks) for other labels just 'cause you can't put everything you do out on your own label.

T: Those who know you know of your passion for coffee. Having returned from Europe somewhat recently, where is the best coffee you've ever had and what is it?

S: Coffee is a staple here at Stickman Records. If you're not a coffee drinker, then something's wrong. (Despite our travels) the best coffee is our own blend of strong Arabian grounds and Swiss Mocha Almond.

T: What do the two of you do when you're not in the studio, making tracks?

S: We like eating good Italian food and chasing women.

T: You've set an example of stylistic diversity in your music and your label. What advice would you give to young DJ/Producer/Remixers coming up in the industry?

S: Go to Europe for three weeks with John Acquaviva and experience **J. Acquaviva's European DJ Boot Camp.** If you can survive, then you got a chance at making it.

dj charts

PAUL VAN DYK
DJ/Remixer/Producer
Berlin, Germany

Glob 007-Do Y'Wanna Dance
Diss-cuss-Save The Day
Housey Doings-Brothers
Lovechild-Time Travellers
Milch-RMX ep
GAD-Starberry
Rise-The Single
Effective Force-My Time Is Yours
Dajae-It's All Over My Face
Point Black-Meng's Theme

ANDREW DUKE
Cognition Audioworks
Halifax, NS

Christian Vogel-Lambda EP
Love The Machines! EP
Jeff Mills-AX009
Freddie Fresh-Gnarl EP
Hardfloor-Mr. Anderson
Pharmakol-Exotherm
Gizz TV + Walker-Live At The Electro
Mooses On Acid-One Day In The Woods
Synesthasia-Slope
V/A-Quarknosis

BRAD SMITH
Spin Club
Tampa, FL

Dub Tribe-Deep Soul
Rebirth-Migration Of Da Party People
DJ Icee-Beats-A-Rockin'
Pan Position-Elephant Paw
Sound Gathering-The Meaning
Union Jack-Two Full Moons & A Trout
Cloud Innovator-Can You Believe
La Luna-The Ethics EP
Crystal Method-Now Is The Time
Future Sound Of London-Lifeforms

dj charts

GREG & PAUL
The Stickmen
Toronto, ONT

P.J. & Saxy-All I Can Give
Nick Holder Project-Get It Up
Pizzaman-Trippin' On Sunshine
Derrick Carter-various cuts
Perks Of Living Society-Body & Soul
Hardtrax-Hardphunk
Digisoul-P
Guys From Philly-Everybody Move
ZigZag-Heaven
Mathumatix-Blue

DJ KELLY D.
The Sensory Collective
Ft. Lauderdale, FL

Tata Box Inhibitors-Plasmids
In 2 Deep-Strange Movement
Technossomy Elektron Bender
Auto Kinetic-Vsepr Theory
Crawlin' Kingsnake-Snake In The System
XP-Groundhog
Sound Enforcer-Re-Enforcement
Alter Ego-Nude Restaurant
Brainscanner-Spiral Trance
Syn-R-G-LSD Experience

DJ JEFFEE
Mobile Junglism/Junglize Mag
Orlando, FL

Ellis Dee-Big Up Your Chest
Morning Rush EP
DJ DMS & Boneman X-Sweet Vibrations
Chaka Demus & Pliers-Gal Wine
King Of The Jungle-Horn EP
Cold Mission-20 Below Zero EP
Kenny Ken & DJ Monk-Good Body Girl
TDK-It Never Rains In California
KingSize-Cosmos EP
Krome & Time-Visions Of Light

dj charts

SASHA
DJ/Remixer/Producer
U.K.

B.T.-Nocturnal Transmission
Tekuana-Thousand Rains
Underground Sound Of Lisbon-Dance With Me
Yum Yum-Three Minute Warning
Quiver-Twist And Shout
Histerya-Love Nature
Lazonby-Wave Speech
Opus III-Hand In Hand
Rhizone-Fragments
C.A.P.-Rising

KIMBALL COLLINS
Made In The USA/Various U.S.
Orlando, FL

Janice Robinson-Children (J.T. Tribe Mix)
Esenem-Dreamstate
Mogo Djolo-Mogo Djolo
Sasha-Magic
Hed Boys-Girls And Boys
B.T.-Posiedon/Nocturnal Transmission
Tony Di Bart-Do It
Waterlillies-Tempted
Lighter Shade Of Brown-Hey DJ
Lovechild And Rolfe-Time Travellers

DALE CHARLES
Space Records
Los Angeles, CA

Anoesis-EP
RAC-Tangents EP
Sedona-Pulsation
Jung Collective-A.D. Astra
Wubble-U-Petal
Empirion-Quark
Crystal Method-Now Is The Time
V/A-Types
CSL-Dub It
Clubzone-Hands Up (Funked Up Dub)

dj charts

MIXMASTER MORRIS
Irresistible Force
London, U.K.

E. A. R.-Mesmerise EP
Wagon Christ-Phat Lab Nightmare
Starseed Transmission-Metamorphic Illumination
Irresistible Force-Global Chillage LP
Terre Thaemlitz-Tranquilizer LP
Tetsu Inoue-Ambient Otaku
Dreamfish II
Sun Kings-Hall Of Heads
No. 9 Dream-Rhythm & Irrelevance
Ash Ra Tempel-Le Berceau De Cristal

CHARLES UZZELL-EDWARDS
(10 Records I Wish I Had Never Bought)
FAX +49-69/450464 (U.S.)
San Francisco, CA

Ryuichi Sakamoto-Adventures of Chatra
Mike Oldfield-Tubular Bells II
Madrigals Across The Centuries
Tangerine Dream-Anything After 1980
Steve Hillage-L
Neil Norman-Greatest S.F. Hits
Mark Isham-Fire In The Sky Soundtrack
San Sebastian Strings-The Sky/The Sea
John McLaughlin-Adventures / Radioland
Jon Hassell v. 808 State-Voiceprint

JAY PATRICK AHERN
Sunset FM/Aquarhythms
Dublin, Ireland

Drexciya-Deep Sea Dweller
Electronic Dub
Jack Of Swords-The Box
Basic Channel-Radiance
Laurie Anderson-Bright Red LP
Bedouin Ascent-Pavilion Of The New Spirit
Viz-Return Of Billy The Fish
Absolutely Anything By Dan Bell
Sammy Davis, Jr.-The Wham Of Sam
Ani-Love Is The Message

dj charts

DARKHORSE
Natural Music
San Francisco, CA

Skylab-#1
Zion Train-Natural Wonders In Dub
Spacetime Continuum-Pressure
Transonic-Downstream Illusion
Another Fine Day-Life Before Land
Namlook VI-The Caves Of Cubik
V/A-Objects d' Art
Moody Boyz-Recycled EP
Electronic Eye-Closed Circuit
Cabaret Voltaire-The Conversation

TINA BEANS
Megadog/Planet Dog
London, U.K.

Orbital-Are We Here?
Smooth Touch-In My House
Kenny Dope-It's An Ill Groove
Banco De Gaia-Heliopolis (Dog RMX)
The Aloof-Society
Tattoo Project-Digital Sex
Dreadzone-Africa (Live)
Flammable-Step Into The Sound
Dr. Fernando-Ruhr Belgium
Dave Clarke-Red 2 RMXS

BRIAN WALTERS
Mental
New York, NY

Joey Beltram-The Next
Dan Curtin-Parallel
Bandulu-Presence
Bam Bam-Spacetrax
S. James-Alien Transmission
Sabres Of Paradise-Wilmot
Pure Gama
Autechre-Anti EP
Hardfloor-Mr. Anderson
Spacetime Continuum-Pressure

TRiPmag CHARTS

UNDERGROUND DANCE MUSIC CHART

compiled by **DJ THREE**

Rebirth-Embryo
Sven Vath-Robot
Safar-Raheem
Emmanuel Top-Escsta-deal
B.T.-Sasha RMX
Underground Sound of Lisbon (Double Pack RMXS)
Jaydee-Music Is So Special
HOTH-System 3
Republica (Dust Brothers RMX)
Frederick Jorio-The Chant

TRiP HOUSE CHART

compiled by **DJ JASK**

PJ & Saxy-All I Can Give
Voices-Voices In My Head
Believers-Who Dares To Believe
Inner City-Share My Life(RMXS)
DJ EFX-Let It Go
Aphrohead-In The Dark (RMXS)
The Boss-Congo
Deee-Lite-Picnic In The Summertime
X-Celo-Feel It
The Thaichild-Red Pepper Trax, Pt.1

OASiS AMBIENT CHART

compiled by **DJ's ORION, GRUMPY, & MATTY**

Electronic Dub
Spacetime Continuum-Pressure (Horizontal Mix)
Ether-Nite Sequence
Global Communications-76:14
Sub Dub-Babylon Unite EP
Namlook VI-Caves Of Cubik
Sabres Of Paradise-Wilmot
Portishead-Dummy
Ebi-Zen
Other World Collective-Artificial World
Main-Motion Pool

COMPETITION

Plink Plonk is an English label founded a few years back by Paul Rip and a famous U.K. pop star who was instrumental in breaking the sound of techno/rave in the U.S. and Europe by combining the concept of rock gig and club atmosphere.

Dedicated to making good experimental house music, Plink Plonk is the home to other successful dance music artists who wish to release music other than what they are best-known for that stands on its own, without hype and fanfare that their name would bring.

The label has given TRiP four smart looking t-shirts and a slew of stickers for the record boxes of discriminating DJ's, trainspotters, and TRiP readers who can....

Name the U.K. pop star who runs Plink Plonk.

Just write the answer on a postcard to:

Plink Plonk Competition, TRiP Magazeen, 100 East MLK Blvd. Suite 5, Tampa, Florida, 33603 U.S.A. Four correct entries will be drawn on **October 15, 1994**, but everyone who enters will recieve a Plink Plonk sticker.

One entry per person, please.

T-shirt winners will be notified by mail.

RECORD REVIEWS 12"/EP

PJ &SAXY-"All I Can Give" (Stickman/ Canada) Now this is the one record I think everybody and their mother should have, even buy two copies and cherish forever. A good record like this comes once every so often and the Stickmen sure know how to deliver them. But the man responsible for the slammin tracks is gifted producer **Paul Jacobs** and one of my favorites as well. With his unique style venturing between house and jazz He's created his own definition of house. Now with this new track "All I Can Give," PJ does more than give, he goes all out and theres four mixes to prove it to ya. One strong vocal mix to fall in love with. One tribal mix with some of the phattest percussion I've ever heard in a long time. One sax dub which consistsof a deep old school baseline but wait til you hear the sax breakdown, simply sweeeeeet! Last but not least, the dub mix which is on the hard side and if your not careful, this mix will put a hurtin' on them feet, cause you're gonna be mad dancin' on the floor nonstop. Trust me, this is just one of those records ya just gots to get. **(Jask)**

CAP'M STARGAZER & COMMANDER MINDFUCK-Cap'm Stargazer v. Commander Mindfuck (Exist Dance) Jeez! Looks like these guys found some GREAT drugs - not too hard to figure out from the names of the mixes: "Battle on the Tundra" (The Initial Citrus Earthquake Confrontation), "the Mindfuck Introspective Ancestral Channeling Pilgrimage," and "Allied Against Nivar the Floor Killer." I don't know what to say except - BUY THIS SHIT!!! This latest release from Exist Dance is most definitely the weirdest most experimental thing I've heard in a while - all three mixes are very useable. Out of 10, this is an 11. Tweaked. **(IR)**

SABRES OF PARADISE-"Wilmot I & II" (Warp/UK) The new one from **Weatherall** and his Boys, Gary and Jagz. The 12" has an extremely weird Clash-like thing with vocals by Wonder on one side and a pounding techno tune with a very good strong melody. I love it! The 10" features two remixes from the 12", one a ska-infested version and a nice reggae mix by**Scruff**, which wouldn't be out of place if played by a good jungle DJ. But just when it gets really good, it ends-but it still rules! Awesome! **(G)**

SUB DUB-"Babylon Unite" EP (White) This four-track EP offers a little something of everything for each genre in a dub stylee. The title track fuses elements of house, dub, ambience, and techno into a down-to-earth mixture spread evenly over 7+ minutes, while part two is a dubby reflection of the current ambient scene. "Vision Quest" is a dubbed-up percussive chugger of an ethno-ambient house track while "Rhythm Collision" is a true-to-form slice of dub reggae. Warm... **(Orion)**

SOUND ENFORCEMENT-"Re-enforcement" (Rising High/UK) Produced by **Dave Angel**, this is one of my favorite tracks right now. Reinforcement One is a fast techno workout with great strings and some tribal drums thrown in for good measure. Reinforcement Two is a more minimal mix that emphasizes the congas a bit more. **(G)**

EX-30-Magenta 12" (Experimental White) Shapechanger's **Cari Lekebusch** and somebody named David Oesterberg come at you with some hard acid in a good way, very straight ahead no-fucking- around trance. Just one song on each side but that's not necessarily a bad thing. The first 30 have been really good so hopefully the best is yet to come! **(G)**

EX-30-Magenta 7" (Experimental White) This bonus 7" is two sides of pure ambient techno- one side is smooth and jazzy with a slow breakbeat, the other is more atmospheric and techno-y. Really nice morning stuff for listening or dancing. Find one if you can. **(Orion)**

YOUNG AFRICAN PIONEER-"Caught In The Act" (Unclassified) This latest release on the Unclassified label is a smooth midtempo deep house track with two mixes. The vocal takes the light bongos and adds a male tribal vocal that sort of uplifts as the track builds subtly. The instrumental drops the vocal and makes the arrangement more driving and thumpy. Also check the bonus beats... **(PW)**

TANZMUSIK-"Tan Tangue" EP (Rising High/UK) Five experimental electronic soundscapes make up this debut ep from this artist from the Land Of The Rising Sun. The first track, "Wood Neckrace/Sinsekai" is a manic electro-influenced thumper of experimental beats that dribbles down into dripping sounds and counterpointed melodies. "Sight" is a beautiful, delicate ambient piece, laced with 808 hi-hats over the top and a steady kick. The flipside's other tracks are excursions in beat-oriented experimental electronics. Unclassifiable but worth listening. **(Orion)**

CRYSTAL METHOD-"Now Is The Time" (City Of Angels) Debut for new label, City of Angels, is quite a nice four track EP. The logoside is a decent trancer with Wax Trax era **GTO** samples and groovy breakbeats. There is also an ambient dub version and two more good dancing tunes. **(G)**

BEDOUIN ASCENT-"Pavilion Of The New Spirit" (Rising High/UK) Six track experimental techno from those mystery men Bedouin Ascent. Nothing that is really for the dance floor here, but definitely for the chillout rooms. **(G)**

SIN-"Overdrive" (Matrix) Another record from**Sean Deason**, one of the most talented new producers. Three separate tracks and one remix. Overdrive comes in two versions, one an up-tempo hard techno tune with the title repeated over and over. The Submix is slower and more bass heavy. Side 2 had two separate songs: one another minimal hard Detroit track and the other a beautiful ambient-ish track. **(G)**

FEEDBACK-"Element" (F Communications/France) Created by **Simon Hartley**, this is four tracks of trippy minimal trance with spiralling atmosphereics. All 4 tracks float around your head long after you've stopped listening to it. **(G)**

X-CELO-"Feel It" (Stickman/Canada) One word for this, "X-Celo-Lente`!" Produced by Jon Denisi and Chris Jordan. It seems these guys have that fresh formula for making good quality house music. "Feel It" is a good example, too. Nothing but hard beats, flaming hi hats, wicked organ stabs, and slammin vocals. The Steelcase Sub Mix is the standout here but one should check out the Klubb Kidz Dub, more in the garagey side, but kickin' much booty!!!!! **(Jask)**

STERAC-"Sitting On Clouds" (100% Pure/NL) Steve Rachmad from Outland/Spiritual in Holland creates a very emotional, mellow, early morning masterpiece. Also included is another version of "Sitting on Clouds" and a second song transpose that is a return to the old days of Detroit. **(G)**

SHAZZ-"A View Of Manhattan" (F Communications/France) Five track EP of beautiful, deep New York house tracks. The best being Ln's remix of "Marathon Man." As usual somethinggreat from F. **(G)**

FREQ-"Green" EP (Matrix) Yet another Freq ep from the mind of Sean Deason. Four tracks on limited edition clear vinyl, Green opens with a sweeping intro track, long synth washes glide over repeating analog blurps, a kick drum and hi-hats coming in almost at the end to push the track into the next phase. Track two is a driving pounder with a bittersweet melody line for your mind that flows behind the drum track and bassline created for your body. On the flip, track 3 is one of those moody mellow tracks that Sean does that I like so much, perfect early morning stuff for dancing or listening. The EP closes out with a slow groovy percussion piece that builds up and twitters off. More excellent stuff from Matrix. **(PW)**

SYNESTHASIA-"Slope" (Harthouse/Germany) Another typical German trance 12" from Harthouse. Pounding beats with a dark, moody feel that has become the norm. Nothing new, but still good. **(G)**

NUW IDOL-"Wu Maze"/"Drimax Phenyl" (Electro Audio Response/UK) The third release in the recently restarted E.A.R. division of Plink Plonk comes from Nuw Idol. The standard here is Drimax Phenyl, a furious hard trancer, that does serious damage on a loud system. Wu Maze is also a harder trance/euro sounding track that speeds up to 200 bpm before breaking down into luscious strings. **(G)**

LOVE AND ROCKETS-"Body And Soul" (American) With various members spotted at L.A. raves and chillout events over the past couple of years, post-goth rockers **Love And Rockets** choose to reinvent themselves for this first single for their American Recordings debut***Hot Trip To Heaven***. The album version is a 14-minute long opus of synthchimes and droning guitars as**Daniel Ash**'s voice seeps in through the mix, before the drums kick in and return us to indie land. Remixes from both**Secret Knowledge** and **Higher Intelligence Agency** are what really make this 12". Kris Needs' Secret Knowledge project turns in a manic trance mix on the A-side while the B-side opens with a slow stomper of a remix with thunderous drums-awesome! HIA's Dark Side Of The 12th Moon mix is a way leftfield whacked out dub. The 12" ends with a non-album track, "Coyote," an odd Spaghetti Western of a track with slide guitar and harmonica and radio edit. L&R did very well with the ep of Swing a couple years back, and I'm interested in exploring this new direction in full-length. **(PW)**

MUSHROOM-"The Fungus Amongus" EP (Magick Eye/UK) Mushroom is the collective name for this collaboration between the **Magic Mushroom Band, Astralasia,** and **UVX.** Using samples from the Magic Mushroom Band's *Spaced Out* album, Astralasia and UVX have created and remixed two new tracks. UVX's Time Just Takes It is a dark bubbling slow acid groover while Astralasia's Slap Tongue Squeaky Bonk is my pick, a bit of upliftiing warm ambience with treated guitar textures and subtle pulsing percussion. **(Orion)**

Jack Of Swords-"The Box" (Sabres Of Paradise/UK) One side is a slow dubbed up twisted tale of lost love. The vocal is from **Velvet Underground's "The Gift."** Not something to listen to while you're alone. The Angel of Death Dub is a normal Sabres trancer with cool effects. This label is still the shit! Each release keeps getting further out there. **(G)**

STEVE FISK-"Express God" (RMXS) (Astralwerks) Nirvana producer **Steve Fisk**'s track from the third installment of *Excursions In Ambience* gets retreated with a mix by Exist Dance's **Cap'm Stargazer and Commander Mindfuck**, a bizarre mix of twisting synth lines, gurgling 303, and breakbeats with Fisk's crazed rantings interspersed. The other side has two other mixes which are more ambient with looped beats run backwards and forwards. Definitely way out there. **(PW)**

AMBIENT TEMPLE OF IMAGINATION-"Mystery School, Vol. 1" (Visible) Richard Sun and Visible's **Seofon** comes up with some very cool ambient tunes. A full length journey through pure ambience, loads of percussion, and spooky atmosphere. Not exactly groundbreaking, but at least worth more than a listen. **(G)**

CHAKA DEMUS & PLIERS-"Gal Wine" (Mango/UK) Here we go! Although not the first dancehall artsts to record a jungle track (i.e. SuperCat & General Levy previously), **Demus & Pliers** have the distinction of having the first jungle record released on a major label. (Mango is a division of Island.) Recruiting **M-Beat**, who are hot off their massive UK track "Incredible" (which featured General Levy's live toasting over speedy, smoking jungle breakbeats), for the mixdown was no slouchy move. This one's got an updated old school breakbeat with all the jungle elements (including a nice, moody keyboard intro) tucked neatly into place. What really makes this track stand out is the soothing, soulful (not to menntion catchy) vocals. Chaka Demus & Pliers' voices are of the lazily, sexy style which instantly sets this jungle track apart from the many others that consist of the more familiar rude-boy dancehall samples. A nice change of pace. Watch for more dancehall artists following this record's footsteps with jungle tracks of their own. **(Jeffee)**

BE-ZET-"Blue Illusion" (Eye-Q/Germany) Three versions of the same song. My favorite being the Flat Horizon mix. Mid-tempo (128 bpm) trance with chilling chords and a beautiful melody. **(G)**

BLAKKAT-"Blakkat" (Bush/UK) Another release for **Felix da Housecat**. Phase 033 is an interesting hard house affair with what sounds like "Strings Of Life" samples cut up and thrown in. **Mark Bell**'s Medic mix on side B is the shit, hard kick, tribal drums and a typical Felix vocal and acid sounds. Full of energy and very loud compared to most of the rest of Felix's productions. **(G)**

DAISY GLOW-"Right On" (Zoe Magik) **Daisy Glow** doing the house swing on us this time. Produced by **Mouse** and **Kelix**, the people responsible for that "Come On" track on La Casa records. "Right On," a feel good vocal house track spreading what's missin in this hectic world, that is unity. That's right Brothers and Sister DJ's - Get with it! Discover this record and don't be fooled over the label. Zoe Magik has gained back my respect for them with this 12" **(Jask)**

ROBOTMAN-"DooDaDoo" (RMXS)

Dancing About Architecture

-A Music Column By DJ Three-

As **Steve Martin** once said, "Talking about music is like dancing about architecture." Through the final days of summer there has been an abundance of great music spinning on turntables. Now more than ever the lines are blurring between styles of music with the 125 to 135 bpm range being the common ground. A sound that sits right on the line between house and techno has taken hold, while House becomes the new buzzword.

Lots of DJ's are back with new music. Most impressive is **Sven Vath**'s ***The Harlequin, The Robot, and The Belly Dancer*** LP. Not at all typical German trance, Sven has created a very original dance music, fusing many elements, yet without obvious influence and interwoven by excellent ambient segments. **Justin Robertson** returns as **Lion Rock** with "Tripwire". 3 mixes by himself, The Prankster's Soundtrack being the most interesting...808 rimshots, backwards electro breaks and dub bassline. A **David Holmes** mix as well, which is far from his best. Holmes has struck gold, however, with his **Robotman-"DooDaDoo"** remixes...the mix entitled David Holmes Mix does the business in a serious acid house way. **Alter Ego-"Nude Restaurant"** on Harthouse features Holmes mixes which will send fans of Detroit smiling. Ambient and experimentalists will love the **Black Dog** mix. **Laurent Garnier** and Co. at **F Communication** have been busy putting out some very diverse and excellent music. St. Germain's "Walk So Lonely" Nova Nova's "Falicpa," and Iberia's "Neuva Era EP"-all musts for fans of house, progressive and techno, respectively. Garnier looks set to drop one bomb of an LP if his single is any indication. The one-sided promo has 2 mixes by Garnier, one very **D-Jax** in sound and one more smooth and trancey-both very underground with Chicago/Detroit influence. Look for these with hot remixes by **LFO** and **Carl Cox** out now. **Sasha** fans take note, the Voodoo Dub of "Magick" (light years better than any of the other mixes) will only be available to the public on CD single!?! Sasha's best work since the Hedingarna Qat Mix is on its way-remixes of Music Now artist **B.T.**'s "Embracing The Future"...but not before the release of B.T.'s new 12" "Nocturnal Transmission," an excellent follow-up that always sends people to the booth looking for info. **Ron Trent**'s "Altered States" remixes on D-Jax have been re-issued, for those who know. For those not familiar, it'd be safe to guess that the **Terrace** remix had major influence on Slam's "Positive Education." **Zach Roberts**, possibly Detroit's most underrated, is back on his **Ind-X** label with "Spy Vs. Spy," three tracks co-produced by Eddie Watson that would fit in anyone's set that's into Soma, Sabres, or Exploding Plastic.

Paul van Dyk has released his 12", "Pumpin'" which is well produced Eurochart oriented trance ala **Quivver** or **Flammable**...a definite crowd pleaser. Dave Beer's **Back To Basics** club is now a label as well and the **HOTH**-Systems EP is the first release. 3 mixes-one for any floor, mix 3 is my favorite. **Jack Prongo** comes back on Fresh Fruit/NL with "K-Ucci". L.A.'s **Taylor** recorded a new track recently, his last being a collaboration on Planet 4/UK called "Ask Me", by GTR. No title on my cassette, but this cut is for the floor...bouncy house percussion, acidy basslines, and wicked breaks. **The Believers**' "Dare To Believe In Me" remix double pack on Ministry Of Sound is worth the price for the Roach Motel Acid Dub if you dig the Plastik/Robotman style house. The highly opinionated **Dave Clarke** hits big with the **Red 2** remixes on Reload...hard to deny this one. **The Waterlillies**' first single from their album "Tempted," features a wonderful remix by **Spooky**, who needs to release a new 12" soon, as "Little Bullet" still stays in my box!

What else...**Underground Sound of Lisbon's "So Get Up"** is a Sound Factory smash now available as a double pack on **Tribal America**. Included is the ominous accapella, the **Vasquez** remix and the eurotrancish, "Age Of Love" sampled "Dance With Me," and the most wicked original, acid pumped mix. The Grid go a step back in the right direction with "Rollercoaster." However its Lion Rock's mixes that are doing the business. A 12" by Emmanuel Top that is better known as "Latex Culture" is a kick-ass acid track. Track it down if you can.

Deja Vu-"Speed Of Love" (Cowboy/UK)...Spruceters Dub is the first on **Cowboy** that has moved us in a long time...progressive house/acid. **The Dust Brothers** have two more remixes out; The **Prodigy**'s "Voodoo People" (XL) and **Republica**'s "Out Of This World." (DeConstruction) which is one of their best, but at this time promo only with no official release date. **Lemon 8**-"Model 8" (Energy 101/Belgium) has slowly but surely become a monster for all types of DJ's...sounds like one heck of a Plastikman record, but I don't believe it's Mr. Hawtin. **Lazonby** is back to follow "Sacred Cycles" with "Wave Speech," which is another epic track, but it doesn't hit with the urgent groove we've become used to from this producer. The only big drawback is the awful sound quality...

Bassex is an L.A. label who give us Rebirth-"Embryo." If you dug the King Size Aphrohead remix, check this out, as it's in the same vein, yet very weird. The b-side is wicked club tempo funk with hip-hop beats (ala Dust Brothers). **Bush** sublabel **Grass Green** have two excellent acid, house, groove-laden 12"'s out, MicroGrooves EP and Housey Doings...a third is out as you read this. **Derrick Carter**'s Shock Therapy is crazy house with wicked, bassy percussion and is also available on import on Exploding Plastic/UK. **Fred Giannelli**'s

continued on Page 36

(Nova Mute) Originally released on Definitive last year and released with a **Plastikman** mix a couple of months ago, **Richard Michaels'** classic gets the big push from Nova Mute. Included on two separate 12" 's are Plastikman's Acid House mix, **David Holmes'** mix, an Exploding Plastic mix, Richie's Drum Dub, Hard House Dub, and 808 Mix. If you don't already have the original, you can't miss it a second time around. **(G)**

ZIG ZAG-"The EP" (Stickman/Canada) Four luscious house tracks from **Ron Allen**. Really tasty feel good cuts on side A to choose from, "Special" and "Everybody Free." Smokin piano riffs and well chosen vocals. Side B goes deeper than deep with "Da Pressure," a solid tribal house track with wicked vocal chants. "Heaven," the last cut is house with a touch of soul. Another great Stickman record is born again...**(Jask)**

FRIENDS, LOVERS, & FAMILY-"Signs Of Rebirth"/"Signals Of Decay" (Rising High/UK) Three tracks of dark and experimental techno ambience. Side A has one song that is similar in style to the Diamond LiL's track from the Forus EP. Side 2 has two songs, one with a jazzy piano and one sparse ambient ditty that is very nice. **(G)**

PROTOTYPE 909-"Karma" (Instinct) New three tracker from New York's **Prototype 909**. Karma is a very solid track with a long intro and good 303 work and a hard kick midway through. The two B side cuts are also good, minimal acid workouts and should not be ignored. **(G)**

SHOCK THERAPY-"Enjoy It" (Blue Cucaracha) A release from **Derrick Carter**'s Intellinet distributed Blue Cucaracha label. Three seriously infectious house cuts that you can't help but dance to. More great stuff from one of the best dj's on the planet. **(G)**

FLOPPY DISC JOCKEYS-"Come On" (La Casa) New house label from San Francisco. Burstin' out on the scene doing some serious damage. For their first release these guys pump out some really good deep dub garage. "Come On," comes in four mixes, all good. Funky horns, chunky vocals, phat beats, slammin strings, smooth organ riffs and bouncin baselines are just a little description of what to expect. Can't wait fot the next follow-up! **(Jask)**

MORNING RUSH EP (Firm Handed/UK) Totally wicked jungle debut from Firm Handed! The breakbeats on the A side are cut-up and pasted in a stop, spurt, stop and go fashion with vicious bass whoomps dropped in between, making your body shake "convulsion style"! Buju Banton bits and obscure vocal samples complete the picture. The B side comtains two totally playable tunes with the second breaking down into a heart-melting Paula Abdul vocal sample! Much respect for this excellent debut! **(Jeffee)**

FUTURE SOUND OF LONDON-"Lifeforms 1-7" (Astralwerks) After all the hype and hassle surrounding this long-awaited collaboration between **Liz Fraser** of the Cocteau Twins and self-proclaimed chaos merchants Future Sound Of London, I fully expected something to knock my socks off. It doesn't. Don't get me wrong, what we have here is choice FSOL-innovative deep beats, mind-altering ambient soundscapes, THAT voice...but it's not the epic masterpiece that hype created. I wonder how the Meat Loaf/ Peter Gabriel duet is? **(PW)**

MUSLIMGAUZE-"Infidel" EP (Extreme) If you're a fan of the ethnic percussive trance of **Exquisite Corpse** and **Psychick Warriors Ov Gaia**, Muslimgauze is another artist recording in the genre well worth checking out. While the Muslimgauze outlook is quite political and the music not always suited to the dancefloor, this EP of remixes of older and new material will surely be the tool to gain some much needed exposure for this talent. Five mixes of "Infidel" (from the forthcoming *Citadel* album) are featured, each maintaining the basic integrity of the song while adding a slight spin. Two of the versions add a house-influenced groove, while the others range from the tribalesque to almost beatless ambience. In an unfortunate era where bad songs are given to big name producers and DJ's to reconstruct and overhaul and essentially create someting out of nothing, it is refreshing to hear how well "Infidel" has been tailored to different settings. Even the three extra tracks, some dating back to as early as January 1990, sound fitting here. This package, and anything else frome Australia's Extreme label, comes highly recommended. **(AD)**

SCHOTOMA-"UV Index" EP (Tape) Six tracks of ambience that range from brooding post-industrial darkness and experimental electronics to slowly ascending minimal pulsing excursions and a bubbling spliffed out (but not dubby) title track. Mostly very deep and chilled out, this ep's tracks average around the 7:00 mark (one clocks in at a hefty 17:29), making for perfect mixing in and out, under and on top of other textures. Excellent production really makes this ep shine. For more info, fax 1+902.422.1262. **(Orion)**

COLD MISSION-"20 Below Zero" EP (Reinforced/UK) Pioneering hardcore breakbeat label, **Reinforced**, has always released music that fits in no category. Not rave. Not jungle. Just music that's ahead of it's time. This latest 4-track ep from Reinforced founder **Dego**, paints a surreal sound, proving that ingenuity is alive and kickin' in the hardcore studios. Live jazz trumprt and uplifting indecipherable vocal samples require close listening, while the off-beat drum measures promote more of a spacy, tribal shuffle as opposed to full-on rave dance. This is one smooth piece of jazzy, intelligent breakbeat. **(Jeffee)**

NICK EAST-"East Of Index" EP (Drop Bass Network) Milwaukee's **Drop Bass Network** is known for heavy-duty techno and their latest release is no exception. After beginning as an outlet for material from **DJ ESP** (Woody McBride) and later other American artists, DBN's first release from an European group is the four-track East of Index EP from **Nick East**, a duo with members from Berlin and Copenhagen. Distorted bass drums that bounce around with the weight of a sledgehammer and dirty percussion that will send running those who like their techno with a glossy sheen is the rule on this no-holds-barred in yer face brand of hardcore. "Increased Outline" takes an acid line and mangles it with reverb, while "Nose Job" is content to the rhythm. "Access" with nothing but percussion with plenty of 32nd and 64th notes to liven things up. "Mood Matcher" ends the EP on a much calmer note after the 165 bpm+ madness of the three previous cuts. Here we have a restrained song that actually grooves along (as opposed to barging straight through!) to bubbling acid bits and an occasional string refrain. A very competent package from a label that deserves your support. **(AD)**

VAPOURSPACE-"Vista Humana" (ffrr) Remixes of a track from the debut Vapourspace LP with mixes by **Nev**, the **Stickmen**, and **Mark Gage** himself. Nev's mix is a pretty much indecipherable bleepy and bloppy digifunk mix, as Gage turns in a minimal Plastikman-esque strip down. The flipside's Sleepwalker Mix by **J. Mark Andrus** (Gage in disguise?) leans a bit more on the house tip but still retains some of the trancy techno feel of the original's synth melody while the Stickmen turn in a chugging stripped hardhouser for their first major label remix gig that is the Stick Guys all the way. Some pretty interesting reinterpretations here that I dare DJ's to fit into their sets. **(PW)**

COSMIC BABY-"Futura" EP (Logic) Three new **Cosmic Baby** tracks composed especially for **Futura**, a 'techno-ballet' devised and produced by Germany's **Pyro Space Ballet** company; "Theme," "Rebirth," and "Transformation." Two of the three tracks are very minimal and ethereal, almost Dead Can Dance-like in tone with droning bass tones and female vocals, while the third is more electronic, building up to a trademark Cosmic trance finish. An interesting effort that is definitely worth a listen. **(Orion)**

EX-29-Diffusion (Experimental White) Side A is an uptempo, pounding trance track that is extremely good while the B side is a little odd sounding but nonether less, still very good. **(G)**

HIGHER LEVEL-"Visions Of Light" (Zodiac/UK) There's currently another music movement resurfacing in Britain. And that music, believe it or not, is 'rave' music! Remember stompin' piano lines and butt-shakin' breakbeats? They're back! There are just as many 'Happy Hardcore' rave tunes coming out of England as there are jungle tunes. And this one isn't jungle! Higher Level are really long-time Suburban Base purveyors of breakbeat, **Krome & Time** (along with their new label, Zodiac) bringing back that feeling of 'rave unity.' Only this time, the music's got more intelligence. The faster beats have more bounce and the samples have that "where have I heard that before' familiarity. Both of these tracks feature irresistible paino lines, girl vocal samples, and some rhythmic, Detroit-style keyboard bleeps. Revved-up and dancy! **(Jeffee)**

DJ SOUL SLINGER & NICK HEAVEN-"Ethiopia" (Tape) This track opens with a blurping, atmospheric 303, a slow, chunky breakbeat, clarinet, and an ethno-tribal chant, before evolving into a jungle break that makes one think of **4 Hero**. Poor production hurts here, but this is nonetheless a way cool track. Ambient jungle, indeed! Some crazy shit from the urban jungle of the Big Apple. For more info, call 1+212.343.0532.**(Orion)**

SAPIANO-"Spike It!" (Sabrettes/UK) Written by **Tony Sapiano** and engineered by **Pete Lazonby,** "Spike It!" is a pounding techno jobber with some good sounds and an interesting breakdown. There is a Weatherall/ David Hedger ambient mix on the flip side. Another consistent quality release from the Pinkies! **(G)**

DJ EFX-"Let It Go" (Strictly Rhythm) Get ready for the acid house throbber of the century. **EFX** at it again and comes through in a big way this time. From beginning to the end, it's a massive 303 journey through Amsterdam to New York to Chicago to San Francisco, and even Tampa. Seriously, this ain't no joke-this track soars like no other, sky is not the limit on this one, due to the fact that this is just wicked. Hands in the air siren sounds, euro-synth stabs , acid basslines, pumping beats- what more is there to say? Vicious! Side B contains a tribalish but funky track called "Feelin Kinda Lovely." Definitely a tribal house stomper with massive proportions. Get this acid freaks! **(Jask)**

BLAKE BAXTER-"Touch Me" (Logic) The sexy one returns with some nasty house, this time with the **X-Press 2** touch. Hard house beats with Blake's 'fuck me' lyrics all wrapped up nicely in a trademark **Rocky & Diesel** remix. **(G)**

ESSER'AY-"Forces" (KMS) Master Reese cooks up a monster old school Detroit classic with altered vocal samples, fierce drums, and heartwrenching synth lines. And I haven't even told you about the **Carl Craig** or **Ron Trent/Chez Damier** mixes... Awesome! **(G)**

AJAX-"Evening Chanting" (Infinite Love) A mysterious slab of white vinyl in a white sleeve limited to 500, this is an Eastern-flavored piece of blippy percussion-driven Eurotrance in six mixes. My advice: check the Technodub, Trancendental Trip, and Evening Drums mixes for best results. **(PW)**

HARDFLOOR-"Mr. Anderson"/"Fish & Chips" (Harthouse/Germany) Though their egos cause them to rail perhaps a bit too loudly against those many copyists that abound, **Bondizio** and **Zenker** definitely do have their own sound that no one can seem to touch. Not content to rest on their laurels, Hardfloor continue to break nw ground when others are still trying to rewrite their "Acperience." On this 12", the duo give us two new tracks, each an oddly-named nine-minute long masterpiece. "Mr. Anderson" ditches the typical builds and extended drum rolls for which they've become known and instead uses a sparse four note bassline along with growling flanged 303's that become quite manic but avoid peaking and striving to be anthemic. "Fish & Chips" is absolutely hilarious in a subtle way. Though tight, plenty funky, and acidic, there is an everpresent clip clopping hook skipping merrily along throughout this cut that leaves me thinking of that old electro hit, "Popcorn," every time I hear this! As expected, another marvelous piece of work from the leaders of the second acid wave. Let's hope a full-length album is soon to come. **(AD)**

PROGRESSION-"Your Mind" (Sorted) Micro and **Vicious Vic** are at the helm of this Sorted but funky breakbeat trance track. Four mixes to choose from here, but the last mix on the B-side is my favorite. Jazzy horns with cool breaks is all you need to know. If you like the harder stuff, than this is your cup of tea. **(Jask)**

VOYAGER 8-"We Left The Planet" (Synewave) The fourth release from **Damon Wild**'s new label is a collaboration between him and **Steve Stoll** (Datacloud). "We Left The Planet" is a bleepy, bubbly trancer that really does the job on the floor. "Planets In Motion" is an elemental mix of "We Left...," while "Transistor Rhythm" is a harder-edged 303 track that is very nice, and "Phobos II" is quite possibly a remix of one of the tracks on Steve's ep on Probe. **(G)**

FIDELITY BITES-"Byte Me" EP (Visible) Three track red vinyl from San Francisco. With a title like "D'Funk," I can tell that this is probably a little too funky for the Grumpster-but I listened to it anyway. Well, it IS too funky for me, but the Subfonic Mix is good-less funk. The **Darwin Chamber** Mix is even better because it is just breakbeats and the ever-so-slight aroma of funk. **(G)**

MUSIC MADNESS-"Confusion" (Power Music Trax) More of that psychotic **DJ Duke** stuff to make your ears rumble for days. With hard tribal beats and that familiar Wild Pitch string, you know what to expect. **(Jask)**

MATH-U-MATIX-"Blue" (Definitive) Starting with an old Black man saying, "Ooo, I ain't got the blues no more, I say..." this record launches into one of the coolest, most hypnotic, deep hard house records I've heard in awhile. Building layer after layer-pounding kick that sounds great on a big system, flaring hi-hats, snare, crying female vocal sample, string synth- that grows and gets more hypnotic with every measure before holding back the intensity and breaking down slightly then building back up to a big finish. That's just the A side. The B-side's two mixes are just slightly different variations on the theme pronouncing different elements. This one's already climbing the charts in Europe-believe the hype and see what the buzz is about! This'll make you feel good! **(PW)**

MOTION LOTION-"The Sound" (Strictly Rhythm) Jason Nevins' newest project is the phattest! Bringing back tthat funky disco sound for your platform pleasure, dancefloors beware when this is played! Be prepared to be danced upon wildly. House with a chunk full of funk! **(Jask)**

PEELO-"Neena"/"I Need Love" (Stickman/Canada) "Neena" is a deep, oscillating Chicago-style minimal acid house track that sweeps and swirls over your head and through your body while "I Need Love" also visits the Windy City with a wicked Trax jack track that reminds me of "I've Lost Control." Produced by **David Alvarado,** this is an awesome pair of tracks that really show his versatility and should help him to earn the props he deserves! **(PW)**

JOHNNY VICIOUS V. M.F.S.B.-"T.S.O.P." (Network/UK) Johnny Vicious is one bad ass producer. He gets much props for this pulsating disco/house stomper injected with venomous stabs, bionic breaks, a slammin' tribal breakdown, and that Soul Train anthem. A great record for the peak of your set. **(Jask)**

CREATIVE FORCE-"I'm Not The Same" (Centrestage/UK) Victor Simonelli is back with vocalist **George Eliezer**. This follow-up to "It's So Good" doesn't have quite the same intensity. Harder and deeper, in a good way, Victor did a good job on the production, but flip to the Lifeforce remixes for harder beats on the dub that'll blow your mind away. **(Jask)**

LP/COMPILATIONS

ORBITAL-Snivilization (ffrr) The Hartnoll Brothers have released their third album and this time it has a title. But don't expect the smooth and flowing Orbital of albums past, Snivilization asks us to listen and accept a harder and more diverse sound. Even with the changes, however, these quality tracks are all uniquely Orbital- no mistaking that! Some highlights include the 1-minute 'jungle' track,"Are We Here?" and "Sad But True" with Alison Goldfrapp's vocals played against a heavy bass line. Listen for Goldfrapp's vocal appearances throughout the album, adding extra warmth and depth in all the right places. A new chapter in Orbital's library well worth checking out. **(JR)**

GLOBAL COMMUNICATIONS-74:15 (Dedicated) After *Pentamerous Metamorphosis*, their amazing rework of Chapterhouse's latest LP, finally comes the long-anticipated full-length debut release from the other side of the celebrated duo **Reload**. The lighter side of human emotion, Global Communications use track times to allow the listeners mind to take them wherever the music leads them without the preconcieved notions that words can give. The result is a luscious journey for the auditory senses that stimulates more than your ears, but your imagination, your heart, and your soul. Simply one of the finest releases of the year. And worth the wait. **(Orion)**

DAN CURTIN-The Silicon Dawn (Peacefrog/UK) Even though Cleveland is 3 (?) hours from Detroit, **Dan Curtin** is one producer that gets honorary citizenship and is a should be considered for membership as one of the 'new breed' of Detroit. Over the last couple of years, Curtin has been releasing splendid Detroit tracks on his own **Metamorphic** label and more recently on **Peacefrog**. ***The Silicon Dawn*** is a complex exercise in melody and percussion, gliding easily from ambient techno and driving classic Detroit tracks to deep techno jazz that even stirred the house heads here at **TRiP** Towers. Nine short soundtracks that sound better listened to as a whole but stand alone just as timelessly. **(PW)**

KEN ISHII-Reference To Difference (Sublime/Japan) Japan's **Ken Ishii**, over his handful of releases on **Apollo, R&S, ESP,** and **Plus 8** has established himself as one of electronic music's leading innovators. Debuting the newly formed **Sublime** label from Japan, here on ***Reference To Difference***, Ishii offers up electronic tracks with a **YMO** influence as well as some strange but beautiful experimental tracks. As always with Ken Ishii, it takes a listen or two to get your head around his work, but once you do, it leaves a lasting impression. **(Orion)**

TIMESHARD-Crystal Oscillations (Planet Dog/UK) The twelve tracks on this CD come together to form one complete sonic journey. The first three songs have a harder techno edge to them. Songs four and five are excursions into dubland. Six is a Middle Eastern thing that makes you think you're actually there. Seven to ten bring down from the heavens a cosmic chill of ambience that will leave you breathless and wanting more. Excellent. **(G)**

SPACETIME CONTINUUM-Sea Biscuit (Astralwerks) Placed into the spotlight after his live collaboration with 'rave guru' **Terence McKenna**, ***Alien Dreamtime***, San Francisco's **Jonah Sharp** aka **Spacetime Continuum** won the admiration of ambientos worldwide for his unique approach to ambience. Now, Sharp returns with ***Sea Biscuit***, Spacetime's proper full-length debut. Without the chatter of McKenna as a distraction, Sharp stretches out, exploring textures that he was only able to touch upon on Dreamtime- floating, soaring, pulsating... A release that moves the body, cleanses the mind, and warms the soul. **(Orion)**

ARPEGGIATORS-Selected Remix Works (Harthouse/Germany) Four of the **Arpeggiators** better known songs are remixed by the likes of **Braincell, Norman,** and **Resistance D.** The stand out here is Norman's version of "Discover Your Innerself". All of the songs are around the 150 range. "Liquid Sky" is a bonus track on CD. **(G)**

DRUM CLUB-Drums Are Dangerous (Instinct) With their first album, ***Everything Is Now***, the **Drum Club** established themselves as a credible force in the ambient and trance arenas on tracks like "Spaced Out, Locked In" and "I Really Feel" with their atmospheric and dubbed up tribal vibe. Now the Drum Club return, possibly influenced by the success of their self-titled club night, with ***Drums Are Dangerous***, an effort that will test the duo of **Charlie Hall** and **Lol Hammond**'s ability to capture the clubs. The first few tracks have a distinctly Drum Club feel but are more on the clubby side, with vocals from **Maxine Harvey** (who sang on "Sound System" from the first LP) and former **N-Joi** singer **Saffron**. *Drums Are Dangerous*' latter half is more chilled out in texture with tracks like the slow, dubby techno of "Reefer" and "De-Lushed," a track made up of samples from indie shoegazers **Lush** leading the way. While this album is a good listening experience, I think it's the remixes that will open this album up to the dancefloor. **(PW)**

V/A-Analog Heaven: A Collection Of NY Acid Tracks (Instinct) Compiled by **Dietrich** and **Taylor** of **Prototype 909**, this twelve track collection is a good representation of the New York acid scene, with tracks licensed from **Experimental, Industrial Strength**, and **Direct Drive**. The tracks range from the blissful acid of "Nightvision" by Nuclear Sun to the demented hardcore of Adam X's "Phull Throttle." Also included is the new Prototype 909 single "Karma" and the wonderful "Propellor" by Tiny Objects in Space. **(G)**

DJ Culture 2: The Stress Records Compilation (Moonshine) Moonshine delivers this second collection of progressive house choons from the **Stress** label, this time tapping L.A's **Steve Loria** and Florida's **Kimball Collins** to fill the shoes of **Sasha** and **Dave Seaman** from an American point of view. Each DJ does a good job of displaying their funky styles, Loria plays more smooth and house-y with vocals while Kimball Collins is deeper, chunkier, faster, and more driving. If you're on this tip, it's a nice travelling CD. **(PW)**

SUSUMU YOKOTA-Acid Mt. Fuji (Sublime/Japan) Also known for his **Frankfurt/Tokyo Connection** project on **Harthouse** and more recently the acclaimed **Ebi** on **Space Teddy, Susumu Yokota** bring us yet another facet of his music, ***Acid Mt. Fuji***. Over 74 minutes, Yokota delivers a range of environmental ambientacid tracks, oscillating ambience with beats, and a couple of slightly uptempo tracks for variety. An interesting release that more people should become more familiar with. **(Orion)**

TERRE THAEMLITZ-Tranquilizer (Instinct Ambient) Earlier this year, New York ambient artist **Terre Thaemlitz** emerged from obscurity releasing a brilliant 12" on his own **Comatonse** label, "Raw Through A Straw"/"Tranquilizer," gaining the attention of **Mixmaster Morris** among others. Now signed to **Instinct**, Terre has released his full-length debut. With a minimal setup, Thaemlitz creates deep mesmerizing soundscapes with a sense of warmth by using dialogue, guitar textures, or subtle percussion to draw in and completely envelop the listener. (If I had to pick) Highlights: "Fat Chair," "Hovering Glows," and "2AM On A Silo". **(Orion)**

DUBTRIBE SOUND SYSTEM-S/T (Organico) After two singles and several cross-country tours, San Francisco's **Dubtribe Sound System** present their first full-length lp. Recorded live, **Sunshine** and **Moonbeam** recreate their interpretation of the true San Francisco sound-a positive, uplifting, decidely funky, jazzy, house-y, and smooth flowing mass of warm, pulsating groove. Mileposted by the singles "Sunshine's Theme" and "Mother Earth," the set never rises too high in intensity, nor low in energy level-elements of acid, soulful vocals, and a few ambient passages helping to keep the vibe moving right along. A fine debut effort from an American act that as they evolve, stands to be huge sooner than you think! **(PW)**

FIERCE RULING DIVA-Revolt Of The Perverse (Astralwerks) American labels, if they hope to gain any sort of credibility for themselves and the genre, need to stop releasing dreck like this. Techno, dance music, and the underground get misunderstood enough by the mainstream media in the U.S. without people running around singing the chorus of shit tracks with titles like "I Need Drugs." "Who's gonna go on a drug run?" Puh-leeze! Is this what we want people to think techno is? I don't think so. **(PW)**

PSYCHONAVIGATION (Subharmonic) I'm glad that this fine collaboration between (cool adjectives here) **Bill Laswell** and German ambiento **Pete Namlook** has been released domestically on Laswell's **Subharmonic** label because I hoped to review it last issue, but we ran out of space... In the epic "Psychic And UFO Revelations In The Last Days," Namlook's synth textures and Laswell's incredible mutating basslines chart the course into the realm of the unexplored, transporting us to the outer reaches of our consciousness. Simply magnificent. The remaining 30+ minutes on the disc help to bring us back to Earth. **(Orion)**

DEEP SPACE NETWORK-Big Rooms (Instinct) Long sought after as an import, the expansive ***Big Rooms*** from **Deep Space Network** gains a domestic release on Instinct's ambient label. DSN's work on their own Heidelburg-based **Source** label plus an appearance on the **Fax** label's ***Replugged*** collection and a collaboration with **Dr. Atmo** as **IF** has established them as one of the rising talents of the genre. *Big Rooms* combines dub and electronic rhythms with spoken word and deep cloudlike synth textures while introducing experimental elements throughout. A full-length release that should not be passed on. (Also check out the duo's other domestic release under the guise of **From Earth To Infinity** on **Silent**.) **(Orion)**

MUSLIMGAUZE-Citadel (Extreme) Often described as raga music with a cyber edge, Manchester-based **Muslimgauze** has for over 10 years, used technology to recontexualize traditional Middle Eastern music. This fourth release for Extreme continues this frame for not only the traditional instruments of MiddleEast culture, but for the politics of the region as well. As with previous Muslimgauze releases the music can e listened to without an appreciation of its political origin and gves a satisfying listening experience as well as insight into the plight of the people of Palestine. **(PW)**

V/A-Kickin' Hardcore Leaders (Instinct) A collection of thirteen hard techno nuggets licensed from various producers of the rough stuff. Songs included are Damon Wild's **303 System Project, Union Jack, Mike Ink, DJ Hell** and the **Hypnotist**. Not really recommended for home listening but could be put to good use on the early morning/late night drives home from Orlando. **(G)**

V/A-Secret Life Of Trance, Vol. 3 (Rising High/UK) This third volume in Rising High's **Secret Life Of Trance** series is simply a must have. A fairly comprehensive collection of top tracks from the key producers in the trance/intelligent techno genre during the past eight, nine months. **Union Jack, Paragliders, Balil (Black Dog), RHC** getting the once over from **Hardfloor** and **Perry & Rhodan, Influx/Cybertrax, Art Of Trance, Pascal FEOS (Resistance D)** and more. In a 3 CD or 4 slab of vinyl package, this is an essential purchase for those interested parties who aren't interested enough to trainspot. **(PW)**

PINK FLOYD-Dark Side Of The Moon (Limited Edition Trance Remix) Well, curiosity got the best of me, so I dropped &27.10 with tax on the Limited Edition Trance Remix of Pink Floyd's Dark Side Of The Moon. From personal experience, I know that Pink Floyd's mechanical rights holders do not allow for any sampling of Pink Floyd's records, so I knew that this was a 100% unauthorized remix project. I heard a rumor that The Orb did this remix. I can definitely say it is **NOT** The Orb! This is truly terrible music. Poor sound quality, poorly edited samples, unimaginative and out of key (!) stock synth chords played over snippets of the original tracks. Really bad percussion. Although this CD was probably made by some skank trying to make a fast buck, I'll give it benefit of the doubt and say it's some overzealous PF fan working out of her/his bedroom, and when s/he played a cassette of her/his tinkerings to her/his pals they encouraged her/him to release it. **(TT)**

V/A-Tox Uthat, Vol. 2 (Silent) The follow-up to Silent's ***Tox Uthat*** trance compilation from last year compies eleven new tracks from Germany's **Toxxikk Trakks** label. Except for **Drome**, who contribute two tracks, the rest of the artists are shrouded in relative obscurity which does not bely the depth of the material they contribute here. An interesting collection of ambient and experimental techno. **(PW)**

UVX-Helix (Magick Eye/UK) Culminating the year of experimentation in the synthesis of 'aural hallucinogenics', UVX publish the results on this full-length debut. Opening with the bubbly, soaring "Elevator," the album climbs to "Ambience 1," where you are transported to a swirling mass of what you think are clouds, but is in fact the thick smoke shrouding the pumping ambient dub of "Myalman." And that's just the A side. .. **(Orion)**

NEW LONDON SCHOOL OF ELECTRONICS-The Deepest Cut (Rising High/UK) The very talented, yet underrated **Laurence Elliott-Potter** (of Friends, Lovers, & Family notoriety) and **Caspar Pound** bestow upon us one of the best LP's of the year. Derived from sessions during the recording of the **Rising High Collective** album, this is a truly marvellous full-length ambient album, quality making up for quantity as Potter and Pound explore the strange side of ambience throughout the the LP's eight tracks. Standouts include "The Queen And The Eclipse" and "The Deepest Cut." **(G)**

MAIN-Motion Pool (Beggars Banquet/UK) Trainspotters and journalists alike talk about this new indie ambient movement, citing post-post-psychedelic drone bands like **Spacemen 3** and their offshoots **Spectrum** and **Spiritualized** along with shoegazer/feedback merchants **My Bloody Valentine** as paving the way for acts like **Seefeel**. One band everyone forgets about is **Loop**. With their aggressive almost grungy approach, Loop was perhaps not arty enough or on enough acid for some to consider as part of this clique. Two years after the dust has settled on Loop comes **Main**, led by ex-members of Loop. Their debut album should scare the shit out bands like Seefeel, taking dark, isolationist ambience to another level with tracks of searing guitar noise and almost motionless tranquility. Those who hail bands like Seefeel, who I really like, as the top of the heap in this new subgenre should reevaluate their position after listening to ***Motion Pool***. **(PW)**

MYSTERIES OF SCIENCE-S/T (Instinct Ambient) Best known for his **United Frequencies Of Trance** material, **Dominic Woosey** debuts his new ambient project, **Mysteries Of Science.** Conceived as a soundtrack to his dreams, Woosey weaves a layered, but not suffocating, emotional yet settling web of gentle string arrangements with breathy flute sounds and piano laying a foundation for other elements to flow I and out of the mix. This album is a mantra to Woosey's higher plane. **(Orion)**

V/A-Mind Expansions (Experimental) As stated on the cover, this compilation is a collection of "rhythmic perceptions and concepts from the minds of Experimental artists." Since the first **EX** release, this is a label that has sought to expand musical horizons, and it is a quest that Experimental has been quite successful and it shows here. Included are several unreleased tracks from **Shape Changer, Cyan, and Morgan**, along with favorites from the rest of the EX camp. An essential purchase from a label that truly has it's heart and soul in the Underground. **(G)**

V/A-Psychotrance (Moonshine) Tastefully mixed and compiled by the **Shamen's Mr. C.,** this journey highlights the deeper side of techno-emotional, energetic, soulful, and Detroit-influenced. With tracks from labels like **HOS, Platipus, Prolekult,** and C's own **Plink Plonk**, Moonshine offers a strong look into another side of dance music that doesn't seem to get enough attention in the U.S. Excellent! **(PW)**

V/A-Brilliance For A Better Future (Flask) Breaking the mold of the same old dance music formula, ***Brilliance For A Better Future*** brings together 8 San Francisco-based artists. Brought up in the hi-tech region known as Silicon Valley, these artists blend house, trance, acid, and ambient textures together to probe technology, creating a raw, lo-fi, DIY approach to techno. Standouts include the ambient "Trance For Plants", 303 Terrorists v. DTS' manic acid and Liquid Nitrogen's" Linear Accelerator". **(PW)**

V/A-Behind The Eye (Planet Earth) Scaled back from its import version, ***Behind The Eye*** is a brief, fleeting domestic glance at the brilliant past and bright future of Frankfurt's **Eye-Q** label. Filled with such memorable anthemic German trance favorites like **Vernon**'s "Wanderer," and **Zyon**'s "No Fate," this collection also guides you through some overlooked but choice Eye-Q tracks by **Oliver Leib, Pascal FEOS,** and **Stevie Be-Zet.** One must know the past if they are to know the future...look behind the eye. **(PW)**

V/A-Septic Cuts (ffrr) Founded by **Lord Sabre, Andrew Weatherall,** to put out interesting music that wasn't being released by other U.K.labels, **Sabres Of Paradise** has released some of the most adventurous, intelligent, and occasionally quirky dance music over the past year. ***Septic Cuts*** is a hand picked assemblage of the diversity and depth of vision that has taken the U.K. underground and turned it on its ear. Leading off with the smooth trance of **Secret Knowledge**'s "Sugar Daddy" and Irishman **David Holmes'** simply epic mix of **Sabres**' "Smokebelch II", *Septic Cuts* deviates from there, serving up an exciting and esoteric sampling of flavors- minimal acid, ethnically-tinged acid-laden digifunk, a **Throbbing Gristle** cover given a brilliant thumper of a reworking for the dancefloor that has to be heard to be believed, hard Eurotrance with style, silky Moroder-esque analog workouts, and deep, driving pulsers. Excellent. **(PW)**

NAMLOOK VI (Fax/Germany) Recorded in a cave at the **Cubik** event in Zurich, Switzerland, **Namlook**'s sixth solo performance CD is of the dark, driving, beat-oriented environmental persuasion. Namlook really explores the range of his equipment with lots of bizarre, strange sounds to create a dark, expansive electronic mood. Definitely a disc to listen to with the lights on...or maybe then again, no. **(Orion)**

+N-Plane (Fax Sublabel/Germany) A pure electronic outing along the lines of German electronic improvisational innovators **Can** from **Atom Heart** and **Victor Sol. (Orion)**

CYMATIC SCAN (Fax Sublabel/Germany) Bill Laswell teams up with **Tetsu Inoue** on this dark, minimal, beatfree excursion cut live in the studio. For listening on a higher plane. **(Orion)**

ZENITH (Fax Sublabel/Germany) Tetsu again with **Carlos Vivanco.** Environmental ambience with slow intense beats and liquid melodies. A nice prelude to Tetsu's upcoming solo LP. **(Orion)**

SAD WORLD 2 (Fax Sublabel/Germany) The conclusion of the Sad World series, a continuation of the ethnic-environmental collaboration between **Dr. Atmo** and **Ramin.** Two tracks that gradually evolve, develop, and unfold over an hour's time. An utterly breathtaking excursion. **(Orion)**

OMICRON-Acrocosm (Instinct Ambient) Symbolis, the initial introduction to Athens, Greece native **Savvas Ysatis' Omicron** project brought critical acclaim and attention from DJ's like New York's **Keoki.** Here on his full-length debut, Ysatis opts for a more tranquil sound yest staying true to his own style of organic sounds and spaced out electronics. **(PW)**

PELICAN DAUGHTERS-Bliss (Silent) Australia's **Pelican Daughters** return, exploring ambient dub, psychedelics, tribal grooves and ambient trance. Drawing influence from early 80's electronic music such as **Nurse With Wound, SPK,** and the **Legendary Pink Dots** along with **Mahler** and **Mozart,** this group brings forth a series of influences rarely touched in today's contemporary ambient scene. For the true experimentalists of the bunch. **(Orion)**

SETI-S/T (Instinct Ambient) SETI stands for Search for Extra Terrestrial Intelligence. Concieved by **Taylor 808** of **Human Mesh Dance** and **Prototype 909** and **Savaas Ysatis** of **Omicron,** SETI ponders the question "Is there anybody out there?" Pairing a minimal soundtrack to the short fiction of author **Madison Blue,** Taylor and Savvas almost silently explore the void of the great beyond, looking for a sign of life in a glittering night sky. Are you listening? **(PW)**

DELERIUM-Semantic Spaces (Nettwerk/ Canada) A side-project of industrialists **Front Line Assembly** dedicated to the band's more atmospheric, or if you will, ambient side. In the past, **Delerium** efforts have emphasized darker, more forboding and/or ethnic textures; **Semantic Spaces** deviates from that sound slightly, still using dark, ethnic textures, but not to the same result as previously enjoyed. This Delerium album seems to attempt to cash in on the popularity of **Enigma,** Gregorian chants, and ambient music. Like FLA's weak 'techno' offshoot, **Inter-Mix,** tried to capture underground techno credibility. Inter-Mix failed miserably except to expose industrial fans stuck in 1989 to techno. Delerium does the same with ambient. **(Orion)**

7 KINGS-Out There (The Record Company) An interesting release that was solicited to me on the Internet. Often times I'm skeptical of artists peddling their wares on the Net, but this one is actually quite fine. At the time of writing this, it escapes me of the artists' namebut they are quite well known in studio and production circles having worked with more 'rock' artists. Dark, soothing synthscapes and trippy spoken word take you through the corridor of this release into the space thatis Out There.

THE GRASSY KNOLL-S/T (Nettwerk/ Canada) The title of this project conjures visions of a warm summer field. This feeling also runs through this debut album, combining digital sampling and drum loops with analog sounds. While not necessarily a new thing, The Grassy Knoll is able to assimilate elements of hip-hop, free jazz, and rock with spacy analog technology, creating a sophisticated blend that crosses over several genres of music. This is not the what I had expected to find here and what I've found is really good and fresh. Listen and you will hear... **(Orion)**

Dancing About Architecture, continued from Page 28

Telepathic label gets better and better with time, now with the acid groover, **Space Grass**. San Francisco Sound Factory DJ **Safar** has released a small batch of white labels called **"Raheem"**- one of my favorites lately with two pumpin', funky, tribal-y house mixes, each with their own identity and a b-side that is on a down tempo (and pardon the expression) 'trip-hop' sound. **(Editor's Note: As we were going to press, this record was signed to Strictly Rhythm) Hallucination Records** is set to release the new **Rabbit In The Moon**, "Deeper," which is the Rabbit's most 'ClassA' work yet. Look for a **RITM/Humate** collaboration entitled **Hemispheres** on **Superstition/Germany** soon, plus, later this fall, a collaboration between the Rabbit and **Nick Simpson of Rhythm Invention....**

ARE YOU A TRAINSPOTTER?

Trainspotting is a hobby from the U.K. People will stand on platforms or near railroad tracks to watch the trains go past, pad and pen in hand, ready to write down the ID numbers of the trains that passed. Their goal is to see every train in existence.

When referred to in a musical sense, it means a person who has to have every track or record by an artist, and related trivia.

Are you a trainspotter?

Check yourself against these few simple questions...

1) Do you create discographies of your favorite artists, spending hours and hours making sure you have that one limited edition white label remix?

2) Do you froth at the mouth when you find that limited edition white label on crunchberry purple vinyl?

3) Do you buy whole CD's or album's for that one certain track?

4) Do you repeatedly call the labels you like begging for updated release schedules?

If you answered, "yes" to most of these questions, you're a trainspotter.

Feet First, continued from page 3

marred almost every party we attended during the week. For example, the Hardkiss' Masquerade Party on Thursday night was shut down at 3 am, just as things were about to get moving. Another promoter had called the police, 'complaining' about the noise emanating from the party down in Alphabet City. A Saturday night party's attendance was affected by the promoter's lame door policy-denying entrance until later that morning to a couple hundred people with Seminar passes and many paying Manhattan partygoers due to the fact that a rival promoter threw a directly competing party.

To paraphrase this fax once again, it seems as if the promoters' greediness has stained the scene that supports them. One would think that these promoters would realize, with hundreds of Seminar delegates from around the world in attendance, that this is their scene's moment in the spotlight. At least South Florida has the sense to put their best foot forward during Winter Music Conference in March.

One of the positives of our trip was that all the non-industry people we met were very nice, friendly, into the scene, had social skills (unlike some people here in Florida), and really went out of their way to make us feel welcome and part of their scene. The industry people were nice, too.

You're probably saying, "Okay, now that I've exposed all these problems, where does one go to find a good party in New York?" It was my impression that to go to a party where the music was top notch and promoter really cared about the people that came, one had to make the long and potentially dangerous journey to Brooklyn, or sometimes difficult to-find-a-ride-to New Jersey. Mental, Under One Sky, Factory- these people really care about the state of the underground and fully make an effort to educate, nurture, and enjoy their scene. I was not able to attend the party that they threw in New Jersey on Saturday night, but I was fully convinced that this was a party with a truly underground spirit.

I can't help but feel bad for the scene in Manhattan. It's sad that you've got to travel so far to go to a decent party when there's so much potential within a short cab ride's distance. Will the scene there ever change, who knows? But just like anything else in this scene, if you don't like how something is-change it. It may not be easy, but it begins with you and the people around you.

Tetsu Inoue, continued from Page 8

lumped in as 'ambient' because they don't know what else to call it. People might get the wrong idea about what ambient really is.

TI: It could be really dangerous. Like at the ambient panel at New Music Seminar, when **Kim (Cascone** of **Silent Records)** was speaking about when 'space music' was so happenning and how it didn't have a label. Then it was categorized as New Age and New Age was categorized as (cheesy fusak yuppie jazz) and that's how it was destroyed. Ambient music could happen like that, I'm afraid, but I hope it won't go in that direction.

T: You were in San Francisco recently to do a record with Jonah from Spacetime...

TI: It went quite well, it's called **Electro-Harmonix**. It'll be on Reflective here and on Fax in Europe. We finished in one day; he was quite stressed out with the Spacetime Continuum album, but once we got together and played, it was quite smooth.

T: Tell us about the 2350 Broadway project with Pete...

TI: The first one, he came over to my place and we didn't even talk, nothing. I didn't know he was recording in the beginning, we just started playing, finished it, and he released everything. He didn't cut anything! I'd never worked like that before. I usually stop and change sounds or reprogram sounds, it was quite an experience. The second one has more structure compared to the first.

T: You've also done a record with Bill Laswell, called Cymatic Scan...

TI: That was recorded in same method as 2350 Broadway, all live. It's very dark. (Bill's) really a great guy, he's done so many different things, and I've always wanted to get together with him.

T: You did a record a couple years ago called OM?

TI: It sounds really old now, but two years ago, it was really refreshing. I put so much energy into that project, I really wanted to mix ambient and beats because then, not many people were doing it.

Fax will be releasing *Electro-Harmonix*, Tetsu's project with Jonah Sharp along with a new solo album entitled *Organic Cloud* by the end of 1994.

-A Selected Tetsu Inoue Discography-

Station Rose-Gunafa 2000 ep (Cyclotron)

Trance Media-"Frequency Sex" (Gyroscopic)

Om-Instant Enlightenment (C&S)

-ON FAX-

2350 Broadway 1 & 2 (w/Pete Namlook)

Ambient Otaku

Zenith (w/Carlos Vivanco)

Cymatic Scan (w/Bill Laswell)

Electro-Harmonix (w/Jonah Sharp)

Organic Cloud

4 years leading the sound of the UNDERGROUND.
send a SASE to be on the INSTINCT RECORDS mailing list
instinct RECORDS
RISING HIGH TRANCE INJECTION
DOUBLE CD featuring ambient and intelligent dance from Rising High Records. includes DREAMFISH, THE IRRESISTIBLE FORCE, BALIL (black dog), RD1, OBX and more.
(EX-265)
KICKIN HARDCORE NATIONS
mutant tinged hardcore and hard acid from the UK's Kickin Records. features the mental sounds of THE HYPNOTIST, DJ HELL, 303 SYSTEM and MIKE INK.
(KX-4106)
TECHNOSONIC VOLUME 4
hard trance from the Belgian underground featuring TRANSFORMER 2 + ADAMSKI, GRALOCK and THE UNDERGROUND GIRLS. also available VOLUME 1 (SNC-2001), VOLUME 2 (SNC-2009) and VOLUME 3 (SNC-2022)
(SNC-2030)
KICKIN HARDCORE LEADERS
the hardest jungle and breakbeat sounds from the UK streets. features OMNI TRIO, THE JUNGLE HOUSE CREW and TANGO & RATTY. also available KICKIN MENTAL DETERGENT VOLUMES 1 (KX-4102) and 2 (KX-4103)
(KX-4105)
POD COMMUNICATION PRESENTS: ATOM HEART
12 twisted, acidic tracks from Germany's most original and innovative label. features tracks from MSO, ONGAKU, LISA CARBON and more.
(SNC-2026)
RISING HIGH TECHNO INJECTION 2
exploring the realms of trance and beyond with BLACK DOG, SEQUENTIAL, THE IRRESISTIBLE FORCE and more spaced out European sounds. also available VOLUME 1 (EX-245)
(EX-252)
TRANCEFUSION
trance from around the world featuring timeless tracks from ORBITAL, NIGHTTRIPPER, HIGH LONESOME SOUND SYSTEM, and PARADISE 3001.
(SNC-2021)
KILLER TECHNO VOLUME 3
slammin hardcore from the European techno community. features tracks from BALD TERROR, GREEN BHUDDA and THE SCIENTIST. also available: VOLUME 1 (SNC-2007) and VOLUME 2 (SNC-2020)
(SNC-2023)
ESP VOL.2: THE TRANCE GROOVE
ethereal ambient house grooves from COSMIC BABY, PARADISE 3001, RISING SUN and NICO. also available: ESP VOL. 1 (SNC-2024)
(SNC-2029)
the above discs can be ordered direct from INSTINCT RECORDS:
RISING HIGH TRANCE INJECTION - double CD = $15
ALL OTHER TITLES = $12 each
please send check or money order to the Instinct address below
instinct records 26 W. 17th St. #502 NY, NY 10011 • compuserve: 72170,1153

underworld
dubnobasswithmyheadman
"A milestone on music's endless road to who knows where. A totem to measure all others by."
I-D
"A head on clash between dance music and rock/pop song culture...an endlessly open, fascinating hybrid that is fast becoming a seminal recording.
CMJ
"The greatest record ever! The drugs! The drugs!"
MELODY MAKER
WAX TRAX! RECORDS
TVT RECORDS
available at cool record stores everywhere or send for a free catalogue to
wax trax!/tvt records 23 e. 4th street ny, ny 10003 tel. 212.979.6410 fax. 212.979.6489

Design: Caroline Maxine Cahill

Project Management: Sean M. Johnson

Blurring Books would like to thank Forest Gilbakian for his persistence with this project and for contributing the missing issues needed to publish *TRiP MAGAZEEN: The Complete Collection 1992-1994.*

First Edition. First Printing.

Printed in China